Approaches to Emotion

APPROACHES TO EMOTION

Edited by

KLAUS R. SCHERER
UNIVERSITY OF GIESSEN
PAUL EKMAN
UNIVERSITY OF CALIFORNIA, SAN FRANCISCO

LEA LAWRENCE ERLBAUM ASSOCIATES, PUBLISHERS
1984   Hillsdale, New Jersey   London

Lawrence Erlbaum Associates, Inc., Publishers
365 Broadway
Hillsdale, New Jersey 07642

Library of Congress Cataloging in Publication Data
Main entry under title:

Approaches to emotion.

  Bibliography: p.
  Includes index.
  1. Emotions. I. Scherer, Klaus Rainer. II. Ekman,
Paul.
BF531.A66 1984   152.4   84–1576
ISBN 0–89859–350–6
ISBN 0–89859–406–5 (pbk.)

Printed in the United States of America
10 9 8 7 6 5 4 3 2 1

Contents

Preface

After many years of neglect during which time only a few scholars were concerned with emotion (among them three contributors to this volume, Plutchik, Pribram, and Tomkins), emotion has become a vital, almost fashionable topic in the social and behavioral sciences. Two pitfalls endanger current work: that it may proceed unaware of earlier work and, that it may not be cognizant of the current work from each of the disciplines now concerned with emotion. There are important older contributions and new activity in anthropology, biology, ethology, philosophy, psychology, and sociology. Although not all are represented in this volume, the authors do represent a number of disciplines and multiple approaches that we believe merit further consideration and study, and newer approaches to emotion.

Even though this book is not a volume reporting conference proceedings, it did emerge from two meetings. In 1979 Peter Marler and Klaus Scherer organized a small meeting in Paris with the help of the Thyssen Foundation and the Maison des Sciences de l'Homme on "Evolutionary Continuity in Affect and Affect Expression." On the basis of this preliminary meeting, Paul Ekman, Peter Marler, and Klaus Scherer prepared a larger conference which was held at the Werner-Reimers Foundation, Bad Homburg in July, 1981 with the support of the Deutsche Forschungsgemeinschaft and the Werner-Reimers Foundation. The purpose of this meeting was to consider a variety of questions about the nature and function of emotion, juxtaposing different theories and empirical approaches. The basis for the transactions at the meeting was a long list of relevant questions that were formulated by Ekman and Scherer on the basis of suggestions of the participants (see Chapter 1). Conference participants also prepared position papers to inform one another about their respective work, because about half were unfamiliar with each other.

The authors' willingly and extensively revised their papers after the conference to reflect discussions that took place, making this volume a better set of readings than the usual conference proceedings. Although some of the material in this volume has been printed before, the majority consists of new, up to date statements of theory and/or empirical findings. In order to provide more coverage of developmental issues—one of the most active areas of theory and research, the editors solicited contributions from Emde and Sroufe who had not been able to attend the meeting.

We make no claim to provide a comprehensive compendium of all current approaches to the study of emotion; it was not practical or possible to attempt this in either the conference or the book. We did, however, obtain participation from most of the classic and new approaches to emotion, and while not every major worker in each approach is represented, the contributions do include samples of biological, ontogenetic, ethological, psychological, and the sociological and anthropological approaches.

At the start of each of the different sections we have briefly reviewed some of the major features of each approach, as well as the particular thrust of the individual contributions. We hope that it will serve as a reader in the best sense of that word: a source book allowing researchers and students alike to examine many different aspects and the widely diverging approaches to the study of emotion.

Giessen/San Francisco   Klaus R. Scherer
September 1983   Paul Ekman

Approaches to Emotion

Questions About Emotion: An Introduction

Paul Ekman
University of California, San Francisco

Klaus Scherer
University of Giessen, West Germany

We believe it is fitting to introduce this book with a set of questions, for it is questions more than either theory or established findings which today character-izes the field of emotion. It is questions such as these that provide the excitement which has reawakened interest in emotion after more than 20 years of quiesence. These questions, we believe, represent the intriguing issues and problems that will stimulate both research and theory.

These questions served as the basis for the conference from which this book originated. The authors of this book were asked in advance of the meeting to describe the questions about the nature of emotion which they would most like to have discussed.[1] We sought to delineate areas of uncertainty and disagreement, intending that discussion might bring forth new formulations or isolate problems for research. We preserved the issues but removed, as best we could, terms specific to a particular theorist. Also, we added questions where gaps were apparent and to include our own concerns.

Only some of these questions were addressed at the conference from which this book arose. Still more are addressed in the chapters to follow, all of which were written or rewritten following the meeting. The names of the authors who address each question, and the specific page numbers, are listed after each question. In addition to providing an agenda for theory and research, this chapter

---

[1]Emde and Sroufe were not among the conference participants and therefore were not asked to submit questions. Levy was invited to participate in the conference after the original set of questions was agreed on and circulated to the participants. He introduced a number of additional questions in his presentation which are listed at the beginning of his chapter.

also provides an index, which allows the reader to compare what different authors have said about each question.

Functions of Emotion

Psychologists have tended to emphasize intraorganismic functions of emotion; many seeing emotion as disruptive, although some arguing that emotions motivate behavior. Sociologists have treated emotion in terms of interpersonal and institutional functions. Anthropologists have emphasized societal functions, and many have focused on cultural differences in different aspects of emotion.

1. What are the intraorganismic, interpersonal, and societal function of emotions, and how do these three sets of functions interrelate? (See Emde, pp. 78–98; Lazarus, pp. 228–230, 232, 254–255; Leventhal, pp. 271–272; Levy, 400–411; Plutchik, pp. 197–198; Scherer, pp. 295–297; Sroufe, pp. 109–117; Tomkins, pp. 163–167; Trevarthen, pp. 130–138.)

(a) Are the functions of emotion the same for every emotion? (See Plutchik, pp. 201–203; Tomkins, pp. 170–182; Trevarthen, pp. 133–138, 153–154.)

(b). Do some emotions have more intraorganismic function, while others have more interpersonal or societal functions? (See Plutchik, pp. 215–217; Trevarthen, pp. 133–138.)

2. At the intraorganismic level how is emotion to be distinguished from motivation, drive, mood, learning, attitude and problem solving, and what is the relationship of emotion to each of these? (See Ekman, pp. 333–341; Lazarus, pp. 225–233; Levy, pp. 409–411; Plutchik, pp. 215–217; Scherer, pp. 297–306.)

3. At the interpersonal level how is emotion to be distinguished from interpersonal style or traits, roles, strategic plans, and group dynamics, and what is the relationship of emotion to each of these? (See Kemper, Ch. 17; Plutchik, pp. 205–207.)

4. On the social structural level, what is the role of emotion in establishing, maintaining or changing social organization and social hierarchies? (See Collins, Ch. 18; Plutchik, pp. 216–217.)

Antecedents of Emotion

Recently evidence from a number of investigations has shown some universals in the association of particular social situations or stimulus configurations and the occurrence of particular emotions. Ekman and Friesen (1969, 1972) found the same social stories associated with the same facial expressions in an isolated preliterate and Western cultures. Boucher (Boucher & Brandt, 1981) has found similarities in the antecedent events described for each of six emotions across a number of non-Western cultures. Scherer and his collaborators (Scherer, Summerfield, & Wallbott, 1983) also found similar antecedent events described for particular emotions across a number of Western Cultures.

1. What explains these apparent universalities in the antecedents for particular emotion? (See Ekman, pp. 339–340; Kemper, pp. 371–376; Levy, pp. 404–409; Plutchik, pp. 212–215; Scherer, pp. 306–311; Sroufe, pp. 112–117; Trevarthen, pp. 130–138.)

(a) Are there such antecedents for only some emotions? (See Lazarus, pp. 253–254.)

(b) Are there similarities in the antecedents for any emotions across the life span or across species? (See Kemper, pp. 371–376; Plutchik, pp. 212–215.)

2. Given the fact that there are also variations across individuals in the antecedents for each emotion, what mechanisms would explain both universals and individual differences? (See Ekman, pp. 339–340; Lazarus, pp. 254–255; Levy, pp. 404–409; Plutchik, p. 212; Tomkins, Ch. 7.)

Emotion and Cognition

No one holds that cognitive processes are irrelevant to emotion, but there is marked disagreement about the nature of those processes, and the precise role of cognition in determining which emotion occurs and the subjective experience of emotion.

1. What are the minimal cognitive prerequisites for the occurence of emotion? (See Lazarus, pp. 230–233, 247–254; Leventhal, pp. 272–279; Levy, pp. 404–409; Plutchik, pp. 208–212; Pribram, pp. 22–24; Scherer, pp. 306–314; Sroufe, pp. 112–117; Tomkins, pp. 167–170; Trevarthen, pp. 130–138; Zajonc, Ch. 12.)

(a) Must there be symbolic representation of some facet of the emotional experience, and if so of which facets? (See Leventhal, pp. 275–279; Sroufe, pp. 112–117; Zajonc, Ch. 12.)

(b) Must the organism be capable of being aware of the self, conscious of its behavior? (See Lazarus, pp. 249–250; Levy, pp. 401–409; Pribram, pp. 30–32; Scherer, pp. 306–308; Sroufe, pp. 116–117; Trevarthen, pp. 148–150.)

(c) Must there be retrieval of related memories or expectations? (See Lazarus, pp. 249–250; Levy, pp. 408–409; Pribram, pp. 22–24; Scherer, pp. 306–308.)

(d) Which species other than humans meet these prerequisites? (See Marler, Ch. 16; Pribram, Ch. 1; Scherer, pp. 313–315; Trevarthen, pp. 130–132, 140–145, 148–150.)

(e) How early in life are these prerequisites met? (See Lazarus, p. 254; Scherer, pp. 313–315; Sroufe, pp. 112–117; Tomkins, pp. 167–170.)

2. Do the cognitive prerequisites vary among emotions? It would seem obvious that startle differs from all other emotions; but what about fear versus anger, or either of those and happiness. (See Ekman, pp. 339–340; Lazarus, pp. 253–254; Plutchik, pp. 208–212; Scherer, pp. 306–314; Sroufe, pp. 112–117; Tomkins, pp. 167–182.)

3. Do the cognitive prerequisites vary as a function of the nature of the social situation, the stimulus configuration, or organismic state? (See Lazarus, pp. 254–255; Levy, pp. 404–409.)

(a) Are there any antecedent events (see following) that require less cognitive processing? (See Emde, pp. 81–85; Lazarus, p. 253; Leventhal, pp. 272–279; Scherer, pp. 306–308; Sroufe, pp. 112–116; Trevarthen, pp. 130–138; Zajonc, Ch. 12.)

(b) Can the organismic state change the cognitive prerequisites for emotion? (See Sroufe, pp. 117–126; Tomkins, pp. 167–182.)

Expression of Emotion

The last decade has seen a rapid growth of evidence about both facial and vocal expressions of emotion. Evidence has been found of universality and of appearance early in life. There are many questions about expression, more than about other aspects of emotion. In part this is because there is so much new evidence about this as compared to other aspects of emotion, evidence which has served to raise additional questions for study and for theory. Also, it is easier because of the observability of expression to generate questions. And, since our own work has focused upon expression, we are more intimately familiar with the variety of unknowns to be explored.

1. What is the nature of the information provided by facial or vocal expressions? (See Emde, pp. 86–98; Levy, pp. 410–411; Marler, Ch. 16; Scherer, pp. 312–313; Tomkins, pp. 187–191; Trevarthen, pp. 138–154.)

(a) Does it refer to antecedents, consequences, intentions, physiological state, etc.? (See Ekman, pp. 333–345; Marler, Ch. 16; Scherer, pp. 312–313.)

(b) Does the information provided vary with the age, sex, species, social role, social situation, culture or emotion? (See Emde, pp. 91–98; Levy, pp. 410–411.)

(c) What is typically conveyed or read into such expressions by others? (See Emde, pp. 94–98; Levy, pp. 410–411; Marler, pp. 350–357; Trevarthen, pp. 138–154.)

(d) Can the measurement of facial or vocal expression provide information beyond that which is readily observed without any measurement? (See Ekman, pp. 323–328.

2. What is the relationship between facial and vocal expressions? (See Ekman, pp. 335–336; Trevarthen, pp. 145–148.)

(a) Is one more differentiated or reliable than the other, or are they redundant, consistent expressive channels? (See Ekman, pp. 337–339.)

(b) Do facial and vocal expressions have equal weight as social signals or does that vary with the individual, setting or culture? (See Trevarthen, pp. 145–148.)

3. What are the roles of ontogenetic or environmental as compared to phylogenetic or evolutionary factors in determining the nature of emotional expressions? (See Emde, Ch. 4; Trevarthen, pp. 134–138.)

(a) Are there emotional expressions found in all humans but not other primates?

(b) Are there emotional expressions found in infancy and childhood but not ever observed in adulthood; and, does the reverse occur, are there emotional expressions evident in adults not ever observed in childhood or infancy? (See Emde, Ch. 4.)

(c) Are there emotional expressions found in only one culture not in any way evident in other cultures?

(d) Can there be emotional expressions which are not named in a given culture? (See Levy, pp. 398–410.)

4. Do emotions typically occur in blends; how are blends manifest? (See Ekman, pp. 334–335; Plutchik, pp. 201–205.)

5. Is every emotional expression graded in intensity; and is the range of intensity variations the same across all emotions, and across both face and voice? (See Ekman, p. 337.)

Autonomic, Central Nervous and Neuro-endocrine Substrates of Emotion

One of the oldest and still unresolved arguments has been about whether autonomic nervous system activity is emotion-specific or more simply varies only with the extent of arousal. Recently research has suggested there might be a difference between emotions in the extent and type of hemispheric electrical activity. Much of the recent studies on the neuro-endocrine system has been in relationship to emotional disturbances, but has relevance also to emotion.

1. Is there emotion specific activity in each of the physiological substrates— ANS, CNS, endocrine, etc? (See Davidson, Ch. 2; Ekman, pp. 328–332; Kemper, pp. 376–381; Lazarus, pp. 230–231; Whybrow, pp. 163–165.)

(a) Is there more differentiation for some emotions than others?

(b) Is there differentiation for some emotions in one physiological substrate, while other emotions are differentiated in another physiological substrate?

2. What are the relationships among physiological substrates of emotions? (See Scherer, pp. 312–313.)

(a) What are the linkages between these substrates? Is it only arousal? (See Davidson, Ch. 2; Pribram, Ch. 1.)

b. Do the linkages between these substrates vary with the emotion, with age, with pathology? (See Davidson, Ch. 2; Pribram, Ch. 1.)

3. How do the physiological substrates of emotion influence the subjective experience of emotion? (See Davidson, pp. 51–54; Pribram, Ch. 1.)

(a) Are all the physiological changes equally well represented in awareness as sensations? (See Davidson, Ch. 2; Ekman, p. 340.)

(b) Does this vary with the emotion?

(c) Do this vary with the individual, social setting or role, or culture.

Control of Emotion

Much recent research has explored how individuals may modify their emotional expression and experience. The term control includes a variety of management procedures such as amplifying, deamplifying, concealing, or simulating. While typically control has referred to expression, there has also been interest in how control of expression influences other emotion subsystems, especially subjective experience and physiology. There has also been interest in the control of these substrates, not just expression. Control may occur because of deliberate choice, habit, or learning, reflecting influences from a variety of sources from those that influence many, through cultural standards (e.g., display rules) to highly personal, idiosyncratic choices.

1. What are the minimal prerequisites for such control of emotion; and do they vary with the emotion, the age or the species? (See Marler, pp. 360–362.)

2. Does control of expressive behavior necessarily produce modifications in the subjective experience and/or the physiology such as ANS activity; and is the reverse true, does control of physiology, through biofeedback for example, necessarily produce modifications in expressive behavior? (See Ekman, Ch. 15; Marler, pp. 360–362; Leventhal, pp. 279–288; Tomkins, pp. 187–191.)

(a) Are there any commonalities across cultures in the types of control techniques and in the particular display rules, or are these all culturally variable? (See Ekman, pp. 321–322; Lazarus, pp. 254–255; Levy, pp. 408–409; Marler, pp. 360–362; Plutchik, pp. 216–217.)

3. How well can emotional expression as compared to the physiological changes in emotion be controlled; does it vary with face as compared to voice, with sympathetic as compared to parasympathetic activity? Or does it depend upon the emotion, the age or the culture? (See Davidson, Ch. 2; Ekman, pp. 338–339.)

Clearly these are not all the questions one could possibly ask about emotion. Yet they are questions which in the opinions of the contributors to this volume are ones that needed discussion and clarification. While no chapter provides definitive answers, they do provide hypotheses, and some indications of the kinds of research and theory which may provide better approaches to these questions.

REFERENCES

Boucher, J. D., & Brandt, M. E. Judgment of emotion from American and Malay antecedents. *Journal of Cross Cultural Psychology*, 1981, *12*(3), 272–283.

Ekman, P. Universals and cultural differences in facial expressions of emotion. In J. Cole (Ed.), *Nebraska Symposium on Motivation,* 1971. Lincoln, Neb.: University of Nebraska Press, 1972.

Ekman, P. Sorenson, E. R., & Friesen, W. V. Pan-cultural elements in facial displays of emotions. *Science,* 1969, *164*(3875), 86–88.

Scherer, K. R., Summerfield, A. B., & Wallbott, H. G. Cross-national research on antecedents and components of emotion: A progress report. *Social Science Information,* 1983, *22*(3), 355–385.

BIOLOGICAL APPROACH

We tremble, sweat, cry, and choke, when emotional, have butterflies in our stomach, goosepimples on our skins, and tears in our eyes. It is not surprising, then, that most emotion theorists have placed great emphasis on the biology of the emotions; in many cases, the physiological mechanisms and processes that were postulated to underly emotional experience and behavior actually preceded the psychological aspects of the theory (e.g., theories by James, Lange, Cannon, McLean, Arnold, Pribram).

There are two major sources of controversy. One issue concerns the relevance of underlying biological factors to psychological theory and research. Some have argued that the search for underlying physiological processes will not be helpful in discovering psychological laws. The proponents of this view decry biological reductionism and call for a clear-cut separation of the different levels of analysis. The opposing view is that psychological phenomena can not be understood without specifying the underlying physiological processes and, if possible, isolating and localizing the structures that are involved. Proponents of this view see the study of the physiology of emotion as the best road to an understanding of emotion.

The second major controversy involves the longstanding dispute between peripheralists and centralists. Whereas the peripheralists hold that most of the important aspects of the

9

physiology of emotion can be found in the autonomic nervous systems, particularly the viscera; the centralists believe that the localization of the cortical and limbic system structures that are involved in mediating emotional processes are far more important.

Increasingly, emotion researchers are rejecting either extreme position. Both peripheral and central processes are relevent to an understanding of emotion. The question is not which is more important, but the way in which these structures interact. Similarly, the question is not whether physiology and psychology are to study emotion in isolation of each other, or whether one or the other has to play the leading role, but rather how each other can benefit from the respective theories and findings in contributing to the accumulation of knowledge on each level of analysis. We need to be certain that psychological theories and research efforts are not at odds with established physiological facts. In addition, theory and research on the biology of emotion can provide very important leads for psychological and sociological (see Kemper, this volume) theorizing. The contributions in this section provide testimony for the important contributions of the biological study of emotion.

In the first chapter, Karl Pribram provides an impressive example of a way in which physiological and neurological research findings can be used to develop a conceptualization of emotional phenomena that is amenable to a comparative analysis with psychological emotion constructs. Based on established findings concerning neurophysiological localization and processes, Pribram postulates four major dimensions of emotions related to arousal and stability, specificity and diffuseness of sensations, affective (emotional) and effective (motivational) feelings, and "self versus world outside." Although speculative, this approach suggests a number of fascinating leads for both theory and research.

The remaining chapters in this section explore specific issues in the biological context in more detail. Richard Davidson deals with an important central phenomenon, the timely issue of lateral asymmetry in hemispheric processing. On the basis of a number of studies in his own laboratory and other research, Davidson concludes that there may be a phylogenetically continuous asymmetry in affective processing, with the right hemisphere specialized for negative emotions characterized by avoidance and the left hemisphere for positive emotions characterized by approach tendencies. Again, this biological issue concerning localization and structure turns out to be very fruitful for the development of psychological theorizing. Davidson shows the relevance of the lateralization issue, and its potential for the development of research hypotheses concerning such issues as cognitive-affective interactions, the development of emotion in the infant, the effect of coping styles and affective disturbances.

Peter Whybrow contributes a detailed exploration of an area that is receiving increasing attention: the neuroendocrine functions and their contribution to emotion. There is mounting evidence of hormonal and neurotransmittor changes in emotional arousal. Whybrow musters impressive evidence for the patterning of such neuroendocrine changes, i.e., the notion that there are predictable patterns of changes on the neurochemical level that correspond to specific kinds of emotions. Given that the notion of patterned physiological responses has been much doubted in recent years (e.g., Schachter & Singer; also, see chapters by Ekman & Kemper), these findings rekindle the interest in looking for emotion specific response patterns.

1 Emotion: A Neurobehavioral Analysis

Karl H. Pribram
Stanford University

Current scientific knowledge regarding the physiology of emotion has its roots in Galenical medicine. Four "humors"—sanguine, choleric, phlegmatic and melancholic—were considered to determine differences in temperament. The humors were believed to be organ secretions, and modern biomedical research has supplemented these primitives with a host of endocrine and exocrine hormones that even today must be seriously considered in any comprehensive treatment of the biological regulations that determine feelings of emotion and motivation.

In addition to the multiplication and specification of humors, several other major developements have occurred in the scientific study of the biology of emotions. The first of these developments points to the role of nonhumoral mechanisms in the emotional process: Lange's "visceral" theory made famous by William James (1890), and Nina Bull's "muscle" based attitude theory (1951) are probably the most important of these. Furthermore, brain mechanisms have been shown to be central to understanding emotions. The realization that the brain is involved in the experience and expression of emotions began with the work of Gall and Spurzheim (1809/1969), at the beginning of the 19th century, and achieved considerable sophistication by its end.

Currently, these developments have become enshrined in two central themes that can be identified in practically all biological approaches to emotion: One theme explores the relationship between visceral-glandular reactions and the brain in producing emotion; the other deals with the quantitative relationship between neural excitation and emotion. As we see later, these relationships, although substantial, by themselves form neither an adequate framework for understanding the complexities of emotional processes nor an outline for understanding the intricacies of the relevant neural apparatus. Nonetheless, they do

13

provide a familiar starting point for inquiry, and the basis for developing a more comprehensive view that encompasses the results of recent neurophysiological research.

A LABILE-STABILE DIMENSION

The Visceral Theme

The impact of the visceral theme has been great and is reflected everywhere in our language. "He couldn't be expected to swallow that"; "she has no stomach for it"; "he broke her heart"; "the guy has no guts"; "he sure is bilious today," and so on. In fact, until 1800 A.D. the Galenic medical world subscribed to the notion that while thoughts circulate in the ventricles of the brain, emotions circulate in the vascular system. Gradually, medical and psychological science has become liberated from this view by the accrual of facts showing it to be in error. But the retreat has been a slow and guarded one, partly because old theories do not die easily, and partly because this view has hold of an important part of the truth. The most famous formulations that signal a step-wise retreat and liberation from this view are those of James and Lange, of Cannon and Bard, and of Papez and MacLean.

James and Lange fully faced the accumulated knowledge of the functions of the circulatory and nervous systems of the previous century. They offered the following postulates: When an organism's reaction to a situation involves visceral structures, the sensations aroused by visceral function are perceived as emotional feelings. This proposition provoked a good deal of experimentation. A summary taken from Cannon's critical examinations of the James–Lange theory (1927) is paradigmatic in showing the theory's weaknesses: (1) Total separation of the viscera from the central nervous system does not alter emotional behavior. (2) The same visceral changes occur in very different emotional states and in nonemotional states. (3) The viscera are relatively insensitive structures. (4) Visceral changes are too slow to be a source of emotional feeling. (5) Artificial induction of the visceral changes typical of strong emotions does not produce those emotions.

In place of the visceral theory, Cannon proposed a brain (thalamic) theory: emotional *expression* results from the operation of hypothalamic structures; emotion *feeling* results from stimulations of the dorsal thalamus. This theory was based on the observations that "sham," emotionlike behavior, could be elicited in decorticated and decerebrated preparations, but not when thalamic structures are additionally ablated (Bard & Rioch, 1937). Further, a variety of expressive and visceral responses were obtained when the thalamus was electrically stimulated (Von Bechterev, 1911). Finally, patients with unilateral lesions in the thalamic regions were described as excessively sensing what were to others ordinary cutaneous stimulations. For example, a pin prick would elicit excruciating pain, warmth, intense delight, and so on (Head, 1920).

Probably more is known about the functions of these core thalamic portions of the brain than about any other. This stems in part from the fact that these mechanisms are relatively "peripheral" in the sense that they are relatively directly connected to the organism's receptor mechanisms. In fact, some of these structures contain receptive elements sensitive to a variety of physical and chemical agents that circulate in the blood stream and cerebrospinal fluid. In addition, the core mechanisms exert considerable direct control over the agent to which they are sensitive. This control through feedback was termed "homeostasis" by Cannon and has proved to be a powerful conception in a variety of biological and engineering applications.

But of equal importance is the fact that the processes which are controlled by these mechanics are highly autonomous, that is, self-regulating. Visceral and endocrine regulation is performed with a light hand via two distinct portions of the autonomic nervous system, the sympathetic and the parasympathetic, which balance each other. Experimental evidence was accumulated, especially by Hess (1954), to demonstrate the existence in the hypothalamic region of a trophotropic, energy-conserving process, working primarily through the parasympathetic peripheral division of the autonomic nervous system, and an ergotrophic or mobilizing system, working through the sympathetic division.

The balance between ergo- and trophotropic is not static, of course. When tipped in one direction or the other, a temporary rebound or an "answering effect" (Fair, 1963) could occur as the balance was restored. And indeed both processes could be activated simultaneously so that they would, in effect, work additively. And this was not all. When such activation occurred, somatic, as well as visceral, musculature was involved.

An assumption that paralleled, if not actually guided, these studies was that an understanding of the organization of thalamically regulated processes would provide the key to an understanding of the organization of emotional processes. Once the thalamus and hypothalamus were identified as the neural substrata of emotions, this assumption followed logically.

But Lashley (1960) tellingly criticized the evidence on which this identity was assumed to rest. He pointed out that the type of disturbance on which the theory is based is as often seen to follow lesions elsewhere in the nervous system. "Hyperalgesia is not a result only of lesions within the thalamus but may arise from damage anywhere along the afferent path [p. 352]." He also raised the question of whether "emotional disturbance" in the true sense ever occurs with thalamic lesions: "In no case was the affect referred to the source of emotional stimulation . . . but always to sensations of somatic reaction to the stimulus [p. 351]." Lashley agrees that "in the hierarchy of motor centers we may recognize the thalamic region, especially the hypothalamus, as the region within which the complex patterns of expressive movements are elaborated. It does not follow from this, however, that the pathological phenomena of hyperexcitability of emotional reactions are due solely to release from cortical inhibition or that the thalamic motor center for expressive movement contributes to the emotional experience [p. 348].'' Clearly, the dissociation between emotional expression and feeling, which is such a common clinical and experimental observation, can be leveled against both the James–Lange and Cannon–Bard theories. Unfortunately, Lashley provided no alternative to the theories he so effectively deprecates.

Recently, the James–Lange and the Cannon–Bard views have been superceded by the one proposed by Papez (1937) and elaborated by MacLean (1950). The earlier theories had been firmly based on the evidence that the hypothalamus and dorsal thalamus were at the apex of the hierarchy of control of visceral or autonomic functions. With the development of modern techniques for electrical brain stimulation, viscera were shown to be under the surveillance of the cerebral cortex (Kaada, Pribram & Epstein, 1949). One portion of this cortex came into focus for special attention: the limbic portion of the forebrain. Papez (1937) suggested that the anatomical interconnections among limbic structures were ideally constituted to handle the long-lasting, intense aspects of experience which are usually associated with emotion. MacLean added to this idea the facts of the relationship between this part of the brain and viscera, thus suggesting that here at last is *the* visceral brain—the seat of emotions. The persuasive power of this suggestion is great: Galen, James and Lange, Cannon and Bard, are all saved; visceral processes are the basis of emotion; and an identifiable part of the brain is responsible for emotional control and experience because of its selective relations with viscera. James and Lange were wrong only in leaving out the brain; Cannon and Bard were wrong only in the part of the brain they had identified with emotion; the limbic forebrain, not the thalamus, is the responsible agent. The path from the "emotions in the vascular system" to "emotions in the forebrain" had finally been completed, and each step along the way freed us from preconceptions popularly current when the step was taken.

Despite its persuasiveness and still-present popularity, there are some important criticisms to be levied against the visceral brain theory of emotions. Just as the theory gains in power from its implicit acceptance of the James–Lange and Cannon–Bard views, so it falls heir to the criticisms leveled against the earlier theories. In the same way that the relationship between thalamic structures and emotion fails to be an exclusive one, so the relationship between limbic structures and viscera, or, for that matter, limbic structures and emotions fails to be exclusive. It has been demonstrated experimentally (Wall & Pribram, 1950) that other parts of the cerebral mantle, when electrically stimulated, also give rise to visceral response. Emotional changes are observed to accompany lesions in parts of the forebrain other than the limbic areas. Further, ablation and stimulation of limbic structures influence problem-solving (cognitive) behavior in selective ways that cannot be attributed to changes in emotion. In humans, in fact, a very obvious and specific "memory" deficiency follows limbic lesions, while changes in "emotion" cannot be ascertained. Obviously, the Papez–MacLean theory, like its predecessors, has only a part of the problem in hand.

The Activation Theme

As one turns from the visceral to the activation theories, one can again distinguish between peripheral and central subtheories. Here, however, the argument has not been so sharp. Peripheralists have gladly accepted the diffuse nonspecific reticular activating system as the central locus on which and from which peripheral excitation focuses. And centralists, in turn, have been as concerned with the peripheral as with the central effects of adrenergic and cholinergic substances (e.g., Arnold, 1960). Activation theory can be said, on the whole, to be less specific, less controversial, and considerably more factually oriented than visceral theories (cf. Lindsley, 1951). For example, a classical visceral theorist would have to say that a certain amount of adrenocortical hormone circulating in the blood stream would be correlated with a specific pattern of peripheral and central neural response (in hypothalamus or visceral brain), which in turn corresponds to one or another of the varieties of emotional experience or expression. An activation theorist merely states that a correlation exists between the amount of hormone, amount of neural excitation, and amount of emotional arousal. Considerable evidence can be marshaled in favor of activation theory.

However, common observation and introspection caution that something may be missing. For example, weeping is not just more laughing; fear is not just more love—although there is some truth to the notion of quantitative continuity within each of these processes. Once more, the suggestion arises that activation theory, although part of the story, is not in itself the whole story.

A New Approach

A part of the difficulty comes from the view of activation as an elementary process opposed only to another elementary process—inhibition. True, activation can be viewed as an indicator of behavioral arousal: a temporary state of disequilibrium; a perturbation of patterns of organism-environment ineractions. Also, disequilibration is often sudden, explosive, and has about it the feel of agitation. But this does not necessarily mean that neural impulse transmission is facilitated; rather a different state of organization or disorganization may suddenly have materialized. This difference is expressed as a difference in configuration and not necessarily as a difference in the amount of neural activity. For instance, heart rate may be slowed, cortical rhythms desynchronized, peripheral blood flow diminished, but cerebral blood flow augmented. Cerebral activation, in this context, is an indicator of a configurational incongruity between input arrival patterns and established ongoing neural events.

This view of activation as an indicator of configurational change implies that the organism is fitted with a mechanism that provides a stable baseline from which such change can take off. This baseline is provided by the process of habituation of the orienting reaction. Experimental evidence has accumulated in the past two decades (Sokolov, 1960) to show that habituation of orienting is not due to a progressive raising of threshold to input, but to the formation of a "neuronal model"—a neuronal configuration against which subsequent inputs to the organism are matched. In essence, such neuronal configurations form the sum of an organism's expectancies. The evidence runs like this: A person is subjected to an irregular repetition of a sound stimulus of constant intensity, frequency, and duration. Initially, the person shows a set of physiological and behavioral reactions that together form the orienting response. Among these reactions is "cerebral activation"—that is, a desynchronization of the electrical rhythms recorded from the brain. As the repetition of the sound stimulus proceeds, less and less orienting takes place. This lessening of orienting is called "habituation." For many years it was thought to be due to a simple rise in threshold to input. But "dishabituation"—that is, a recrudescence of the orienting responses—occurs when the intensity of the sound stimulus is decreased or if the duration of sound is shortened. In this latter situation, the orienting reaction occurs at the offset of the stimulation—to the "unexpected" silence.

There can thus be no question about the configurational nature of activation. But these experiments, and the many everyday experiences that they confirm, also account for the importance of visceral and autonomic functions in providing the stable baseline from which the organism's reactions can take off.

Each interaction between environment and organism involves at least two components: (1) discrete interaction by way of the brain's sensory-mode specific classical projection systems and its core homeostats, and (2) a "nonspecific," relatively diffuse interaction by way of reticular and related formations. These nonspecific systems act as a bias on the specific reactions; the set point or value toward which a specific interaction tends to stabilize is determined by the nonspecific activity. Visceral feedback, by the nature of its receptor anatomy and diffuse afferent organization, constitutes a major source of input to this biasing mechanism; it is an input that can do much to determine set-point. In addition, visceral and autonomic events are repetitiously redundant in the history of the organism. They vary recurrently, leading to stable habituations; this is in contrast to external changes that vary from occasion to occasion. Therefore, habituation to visceral and autonomic activity makes up a large share, although by no means all, of the stable baseline from which the organism's reactions can take off.

Another major source of recurrent input that determines bias or sets the level at which change can be sensed is input from the somatic musculature and skin. These somesthetic and proprioceptive inputs give rise to baseline configurations that have been conceptualized in terms such as "body image" and "perceptual-motor organization." Configurational changes in these inputs can also give rise to incongruities that disturb the stable baseline.

Whenever the reaction to incongruous input is sufficient to disturb these baselines, the orienting reaction will include the dishabituation of visceral and autonomic activities. Such dishabituation may be subjectively felt as a mismatch between expected and actual heart rate, sweating, "butterflies," and so on. The sensing of such discrepencies is the basis for the visceral theories of emotion.

If cerebral activation is conceived as a change in the state of organization of neural patterns related to the configurational inconruity between input and established neural activity, what then is its converse? As already indicated, overall neuronal facilitation or inhibition are not involved. Rather some indicator of congruity, of unperturbed, smoothly progressing neuronal activity must be sought. This indicator, at present, is found in the patterns of electrical activity recorded from the central nervous system. There is considerable evidence (Adey, Kado, & Didio, 1962; Li, Cullen, & Jasper 1956a, 1956b) that the slow graded activity of neural tissue, rather than the overall inhibition or facilitation of nerve impulse transmission per se, is involved in the generation of such electrical patterns. The assumption is that the graded electrical activity recorded from the brain reflects the relative stability of the neural system. Such stability would admit increments of change provided these did not disrupt the system. Nor is it implied that incongruity, and therefore activation, are necessarily limited by input. An input that may ordinarily be processed smoothly may perturb the system if that system is already unstable; or an internal change in the organism may initiate incongruity where match had previously existed. Thus, the configuration of activation of the nervous system can predispose the organism toward perturbability or imperturbability.

A considerable body of evidence has recently accrued about the neurophysiological and biochemical mechanisms that regulate these predispositions. As already noted, the nonspecific neural systems are primarily involved in setting the bias toward which more specific organism-environmental interactions tend to stabilize. These diffuse systems are largely made up of fairly short, fine fibers with many branches. Such neuronal organizations are especially sensitive to the chemical influences in which they are immersed. A potent set of such chemical influences are the catecholamines, and they have been shown to be the important locus of action of the pharmacological tranquilizers and energizers that have been so successful an adjunct in altering maladaptive emotional reaction.

But these are not the only chemical influences at play. The importance of humoral factors in determining emotional states has already been noted. *Hormones* are chemicals that exert their influence on the brain via receptors located in its core. In addition to this sensitivity to hormones produced by glands such as the gonads, thyroid, adrenal medulla, and cortex, the core brain receptors monitor a host of other chemical and physical constitutuents of the internal environment of the organism. A respiratory control mechanism is sensitive to the partial pressure of CO_2; a temperature sensor monitors the warmth of the blood stream; sex hormones are selectively absorbed at one location and adrenal steroids at another; the difference in the concentration of sugar in the venous and arterial circulation is monitored as is the concentration of salt and therefore, reciprocally, the concentration of water. Peptides secreted by the walls of the gut and by the kidney and a host of others are being investigated because some experiments indicate that they too are sensed by cells in the core of the brain (see Pribram, 1971/1982, chaps. 9 & 10, for review).

Further, this part of the brain is a veritable cauldron of chemicals locally secreted by aggregates of cells in one or another location. Catecholamines such as norepinephrine (closely related to the hormone epinephrine—adrenaline— secreted by the adrenal medulla) and dopamine (which metabolizes into nor- epinephrine); indole amines such as serotonin; and peptides such as endorphine (an endogenous morphine-like substance) abound. As might be expected, sen- sitivities to these neurohumors are also built into the mechanism.

As noted earlier, Walter Cannon, in his classical studies (1927), determined that the relationship between the sensor and its chemical was such that the concentration of the chemical, although fluctuating, was maintained constant around some set point. He enunciated this relationship as the principle of home- ostasis. The sensor monitors the quantity of the variable and signals, by ways of neural pathways or chemical secretions, when the variable rises above or falls below a certain level. Such signals compose a negative feedback because their sign is opposite to that which characterizes the deviation of the quantity of the variable from the baseline. Often the mechanism that counteracts the decrease of the variable—the appetitive phase—is separate from that which counteracts the increase—the satiety phase.

Individual homeostatic mechanisms are multiply interlinked into complex organizations. Thus, the thermostat regulating temperature is linked to the glucostat regulating food intake and both of these in turn are linked to os- moreceptors (the salt-water receptors) which control thirst. This set of linkages is additionally connected to the thyroid sensitive mechanism controlling activity. Through various metabolic interrelationships, such as breathing, that take place in the body these homeostatic mechanisms also regulate the partial pressure of CO_2, and so on (see Brobeck, 1963 for review).

In short, the core of the brain (mesencephalon, diencephalon, and the basal ganglia and limbic systems of the forebrain) uses chemical regulations to control body functions. The configuration of concentrations of these chemicals, although fluctuating around some set point, is sufficiently stable over periods of time to constitute steady "states." These states apparently are experienced as hunger, thirst, sleepiness, elation, depression, effort, comfort, and so on. Although the chemical characteristics of each state are as yet incompletely specified, enough is known to allow one to say that the concentration of glucose is involved in the hunger mechanism; the concentration of salt in the thirst mechanism; the concentrations of the indole amine serotonin and norepinephrine (a catecholamine) in the sleep mechanism (norepinephrine in dreaming); the concentration of dopamine (another catechol) in feelings of effectiveness—that is, of elation and depression; the concentration of endorphins in those of temperature, novelty, and pain; and the concentrations of the enkephalins (adrenocorticotrophic hormones of the pituitary) in those of effort and comfort (for reviews, see Pribram, 1971/1982, 1977a; Stein, 1978).

AN EPICRITIC-PROTOCRITIC DIMENSION: BRAIN STEM SHELL AND CORE

Pain and Temperature as Protocritic Processes

The control of temperature and of pain falls into the homeostatic mold. But temperature and pain are also skin senses that share a common spinal pathway; thus the question arises about whether the skin components of these sensitivities are processed separately from those involved in internal regulations. The answer to this question is that part of the skin components of temperature and pain are processed separately and part in conjunction with the chemical homeostats of the core brain.

The part of the skin components of temperature and pain sensitivity processed separately (in the parietal lobes of the cortex) from the homeostatic mechanism is characterized by what is called in neurology the "local sign." This means that the sensation can be located on the skin, and that the duration of the sensation is limited. Henry Head (1920) labeled such sensory experiences "epicritic" to distinguish them from more diffuse experiences that are obtained during early regrowth of severed nerves.

The remainder of the skin's temperature and pain sensitivities are processed in conjunction with the chemical core homeostatic mechanisms. The spinal temperature and pain tracts end in structures (such as the substantia gelatinosa of the dorsal spinal cord, the periqueductal grey of the midbrain, and the amygdala of the forebrain) loaded with endorphins. Responses to hot and cold and pain are dramatically altered by electrical stimulations of these core portions of the spinal cord, brain stem (Liebeskind, Mayer, & Akil, 1974), and forebrain and are not affected by stimulations of the parietal cortex or the tracts leading to it (Chin, Pribram, Drake & Greene, 1976; Richardson & Akil, 1974). The assumption is that the stimulations increase the local (and perhaps general) secretions of endorphins.

What is common to the homeostatic internal mechanisms and these aspects of pain and temperature processing is that they are simply sensitive to amounts, to quantities, of chemical and neural excitation. Processing does not lead to identification of location in time and space (or to other qualitative aspects of the stimulus such as color). Head (1920) termed the quantitative "diffuse" aspects of sensitivity "protopathic" because in his experiments they arose while the regenerating nerves were in a pathological condition. The term should be modified to "protocritic" in order to include current evidence that such sensitivities are part of the normal control of the temperature and pain (and probably other sensory) mechanisms. As noted, protocritic processes are homeostatic—that is, they control the quantitative aspects of stimuli and are thus determinants of neural states. Chin et al. (1976) and Pribram (1977a) provide a more complete review.

The protocritic dimension of experience, devoid of epicritic local sign, is therefore characteristically dependent on the quantity, the intensity of the stimulus. Quantity [intensity] in a homeostatic system is, in turn, dependent on change and rate of change of the state of that system. Controlled changes of moderate amounts are apparently experienced positively, whereas more abrupt and overly intense changes of state lead to negative feelings (the Yerkes– Dodson Law, see Hebb, 1955). Here we are at the frontier of knowledge. As noted, the pain and temperature systems run together in the spinal cord and brain stem to terminate in and around the amygdala and frontal cortex. Brain stimulations in human beings that protect against pain are accompanied by the feeling of cold (Richardson & Akil, 1974). Do the elaborations of the temperature systems accrue to the experiencing of comfort as the elaborations of the pain systems accrue to suffering? Or, is suffering experienced only when the limits of tolerable comfort are exceeded? In short, are there two neural systems—one for pain and one for temperature, or is there only one? And if there are two, how do they interact to produce a more or less unitary experience along a hedonic dimension?

Although there are no definitive answers to these questions yet, it has become clear that a host of neural systems become engaged in the rostral extensions of the pain and temperature mechanisms. At the brainstem level up to the forebrain, electrical excitations of these systems produce self-stimulation in animals and hedonic experiences in man. Closely intertwined, but perhaps more laterally placed, are locations from which electrical stimulations produce aversive effects—turning off the stimulus and, in the more caudal placements, evidence of discomfort in animals.

Arousal, Activation and Effort

In the forebrain, these systems focus on structures such as the basal ganglia and limbic formations about which we have a considerable amount of information regarding their relationship to emotion (and motivation). The evidence involved can be organized (detailed by Pribram & McGuinness, 1975) to show that three separate categories of systems can be discerned to influence electrocortical desynchronization—evidence that goes beyond that reviewed in the previous sec-

tion, of "The Activation Theme." One system regulates phasic desynchronization (i.e., brief, lasting at most several seconds), another tonic (on the order of
minutes) desynchronization, while a third system coordinates the other two (over
a longer period of time—the duration of an attention span).

Phasic desynchronization we called "arousal." The system responsible for
arousal centers in the forebrain on the amygdala, a basal ganglion of the limbic
forebrain. Removal of the amygdala eliminates the visceral and autonomic responses that ordinarily accompany orienting and alerting to a change in stimulus
conditions (Bagshaw & Benzies, 1968; Bagshaw, Kimble, & Pribram, 1965;
Kimble, Bagshaw, & Pribam, 1965; Pribram, Reitz, McNeil, & Spevack, 1974,
reviewed by Pribram & McGuinness, 1975). Furthermore, this elimination of the
visceroautonomic responses apparently leads to a failure of behavioral habituation that normally occurs when the novel stimulus is repeated. The visceroautonomic reaction appears necessary for familiarization with the stimulus to
occur. Thus, contrary to Lange and James, the visceral input appears not to be
experienced directly as an emotion, but leads to rapid habituation of the input. As
noted, Sokolov showed that (1960) habituation forms a stable neural representation. Such a stable state is necessary for appreciating subsequent change—the
novelty which then arouses (emotional) interest and when the novelty exceeds
certain limits, the experiencing of (emotional) upset. James and Lange were
correct in suggesting that visceral input is important to emotion, but erroneous in
the specific role they assigned to it in the emotional process.

The second system involved in the desynchronization of cortical electrical
activity (in this instance a tonic—minute long—activation) is centered on the
nonlimbic basal ganglia of the forebrain—the caudate nucleus and putamen
(reviewed by Pribram, 1977b). These structures are concerned with maintaining
the (motivational) readiness of the organism: postural readiness, motor readiness, and the readiness produced by the establishing of sensory (i.e., attentional)
sets (Lassonde, Ptito, & Pribram, 1975; Reitz & Pribram, 1969; Spinelli &
Pribram, 1966, 1967). It is this second system that forms the neural basis for
"attitudes"—much as suggested by Nina Bull (1951).

A third system centers on the hippocampus and coordinates arousal and readiness. Arousal phasically interrupts ongoing tonic readiness. The balance between
interruption and continuation must be coordinated, and neurobehavioral and
neurophysiological evidence points to the hippocampal system as serving this
function (Isaacson & Pribram, 1976). Coordination has been shown to involve
neural work, that is, to take effort (Benson, 1975).

Neurochemically, the three systems also differ (reviewed by Pribram, 1977a).
As already noted the amygdala is rich in endorphins and the caudate and putamen
are characterized by dopamine. The hippocampal system is involved in pituitary–adrenal hormonal controls, selectively absorbing adrenocortical hormone
(Bohus, 1976; McEwen, Gerlach, & Micco, 1976) and being acted on by the
adrenocorticotrophic hormone (ACTH) and related enkephalins (Riezen et al.,
1977).

A Comprehensive Physiological Theory of Emotion

The humoral, visceral, and activation theories of emotion (and motivation) are thus converging into a more comprehensive view that subsumes the earlier ones. The momentary arousal produced by novelty (or its complement, familiarity) appears related to endorphin homeostasis; the activation of motivational readiness is based on a dopaminergic system, and coordinating effort (or its inverse, comfort) is experienced as a result of operations of the brain representation of the pituitary–adrenal hormonal stress mechanism.

The model of emotional feelings that emerges from these data centers on a set of corebrain neurochemical states that comprise the experience of "familiarity." Familiarity implies equilibrium, a feeling of reasonable amount of stability and smooth transition from one state to another. This set of stable states can be altered by novel or pain producing events and what is perceived as novel—or painful—is dependent on the configuration of the states that determine what is familiar. The distinction between novelty and pain is one of intensity *only* [e.g., electrical stimulations of the amygdala in animals and man produce orienting (interest), avoidance (fear), attack and escape (pain) as a function of ascending stimulus intensity (Gastaut, 1954]. In contrast to the arousing disequilibrations produced by the novelty–pain mechanisms, the maintenance of states is effected by tonic operations of the readiness system. As noted earlier, there is a considerable body of evidence that the maintenance of a stable basal temperature involves the food appetitive, water balance, and tonic muscular readiness systems, among others (see Brobeck, 1963, for review). When the demands of arousal are pitted against those of continuing readiness, the feelings of stress and effort are experienced. These experiences are allayed by a coordinating mechanism that adjudicates smooth transition from state to state within some confortable band width of tolerance.

The data briefly noted in this section make it necessary to look carefully at another often neglected distinction. Ordinarily, we use the terms emotion and feelings synonymously. Feelings generated by readiness to respond are more akin to motivations and intentions than to emotions, however. The next section makes explicit therefore a distinction between emotions and motivations and the feelings that are generated by both.

AN EFFECTIVE–AFFECTIVE DIMENSION: BASAL GANGLIA AND LIMBIC FOREBRAIN

The Experiencing and Expressing of Emotions

Since Darwin's classical treatise on the expression of emotion (1965), it has been customary to separate emotional experience from emotional expression. Emotional experiences are classes of feelings, and I have elsewhere (Pribram, 1970,

1971/1982) made the case for using the category "feelings" to encompass a range of experiences which can be separated from those that allow us to perceive objects beyond our skin:

> I once had the opportunity to examine some patients in whom the medial part of the temporal lobe—including the amygdala—had been removed bilaterally. These patients, just as their monkey counterparts, typically ate considerably more than normal and gained up to a hundred pounds in weight. At last I could *ask* the subject how it felt to be so hungry. But much to my surprise, the expected answer was not forthcoming. One patient who had gained more than one hundred pounds in the years since surgery was examined at lunch time. Was she hungry? She answered, "No." Would she like a piece of rare, juicy steak? "No." Would she like a piece of chocolate candy? She answered, "Umhumm," but when no candy was offered she did not pursue the matter. A few minutes later, when the examination was completed, the doors to the common room were opened and she saw the other patients already seated at a long table eating lunch. She rushed to the table, pushed the others aside, and began to stuff food into her mouth with both hands. She was immediately recalled to the examining room and the questions about food were repeated. The same negative answers were obtained again, even after they were pointedly contrasted with her recent behavior at the table. Somehow the lesion had impaired the patient's *feelings* of hunger and satiety and this impairment was accompanied by excessive eating!

As yet we understand little of how this impairment comes about. Nevertheless, this example points clearly to the folly of believing that a direct match exists between observations of any particular type of behavior and introspectively derived concepts. Are we to say that the patient *felt* hungry because she ate ravenously despite her verbal denial? Or are we to take her statements at face value and seek elsewhere for an explanation of her voracious eating? The paradox is resolved if we consider the behavioral function to be composed of several processes, one of which is the feeling state reported verbally.

At the hypothalamic level a similar paradox has plagued investigators. As already noted, when lesions are made in the region of the ventromedial nucleus of the hypothalamus, rats will eat considerably more than their controls and will become obese. But this is not all. Although rats so lesioned ate a great deal when food was readily available, they worked less for food whenever some obstacle interfered (Miller, Bailey, & Stevenson, 1950).

It was also found that the more palatable the food, the more the lesioned subject would eat (Teitelbaum, 1955), giving rise to the notion that the lesioned animals did not show greater "drive" to eat but were actually more "finicky" than their controls. Recent experimental results obtained by Krasne (1962) and by Grossman (1966) added to the paradox: Electrical stimulation of the ventromedial nucleus stops both food and water intake in deprived rats and produces fighting if the animal is provoked (King & Hoebel, 1968).

Grossman (1966) summarizes these results with the succinct statement that medial hypothalamic manipulations change affect not appetite. But we are once again faced with our earlier dilemma. If the medial hypothalamic mechanism does not deal with motivation, how does eating, drinking, etc., come about? The data hold the answer. The ventromedial and lateral hypothalamic regions form a couplet, the lateral portion serving as a feeding, a ''go'' mechanism (which, when ablated, will produce rats that tend to starve), and the medial portions contain the ''stop'' mechanism, the interruption of behavior which we have identified as leading to emotional arousal.

The paradox is thus resolved by the hypothesis that processes ordinarily involved in taking the organism ''out of motion'' also generate affects or feelings of emotion. In this fashion, an important distinction between motivation and emotion becomes clarified: The term ''motivation'' can be restricted to the operations of appetitive ''go'' processes (such as those converging in the lateral hypothalamic region) that ordinarily result in behavior which carries forward an action, and the term ''emotion'' to the operations of affective ''stop'' or satiety processes of reequilibration (Pribram, 1971/1982 pp. 192–194).

Emotion and Motivation

These neurobehavioral data make imperative a reference to an encompassing category, feelings, with the subcategories emotion and motivation clearly distinguished. Emotion is found to be derived from processes that *stop* ongoing behavior: affective reactions accompanying the satiety mechanisms as in the foregoing quotation, arousal as in the orienting reaction to distracting stimuli, and more generally when behavior is interrupted (Mandler, 1964). By contrast, the organism is considered motivated when his readiness mechanisms are activated, when he is ready to ''go'' and to continue ''going.'' These responses are (as noted in the previous section) critically organized by the basal ganglia (Pribram, 1977b) and have as their physiological indicators the CNV (Walter, 1967) and heart rate slowing (Lacey & Lacey, 1974).

The distinction between emotion and motivation is not a novel one. In his opening paragraph on emotions William James (1890) suggests that ''emotional reaction usually terminates in the subject's own body,'' while motivation ''is apt to go farther and enter into practical relations with the exciting object [p. 442].'' In a similar fashion, J. R. Kantor (Kantor & Smith, 1975), whose interbehavioral analyses of psychological processes influenced B. F. Skinner so profoundly, distinguishes between affective and effective interactions: In affective interactions the person is responding primarily with internal body mechanisms, while effective interactions generate readiness or overt responses toward the stimulating object.

In short, for behavior, as well as for the neurophysiology of feelings, it becomes useful to distinguish emotional from motivational antecedents. Motivational antecedents imply that the organism is preparing to or actually acting on the environment, whereas emotional antecedents imply only that internal processing, internal control mechanisms, are in force. The distinction becomes manifest in the connotative differences between the meaning in English of the term "behavior" and its continental counterpart in German and French: *Verhaltung* and *comportment* both connote how one "holds oneself"—one's positive and negative attitudes, whereas the English "behavior" has the more pragmatic and active meaning of "entering into practical relations with the environment."

The Expression of Emotions in a Social Context

An important consideration arises at this point. If the expression of emotions is affective (rather than effective), that is, emotional expression terminates in the subject's own body, how then can we observe and work with such expressions in terms of behavior? Ordinarily, an experimentalist is concerned with the environmental consequences of behavior (e.g., the cumulative record in an operant situation). In this situation, according to our definition, behavior is motivated, not emotional. Thus the behaviorist has had some difficulty in finding measures of emotional expression. Conditioned suppression of responses, bolles of rat feces and the like have been used, but they fail to reflect the richness of (especially the pleasant and positive) emotional (internal) states (reactions that terminate at the skin) which the observed organism can experience. Furthermore, ethologists working with social behavior have followed Darwin's lead and shown that organisms can "read" each other's emotional expressions and be influenced by them.

Thus, emotional expression does have a practical influence beyond the emoting organism, but only in a social communicative setting. In such a setting the practical influence is completely dependent on the ability of other socially receptive organisms to sense the meaning of expression. Effectiveness therefore does not depend on what the emoting organism does, but on what the socially sensitive recipient is able to do. However, an intelligent self-aware organism such as Homo sapiens can use these emotional expressions motivationally—that is, to manipulate the social situation. Such manipulations, when deliberate and planned characterize the "con" artist, actor, and administrator. But often, through imitation and conditioning, the emotional expressions become automatic, leading to stereotyped interactions. Much of the social display behavior of animals (e.g., birds) is apparently of this type: internal and/or external stimuli set in motion an emotional reaction, which, when expressed, triggers another emotional reaction in a socially receptive conspecific (e.g., Hinde, 1954a, 1954b, 1960). In these animals, behavior sequences are thus concatenated of emotional expressions (and labeled "instinctive"). Such concatenations comprising instincts can also be elicited when an organism becomes completely adapted to an ecological niche in the nonsocial environment (Miller, Galanter, & Pribram, 1960, Chap. 5). By contrast, organized motivations ("plans") are constructed within the organism's brain and "mean to enter into practical relations with the exciting object." The adaptive consequences of motivated behavior is a function of that behavior. The adaptive consequence of emotional expression is a function of the social matrix in which it occurs or of a stability attained in the evolutionary process, which eliminates the occurrence of the expression of nonadaptive situations.

In summary, *emotional behavior* is defined as an expression of positive and negative emotional feelings that are inferred to reflect certain internal neurological states of the organism. The term "feelings" is therefore not synonymous with the term "emotion," since it is possible to identify additional internal neurological states and the experiences and behaviors they determine. One such additional category encompasses motivational feelings and behavior. Emotions are distinguished from motivations in that emotional reactions ordinarily "terminate within the organism's body," whereas motivations are "apt to go farther and enter into practical relations with the exciting object." An exception arises in social behavior, however. When a socially sensitive organism can be influenced by the expression of emotions or when an organism is totally adapted to his ecological niche, the sequential triggering of emotional expressions can lead to automatic (instinctive) behavior that is often, although not always, highly adaptive. Note, however, that the adaptation is due not directly to the expression of emotion but to the forces operating in the social and physical environment. We have already dealt with these "triggering" stimuli for emotional expression: The protocritic dimension was seen to be critical. But what neural control mechanisms determine how an emotional feeling will be experienced?

AN ETHICAL-ESTHETIC DIMENSION

The Cortical Contribution to a Labeling of Feelings

The biological contribution to an understanding of feelings in general and emotional feelings in particular can therefore not rest here. A basic problem set out by William James and also by Freud has to be faced. Freud (1895/1966) proposed that the critical neurological mechanisms involved in emotion are neurochemical and derive from body stimulation (the endogenous paths), which affect a certain portion of the brain. The work reviewed here has given substance to Freud's proposal and enlarged it: a protocritic dimension of stimulation was identified, a dimension describing much of the input through visceroautonomic (endogenous) paths, but also receiving a contribution from exteroceptors (exogenous paths), especially those of the pain and temperature senses. Further, the processing of this protocritic dimension was found to take place in limited portions of the brain—the core brain systems of the brain stem and the limbic forebrain.

William James (1890) faces the possibility that such separate neural processing of emotion occurs:

> And yet it is even now certain that of two things concerning the emotions, one must be true. Either separate and special centres, affected to them alone, are their brainseat, or else they correspond to processes occurring in the motor and sensory centres already assigned, or in others like them, not yet known. If the former be the case, we must deny the view that is current, and hold the cortex to be something more than the surface of "projection" for every sensitive spot and every muscle of the body. If the latter be the case, we must ask whether the emotional *process* in the sensory or motor centre be an altogether peculiar one, or whether it resembles the ordinary perceptive processes of which those centres are already recognized to be the seat. Now if the theory I have defended be true, the latter alternative is all that it demands [pp. 472–474].

Thus, James opts for the cortex. Was he wrong? I do not believe so. There is more to feeling that the protocritic dimension. Schachter (Schachter & Singer, 1962) has delineated two aspects to feeling: one that devolves on its intensity and the other that "labels" the feeling. With regard to his intensity dimension, Schachter, using only adrenalin, was trapped by this unidimensional approach in the activation theme current at the time he performed his experiments. As previously detailed, a richer protocritic dimensionality better describes this aspect of his experimental results. But Schachter's data do provide evidence for another set of dimensions, those that determine whether an emotional or motivational feeling or expression is "good" or "bad." Such evaluative labels are specific; they identify the feeling with respect to a qualitative context. In short, labeling can encompass epicritic as well as protocritic factors, and we should turn, as James proposed, to the cerebral convexity in the search for the neural mechanisms that are involved.

According to James (1890b), what needs to be demonstrated is that "the reflex currents pass down through their preordained channels, alter the condition of muscle, skin and viscus; and these alterations, perceived, like the original object, in as many portions of the cortex, combine with it in consciousness and transform it from an object-simply-apprehended into an object-emotionally felt [pp. 472–474]."

Review of the foregoing work has demonstrated that "the condition of muscle, skin and viscus" need not, in fact, be altered. A stable representation, a neural representation of bodily function, including its quantitative hormonal composition, is interposed between "muscle, skin and viscus" and the cortex. All that needs to be established is that the representation (and its potential or actual perturbance) be addressed. The pathways whereby this can occur have now been thoroughly established both anatomically and physiologically (Goldman & Nauta, 1977; Kemp & Powell, 1970; Lassonde, Ptito, & Pribram, 1981; Nauta, 1964; Reitz & Pribram, 1969).

Personal and Extrapersonal Processes

The cortical contribution to the regulation of more primitive functions is, as might be expected, complex. Sense can be made of this complexity, however, by relating the myriad of observations on the effect of cortical lesions and excitation to the two simpler dimensions that have been delineated thus far. The cerebral isocortex is directly connected both to brain stem (core and shell portion) and to the remainder of the forebrain (basal ganglia and limbic formations). These connections can therefore modulate the epicritic–protocritic and the affective–effective dimensions of experience and behavior that are regulated by the more primitive structures.

The far frontal cortex receives abundant connections from both the limbic and basal ganglia systems (Pribram, 1954, 1958a). Anatomically the far frontal (frontal intrinsic) cortex receives projections from the n. medialis dorsalis of the thalamus (an "intrinsic" nucleus, since it is only indirectly connected with extracerebral inputs), which lies embedded within nuclei that project to limbic cortex. Behaviorally, resections of far frontal cortex result in deficits in delayed alternation performance, deficits also obtained when lesions are made of limbic and basal ganglia (caudate) structures but not when the posterior cortical convexity is damaged. By contrast, damage to regions located in the posterior cortical convexity (the posterior intrinsic cortex that receives its input from the pulvinar, another intrinsic thalamic nucleus) produces deficits in discrimination learning and performance, which remain unaffected by frontal, limbic and caudate lesions. The difference between alternation and discrimination has been conceptualized to reflect the difference between context-sensitive reactions on the one hand, and context-free information processing on the other (Pribram, 1978).

The far frontal cortex thus operates to combine the protocritic with the effective poles of the protocritic–epicritic and affective–effective dimensions. This combination produces one pole of a new dimension that I have labeled esthetic–ethical (Pribram, 1967), based on the distinction between the processing of "external space" and the processing of a "body image" or "self." Processing that results in the effective use of local sign (the epicritic dimension) is a function of a band of cortex surrounding the three major cerebral fissures: sylvian, rolandic (central), and calcarine. (The continuity between perirolandic and periocalcarine cortex is established at the apex of the cortical convexity: In the monkey brain this is at the confluence of the intraparietal, superior temporal and lunate sulci. The continuity between perisylvian and perirolandic cortex lies at the foot of the central fissure.)

In primates, including man, the growth of the cortex surrounding these major fissures has split the remaining cortex into two divisions:

1. the far frontal cortex discussed earlier which is interconnected by the fibers of the uncinate faciulus to the adjacent orbitofrontal, anterior insular and periamygdaloid cortex of the temporal pole, which are a part of the limbic system.

2. a posterior division focused on the inferior parietal lobule on the lateral surface and the precuneus on the medial which is connected to the inferior parietal lobule via the medial extension of the confluence between intraparietal and lunate sulci. The functional connectivities of these divisions of the cortical mantle have been most clearly demonstrated by strychnine neuronography (Pribram & MacLean, 1953; Von Bonin & Bailey, 1947) and have been confirmed histologically by the use of silver staining techniques (Jones, 1973; Nauta, 1964).

The behavioral evidence showing that the perifissural cortex processes "external space," while the remaining cortex processes "self" is so extensive that only the highlights can be listed here: (1) Beginning with the precentral (prerolandic) cortex, Pribram, Kruger, Robinson, and Berman (1956) showed that the environmental consequences of movement, not movements or muscle constructions per se, are encoded in this "motor" cortex (see review by Pribram, 1971/1982). (2) The postcentral and superior parietal cortex deals with the somatosensory (haptic) discrimination of objects in external space (Brody & Pribram, 1978; Kruger & Michel, 1962; Mountcastle, Lynch, Georgopoulos, Sakat, & Acuna, 1975; Pribram & Barry, 1956; Wilson, 1957). (3) The pericalcarine cortex deals with visual processing (see Weiskrantz, 1973, for review) and its extension into the inferior temporal gyrus, with making visual discriminations (see Pribram, 1974, for review). (4) The posterior perisylvian cortex is involved in auditory processing (see Neff, 1961, pp. 259–278 for review) and its extension into the superior temporal gyrus with auditory discriminations (Dewson, 1977; Dewson & Cowey, 1969; Dewson, Pribram, & Lynch, 1969). (5) The anterior perisylvian cortex in the depths of the fissure and extending forward to the temporal pole and orbital surface of the frontal lobe processes gustatory information (Bagshaw & Pribram, 1953; Pribram & Bagshaw, 1953) and is also involved in olfactory (Brown, 1963; Brown, Rosvold, & Mishkin, 1963), and, as noted earlier, temperature discriminations (Chin, Pribram, Drake, & Green, 1976).

By contrast to these clear-cut results of experiments relating the perifissural cortex to processing of "external space," the evidence for processing "self" by the remaining cortex is somewhat more difficult to interpret. Initially, data were believed to point to the far frontal cortex as the sole source of an image of self. Recent experimental results show, however, that this conclusion was oversimplified and to a large extent erroneous (Brody & Pribram, 1978). Furthermore, clinical evidence has shown the inferior parietal lobule to be concerned with body image: Lesions of this cortex lead to severe "neglect" of the opposite side of the body and this is especially severe when the lesion is in the right hemisphere. The lesions are often deep involving the precuneus and its connections (Pribram & MacLean, 1953) with the cingulate and retrosplenical portions of the limbic cortex (Geschwind, 1965).

What seems to be a more accurate reading of current available evidence is that there is a balance between the parietal and far frontal and temporal polar portions of this cortex which processes self. While lesions of the parietal cortex lead to neglect, lesions of the frontal and temporal poles lead to its opposite (Geschwind, 1965; Teuber, 1972). Patients with far frontal and temporal lobe involvement tend to talk and write voluminously about themselves and, as noted, to lose control over behavior that is context-sensitive, that is, behavior which depends on some stable mnemonically organized self. These observations fit the suggestion made earlier on anatomical grounds that the far frontal and temporal cortex operates to combine the protocritic and effective poles of the respective dimensions.

The cortical contribution to emotion thus relates the affective–effective dimension to the protocritic–epicritic in such a way that a new dimension, labeled ethical–esthetic, emerges. This new dimension is based on the construction of a self-concept, which is organized and enhanced by parietal—and selectively inhibited (made context sensitive) by frontal cortical functioning. The construction is achieved in human beings by combining a frontolimbic protocritic versus cortical convexity epicritic axis with limbic affective versus a basal ganglia effective axis. The poles of each axis have been found to oppose each other (Lassonde, Ptito, & Pribram, 1981; Pribram, Lassonde, & Ptito, 1981; Spinelli & Pribram, 1967) in such a way that a combinatorial balance of control is achieved (Jackson, 1873).

CONCLUSION

Current physiological data support a multidimensional view of the organization of emotional and motivational feelings and expressions. A *labile-stabile dimension* is discerned as operating by virtue of corebrain homeostatic feedback mechanisms. However, homeostats become biased by brain stem activation. This results in mechanisms which can be reset by a variety of internal and external contingencies.

Neither the homeostats nor the mechanisms that determine their setpoints are unimodal. A variety of emotional and motivational processes (e.g., elation, depression, hunger, thirst) have been shown to be intimately related to specifyable neurochemical organizations. This is a very active field of investigation which holds that the neurochemistry of many more feeling states will be specified.

The determination of setpoints has been shown to be guided by at least three distinct processes: phasic arousal, chronic activation, and tonic effort. The mechanisms involved are located in the forebrain; all of them regulate and are regulated by structures which compose the territory of the mesencephalic reticular formation.

The forebrain arousal, activation and effort mechanisms which determine setpoints on homeostatic regulations are intimately connected, as well, with spinal and brainstem pain and temperature systems. Sensory processes can be divided into those which display local sign (can be located in time and place) and those which do not. Following Henry Head (1920), those which display local sign are called epicritic. These sensory processes have been traced to the parieto-temporo-occipital portion, i.e., the posterior convexity of the cerebral hemisphere.

By contrast, those aspects of pain and temperature sensibility (and perhaps these same aspects of other senses) which do not display local sign, have been traced to the far frontal and temporal polar portions of the cerebral hemispheres. In a slight modification of Head's terminology, these aspects of sensation are called protocritic.

Thus, the second dimension of the organization of emotional and motivational feelings and expression is the *epicritic–protocritic*. As in the case of the labile–stabile dimension, the epicritic–protocritic dimension applies to the variety of specific emotional and motivational feelings and expressions.

A third dimension is embodied in the distinction between emotion and motivation, between feelings and expressions, and between arousal and activation. This dimension is an *affective–effective dimension*. Neurologically it is manifest in the distinction between limbic (including the amygdala, n. accumbeus and mesolimbic systems) forebrain and the caudate nucleus of the basal ganglia.

Finally, at the cortical level, still another dimension is introduced. I have called this an *esthetic–ethical dimension* but a somewhat more descriptive term would be a dimension which at one pole constructs a world beyond the skin and at the other, a self-reflective world within. The construction of the external pole of this dimension is based on the cortical systems composing and surrounding the major cerebral fissures. Its internal pole is based on the cortex that lies between the perifissural cortex with strong connections to the limbic forebrain.

The identification by neurophysiological and neuropsychological methods of these dimensions still leaves unexplained how it is that we can distinguish anger from fear, acceptance from rejection, joy from sadness, and each of these pairs from one another. Schachter and others have suggested that environmental context determines the labels that we place on some more basic physiological processes. But, as noted, Schachter (1967), by using only adrenalin in his experiments, came to focus on only one such basic process, one which determines the intensity of experience. Others, e.g., Tomkins (this volume) and Koestler (1967) have also called attention to the amplifying dimension which emotions and motivations exercise. But as we have seen this amplifying, intensive aspect of emotions and motivations, subsumed here under the rubric "protocritic," is only one of a set of dimensions that characterize these processes.

A more promising lead (which also takes situation into account) for relating the dimensions identified by neuroscience research to the nuances of feelings comes from the work of Plutchik, Tomkins, Ekman and others (this volume) who have used scaling techniques and facial expression in an attempt to classify the indicators of feelings and to relate this classification to the psychophysiological variables (such as GSR and heart rate) which were also used in the neuroscience studies reviewed here. Plutchik, for example, has identified four processes basic to his classification: (1) control–dyscontrol; (2) toward–away; (3) gain–loss; and (4) in–out. It is tempting to identify the control–dyscontrol process with the stabile–labile dimension; the toward–away process with the effective–affective dimension; the gain–loss process with the protocritic–epicritic dimension; and the in–out process with the ethical–esthetic dimension. Ekman is currently linking facial expression of specific emotional and motivational experiences to *patterns* of psychophysiological indicators. This research is in a position to validate the identity between Plutchik's processes (derived from factoring the reports of specific emotional and motivational experiences) and the neurologically based dimensions described in this chapter (which were derived by relating manipulations of neural systems to patterns of psychophysiological indicators). Should such a convergence of results of different research programs materialize a major step will have been achieved in understanding the physiology of the emotions and motivations which so enrich our personal and interpersonal lives.

REFERENCES

Adey, W.R., Kado, R.T., & Didio, J. Impedence measurements in brain tissue of animals using microvolt signals. *Experimental Neurology*, 1962, 5, 47–66.

Arnold, M.B. *Emotion and personality, Vol. II. neurological and physiological aspects.* New York: Columbia University Press, 1960.

Bagshaw, M. H., Benzies, S. Multiple measures of the orienting reaction and their dissociation after amygdalectomy in monkeys. *Experimental Neurology*, 1968, 20, 175–187.

Bagshaw, M.H., Kimble, D.P., & Pribram, K.H. The GSR of monkeys during orienting and habituation and after ablation of the amygdala, hippocampus and interotemporal cortex. *Neuropsychologia*, 1965, 3, 111–119.

Bagshaw, M.H., & Pribram, K.H. Cortical organization in gustation (Macaca mulatta). *Journal of Neurophysiology*, 1953, 16, 499–508.

Bard, P., & Rioch, D. A study of four cats deprived of neocortex and additional portions of the forebrain. *Johns Hopkins Hospital Bulletin 60*, 1937, 73–147.

Benson, A. Symposium VIII, Munksgaard, 1975, *Brain Work.*

Bohus, B. The hippocampus and the pituitary adrenal system hormones. In R.L. Isaacson & K.H. Pribram (Eds.), *The hippocampus.* New York: Plenum, 1976.

Brobeck, J.R. Review and synthesis. In M.A. Brazier (Ed.), *Brain and Behavior* (Vol. II). Washington, D.C.: American Institute of Biological Sciences, 1963.

Brody, B.A., & Pribram, K.H. The role of frontal and parietal cortex in cognitive processing: Tests of spatial and sequence functions. *Brain*, 1978, 101, 607–633.

Brown, T.S. Olfactory and visual discrimination in the monkey after selective lesions of the temporal lobe. *Journal of Comparative and Physiological Psychology*, 1963, 56, 764–768.

Brown, T.S., Rosvold, H.E., & Mishkin, M. Olfactory discrimination after temporal lobe lesions in monkeys. *Journal of Comparative Physiological Psychology*, 1963, *56*, 190–195.

Bull. N. The attitude theory of emotion. *Nervous and Mental Disease Monographs*, 1951(*81*).

Cannon, W.B. The James-Lange theory of emotions: A critical examination and an alternative theory. *American Journal of Psychology*, 1927, *39*, 106–124.

Chin, J.H., Pribram, K.H., Drake, K., & Greene, L.O., Jr. Disruption of temperature discrimination during limbic forebrain stimulation in monkeys. *Neuropsychologia*, 1976, *14*, 293–310.

Darwin, C. *The expression of the emotions in man and animals*. Chicago: University of Chicago Press, 1965.

Dewson, J.H., III. Preliminary evidence of hemispheric asymmetry of auditory function in monkeys. In S. Harnard, R.W. Doty, J. Jaynes, L. Goldstein, & G. Crauthamer (Eds.), *Lateralization in the nervous system*. New York: Academic Press, 1977.

Dewson, J.H., III, & Cowey, A. Discrimination of auditory sequences by monkeys. *Nature*, 1969, *222*, 695–697.

Dewson, J.H., III., Pribram, K.H., & Lynch, J. Effects of ablations of temporal cortex on speech sound discrimination in monkeys. *Experimental Neurology*, 1969, *24*, 579–591.

Fair, C.M. *The physical foundations of the psyche*. Middletown, Conn.: Wesleyan University Press, 1963.

Gall, F. J., & Spurzheim, G. [Research on the nervous system in general and on that of the brain in particular.] F. Schoell, Paris, 1809. In K.H. Pribram (Ed.), *Brain and Behavior I*. Middlesex, New Jersey: Penguin Books, 1969.

Gastaut, H. Interpretation of the symptoms of ''psychomotor'' epilepsy in relation to physiologic data on rhinencephalic function. *Epilepsia*, Series III, 1954, *3*, 84–88.

Geschwind, N. Disconnexion syndromes in animals and man: Part I. *Brain* 1965, *88*, 237–294.

Goldman, P.S., & Nauta, W.J.H. An intricately patterned prefrontocaudate projection in the rhesus monkey. *Journal of Comparative Neurology*, 1977, *171*(3), 369–384.

Grossman, S.P. The VMH: A center for affective reaction, satiety, or both? *Physiology and Behavior*, 1966, *1*;10.

Head, H. *Studies in neurology*. Oxford: Medical Publications, 1920.

Hebb, D.O. Drives and the CNS (conceptual nervous system). *Psychological Review*, 1955, *62*, 243–254.

Hess, W.R. *Diencephalon: Autonomic and extrapyramidal functions*. New York: Grune & Stratton, 1954.

Hinde, R.A. Factors governing the changes in strength of a partially inborn response, as shown by the mobbing behavior of the chaffinch (Fringilla coelebs). I. The nature of the response, and an examination of its course. *Proceedings of the Royal Society*, 1954, *142*, 306–331.(a)

Hinde, R.A. Factors governing the changes in strength of a partially inborn response, as shown by the mobbing behavior of the chaffinch (Fringilla coelebs). II. The waning of the response. *Proceedings of the Royal Society*, 1954, *142*, 331–358.(b)

Isaacson, R.L., & Pribram, K.H. (Eds.) *The hippocampus, Vol. II: neurophysiology and behavior*. New York: Plenum, 1976.

Jackson, J.H. *Clinical and physiological researches on the nervous system*. London: J. and A. Churchill, 1873.

James, W. *Principles of psychology* (Vol. I). New York: Dover, 1890.(a)

James, W. *Principles of psychology* (Vol. II). New York: Dover, 1890.(b)

Jones, E.G. The anatomy of extrageniculostriate visual mechanisms. In F.O. Schmitt & F.G. Worden (Eds.), *The neurosciences third study program*. Cambridge, Mass.: MIT Press, 1973.

Kaada, B.R., Pribram, K.H., & Epstein, J.A. Respiratory and vascular responses in monkeys from temporal pole, insula, orbital surface and cingulate gyrus. A preliminary report. *Journal of Neurophysiology*, 1949, *12*, 347–356.

Kantor, J.R., & Smith, N.W. *The science of psychology: An interbehavioral survey*. Chicago: Principia Press, 1975.

Kemp, J.M., & Powell, T.P.S. The cortico-striate projection in the monkey. *Brain*, 1970, *93*, 525–546.

Kimble, D.P., Bagshaw, M.H., & Pribram, K.H. The GSR of monkeys during orienting and habituation after selective partial ablations of the cingulate and frontal cortex. *Neuropsychologia*, 1965, *3*, 121–128.

King, M.B., & Hoebel, B.G. Killing elicited by brain stimulation in rats. *Communications in Behavioral Biology*, Part A., 1968, *2*, 173–177.

Koestler, A. *The ghost in the machine*. London: Hutchinson of London, 1967.

Krasne, F.B. General disruption resulting from electrical stimulation of ventro-medial hypothalamus. *Science*, 1962, *138*, 822–823.

Kruger, L., & Michel, F. A single neuron analysis of buccal cavity representation in the sensory trigeminal complex of the cat. *Archives of Oral Biology*, 1962, *7*, 491–503.

Lacey, B.C., & Lacey, J.I. Studies of heart rate and other bodily processes in sensorimotor behavior. In P.A. Obrist, A. Black, J. Bruner, & L. DiCara (Eds.), *Cardiovascular psychophysiology: Current issues in response mechanisms, biofeedback and methodology*. Chicago: Aldine-Atherton, 1974.

Lashley, K. *The thalamus and emotion. In F.A. Beach, D.O. Hebb, C.T. Morgan, & H.W. Nissen (Eds.), The neurospsychology of Lashley*. New York: McGraw-Hill, 1960.

Lassonde, M.C., Ptito, M., & Pribram, K.H. Are the basal ganglia only motor structures? *Programs and Abstracts*, American Physiological Society, 1975.

Lassonde, M., Ptito, M., & Pribram, K.H. Intracerebral influences on the microstructure of receptive fields of cat visual cortex. *Experimental Brain Research*. 1981, *43*, 131–144.

Li, C.L., Cullen, C., & Jasper, H.H. Laminar microelectrode analysis of cortical unspecific recruiting responses and spontaneous rhythms. *Journal of Neurophysyiology*, 1956, *19*, 131–143.(a)

Li, C.L., Cullen, C., & Jasper, H.H. Laminar microelectrode studies of specific somatosensory cortical potentials. *Journal of Neurophysiology*, 1956, *19*, 111–130.(b)

Liebeskind, J.C., Mayer, D.J., & Akil, H. Central mechanisms of pain inhibition: Studies of analgesia from focal brain stimulation. In J.J. Bonica (Ed.), *Advances in neurology, Vol. 4: Pain*. New York: Raven Press, 1974.

Lindsley, D.B. Emotion. In S.S. Stevens (Ed.), *Handbook of experimental psychology*. New York: Wiley, 1951.

MacLean, P.D. Psychosomatic disease and the "visceral brain," recent developments bearing on the Papez theory of emotion. *Psychosomatic Medicine* II, 1950, 338–353.

Mandler, G. The interruption of behavior. In D. Levine (Ed.), *Nebraska Symposium on Motivation*. Lincoln: University of Nebraska Press, 1964.

McEwen, B.S., Gerlach, J.L., & Micco, D.J. Putative glucocortical receptors in hippocampus and other regions of the rat brain. In R.L. Isaacson & K.H. Pribram (Eds.), *The hippocampus*. 1976.

Miller, G.A., Galanter, E.H., & Pribram, K.H. *Plans and the structure of behavior*. New York: Henry Holt & Co., 1960.

Miller, N.E., Bailey, C.J., & Stevenson, J.A. Decreased "hunger" but increased food intake resulting from hypothalamic lesions. *Science*, 1950, *112*, 256–259.

Mountcastle, V.B., Lynch, J.C., Georgopoulos, A., Sakata, H., & Acuna, C. Posterior parietal association cortex of the monkey: Command functions for operations within extrapersonal space. *Journal of Neurophysiology*, 1975, *38*, 871–908.

Nauta, W.J.H. Some efferent connections of the prefrontal cortex in the monkey. In J.M. Warren & K. Akert (Eds.), *The frontal granular cortex and behavior*. New York: McGraw-Hill, 1964.

Neff, D. Neural mechanisms of auditory discrimination. In W.A. Rosenblith (Ed.), *Sensory communication*. New York: Wiley, 1961.

Papez, J.W. A proposed mechanism of emotion. *Archives of Neurological Psychiatry* Chicago, 1937, *38*, 725–743.

Pribram, K.H. Toward a science of neuropsychology (method and data). In R.A. Patton (Ed.),

Current trends in psychology and the behavioral sciences. Pittsburgh: University of Pittsburgh Press, 1954.

Pribram, K.H. Comparative neurology and the evolution of behavior. In A. Roe & G.G. Simpson (Eds.), *Behavior and evolution.* New Haven: Yale University Press, 1958. (a)

Pribram, K.H. The new neurology and the biology of emotion: A structural approach. *American Psychologist,* 1967, *22,* 830–838.

Pribram, K.H. Feelings as monitors. In M.B. Arnold (Ed.), *Feelings and emotions.* New York: Academic Press, 1970.

Pribram, K.H. *Languages of the brain: Experimental paradoxes and principles in neuropsychology.* Englewood Cliffs, N.J.: Prentice Hall, 1971. (Reprinted 1977 Brooks-Cole; 1982 Brandon House Press.)

Pribram, K.H. How is it that sensing so much we can do so little? In F.O. Schmitt (Ed.), *The neurosciences third study program.* Cambridge, Mass.: MIT Press, 1974.

Pribram, K.H. Peptides and protocritic processes. In L.H. Miller, C.A. Sandman, & A.J. Kastin (Eds.), *Neuropeptide influences on the brain and behavior.* New York: Raven Press, 1977. (a)

Pribram, K.H. New dimensions in the functions of the basal ganglia. In C. Shagass, S. Gershon, & A.J. Freidhoff (Eds.), *Psychopathology and brain dysfunction.* New York: Raven Press, 1977. (b)

Pribram, K.H. Modes of central processing in human learning. In T. Teyler (Ed.), *Brain and learning.* Stamford, Conn.: Greylock, 1978.

Pribram, K.H., & Bagshaw, M. Further analysis of the temporal lobe syndrome utilizing fronto-temporal ablations. *Journal of Comparative Neurology,* 1953, *99,* 347–375.

Pribram, K.H., & Barry, J. Further behavioral analysis of the parieto-temporo-preoccipital cortex. *Journal of Neurophysiology,* 1956, *19,* 99–106.

Pribram, K.H., Kruger, L., Robinson, F., & Berman, A.J. The effects of precentral lesions on the behavior of monkeys. *Yale Journal of Biology and Medicine,* 1956, *28,* 428–443.

Pribram, K.H., & MacLean, P.D. Neuronographic analysis of medial and basal cerebral cortex. II. Monkey. *Journal of Neurophysiology,* 1953, *16,* 324–340.

Pribram, K.H., Lassonde, M.C., & Ptito, M. Classification of receptive field properties in cat visual cortex. *Experimental Brain Research,* 1981, *43,* 119–130.

Pribram, K.H., & McGuinness, D. Arousal, activation and effort in the control of attention. *Psychological Review,* 1975, *82*(2), 116–149.

Pribram, K.H., Reitz, S., McNeil, M., & Spevack, A.A. The effect of amygdalectomy on orienting and classical conditioning. In *Mechanisms of Formation and Inhibition of Conditional Reflex.* (Asratyan Festschrift). Moscow: Publishing office "Nauka" of the USSR Academy of Sciences, 1974.

Reitz, S.L., & Pribram, K.H. Some subcortical connections of the inferotemporal gyrus of monkey. *Experimental Neurology,* 1969, *25,* 632–645.

Richardson, D.E., & Akil, H. Chronic self-administration of brain stimulation for pain relief in human patients. *Proceedings of the American Association of Neurological Surgeons,* St. Louis, Missouri, 1974.

Riesen, H., Rigter, H., & Geven, H.M. Critical appraisal of peptide pharmacology. In L.H. Miller, C.A. Sandman, & A.J. Kastin (Eds.), *Neuropeptide influences on brain and behavior.* New York: Raven Press, 1977.

Schachter, S. In D.C. Glass (Ed.), *Neurophysiology and emotion.* New York: Rockefeller University Press—Russell Sage Foundation, 1967.

Schachter, S., & Singer, T.E. Cognitive, social and physiological determinants of emotional state. *Psychological Review,* 1962, *69,* 379–397.

Sokolov, E.H. Neuronal models and the orienting reflex. In M.A.B. Brazier (Ed.), *The central nervous system and behavior.* New York: Josiah Macy Jr. Foundation, 1960.

Spinelli, D.N., & Pribram, K.H. Changes in visual recovery functions produced by temporal lobe stimulation in monkeys. *Electroencephalography and Clinical Neurophysiology*, 1966, *20*, 44–49.

Spinelli, D.N., & Pribram, K.H. Changes in visual recovery functions and unit activity produced by frontal and temporal cortex stimulation. *Electroencephalography and Clinical Neurophysiology* 1967, *22*, 143–149.

Stein, L. Reward transmitters: Catecholamines and opioid peptides. In M.A. Lipton, A. DiMascio, & K.R. Killam (Eds.), *Psychopharmacology: A generation of progress*. New York: Raven Press, 1978.

Teuber, H.L. Unity and diversity of frontal lobe functions. In J. Konorski, H.L. Teuber, & B. Zerniki (Eds.), *ACTA Neurogiologiae Experimentalis: The Frontal Granular Cortex and Behavior*, 1972, *32*(2), 615–656.

Von Bechterev, W. *Die Funktionen der Nervencentra*. Berlin: Fischer-Verlag, 1911.

Von Bonin, G., & Bailey, P. The neocortex of Macaca mulatta. *Illinois Monographs in the Medical Sciences*. Urbana: University of Illinois Press, 1947, *5*(4).

Wall, P.D., & Pribram, K.H. Trigeminal neurotomy and blood pressure responses from stimulation of lateral cortex of macaca mulatta. *Journal of Neurophysiology*, 1950, 25, 258–263.

Walter, W.G. Electrical signs of association, expectancy, and decision in the human brain. *Electroencephalography and Clinical Neurophysiology* 1967, *25*, 258–263.

Weiskrantz, L. Striate and posterior association cortex interactions. *The Neurosciences*, 1973, *3*.

Wilson, M. Effects of circumscribed cortical lesions upon somesthetic and visual discrimination in the monkey. *Journal of Comparative Psychology*, 1957, *50*, 630–635.

2 Hemispheric Asymmetry and Emotion

Richard J. Davidson
State University of New York, Purchase

INTRODUCTION

Although not as well-studied as asymmetries for cognition, affective asymmetries have been receiving increasing attention in the literature (e.g., Davidson, 1983a; see also Denneberg, 1981 for a review of relevant animal data), and most investigators would now agree that the two hemispheres of the human brain differentially contribute to certain forms of affective behavior. The specific nature of these hemispheric differences and the particular parameters of emotion which are asymmetrically organized in the cortex are not fully known.

The principal purpose of this chapter is to selectively review data from my laboratory in this area. These findings, primarily derived from the study of normal subjects, are preceded by a brief review of portions of the clinical literature which provided the impetus for much of our own research. These reviews are followed by a general discussion of what the asymmetries for emotion reflect. Speculations on which components of emotion are associated with differential activation of specific hemispheric regions are provided. In addition, suggestions concerning the essential continuum along which the hemispheres are lateralized in the affective domain are offered.

Recent studies on both normal and clinical populations are beginning to challenge an early hypothesis which regarded the right hemisphere as the "seat of emotion" in humans. The data are more consistent with the notion of differential lateralization for at least certain positive and negative emotions. This latter view holds that certain regions of the left hemisphere are specialized for the processing of certain forms of positive affect while corresponding regions of the right hemisphere are specialized for the processing of certain forms of negative affect.

As the reader shall note, several ambiguities are contained in the position described earlier: (1) The specific hemispheric regions associated with the affective asymmetry are left unstated; (2) the precise emotions for which this asymmetry exists is not indicated; and (3) the specific parameters of emotion that are asymmetrically lateralized are not specified. In other words, is the asymmetry associated with the perception of emotion? The experience of emotion? The expression of emotion? The available data allow us to tentatively provide an answer to the first source of ambiguity—the specific regions within the hemispheres which show functional asymmetries during emotion. No direct evidence exists on the remaining two questions. Preliminary responses to these questions are provided in the final section of the chapter.

DATA ON CLINICAL POPULATIONS

Numerous early reports have noted a high incidence of negative affect and "catastrophic reactions" among patients with unilateral left hemisphere damage (Alford, 1933; Goldstein, 1939), and predominantly indifference or euphoric reactions among patients with unilateral right hemisphere damage (e.g., Denny-Brown, Meyer & Horenstein, 1952; Hécaen, Ajuriaguerra & Massonet, 1951). The catastrophic reaction is characterized by excessive negative affect, fear, and pessimism about the future; the indifference reaction is associated with a lack of emotional responsivity as well as anosognosia; the euphoric reaction includes inappropriate displays of positive affect, joking, and laughing.

Gainotti (1969, 1972) was one of the first investigators to systematically compare the emotional behavior of patients with left versus right unilateral lesions. In a large series of patients he found that those with left-sided lesions more frequently displayed the catastrophic reaction whereas patients with right-sided lesions were found to display inappropriate positive affect and indifference. The category of behavior most frequent among right damaged patients was joking.

Consistent findings were obtained in a recent review of 109 cases of pathological laughter and crying (Sackeim, Weinman, Gur, Greenberg, Hungerbuhler & Geschwind, 1982). These investigators found that left-sided lesions were more frequently associated with crying; right-sided lesions were often associated with laughing.

Research on other clinical populations using different methods is also generally consistent with the brain damage evidence. Relevant findings on the effects of intracarotid sodium amytal and unilateral and bilateral ECT on emotional processes have been reviewed elsewhere (see Davidson, 1983a).

An important series of studies has been recently performed which evaluated the effects of location of lesion within the left hemisphere and its relation to the severity of depression (Benson, 1973, 1979; Robinson & Benson, 1981; Robinson & Szetda, 1981). Benson (1973) found that depression was more severe in patients with anterior aphasias and Robinson and Szetda (1981) reported that proximity of injury to the frontal lobe was strongly correlated with the severity of depression. Robinson and Benson (1981) observed that depression among nonfluent aphasic patients was both more frequent and more severe compared with both fluent and global aphasics. Patients with nonfluent aphasias had lesions which were more anterior as assessed by CT scan compared with the other two groups. All patients with nonfluent aphasias had frontal lobe lesions. Importantly, lesion size was equivalent in the nonfluent and fluent aphasic groups. These findings indicate that damage to the left frontal region is most likely to be associated with depression. Posterior left hemisphere damage is less likely to be associated with depression.

These latter findings have important implications for uncovering possible hemispheric dysfunctions associated with depression. It is logical to assume that "psychiatric" forms of depression may have certain core neural substrates similar to those that produce depression in primary neurological illness.

Using bilateral EEG as a dependent measure of hemispheric engagement, Flor-Henry and his colleagues (Flor-Henry, Koles, Howarth, & Burton, 1979) found that psychotically depressed patients showed a bilateral increase in temporal power in the 13-20Hz (beta) band while at rest with eyes closed, relative to controls, with the energy distribution lateralized to the right hemisphere. A number of other investigators have observed relations between increased right-sided activation in anterior scalp leads and depression (e.g., Perris & Monakhov, 1979; Tucker, Stenslie, Roth, & Shearer, 1981). Some workers also reported a higher percentage of right- versus left-sided EEG abnormalities among depressed patients compared with controls (e.g., Abrams & Taylor, 1979).

We (Schaffer, Davidson, & Saron, 1983) have recently studied resting frontal and parietal EEG asymmetry in a group of subclinically depressed subjects and matched normal controls. We began by administering the Beck Depression Inventory (BDI; Beck, Ward, Mendelson, Mock, & Erbaugh, 1961) along with a number of other psychometric tests to 415 individuals. We then selected a group of depressed and nondepressed subjects who fell at the extremes of the distribution on the BDI. Subjects scoring 20 or above were asked to come to the laboratory as potential depressed subjects. Prior to the laboratory sessions, they were re-administered the BDI in two forms: one assessing trait characteristics and the other assessing state characteristics (i.e., according to how they felt at the moment). In order to participate further, the depressed subjects were required to score 14 or above on the trait scale. After excluding subjects for failing to meet these criteria and for excessively confounded EEG records, we were left with six depressed individuals. These subjects had a mean score of 29.7 (SD = 7.84) on the initial BDI, 25.7 (SD = 8.26) on the trait scale and 18.0 (SD = 5.9) on the state scale, the latter two administered just prior to the experimental session.

In selecting the control group, we wanted to obtain a sample of truly nondepressed subjects who were matched to the depressed group on sex, age, and marital status. Individuals were required to score 6 or below on the BDI to meet the initial criterion of nondepression. In order to screen out subjects who were defensively denying depression in their self-reports, we administered the Marlowe-Crowne Scale of Social Desirability (MC) (Crowne & Marlowe, 1964). By eliminating subjects who scored low on the BDI and high on the MC, we would be able to restrict our nondepressed sample to individuals who were nondefensively reporting nondepression. Subjects had to score 11 or below on the MC to meet the criterion for nonrepression. Therefore, subjects scoring 6 or below on the BDI *and* 11 or below on the MC were invited to the laboratory, if they also met the other subject characteristic criteria (i.e., sex, age, marital status, etc.). At the time of the laboratory session, the BDI was again readministered in both forms and subjects had to score 8 or below on trait scale to be tested. After eliminating subjects who failed to meet the criteria presented above, and subjects whose EEG records were excessively confounded, nine nondepressed subjects remained in the control group. All subjects were right-handed as assessed by the Edinborough Inventory (Oldfield, 1971). The psychometric characteristics of the final groups are summarized in Table 2.1.

Resting EEG was recorded both for eyes open and eyes closed for 30 sec periods prior to the administration of various cognitive and affective tasks. Alpha activity from left and right frontal and left and right parietal regions (F3, F4, P3 and P4) referenced to a common vertex (Cz) was extracted for all artifact-free epochs. The results revealed no group differences for either frontal or parietal EEG during the eyes open baseline period. However, for the eyes closed resting period, a significant ($p = .05$) group effect was obtained on a measure of frontal alpha asymmetry (($R-L/R+L$) alpha; higher numbers on this index reflect greater relative left-sided activation). The relevant means are presented in Table 2.2 and indicate that depressed subjects show greater relative right frontal activation compared with nondepressed subjects. Importantly, no significant group effects were obtained on the parietal ratio score, indicating that the group difference was specific to the frontal recordings.

TABLE 2.1
Psychometric Characteristics of the Depressed and Nondepressed
Groups[a]

		Initial BDI[b]	Trait BDI[c]	State BDI[c]	MC[d]
Depressed	X̄	29.7	25.7	18.0	12.8
(N = 6)	SD	7.84	8.26	5.9	.84
Nondepressed	X̄	4.2	4.8	4.3	8.4
(N = 9)	SD	1.39	2.11	2.35	2.65

[a]Adapted from Schaffer, Davidson and Saron, 1983.
[b]Administered 3 to 6 months prior to lab session.
[c]Administered at the lab session.
[d]Administered with the initial BDI.

TABLE 2.2
EEG Laterality Ratio Scores For Eyes Closed Rest for Depressed and
Nondepressed Subjects[a,b]

	Depressed		*Nondepressed*	
	F-Ratio[c]	*P-Ratio[d]*	*F-Ratio*	*P-Ratio*
$\bar{X}$	−.015*	.158	.034*	.072
SD	.059	.110	.031	.080

*p = .05.
[a]From Schaffer, Davidson and Saron, 1983.
[b]The ratio scores were computed with the following formula: R−L/R+L alpha. Higher numbers on this ratio are indicative of greater relative left-sided activation.
[c]F-Ratio was derived from left and right frontal leads.
[d]P-Ratio was derived from left and right parietal leads.

Figure 2.1 presents the individual subject means for the frontal region score derived from the eyes closed baseline, separately for each group. All nondepressed subjects showed frontal ratio scores indicative of relative left-sided activation, whereas 5 out of 6 depressed subjects showed the opposite pattern. This difference is significant ($X^2=7.81$, df=1, p < .01 with Yates' correction for continuity).

We examined the separate contributions of the left and right hemisphere to the frontal ratio score differences between groups and obtained a significant Group X

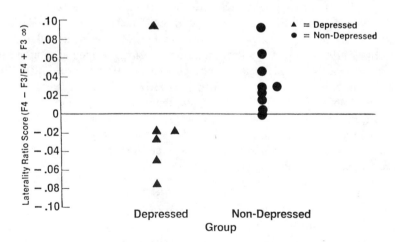

FIG. 2.1   Frontal laterality ratio (R-L/R+L alpha power) scores for individual subjects split by group. Positive numbers on this score are indicative of left-sided frontal activation while negative numbers are indicative of right-frontal activation. From Schaffer, Davidson and Saron (1983).

Hemisphere interaction (p=.007) which was a function of depressed subjects showing less alpha activity in the right versus left frontal region (p=.004); nondepressed subjects showed slightly less alpha in the left versus right frontal regions (p < .02). Thus, the major difference between groups is that depressed subjects show right frontal activation while nondepressed subjects show slight left frontal activation.

Three important conclusions emerge from the clinical data: (1) Left hemisphere damage is more likely than right to lead to an accentuation of negative affect and to the display of a catastrophic-depressive reaction; right hemisphere damage is more often associated with indifference or euphoria. (2) Individuals exhibiting depression have accentuated right hemisphere activation in particular cortical regions relative to controls. (3) These hemispheric differences are most apparent in the frontal region. It is likely that unilateral cortical damage results in a disturbance of the normal reciprocal inhibitory feedback between homologous hemispheric regions so that, for example, left frontal damage results in hyperactivation in the corresponding region on the right side (Flor-Henry, 1979).

The association of frontal lobe asymmetry with affective behavior is not surprising based upon the anatomical situation of this brain region as well as previous empirical findings relating the frontal lobes to affective regulation. The frontal lobes have more extensive anatomical reciprocity with limbic structures than any other cortical region (e.g., Kelly & Stinus, in press; Nauta, 1964; 1971). A variety of neuropsychological evidence links damage to particular areas of the frontal lobes to deficits in affective regulation (e.g., Akert, 1964; Baranovskaya & Homskaya, 1973; Luria, 1966; 1973; Pribram, 1973; Simernitskaya, 1973). In recent research, frontal lobe lesions have been found to markedly impair both voluntary and spontaneous facial expressions (Kolb & Milner, 1981 a,b). Interestingly, although they failed to comment on this, Kolb and Milner (1981a) found that left-sided frontal lesions resulted in significantly less spontaneous smiling compared with right-sided lesions. The specific manner in which the frontal lobes are asymmetrical is currently unknown. For example, it is possible that the frontal lobes are themselves structurally and neurochemically symmetrical but have asymmetrical connections with certain subcortical structures. It is also possible for the asymmetry to be entirely cortical. Answers to some of these questions may emerge from the various programs of animal research currently in progress (see Denenberg, 1981).

DATA ON NORMALS

Although the findings on clinical populations reviewed earlier provide important information on hemispheric involvement in affective regulation, the data are not always generalizable to the intact organism. In the study of brain-damaged patients, the lesions are often not discretely localized, introducing unwanted variability. Other problems exist in the study of psychiatric patients. The emotional landscape of individuals with affective disorders is complex and far from homogeneous. Therefore, it is never really clear which emotion one is assessing the neurophysiological substrates of, in studies of psychiatric patients.

Behavioral and electrophysiological data on normals from our laboratory are reviewed in the remainder of this section.

Our first efforts in this area used lateral eye movements as a dependent measure of hemispheric engagement (Schwartz, Davidson, & Maer, 1975). Problems surrounding the validity of this index as a measure of hemispheric engagement (e.g., Ehrlichman & Weinberger, 1978) have led us to abandon its use except as an exploratory tool (see Davidson, 1983a for a review of our early studies with this method).

A number of studies have utilized lateralized presentation of visual stimuli to study hemispheric differences in both the perception of and reactivity to emotional stimuli.

Suberi and McKeever (1977) studied recognition memory for emotional and nonemotional faces in each visual field. They found a greater left visual field (LVF) advantage (faster reaction time) in the recognition of emotional compared with nonemotional faces. Importantly, they also observed that sad faces produced the greatest left-visual field (right hemisphere) advantage while happy and angry faces were associated with the least LVF superiority.

In a similar vein, Ley and Bryden (1979) reported on a study where subjects were required to recognize schematic emotional faces that were tachistoscopically exposed to each visual field. Across all emotions, subjects on the average showed a left visual field advantage for this task. However, when the separate emotions were examined, it was found that subjects made more errors when extremely positive expressions were presented to the LVF compared with the presentation of extremely negative expressions to the same visual field.

In an experiment explicitly designed to assess differences in the perception of positive and negative affective stimuli, we (Reuter-Lorenz & Davidson, 1981) exposed subjects to a neutral and an emotional face of the same individual simultaneously, with one stimulus presented to the LVF and the other presented to the RVF. On each trial, subjects were required to indicate on which side the emotional face had been presented. Reaction time to the button press was obtained. We found that happy faces were responded to more quickly when presented to the RVF than when presented to the LVF. The opposite pattern of results was obtained in response to the sad faces (see Fig. 2.2).

In general, the data on differential lateralization in the perception of positive and negative emotional stimuli are somewhat inconsistent (e.g., Hirschman & Safer, in press). Laterality differences in the perception of stimuli differing in valence are not always found. It may be that such asymmetries in studies of the perception of affective stimuli obtain insofar as subjects covertly (or overtly) produce the affective expression that matches the stimulus in the act of percep-

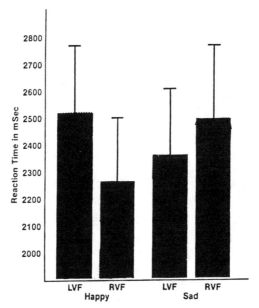

FIG. 2.2.   Mean reaction time (bars indicate standard errors) for happy and sad stimulus presentations, for each visual field. From Reuter-Lorenz and Davidson (1981).

tion. Recent data on the perception of emotional faces (Dimberg, 1982) indicates that subjects sometimes make a covert facial expression (as assessed with facial EMG) which mimics the expression to be perceived in a task requiring facial expression identification.

In addition to assessing asymmetries in the perception of emotional stimuli, lateralized visual stimulation techniques can be used to study differences in emotional response elicited by identical stimuli presented initially to the left versus right hemisphere. Dimond and his colleagues were explicitly concerned with examining left versus right hemisphere specialization for positive and negative affect (Dimond & Farrington, 1977; Dimond, Farrington, & Johnson, 1976). They developed a contact lens system whereby prolonged visual input can be projected to either the left or the right visual fields. Using such a system, films were projected separately to each visual field and were then subsequently rated on the nature of the affect elicited. Heart rate was recorded as a measure of autonomic reactivity. Dimond et al. (1976) found that when films were projected to the right hemisphere first (LVF) they were judged to be significantly more unpleasant than the same films initially projected to the left hemisphere (RVF). Moreover, Dimond and Farrington (1977) found that cartoons produced the greatest change in heart rate when projected to the left hemisphere, while more unpleasant or threatening films evoked the greatest heart rate changes when projected to the right hemisphere.

We have recently conducted an experiment (Davidson, Moss, Saron, Schaffer, & Mednick, 1983) in which 19 right-handed subjects were presented with affective or neutral faces unilaterally to either the left or right visual field for a prolonged 8 sec exposure. The stimuli were exposed for this duration because of pilot work that indicated subjects were unable to make the kinds of complex judgments asked for with durations that were any shorter. In order to ensure that subjects were centrally fixating throughout stimulus exposure, EOG was recorded and any trial associated with an eye movement of greater than 1° was omitted. Following presentation of the faces, subjects were asked to rate each face on the degree to which it expressed various emotions as well as on the degree to which it evoked various emotions in themselves (on 7 point scales). The reason for both types of questions was based on our belief that the asymmetry would be much stronger for ratings of subject's emotional *experience* compared with ratings of the stimulus.

Subjects' ratings of the degree to which each face *expressed* various emotions was uninfluenced by the hemifield to which the face was presented. However, when subjects were asked to rate the degree to which the face evoked various emotions in *themselves,* significant visual field effects emerged. Specifically, when asked to rate how happy they felt in response to the stimuli, subjects reported experiencing significantly more happiness in response to faces presented to the RVF (i.e., initially to the left hemisphere) compared with responses to the *identical faces* when presented to the LVF. This effect held irrespective of the valence of the face. That is, more happiness was reported in response to RVF presentations of all faces, compared with LVF exposures. The data on ratings of happiness and sadness in response to happy and sad faces exposed to the RVF and LVF are presented in Table 2.3. Subjects report more happiness in response to RVF presentations of happy and sad faces compared with LVF presentations of these identical faces. The data on sadness ratings are in the predicted direction, i.e., higher ratings of sadness in response to LVF compared with RVF presentations. However, these latter findings are clearly nonsignificant.

The findings on asymmetries in self-reports of emotional experience suggest that the hemispheres may differ in their characteristic affective bias. When input initially goes to the left hemisphere, subjects' respond slightly but consistently more positively, irrespective of the valence of the stimuli.

In order to more precisely pinpoint the locus of the asymmetry for affect in normal subjects, we have recorded the spontaneous EEG from homologous left and right scalp leads in different regions to infer asymmetrical patterns of brain activation along the anterior–posterior plane. This methodology has a number of important advantages in the study of asymmetries associated with affect. It does not require special constraints on stimulus exposures as do the behavioral methods of inferring hemispheric involvement. The procedure allows the investigator to present continuous stimulation which is likely to actually elicit emotion in the observer. For example, emotional films can be presented while EEG is recorded from various scalp loci. Differences in patterns of EEG activation can then be

TABLE 2.3

Self-ratings of Happiness and Sadness in Response to Happy and Sad
Faces Presented to the Left and Right Visual Fields[a,b]

		Rating of Happiness		Ratings of Sadness	
		Face		Face	
		Happy	Sad	Happy	Sad
Hemifield					
Left	$\bar{X}$	3.19	1.95	1.98	2.65
	SD	1.26	.91	.91	.86
Right	$\bar{X}$	3.26	2.31	1.92	2.59
	SD	1.30	.86	.82	1.06

[a]Adapted from Davidson et al., 1983.
[b]Ratings are based on a 7 point scale.

examined as a function of subject self-reports of their affective response to the stimulation.

This is a strategy we have used in a number of studies conducted in our laboratory. We have been specifically interested in comparing frontal and parietal EEG asymmetries in response to various positive and negative affective stimuli. Based upon the literature previously reviewed, we hypothesized that epochs during which subjects report positive affect would be associated with greater relative left frontal activation compared with epochs during which subjects report negative affect. We also predicted that parietal EEG asymmetry would not differentiate between positive and negative epochs.

In one study (Davidson, Schwartz, Saron, Bennett, & Goleman, 1979), 16 right-handed subjects were exposed to videotaped segments of popular television programs which were judged to vary in affective content. While viewing the videotapes, subjects were instructed to continuously rate the degree to which they experienced positive versus negative affect by pressing up and down on a pressure sensitive gauge. The output of this pressure transducer was digitized to provide a quantitative measure of affective self-report.

EEG was recorded from the left and right frontal (F3 and F4) and left and right parietal (P3 and P4) regions referred to a common vertex (Cz). Activity in the alpha band was extracted from the EEG, integrated and digitized. EOG was also recorded and epochs confounded by eye movement artifact were eliminated. In order to obtain an independent measure of the subject's affective response to the video stimuli, two channels of facial EMG were also recorded, one from the zygomatic major region (the "smile" muscle), and one from the frontalis region (Schwartz, Fair, Salt, Mandel, & Klerman, 1976). EMG data were also integrated and digitized.

In order to test our major hypotheses, we compared the 30 sec epoch each subject judged to be most positive with one rated as most negative. This information was derived from the pressure transducer data. The positive and negative epochs deviated from the central neutral position by comparable amounts. It is important to emphasize that the positive and negative epochs were individually obtained for each subject on the basis of his or her self-reports. We believe that this methodological approach is superior to analyses based upon a priori classification of stimulus conditions.

We first compared the positive and negative epochs on the laterality alpha ratio score (R−L/R+L alpha power). Higher numbers on this score indicate greater relative left-sided activation. We found that positive epochs elicited significantly greater relative left frontal activation compared with negative epochs (p=.02). Parietal asymmetry did not distinguish between conditions. These data are displayed in Table 2.4. Interestingly, parietal EEG indicated that subjects showed right-sided activation in both positive and negative epochs. Analysis of the separate contributions of the left and right frontal sites to the ratio score difference revealed that positive epochs were associated with less left hemisphere and more right hemisphere alpha compared with negative epochs.

To independently examine the impact of self-rated positive and negative epochs on a physiological system which has been found in previous research to discriminate between self-generated positive and negative imagery, we examined the integrated EMG recorded from the zygomatic and frontalis muscle regions. As Table 2.5 reveals, positive segments elicited more zygomatic and less frontalis activity than negative segments (p=.04). The EMG data confirm that subjects self-reports were indeed associated with expected changes in facial muscle activity.

We have confirmed this general pattern of results in a second study using the generation of affective imagery as the independent variable (Bennett, Davidson,

TABLE 2.4
Frontal and Parietal Laterality Ratio Scores for
Self-rated Extreme Positive and Negative
Epochs[a,b]

		Positive	Negative
Frontal Ratio[c]	X̄	.102	−.154
	SD	.358	.365
Parietal Ratio	X̄	−.046	−.119
	SD	.236	.209

[a]Adapted from Davidson et al. (1979).
[b]N = 16.
[c]The ratio scores consist of R−L/R+L alpha.

TABLE 2.5
Zygomatic and Frontalis EMG for Self-rated
Extreme Positive and Negative Epochs[a,b]

		Positive	Negative
Zygomatic EMG[c]	X̄	263.63	222.19
	SD	157.71	150.46
Frontalis EMG	X̄	188.88	201.50
	SD	39.52	44.68

[a]Adapted from Davidson et al. (1979).
[b]N = 16.
[c]Units are arbitrary.

& Saron, 1981). Other investigators have also found that frontal (e.g., Tucker, Stenslie, Roth, & Shearer, 1981) and temporal (Karlin, Weinapple, Rochford, & Goldstein, 1978) EEG asymmetry discriminates between positive and negative affective states in the same direction.

We have recently been studying EEG asymmetries in response to emotional stimuli in infants to explore the ontogeny of affective lateralization. Our initial studies (Davidson & Fox, 1982) focused on 10-month old babies since, by this age, the infant is capable of expressing a wide range of both positive and negative affects. We expected 10 month olds to show the same pattern of frontal lobe asymmetry as adults in response to positive and negative stimuli.

Thirty-eight 10-month old female infants were seen in the two studies. From these, we were able to obtain artifact-free data from 24 infants. Only infants born to right-handed parents were tested. The methods for both studies were virtually equivalent. The infant sat in her mother's lap facing a 21″ (diagonal) video monitor. EEG was recorded from the left and right frontal and parietal regions referred to a common vertex and stored on separate channels on FM tape.

The positive and negative affective facial stimuli were embedded in a video recording of Sesame Street. The stimulus tape was sequenced in the following manner: 10 sec of a Sesame Street segment followed by 90 sec of an affective face segment, which was either happy or sad (counterbalanced across subjects). Following the first affective segment the infant viewed 90 sec of Sesame Street after which the second 90 sec affective segment occurred. Each affective segment consisted of a female actress who maintained a neutral face for 15 sec and then spontaneously broke into either smiling and laughing (happy segment) or frowning and crying (sad segment). The audio portion was edited out so as to match the happy and sad segments.

EEG in response to each segment from each of the four leads was reviewed and edited for gross eye movement, muscle and movement artifact. Artifact-free epochs were then filtered for 1–12 Hz activity. The filtered output was digitized and energy (in uv sec) in the 1–12 Hz band was computed separately for each of the four leads and each of the affective epochs.

TABLE 2.6
Frontal Ratio Scores (R−L/R+L 1–12 Hz
Activity) by Affect Condition for Studies I and II[a]

	Study I[b]		Study II[c]	
	Happy	Sad	Happy	Sad
X̄	.021	−.001	.073	.032
SD	.051	.032	.100	.115

[a]From Davidson and Fox, 1982.
[b]N = 10.
[c]N = 14.

In the second study (Davidson & Fox, 1982), an observer blind to the affective condition coded the infant's visual fixation and EEG was examined only for artifact-free epochs during which the infant was fixating on the monitor.

Laterality ratio scores (R−L/R+L 1–12 Hz power) were computed for frontal and parietal scalp leads. Parietal asymmetry did not discriminate between the happy and sad segments. The frontal ratio score data are presented in Table 2.6 and indicate that happy epochs are associated with greater relative left frontal activation compared with sad segments in both studies.

Across both studies, 20 of the 24 infants showed equal or greater relative left frontal activation during happy versus sad epochs.

These findings are consistent with the adult literature on frontal asymmetries in response to affective stimuli. It should be noted that one important difference exists in the pattern of data at each of the two age groups. In the adult study, the positive epochs were associated with left frontal activation *and* the negative epochs were associated with right frontal activation. In the infant data, the happy segment produced left frontal activation. In Study I, the sad segment produced hemispheric symmetry whereas in Study II, it simply produced less left frontal activation compared with the happy segment. It is not clear whether this difference is a function of age, or rather, a function of the different emotional states that were presumably elicited by the different stimulus conditions.

EMOTION SUBSYSTEMS AND AFFECTIVE ASYMMETRIES

The data previously reviewed clearly indicate that hemispheric differences exist in the affective domain. The findings strongly argue against the position that the right hemisphere is predominantly involved in all emotional behavior. The argument that the differences we and others have observed in EEG asymmetry between positive and negative affective stimulus conditions are due to intensity effects with the negative stimuli eliciting a more intense response is simply inadequate to account for the data. First, if this were true, we would expect to obtain main effects for Emotion condition (across hemisphere). Such a main effect would suggest that the conditions produced differences in overall cortical arousal, presumably as a function of differences in intensity. In none of our EEG studies have we obtained such effects. Moreover, in the adult data described earlier (see Table 2.4), the positive and negative epochs were judged to deviate from neutrality by comparable amounts. Finally, our behavioral data on self-ratings of emotion following lateralized exposure of affective stimuli indicates that subjects report more intense feelings of happiness in response to stimuli initially presented to the *left hemisphere*. Collectively, these data should finally put to rest the claim that the right hemisphere is the seat of emotion in man.

The electrophysiological data on clinical and normal adult samples, as well as infant samples, convincingly argue that the frontal region is an important site for affective asymmetry. Studies on all three populations have indicated that frontal lobe activation asymmetry discriminates between certain positive and negative emotion conditions. The data do not exclude the possibility that other cortical regions will also show similar patterns of activation asymmetry. In fact, a number of studies were briefly described (e.g., Flor-Henry et al., 1979; Karlin et al., 1978) which found similar asymmetries in the temporal region. Unfortunately, almost no information is currently available on tbe scalp topography of these asymmetries. However, based on anatomical evidence, it is likely that the frontal and temporal regions will be the two cortical sites for affective asymmetries since these areas have extensive anatomical connections to limbic structures which have been implicated in emotional behavior.

Based upon animal data, it is the orbital area of the frontal cortex that is most involved in the affective asymmetries as damage to this region produces more extreme emotional consequences than dorsolateral frontal lesions (see Fuster, 1980, for a review). Monkeys with orbital frontal lesions display a loss of vocalization, facial expression, and other forms of communication. After such frontal surgery, both male and female monkeys become generally less aggressive and lose both the zest and ability to compete for food, shelter, sex, and the company of others (e.g., Myers, 1972, 1975). Moreover, the orbital frontal-cortex is functional at an earlier age compared with dorsolateral frontal cortex. Frontal EEG in infants probably contains a significant orbital contribution although techniques are not currently available to disentangle orbital versus dorsolateral influences on scalp-recorded frontal EEG.

The current evidence on affective lateralization does not allow the precise specification of the discrete emotions that are most asymmetrically localized. Investigators have paid insufficient attention to precise definition of subjects' emotional states and have only used relatively crude self-report scales to index emotional experience. In our own studies (Davidson et al., 1979; Davidson & Fox, 1982) left frontal activation was observed: (1) in response to video stimuli that elicited self-reports of positive affect; (2) during eyes closed rest in normal subjects; and (3) during presentation of a videotape depicting an actress laughing and expressing happiness in 10-month old infants. At this point in our research program, the underlying commonality among these situations is not entirely apparent. It appears that left frontal activation is elicited when subjects are happy although we have not, up until now, utilized sufficiently precise behavioral methods to discriminate among other positive emotions.

We have observed absolute right frontal activation in two situations: (1) in response to video segments during which subjects reported experiencing intense negative affect; and (2) in depressed subjects during eyes closed rest. The sad video stimulus in our infant studies did not elicit absolute right frontal activation. Again, we currently have no basis for specifying more precisely which negative emotions are most strongly associated with right frontal engagement.

I have previously proposed (Davidson, 1983a) that approach/avoidance may be a more appropriate continuum than positive/negative on which to describe the affective asymmetries because anger, for example, appears to be lateralized in a manner similar to happiness (Suberi & McKeever, 1977). Anger is a negative emotion, probably often associated with approach behavior.

It is clear that the overt activation of approach or withdrawal behavior is *not* required to produce frontal activation asymmetries. In all of our studies which revealed significant EEG asymmetry differences between conditions, subjects were sitting in a chair and exhibited little overt action of any kind.

This observation is relevant to the question concerning which emotion sub-system is most strongly associated with the affective asymmetries discussed in this chapter. It seems apparent that the perception of emotion is inconsistently lateralized as a function of the valence of the stimulus to be perceived. Some studies have uncovered reliable differential asymmetries for the perception of certain positive and negative affective stimuli while others have not. In all of our EEG studies where visual stimuli have been used, we found that parietal EEG showed right-sided activation during negative *and* positive stimulus conditions. These findings suggest that the perception of at least visual emotional stimuli is associated with right parietal activation irrespective of the valence of the stimulus. Consistent with this view is the data on the effects of right parietal damage (e.g., Luria, 1973). Lesions in this region commonly produce deficits in affective facial recognition.

Thus, the frontal asymmetry is not likely to reflect the perception of emotion. Nor is it likely to directly reflect its expression. This statement is based upon many, but anecdotal observations of our subjects during conditions we have found to be associated with differential frontal lobe activation asymmetries. Because these impressions are anecdotal and not based upon rigorous examination of facial behavior during these situations, this claim must be treated cautiously at the present time. However, we observed little change in the facial expression of the 10-month old infants when they were exposed to the happy versus sad video segment, yet robust frontal asymmetry differences were obtained. Similarly, little difference in overt facial expression was apparent between the depressed versus nondepressed subjects during rest in the Schaffer et al. (1983) study described earlier. These admittedly preliminary observations suggest that expression changes are *not required* in order to observe differences in frontal activation asymmetry between two conditions.

Now that perception and expression have been at least tentatively ruled out as the subsystems which are most directly associated with the frontal asymmetries, what remains? I propose that what the frontal asymmetry most directly reflects is a central hedonic state that is often, although not always, correlated with emotional experience and which may be sometimes associated with expressive changes, the latter of which is dependent upon certain situational and contextual variables. This view holds that frontal asymmetries are correlated with emotional experience in individuals who are capable of veridically reporting on their internal states. In other research, we have demonstrated that individuals who exhibit repressive defensiveness show large dissociations between their verbal reports of internal states and other indices that more directly reflect these states (e.g., Davidson, 1983b; Weinberger, Schwartz, & Davidson, 1979). We would not expect repressors to show high correlations between their self-reports of emotional experience and frontal activation asymmetries.

The experiential differences between situations which elicit left versus right frontal lobe activation may also be associated with the initial activation of motor programs designed to initiate action sequences which reflect these emotional states. These motor programs may be expressed as both facial expressions and/or approach/withdrawal reactions. However, as I previously indicated, the overt expression of these actions is probably not necessary for the frontal asymmetries to be elicited. However, the presence of the frontal asymmetries may index the covert activation of these motor programs which in turn reflect a state of response preparedness. Definitive answers to these proposals probably must await studies on various neurological populations with paralysis of particular components of the skeletal-musculature.

The findings on affective lateralization indicate that an important cortical system which differentiates between certain positive and negative emotions exists in man. The presence of such a system provides a potentially important basis on which to differentiate among certain emotions. It is clear that a neurobiological/neuropsychological approach to emotion has much to contribute to understanding its basic nature.

ACKNOWLEDGMENT

Preparation of this chapter was supported in part by grants from the John D. and Catherine T. MacArthur Foundation and the Foundation for Child Development. I would like to thank Paul Ekman for sensitizing me to certain issues which I address in this chapter and Diana Angelini for her secretarial assistance.

REFERENCES

Abrams, R., & Taylor, M.A. Differential EEG patterns in affective disorder and schizophrenia. *Archives of General Psychiatry,* 1979, *36,* 1355–1358.

Akert, K. Comparative anatomy of frontal cortex and thalamofrontal connections. In J.M. Warren & K. Akert (Eds.), *The frontal granular cortex and behavior.* New York: McGraw-Hill, 1964.

Alford, L.B. Localization of consciousness and emotion. *American Journal of Psychiatry,* 1933, *12,* 789–799.

Baranovskaya, O.P., & Homskaya, E.B. Changes in the electroencephalogram frequency spectrum during the presentation of neutral and meaningful stimuli to patients with lesions of the frontal lobe. In K.H. Pribram & A.R. Luria, (Eds.), *Psychophysiology of the frontal lobes.* New York: Academic Press, 1973.

Beck, A.T., Ward, C.H., Mendelson, M., Mock, J., & Erbaugh, J. An inventory for measuring depression. *Archives of General Psychiatry,* 1961, *4,* 561–571.

Bennett, J., Davidson, R.J., & Saron, C. Patterns of self-rating in response to verbally elicited affective imagery: Relation to frontal vs. parietal EEG asymmetry. *Psychophysiology,* 1981, *18,* 158.

Benson, D.F. Psychiatric aspects of aphasia. *British Journal of Psychiatry.* 1973, *123,* 555–566.

Benson, D.F. *Aphasic, alexia and agraphia.* New York: Churchill-Livingstone, 1979.

Crowne, D.P., & Marlowe, D. *The approval motive: Studies in evaluative dependence.* New York: Wiley, 1964.

Davidson, R.J. Affect, cognition and hemispheric specialization. In C.E. Izard, J. Kagan, & R. Zajonc (Eds.), *Emotion, cognition and behavior.* New York: Cambridge University Press, 1983. (a)

Davidson, R.J. Affect, repression and cerebral asymmetry. In C. Van Dyke & L. Temoshok (Eds.), *Emotions in health and illness: Foundations of clinical practice.* New York: Academic Press, 1983. (b)

Davidson, R.J., & Fox, N.A. Asymmetrical brain activity discriminates between positive versus negative affective stimuli in human infants. *Science,* 1982, *218,* 1235–1237.

Davidson, R.J., Moss, E., Saron, C., Schaffer, C.E., & Mednick, D. *Self-reports of emotion are influenced by the visual field to which affective information is presented.* Submitted for publication, 1983.

Davidson, R.J., Schwartz, G.E., Saron, C., Bennett, J., & Goleman, D.J. Frontal versus parietal EEG asymmetry during positive and negative affect. *Psychophysiology,* 1979, *16,* 202–203.

Denenberg, V.H. Hemispheric laterality in animals and the effects of early experience. *The Behavioral and Brain Sciences,* 1981, *4,* 1–49.

Denny-Brown, D., Meyer, S.T., & Horenstein, S. The significance of perceptual rivalry resulting from parietal lesion. *Brain,* 1952, *75,* 433–471.

Dimberg, U. Facial reactions to facial expressions. *Psychophysiology,* 1982, *19,* 643–647.

Dimond, S., & Farrington, L. Emotional response to films shown to the right or left hemisphere of the brain measured by heart rate. *Acta Psychologia,* 1977, *41,* 255–260.

Dimond, S., Farrington, L., & Johnson, P. Differing emotional response from right and left hemispheres. *Nature,* 1976, *261,* 690–692.

Ehrlichman, H., & Weinberger, A. Lateral eye movements and hemispheric asymmetry: A critical review. *Psychological Bulletin,* 1978, *85,* 1080–1101.

Flor-Henry, P. On certain aspects of the localization of the cerebral systems regulating and determining emotion. *Biological Psychiatry,* 1979, *14,* 677–698.

Flor-Henry, P., Koles, Z.J., Howarth, B.G., & Burton, L. Neurophysiological studies of schizophrenia, mania and depression. In J. Gruzelier & P. Flor-Henry (Eds.), *Hemisphere asymmetries of function in psychopathology.* New York: Elseview/North Holland, 1979.

Fuster, J.M. *The prefrontal cortex.* New York: Raven Press, 1980.

Gainotti, G. Réactions "Catotrophiques: et manifestations d'indifférence au cours des atteintes cérébrais. *Neuropsychologia,* 1969, *7,* 195–204.

Gainotti, G. Emotional behavior and hemispheric side of lesion. *Cortex,* 1972, *8,* 41–55.

Goldstein, K. *The organism.* New York: Academic Book Publishers, 1939.

Hécaen, H., Ajuriaguerra, J.D., & Massonet, J. Les troubles visuo constructifs pars lesions parieto-occipitales droites. Roles des perturbations vestibulaires. *L'Encephale,* 1951, *1,* 122–179.

Hirschman, R.S., & Safer, M. Hemisphere differences in perceiving positive and negative emotions. *Cortex,* in press.

Karlin, R., Weinapple, M., Rochford, J., & Goldstein, L. *Quantitative EEG features of negative affective states: Report of some hypnotic studies.* Paper presented at the Society of Biological Psychiatry, Atlanta, Georgia, 1978.

Kelly, A.E., & Stinus, L. Neuroanatomical and neurochemical substrates of affective behavior. In N. Fox & R.J. Davidson (Eds.), *The psychobiology of affective development.* Hillsdale, N.J.: Lawrence Erlbaum Associates, in press.

Kolb, B., & Milner, B. Observations on spontaneous facial expression after focal cerebral excisions and after intracarotid injection of sodium amytal. *Neuropsychologia,* 1981, *19,* 505–514. (a).

Kolb, B., & Milner, B. Performance of complex arm and facial movements after focal brain lesions. *Neuropsychologia,* 1981, *17,* 491–503. (b)

Ley, R., & Bryden, M. Hemispheric differences in processing emotions and faces. *Brain and Language,* 1979, *7,* 127–138.

Luria, A.R. *Higher cortical functions in man.* New York: Basic Books, 1966.

Luria, A.R. *The working brain.* New York: Basic Books, 1973.

Myers, R.E. Role of prefrontal and anterior temporal cortex in social behavior and affect in monkeys. *Acta Neurobiologica Experimentalis,* 1972 *32,* 567–579.

Myers, R.E. Neurology of social behavior and affect in primates: A study of prefrontal and anterior temporal cortex. In K.J. Zuelch, O. Creutzfeldt, & G.C. Galbraith (Eds.), *Cerebral localization,* New York: Springer, 1975.

Nauta, W.J.H. Some efferent connections of the prefrontal cortex in the monkey. In J.M. Warren & K. Akert (Eds.), *The frontal granular cortex and behavior.* New York: McGraw-Hill, 1964.

Nauta, W.J.H. The problem of the frontal lobe: A reinterpretation. *Journal of Psychiatric Research,* 1971, *8,* 167–187.

Oldfield, R.C. The assessment and analysis of handedness: The Edinborough Inventory. *Neuropsychologia,* 1971, *9,* 97–113.

Perris, C., & Monakhov, K. Depressive symptomatology and systemic structural analysis of the EEG. In J. Gruzelier & P. Flor-Henry (Eds.), *Hemisphere asymmetries of function in psychopathology.* New York: Elsevier/North Holland, 1979.

Pribram, K.H. The primate frontal cortex—executive of the brain. In K.H. Pribram & A.R. Luria (Eds.), *Psychophysiology of the frontal lobes.* New York: Academic Press, 1973.

Reuter-Lorenz, P., & Davidson, R.J. Differential contributions of the two cerebral hemispheres to the perception of happy and sad faces. *Neuropsychologia,* 1981, *19,* 609–613.

Robinson, R.G., & Benson, D.F. Depression in aphasic patients: Frequency, severity and clinical-pathological correlations. *Brain and Language,* 1981, *14,* 282–291.

Robinson, R.G., & Szetda, B. Mood change following left hemispheric brain injury. *Annals of Neurology,* 1981, *9,* 447–453.

Sackeim, H.A., Weinman, A.L., Gur, R.C., Greenberg, M., Hungerbuhler, J.P., & Geschwind, N. Pathological laughing and crying: Functional brain asymmetry in the experience of positive and negative emotions. *Archives of Neurology,* 1982, *39,* 210–218.

Schaffer, C.E., Davidson, R.J., & Saron, C. Frontal and parietal electroencephalogram asymmetry in depressed and non-depressed subjects. *Biological Psychiatry,* 1983, *18,* 753–762.

Schwartz, G.E., Davidson, R.J., & Maer, F. Right hemisphere lateralization for emotion in the human brain: Interaction with cognition. *Science,* 1975, *190,* 286–288.

Schwartz, G.E., Fair, P.L., Salt, P., Mandel, M., & Klerman, G.L. Facial muscle patterning to affective imagery in depressed and non-depressed subjects. *Science,* 1976, *192,* 489–491.

Simernitskaya, E.G. Application of the method of evoked potentials to the analysis of activation processes in patients with lesions of the frontal lobes. In K.H. Pribram & A.R. Luria (Eds.), *Psychophysiology of the frontal lobes.* New York: Academic Press, 1973.

Suberi, M., & McKeever, W.F. Differential right hemispheric memory storage of emotional and non-emotional faces. *Neuropsychologia,* 1977, *15,* 757–768.

Tucker, D.M., Stenslie, C.E., Roth, R.S., & Shearer, S.L. Right frontal lobe activation and right hemisphere performance decrement during a depressed mood. *Archives of General Psychiatry,* 1981, *38,* 169–174.

Weinberger, D.A., Schwartz, G.E., & Davidson, R.J. Low anxious, high anxious and repressive coping styles: Psychometric patterns and behavioral and physiological responses to stress. *Journal of Abnormal Psychology,* 1979, *88,* 369–380.

3 Contributions from Neuroendocrinology

Peter Whybrow
Dartmouth Medical School

The perspective that I bring to this volume is that of the psychopathologist. For several years, my major research interest has been the abnormal mood states of depression (Melancholia) and elation (mania). I have focused upon the psychobiology of these states with a particular emphasis upon the neuroendocrinology, especially the modulating influence of thyroid metabolism on the behavioral and biological phenomena observed. Although one might reasonably conclude from this that my interest in emotion is dangerously esoteric, I believe that the underlying psychobiologic principles which serve to organize my thinking plus some of the details of my particular work suggest a useful contribution to the study of emotion. Here, in this general overview, I draw together the elements of the philosophical roots of my perspective, provide some general background in concepts of central nervous system and endocrine function, and discuss briefly steroid metabolism in affective illness. Finally, I outline a postulate that thyroid metabolism is an important modulator of mood and disorders of mood.

SOME WORKING DEFINITIONS

Affective state is a term in common parlance among psychopathologists. It tends to be used interchangeably with the generic terms feeling and emotion. When an affective disorder is referred to, however, the major focus is upon the emotions of elation and despair—these being central features of the disease syndrome. An emotion sustained in time is considered a mood. If of sufficient quantitative change or sustained over a sufficient time period, despite environmental changes that make it inappropriate, the mood is considered pathologic.

PHILOSOPHICAL CONSIDERATIONS

A fundamental characteristic of successful living organisms is a high degree of order and their ability to maintain that order in the face of the physical world, which, being governed by thermodynamic law, tends towards disarray. Sustaining life is essentially the maintenance of this organized autonomy, an energy-consuming struggle against entropic law. If relative autonomy from the environment is necessary for life, then when the environment changes, adaptation is necessary to preserve that autonomy. Such processes are central, not only to our individual existence as biological organisms but also to our social organization and the intrapsychic symbolism upon which in part that organization is built. Because the social and physical environment is in flux, the demand for change is constant and dependent upon accurate information.

In simplification, emotion may be considered a generic term used to describe from a subjective reference point a set of signal functions, which both monitor and modulate an individual's ongoing interaction with the environment. Emotion may thus be considered a composite of functions that assist in the essential maintenance of psychobiologic order.

Whether the entity of emotion is first described from the reference point of subjective experience or from some other intellectual paradigm is a matter of research preference and opportunity. However, regardless of the level of psycho-biologic organization focused upon, the research paradigm will ideally be structured to accommodate the dynamic flux which we know to be characteristic of living things. Claude Bernard (1927) put it thus:

> We really must learn then that if we break up a living organism by isolating its different parts, it is only for the sake of ease in experimental analysis and by no means in order to conceive them separately. Indeed, when we wish to ascribe to a physiological quality, its value and true significance we must always refer to this whole and draw our final conclusion only in relation to its effects in the whole. Physiologists and physicians must, therefore, always consider organisms as a whole and in detail at one and the same time without ever losing sight of the peculiar conditions of all the special phenomena whose resultant is the individual [p. 91].

Thus while behavior may be viewed at multiple levels, each of which interacts dynamically with the others, an organizing principle is essential in attempting to integrate these levels. Even though in the mental sciences many have come to consider behavior as purely the motoric component of the total organism (be that speech reflecting symbolic thought in humans or the fight and flight associated with the emotion of fear in the laboratory animal), in fact the concomitant biochemical and physiological behavior of the organism, especially in the face of a provocative stimulus, is of comparable interest (Stolk & Whybrow, 1977). Furthermore, it is the assessment of the adaptive value of that behavior in the context of the psychobiological environment that can offer an important if not vital organizing principle and one which is capable of bridging specific research paradigms.

I do not subscribe to a theory that attributes causation of a behavioral syndrome or emotion to an individual physiological or biochemical system. Thus I do not consider a discrete biological lesion as being the cause, for example, of depressed mood. Rather, I view physiological and biochemical responses to potentially disabling psychosocial stimuli as indices of biological change capable of influencing the behavioral outcome of the total organism. Furthermore, I believe it is the *patterns* of these responses, kaleidoscopically changing through time, which are subjectively recognized as emotion and mood. Particularly intriguing is the potential delineation of adaptive and nonadaptive biologic response which may facilitate, respectively, the probability of behavioral recovery or decompensation during a period of challenge, such as a personal loss or any event that destabilizes adaptation. Theoretically, exploration of those biologic patterns which appear concomitant with various mood states or are capable of precipitating specific emotions thus becomes a powerful research paradigm. Neuroendocrine patterns become of interest in this context.

NEUROENDOCRINE MECHANISMS OF COMMUNICATION

Successful adaptation demands accurate information. The sophistication of the mechanisms that have developed for the transfer of information between the cells of a multicellular organism are thus critical in survival. The nervous system and the endocrine system are both highly complex mechanisms for information transfer.

The endocrine system may be viewed as an evolution of the simplest form of communication between cells in a multicellular organism. A chemical substance liberated from one cell is transported via the blood stream and arrives at the surface of a second cell modifying the behavior of the latter. Despite its further evolution, the nervous system retains this same basic principle of communication (Whybrow & Silberfarb, 1974). Although there has been considerable adaptation of cell shape and function, promoting intimate physical contact between cells and dispensing with the need for the circulating blood to convey the messenger, the actual transfer of information from one cell body to another remains dependent on the release of the chemical transmitter passing across the cell gap or synapse. The nervous system and the endocrine system share many common "messengers." Norepinephrine is a good example. Furthermore, although both are self-regulating or homeostatic dynamic systems, each is intimately dependent upon the other and influences the behavior of the other.

ORGANIZATION OF NEUROENDOCRINE FUNCTION

A disturbance of neuroendocrine function represents a fascinating experiment in nature. Our specific understanding began in 1786 in Bath, England, when Caleb Parry noted with curiosity the acute development of anxiety and nervousness in a young woman who had fallen from a wheelchair. Her distressed mental condition was clearly associated with a large swelling of a thyroid gland in her neck (Whybrow & Ferrell, 1974).

Probably the first experiment in endocrinology was conducted by Berthold, who in 1849 transplanted the testis into the abdominal cavity of a castrated cockeral. The birds over time returned to their normal behavior and appearance—growing combs and wattles, fighting, crowing, and showing an interest in hens. Upon sacrificing the animals, it was found that the testis had gained a blood supply from the intestine and Berthold correctly concluded that the living testis produced a hormone that influenced the behavior; previously it had been thought that such behavior was directly under the control of the central nervous system. Many neuroendocrine connections are now recognized, but in all instances, the interaction between the central nervous system and the endocrine system is similar. The brain is both crucial in the release of the endocrine hormones and is also a target organ for their effect. An important common denominator in these systems is the closed homeostatic loop where the controlled variable itself, usually the plasma hormone level, determines the rate of secretion of that hormone. This major loop is usually of a negative feedback type so that the output of the system, the hormone itself, produces an inhibition of production. Through a series of transducer cells, peptides known as releasing factors, are secreted in the hypothalamus and preoptic area and later released under stimulation to trigger in turn the release of the corresponding pituitary trophic hormones. These trophic hormones act on the peripheral endocrine glands, be they the adrenal cortex, the thyroid gland, gonads, etc., and in turn the target gland hormones released by these organs act on the brain influencing the neuronal events which control the secretion of the peptides.

However, there is also another potent determinant of neuroendocine function—that of the "open loop" where hormone production is increased secondary to events external to the individual. As has been clearly demonstrated by Mason in primates (Mason, 1968), and by a large number of different workers in human beings, psychological and physical environmental challenge has a powerful influence upon the neuroendocrine system through this mechanism (see Friedman, Mason, & Hamburg, 1963; Levi, 1974; Rubin, 1974; Von Euler & Lundberg, 1954). It is the factoring out of these many influences and their homeostatic regulation through time that determines the psychobiologic behavior of the individual at any instant. At the biological level, the enzymes responsible for the manufacture of the hormones or neurotransmitters are under genetic control, and this adds a further governance to the capability of the system to respond to challenge. Such an individual difference may, therefore, underly differences in performance and mood (Hamburg & Lunde, 1967).

PATTERNS OF NEUROENDOCRINE RESPONSE

The adrenal medulla was the first endocrine system to be studied experimentally with regard to the influence of psychically mediated environmental influences. Walter Cannon's (1914) early experiments showing the Epinephrine appeared in blood when a cat was frightened by a barking dog have been confirmed and amplified in various animals, including man. Catecholamine levels in blood and urine appear to be sensitive indices of everyday events, tasks, and activities. Dissociation between E and Norepinephrine levels, deriving predominantly from adrenal medulla and sympathetic nerve terminals, respectively, has been clearly demonstrated in relation to psychological influences (Frankenhaeuser, 1971b).

Enormous stimulus to a research interest in neuroendocrine response as a mechanism of adaptation was provided by the second world war. The war had heightened general awareness to disorder induced by stressful experience, and technology was also moving rapidly ahead greatly improving the methods for the measurement of peripheral hormone levels.

The early evidence of the existence of hypothalmic-releasing factors also came at about this time, when in 1947 Green and Harris put forward their original hypothesis (Green & Harris, 1947), and in 1955, corticotrophin-releasing factor was identified (Saffran & Schally, 1955).

At a mundane, if not practical, level Thorn was studying Harvard oarsmen in the annual boat race against Yale and found that there was a marked increase of 17 hydroxycorticosteroids prior to the race. That was in 1951 (see Renold, Quigley, Kennard, & Thorn, 1951). There rapidly followed a series of investigations showing that anticipation of parachute jumping, of dentists, surgical operations, and hospitalization were all a potent stimulus to the adrenal cortex (Rubin, 1974).

In these general studies of "stress," some very interesting points were emerging. In situations where physical exertion was demanded, certainly hydroxycorticosteroids rose. But it was in those situations where individuals were called upon to make complex decisions under a certain time pressure (such as, for example, when landing an airplane on an aircraft carrier deck) that the truly high output of these steroids occurred. In one rather amusing report, crossing a polar region was found to produce nowhere near the output of 17 hydroxycorticosteroids as did the demand of the daily routine teaching in Edinburgh Medical

School! (See Simpson, 1967.) Subsequently, direct comparisons were made between the responses of officers and enlisting men in battle situations, and it was clearly demonstrated that the 24-hour urinary excretion of corticosteroids was far higher in those held responsible for the success and safety of the group as a whole—the officers (Elmadjian, 1955).

Thus the perception of the environment and the symbolic nature of the task were emerging as important variables in determining the physiological arousal. Rose, Poe, and Mason (1968) in a very careful study of army recruits showed that not only did weight correlate with the urinary output of 17 hydroxycorticosteroids but also a global psychological assessment showed a high correlation between successful social adaptation and a minimal rise in corticosteroids under stress. Individual differences in the psychological management of the environment appear to play a key role in the individual's physiological response—observations that have profound implications for our understanding of the genesis of psychopathology.

It is not only in the area of steroid metabolism that individual differences have been found to play a major role in response to challenge. In an elegant series of experiments spread over many years, Frankenhaeuser (1971a, 1971b) and her colleagues in Scandanavia have studied the changes in peripheral levels of epinephrine and norepinephrine derived from the adrenal medulla and sympathetic nerve terminals in response to a wide variety of psychological influences. Most of their experiments have been well controlled and undertaken in a laboratory, and it is worthwhile summarizing some of the important points. Both epinephrine secretion and norepinephrine secretion rose when normal subjects performed mental work under mild conditions of external control or heavy physical work or even in the face of unpleasant stimuli such as electric shock. However, when subjects were given control over their environment, there was an interesting splitting of the epinephrine and norepinephrine responses. Epinephrine progressively decreased as control over the situation was exerted, whereas norepinephrine remained high. These findings have some support from primate work by Mason (1968) where it is suggested that epinephrine output increases in situations characterized by novelty and uncertainty but falls as familiarity occurs. The norepinephrine excretion continues to elevate, however, regardless of the familiarity and seems to be a correlate of any attention-demanding activity.

In regard to the individual differences, Frankenhaeuser (1971a) was able to identify indices of behavioral efficiency. Normal subjects with higher than average excretion rates of epinephrine performed significantly better than those who had low epinephrine excretion rates making significantly fewer errors and having a consistently shorter response time in the face of similar tasks. There was also a diurnal pattern which could be detected with those individuals who preferred to work in the morning, rising early and going to bed early, tending to have a shift of their epinephrine secretion toward the morning hours, this correlating with their behavioral efficiency. Evening workers likewise tended to have higher levels of epinephrine in the evenings when they preferred to work.

NEUROENDOCRINE BALANCE

Mason (1968), in studies conducted mainly in primates, has clearly shown that the scope of psycho-neuroendocrine response to the environment is very broad. He has presented convincing evidence in the monkey that there is a complicated pattern of organization or clustering of responses that suggest a functional alignment of the hormonal response, a hierarchy and an orchestration similar to that predicted by Claude Bernard. The timeframe of each response is different, and the result is the occurence of a complex catabolic, anabolic sequence of the endocrine changes. Using the criterion of the role of each hormone in energy metabolism, Mason has attempted to provide a unifying explanation of the many hormonal responses which comprise the overall pattern. He suggests that in the first group, that of the catabolic or energy-releasing agents, there cluster corticosteroids, epinephrine, norepinephrine, growth hormone, and thyroxin. While the timeframe for each is different, their peak of response is earlier than for the second group which provides predominantly an anabolic effect—the regeneration of energy stores. In the second group fall insulin, estrogens, testosterone, and the androgenic metabolites.

Many systems in biology that are capable of being finely tuned, employ the common principle of two or more mechanisms, working in opposition to each other. A familiar example is that of the peripheral nervous system, where sympathetic nervous stimulation speeds the heart rate while stimulation of the parasympathetic pathway slows it down. The actual rate of the heart is then a function of the prevailing tone of these two mechanisms.

Similar ideas applied to the central nervous system were introduced by Hess of Zurich, one of the first individuals to demonstrate that emotions could be generated by electrical stimulation of particular regions of the hypothalamus in the cat. He suggested there were two opposing mechanisms—one which he termed ergotropic or arousal system and the other a quieting system which he termed trophotropic—these being essentially equivalent to the parasympathetic and sympathetic systems of the periphery but located in the diencephalon (Hess, 1924). This creative idea has retained considerable validity, and in the 1950s Brodie and Shore (1957) suggested that catecholamines are messengers of the ergotropic system while the indolamines, specifically serotonin, serves as the messenger of the trophotropic system. Animal studies have accumulated considerable evidence that these two amine systems are involved in mechanisms capable of generating opposite kinds of behavior; thus serotonin may be predominantly responsible for behaviors related to tranquility, to deep sleep, and to hibernation, whereas the catecholamines facilitate aggressive behavior and activity.

NEUROENDOCRINE PATTERNS IN AFFECTIVE ILLNESS

There is evidence that hormonal balance may contribute in a special way to some elements of mood dysfunction. It seems, for example, that a major decrease in circulating thyroid hormone, in otherwise normal individuals, fosters depressive affect and that a rise in circulating thyroid hormone protects the individual from that affect (see Whybrow & Ferrell, 1974). Similarly, euphoria is associated with a rising level of corticosteroids, whereas depressive affect appears as these levels are maintained. In addition, with increasing severity, all endocrinopathies appear to promote a final common path of psychopathology—that of delirium (Whybrow & Hurwitz, 1976).

Thus these experiments of nature provide intriguing leads. If the pattern of neuroendocrine change and mood were indeed to have some correlation in time then one would expect a change in endocrine function in affective illness. Such indeed does occur. Here I shall focus upon the adrenal cortex and the thyroid axes.

An enormous body of work has accumulated over the past 20 years in relation to the metabolism of *steroids in depression and mania* (Whybrow & Parlatore, 1973). In fact, it has probably been the most extensively studied of all the hormone systems in the affective disorders. Most of the studies have concerned themselves with the 17 hydroxycorticosteroids, measured in blood or urine. More recently, ACTH has also been assayed, but this is a difficult procedure, and the focus has been largely upon the peripheral hormones. Initially, the dynamics of the system were not explored as in the case of the early paper by Board which reported elevated plasma cortisol levels at hospital admission in depressed individuals which subsequently subsided after two weeks (Board, Wadeson, & Persky, 1957). Board considered these to be secondary to psychological turmoil. Sachar, in a series of studies, confirmed this but established that it was a subgroup of depressed patients that were truly hyper-secreters of cortisol and that in these individuals, even after they are adapted to hospitalization, cortisol levels continue to be elevated in their blood and urine (Sachar, Hellman, Fukushima, & Gallagher, 1970) Some of the clinical characteristics of these individuals appear to be active suicidal thought, severe anxiety, and acute psychotic decompensation. Individuals who have developed a "fixed" depression where there is less psychological turmoil appear to have lower levels of cortisol, but this is not necessarily always the case.

The development of the research in this area and the increasing sophistication of the studies undertaken is a good example of a progressive effort to improve the nature of the evidence upon which our knowledge is based. Early studies tended to compare serum levels of cortisol in depression with control populations or normals in other psychiatric disturbances. Subsequently, individuals were followed through the illness and into normality and studies were also undertaken in those individuals who had bipolar (i.e., depression and mania) illness. Here, the evidence suggests that the excretion of corticosteroids is generally less in bipolar depression than in unipolar depression of comparable severity. However, in mania itself, reports are conflicting, and only some investigations record an increasing level of cortisol as mania occurs (Sachar, Hellman, Fukushima, & Gallagher, 1972).

In a sophisticated series of studies, Sachar (1973) undertook pioneering work in an assessment of the 24-hour secretion of cortisol and its pattern in relation to the sleep-wake cycle. Studies of ACTH production also were undertaken, and it became clear that normally cortisol is secreted episodically in a series of bursts throughout the day—these being synchronized with the sleep-wake cycle. In normal individuals sleeping from 12 midnight to 8 A.M., there is very little secretion of cortisol during the late evening and early morning hours, but after about 2 A.M., a rapid rise occurs so that there is a peak of excretion between 5 and 9 in the morning. This clearly defined circadian rhythm is retained in depression but is phase shifted to the left that is the peak occurs earlier than in normal individuals and is usually elevated in addition. These changes are important as they tie closely to changes which we discussed earlier in the sleep-wake cycle itself and in the circadian variation in REM sleep plus changes in the circadian body temperature.

Cortisol hypersecretion during depressive illness almost certainly reflects hypersecretion of ACTH, and this would suggest in turn that there is hyperactivity of the hypothalamic neuroendocrine centers which secrete cortisol-releasing hormone.

Evidence that this hypersecretion is driven by an abnormally high level of hypothalamic hormone is demonstrated by the dexamethasone suppression test. Dexamethasone is a potent synthetic corticosteroid which normally suppresses the early morning rise in ACTH secretion by fooling the hypothalamus into thinking that there is sufficient cortisol already circulating. Studies by Carroll (1982) and others have shown that this suppression is lost during depression. The cortisol excretion "escapes" from the dampening effect of the dexamethasone during the illness but is suppressed normally after recovery from the depression. Furthermore, during the actual phase of recovery, Carroll has been able to show that the dexamethasone patterns of secretion move towards normal profiles in a predictable fashion. Individuals who have minimal depressive syndromes without the disturbances of "biologic signs" such as sleep disturbance, appetite loss, and thinking disability, do not show the rapid escape characteristic of the severely depressed individual. Carol concludes that in severe depressive illness, the steroid sensitive neurons of the hypothalamus—the steroid tranducer cells—

are subjected to an abnormal drive from other limbic areas. What we know of the mechanism of secretion of ACTH suggests that it is a noradrenergic system which tonically inhibits the secretion. In other words, if there is a reduction in norepinephrine, cortisol-releasing hormone (CRH) and subsequently ACTH are increased because the inhibition secondary to the high levels of norepinephrine has been removed. Serotonin and acetylcholine are also thought to play a role, however, in the release of CRH. Hence at the moment we almost certainly have an oversimplified view of this particular mechanism (Sachar, Asnis, Naltan et al., 1980).

The possibility that the elevated cortisol levels in some depressives are in themselves contributory to the depressive syndrome has been suggested by several workers. One specific mechanism postulated by Curzon (1969) in England and Lapin and Oxenkrug (1968) in the U.S.S.R. has been that the raised cortisol levels inducing the enzyme tryptophan-pyrolaze in the liver tend to increase the metabolism of tryptophan, the serotonin precursor, along the kyurenine pathway, causing a relative depletion of central nervous system serotonin.

Certainly the raised level of circulating steroid hormones, which in some individuals can be close to those very high levels found in Cushing's Disease, highlight consideration of what we know to be usually an adaptive mechanism in the face of environmental challenge as actually working in a counterproductive way in severe depression. The pervasive effects of the steroid hormones make this a question which continues to need close attention. What is adaptive in most individuals may be maladaptive in a continuing depressive disturbance.

The whole question as to whether there are physiologic mechanisms which occur in defense of the individual against a developing affective disorder is brought into sharp focus by my own research into the *brain thyroid axis* and the changes which occur during depressive illness. Levels of thyroxin in the blood do not vary as quickly in response to environmental challenge as do the 17 hydroxycorticosteroids. This is in part because thyroxin has a half life of 8 days but is largely secondary to the dynamics of cellular metabolism. Thyroxin is converted to T_3, (triiodothyronine), before actually being utilized by the cells. This latter molecule has a half life of some 8 hours and is four times as potent as thyroxin which serves as its circulating reservoir (see Whybrow, Coppen, Prange et al., 1972).

Nonetheless, changes in thyroid gland output in response to environmental challenge, be that temperature change or a perceived threat, are well established.

A lack of thyroxin, either because of reduced pituitary secretion of TSH or secondary to thyroid gland dysfunction itself, produces a profound syndrome including a disturbance of mental function, the predominant feature of which is depression and cognitive disability (see Whybrow, Prange, & Treadway, 1969). It has also been known for a long time that such individuals are comparatively insensitive to catecholamine infusion and contra-wise, hyperthyroid individuals are more sensitive. That the two molecules, the catecholamines and thyroxin come from the same parent amino acid tyrosine, makes their interrelationship highly probably from the evolutionary standpoint. It has long been thought that in some way the thyroid molecules modulate the action of the catecholamines (Whybrow & Prange, 1981).

A whole series of studies now suggest that there are indeed intimate links between these two systems (Whybrow & Prange, 1981). Nor is this linkage of a purely academic interest, for in 1969 Prange (Prange, Wilson, Wabon et al., 1969) demonstrated that in some individuals, (we found later that is was largely women, Whybrow et al., 1972), a small dose of triiodothyronine given with tricyclic antidepressants speeded the individual's response to these latter medications. That, in combination with the evidence that lithium, a potent antimanic agent is also an antithyroid agent producing hypothyroidism in some predisposed individuals, has led to a rising research interest in the brain-thyroid axis in regard to the affective disorders (see Rogers & Whybrow, 1971).

What happens to this axis during depression? It would appear that as in the case of peripheral cortisol, thyroxin rises during depressive illness in some individuals with these higher levels of a circulating hormone falling back toward normal as the depression improves. In addition, recent studies of the hypothalamic mechanisms involved show that there is a blunting of the usual TSH response to TRH challenge during depression. This is a remarkably consistent finding across many different studies, and the explanations for it are several (e.g., Loosen & Prange, 1982).

One possibility is that the already raised levels of circulating thyroxin are feeding back negatively upon the hypothalamus and so the individual is essentially in a mild state of hyperthyrosis. Another possibility, for it is known that raised levels of cortisol interfere with the pituitary TSH response to TRH, is that the elevated cortisol itself is the cause of the blunting. I have suggested that these changes in thyroid function in depression may be a mechanism of physiological defense offsetting changes in biogenic amine metabolism, specifically catecholamine function, in the affective disorder. There is evidence that the higher the level of circulating thyroid hormone, the faster the ankle reflex and the lower the level of cholesterol (these latter two being dependent variables of thyroid metabolism), then the faster does the individual respond to tricyclic antidepressants. Thyroid state thus appears to be of prognostic significance. That triiodothyronine given adjunctively speeds recovery fits with this hypothesis.

Most recently, evidence has been developed that the thyroid hormones act by increasing beta-adrenergic receptor function at the postsynaptic site (Whybrow & Prange, 1981), with this enhancing the effect of available catecholamines. The thyroid hormones, therefore, modulate the action of the catecholamines and the two work synergistically. This is an explanation for the long-standing physiological evidence of hyperthyroid individuals being more sensitive to catecholamines. It also explains why in a study giving adjunctive triiodothyronine to depressives who were also receiving tryptophan no potentiation of the tryptophan as an antidepressant was found. The thyroid hormones work specifically with the catecholamine system with which they share a common amino acid precursor but do not influence the indoleamine system, where no such common progenitor exists.

Within the normal range of thyroid hormone levels fluctuations may have adaptive value so that with "demand" on the normal organism, physiological adaptation to stress is aided. If Thyroid hormones indeed are a mechanism whereby catecholamine function can be enhanced, then presumably such mechanisms would usually come into play to off-set changes in biogenic amine metabolism developing during depressive illness. Thyroid hormones by increasing β-adrenergic receptor activity may thus provide a physiological advantage to persons who face the adaptive demand of events that would otherwise be likely to lead to depressive illness. In persons predisposed to bipolar illness, however, the advantage gained in recovering from depression may become maladaptive in that manic illness may be precipitated by the same physiological mechanisms.

The thyroid axis is thus postulated as a major modulator of mood, acting in synergism with its sister mechanism the catecholaminergic messenger system. It is the pattern of interaction of the thyroid and adrenergic systems through time which is important. I suspect a search for similar neuroendocrine underlays of mood, especially as our biologic understanding and technical abilities improve, will be fruitful.

REFERENCES

Bernard, C. *An introduction to the study of experimental medicine.* (H.C. Green trans.). New York: Macmillan Publishing Co. Inc., 1927.

Board, F., Wadeson, R., & Persky, H. Depressive affect and endocrine functions. *Archives of Neurology and Psychiatry,* 1957, *78,* 612–620.

Brodie, B.B., & Shore, P.A. A concept for the role of serotonin and norepinephrine as chemical mediators in the brain. *Annals of the New York Academy of Science,* 1957, *66,* 631–662.

Cannon, W.B. The emergency function of the adrenal medulla in pain and the major emotions. *American Journal of Physiology,* 1914, *33,* 356–372.

Carroll, B.S. The Dexamethasone Suppression Test for Melancholia. *British Journal of Psychiatry,* 1982, *140,* 292–304.

Curzon, G. Tryptophan pyrrolase—a biochemical factor in depressive illness. *British Journal of Psychiatry,* 1969, *115,* 1367–1374.

Elmadjian, F. Adrenocortical function of combat infantry men in Korea. In *Ciba Coloquium–Endocrinology,* 1955, *8,* 627–655.

Frankenhaeuser, M. Behavior and circulating catecholamines. *Brain Research,* 1971, *31,* 241–262. (a)

Frankenhaeuser, M. Experimental approaches to the study of Human Behaviors as related to neuroendocrine functions. In L. Levi (Ed.), *Society stress and disease,* London: Oxford University Press, 1971. (b)

Friedman, S.B., Mason, J.W., & Hamburg, D.A. Urinary 17-Hydroxy cortico steroid levels in parents of children with neoplastic disease. *Psychosomat Medicine,* 1963, *25,* 364–76.

Green, J.D. & Harris, G.W. The neurovascular link between the neurohypophysis and adenohypophysis. *Journal of Endocrinology*, 1947, *5*, 136–145.

Hamburg, D.A., Lunde, D.T. Relation of behavioral genetic and neuroendocrine factors in thyroid function. In J.N. Spuhler (Ed.), *Genetic diversity and human behavior*. Chicago: Aldine Publishing Co., 1967.

Hess, W.R. Uber die wechselbeziehungen zwischen psychischen and vegetatiwen funktionen. *Schweizer Archiv fur Neurologie und Psychiatrie* 1924, *15*, 260–64.

Lapin, I.P., & Oxenkrug, G.F. Intensification of the central serotoninergic processes as a possible determinant of the thymoleptic effect. *Lancet* 1968, *I*, 132–136.

Levi, L. Stress, distress and psychosocial stimuli. In A. McClean (Ed.), *Occupational stress*. Springfield, Ill.: Charles C Thomas, 1974.

Loosen, P.T., & Prange, A.J. Serum thyrotopin response to TRH in psychiatric patients. *American Journal of Psychiatry*, 1982, *139*, 405–416.

Mason, J.W. Organization of the multiple endocrine responses to avoidance in the monkey. *Psychosomatic Medicine*, 1968, *30*, 744–790.

Prange, A.J., Wilson, J.C., Wabon, A.M. et al. Enhancement of imipramine antidepressant activity by thyroid hormone. *American Journal of Psychiatry*, 1969, *126*, 457–469.

Renold, A.E., Quigley, T.B., Kennard, H.E., & Thorn, G.W. Reaction of the adrenal cortex to physical and emotional stress in college oarsmen. *New England Journal of Medicine*, 1951, *244*, 756–757.

Rogers, M., & Whybrow, P.C. Clinical hypothyroidism occurring during lithium treatment: Two case histories and a review of thyroid function in 19 patients. *American Journal of Psychiatry*, 1971, *128*, 158–162.

Rose, R.M., Poe, R.O., & Mason, J.W. Psychological state and body size as determinants of 17-OHCS excretion. *Archives of Internal Medicine*, 1968, *121*, 406–413.

Rubin, R.T. Biochemical and neuroendocrine responses to severe psychological stress. In E.K.E. Gunderson & R.H. Rahe (Eds.), *Life stress and illness*. Springfield, Ill.: Charles C Thomas, 1974.

Sachar, E.S. Disrupted 24 hour patterns of cortisol secretion in psychotic depression. *Archives of General Psychology*, 1973, *28*, 19–26.

Sachar, E.S., Asnis, G., Naltan, R.S. et al. Dextroamphetamine and cortisol in depression. *Archives of General Psychology*, 1980, *37*, 755–757.

Sachar, E.S., Hellman, L., Fukushima, D.K., & Gallagher, T.F. Cortisol production in depressive illness. *Arch Gen Psychiat*, 1970, *23*, 289–298.

Sachar, E.S., Hellman, L., Fukushima, D.K., & Gallagher, T.F. Cortisol production in mania, *Arch Gen Psychiat*, 1972, *26*, 137–139.

Saffran, M., & Schally, A.V. The release of corticotrophin by anterior pituitary tissue in vitro. *Canadian Journal of Biochemistry and Physiology*, 1955, *33*, 408–15.

Simpson, H.W. Field studies of human stress in polar regions. *British Medical Journal*, 1967, *1*, 530–533.

Stolk, J.M., Whybrow, P.C. Peripheral physiologic systems as potential indicators of liability to behavioral dysfunction. *Neuroregulators and Psychiatric Disorders*. E. Usdin (Ed.), 1977.

Von Euler, U.S., Lundberg, U. Effect of flying on the Epinephrine excretion in Air Force personnel. *Journal of Applied Physiology*, 1954, *6*, 551–555.

Whybrow, P.C., Ferrell, R.B. Thyroid state and human behavior: Contributions from a clinical perspective. In A.J. Prange (Ed.), *The thyroid axis, drugs, and behavior*. New York: Raven Press, 1974.

Whybrow, P.C., & Hurwitz, T.C. Psychological disturbances associated with endocrine disease and hormone therapy. In E.J. Sachar (Ed.), *Hormones, behavior, and psychopathology*. New York: Raven Press, 1976.

Whybrow, P.C., & Parlatore, A. Melancholia, a model in madness: A discussion of recent psychobiologic research into depressive illness. *Psychiatry in Medicine*, 1973, *4*, 351–378.

Whybrow, P.C., & Prange, A.J. A hypothesis of thyroid catecholamine receptor interaction *Archives of General Psychology* 1981, *38,* 106–112.

Whybrow, P.C., Silberfarb, P.M. Neuroendocrine mediating mechanisms: From the symbolic stimulus to the physiological response. *International Journal of Psychiatry in Medicine,* 1974, *5,* 531–539.

Whybrow, P.C., Coppen, A., Prange, A.J., Jr. et al. Thyroid function and the response to liothyronine in depression. *Archives of General Psychiatry,* 1972, *26,* 242–245.

Whybrow, P.C., Prange, A.J.Jr., & Treadway, C.R. Mental changes accompanying thyroid gland disfunction: A reappraisal using objective psychological measurement. *Archives of General Psychiatry,* 1969, *20,* 48–63.

II

DEVELOPMENTAL APPROACHES

The scientific investigation of living systems often resorts to two major strategies of discovery: (1) the destruction or suppression of specific system structures to observe the resulting changes in function; and, (2) the detailed observation of the development of system structures and functions. As described in the preceding chapters on biological approaches, the first discovery strategy has been very successfully used in neurophysiology to investigate the role of various structures of the brain in the occurrence and regulation of emotion. This strategy is, of course, very difficult to apply to human subjects because of serious ethical constraints that rule out the use of experimental manipulation of any bodily structures and place very rigid limits on the use of drugs to produce temporary changes in function. The "experiments of nature" which can be found in a large number of pathologies and diseases that affect specific structures of the organism, provide interesting insights but are usually not well enough controlled to allow clear-cut conclusions.

Therefore, the use of the second discovery strategy, the observation of developmental processes, has increasingly become one of the most popular approaches to the study of many different aspects of human behavior. The study of both phylogenetic and the ontogenetic development is especially important for understanding of emotion. In recent years, study of the development of emotions has spurred a great deal of research activity. In tracing the development of both structures and functions from simple to complex, the developmental approach not only produces research findings that are important in their own right, but also provides pertinent clues for theory and research on emotion in general.

Evolutionary aspects of the phylogenetic development of emotion are referred to in several chapters in various sections of this volume. The three contributions in this section convincingly demonstrate the importance of emotion for the development of the human organism and its integration into the social world. While research in the past few years has resulted in a large number of interesting findings, the following general trends seem to be of particular importance for the phenomenon of emotion generally and with respect to the chapters to follow in the remaining sections of this volume: (1) The capacity for emotion seems to be innate and appears to rapidly unfold in the very few first days, weeks, and months of the infant's life. In addition, both the available structures and their functions seem to be much more complex than had been previously thought. (2) Emotional development appears to be very closely linked to cognitive and social development and seems to play a major role in the development of these other modes of functioning and in the general adaptation of the organism to the environment, both internally and externally. Finally, (3) far from being an exclusively individual phenomenon, emotion plays a major role in the interaction between infant and caretaker, thereby constituting emotion as one of the most important interpersonal phenomena in human behavior.

The three contributions in this section highlight different aspects of these general trends. Robert Emde provides an overview of the development of emotion as "complex system of organized functioning" which, according to his view, needs to be studied on several "levels of meaning": the biological response, the organizational state, and the enduring trait, both in the individual and the social domain. In the course of showing the importance of emotion on each of those levels of meaning, Emde not only summarizes recent research by others on the development of emotion but also provides an in-depth survey of some of the research conducted in his own laboratory. Emde particularly stresses the role of expressive behavior in the infant as a signaling device; signals both for the organism in terms of bodily responsiveness and to the social environment.

Alan Sroufe, while acknowledging the importance of affect as a signaling system, concentrates in his chapter on his model of emotion as a system that modulates arousal and tension in the infant. He sees tension management as a mediating mechanism between environmental stimulation and the organismic response. In addition, Sroufe stresses important relationships in the developmental sequence between emotion and cognition and between emotion and social development. In discussing the importance of different attachment relationships as the basis for long-term adaptation and tension management Sroufe exemplifies what Emde described as the enduring trait level of meaning.

Colwyn Trevarthen critiques past theories of emotion as neglecting the essential role of emotions as the basic mechanism that regulate direct interaction between persons. He stresses the importance of distinguishing between the infant's behavior toward objects and toward persons. Trevarthen demonstrates with observations and experiments in his own laboratory that emotional expression is used by infants as an unlearned mechanism to regulate their relationship and interaction with significant others, particularly their mother, and that these adults similarly use emotional expression to maintain and develop their relationship with the infant and foster development. Developments in interpersonal engagement exercise control of cognitive development and cooperative action from birth throughout infancy. In addition to a detailed description of the development of emotional behavior, particularly expression, Trevarthen refers to a number of interesting research issues that so far have been neglected in developmental research. One particularly intriguing area is the role of vocal communication between infants and adults, which compared to facial expression, has received little attention so far.

4 Levels of Meaning for Infant Emotions: A Biosocial View[1]

Robert N. Emde
University of Colorado Medical Center

I believe we stand on the threshold of a new era in our scientific understanding of the emotional life of the infant. Cross-cultural studies of adult facial expression and a renewed emphasis on analyzing patterned emotional responses (Ekman, Friesen, &Ellsworth, 1972; Izard, 1971) have given a dramatic impetus to the psychological study of emotions. At the same time our burgeoning knowledge of the human infant as a biologically active and socially interactive being has increased our awareness of a lag in our knowledge of emotional development. We know much more about the domains of perception and cognition than we do about emotion, as several recent reviews have documented (Charlesworth & Kreutzer, 1973; Haith & Campos, 1977; Lewis & Rosenblum, 1978; Oster & Ekman, 1978; Sroufe, 1979). This lag is especially dramatic for clinicians, for whom emotional expressions are an essential orienting feature of our everyday work with patients of all ages. Even though infants cannot tell us how they feel, they have other ways of communicating emotions; and we should be able to understand more.

But a lag in knowledge does not ensure an advance, and the reader may wonder about the source of my optimism. More than anything else, such optimism stems from today's scientific climate of multidisciplinary endeavor. Kessen (1965) has documented how, earlier in this century, different theoretical approaches to child study selfconsciously fostered isolation and polemicism. In

---

[1]This chapter is drawn from a longer report which appeared as a chapter in Development of Cognition, Affect and Social Relations. W. A. Collins (Ed.) *Minnesota Symposia in Child Psychology,* (Vol. 13), Hillsdale, N.J., Lawrence Erlbaum Associates, 1980, 1–37.

contrast, as I see it, progress today in a discipline is most often facilitated by challenges from other disciplines. Alternative points of view are sought not just for critical tests of hypotheses, but for novel ideas and for approaches found only at the boundaries between disciplines.

This essay presents a view about infant emotions that has emerged from our laboratory in recent years. It is entitled "biosocial" for simplicity (our frame of reference obviously being developmental psychology) and for emphasis of a neglected interface between biological and social aspects of emotional development. In appreciation of the high degree of organized complexity in human functioning, I argue for the usefulness of a "levels of meaning" approach for understanding infant emotional development. Although the paper highlights aspects of our own work, a special plea is made for interdisciplinary *collaborative* research efforts at a critical time in the development of our field. I conclude with some thoughts about the adaptive nature of infant emotions and their signaling functions.

THE EVOLUTION OF ORGANIZED COMPLEXITY
AND VIEWING EMOTIONS

The extraordinary extent of organized complexity in human functioning is an essential background for our thinking about development. Indeed, modern biology has been characterized as the biology of organized complexity, in contrast to a biology of former times that was mainly concerned with linear and noninteractive effects. Platt (1966) has emphasized that an evolutionary perspective shows man to be the most complex entity of the universe; and, for scientists, such complexity forever ensures a large amount of indeterminacy and privacy with respect to understanding human behavior. As aspects of an individual's complex functioning, it is not surprising that human emotions elude precise or comprehensive definition.

One thing is certain: In the field of infant emotions, in the study of increasingly organized complexity, we cannot proceed from isolation. We need multiple views that tap different levels of meaning. Emotions are parts of an array of complex human systems that are in continuous interaction, that are often hierarchically arranged at different levels of organization, and that can be characterized as having varying degrees of stability or change.

In this connection, I believe there is one view about emotions that can be misleading. In this view, verbal designations of emotion states offer temporary shortcuts for description before scientific specification is possible. In one form or another, this has been put forth by Hebb (1946) and his work with chimpanzees, by Mandler (1975) in a general way, and by Bowlby (1969) and Kagan (1978) in consideration of work with human infants. An implication of this view is that emotion terms are useful *only* at an early stage of investigation, that they represent *only* global, intuitive, and inexact formulations, and that with the advance of science, designation of "emotion states" will become unnecessary. We think there is more to it (Emde & Gaensbauer, in press). A biosocial view, incorporated by many (e.g., Chevalier-Skolnikoff, 1973; Darwin, 1872; Izard, 1977; Kaufman & Rosenblum, 1967; Tomkins, 1962, 1963) leads to the conclusion that emotional states represent complex systems of organized functioning inherent in the human person, states that are generally advantageous to the species as well as to the individual in the course of development. Evolutionary considerations seem to highlight both the complexity of emotions and their centrality in social adaptation.

Hamburg (1963) concluded that human emotions evolved because of a selective advantage in facilitating social bonds. In reviewing the course of primate evolution, he speculated that group living operated as a powerful adaptive mechanism and that, because of this, the formation of social bonds has been experienced as pleasurable and their disruption as unpleasurable. He pointed to the widespread prominence of psychophysiological changes associated with the disruption of social bonds and of instrumental behaviors that are mobilized for restoring such bonds. The research of Myers (1976) involving free-ranging and laboratory macaques provides some experimental support for the close relations between emotions and social life. Myers found that emotional and social behaviors are controlled by the same forebrain areas (prefrontal, anterotemporal, and orbitofrontal cortex), and when these regions were surgically ablated, facial expressions and vocalizations ordinarily used in emotional behavior and in social communication were unavailable for these purposes. When released from captivity, ablated animals wandered through their social groups without interacting; all indications pointed to the fact that they did not survive in what amounted to an emotionless state of aloneness.

When one looks at the evolution of primate facial expressions, one perceives a continuation of this theme: Such evolution may have occurred concomitant with the enhancement of visual capacity that brought advantageous functions of social communication for group-living species (see Andrew 1964; vanHooff, 1962; and especially the extensive review of Chevalier-Skolnikoff, 1973). Chevalier-Skolnikoff points out that in monkeys there is a shift from the prosimians to the old world monkeys and beyond—a shift marked by increasing facial expressiveness and visual function concomitant with decreasing emphasis on olfaction, touch, and sound reception. Such a shift also corresponds to a change from a nocturnal to a diurnal ecological niche and to engagement in a more complex social world.

In the evolutionary step to man, facial muscles became further differentiated in connection with speech and, as Chevalier-Skolinikoff emphasizes (1973), social communication of more subtle internal states occurs more through language than through facial expression of emotion. Nonetheless, cross-cultural evidence that a number of discrete facial expressions, representing qualitatively separable emotional response systems, are universally recognized and expressed throughout the human species would indicate that facial expressions have continued adaptive importance (Ekman, 1971; Ekman, Friesen, & Ellsworth, 1972; Izard, 1971, 1972, 1977). Indeed, the case could be made that emotional expressions persist in the human as a universal "language," one that is clarified and modulated by speech.

A biosocial view highlights that in human infancy, without language, emotional expressions are prominent and provide a medium of messages in the infant–caregiver system. Some messages are unequivocal and biologically necessary to the infant's survival. Crying communicates distress and gives a universal peremptory message, "come, change something"; whereas smiling communicates pleasure to caregivers and conveys, "keep it up, I like it" (Stechler & Carpenter, 1967). Further, an expression of interest reveals a readiness for learning and, for the infant, the emotion of surprise may have a basic role in facilitating the assimilation of new information (Charlesworth, 1969). Whatever specific messages such expressions as fear, anger, sadness may give in later infancy, it is certain that cognitive development increasingly alters the meaning of emotional states both before and during language development.

MEANING AND EMOTIONAL DEVELOPMENT

More than 15 years ago at a symposium on emotions, Knapp (1963) reminded participants that emotions could be viewed from three aspects—physiology, expression, and private experience. Such a scheme is useful and points out our limitations in researching emotions of preverbal infants who cannot tell us how they feel. I would now like to offer another scheme, a developmental one, that emerges from a biosocial view and emphasizes levels of meaning useful for multidisciplinary research. This scheme can be superimposed on Knapp's and has the advantage that levels of meaning apply to all aspects of behavior and serve as a guide for research questions.

The scheme has two major domains, the individual and the social. Each domain has three levels of meaning: the level of biological response, the level of organizational state, and the level of enduring trait. Further, each level of meaning has two aspects. The first is a description of patterns of behavior, and the second is a context analysis. Since contemporary researchers are interested in more than linear effects and concern themselves with interactions between levels, a context analysis explores the "boundary conditions" of phenomena, the operational principles of the system, and the especial defining conditions wherein the described patterns may or may not occur (Polanyi, 1965/1974). I now discuss the scheme, highlighting some thoughts emerging from our own research.

The Individual Domain of Meaning

At the Level of Biological Response

Sound, scientific understanding begins with a full description of species-wide behavioral patterns and how they occur. Much has been learned at this level of meaning about smiling, crying, responses to maternal separation, and other infant emotional responses (see reviews of Charlesworth & Kreutzer, 1973; Sroufe, 1979). Still, as Oster and Ekman (1978) remind us, there is much to be investigated in the area of facial-action patterns related to infant emotion. Further, patterns of posture, gaze behavior, vocalization, and temporal patterns of emotion are in need of study.

Another area hardly touched by our investigative probes relates to "spontaneous" emotional activity. In a recent study of fear, surprise, and happiness in 10–12 month-old infants, Hiatt (1978) found that control groups of infants who were not placed in emotion-eliciting situations displayed a variety of emotional activities. There was no "zero baseline" for facial expressions of emotion. In the experimental and naturalistic investigation of emotional elicitation, perhaps we ought to pay more attention to studying base rates of emotional activity. It seems to me that the human organism is primed to be emotional, that emotional activity is ongoing and fluctuates in accordance with a variety of stimulus circumstances or "incentive events," as Kagan (1978) has put it. Stimuli can be internal, from rhythmic pacemakers and internal disturbances, as well as external.

Such considerations bring us to context analysis—defining the conditions under which patterns may occur. Context analysis necessarily penetrates to other levels of meaning, forces us beyond our isolated territory of description and provides the technical basis for the replicability and generalizability of findings. First, context analysis rests on an adequate description of one's study population and the conditions under which observations were made. Beyond this, it involves modes of sampling. I like to think that in a context analysis, one must consider the triad of *performance, competence, and relevance*. In other words, for an organized behavior, one must consider what is usual, what occurs under optimal (or special) conditions, and also what is naturalistically relevant or "ecologically valid." The field of infant developmental assessment may be illustrative. For years, there has been a focus on competence, often to the exclusion of other aspects; now, as assessment instruments are used to document more about what is so, as opposed to what can be so, investigators are beginning to turn their attention to the other two aspects of context analysis (see Sameroff, 1978).[2]

---

[2]Two other examples of context analysis from the literature on infant emotional development are contained in the longer version of this chapter (cf. Footnote 1).

At the Level of Organizational State

Organizational state is usually considered in terms of psychophysiology (e.g., see Lewis & Rosenblum, 1978). Thus, one can think of state as referring to patterns of behavior and/or physiology which tend to repeat themselves over time and can lead to an inference about a central organizing tendency from which we can predict. Although interpretations about criteria may vary, the description of patterns that underlie inference about state in such a scheme are fairly clear (see, e.g., Hutt, Lenard, & Prechtl, 1969, and Anders, Emde, & Parmelee, 1971, for discussion of these issues with respect to the states of newborn sleep and wakefulness).

In our initial work on early emotional development, we became engrossed with matters of state. Viewing expressions at this level of meaning seemed to capture a readiness to act as well as to react; and, in work inspired by previous findings of Wolff (1959, 1966), we began to study emotional expression as aspects of state. In the infant's first two postnatal months, we found that smiling and frowning occurred as "spontaneous behaviors," as concomitants of patterns of rapid eye movement (REM) state physiology (Emde & Koenig, 1969a, b; Emde & Metcalf, 1970). REM smiling occurred more often in the premature, where it had a negative correlation with gestational age (Emde, McCartney, & Harmon, 1971); and it was found at characteristic fullterm rates in an infant whose forebrain and limbic cortex were virtually absent (Harmon & Emde 1972). In these early studies, newborn frowning was found not only linked to conditions from which we would infer distress (e.g., time since last feeding, noxious stimulation), but also linked to the rhythmically repeating internally organized REM state. Newborn smiling was most often seen as "spontaneous behavior" during the REM state and was uncommonly related to external stimulation.

This brings me to the reason I wish to consider organizational state in terms broader than the above—namely, in terms of developmental level. We found that after two postnatal months, behavior cannot easily be accounted for by internal state and endogenous rhythms. There is a shift away from endogenous control with more of life in wakefulness and less in sleep (Emde, Gaensbauer, & Harmon 1976). Further, as Dittrichova and Lapackova (1964) have observed, wakefulness becomes used in a new way. There is a developmental shift in organization.

For parents, the developmental shift is most obvious in affective development. The dramatic flowering of a baby's social smile around two months, soon to be accompanied by cooing, is well known. The newborn period of irregular smiling to external stimulation is followed by an upsurgence of smiling to stimuli in a wide variety of modalities (Emde & Harmon, 1972). REM smiling, which we have characterized as "endogenous smiling," declines during the first two postnatal months at the same time that "exogenous smiling," that form of smiling elicited from outside stimulation, increases. Such a developmental change is also concomitant with the decline of nonhunger (or endogenous) fussiness, a decline that has been documented by Brazelton (1962), Dittrichova and Lapackova (1964), and by two longitudinal studies of our own (Emde, Gaensbauer, & Harmon, 1976; Tennes, Emde, Kisley, & Metcalf, 1972).

That there is a developmental organizational state change that can be described as a biobehavioral shift from endogenous control to exogenous control is indicated by a host of changes in other sectors. These have been reviewed elsewhere (Emde, Gaensbauer, & Harmon, 1976; Emde & Robinson, 1979) and will be briefly noted here. In terms of sleep, quiet sleep increases markedly during the first two months (Parmelee, Wenner, Akiyama, Schultz, & Stern, 1967, Dittrichova, & Lapackova, 1969), there is a decrease in behavioral activity during sleep, and "behaviorally undifferentiated REM states" diminish (Emde & Metcalf, 1970). Further, the pattern of sleep onset shifts, there is an increase in the ability to sustain long periods of sleep, and there is a shift to a diurnal pattern of nighttime sleep. The interpretation that such changes reflect the maturation of forebrain inhibitory areas is bolstered by our knowledge that a variety of "transitory neurological reflexes" become inhibited during this same developmental period (see reviews in Paine, 1965; Parmelee & Michaelis, 1971; Peiper, 1963).

In the area of perception, significant scanning of the face becomes apparent around seven weeks of age when there is a prominent scanning of the eye region (Bergman, Haith, & Mann, 1971; Haith, Bergman, & Moore, 1977), a finding that corresponds to naturalistic observations of enhanced eye-to-eye contact and expressions of interest at this age. Perhaps related to this is the fact that the visual cortical evoked response undergoes rapid maturational change between 4–8 postnatal weeks (Ellingson, 1960). There also appears to be a change in organization around two months with respect to orienting and attentiveness, one illustrated by heartrate responsiveness (Graham & Jackson, 1970) and visual attention (Kagan 1970a, b).

Conditioning and habituation studies indicate different results before and after two months. Before that time, classical avoidance conditioning is difficult and operant conditioning effects are shortlived. After two months, this is not the case. The same is true with habituation, wherein almost "heroic" measures are needed before two months for a successful experiment, whereas habituation can readily be established in auditory and visual modalities after that (see Jeffrey & Cohen, 1971; Sameroff & Cavanagh, 1979).

Another developmental shift in organization occurs during the age period of 7–9 months. In social-affective development, the differential responsiveness to stranger and caregivers, with fearfulness being shown to the stranger, is prominent. A similar shift, involving both behavior and heartrate, is apparent using the stimulus conditions of the visual cliff (Campos, Hiatt, Ramsay, Henderson, & Svejda, 1978). As was the case with social smiling and the first shift, we found that stranger fearfulness does not emerge without antecedents; certain behaviors (comparing faces and sobering to the stranger's approach) regularly precede it in development. Other changes, including those involving cognition, sleep-state organization, and heartrate organization, have been reviewed elsewhere (Emde, Gaensbauer, & Harmon, 1976).

Our longitudinal research indicates a developmental curve with respect to amounts of wakefulness during the first year. We have found an increase of wakefulness during the first two postnatal months, followed by a plateau that is then followed by a further increase in wakefulness in the two-month period immediately preceding 7–9 months. This is in turn followed by a second plateau lasting until the end of the first year. We believe such a curve can represent a model for times of developmental shift. In contrast to our previous conceptualization, we no longer think of these shifts primarily as times of rapid change. Preceeding each, and roughly corresponding to the times-of-wakefulness increment, there are approximately two months of preparation during which components of new behaviors appear. These are integrated into a new emergent organization at nodal times (two months and 7–9 months) and are followed by periods of developmental consolidation. Two other investigators have recently reported a major qualitative transition in infant behavior at similar age periods. McCall (1977), in reanalyzing data from the Berkeley Growth Study, found qualitative transitions at precisely these two age points. Kagan (1977), in summarizing his research program on cognitive development, presented compelling evidence for a behavioral reorganization at the time of the second shift.

Description of patterns leading to inferences about cognitive state in infancy as they relate to emotion are extremely important at this level of meaning. They have been given programmatic attention by Decarie (1965; 1978), Kagan (1971), Campos et al. (1978) and especially by Sroufe (1979; Sroufe & Waters, 1976). Sroufe presents a scheme for relating emotional, cognitive, and social development that integrates ideas from Piaget and Sander and is consistent with the scheme advocated in this essay. In our own work, we have become particularly interested in the signalling aspects of emotional expressions and the developmental progression from biologically organized states of social signalling to psychologically organized states of cognitive-affective signalling.

In terms of context, analyzing performance, competence, and relevance for organizational state are as important as they were for the level of biological response. Descriptive patterns must be anchored according to what usually occurs, what can be shown to be available under optimal or special conditions, and what has meaning in the lives of particular infants and families. There seems to be little controversy in the current literature related to these contextual questions, perhaps because investigators are apt to stay at one mode of sampling. Patterns of response related to psychophysiology, cognition and broader aspects of developmental state are typically tested in standardized laboratory conditions or under presumed "optimal" conditions for performance. Restricting this sampling mode can be misleading, as we found when studying infant sleep-onset patterns that differed drastically in our laboratory as compared with the usual home environment (Bernstein, Emde, and Campos, 1973; Kligman, Smyrl, & Emde, 1975). Lewis, Brooks-Gunn, and Haviland (1978) have pointed out that little work has been done integrating different measurements of emotional state, and have shown the complexities which arise when one attempts to relate changes in heartrate to facial expression in individual infants. In terms of exploring the context of sampling due to biological variation, studies of emotional state in Down's syndrome infants promise to advance our knowledge of such processes in relation to the organization of both cognitive and social development (Cicchetti & Sroufe, 1978; Emde, Katz, and Thorpe, 1978).

At the Level of Enduring Trait

At the previous level of meaning, we considered emotional state as a *relatively* stable organization of emotions which appears at a biologically appropriate developmental level, and which is supplanted with further development. Such a designation of "state" reflects a basic developmental process involving change. Thus endogenously determined REM smiling gives way to exogenously determined smiling which conveys pleasure and reinforces parental approach behavior; this in turn becomes less automatic as social smiling becomes more situation and person-specific. The process is also seen with the smile of recognitory assimilation which becomes prominent and fades when recognitory assimilation ceases to become effortful (McCall, 1972). Similarly, stranger fearfulness is over-ridden by further developmental factors along the lines of "separation-individuation" (Mahler, Pine, & Bergman, 1975). In other words, although the inference of organizational state is based on observations of repetitive patterns of behavior, these patterns shift as development proceeds. What endures is therefore at a different level of meaning.

Enduring emotional traits have to do with individual differences in response tendencies, moods, and temperament; they also lead to questions of pathology. We might assume that an "average expectable" individual would be predisposed by biology towards a basic ongoing mood of happiness with some outgoing engagement of the world. Yet it would also be true that such a person's affective response tendencies would vary within each day in characteristic dynamic modes. Many questions exist about the dynamic features of emotional traits. How do emotional traits vary with endogenous biological rhythms such as sleep-wakefulness rhythms, basic rest activity rhythms, and hormonal rhythms? Do emotion traits typify characteristic ways of responding to stress?

Thomas, Chess, Birch, Hertzig, and Korn (1963) used "mood" as one of their nine categories of behavioral functioning for looking at temperament in individual infants. With data derived from mothers' reports, they defined mood as "the amount of pleasant, joyful and friendly behavior, as contrasted with unpleasant, crying and unfriendly behavior [p. 41]." Not only did they find that most babies were regarded as ''preponderantly positive in mood,'' but that from one period to another (from 6–27 months) the patterning of mood showed the greatest stability of their categories. In spite of these promising beginnings with respect to maternal perceptions of moods in early childhood, little research attention has been given to the direct measurement of such moods and their individual differences (see Cytryn, 1976, and Pedersen, Anderson, & Cain, 1976).

Aside from mood, it seems likely that a number of affectively related childhood traits or personality variables such as sociability, impulsivity, and perhaps even ego-control and ego-resiliency (Block & Block, this volume) would have their roots in infancy. In addition, a biosocial view might lead to the hypothesis that adaptively important affective structures having to do with learning, approach–avoidance, access to consciousness, and sociability would be recognizable as modes of behaving in infancy; these have to do with the general modulating functions of emotions and enduring individual differences in behavior might be expected.

Prediction of behavior from infancy to childhood has been poor in general, and there is compelling need for further longitudinal research to understand developmental transformations of emotional activity within individuals. Prospective studies often yield surprises that can correct limited impressions gleaned from retrospective study and from clinical populations. (For an account of some of our surprises, see the longitudinal study of infantile depression reported in Emde & Harmon, in press.)

The Social Domain

Increasingly, our research efforts have been devoted to the study of infant emotion in the social domain. Whatever else, our definition of an emotion is a social one. Further, although a baby cannot tell us how he or she feels, there is a communication of feelings to caregivers who can tell us how they feel in response to babies and who guide caregiving responses accordingly.

At the Level of Biological Response

Because they so directly communicate feelings and messages about need states, emotional expressions have been called the language of infancy. Although our longitudinal observations gave us certain convictions about regularities in caregivers' interpretations and responses to infant expressions, more systematic study was called for. Further, the adult cross-cultural work with facial expressions suggested ''species-wide'' messages about specific emotions and focused our attention on questions of biological response patterns involved in infant-caregiver messages. What are the species-wide messages in emotional language? Who can send and receive what? What are the universals of patterned messages between infants and caregivers? Although the research described next centers on the face, this is only a beginning. We know for example that the dynamics of endogenously and exogenously determined eye behavior are complexly organized (Haith et al., 1977) and involved in a high degree of meaningful communication with caregivers (Brazelton, 1974; Emde & Brown, 1978; Robson, 1967; Stern, 1974; Tronick, Als, Adamson, Wise, & Brazelton, 1978) and that intriguing findings have appeared suggesting early postural communication systems (Condon & Sander, 1974; Meltzoff & Moore, 1977).

Adult Judgments of Infant Facial Expressions. A previous report (Emde, Katz, & Thorpe, 1978) describes our initial studies using modifications of the Ekman and Izard forced-choice procedure for adults judging still photographs of facial expressions of infants. Not surprisingly, we found that forced judgments using categories derived from adult peak emotional expressions appeared inappropriate for the 3-month-old, whereas encouraging consistencies emerged from free-response choices. Mothers understood more and wanted to tell us more than they could in the forced-choice task. We therefore pursued two approaches for global judgment studies of infant facial expressions. One involved sorting of pictures by similarities and subsequent multidimensional scaling analysis, and another involved free responses and subsequent analysis by categorizing. In all our studies, we have used adult women experienced with children as independent judges.

The multidimensional scaling approach adapted from Shepard (1962a, b; 1974) employs 25 judges who are asked to sort stimulus cards that may either be infant pictures or verbal responses of mothers to their own infants' pictures. Judges are asked to sort these into one or more piles, putting those that seem to belong together in the same pile.

Sampling of infant facial expressions was begun in a limited fashion using 10 normal infants. Photographs were taken in standardized home sessions, beginning with infants in a wakeful state. A mother was asked to talk and play with her baby and the first five photos were taken at 30-sec intervals. The next two photos were taken with a stranger talking to the baby, and this was followed by two more photos taken during the presentation of a standard inanimate visual pattern. Next, 10 photos were taken at 30-sec intervals without any stimulus presentation. A final photo was taken during a loss-of-support stimulus (moro response). The procedure was modified at 12 months in the following manner: Four pictures were taken during maternal separation, four pictures during a stranger approach, five pictures when mother returned and greeted her infant, three more pictures when the infant was shown an inanimate object, five pictures during the infant playing peek-a-boo with mother, 10 pictures at 30-sec intervals with the infant left in an unstimulated condition, and three pictures when the infant was asleep.

One week after the taking of photographs, a visit was made to each mother and an interview conducted in order to get a mother's responses to her own baby's pictures. Interview responses were tape recorded and later transcribed.

This latter procedure allowed us to do multidimensional-scaling analyses of mothers' responses, as well as of original pictures. The results of both kinds of analyses have been consistent. Similarity sortings have been done for infants' expressions at 2½ months, 3½ months, 4½ months, and 12 months of age and have involved eight different experiments each using 25 judges (Emde, Kligman, Reich, & Wade, 1978). At 2½ months, scaling solutions have been two-dimensional, with the first dimension easily characterized as "hedonic tone" and the second best characterized as "state." After 3 months, three-dimensional scaling solutions predominate. In three-dimensional solutions, hedonic tone carries the most variance, activation appears as the second dimension, and an internally oriented/externally oriented dimension is the best description for the third dimension.[3]

Our free-response approach is one that also makes use of multiple judges who are asked to give responses to the same infant pictures. As in our multidimensional scaling studies, all judges have been women experienced with children. They are given a set of instructions modified from the free response technique of Izard (1971), who devised this technique for cross-cultural studies of adults. Judges are asked to record in one word or phrase "the strongest and clearest feeling that the baby is expressing." Izard found that the words used by adult subjects responding to photographs were relatively limited in number and obtained a large pool of judges to categorize such words in accordance with his scheme of fundamental emotions. We began with Izard's accumulated lexicon of words for eight emotional categories and added a ninth, "bored-sleepy." Over 99% of our responses are categorized automatically into one of these nine categories plus a 10th of "no emotion."

At the earlier age, photos meeting our one-third criterion for agreement included: interest (33%), joy (41%) distress (9%) sleepy (6%) and anger and fear (1% each). Nine percent of the pictures were blends; most of these were of interest combined with joy. At 12 months of age, 39% of pictures were classified as interest, 19% as joy, 12% as distress, 4% as surprise, 1% as sleepy and 1% each for anger, fear, and disgust. Fifteen percent of the pictures were categorized as blends; 6% were interest and joy, 5% sleepy and joy, 2% fear and interest, and 1% each for distress/anger and interest/surprise.

As a result of our experience in longitudinal study, we (Emde, Kligman, Reich, & Wade, 1978) along with Sroufe (1977) speculated that expressions of fear, surprise, and anger were prominent only in the latter half of the first year. It seemed to us that this would be consistent with an epigenetic view of these emotions that might require more experience and cognition. The free-response data are inconclusive concerning age effects. Anger and fear were judged for one

---

[3]These results are similar to those reported for adult emotional expression. See comparison in the longer version of this chapter (cf. Footnote 1).

picture at 3½ months, and surprise appeared as a blend with interest. However, these judgments of categories did not replicate in our second study. At 12 months, there were similar findings with respect to anger and fear; and there were more pictures that reached criterion for surprise.[4]

The reliability findings about emotional messages in these pictures are encouraging and point to the robustness of their signalling features. But there are many context questions. First, are these categories of messages wholly dependent on verbal mediation? Would they appear together in similarity sortings of pictures? The answer appears to be yes. In a study in which 50 raters were randomly assigned to either a similarity sorting task or a free-response labelling task, we found a strong tendency for pictures similarly labelled in the free-response paradigm to be close together in the three-dimensional space generated from multidimensional scaling (Emde, Kligman, Reich & Wade, 1978). There are of course multiple questions that need to be answered about sampling. We sampled infants' facial expressions under special and somewhat arbitrary conditions and represented them in still photographs. "Usual performance" must be at some distance from these special conditions. One question in this area concerns the use of still photographs. Is the still photograph a meaningful unit when we know that emotional life is embedded in temporal patterns of activity? A study compared still photographs with movies. The movies contained 30-sec sequences of the infant's face and upper torso which led up to each still photograph. In three separate experimental sessions, we found that more than 75% of our photographs that met criteria for stability were judged to be in the same category using our free-response categorizing technique, regardless of whether they were presented by movies or by slides. Disagreements were explained readily by the addition of new information occurring during the 30-sec movie segment; these included discrete events such as a yawn, eye closure, and smile. It seemed to us that within the 30 sec and under the conditions of our sampling, discrete events of emotional expression were reasonably well captured by our still photographs and that such expressions seemed to be communicated in small time units that may or may not depend upon sequential coding for their interpretation.

Another question about "usual performance" had to do with the infant's "behavioral day." We had reason to believe from our prior naturalistic studies that our sampling of pictures underestimated sleep, underestimated periods around feeding, and overestimated periods with positive affective engagement. We therefore did a time-lapse video recording of an infant's face and upper torso during a continuous 12 hour period from 8 a.m. to 8 p.m. The infant was 3½ months of age, and filming was done in the home with mother and infant instructued to carry on a "typical day." Both were previously familiarized with

---

[4]Tabular presentation of these results, results on reliability and comparison with the reliability in judgments of adult expressions are given in the longer version of this chapter (cf. Footnote 1).

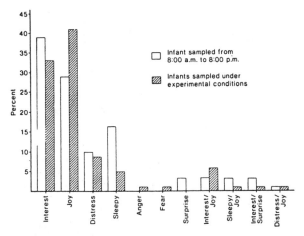

FIG.4.1   Emotions observed at 3½ months of age.

the photographer and equipment and we subsequently established that the day of filming was typical for the baby in terms of sleep, wakefulness, and feeding when compared with records of the previous week. Further, we were able to compare amounts of wakefulness for 12 2-hr intervals of the 24 hr surrounding the filming with normative data previously collected from longitudinal studies involving 25 infants. For 11 of 12 2-hr intervals, the individual infant's sleep was within one standard deviation of our normal group means. (The single exception was from 8 to 10 p.m., when the individual infant's sleep was 1.7 standard deviations below the group mean.) After completion of filming, we sampled still photographs from our videotape at 10-min intervals throughout the 12-hr period. These photos were then judged by 25 women, as in our previous free-response categorizing studies. Figure 1.1 compares emotions derived from this infant with mean values derived from five infants of the same age previously sampled under our more arbitrary conditions. Comparison suggests that the previous conditions over-represented joy and under-represented sleep, and that blends were prominent in both methods of sampling. It should be mentioned that 77% of the remaining 12 unfilmed hours in the 24-hr day of our individual infant consisted of sleep; therefore, ours is undoubtedly a conservative estimate of that expression.

What about optimal performance for emotional messages? Such a question might be phrased in terms of analyzing peak emotional expressions for infants. We are engaged in a collaborative study with Izard in which he has selected still pictures representing peak emotional expressions from videotapes of his infant studies. Our free-response categorizing indicates that blends are common, even among these pictures that were selected as examples of peak emotions. We are now estimating the extent of agreement between free-response categorizing experiments, whether done in Delaware with students (Izard's judges) or in Denver with adult women experienced with children. The study is ongoing, but we are already gaining increasing conviction concerning the robustness of these messages, even with diverse groups of judges and with still photographs that do not offer sequential cues related to movement and that do not offer the multiple feedback confirmation for the kinds of affective messages we experience in real life.

Emotional Signalling.   The study of deviation and individual differences are useful strategies for understanding the relevance of emotional signalling. One deviant infant group we have studied consists of those with Down's syndrome and their caregivers. We found evidence that Down's syndrome messages are noisier (Emde, Katz, & Thorpe, 1978) and are often disappointing to parents (Emde & Brown, 1978). As the result of multidimensional scaling analyses of mothers' original responses to their own Down's infants' pictures and of separate analyses of the pictures themselves, we were able to show that the noise originated in the infant signals rather than in the mothers' original interpretations of these signals. Down's syndrome emotional expressions are more ambiguous and apt to be less intense. There is a few weeks' delay in the onset of the social smile, but parental disappointment typically results from its dampened intensity. There is a bilateral upturning of the corners of the mouth, but cheeks and eyes typically do not participate. There is no brightening of the eyes, there is poor eye-to-eye contact, and there is little activation or bicycling of the arms and legs as one would expect from the normal 3–4-month-old. Individuals experiencing this sequence feel let down. Instead of rewarding a social interaction, instead of engaging and ''being fun,'' it tends to disappoint because it violates our expectations. That there may be a general deficit in the activation of emotional expression in Down's syndrome is the subject of further study, and it is noteworthy that Cicchetti and Sroufe (1978) found a dampening of negative as well as positive expressions during the first two years of Down's syndrome development, a finding that could not be accounted for strictly in terms of delayed cognitive development.

Thinking about relevance and meaning leads us to the more general question of understanding ''signal-operating'' features as opposed to ''receiver-operating'' features (Green & Swets, 1966) of emotional messages between infants and caregivers. Such an understanding is crucial for any analysis of individual differences. Perhaps one could assume there is a biological potential for both species-wide expression and species-wide recognition of infant emotional expressions. If so, a masking experiment in which an ambiguous facial signal was presented to judges might result in regularities for defining receiver-operating features. This experiment has yet to be done for infant signalling. The other side of the system, that of caregiver signalling to infants and of infant receiver-operating features, is uncharted territory (Hoffman, 1978).

Our understanding of meaning will also be enriched by studying the adaptive significance of variations in infant-caregiver messages, especially when attention is given to groups "at risk" for deviant communication. As a start in this direction, we are seeking to characterize individual differences in mothers' interpretations of infant signals and also in infant signals themselves. We have developed standard sets of infant pictures at 3 and 12 months and have generated computerized normative data for an appropriate form of multidimensional scaling (INDSCAL of Carroll & Chang, 1964) and for free-response categorizing. Studies are under way with teenage mothers, parents of infants wherein there has been prolonged neonatal separation, and parents who are referred for evaluation of child abuse and child neglect. Other studies with parents of children with known psychopathology are planned.

Much work needs to be done to describe and understand individual differences with respect to infant signals. Individual features of Down's syndrome infants and other handicapped infants, because of wide intragroup variation, offer opportunities for understanding developmental consequences. In addition, autistic infants who have been hypothesized to have an early defective "sending power" with respect to emotional messages (Schopler, 1965), may offer opportunities for understanding processes involved in the pathogenesis of that disorder.

Another intriguing aspect of our understanding the context for emotional signalling has been opened up by a recent study that found a positive relationship between the frequency of predicted facial components for expression of an emotion and the independent global judgment of that emotion (Hiatt, Campos, & Emde, 1977). An ongoing study seeks to pursue these findings with several independent judgment tasks. As important as it is to study the instances of positive relationship between global judgments of emotion and predicted facial components, we are especially intrigued with findings where reliable global judgments of emotion occur in the absence of predicted components. Global judgments of emotion, even from still photographs, appear to be based on more information than we currently capture from our facial pattern analysis.

At the Level of Organizational State

In the social domain, the level of organizational state is interaction rather than internal. The description of behavioral patterns is intended to answer questions about the level of communication that has evolved between partners within an infant-caregiver system. Our own research program has barely approached the threshold of this level of meaning; but it has been discussed by others in terms of what has been negotiated (Sander, 1975), what has been transacted (Sameroff, 1975), and in terms of the characteristics of mother–infant synchrony (Brazelton, 1974; Tronick et al., 1978).

Theodore Gaensbauer, working in our infancy laboratory, has developed a program for assessing organizational states of emotional interaction in infant-caregiver pairs wherein there is documented or suspected child abuse or neglect (Gaensbauer & Sands, 1979). Robert Harmon has developed a research program for assessing similar features in the emotional interaction and play of infant-caregiver pairs in a longitudinal study of premature and full-term infants.

In terms of context analysis, one must ask the logical questions about such patterns: To what extent are the described patterns usual, to what extent are they special, and to what extent are they relevant in the life of a particular infant and his family? Questions about how these states of organization came about shade into questions at the level of enduring trait. Nonetheless, there are indications that such states involve intricate moment-to-moment reciprocal exchanges of affective expressions for their maintenance. If 1–4-month-old infants do not receive normal feedback from caregivers in face-to-face interaction, if their mothers remain still-faced for example, they may react with distress and withdrawal (Tronick et al., 1978). Of equal importance is the fact that mothers find it very uncomfortable to sit still-faced and not respond to their infants' overtures during a 3-min experimental period. An implication of this work and that of Stern (1974) is that each partner has a lot at stake in the maintenance of a continued level of organization for affective reciprocity.

At the Level of Enduring Trait

We are at the earliest phases of being able to describe and analyze enduring traits of interaction. Yet I think the prospects are for major advances. The work of Thomas, Chess, and Birch (1963, 1968) on infant temperament actually concerns parental perception of infant temperament. Following their innovative lead, a number of second-generation parental perception scales are now being developed that have advantages in terms of known psychometric properties, usefulness at different ages, and convenience for studying individual differences (Carey, 1970; Pederson, Anderson, & Cain, 1977; Rothbart, 1978). Parental perceptions are worthy of study in their own right, and it is important to realize they are not the same as infant temperament. However, I believe that Thomas et al. may have tapped a more complex *interactional* system in demonstrating their developmental continuities; perhaps they have discovered enduring interactional traits. Perhaps what has been called "infant temperament" refers to fundamental adaptational modes, to dynamic equilibria characterizing parent-infant relational systems over the course of development. Individual differences of infants are not stable in any simple way; perhaps there are relational "constants" that will give us a research handle on developmental continuities. I believe the work of Sroufe and Waters (1977) showing organizational continuities in post-separation reunion behaviors between infants and mothers at 12 and 18 months illustrates the promise of such an approach. In addition Sander (personal communication) in a 20-year followup of families originally studied in the Boston infant development study (Sander, 1962; 1964) has been most impressed by the remarkable continuity of family styles of interaction over this time span.

SOCIAL DEFINITION OF INFANT EMOTIONS
AND CHALLENGES FOR UNDERSTANDING
MEANING

At this point I would like to offer some thoughts about the ways we attribute emotion to infants. Broadly speaking, such a discussion belongs in the social domain of our biosocial scheme, but I offer it separately since it offers a number of challenges for understanding meaning.

Parental Attribution

We have taken the position that the best starting point for defining infant emotions is in terms of what is seen by parents, since their interpretations are likely to make a difference in an infant's life. Let us consider the example of anger. As scientists, we may choose to say that anger occurs in development when an infant shows a particular facial expression, has a particular posture, and/or demonstrates an instrumental behavior such as banging a frustrating object. But in our longitudinal studies we have encountered mothers who interpret an "angry cry" during the newborn period, a cry that is intense, prolonged, and occurs in a particular context. The context is usually one in which the mother feels her infant is expressing a need that she is unable to meet; in other words, she feels she is the cause of frustration. A common example occurs with a hungry infant who cannot be attended to immediately because mother is preparing the family meal. Still other mothers have told us that their babies do not express anger until the end of the first year when they have temper tantrums. Similar observations could be made concerning individual differences for maternal interpretations of surprise, fearfulness, and other emotions. It seemed to us that there is need for a systematic developmental study of parental attributions of emotions in their infants. We have begun such a study, surveying mothers of infants of different ages in the Denver area using both face-to-face interviews and a mail-survey approach. The initial part of this study is cross-sectional, with mothers of infants ranging in age from 1–18 months (N = 30 at each infant month). In addition to obtaining demographic information, we ask mothers if their babies have shown any of a variety of different emotions. Each mother is then asked to fill out the Differential Emotions Scale (DES) of Izard (1972) as it applies (1) to her baby, and (2) to herself. The DES lists 30 words that describe feelings, three for each of 10 emotions. Mothers are requested to indicate the frequency with which these feelings have been *expressed* (by her baby) or *experienced* (by herself) during the past week.

A factor analysis of maternal DES responses of 230 subjects (for experienced emotions) gave support to our assumption that words were understood by mothers. The factor structure originally obtained by Izard (1977) was closely duplicated, with eight clear factors emerging in our analysis. One factor combined items for anger and distress; and separate factors were obtained for joy, fear, surprise, interest, shyness, contempt, and guilt. There was no clear factor corresponding to disgust, and two of the 30 items did not load on any factor.

Although data collection is incomplete, Table 4.1 gives some preliminary findings with respect to the age of first occurrence of infant emotions. Groupings are according to infant age at the time of the survey and are for 2–4 months, 5–6 months, 7–8 months, 11–12 months and 17–18 months. All mothers felt that interest and joy were present in their infants, regardless of the baby's age. Further, there was high attribution of emotion at the early months for surprise, anger, fear, and distress. Shyness and sadness were attributed much less and, throughout the age range surveyed, disgust, contempt, and guilt were never seen as present by a majority of mothers for their infants. When comparing the onset of emotions for different infant ages, one is confronted with confounding factors resulting from differences in maternal observation time and differences in maternal memory. Mothers of older infants will have more observation time, but will have more to remember. In spite of these problems, the mean age for the first occurrence of emotions by age suggests that there are differences among emotions. The table illustrates that these differences persist even when some emotions are judged as present by a minority of mothers.

When one looks at the mean month of onset for emotions for those infants one year and over and includes only those emotions for which a majority of mothers felt their infants had exhibited them, one finds similar trends. The mean age of the first occurrence for interest is 2.6 montbs, for joy 2.9 months, for surprise 5.6 months, anger 6.3 months, fear 8.1 months, shyness 9.1 months, and distress 8.9 months.

It seems likely that mothers who attribute a variety of emotions early in infancy probably respond to different features of their infants' behaviors than they do at later ages. Perhaps stimulus-related features are more important early and response-related features are more important later. Analyses of correlations between maternal and infant DES scores and analyses for effects of amount of maternal experience with infants are geared to understand such age-related differences. An intriguing finding across ages is that mothers see their infants as having significantly more of most emotions than themselves. They see their infants as having more joy, interest, surprise, fear, anger, and shyness. An exception concerns distress, wherein they see themselves as having significantly more of that emotion than do their own infants.

Scientific Attribution

Up until recently, the designation of infant emotions had less to do with infants and more to do with researchers who looked for early forms of emotions in terms of one general theory or another. The difference today is not that we discount earlier ways of viewing emotions—for example, in terms of external stimulus conditions or in terms of retrospective constructions from subjective reports of adults—but that we insist on appreciating the infant *as infant* and that

TABLE 4.1
Age of First Occurrence of Infant Emotions

Emotion	Age (in months)	N	% Answering That Emotion Has Appeared	$\bar{X}$ Occurrence, if Present (in months)
Interest	2–4	37	100	1.6
	5–6	61	100	1.5
	7–8	90	100	2.0
	11–12	63	100	2.4
	17–18	59	100	2.8
Joy	2–4	37	100	1.8
	5–6	61	100	1.9
	7–8	90	100	2.0
	11–12	63	100	3.1
	17–18	59	100	2.7
Surprise	2–4	37	73	1.7
	5–6	61	95	2.3
	7–8	90	94	2.8
	11–12	63	94	4.5
	17–18	59	100	6.7
Anger	2–4	37	86	1.5
	5–6	61	93	2.6
	7–8	90	96	3.4
	11–12	63	95	5.5
	17–18	59	98	7.1
Fear	2–4	37	68	1.7
	5–6	61	74	2.8
	7–8	90	69	3.8
	11–12	63	83	6.8
	17–18	59	92	9.3
Distress	2–4	37	62	0.9
	5–6	60	77	1.3
	7–8	66	76	2.9
	11–12	63	73	4.1
	17–18	59	78	7.6
Sadness	2–4	37	38	1.9
	5–6	60	42	3.0
	7–8	90	49	4.6
	11–12	63	70	7.4
	17–18	58	55	10.1

(continued)

TABLE 4.1 (*Continued*)

Emotion	Age (in months)	N	% Answering That Emotion Has Appeared	$\bar{X}$ Occurrence, if Present (in months)
Shyness	2–4	37	19	2.4
	5–6	61	46	3.8
	7–8	90	64	5.1
	11–12	63	78	7.6
	17–18	59	90	10.6
Disgust	2–4	37	27	2.1
	5–6	61	34	4.1
	7–8	90	29	5.0
	11–12	63	40	7.6
	17–18	59	49	12.3
Contempt	2–4	37	11	1.3
	5–6	61	23	3.3
	7–8	89	19	4.2
	11–12	62	35	8.3
	17–18	57	32	8.5
Guilt	2–4	37	3	3.0
	5–6	61	3	4.0
	7–8	90	6	6.2
	11–12	63	32	9.0
	17–18	58	48	13.3

we are unsatisfied with single views. Single views are partial at best. In former times, it seemed as if we had to choose a psychological view, whether behavioristic or psychoanalytic, to the exclusion of a biological or social one. Today, as we integrate multiple views, we find advantages for both naturalistic relevance and scientific understanding. Further, knowing the boundary conditions of our observational field leads to a sharper picture and enhances replicability of findings.

But since the viewpoints and methods of today are so diverse, the process of scientific attribution of infant emotions is complicated. Multifaceted views lead to different terminologies. Methods of observation are various and differing populations in differing environments are under study. Under these circumstances, and when a multidisciplinary field such as this is beginning to flourish, there is a need for ensuring consistent and accurate communication. A standardized terminology with a few agreed-upon standardized techniques or "merker variables" (see Bell & Hertz, 1976) would be extremely helpful in comparing results of different investigators. Such an effort was successfully carried out for multidisciplinary sleep research both for adults (Rechtschaffen & Kales, 1968) and for newborn infants (Anders, Emde, & Parmelee, 1971). But most of all, I feel that the time is critical for collaborative studies, involving different laboratories, different techniques, and different populations. Such studies could ensure the sharing of data and methods and advance programmatic goals for the field while, at the same time, not discouraging unique approaches.

THE ADAPTIVE NATURE OF INFANT EMOTIONAL STATES

Our biosocial view highlights that infant emotional states are rooted in biology and central in biobehavioral development from the outset. Aside from evolutionary and clinical evidence that emotions facilitate social relations in general, there is also evidence for emotions being continuous factors in the lives of infants and caregivers. They provide a medium for development, with mother and infant normally establishing modes of reciprocal adjustment over constantly occurring sequences of interaction that leave both of them with a preponderance of pleasurable and positively toned expectations rather tban negative ones. Early separation that denies opportunity for mutually rewarding affective reciprocity can have devastating consequences and correction of early separation can enhance affective parent-infant relations. (See reviews in Emde & Robinson, 1979; Klaus & Kennell, 1976). Also, as has been reviewed, brief interruptions in face-to-face affective reciprocity between young infants and caregivers can lead to distress for both partners. Social smiling and enhanced eye-to-eye contact are important incentives for caregiving, and disappointment results when early smiling is dampened.

A biosocial view brings into focus that emotional states are complex. They involve aspects of appraisal and motivation with centered aspects being relations to pleasure and unpleasure—a point of view that is consistent with that of Arnold (1970). State complexity would seem to assure considerable variation and, considering this, it is all the more remarkable that evolution has wrought certain species-wide biological features. These features include the tendency for certain kinds of behavior to be experienced as pleasurable and rewarding, behavior not only related to drive satisfaction but exploratory activity and, most importantly, social interaction. The converse, that there is a tendency for certain other behaviors to be experienced as unpleasant, is equally true and is discussed further under cognitive-dynamic considerations.

We feel that soon after the neonatal period, human affective expressions can be represented in a three-dimensional space. These dimensions, especially ones of hedonic tone and activation, appear to characterize the emotional system throughout the lifespan. Since they appear to represent dimensions of biologically meaningful messages vital for adaptation and survival, we feel it is appropriate to speculate about neurophysiological underpinnings. The first two dimensions would likely involve diencephalic-reticular core brain structures, including reward and aversion systems, mediating "hedonic tone" (Olds & Olds, 1963) and the reticular activating system, mediating "activation" (Lindsley, 1951). Consistent with the early and persistent appearance of these dimensional functions is the fact that core brain structures regulate a variety of homeostatic survival systems and tend to mature early in ontogenesis (Bergstrom, 1969). The third dimension, one which has been somewhat more difficult to interpret in our studies, may represent a motivational aspect of affect, perhaps concerning regulation of incoming stimulation (see emotions as regulators of input in Pribram, 1967). On the other hand, it may also represent a general aspect of systems functioning (Fentress, 1976). Either way, its neurophysiology would be less certain, but it would not be far fetched to think of it as involving early-maturing and related core brain structures.

Discrete emotions, which could be represented as areas in our three-dimensional space, would appear to be more complex. Since they are species-wide, one would surmise that they must represent biologically meaningful messages that may reflect phylogenetically derived central nervous system "affect programs" for modes of experiencing and expressing discrete emotions (Izard, 1977). Based on our previous experience in longitudinal studies, we had thought that such expressions were not present at birth and appeared according to an epigenetic sequence. We thought such a sequence might be similar to what Redican (1975) had found in his review of facial expressions of nonhuman primates—a developmental sequence in which social cohesive expressions preceded fearful expressions which, in turn, preceded aggressive expressions. It also made sense to us that discrete expressions would require more complex organization than those regulating dimensional aspects and would necessitate feedback relationships among hypothalamic, thalamic, and autonomic nervous system regulatory centers as well as forebrain cortical areas for cognition. As such, we presumed they would be later developing.

In view of the fact that early infancy contains such a high maternal attribution of discrete emotions and also contains such a rich repertoire of facial activity patterns, we must say that the matter is not so simple. Our experimental study of fear, surprise, and happiness indicated that infants may have been judged as fearful in response to the visual cliff or the approaching stranger and yet not have facial expressions of fearfulness with predicted activity patterns (Hiatt, Campos, & Emde, 1977). Judgments can be made on bases other than what we have been studying so far. Many questions remain. What are the conditions under which a mother sees fear or anger in early infancy? To what extent are early attributions of emotion related to facial patterns of activity or other behaviors? To what extent are they related to stimulus events in the life of the baby and/or the life of the mother? Which emotional expressions make a difference in the life of the baby in terms of caregiving responses, and which are ignored?

Cognitive-Dynamic Considerations

A fascinating feature in the development of infant emotional states has to do with signalling. In early infancy, signalling is predominantly social. Crying and smiling provide appealing guides for caregiving activity. Later in infancy, with the advance of cognitive development, emotional states involve psychological signalling as well as social signalling. At approximately 7–9 months, with the attainment of stage IV of sensorimotor development (Piaget, 1936/1952), an infant's cognition reaches the point where it is more independent of action. Intentionality exists in the sense of an ability to interpose a delay between an initial perception of a goal and in terms of the capacity for circumventing detours such that we can infer the existence of means-ends relationships. As has been so nicely discussed by Sroufe (1979), anticipation beyond the motor act extends to affectivity. By 9 months, the infant laughs in anticipation of mother's return in a peek-a-boo game instead of after a completed sequence, and expresses fearfulness at moderate levels of stimulation in advance of avoidance behavior. (Also see discussion in Emde, Gaensbauer, & Harmon, 1976). At this point it can be said that affective expression leads to behavior; it may be motivating subsequent instrumental behavior on the part of the infant instead of merely motivating subsequent instrumental behavior on the part of the caretaker. Now there is psychological signalling, and a two-phased affective response sequence that bears comparison with adult emotional responses as conceptualized by Arnold (1970). In the case of fear, such a two-phased affective sequence involves an initial phase of appraisal and a subsequent phase of expressed distress with attempts at avoidance (Emde, Gaensbauer, & Harmon, 1976).

Obviously, there are internal feedback processes before stage IV of cognitive-affective development, and internal signalling becomes more complex and subtle after stage IV. A world of questions are awaiting investigators in this area (Sroufe, 1979).

Another related area awaiting programmatic study has to do with emotional dynamics. Our biosocial view indicates emotions are ongoing processes. They are not primarily intermittent or disruptive. Rather, they vary over time and influence behavior in a variety of ways. It seems to me that emotional states in dynamic perspective operate at three levels. These include *ongoing set processes* (moods), *ongoing monitoring processes* (background activity), and *episodic salient processes* (signal affects and peak reactions).

Set processes of emotion involve everyday moods that could be said to have long time constants. They are influenced by slower acting hormones and biochemical imbalances as well as prolonged situations and psychological conflict; in short, they are influenced by relatively enduring aspects of biological and psychological structures. They operate over days and weeks and are involved in setting and resetting baseline parameters for emotional reactivity. Because of their centered relations to pleasure and unpleasure and additional relations with a wide variety of other psychological and organismic processes, moods have been considered indicators of ego functioning (Jacobson, 1957).

Ongoing monitoring processes of emotion consist of oscillating emotional activities. I postulate that a certain amount of ongoing endogenous activity of this sort keeps emotional functioning "in tune" and sets ranges for emotional responsiveness; it also accommodates to minor perturbations from either internal or external incentive events.

The first two levels of emotional-cognitive dynamics have received little attention in infancy research. Instead, most research has been concerned with the third level, that of episodic salient processes. Such processes include reactions to dramatic episodic events, which can be internal or external. Functions of episodic salient processes include mobilizing plans for action and mobilizing communications to others. A variety of anticipatory signal affects are included at this level, as well as peak emotional reactions. That some peak reactions may be maladaptive should not surprise us when we consider the inverted-U relationship that usually characterizes activation and performance. In extreme situations, and with high activation, emotions may be so intense that mobilized plans are disrupted and adaptive action (performance) declines.

As a psychoanalyst, I have a major interest in the theoretical development of affective-cognitive dynamics and a clinically useful theory of signal affect systems. Signal affects act as monitors of bodily processes and provide evaluation of where we stand in our social world. But there are not only anticipatory affects of pleasure and unpleasure and of anger, fear, and surprise as we imagine outcomes; there are also more complex combinations of affective-cognitive experience that have similar dynamic properties. These receive clinical attention in the form of "signal anxiety" and "signal depression."[5] Such anticipatory affects give us small doses of painful feelings along with relevant thoughts. Signal anxiety may have to do with uncertainties about future events and the potentiality for physical danger and helplessness. Signal depression may have to do with real or imagined disappointments and loss as well as the potentiality for a decline in self esteem. As contemporary psychoanalytic theorists have emphasized (Brenner, 1974; Emde & Robinson, 1979; Engel, 1962; Engel & Schmale, 1972; Kaufman, 1976), these complex signal affect systems are important for adaptive functioning. When solutions to problems are seen as possible, appropriate plans are mobilized; but when solutions are not perceived, pathological outcomes with defensive activity, clinical anxiety, or sustained depression may occur. It is obvious that we have much to learn about the development of signal affect systems as the infant moves from sensorimotor to representational intelligence and as meaning widens during the preschool years.

---

[5]It is interesting that Izard (1972), from his investivative stance, conceptualizes anxiety and depression as patterns of emotion that are made up of combinations of other more fundamental discrete emotions.

REFERENCES

Abelson, R.P., & Sermat, V. Multidimensional scaling of facial expressions. *Journal of Experimental Psychology*, 1962, *63*, 546–554.

Anders, T., Emde, R.N., & Parmelee, A. *A manual of standardized terminology, techniques, and criteria for use in scoring states of sleep and wakefulness in newborn infants.* University of California at Los Angeles Brain Information Service, NINDS Neurological Information Network, 1971.

Andrew, R.J. The displays of the primates. In J. Buettner-Janusch (Ed.), *Evolution and genetics (Vol. 2)*. *New York: Academic Press, 1964*.

Arnold, M. *Perennial problems in the field of emotion. In M. Arnold (Ed.), Feelings and emotion: The Loyola Symposium.* New York: Academic Press, 1970.

Bell, R.Q., & Harper, L.V. *Child effects on adults.* Hillsdale, N.J.: Lawrence Erlbaum Associates, 1977.

Bell, R.Q., & Hertz, T.W. Toward more comparability and generalizability of developmental research. *Child Development*, 1976, *47*, 6–13.

Bergman, T., Haith, M., & Mann, L. *Development of eye contact and facial scanning in infants.* Paper presented at the biennial convention of the Society for Research in Child Development, Minneapolis, Minn., April 1971.

Bergstrom, R.M. Electrical parameters of the brain during ontogeny. In R.J. Robinson (Ed.), *Brain and early behavior.* New York: Academic Press, 1969.

Bernstein, P., Emde, R.N., & Campos, J. REM sleep in 4-month-old infants under home and laboratory conditions. *Psychosomatic Medicine*, 1973, *35*, 322–329.

Bowlby, J. *Attachment and loss, Volume I: Attachment.* New York: Basic Books, 1969.

Brazelton, T.B. Crying in infancy. *Pediatrics*, 1962, *29*, 579–588.

Brazelton, T.B. The origins of reciprocity: The early mother-infant interaction. In M. Lewis & L. Rosenblum (Eds.), *The effect of the infant on its caregiver.* New York: Wiley, 1974.

Brenner, C. On the nature and development of affects: A unified theory. *Psychoanalytic Quarterly*, 1974, *43*, 532–556.

Caldwell, B. Mother-infant interactions in monomatric and polymatric families. *American Journal of Orthopsychiatry*, 1963, *33*, 653–664.

Campos, J., Emde, R.N., Gaensbauer, T.J., & Henderson, C. Cardiac and behavioral interrelationships in the reactions of infants to strangers. *Developmental Psychology*, 1975, *11*, 89–601.

Campos, J., Hiatt, S., Ramsay, D., Henderson, C., & Svejda, M. The emergence of fear on the visual cliff. In M. Lewis & L. Rosenblum (Eds.), *The development of affect.* New York: Plenum Press, 1978.

Carey, W.B. A simplified method for measuring infant temperament. *Journal of Pediatrics*, 1970, *77*, 188–194.

Carroll, J.D., & Chang, J.J. *Non-parametric multidimensional analysis of paired-comparison data.* Paper presented at joint meeting of Psychometric and Psychonomic Societies, Niagara Falls, N.Y. October, 1964.

Charlesworth, W.R. The role of surprise in cognitive development. In D. Elkind & J.H. Flavell (Eds.), *Studies in cognitive development.* New York and London: Oxford University Press, 1969.

Charlesworth, W.R., & Kreutzer, M.A. Facial expressions of infants and children. In P. Ekman (Ed.), *Darwin and facial expression.* New York: Academic Press, 1973.

Chevalier-Skolnikoff, S. Facial expression of emotion in nonhuman primates. In P. Ekman (Ed.), *Darwin and facial expression.* New York: Academic Press, 1973.

Cicchetti, D., & Sroufe, L.A. An organizational view of affect: Illustration from the study of Down's syndrome infants. In M. Lewis and L. Rosenblum (Eds.), *The development of affect.* New York: Plenum Press, 1978.

Condon, W.S., & Sander, L.W. Neonate movement is synchronized with adult speech: Interactional participation and language acquisition. *Science,* 1974, *183,* 99–101.

Cytryn, L. Methodological issues in psychiatric evaluation of infants. In E. Rexford, L. Sander, & T. Shapiro (Eds.), *Infant psychiatry: A new synthesis.* New Haven: Yale University Press, 1976.

Darwin, C. *Expression of emotion in man and animals.* London: John Murray, 1904. (Originally published, 1872.)

Decarie, T. *Intelligence and affectivity in early childhood.* New York: International University Press, 1965.

Decarie, T. Affect development and cognition in a Piagetian context. In M. Lewis & L. Rosenblum (Eds.), *The development of affect.* New York: Plenum Press, 1978.

Dittrichova, J., & Lapackova, V. Development of the waking state in young infants. *Child Development,* 1964, *35,* 365–370.

Dittrichova, J., & Lapackova, V. Development of sleep in infancy. In R.J. Robinson (Ed.), *Brain and early behavior.* London and New York: Academic Press, 1969.

Ekman, P. Universals and cultural differences in facial expressions of emotion. In J.K. Cole (Ed.), *Nebraska Symposium on Motivation.* Lincoln, Nebraska: University of Nebraska Press, 1971.

Ekman, P., Friesen, W.V., & Ellsworth, P. *Emotion in the human face.* New York: Pergamon Press, 1972.

Ellingson, R.J. Cortical electrical responses to visual stimulation in the human heart. Electroencephalographic Clinical Neurophysiology, 1960, *12,* 663–677.

Emde, R.N., & Brown, C. Adaptation to the birth of a Down's syndrome infant: Grieving and maternal attachment. *Journal of the American Academy of Child Psychiatry,* 1978, *17,* 299–323.

Emde, R.N., Gaensbauer, T.J., & Harmon, R.J. Emotional expression in infancy: A biobehavioral study. *Psychological Issues, A Monograph Series, Inc.* (Vol. 10). New York: International University Press, 1976.

Emde, R.N., & Gaensbauer, T.J. Modeling emotion in human infancy. In K. Immelmann, G. Barlow, M. Main, & L. Petrinovitch (Eds.), *Behavioral development: The Bielefeld interdisciplinary project.* Cambridge University Press, 1980.

Emde, R.N., & Harmon, R.J. Endogenous and exogenous smiling systems in early infancy. *Journal of the American Academy of Child Psychiatry,* 1972, *11,* 177–200.

Emde, R.N., & Harmon, R.J. *Towards a strategy of studying mood in infants.* NIMH Workshop on the Origin and Development of Mood and Related Affective States in Infants and Young Children. Washington, D.C. November 12 and 13, 1976.

Emde, R.N., Katz, E.L., & Thorpe, J.K. Emotional expression in infancy: II. Early deviations in Down's syndrome. In M. Lewis & L. Rosenblum (Eds.), *The development of affect.* New York: Plenum Press, 1978.

Emde, R.N., Kligman, D.H., Reich, J.H., & Wade, T.D. Emotional expression in infancy: I. Initial studies of social signaling and an emergent model. In M. Lewis & L. Rosenblum (Eds.), *The development of affect.* New York: Plenum Press, 1978.

Emde, R.N., & Koenig, K.L. Neonatal ssmiling and rapid eye movement states. *Journal of Child Psychiatry,* 1969, *8,* 57–67. (a).

Emde, R.N., & Koenig, K.L. Neonatal smiling, frowning, and rapid eye movement states. II. Sleep-cycle study. *Journal of American Academy of Child Psychiatry,* 1969, *8,* 637–656. (b)

Emde, R.N., McCartney, R.D., & Harmon, R.J. Neonatal smiling in REM states: IV. Premature study. *Child Development,* 1971, *42,* 1657–1661.

Emde, R.N., & Metcalf, D.R. An electroencephalographic study of behavioral rapid eye movement states in the human newborn. *Journal of Nervous and Mental Disorders,* 1970, *150,* 376–386.

Emde, R.N., & Robinson, J. The first two months; Recent research in developmental psychobiology and the changing view of the newborn. In J. Call & J. Noshpitz (Eds.). *Basic handbook of child psychiatry* (Vol. 1). New York: Basic Books, 1979.

Engel, G. Anxiety and depression-withdrawal: The primary affects of unpleasure. *International Journal of Psycho-Analysis*, 1962, *43*, 89–97.

Engel, G., & Schmale. A. Conservation-withdrawal: A primary regulator process for organismic homeostasis. *Physiology, Emotion and Psychosomatic Illness*. CIBA Foundation Symposium 8, Amsterdam: Elsevier, 1972.

Fentress, J.C. System and mechanism in behavioral biology. In J.C. Fentress (Ed.), *Simpler networks and behavior*, Sunderland, Mass.: Sinauer Associates, 1976.

Freud, S. *Instincts and their vicissitudes. Standard Edition* (Vol. 14). London: Hogarth Press, 1968 (Originally published, 1915.)

Frijda, N. Emotion and recognition of emotion. In M.B. Arnold (Ed.), *Feelings and emotions*. New York: Academic Press, 1970.

Frijda, N., & Philipszoon, E. Dimensions of recognition of expression. *Journal of Abnormal and Social Psychology*, 1963, *66*, 45–51.

Gaensbauer, T., Emde, R., & Campos, J. "Stranger" distress: Confirmation of a developmental shift in a longitudinal sample. *Perceptual and Motor Skills, 1976, 43,* 99–106.

Gaensbauer, T.J., & Sands, K. Distorted affective communication in abused/neglected infants and their potential impact on caretakers. *Journal of the American Academy of Psychiatry, 1979, 18,* 236–250.

Gladstone, W.H. A multidimensional study of facial expression of emotion. *Australian Journal of Psychology*, 1962, *14*, 19–100.

Graham, F., & Jackson, J. Arousal systems and infant heart-rate responses. In H.W. Reese & L.P. Lipsitt (Eds.), *Advances in child development and behavior* (Vol. 5). New York: Academic Press, 1970.

Green, D.M., & Swets, J.A. *Signal detection theory and psychophysics*. New York: Wiley, 1966.

Greenberg, M., Rosenberg, I., & Lind, J. First mothers rooming-in with their newborns: Its impact upon the mother. *American Journal of Orthopsychiatry*, 1973, *43*, 783–788.

Haith, M.M., Bergman, T., & Moore, M.J. Eye contact and face scanning in early infancy. *Science*, 1977, *198*, 853–855.

Haith, M.M., & Campos, J.J. Human infancy, In M.R. Rosenzweig & L.W. Porter (Eds.), *Annual review of psychology* (Vol. 28). Palo Alto: Annual Review Inc., 1977.

Hamburg, D.A. Emotions in the perspective of human evolution. In P.H. Knapp (Ed.), *Expression of the emotion in man*. New York: International University Press, 1963.

Harmon, R.J., & Emde, R.N. Spontaneous REM behaviors in a microcephalic infant: A clinical anatomical study. *Perceptual and Motor Skills*, 1972, *34*, 827–833.

Hebb, D.O. On the nature of fear. *Psychological Review*, 1946, *53*, 259–276.

Hiatt, S., Campos, J., & Emde, R. *Fear, surprise and happiness: The patterning of facial expression in infants. Child Development*, 1979, *50*(4), 1020–1035.

Hiatt, S. *The patterning of facial expressions of fear, surprise and happiness in 10–12 month infants*. Doctoral dissertation submitted as partial fulfillment for Ph.D., University of Denver, Colorado, 1978.

Hoffman, M.L. Toward a theory of empathic arousal and development. In M. Lewis & L. Rosenblum (Eds.), *The development of affect*. New York: Plenum Press, 1978.

Horner, T.M. Two methods of studying stranger fearfulness in infants: A Review. *Journal of Child Psychology*, 1980, *21*, 203, 219.

Hutt, S.J., Lenard, H.G., & Prechtl, H.F.R. Psychophysiological studies in newborn infants. In L.P. Lipsitt & H.W. Reese (Eds.), *Advances in child development and behavior*. New York, Academic Press, 1969.

Izard, C. *The face of emotion*. New York: Appleton-Century-Crofts, 1971.

Izard, C. *Patterns of emotion*. New York: Academic Press, 1972.

Izard, C. *Human emotions*. New York: Plenum Press, 1977.

Jacobson, E. Normal and pathological moods: Their nature and functions. *Psychoanalytic Study of the Child,* 1957, *12,* 73–126.

Jeffrey, W.E., & Cohen, L.B. Habituation in the human infant. In H.W. Reese (Ed.), *Advances in child development and behavior* (Vol. 6). New York: Academic Press, 1971.

Kagan, J. Attention and psychological change in the young child. *Science,* 1970, *170,* 826–832. (a)

Kagan, J. The distribution of attention in infancy. In D.H. Hamburg (Ed.), *Perception and its disorders.* Baltimore: Williams and Wilkins, Research publication ARNMD (Vol. 48), 1970. (b)

Kagan, J. *Change and continuity in infancy.* New York: Wiley, 1971.

Kagan, J. *The growth of memory and the fears of infancy.* Paper presented at the biennial Convention of the Society for Research in Child Development, New Orleans, La., March, 1977.

Kagan, J. On emotion and its development: A working paper. In M. Lewis & L. Rosenblum (Eds.), *The development of affect.* New York: Plenum Press, 1978.

Kaufman, I.C., & Rosenblum, L.A. The reaction to separation in infant monkeys: Anaclitic depression and conservation withdrawal. *Psychosomatic Medicine,* 1967, *29,* 648–675.

Kaufman, I.C. Developmental considerations of anxiety and depression: Psychobiological studies in monkeys. *Psychoanalysis and Contemporary Science* (Vol. 4). New York: International University Press, 1976.

Kessen, W. *The child.* New York: Wiley, 1965.

Klaus, M.H., & Kennell, J.H. *Maternal-infant bonding.* St. Louis: C.V. Mosby, 1976.

Kligman, D., Smyrl, R., & Emde, R. A "non-intrusive" home study of infant sleep. *Psychosomatic Medicine,* 1975, *37,* 448–452.

Knapp, P. *Expression of the emotions in man.* New York: International University Press, 1963.

Lewis, M., Brooks, J., & Haviland, J. Hearts and faces: A study in the measurement of emotion. In M. Lewis & L. Rosenblum (Eds.), *The development of affect.* New York: Plenum Press, 1978.

Lewis, M., & Rosenblum, L. Introduction: Issues in affect development. In M. Lewis & L. Rosenblum (Eds.), *The development of affect.* New York: Plenum Press, 1978.

Lindsley, D. Emotion. In S.S. Stevens (Ed.), *Handbook of experimental psychology.* New York: Wiley, 1951.

Mahler, M.S., Pine, F., & Bergman. A. *The psychological birth of the human infant.* New York: Basic Books, 1975.

Mandler, G. *Mind and emotion.* New York: Wiley, 1975.

McCall, R.B. Smiling and vocalization in infants as indices of perceptual-cognitive processes. *Merrill-Palmer Quarterly,* 1972, *18,* 341–348.

McCall, R.B. *Stages in mental development during the first two years.* Paper presented at the biennial Convention of the Society for Research in Child Development, New Orleans, La., March, 1977.

Meltzoff, A.N., & Moore, M.K. Imitation of facial and manual gestures by human neonates. *Science,* 1977, *198,* 75–78.

Morgan, G., & Ricciuti, H. Infants' responses to strangers during the first year. In B.M. Foss (Ed.), *Determinants of infant behavior* (Vol. 4). London: Methuen, 1969.

Myers, R.E. *Cortical localization of emotion control.* Invited lecture of the American Psychological Association, Washington, September, 1976.

Olds, M.E., & Olds, J. Approach-avoidance analysis of rat diencephalon. *Journal of Comparative Neurology,* 1963, *120,* 259–295.

Osgood, C. Dimensionality of the semantic space for communication via facial expression. *Scandinavian Journal of Psychology,* 1966, *7,* 1–30.

Oster, H., & Ekman, P. Facial behavior in child development. In A. Collins (Ed.), *Minnesota Symposia on Child Psychology* (Vol. 11). New York: Crowell, 1978.

Paine, R.S. The contribution of developmental neurology to child psychiatry. *Journal of the American Academy of Child Psychiatry,* 1965, *4,* 353–386.

Parmelee, A., & Michaelis, R. Neurological examination of the newborn. In J. Hellmuth (Ed.), *The exceptional infant, studies in abnormalities,* (Vol. 2). New York: Brunner/Mazel, 1971.

Parmelee, A., Wenner, W., Akiyama, Y., Schultz, M., & Stern, E. Sleep states in premature infants *Developmental Medicine and Child Neurology,* 1967, *9,* 70–77.

Pedersen, F., Anderson, B., & Cain, R. *A methodology for assessing parental perceptions of infant temperament.* Paper presented at the 4th Biennial Southeastern Conference on Human Development, April, 1976.

Pedersen, F.A., Anderson, B.J., & Cain, R.L. *An approach to understanding linkages between the parent-infant and spouse relationships.* Paper presented at the biennial Conference of the Society for Research in Child Development, New Orleans, La., March, 1977.

Peiper, A. Cerebral function in infancy and childhood. In J. Wortis (Ed.), *The international behavioral sciences series.* New York: Consultants Bureau, 1963.

Piaget, J. *The origins of intelligence in children.* (2nd ed.). New York: International University Press, 1952. (Originally published, 1936.)

Platt, J.R. *The step to man.* New York: Wiley, 1966.

Polanyi, M. On the modern mind. *Encounter,* 1965, *15,* 12–20. Reprinted in F. Schwartz (Ed.), *Psychological Issues (Vol. 8) Scientific thought and social reality. Essays by M. Polanyi.* New York: International University Press, 1974.

Pribram, K.H. Emotion: Steps toward a neuropsychological theory. In D.C. Glass (Ed.), *Neurophysiology and emotion.* New York: Rockefeller University Press and Russell Sage Foundation, 1967.

Rechtschaffen, A., & Kales, A. *A manual of standardized terminology, techniques, and scoring system for sleep stages of human subjects.* Los Angeles: University of California at Los Angeles, Brain Information Service, NINDS, Neurological Information Network, 1968.

Redican, W.K. Facial expressions in nonhuman primates. In L. Rosenblum (Ed.), *Primate behavior.* New York: Academic Press, 1975.

Rheingold, H.L., & Eckerman, C.O. Fear of the stranger: A critical examination. In H.W. Reese (Ed.), *Advances in child development and behavior* (Vol. 8). New York: Academic Press, 1973.

Ricciuti, H. Fear and the development of social attachments. In M. Lewis & L. Rosenblum, (Eds.), *The origins of fear.* New York: Wiley, 1974.

Robson, K.S. The role of eye-to-eye contact in maternal-infant attachment. *Journal of Child Psychology and Psychiatry,* 1967, *8,* 13–25.

Rothbart, M. Workshop presented at the International Conference on Infant Studies, Providence, R.I., March, 1978.

Sameroff, A. Transactional models in early relations. *Human Development,* 1975, *18,* 65–79.

Sameroff, A. (Ed.) Organization and stability of newborn behavior: A commentary on the Brazelton neonatal behavioral assessment scale. *Monographs of the Society for Research in Child Development,* Vol. 43 (5–6), 1978.

Sameroff, A.J., & Cavanagh, P.J. Learning in infancy: A developmental perspective. In J. Osofsky (Ed.), *Handbook of infant development.* New York: Wiley, 1979.

Sander, L. Adaptive relationships in early mother-child interaction. *Journal of the American Academy of Child Psychiatry,* 1964, *3,* 231–264.

Sander, L.W. Infant and caretaking environment. In E.J. Anthony (Ed.), *Explorations in child psychiatry.* New York: Plenum Press, 1975.

Schopler, E. Early infantile autism and receptor processes. *Archives of General Psychiatry,* 1965, *13,* 327–335.

Shepard, R. The analysis of proximities: Multidimensional scaling with an unknown distance function. *Psychometrika,* 1962, *27,* 125–140. (a)

Shepard, R. The analysis of proximities: Multidimensional scaling with an unknown distance function: II. *Psychometrika,* 1962, *27,* 219–246. (b)

Shepard, R. Representation of structure in similarity data: Problems and prospects. *Psychometrika,* 1974, *39,* 373–421.

Skarin, K. Cognitive and contextual determinant of stranger fear in six- and eleven-month old infants. *Child Development,* 1977, *48,* 537–544.

Spencer, H. *The principles of psychology* (Vol. 1). New York: Appleton, 1890.

Spiro, M.E. *Children of the kibbutz.* Cambridge: Harvard University Press, 1958.

Sroufe, L.A. Wariness of strangers and the study of infant development. *Child Development,* 1977, *48,* 731–746.

Sroufe, L.A. Socioemotional development. In J. Osofsky (Ed.), *Handbook of infant development.* New York: Wiley, 1979.

Sroufe, L.A., & Waters, E. The ontogenesis of smiling and laughter: A perspective on the organization of development in infancy. *Psychological Review,* 1976, *83,* 173–189.

Sroufe, L.A., & Waters, E. Attachment as an organizational construct. *Child Development,* 1977, *48,* 1184–1199.

Stechler, G., & Carpenter, G. Theoretical considerations. In J. Hellmuth (Ed.), *Exceptional infant* (Vol. 1). New York: Bruner/Mazel, 1967.

Stern, D.N. Mother and infant at play: The dyadic interaction involving facial, vocal, and gaze behaviors. In M. Lewis & L. Rosenblum (Eds.), *The effect of the infant on its caregiver.* New York: Wiley, 1974.

Stevens, A.G. Attachment behavior, separation anxiety, and stranger anxiety in polymatrically reared infants. In H.R. Schaffer (Ed.), *The origins of human social relations.* New York: Academic Press, 1971.

Tennes, K., Emde, R.N., Kisley, A.J., & Metcalf, D.R. The stimulus barrier in early infancy: An exploration of some formulations of John Benjamin. In R.R. Holt, & E. Peterfreund (Eds.), *Psychoanalysis and contemporary science.* New York: Macmillan, 1972.

Thomas, A., Chess, S., Birch, H., Hertzig, M., & Korn, S. *Behavioral individuality in early childhood.* New York: New York University Press, 1963.

Thomas, A., Chess, S., & Birch, H.G. *Temperament and behavior disorders in children.* New York: New York University Press, 1968.

Tomkins. S.S. *Affect, imagery, consciousness. The positive affects.* New York: Springer, 1962.

Tomkins, S.S. *Affect, imagery, consciousness. The negative effects.* New York: Springer, 1963.

Tronick, E., Als, H., Adamson, L., Wise, S., & Brazelton, T.B. The infant's response to entrapment between contradictory messages in face-to-face interaction. *Journal of the American Academy of Child Psychiatry,* 1978, *17,* 1–13.

vanHooff, J. Facial expression in higher primates. *Symposium of Zoological Society of London,* 1962, *8,* 97–125.

Wolff, P. Observations on newborn infants. *Psychosomatic Medicine,* 1959, *21,* 110–118.

Wolff, P. The causes, controls, and organization of behavior in the neonate. *Psychological Issues, Monograph No. 17.* New York: International University Press, 1966.

Woodwoth, R.S., & Schlosberg, H.S. *Experimental psychology.* New York: Holt, 1954.

Wundt, W. Grundriss der psychologie (C.H. Judd, Translator). As quoted in Izard, 1971. (Originally published, 1896.)

5

The Organization
of Emotional
Development[1]

L. Alan Sroufe
University of Minnesota

The domain of emotional development is extensive. Obviously, it includes the evolution of the various affect systems, from precursors in early infancy to the forms we recognize in children. But it also includes the changing capacity of the infant to modulate arousal and to mediate affective response. And, in addition, it includes the role of emotions in individual development. Development in general may be viewed as organized around a series of issues, each with an emotional core. Individual differences may be assessed in terms of the quality of adaptation with respect to these developmental issues, and the consequences of early adaptation for later emotional development may be examined.

Each of these aspects of the organization of emotional development are briefly sketched in various parts of this paper. Recent research has helped to clarify the meaning of affective expressions, the relationship between early and later affective expression, and the determinants of emotional reactions. It has enabled a beginning integration of affect, cognition, and social behavior (e.g., Sroufe, Schork, Motti, Lawroski, & LaFrenier, in press). And it has provided the first *predictions* of the young child's functioning from assessments of infant adaptation, independent of IQ or temperament.

Subjective Factors in Emotion

Meili (1955) and others (Sroufe, Waters, & Matas, 1974; Stechler & Carpenter, 1967) have emphasized that the explanation of emotional reactions is not to be

---

[1]This chapter was reprinted, with slight expansion, from *Psychoanalytic Inquiry,* 1982, Vol. 1, (No. 4), 575–599.

109

found in external information alone. Emotions always involve a person interacting with the surrounding environment. Meili has described how with prolonged, "insistent" stimulation there is a buildup of tension, with consequent changes in the infant's motor and facial behavior. It is the tension, reflecting a transaction between infant and event, that results in affect, not the stimulation per se.

Likewise, Stechler and Carpenter (1967) point out that quantitative aspects of incoming stimulation (amount of change, novelty, complexity, intensity, etc.) provide no implication of directionality; that is, whether the resulting affect will have a positive or negative quality. Beyond these quantitative factors, one must also consider the experienced-based *meaning* of the event *for the child*. The same event can produce widely differing emotional reactions in different infants and in the same infant on different occasions, under different circumstances, or at different points in development.

Novel or salient stimulation produces arousal or tension, but whether this tension is expressed in positive or negative affect depends on the infant's context-based evaluation of the event. Previous research has shown that the same stimulus (e.g., mother approaching with mask) can produce the entire range of affective reactions in the 10-month-old infant, from smiling and laughter to sobriety and distress (Sroufe, Waters, & Matas, 1974; Sroufe & Wunsch, 1972). In a playful home context nearly all infants tested smiled at mother approaching wearing the mask; 50% laughed, and none cried. In the laboratory, however, following a separation experience, no infants laughed, only some smiled, and some even became distressed. The event is arousing in both contexts (according to overt behavior and physiological recordings), but in the playful home context the infant's evaluation of the event is positive. Its threshold for threat is higher. *Within broad limits no amount of tension is necessarily aversive.* Herein lies a key to tbe study of individual differences.

In our tension model we hypothesize a dynamic threshold range for affective response (see Fig. 5.1). For positive affect to occur the level of tension must exceed Threshold 1, but not remain above that threshold. Smiling has been interpreted as oscillations around the threshold; laughter as a steeper tension fluctuation (Sroufe & Waters, 1976; see following). Negative affect would occur only when the tension remains above Threshold 1 or exceeds Threshold 2. The critical feature of the model, however, is that neither threshold is stationary. Both the thresholds for positive affect and negative affect may shift. Such a model can account for individual differences in wariness, for changing sensitivities in different contexts (Fig. 5.1c), and for developmental changes. With development, for example, the infant can maintain organized behavior (and positive affect) in the face of increasing amounts of tension (Sroufe, 1979; Sroufe & Waters, 1976). The model can also account for infants changing from laughter to crying following prolonged stimulation (Fig. 5.1d) or crying at an event which had produced laughter only moments before, if a threatening event occurred in the interim (Fig. 5.1e).

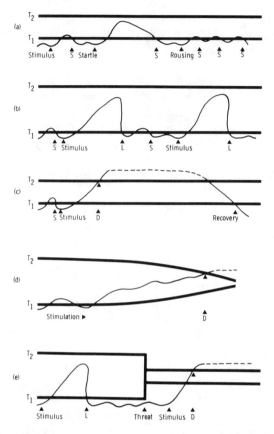

FIG. 5.1.   Hypothetical tension thresholds, illustrating the occurence of smiling (S), laughter (L) and distress (D). Both thresholds may shift due to the infant's changing evaluation, changing state, or changing capacities with development. Part (a) describes the case of the endogenous sleep smile of the newborn. Part (b) represents an older infant and part (c) the same infant in a threatening context. Sections (d) and (e) represent the consequences of changing thresholds within an observational session.

For example, a mother picks up her 14 month old by the ankles. The infant squeals with laughter. Then the mother briefly leaves the baby and the infant is upset. Mother returns and fully calms the baby. Nonetheless, when she picks the infant up once again by the ankles, the infant now cries. The amount of tension produced by this vigorous event now is not tolerable.

In this model tension is not viewed as negative or as something to be avoided.It is a natural consequence of engaging the environment. In some circumstances a great deal of tension may be tolerated. It may even be sought, as when infants reproduce arousing events which delight them (e.g., peek-a-boo). Tension plays an important role in positive affect as well as negative affect. Individuals differ in their capacity to tolerate tension or their ability to manage tension, but the experience of tension per se is a normal part of living and developing for every child.

Before considering individual differences in development, let us examine implications of the tension model for developmental changes in affect across the early years. Subjective factors and the increasing relevance of meaning play a central role in developmental definitions of the various emotions.

EMOTIONS AS EVOLVING SYSTEMS

Within an organizational perspective, emotions are viewed as evolving systems (Sroufe, 1979). Rather than simply trying to demonstrate the appearance of anger, fear, or joy at a particular age, the roots of those reactions are traced and their continuing development and elaboration are followed. When this is done, striking parallels are noted among the basic emotional systems.

I have outlined the development of three basic emotional systems in Table 5.1: (1) rage-anger, (2) wariness-fear, and (3) pleasure-joy. The same cognitive development is considered to underlie each system. In each case there is increasing importance of the specific content of the event and its *meaning* for the infant. Arousal or tension is involved in all affective expression, but in the early months arousal is due to stimulation per se. Later the arousal or "tension" is due to the infant's cognitive effort with regard to the event or to its interpretation of the event (Sroufe, Waters, & Matas, 1974). An emotion is defined as a subjective relationship between infant and event. Therefore, the infant's capacity for anticipation, intentionality, and evaluation are crucial in the evolution of the emotions.

Rage-Anger System

In the newborn period the infant, distressed for any reason, may work up to an intense crying and flailing, which may be considered the prototype of *rage*. One stimulus for this reaction is head restraint. Merely blocking the normal flow of behavior is sufficient for the provocation of rage. But it is not until several months later (about the fifth month) that the rage reaction is due to "disappointment"—the failure of a *motor* expectation or the interruption of *specific* ongoing activities; for example, the failure of a well-established action sequence to be continued. In our scheme it is only now that one may speak of a genuine emotional reaction, because here the reaction derives from the infant's involvement with a *particular* event; for example, being unable to reach a visible object. I call this emotion rage. Specific "anger" emerges out of rage in the second half year with qualitative advances in other aspects of development. The infant now perceives in a new sense the *cause* of the interruption, as when a sought-after

TABLE 5.1
Emotional Development and Developmental Issues

Month	Pleasure-Joy	Wariness-Fear	Rage-Anger	Issues (Periods) in Emotional Development
0	endogenous smile	Startle/pain obligatory attention	distress due to: covering the face, physical restraint, extreme discomfort	Absolute Stimulus Barrier Period 1 Physiological Regulation Period 2
1	turning toward			
2				
3	pleasure		rage (disappointment)	Regulation of Tension (positive affect) Period 3
4	delight active laughter	wariness		
5				
6				Development of Reciprocity (Active Participation) Period 4
7	joy		anger	
8				
9		fear (stranger aversion)		Formation of an Effective Attachment Relationship Period 5
10				
11				
12	elation	anxiety immediate fear	angry mood, petulance	Practicing (Exploration and Mastery) Period 6
18	positive valuation of self affection	shame	defiance	Emergence of Self Period 7
24			intentional hurting	
36	pride, love		guilt	Mastery through Play and Fantasy Period 8
54				Identification, Sex-role development and peer competence Period 9

(but not visible) toy cannot be obtained. Situations much more subtle and diverse than physical restraint or disruption of an ongoing action pattern can now produce anger and rage, including disruption of an *intended* and perhaps novel action. It is not disruption of an habitual action pattern, but the inability to carry out a specific, intended act that produces anger. *The anger reaction may be immediate and need not build as was the case with the earlier rage.* It also may be divorced from the event, as when an infant shows anger at mother *upon her return* following a separation, rather than when she leaves. Investigators may differ as to what age they would use the term anger. Some would use it in describing the early reactions; some would place it even later than we have. The important thing, however, is an appreciation of the developmental sequence, whatever the semantics.

Wariness-Fear System

A similar course may be seen in the wariness-fear system (see Table 5.1). Even in the newborn period arresting *visual stimulation* may lead to distress (as in Stechler & Latz', 1966 "obligatory attention"). The situation is analogous to distress due to head restraint, though here the blocking of behavior and the consequent buildup of arousal is due to distal intrusion on and interference with the child's freedom of response. Only later (again between 3–6 months) does the *particular content* of the event become important, however. For example, *prolonged* study of a stranger's face (arresting because it is a familiar—yet unfamiliar event), leads to distress (Meili, 1955). By this age infants *can* disregard visual events, but not this *particular* event, which has an insistant quality. This is therefore a true emotion, representing a connection between the infant and the event. Later, in the second half year, the negative reaction may be rather immediate, as was the case with anger reactions. It is now not a failure to "let go," with a buildup of tension due to arrest; rather, the reaction is due to the negative *meaning* of the event, as when the infant shows immediate aversion to a stranger following a trip to the doctor.

Pleasure-Joy System

The pleasure-joy system is perhaps the best worked out and most revealing. Neonatal smiles *cannot* reflect the emotion of pleasure, because, as Emde (Emde, Gaensbauer, & Harmon, 1976) and others have shown, they most commonly occur during sleep. They also are more common in premature infants, and occur in newborn microcephalics, as well as normal infants. In our view, however, these newborn smiles must be the precursor or prototype of later pleasure.

In our research we have traced the trail from newborn spontaneous sleep smiles, to elicited sleep smiles, to elicited smiles while drowsy, then to elicited smiles while alert, and finally to smiles produced by the infant's engagement of a purely visual event. We proposed a model (Sroufe & Waters, 1976) in which smiles occur whenever arousal or tension exceeds, then drops below a variable critical threshold. For example, when the sleeping newborn is startled it cannot again smile for some time (Fig. 5.1a). Likewise, a newborn in deep sleep will not smile. A *gentle* chime, however, may produce a smile some 5–8 seconds later, and then, gently rousing the infant from deep sleep produces a chain of smiles (Emde et al., 1976; Sroufe, 1979). In the early weeks gentle stimulation is required so that the rather labile system can recover back below the threshold. Later, when the infant's assimilative capacities are increased, more vigorous stimulation (sharper tension swings) produces broad, full-face smiles.

Pleasure is located at about 3 months in Table 5.1 because by that time the infant will smile at static visual events; for example, after three or four presentations of a dangling clown (Zelazo, 1972). This is a true emotion because, as before, it is in response to a particular event; it reflects a *subjective relationship* between the infant and the event. If a different object is presented, the smile is disrupted. Only if the clown is repeatedly presented, so that the infant comes to assimilate it, does the smile occur. As was the case with rage and wariness, the content of the event is important for eliciting the emotion. Somehow, the infant's *own cognitive effort* produces the tension-relaxation process here. With further presentations the smile wanes, because effort (tension) is no longer involved in assimilating the clown. (See Sroufe, 1979; Sroufe & Waters, 1976). As in the other systems, *joy* is located in the second half year, when there is laughter in *anticipation* of events and when laughter reflects the increasingly *active* involvement of the infant in the event. For example, laughter to playing tug (back and forth pulling on a string by mother and infant) occurs only when the infant is capable of reciprocal tugging (Cicchetti & Sroufe, 1976). As in the other two systems, there is a development from affective expression based on physical characteristics of the event and purely physiological reactions toward expression based on meaning.

In considering each of these systems, the close ties between tension, emotional development and cognitive development should be clear. Emotional development is in part the development of awareness, anticipation, intentionality, and meaning; the subjective relationship between the infant and the event; and changing sources of arousal or tension. When the specific content of the event becomes important—when the reaction is dependent on the infant's cognitive processes— we have the early emotions of rage, wariness, and pleasure. When, in addition, the *specific meaning* of the event *for the infant* ascends, we have the more mature emotions of the second half year.

At the same time, the experienced affect is an important part of the meaning of the event for the infant, and it promotes cognitive growth. As Piaget has stated often, affect and cognition are nondissociable, two aspects of the same process (e.g., Piaget & Inhelder, 1969).

EMOTION AND THE ORGANIZATION OF
DEVELOPMENT

As we have seen, there is organization in the development of the emotions. At the same time, emotional growth reflects the organization of development more generally. Along with Sander (1962), Spitz (1965), Emde (Emde et al., 1976), and others, we view development with respect to a series of issues around which development is organized. Each of these issues has an affective core, though they reflect and foretell important cognitive development as well.

In the right-hand column of Table 5.1, I have divided early development into nine periods. The following discussion is focused upon four of these, Periods 3, 5, 6, and 7. They encompass three major developmental issues: (1) early regulation of tension, (2) formation of an effective attachment relationship, and (3) emergence of the autonomous self. Like other developmentalists, I wish to stress the way in which one issue paves the way for the next and, ultimately, how the individual's adaptation with respect to one issue influences subsequent adaptation. At the same time each earlier issue is embodied in the later issues (Erikson, 1963; Sroufe, 1979).

After the early months, in which the crucial issue is physiological regulation (establishing smooth, harmonious routines), a major task in the 3–6 month period is the management and regulation of tension—learning to maintain organized and coordinated behavior in the face of high levels of arousal. As Brazelton (Brazelton, Kowslowski, & Main, 1974), Stern (1974), and others have suggested, the caregiver (partly through face-to-face interaction) helps the infant to remain engaged, to tolerate increasing levels of tension, and to maintain organized behavior in the face of such tension. By not overexciting the infant, yet by bringing the infant to new levels of organized excitement, the caregiver expands the infant's capacity for differentiated emotional reaction. Laughter can occur, for example, where such a level of tension previously would have produced only crying. At the same time, such interaction paves the way for the infant's active participation in a truly reciprocal relationship (Period 4).

The responsiveness and sensitivity of the caregiver in the earlier period lays the groundwork for a secure attachment relationship (Period 5). As Ainsworth (e.g., Ainsworth, Blehar, Waters, & Wall, 1978) has described, security of attachment is the deelp-felt knowledge that the caregiver is available and responsive, that stimulation in the context of the caregiver is not strident or overarousing, and that relatively high levels of tension in the context of the caregiver will not lead to behavioral disorganization. For the infant secure in his attachment, not only the ministrations but the mere presence of the objectified caregiver is a source of reassurance by the end of the first year. In contrast, a chronically rejecting, unavailable caregiver, or an inconsistently available or overcontrolling caregiver, will contribute to an insecure attachment relationship by not helping the infant learn to manage tension effectively. Within our system, this would be revealed by a lowered threshold for threat, a lowered tolerance for novelty-produced excitation, a consequent poverty of exploration, an inability to be comforted, or a failure to seek comfort when distressed. The infant would be unable to use the caregiver to support exploration, because her presence or interaction would not increase the threshold for threat and would not aid the infant in maintaining organized behavior in the face of novelty.

The formation of a secure attachment relationship, in turn, lays the ground-work for moving out from the caregiver (Period 6) and thereby the emergence of a healthy *self*-concept (Period 7). From the secure base of the attachment relationship the infant explores the environment. And in exploring, manipulating, and mastering the environment, *on his own*, the infant inevitably develops an awareness of separateness and autonomy. In Margaret Mahler's (Mahler, Pine, & Bergman, 1975) scheme, this leads to the major crisis of early development: The conflict between maintaining the new-found autonomy and leaving behind the former closeness of the symbiotic relationship. (Positive self-evaluation, shame, and defiance are emotions of this period.) The child must find new ways of maintaining a connection with the caregiver (e.g., through the affective sharing of play), while developing confidence in it *own* capacities for coping with tension. A new, more complex responsivity is required of the caregiver now, in which self-assertion on the part of the infant is accepted, but assistance also is provided when necessary. In providing firm, clear limits during this period, the caregiver helps the infant deepen trust in their relationship, and to establish the foundations of self-control and self-confidence (Erikson, 1963).

EMOTIONAL DEVELOPMENT AND CONTINUITY (COHERENCE) IN ADAPTATION

The power of an organizational perspective is revealed in predictions of individual differences in adaptation across developmental periods marked by rapid growth. Previously, this has proved difficult to accomplish. Because of the dramatic changes with development, efforts to establish homotypic continuity (identical behavior over time) have failed. The roots of preschool aggression, for example, are not likely to be found in similar behavior in early infancy (e.g., vigorous nursing). But the manner in which tension was managed within the caregiver-infant dyad may well be predictive of later aggression, dependency, overcontrol, and so forth. Within an organizational perspective, the problem of continuity in personal adaptation becomes a problem of assessing adaptation with respect to each developmental issue and examining individual differences in the continuing quality of adaptation, however different the observation procedures must be.

Attachment (the affective bond between infant and caregiver) is a key construct in this organizational view of infant emotional development, because it lies at the intersection of affect and cognition, and because it rests upon all earlier development. The quality of this relationship is the cornerstone for the study of individual differences in emotional development. The attachment relationship serves the dramatic social, emotional, and cognitive development of the second year and beyond, including emergence of the self-concept.

Ainsworth (Ainsworth, Blehar, Waters, & Wall, 1978) has described how one may assess the quality of the attachment relationship in the 12–18 month-old-infant. Not frequencies or duration of particular behaviors, but the organization of attachment behavior around the caregiver and the balance of attachment and exploration are assessed; that is, individual patterns of behavior across stressful and nonstressful contexts. Commonly, these assessments involve a 20-minute laboratory visit, which includes play in a novel room in mother's presence, engaging a stranger, and two brief departures by the mother.

The infant secure in his/her attachment is able to leave the caregiver's side with ease in a novel playroom and to become engaged in exploration. He is not threatened by novelty in the presence of the caregiver. On the other hand, when threatened or distressed, for example by a brief separation, the secure infant actively seeks proximity and contact with the caregiver upon her return. Moreover, this contact is effective in relieving the distress so that the infant can return to play. Although this infant may be friendly toward a stranger, clear preference is shown for the caregiver when distressed. Even when not distressed these infants show positive greeting behavior and are active in seeking interaction upon reunion. One cannot reduce the quality of attachment to any single behavior. Securely attached infants may cry a little or a lot. They may seek relatively little physical contact or a great deal of contact. Sometimes they are friendly to strangers; sometimes they are not. They may or may not seek *physical* contact upon reunion, depending on the degree of distress. The secure attachment is revealed in the organization of behavior across circumstances—actively seeking contact or interaction when the bond is threatened, being able to separate and explore when it is not—and in the active way the caregiver can be used to modulate tension (Sroufe & Waters, 1977).

The infant secure in attachment can use the relationship as a base of confidence for engaging novel or threatening aspects of the environment. The ability to maintain behavioral organization in the face of tension producing novelty, which of course draws on the history of earlier negotiation of salient issues, allows the infant to expand his or her flexibility and self-sufficiency. Ultimately, the infant is able to engage novel and challenging circumstances more independently.

Other infants are not so well prepared for flexible, autonomous functioning by their attachment relationships. One group (15%) does little exploring in the playroom situation, even when mother is present. They are wary of the stranger and the novel surrounding and may seek contact even prior to separation. They are extremely distressed by separation and are difficult to settle when mother returns. Some clearly reveal their ambivalence by mixing contact resistance with contact seeking. They seek to be picked up, then push away, squirm, or kick. They may bat away offered toys or simply continue fretting. Because these infants are not reassured by their mother's presence or comforting, partly because their anxiety and explicit anger interferes with the contact-seeking they need, they are not effectively moving toward successful management of tension on their own. They are not acquiring the flexibility of behavioral organization, the ability to stay organized under stress, and the positive attitude concerning challenges that will serve them well in the next phase. With Ainsworth, we assume that these infants have not experienced a history of consistent responsiveness and assistance in managing tension within the dyad.

Another group of infants (18%) shows a different maladaptive attachment pattern. These infants separate readily and engage the toys. They are not wary of the stranger, and they are not upset when left with the stranger (which is also true of some securely attached infants). The striking thing about these infants is that when mother returns they fail to actively initiate interaction or seek contact with her. This avoidance is more striking when they are distressed following being left alone in the second separation. In this case, the infant is dealing with the arousal inherent in this situation by a precocious over-control. Anger at the mother is expressed only indirectly, through nonresponsiveness or avoidance. Still, the failure to actively seek renewed psychological contact has the consequence of preventing the return to active exploration. Even though not obviously overdependent, in the sense of preoccupation with mother, this infant, too, is seen to be at a disadvantage for later autonomous functioning. The precocious control of affect is predicted to lead to a failure to become emotionally involved in environmental challenges and opportunities, a lack of trust in the availability of adult support, limited mastery skills and an avoidance of emotionally laden situations.

In summary, the securely attached infant can stay organized in the face of stress, directly expresses affect, and may smoothly regain equilibrium given support by trusted persons. The ambivalent/resistant infant has a low threshold for threat, becomes quickly disorganized, and cannot readily regain equilibrium. The avoidant infant has already learned to guard against strong affect, expresses affect indirectly, and avoids contact when it is most needed, presumably because of a history of rejection or chronic unavailability of the caregiver (Ainsworth et al., 1978).

To test the validity of these propositions, we have observed large numbers of children longitudinally, both prior to and, as will be described, following the assessments of attachment. If basic differences in the quality of adaptation—the style of behavioral/affective organization—have been captured, then these assessments should strongly predict later differences in functioning.

We first developed an assessment of adaptation or competence for the early toddler period comparable to Ainsworth's assessment of effective attachment (see Matas, Arend, & Sroufe, 1978). We elected to use a tool-using, problem-solving situation (developed by William Charlesworth and his colleagues at Minnesota). Some of the problems used were readily solved. Others were well beyond the capacity of the 2-year-old (such as weighting down the end of a lever with a block to get candy out of a Plexiglas box), but the child's mother was available for assistance. Thus, as in the Ainsworth paradigm, this situation taxed the child's cognitive and motivational capacity, and his capacity for drawing upon personal and environmental resources. By focusing on task involvement, persistence, ability to use adult resources, frustration tolerance, aggression, and other aspects of problem-solving *style,* rather than success or failure per se, it was felt that the quality of adaptation could be defined in functional terms within a real-life context.

In an initial study, then, the link between quality of attachment in infancy and quality of problem-solving behavior at age 2 was examined in 48 infants. Based on completely independent assessments, with good interrater reliability, infants assessed as securely attached at 12 or 18 months were found to be more enthusiastic, persistent, cooperative, and in general, more effective than insecurely attached infants in the 2-year assessment. (The means and standard deviations for all 2-year measures are found in Table 5.3. Major criteria for the attachment classifications are found in Table 5.2.)

In a later study we again showed that infants who were secure in their attachments were more effective in the problem-solving situation. Moreover, toddlers who had been ambivalent/resistant as infants were specifically characterized by anger and frustration directed toward the mother coupled with contact seeking during even the easier tool problems. Toddlers who had been avoidant as infants expressed explicit anger as toddlers, but they did it more indirectly through noncompliance and object-directed aggression. They sought little physical contact.

Interestingly, in both of these studies, the attachment grouping of the infant, based solely on infant behavior, also predicted the behavior of the mothers in the 2-year situation. Toddlers who were securely attached as infants had mothers who gave more emotional support and more responsive and helpful assistance in the tool problem situation. This suggests that the competence of the dyad is being captured in each of our assessments. The security of the infant's attachment reflects the sensitivity and responsiveness of the care and, not surprisingly, also predicts such care later.

In these and other studies, it has been possible to show that such continuity or coherence in development is not due to differences in what is usually described as temperament, or to intelligence, or simply to the presence of the mother in our measurement situations. Our measures are much broader and more integrative than usual temperament dimensions (activity level, irritability, etc.) and they have an affective core not captured by standard intelligence tests. Recall that securely attached children may cry a lot or a little, cuddle and cling or use distance interaction to establish contact, and so forth. Securely attached infants

TABLE 5.2

Patterns of Interactive Behavior and Crying in the Strange Situation

	Behavior to Mother on Reunion[a]				Crying	Additional Characteristics
	Proximity Seeking	Contact Maintaining	Proximity Avoiding	Contact Resisting	Preseparation/ Separation/ Reunion	
Avoidant						
A1	Low	Low	High	Low	Low/Low or High/Low	Avoidance is the same or greater on 2nd reunion.
A2	Moderate to High	Low	High	Low to Moderate	Low/Low or High/Low	Avoidance is the same or greater on 2nd reunion.
Secure						
B1	Low to Moderate	Low	Low	Low	Low/Low/Low	Positive greeting to mother on reunion and active distance interaction.
B2	Low to Moderate	Low to Moderate	Low to Moderate	Low	Low/Low to Moderate/Low	Avoidance decreases on 2nd reunion. May show proximity seeking in pre-separation episodes.

(continued)

TABLE 5.2 *(Continued)*

	Behavior to Mother on Reunion[a]				Crying	Additional Characteristics
	Proximity Seeking	*Contact Maintaining*	*Proximity Avoiding*	*Contact Resisting*	*Preseparation/ Separation/ Reunion*	
B3	High	High	Low	Low	Low/Moderate to High/Low	Proximity seeking and contact maintaining vary directly with separation distress. Recovery from distress before 2' and return to play is typical.
B4	High	High	Low	Low	Low/High/Low to Moderate	Proximity and attention to mother throughout.
Ambivalent						
C1	High	High	Low	High	Low to Moderate/ High/Moderate to High	Difficult to comfort on reunion. Strong resistance of contact with stranger during separation. Often angry toward mother on reunion.
C2	Low to Moderate	Low to Moderate	Low	High	Low to Moderate/ High/Moderate to High	Exploratory behavior is weak throughout. Difficult to comfort on reunion.

[a]Scored on 7-point scales, odd points anchored to behavior descriptions selected from typed transcripts of the behavior of one-year-olds in the Strange Situation.

TABLE 5.3
Means and Standard Deviations for Dependent Variables At Age 24 Months for the Three Attachment Groups

Measures	Sample		Group B (securely attached)		Group A (avoidant)		Group C (resistant)	
	$\bar{X}$	SD	$\bar{X}$	SD	$\bar{X}$	SD	$\bar{X}$	SD
1. Bayley MDI	115.25	18.31	118.96	17.52	108.89	18.95	108.25	20.27
2. % comply	.28	.15	.36	.17	.22	.08	.26	.08
3. % comply or attempt comply	.45	.19	.57	.22	.39	.12	.40	.12
4. % active noncompliance	.05	.06	.04	.08	.07	.04	.05	.04
5. % ignoring	.36	.18	.26	.18	.44	.13	.46	.11
6. % time away from task	.17	.15	.12	.12	.24	.17	.17	.14
7. # help-seeking	6.15	6.06	4.48	3.50	7.60	7.52	7.80	7.74
8. Enthusiasm rating (both tools combined, 7-point scales)	7.96	2.95	9.22	2.63	6.08	2.92	7.70	2.36
9. Proportion saying ''no''	.35	.14	.22	.14	.60	.14	.30	.14
10. # frustration behavior	1.50	2.79	.65	.98	2.67	4.29	1.70	2.36
11. Proportion engaging in aggressive behavior	.13	.09	.00	.09	.33	.09	.10	.09
12. Proportion cry or whine	.65	.14	.52	.14	.72	.14	.80	.14
13. Proportion help-seeking within 30 secs.	.44	.18	.30	.18	.53	.18	.60	.18
14. Proportion = ''3'' on positive affect	.15	.10	.26	.10	.07	.10	.00	.10
15. Proportion = ''3'' or ''4'' on negative affect	.23	.12	.13	.12	.43	.12	.20	.12
16. Mother's supportive presence (two tools, combined, 7-point scale)	7.82	3.43	10.04	2.51	5.53	2.67	6.20	3.26
17. Mother's quality of assistance (two tools combined, 7-point scale)	7.56	3.47	10.04	2.64	5.00	2.59	5.70	2.21

differ greatly in terms of temperament. It is not that they cry more or less than others (or are slow or fast to warm up) but that the caregiver is an effective source of comforting and security for them. Similarly, securely attached toddlers may be quite negativistic, for example when asked to put away attractive toys, but they do not tend to be noncompliant when seeking help in solving a problem. It is the organization of behavior that illustrates the quality of adaptation. Children with varying temperaments and with only modest intelligence may be well organized (Cicchetti & Sroufe, 1978).

Two other published reports document some of these points (Arend, Gove, & Sroufe, 1979; Waters, Wippman, & Sroufe, 1979). In the first study we examined preschool follow-up data on a group of infants classified as securely or anxiously attached at 15 months. The groups were matched on IQ. Based on observations made without knowledge of attachment history, securely attached infants were found to be more effective with peers and more able to engage opportunities and challenges in the preschool setting at age $3\frac{1}{2}$ years. For example, they were more frequently described as peer leaders, as engaged, as attractive to other children and as empathic, as well as curious, self-directed, and pursuant of goals (see Table 5.4). Effectiveness with peers is again a broad construct, not reducible to specific dimensions of behavior such as activity level. And it is to be noted that it refers to a domain of function far removed from the mother-infant separation paradigm in the laboratory.

We replicated and extended these findings (Arend, Gove, & Sroufe, 1979) with another group of children followed to kindergarten. We again found that children with histories of secure attachment were more flexible, resilient, curious, and socially able than anxiously attached infants, based both on teacher observations and on objectively scored laboratory tasks, including tests of planfulness, curiosity, imaginativeness, and self-control (Block & Block, 1980). In neither of these latter studies was mother present during the outcome assessment.

Finally, we have conducted a detailed follow-up study of 40 children followed from birth (in collaboration with Byron Egeland and Amos Deinard). The children participated in two consecutive preschool classes (one 10 weeks, one 20 weeks), and it was possible to observe them daily as well as obtain extensive information from their teachers.

Children who had histories of anxious attachment were judged by their teachers (who had no knowledge of attachment history) as being more dependent, less emotionally healthy and less socially competent, and as having lower self-esteem. Teacher Q-sort data again confirmed the high "ego-resiliency" (flexible management of impulses) of the securely attached children, with little overlap between the secure and anxious groups. The children with a history of secure attachment also were found to be higher on empathy (with avoidant children lowest). Finally, behavior problem checklist data revealed a greater frequency of disturbance in the anxious groups, including aggressiveness (characteristic of the avoidant group) and impulse control problems (Sroufe, 1983).

TABLE 5.4
Mean Placements ("Ratings") of Peer Competence and Ego Strength
Items Securely and Insecurely Attached Subjects at Age 3½ Years[a]

	Means		
	Securely Attached	Insecurely Attached	P (one tail)
Peer Competence Q-Sort			
Sympathetic to peers' distress	16.7	8.3	.01
Spectator in social activities	8.2	12.2	.02
Hesitant with other children	6.8	10.8	.03
Characteristically unoccupied	7.3	9.4	.14
Hesitates to engage	7.7	12.4	.007
Peer leader	10.4	6.5	.01
Other children seek his company	12.4	7.5	.001
Attracks attention	11.2	6.8	.02
Suggests activities	12.3	6.9	.005
Socially withdrawn	6.7	12.1	.002
Withdraws from excitement and commotion	5.3	8.2	.03
Typically in role of listener (not full participant in group activities)	8.3	11.8	.05
Ego Strength Q-Sort			
Forcefully goes after what he wants	13.2	10.2	.04
Likes to learn new cognitive skills	11.8	10.0	.05
Does not persevere when nonsocial goals are blocked	5.3	6.2	.25
Suggestible	8.8	9.6	.36
Becomes involved in whatever he does	14.2	13.0	.23
Confident of his own ability	13.2	11.4	.15
Uncurious about the new	4.8	7.4	.01
Self-directed	12.8	8.3	.01
Unaware, turned off, "spaced out"	5.6	8.4	.03
Sets goals which stretch his abilities	12.5	11.0	.19
Samples activities aimlessly, lacks goals	6.3	7.5	.25
Indirect in asking for help	6.4	7.0	.38

[a]Items were placed in categories from 1 (least characteristic) to 9 (most characteristic). Scores from 2 independent judges were combined.

The teacher data was corroborated by independent observational data. Those children with histories of anxious attachment elicited more support, guidance, and discipline from the teachers, and when observed in circle time more frequently sat next to teachers and on teachers' laps. In contrast to the secure group, they also showed more impulsive behavior and negative affect, and less often showed positive affect when initiating contact with others or responding to their overtures. They were less popular with other children (as assessed through so-ciometric techniques) and formed fewer friendships. Given their management and expression of affect and impulses, these latter results are not surprising.

These findings are completely reasonable from an organizational perspective. The child with a secure attachment relationship should learn object mastery skills, a sense of effectance, and positive attitudes concerning people because exploration, mastery, and affective sharing are all part of such a relationship. It is not surprising then that this child is enthusiastic, self-confident, flexible, socially skilled, and well liked by peers and teachers. Thus, what began in the first year as the caregiver's flexible responsivity to the infant—helping it learn to remain organized in the face of increasing tension, without over-stimulation—ultimately results in a child with flexible *self-control*. This child can engage the social and object world enthusiastically, being curious and spontaneous when circum-stances permit. At the same time, he or she does not behave impulsively or become disengaged in the face of novel or complex experiences, but, when circumstances require, can remain planful and organized, even in the face of considerable tension.

CONCLUSION

No investigators had previously demonstrated continuity for groups of indi-viduals across the early years. Attempts to demonstrate consistency in individual functioning had repeatedly failed (see, for example, the summary by Kagan, Kearsley, & Zelazo, 1978). Yet the relationships we obtained from infancy through the preschool years were quite strong. I would like to emphasize the role of theory, in general, and a dynamic tension construct, in particular, in this achievement.

First, the model of continuity underlying this research allowed for dramatic behavioral change. Individuals might behave quite differently from age to age, but there would be a predictability and coherence to their behavior over time. The quality of adaptation at one period, in fact, promotes *very different* behaviors in the next period and, yet, a similar quality of adaptation. For example, depen-dency is the norm in early infancy; effective dependency in the first year helps to bring about autonomous functioning later (Mahler et al., 1975). Each phase of development must be considered in its own right, in terms of issues salient for that period, rather than in terms of fixed categories of response (e.g., aggres-sion).

Second, a dynamic tension contruct is the thread that ties together the various issues in early development. Parallel to the emergence and differentiation of the self, one may view early development in terms of the increasing ability of the child to modulate tension, first with the caregiver and later on his or her own. Individual differences in the style of managing tension may emerge early and then interact with subsequent experience. Style of tension management, which is not wedded to drive reduction or fixed quantities of energy, may be a more viable construct than constructs which assume a single motive of keeping tension low and which emphasize amount of gratification of drives. Although research in the last three decades has called into question drive reduction and energy conservation concepts, the dynamic tension model proposed here is completely congruent with recent developmental literature. Affect and dynamic concepts will have a clear role in the continued evolution of personality development theory.

ACKNOWLEDGMENT

This paper is reprinted, with some expansion, from *Psychoanalytic Inquiry,* 1983. The preparation of this paper was supported in part by a program project grant from the National Institute of Child Health and Human Development, University of Minnesota, Minneapolis, Minnesota, 55455.

REFERENCES

Ainsworth, M., Blehar, M., Waters, E., & Wall, S. *Patterns of attachment: A psychological study of the strange situation.* Hillsdale, N.J.: Lawrence Erlbaum Associates, 1978.

Arend, R., Gove, F., & Sroufe, L.A. Continuity of early adaptation: From attachment in infancy to ego-resiliency and curiosity at age 5. *Child Development,* 1979, *50,* 950–959.

Block, J.H., & Block, J. The role of ego-control and ego-resiliency in the organization of development. In W.A. Collins (Ed.), *Minnesota symposia on child psychology* (Vol. 13). Hillsdale, N.J.: Lawrence Erlbaum Associates, 1980.

Brazelton, T., Koslowski, B., & Main, M. The origins of reciprocity: The early mother-infant interaction. In M. Lewis & L. Rosenblum (Eds.), *The effect of the infant on its caregiver.* New York: Wiley, 1974.

Cicchetti, D., & Sroufe, L.A. An organizational view of affect: Illustration from the study of Down's syndrome infants. In M. Lewis & L. Rosenblum (Eds.), *The development of affect.* New York: Plenum, 1978.

Emde, R., Gaensbauer, T., & Harmon, R. Emotional expression in infancy: A bio-behavioral study. *Psychological Issues,* 1976, *10* (1, Whole No. 37).

Erikson, E. *Childhood and society,* 2nd edition. New York: Norton & Co., 1963.

Kagan, J., Kearsley, R., & Zelazo, P. *Infancy: Its place in human development,* Cambridge, Mass.: Harvard University Press, 1978.

Mahler, M., Pine, F., & Bergman, A. *The psychological birth of the infant.* New York: Basic Books, 1975.

Matas, L., Arend, R., & Sroufe, L.A. Continuity of adaptation in the second year: The relationship between quality of attachment and later competent functioning. *Child Development,* 1978, *49,* 547–556.

Meili, R. Angstentstehung bei Kleinkindern. *Schweizerische Zeitschrift fur Psychologie und ihre Anwendungen,* 1955, *14,* 195–212.

Piaget, J., & Inhelder, B. *The psychology of the child.* New York: Basic Books, 1969.

Sander, L. Issues in early mother-child interaction. *Journal of the American Academy of Child Psychiatry,* 1962, *1,* 141–166.

Spitz, R. *The first year of life. A psychoanalytic study of normal and deviant development of object relations*. New York: International Universities Press, 1965.

Sroufe, L.A. Socioemotional development. In J. Osofsky (Ed.), *Handbook of infant development*. New York: Wiley, 1979.

Sroufe, L.A. Patterns of individual adaptation from infancy to preschool: The roots of maladaptation and competence. In M. Perlmutter (Ed.), *Minnesota symposia in child psychology* (Vol. 16). Hillsdale, N.J.: Lawrence Erlbaüm Associates, 1983.

Sroufe, L.A., Schork, E., Motti, F., Lawroski, N., & LaFrenier, P. The role of affect in emerging social competence. In C. Izard, J. Kagan, & R. Zajonc (Eds.), *Emotion, cognition and behavior*. New York: Plenum, in press.

Sroufe, L.A., & Waters, E. The ontogenesis of smiling and laughter: A perspective on the organization of development in infancy. *Psychological Review*, 1976, *83*, 173–189.

Sroufe, L.A., & Waters, E. Attachment as an organizational construct. *Child Development*, 1977, *48*, 1184–1199.

Sroufe, L.A., Waters, E., & Matas, L. Contextual determinants of infant affective response. In M. Lewis & L. Rosenblum (Eds.), *The origins of fear*. New York: Wiley, 1974.

Sroufe, L.A., & Wunsch, J.P. The development of laughter in the first year of life. *Child Development*, 1972, *43*, 1326–1344.

Stechler, G., & Carpenter, G. A viewpoint on early affective development. In J. Hellmuth (Ed.), *The exceptional infant, Vol. 1*. Seattle: Special Child Publications, 1967.

Stechler, G., & Latz, E. Some observations on attention and arousal in the human infant. *Journal of the American Academy of Child Psychiatry*, 1966, *5*, 517–524.

Stern, D. The goal and structure of mother-infant play. *Journal of the American Academy of Child Psychiatry*, 1974, *13*, 402–421.

Waters, E., Wippman, J., & Sroufe, L.A. Attachment, positive affect and competence in the peer group: Two studies in construct validation. *Child Development*, 1979, *50*, 821–829.

Zelazo, P.R. Smiling and vocalizing: A cognitive emphasis. *Merrill-Palmer Quarterly*, 1972, *18*, 349–365.

6

Emotions in Infancy: Regulators of Contact and Relationships with Persons

Colwyn Trevarthen
University of Edinburgh

INTRODUCTION

The study of infants can contribute vital evidence on the nature and function of human emotion. It can help resolve four classical problems which challenge all attempts to understand empathic communication between persons. First, accurate description of the expressive movements of infants can give evidence on the inherent motor coordinating mechanisms of affect and on the process of their development. Second, analysis, both descriptive and experimental, of the changes of affective expression of infants when they are communicating with adults can reveal the extent to which infants are sensitive to emotions of others and able to regulate their own affective states by eliciting supportive responses from others. This leads to analysis of the role of affective communication in the formation and maintenance of relationships between infants and persons with whom they have different degrees of familiarity. Third, developments in expressive behavior may be related to orienting and focusing on objects, interest for the displacements, appearances and disappearances of objects and abilities to grasp, manipulate and combine objects with recreation of experiences, all of which show large and systematic advances in infancy. This comparison between affective and cognitive development may resolve the problem of how the infant gains awareness of persons as entities separate from themselves. Do infants have to build a universal concept of self and object before they can be emotional about their relationships to persons? Or, are persons conceived by a different mechanism from that which masters manipulable objects? Finally, an accurate estimation of the use of emotional expressions in communication by infants of different ages can provide information on the role of language in the formation of emotions. If infants' acts of emotional communication are comparatively well-differentiated and similar in form to those of adults, then the idea that emotions are first defined verbally, or by thoughts or reflections mediated verbally, must be rejected. A similar argument about how far the development of awareness of a social self by imitation of adults and by learning of an independent and consistent social role contributes to definition of emotional states may be resolved by observing how the expressions of affective states of mind develop in the first few months, before the child has significant social autonomy.

Darwin led the way in careful description of infant expressions, presenting accurate eye witness accounts and excellent photographs of facial, vocal, and gestural signs of feeling in infants in particular situations (Darwin, 1872, 1877). He used this evidence to support the argument that human expressions of feeling were largely innate and that they had morphological similarity to the signals by which animals regulate adaptive social behaviours. Subsequent descriptive accounts have added little to Darwin (Charlesworth & Kreutzer, 1973; Peiper, 1963) until, over a century after Darwin's publications, Oster and Ekman (1977) applied a minute descriptive technique to facial muscle movements of newborns. They confirmed elaborate differentiation of the neuro-motor elements and a high degree of inborn coordination between them to form patterns of expression essentially the same as those of adults.

Darwin noted age-related changes in emotional expression in infants and most subsequent observers have been persuaded that he observed the earliest signs of each feeling (Bridges, 1932; Charlesworth & Kreutzer, 1973). Nevertheless, there are a number of observations that indicate expressions may make their appearance earlier than Darwin perceived them, a possibility he would certainly have allowed (e.g., Izard, 1978; Peiper, 1963; Wolff, 1963). Oster and Ekman (1977) concluded that initially all the elementary movements of human expression and many of the expressive patterns are emitted by newborns. They believe their minute observations "suggest a richness and complexity of affective and cognitive experience that might not otherwise have been suspected." Like Darwin, Oster is inclined to infer emotional states from the patterns of emotional expression, but she observed expressions in newborns which Darwin noted only in older infants.

Little is known about the effects that infant expressions have on other persons, or how far the interior emotional states are sensitive to particular stimuli from persons. Most authors can, therefore, give little evidence on the systematic use of expressions to convey information about emotional states that are reactive to persons. Until recently the emotional expressions of infants made while they are interacting with persons have not been studied as an essential part of the interaction. It has been felt necessary to explain early expressive behaviours of young infants, even their oriented reactions when older to persons who are recognized as individuals, entirely in terms of their broadcast signaling value for regulation of protective and nutritive maternal care. Correspondingly the mother has been described as adapted to respond to infant expressions with caretaking behaviors rather than manifestations of feeling. However, in the last two decades micro-analyses of film and video records of communication between mothers and infants has revealed a high degree of patterning and mutual control in movements of many kinds, even with newborns (Brazelton, Koslowski, & Main, 1974; Stern, 1974; Stern & Gibbon, 1980; Trevarthen 1977, 1979a; Tronick, Als, & Brazelton, 1979). After 6 weeks normal infants readily engage in precise interaction with their mothers by means of facial, vocal and gestural expression. They stimulate elaborate expressions of interest and feeling in others and respond by coordinating their own expressions of interest and feeling so as to produce coincident or reciprocal displays. Experimental studies prove that even newborns have numerous alternative perceptual channels capable of selective recognition of a human being and its body movements, face expressions, vocalizations (Trevarthen, Murray, & Hubley, 1981) Then in the second month, when the visual system is capable of maintained focalization on an external object, infants show a strong preference for looking towards human beings and for establishing interactions that are precisely regulated by facial and vocal expressions of affect. Detailed analysis of how a young infant may regulate expressions of feeling when oriented to a person who is in turn responding emotively to the baby strongly suggest that a special ability to perceive persons and to engage in affective interactions with them is present before the baby can carry out controlled manipulation of objects.

Piaget is responsible for the widely accepted theory that the infant mind constructs representations of extracorporeal reality by retaining experiences obtained through performing acts of manipulation on objects. Exteroceptive awareness is, according to Piaget, created by manipulations which have sufficient coordination with vision only after an infant is 4 months of age. In his rare and abbreviated discussions of affective processes (e.g., Piaget & Inhelder, 1969) he is firm about the absolute coincidence of affective development with his scheme for stage-by-stage development of the object concept. His attempts to explain the growth of interpersonal communication as a rational process, no different in principle from development of mental representations of operations that can be performed on nonliving objects, are obscure on many points and little evidence is presented. Emotion, according to Piaget, is an aspect of mental activity concerned with "energetics" or "economy."

As shall be explained, the facts of development in infancy suggest that early development of behavior appropriate to exploration and use of objects is to a high degree separate from development of mental engagement with persons. Moreover, this inherent duality of the human mind appears to be responsible for the generation of the unique human awareness of the possibilities of cooperation and shared consciousness. If affective or interpersonal and rational or practical forms of intelligence are assumed to be one and the same, cooperation, involving as it does representation of complementary motives for action in a common world, is unintelligible.

Bowlby's Attachment Theory, (Bowlby, 1958) has led psychologists to give attention to the importance of affectional ties in childhood, and research stimulated by it has discovered strong interactions between motivation to explore the world cognitively and the formation of consistent supportive relationships (Ainsworth, 1973; Ainsworth, & Wittig, 1969). Unfortunately, the theoretical basis of Attachment Theory is too simple (Trevarthen, 1980). The mother's face was first described by Bowlby as a "sign stimulus" which triggered the infant smile, an instinctual behavior pattern that, in turn, gives reward to the mother for her attentions. Following criticism of cognitive psychologists whose experiments seek to obtain a physical description of stimuli, the imprinting of an infant to the mother's face is now most frequently stated to occur because a face is, in some undefined physical sense, the most complex and therefore most interesting stimulus the infant encounters. The infant's expressions of distress (crying, seeking eye contact, clinging, running to the mother) by which the strength of attachment is measured are described as maintaining the proximity needed for protection. Thus, in spite of its foundation in evolutionary theory, the concept of attachment has small appreciation of the adaptive advantage to a growing human mind of the consistent affectionate companionship between the child and one or a few attentive older persons who are capable of sharing consciousness and intentions as well as taking care of physical or physiological needs.

Research on prelinguistic communication in the past decade has established that older infants exercise specifically human forms of sharing of interests and awareness with those persons that maintain an intimate warm relationship with them (Bates, 1976; Bruner, 1975; Trevarthen, 1979b; Trevarthen & Hubley, 1978). This sharing by means of coordinated orientations to surroundings and to each other allows the growth of meanings. Without joint determination of action in a friendship that is sustained by means of expressions of emotion the child's language can discover nothing to refer to and can find no purpose in communication. But this raises psychological questions outside the scope of the clinical fields which give most support to studies of attachment.

Piaget greatly enriched developmental psychology by demonstrating that infants could, indeed had to, acquire the rudiments of practical reasoning before they learned to represent the contents of their consciousness symbolically in language. In recent years research on communication before language has shown that the affective or interpersonal component of intelligence is also highly active long before the first words are uttered. Rational and informative use of language is carried by intersubjective processes that require the infant to make emotional use of relationships to persons. Unfortunately Piaget's rationalist theory is so dominant in developmental psychology that significant steps towards communication by gesture and vocalization are usually interpreted as consequences of advancement through stages in development of the ''object concept'' (e.g., Bates, 1976; Sroufe, 1978). This conclusion results from a scholastic form of reasoning and it puts untenable weight on certain coincidences of developments in communicative expression with critical stage-transition periods in development of the object concept that, while they undoubtedly reflect advances in the child's control of his actions, do not necessarily situate interpersonal awareness in a subordinate position to awareness of passive things. Observation of natural interactions between infants and parents do not support that view.

As for the development of consistent modes of presentation of a self in society, this too appears to occur because the child's awareness of other persons as individuals with different degrees of familiarity and different kinds of personal relationsbip undergoes systematic intrinsically generated changes. Evidence can be presented (see below) that the beginning of one easily recognized kind of self-consciousness is tied in with the coming into effect of an inherent interest in other people's use of conventional and therefore usefully imitated gestures and poses. These developments have, I believe, great significance for emergence of linguistic understanding, and they change the possibilities for acting on objects too. They are more than developments in cognitive representation of an object (any object) as separate from the self (cf. Lewis & Brooks, 1975). Important for our purpose is evidence, which shall be discussed, that these developments occur after infants have manifested a rich array of spontaneous emotional expressions and developed effective use of emotions to regulate interactions with those most familiar to them, and also acquired the ability to fend off intruders to this intimate circle.

The changes in use of emotions in communication do not mean that emotions themselves or their effects on others are defined by social imitation. As we have seen, infants use emotional expression and sensitivity to emotions months before they show an interest in imitating gestures or expressions of others. Developing social awareness may transform the use of emotional expression without changing the basic function of emotions to regulate interpersonal relations.

DIFFERENT CONCEPTS OF EMOTIONAL STRUCTURES

It seems evident that two kinds of conceptual barrier, poles of a dualist dilemma, have led psychologists to perceive emotion as second order processes which import their structure from other levels of the mental or behavioral systems. These ideas would appear to make the emotional processes of infants more obscure than they need be (see Trevarthen, Murray & Hubley, 1981).

In an evolutionary perspective attention has been concentrated on the peripheral problem of how certain innate motor systems have changed from an autonomic function to contribute to more effective social communication. This preoccupation with expressive mechanisms may be traced to Darwin's theory (Darwin, 1872).

Darwin was, of course, working within the limitations of 19th century knowledge of neural systems. His psychological insights, the fruits of patient observation of behavior, were not supported by adequate evidence on how an evolved organic mechanism, namely the brain, might represent interpersonal situations, and he reduced the function of feelings to the satisfaction of bodily needs. He believed that expressive behavior must have originated by natural selection acting on already existing muscular or circulatory adjustments that served to regulate body processes usefully when the organism is moving to get sensory information or to perform some act, or is preparing to start a form of action. He was able to relate nearly all expressions to his famous principles of "serviceable associated habits," "antithesis," and "direct action of the nervous system"— all mechanical or physiological principles, none of which require emotion to be part of a psychological concept of other beings, of relationships, or of a self with a particular place or role in society.

Darwin (1877) did give meticulous interpretations of the expressive behaviors of infants and children in relation to the interpersonal circumstances in which the expressions occurred, concluding that, "an infant understands to a certain extent, and as I believe at a very early period, the meaning or feelings of those who tend to him, by the expression of their features." His classification of emotional states in terms such as suffering, anxiety, grief, despair, joy, love, tenderness, meditation, sulkiness, determination, hatred, anger, contempt, disgust, guilt, pride, patience, surprise, fear, and shame shows that he was ready to accept a cognitive and motivational context for emotional feeling as an essential factor in interpersonal communication. Nevertheless, he failed to state how he thought the psychological processes that represent persons and relationships could enter into the determination of emotional states.

There is thus a deep fault in Darwin's logic which renders difficult the task of relating his theory of the evolution of emotions to the part emotional expression plays in normal discourse and cooperative life. It also leaves the emotional expressions of infants, which Darwin documented with great patience and care, without psychological content.

It is of interest that Darwin concluded that blushing is "the most human of all expressions" because the shyness, shame, or modesty that accompany blushing have self-attention as an essential element. He noted a claim that infants do not blush, though they express other emotions. He collected evidence that the perception of others as attending to one's person can cause circulatory and other changes in "parts and organs not properly under the control of the will." But what mental mechanism is needed to perceive that another person has directed interest too pointedly to oneself? Apparently, Darwin was put in difficulty by the inevitable conclusion that blushing for shyness, unlike other expressions, could never have had in the evolutionary past an immediate organic value. It relates to a self-awareness and to attention from others, and to no body-preserving function. As Darwin says "it is the mind which must be affected" to induce blushing.

Darwin (1872) concludes his book with the following remarks:

> The movements of expression . . . whatever their origin may have been, are in themselves of much importance for our welfare. They serve as the first means of communication between the mother and her infant; she smiles approval, and thus encourages her child on the right path, or frowns disapproval. We readily perceive sympathy in others by their expression; our sufferings are thus mitigated and our pleasures increased; and mutual good feeling is thus strengthened. The movements of expression give vividness and energy to our spoken words. They reveal the thoughts and intentions of others more truly than do words, which may be falsified . . .
>
> Expression in itself, or the language of the emotions, as it has sometimes been called, is certainly of importance for the welfare of mankind. To understand, as far as is possible, the source or origin of the various expressions which may be hourly seen on the faces of the men around us, not to mention our domesticated animals, ought to possess much interest for us.

These modest statements may conceal disappointment, for Darwin did not succeed in explaining how emotions evolved to be an essential part of the mental equipment for interpersonal communication and cooperative human life. He was puzzled to the end about how feelings are perceived, but thought it most likely that recognition had "become instinctive" along with the power of expression.

The second way of seeing emotions, often linked with the first, is a rationalist explanation of emotions as by-products of cognitive mastery of stimuli. This concept may be couched in mentalistic terms and be related to the work of thinking, reasoning, and problem solving, or be paraphrased in physical terms as rate or density of neural excitation in cognitive networks, information processing, etc. The mind is said to bring primitive excitatory states under an acquired cognitive control; we like what we have learned to present prospects of pleasure and fear what we have learned to be dangerous. Descartes (1650) enunciated such a rational/cognitive explanation of emotions in his *Traité des Passions de l'Ame*. He stated that the primary emotion is admiration or curiosity because the mind feels this immediately it encounters a new experience, before recognition occurs. All other feelings arise out of elaboration of the awareness of things in the light of past experience, with added feedback effects to the mind from bodily adjustments (circulation of the blood, beating of the heart, breathing, trembling of the limbs, etc). According to this interpretation, infants, because they are inexperienced, must have at best crude states of excitement which are given polarity by the principle of pleasure and pain. This adaptive principle enables an organism to maintain the physiological system of its body by controlling repetition of behaviors that give organic benefits and cessation of behaviors that cause damage. Such a pleasure/pain system is part of the constitution of all active creatures and so infants are not to be distinguished in this respect from lowly organisms, except that they must signal their pleasure or pain to control aid from caretakers. They can record the state of their bodies without making any representation of the external world, and without awareness of other persons' feelings as separate from their own. The special human features of emotional life must be acquired after the development of cognitive functions and these functions will progressively define the emotions by which they are regulated.

It will be appreciated that such a theory of how human emotions develop assumes that the infant begins living as a self-maintaining organic isolate, one that experiences or shows pleasure and pain only with respect to its existence as a separate unsocialized "biological" system.

An alternative theory of how human social life is regulated by emotions may furnish us with a more receptive attitude towards emotional behaviors in infants. Human behavior appears to be governed by an organised community of motives which may or may not be conscious. The obvious benefits of living in culturally contrived societies with all their artifacts and techniques requires that each person's actions be directed to cooperate with or complement the actions of others. The world we create together and build by an effort extending over many generations requires exchange of information about knowledge, intentions, reasons, meanings and the like. This exchange is made possible by the formation of stable but developing relationships that are regulated by emotions.

If motives of each individual are defined as the intramental processes which generate and regulate acts in relation to an awareness of the environmental conditions for their execution (a concept discussed more fully in Trevarthen, 1982a), then emotions may be defined as direct intermental manifestations of motives between individuals who in their relationships are persons. Emotions communicate about, and give value, to the probable action of a person in relation to other persons. They do not necessarily specify what motives are related to in the unpersonal world. They bring persons into motivational relationship. Whereas motives are organized in a coherent conscious and intending self, emotions define a person in relation to other persons, and characteristics of personality for each individual are defined by the emotions they habitually show in relation to others.

Because we have experience of how others feel about us, emotions may describe oneself as perceived by other persons, but this self-sensing is not essential to a primary coordination of motives by emotional expressions. Self-awareness assists in the definition of one's cooperative role by creating a particular consistent and controlled personality which others will recognize, but emotions may regulate relationships between persons without this reflective representation just as intelligent action may be performed without rational analysis of motives.

From these definitions it follows that emotions are inseparable from contacts or relationships between persons. Where there is an emotion expressed or felt, this will relate to a mental representation of another person who may be affected by that emotion. Emotions are not part of the mental processes of isolated subjects as such.

A clear distinction must be drawn between emotions that apply directly to engagements between persons and all other behaviors that give evidence of changing motivation. The latter include messages that are transmitted to other persons incidentally while one is engaged in autonomous mental work, such as signs of interest, concentration, tiredness, vigilance, vigour, urgency, etc. It is difficult to find a suitable word to make this distinction because modern dictionaries give very flexible definitions to the words "emotion" and "affect." However, there is a clear psychological difference between expressions of happiness, sadness, and anger on the one hand, which have direct interpersonal value, and an expression of curiosity or avoidance that shows the quality of cognitive involvement with an impersonal event. In the theoretical perspective argued for here, interpersonal expressions of feeling have primary functions in human mental life to regulate contacts and relationships.

Emotions can effectively control interactions of motives only if expressions of feeling have consistent effects in other persons. The interpersonal meaning of seen or heard expressions and of changes in orientation or proximity between persons have to be perceived without ambiguity if they are to communicate feelings in a way that assists formation of joint motives or controlled separation of motives. This requires a person to possess a specific cognitive system with capacity to represent feelings in empathic response to the expressive movements of other persons. Again, it is by no means essential that the emotional subject be able to perceive directly his or her own emotional state. One might successfully communicate affection or dislike, with appropriate effect on the feelings and behavior of another person, without being aware of one's expression. The feeling in oneself is of that other person having likeable or unpleasant characteristics or expressions. On the other hand, effective transmission of emotion to another does require an ability to detect and identify any consequent sign of emotion in that person. Being able to know or describe emotional states in oneself is thus of secondary importance and it is therefore not surprising that psychological research on introspective emotion has produced confused results. Studies of the emotions people perceive in others and of the words used to describe emotions as these may be observed in others have yielded much clearer findings indicating that people use an orderly conceptual scheme of emotions to regulate their interpersonal life (Plutchik, 1980).

There are consistent bodily or physiological changes with different emotions, related to the kinds of behaviors likely to be evoked in interpersonal situations of different degrees of animation or antagonism. But these effects do not constitute emotions. Some may contribute to emotional expression, but forms of expression that make no discernable contribution to autonomic regulations give more reliable indication about the mental representations of relationships to persons. Humans would appear to have the richest repertoire of pure expressive movements including many like the smile, which function only to qualify interpersonal engagements.

EMOTIONAL EXPRESSION FROM BIRTH TO SIX MONTHS

The following account summarizes expressive behaviors observed in film and video recordings of interactions between infants and adults. Recordings were made in studio conditions in such a way that all changes of posture, gestures, facial expressions and vocalizations of both partners could be clearly distinguished. The infant was supported in a baby chair designed to give freedom of limb and head movements and the adult was seated in front with eyes level with those of the baby. Observers and cameras were in an adjacent room and concealed from the subjects.

Observations of facial expressions, gestures, and postural changes have been greatly aided by examination of 6000 still photographs taken with a Nikon motor-drive camera concurrently with the video recordings. These methods are described and findings are discussed and illustrated in the following publications that also present the thesis that human preverbal communication develops on a basis of an inherent system that distinguishes persons from objects and permits the baby to engage in affective interaction with persons from birth (Hubley & Trevarthen, 1979; Trevarthen, 1975, 1977, 1979a, 1979b, 1982a, 1982b, 1983; & Trevarthen & Hubley, 1978; Trevarthen, Murray & Hubley, 1981).

An infant may be alert and responsive immediately after birth and may orient with eyes to sights and sounds and show interest by stilling of movements. Preferential orientation is shown to many stimuli from human beings, the infant being particularly sensitive to gentle vocalizations and to stimuli associated with holding, including odor, warmth, rocking, soft tactile stimulation, and patting. Newborns may be calmed from an agitated state and steadied in their orientation by the above stimuli, as well as being satisfied by feeding and by maternal comforting that is timed to respond to the infant's tenseness, relaxation, and orientation. However, newborns do not move to sustain face-to-face orientation with their eyes open and fixated and, in general, their expressions and movements do not appear to be sensitive to emotions that may be seen in a person's face. A newborn baby also responds poorly to support in a near upright position at a distance from the mother in a strange place, and for this reason they are difficult subjects in our recording situation throughout the first month. Nevertheless, we have observed 1 week olds alerting to and fixating on to a mother's face and voice, and they rarely smile when so oriented. Visual habituation tests show that newborns can exhibit preferential looking and that faces have high salience even though the gaze is poorly focalized.

In the second month infants become more precisely alert to the human voice and they exhibit subtle responses in expression to the flow of maternal speech. They are frequently content to engage in expressive exchanges for many minutes on end by means of sight and sounds alone. Most conspicuous is the improvement in visual orienting and the manifestation of a preference for fixing gaze in the direction of the upper part of the mother's face. Definite eye contact is sought by most infants about 6 weeks after full term birth. Once this orientation is achieved, and in response to a complex array of maternal expressive signals, many 4- to 6-week-olds smile and coo. They also make a variety of other expressive movements that, while perceived as communications by the mother, are not emotional in the strict sense. These include rudimentary articulatory movements of lips and tongue (prespeech) and a wide variety of gesture-like movements of the hands.

Mothers align their faces with the baby, adjusting position to the least distance of clear vision for an adult, and making modulated vertical and horizontal head rotations. Their faces are exaggeratedly mobile in every feature and these movements are synchronized with gentle but rhythmically accentuated vocalizations. All this behavior responds to the infant's evident awareness and acts to draw out signs of interest and pleasure. The infants show intent interest with fixed gaze, knit brows and slightly pursed lips or relaxed jaw, and immobility of the limbs. They exhibit an affectionate pleasure, closely linked to fixation on the mother's face and responsive to her expression, with smiles of varied intensity, coos, and hand movements. In distress they lower their brows and draw their mouths down at the corners and pout. Some expressions look sad and these elicit sympathetic tones and expressions of sad comforting from the mother. Other expressions are angry and avoidant, which may elicit a sterner mocking response from the mother. When the baby is confronted with a stranger, a 4- or 5-week-old may stare soberly even if smiling immediately before to the mother. If the mother presents an object, the baby may show intent knit-brow visual focalization without smiling and various concentrated pursed lip expressions accompanied by "prereaching" arm and hand movements. When the mother makes her face immobile the baby ceases smiling and may exhibit distress with grimaces, pouting, wringing of the hands, large forceful gestures with fisted hands, and gaze avoidance (see next section).

It is evident that by 6 weeks infants may express intent interest in an object, pleasure at recognition of the mother, and a withdrawn unease in front of a stranger. In a "good mood" the baby may engage in elaborate interactions of affective expression with the mother, alternating intent regard with smiling, accompanied by other kinds of communication movement. Expressions indicative of sadness or anger are made without maintaining eye contact, that is to say they are made as "broadcasts." If the mother confronts the baby without show-ing positive affection and a watchful and responsive gentleness the baby exhibits withdrawal and distress.

In the next 2 or 3 weeks these forms of behavior become more clearly defined and the mother and other family members become used to brief face-to-face exchanges of expression of feeling with the baby. There are subtle differences in the smile indicating, for example, that positive recognition and liking of a person may be mingled with doubt or with a teasing aggressiveness. When confronted with a stranger a 2- or 3-month-old may exhibit a complex conflict between friendliness and fear. Smiling in this situation frequently has a challenging straight upper lip form that becomes the typical play smile of a 3-month-old. From films and videorecords it is clear that a 2-month-old is able to scan a person's eyes or mouth and that expressions of feeling are instantly perceived. The expressions of the baby are appropriately reactive and capable of transmit-ting contingent feelings of liking, dislike, shyness, sadness or annoyance, as well as inattention and sleepiness.

In the third and fourth month infants become more interested in objects that are potentially graspable in mouth or hands. In our recordings they will often remove attention from the mother in front of them to look elsewhere and explore the room. When looking at persons they may smile or look worried, distressed, etc. When attentive to objects they generally have a serious, totally unsmiling expression, with lips often pursed and pushed forwards whether closed or parted. They begin to reach out with increasing control of the proximal arm muscles, then, at about 16 weeks, master well-aimed reaching and grasping.

In interactions with a familiar person, such as the mother, 3-month olds exhibit more vigorous playfulness. That is to say they enjoy particular forms of stimulation that serve to excite intense tight-lipped smiling or laughter. Key features of maternal playful activity are rhythmic bouncing of the baby or his limbs, chant-like vocalizations, looming and stalking with a climax that is mildly threatening (poking the baby's body, blowing, shouting, etc). This kind of behavior will attract an infant's attention back to the mother after her gentler forms of attention have been avoided in favor of looking at nearby objects.

Three- and four-month-old infants may be friendly and playful with strangers, but equally often show suspicion or fear by staring or avoiding eye contact, hunching the head down into the shoulders, handling the clothes or clasping hands, staring at hands or feet, chewing hands, pouting and grimacing. Some playful smiles may be combined with awkward posturing with the hands and a wrinkled nose expression that appears both tense and aggressive. When a mother withdraws her communication and sits with an immobile face in front of a 3- or 4-month old, the baby is less likely to be distressed than at 2 months, but looks away exploring the surroundings, seeking to handle objects, and may vocalize repeatedly in an apparent attempt to solicit attention, but without looking at the mother. The expression may be vacant or sad.

By 5 and 6 months most infants have learned to recognize a number of play routines. They enjoy tickling games, which often involve stimulation of their hands, they watch hand clapping and may imitate it. They also enjoy games such as peek-a-boo, which involve deliberate regulation of eye contact. Their own expressive behavior is coupled to subtle use of the gaze both to monitor what a partner is expressing and to regulate the partner's expressions. At this stage infants begin to look at their faces in a mirror though they do not show much affective interaction with the image. Playfulness is more limited with strangers who frequently cause a 5-month-old to exhibit fear and crying. Individual babies differ in their reactions to strangers but most show increasing fear from 3 to 6 or 7 months in our recordings.

The most important conclusion from our developmental studies over these early months is that comprehension of emotions in other persons and use of expression of emotions to regulate affectional interaction with them is highly elaborate before infants master prehension of objects. It appears as if interest in communication with persons regulated by visible and audible expressions develops in the second month (Primary Intersubjectivity). Then, in the third and fourth month interest in objects and surroundings, and an interest in strangers that is at first positive then more negative, competes with interest in simple diadic communication. Playfulness allows the mother to regain intense communication with kinds of action that are highly responsive to the infant's sensitivity to rhythmic events, and response to dramatic displays that have a high degree of emotional coloring. Teasing in play combines affectionate and aggressive expressions; it seems to exercise a more combatitive motivation. The importance of emotional signaling is heightened in play and it has a metacommunicative function (Bateson, 1955), as in play fighting.

By the end of the first month it is easy to discriminate in an infant's expression signs of cognitive effort and to distinguish them from signs of feeling with respect to another person. By the fourth month infants express pleasure in a humourous way that may qualify all kinds of action. Thus, although moods appropriate to mastering problems of awareness or action, and those that draw directly on the feelings of others, can be distinguished in the earliest expressive behavior, they soon become combined as infants begin to develop sharing of their awareness and intentions.

Mothers describe their children as having consistent personalities from early infancy and our recordings with a number of subjects over the first 3 years would support their judgments. Timidity or defiance with strangers, relative interest in persons and objects, playfulness, willfullness, affectionateness—these kinds of attributes vary because the infants have consistent tendencies to maintain a personal style of affective reaction in particular circumstances.

Two-month-olds differ in their reactions to loss of communication with the mother, for example, when the mother withdraws her expressions of interest and affection and keeps a straight face. Some infants become withdrawn and silent, others become angry and vocal (Murray, 1980). Similarly, 1-year-olds react with stolid defiance to strangers, or they are timid and fearful. Such evaluations of temperamental differences, whatever their cause, rest upon an assumption that there is one code of expressions interpretable as unambiguously signifying a range of emotions that have the same interpersonal function for infants as for older children and adults. Indeed, the patterns of infant expression are coherent and predictable and they respond in predictable ways to attentions from the mother. They function reliably in this ongoing interpersonal context. Different infants evidently share the common code of affect, but adopt different strategies in their relations with their mothers, just as mothers employ a variety of approaches to the task of communicating with and caring for their infants. The affective regulation of the mother-infant relationship is therefore two-way.

EXPERIMENTAL PROOF THAT TWO-MONTH-OLDS REGULATE EMOTIONS IN RELATION TO THEIR MOTHERS' EXPRESSIONS OF FEELING

Detailed descriptions of the expressive behaviors of infants in interaction with their mothers produce abundant evidence that both mother and infant are perceiving affect in each other, and that both of them also mirror what they perceive by complementary generation of affective responses within themselves (Trevarthen, 1975, 1977, 1979a, 1979b; Trevarthen, Murray & Hubley, 1981). This would seem to require an elaborate person-representing structure and an affective control process or evaluator of interpersonal feelings. However, with only photographic and audiographic data on spontaneous behaviors one cannot persuade an experimentalist that the infant has not learned a set of movements by conditioning of reflex actions that have in their original state no affective organization. Interpretation of whole behavior is relatively simple with a natural empathic or subjective response on the part of the observer (perceiving the happiness, sadness, etc), but very difficult in terms of more "objective" definition of isolated behavioral elements (such as eyebrow movements, mouth opening, smiles, gaze avoidance or vocalization). It is difficult to counter the hypothesis that coordinated patterns of affective response have been constructed by conditioning.

Consider how one might test the following line of reasoning. It has been observed that neonates make smile-like movements when alone, with eyes closed, or when in REM sleep, but not when they are distressed; then at 2 months they smile after orienting to a mother's eyes with an unsmiling face. Given that every mother observes her infant from birth and "rewards" with caressing touches or gentle vocal stimulation, and smiles in immediate contingent or even synchronous response to any movement that can be interpreted as a recognition of herself, the infant could have been trained to smile to the mother. The infant could come to direct the smile to the mother by associating the act with pleasurable recognition of her stimulation. The feeling of pleasure has been transferred to the smile by association with some inherently hedonic response to tactile stimulation.

The argument can be taken a step further back (or further into the infant's body), explaining the reward function of contingent maternal responses by their early association with the reflexes of suckling for food reward. Thus, it has been claimed that the primary learning process, which sets the acquisition of social interaction on the road, is one that associates the food reward from reflex sucking on the mother's breast or on a bottle she is holding with her responsive jiggling of the nipple, hand stroking, or speaking, actions that mothers commonly used to stimulate feeding. The infant learns to associate the mother's face and touch with feeding, and then acquires discrimination of her expressions of pleasure and ultimately of her speech, linking these with the particular characteristics of her face and voice that accompany giving of oral and bodily comfort.

Recent evidence (Field, Woodson, Greenberg, & Cohen, 1982) that newborns can imitate exaggerated face movements resembling expressions of cardinal emotions (joy, sadness, surprise) would seem to disprove that at least visual perception of faces and an empathic (imitative) response of the infant's face-moving system, requires to be learned. But, how does one examine the suggestion that newborns imitate because they are incapable of perceiving others as separate from themselves and with a distinct set of feelings?

There are logical flaws in such explanations of how emotional reactions are acquired—they are based upon arbitrary selection of criteria for awareness and arbitrary assumptions about the generation and function of expressive movements. However, merely pointing out these flaws of data selection is not sufficient. It is necessary to carry out experiments that observe how infants react with all their expressive systems together to systematic perturbations of maternal communication behavior. If the infant reacts to changes in the mother's expressive behavior with organized affective states, coordinating many expressions in appropriate and nonimitative relation to what the mother does, and if these expressions of the infant generate strong and predictable affective responses in adults of a supportive kind, then one must conclude that the infant possesses an internal representation of the *interactive relationship and its possible productive states*. In other words, this representation is such that it sets up criteria for a "good" interaction, and it functions to elicit the mother's aid to correct "bad" interactions.

In 1974, Tatam carried out such an experiment in Edinburgh (Tatam, 1975; Trevarthen, 1975). He showed that three 9-week-old babies acted puzzled, then agitated and depressed when, by means of a partial mirror, each baby saw its mother through the glass, with her eyes directed to the baby, but actually carrying on a conversation with another adult who was silently presenting written questions to the mother with the aid of the mirror. Such behavior, i.e. talking to an adult, contrasts with the normal baby talk of the mother in that it is less repetitive and affectionate, more complex in organization and informative in message form. It differs in many features of patterning as well as in emotional or emotive quality and communicative intent. Of course, the mother was also not seeing or hearing the infant while she was looking at the mirror reflection of the other adult, so she could not act in a responsive manner to the infant. Tatam observed the infants become markedly distressed in this situation, withdrawing gazes from mothers, ceasing to smile and looking sad, even becoming pale and inert.

Murray carried out a similar kind of experiment with more detailed examination of the behavior of five infants 6- to 19-weeks-of-age (Murray, 1980; Murray & Trevarthen, 1983). She asked mothers to change from affectionate face-to-face play and, in response to a signal, to hold their faces motionless for 1 minute while they continued to look quietly at their babies. Murray analyzed the infants' facial expressions, mouth and hand movements, and direction of gaze from film, measuring behavior in 0.5 second intervals and making comparisons between the still-face episode and periods of normal communication just before and just after it. There were highly significant changes in the infant behaviors and close agreements were obtained between independent observations of two observers. In both periods of normal interaction the infants looked at their mothers' eyes most of the time and sustained this regard uninterrupted for many seconds, smiled with relaxed or raised brows, vocalized with tonguing movements and made hand and arm movements. When the mother withheld communication the infant looked less time at her and for much shorter intervals, often looking away into the room or down; infants stopped smiling and frowned, grimaced and pouted, looked sad, yawned and touched their clothes with the left hand significantly more than before.

The aforementioned infant behaviors communicated either happy enjoyment combined with an impulse to transmit a message by vocalization, or sadness, distress, and withdrawal. In other words there were two highly coordinated, statistically improbable complexes of motor activity, evidently held together by emotional "states of mind." The infants' *moods*, which changed in line with the mother's behavior, had pronounced effects on the mothers who became either cheerful, interested and playful, or concerned and comforting. A similar experiment performed by Tronick, Als, Adamson, Wise & Brazelton (1978) produced essentially the same results.

Murray also developed a double closed-circuit television system by which, with the aid of partial mirrors, mother and baby saw each other as a full-face and natural size image on a television monitor (Murray, 1980; Trevarthen, Murray & Hubley, 1981; Trevarthen & Murray, 1983). She obtained happy interactions in this apparatus between mothers and infants, then she replayed to the infants videotapes made of the mother's immediately preceding cheerful and encouraging communications. This produced in the infants the same change to negative emotional expression as in the "still face" experiment. Therefore, even though the infant saw the same evidence of maternal feelings, the fact that the mother's image was not responding sensitively or supportively, but instead was acting out of relation to what the baby did was enough to make the baby distressed.

Murray also compared the infant's avoidant and sad behavior with a still-faced mother or a video image behaving without sensitivity, to that which occurred when the mother was interrupted in a natural way, i.e., caused to turn from her baby to speak to an adult who approached from the side. In this situation babies ceased to smile and to vocalize, but they did not become distressed. They simply watched their mothers, exhibiting faces in repose, with 'raised frowns' or enquiring looks.

One further experiment by Murray (1980) showed that mothers expected their 2-month-olds' affective behavior to be sensitive and comprehensible. When mothers viewed videotapes of infants, recorded during a normal happy interaction, only a few minutes after the real event, they perceived their infants to be behaving in an odd way. They thought their babies were avoiding and strangely unaware; some mothers felt there was something wrong with their own behavior that had disturbed their infants. They were unaware they had seen the same behavior a short time before, and communicated happily with it. The complementary replay experiments with double video communication show that, for both mother and baby, the form and responsiveness of expressive behavior determines its affective message. Emotions were in the interactive relationship of expressive behaviors.

Detailed observations made by Murray (1980) of a profoundly depressed mother communicating with her 2-month-old infant in an abnormal clinging way revealed that the apparently normal baby was acting with avoidance, and distress, like that of a baby confronted with a brief episode of inexpressive or insensitive behavior from a normal mother. The clinical literature contains records of similar breakdowns of affective contact between depressed or mentally ill mothers and infants of this already highly responsive age (e.g., Fraiberg, 1980; Robertson, 1963). Sylvester-Bradley (1981) presents evidence of defensive or negative behavior in infants confronted with spontaneously produced insensitive or inappropriate communication by their normal mothers.

EXPRESSION OF EMOTIONAL EMPATHY IN MATERNAL SPEECH TO INFANTS

Mothers' speech to infants has many special qualities. The linguistic features of this "baby talk" are interesting in relation to later acquisition of speech and it has been suggested that they form a kind of tutorial medium for infant vocalizations, training them into a vocabulary and giving them grammatical form (e.g.,

Snow, 1977). However, baby talk to infants under 6 months of age, when the child has no trace of verbal behavior, is remarkable mainly for its nonverbal, affective features. Evidently, mothers are producing speech of a particular emotional quality from the start of their infant's lives. Presumably they do this to sustain affective needs of their infants.

The emotional processes of the mother are revealed in what they say. When trying to communicate with a newborn, mothers slowly repeat many brief questions about the infant's feelings and impulses. They express subtle reflections of the perceived happiness, excitement, sleepiness, sadness, etc., of their babies. They match sudden alerting movements, smiles, wimperings of their infants with statements of surprise, gladness, or sympathy, etc. With 2-month-olds mothers ask the infant to look at them and to smile, and they give praise and say they are glad when the infant appears to comply. Their questions ask about the infant trying to say things to them or tell stories. They make approving comments like "Ooh, that was a big story!" All this speech can be thought of as an automatic attempt to explain or comment on an intense identification or empathy with the infant's motives, especially any that appear to be aimed at communication with the mother. After 3 months mothers talk increasingly about what the infant is trying to look at or handle. This reflects the infant's widening curiosity and reduced interest in direct attention to the mother's face.

Throughout these early months the quality of the mother's speech to her infant is obviously charged with feeling and equally obviously there are changes in the range of her feelings as the baby develops more complex behavior. To describe these changes it is necessary to introduce some objective description for vocal control. Little systematic work has been done on the way emotion is expressed in the human voice, but we have found that Laver's phonetic system to describe voice quality is perfectly adapted to this task (Laver, 1980). This system distinguishes positions of the larynx and supralaryngeal tract and it is intended to describe long-term habitual settings of an individual that restrict the range of operation of the vocal tract in speaking. Laver has related voice quality settings to social roles and classes and voluntarily adopted poses, as well as to speech disorders. However, his system is inherently suited to describe momentary changes in voicing that superimpose a range of attitudinal or affective tones on utterances.

Marwick, in an unpublished study, trained herself in this system for identifying changes in the sounds of speech related to positioning of lips, tongue, jaw, and larynx. She and Laver's group applied the analysis to each syllable of a mother's speech during 40 seconds of a video record of a fairly aggressive playful interaction with an 18-week-old girl. They identified 16 different voice quality settings. Voice quality changes occurred in pauses between speech segments. The visible behavior of mother and infant were analyzed independently in terms of a comprehensive system of categories to define interpersonal engagement, affect, and intention, to an accuracy of .02 seconds. All changes of voice quality were found to be synchronous with changes of interpersonal engagement and affect of the mother. When compared to facial expression, direction of gaze, and actions and gestures, changes of voice quality gave far more direct and complete information on the mother's communicative intentions and affect— 90% of all utterances accompanying a change of state of interpersonal engagement (judged from visible behavior) were accompanied by a significant change in voice quality, whereas only 57% were accompanied by changes in facial expression. It was concluded that the most direct expression of the mother's affect and attention available to the infant was that carried in changes of voice quality. When the mother was happy, affectionate, playful or flirting her voice was "breathy," with "lax and lowered larynx," "nasal," and she spoke with her tongue more "fronted" in her mouth. When she was aggressive and exasperated her voice was "whispery" with "tense larynx." However, as with movements of facial muscle in interpersonal engagements, voice quality settings can give no simple description of affect—it is the configuration of settings and their changes which carries the clear message of emotion to the partner.

Marwick also found that when speaking to an 8-week-old infant a mother normally uses far fewer voice quality groupings and maintains a single grouping for a longer time as well as holding longer pauses between utterances, as compared to the above described speech with a 4-month-old. With the younger baby the interaction is directly affective, mirroring the infants feelings. The mother carefully paces her supportive, responsive behavior, encouraging attention to herself and imitating the infant's expressions of pleasure and excitement. At 4 months the mother is trying to draw the child into rapid exchanges, using surprising teasing and rhythmic action routines to entice the baby into games and attempting to excite his interest and pleasure in relation to actions and things.

These preliminary studies reveal the orderly control of emotional expression by settings of the vocal tract that are capable of instantaneous changes in parallel with movements of the face. Indeed, placings of lips, tongue, and jaw simultaneously effect facial expression and voicing. The systematic regulation of these expressions by mothers when they speak to their infants shows that important indications of affect are transmitted through these channels. Marwick's microanalysis of mothers' communicative behaviors indicates that affect is expressed in the total coordinated behavior of the mother, but that face and voice carry the bulk of information about the mother's feelings, voice quality being the most informative single channel.

It is of interest that newborns demonstrate high sensitivity for features of human speech, especially female speech, that they direct affective expressions including smiling in reaction to vocalization, and that they may have formed a preference for the distinctive habitual features of their own mother's voice before birth. Clearly, further research is required to elucidate transmission of affect by means of the mother's voice and to discover how infants develop vocal expression of affect in interactions.

SOME DEVELOPMENTS IN AFFECTIVE EXPRESSION
AFTER SIX MONTHS

Older infants exhibit expressions of greater complexity which appear to signal more elaborate combinations of feelings. This is explained by their more elaborate motives for controlling themselves in relation to other people (Trevarthen, 1982a, 1983). Towards the end of the first year contented infants are very playful, enjoying teasing games with familiar persons. They are simultaneously becoming more aware of the possibilities of having their own viewpoint on actions and events, which may differ from the perspective of another. This increasing self-awareness is linked to the growth of an awareness of the other's intentions to communicate about how objects are to be attended to or manipulated (Hubley & Trevarthen, 1979; Trevarthen & Hubley, 1978). Looking to the other's face with an inquiring expression when requested to do something, and smiling when agreement has been reached, are two behaviors that become more common after an infant is 10 months of age (Bretherton & Bates, 1979). At the same time expressive vocalizations begin to have clear protolinguistic function—they are modulated and combined with orientations and gestures to constitute a variety of "acts of meaning" made in orientation to others, and with reference to the shared milieu. (Halliday, 1975). Apparently, a clearer awareness of a self as the one expressive agent with whom one cannot have a complementary or cooperative interaction also develops at this age (Lewis & Brooks, 1978).

Whereas infants 3- to 5-months-of-age enjoy play with eye-to-eye contact, vocalization, touching, and movements of the body, all accented by affectionate and inviting expressions, 6 month olds begin to add a playfulness in interactions with objects that people present to them in a lively way. They happily chase a ball dangled in front of them, and laugh when the ball is made to evade their grasp, or rushes towards them in an attacking way. They also begin to act jokingly when their mothers stop speaking to them and keep a straight face. They appear indifferent to this kind of break in communication. They enjoy jokes about the way they handle objects themselves using banging, dropping, and the like to tease their mothers in play. Self-satisfied amusement is often evident in the way the baby maintains eye contact with his or her own image in the reflecting surface of the camera window, making gestures, laughter, and comical faces to amuse themselves. Infants of this age appreciate direct evidence of their own comical behavior.

At the same age infants may show a deliberate willful disobedience and a 6-month-old is capable of aggressively scowling at his mother with gaze directed steadily to her eyes when refusing to comply with an instruction or prohibitive. Vocalizations at this age commence to carry a wide range of expressive tones—laughter, singing, calling, growling, and shouting being used to convey feelings that are signaled at the same time by posture and facial expression. Expressive behavior frequently gains the infant a communicative initiative *vis à vis* their partners.

The capacity of young infants to protest and to act with aggressive self-assertion can be expressed at earlier ages, but this manifestation of feeling develops markedly at 6 months. Babies become strongly independent and un-cooperative wth their caretakers in certain *difficult* periods (e.g., in Spitz' period of *No!* at about 15 months; Spitz, 1957). Such changes in expression of affect apparently reflect changes in underlying motives for communication, which are revealed in all aspects of the child's communication (Trevarthen, 1982a). They also give indication of the quality of relationship between each baby and mother and the habitual forms of affective regulation of the relationship (Blehar, Lieberman, & Ainsworth, 1977).

A greater self-awareness and more subtle sense of the comical in infants near 1 year of age may be seen in the way they share jokes about particular performances. They frequently appear conscious of their mothers' appreciative interest or mockery and conscious of their own imitative or posturing responses, identifying them immediately in a mirror. We find them turning to amuse themselves in the mirror when their mothers keep a straight face, and sometimes they present play routines to strangers in apparent defiance. A sense of the ridiculous would appear to combine self-consciousness with a desire to excite another. Joking expressions of the 9- to 12-month-olds include artificially harsh vocalizations, high-pitched noises, "silly" faces with wrinkled nose and pursed or twisted mouth, tight closed or wide open eyes. One year olds also learn performances like clapping hands, bouncing, hiding and reappearing (peek-a-boo), popping the finger from the mouth, blowing "raspberries" through closed lips, etc.

Expressions of self-observation in a mirror are not simple ones of pleasure or interest; they are conflicted and either fascinated or tense. It would appear that the 1-year-old is instantly aware of the trap-like situation a mirror affords for an affective resonance with the self. Mothers echo and reply to a wide variety of the affective expressions in voice, face movement, gesture, and posture. Evidently they are playing with the infants' increased self-awareness.

At the same time as a cooperative awareness is emerging in playful use of objects with familiar persons (Hubley & Trevarthen, 1979), and the child is beginning to vocalize a variety of protolinguistic messages eliciting interest and greetings or concessions from these same persons (Dore, 1975; Halliday, 1975), strangers are perceived as more threatening. Evidently their strangeness is due to their unfamiliarity, and recognition that trust or common knowledge of communication is limited. One-year-olds often cry in spite of gentle and kind attention from a stranger, or they stare with sadness and fear, or scowl with defiance, fingering their clothes or wringing their hands, or covering their mouth or eyes with them. When the mother returns after the baby has been 2 minutes with a stranger, the baby often cries in anger and may act in a rejecting way, refusing to look at the mother. Infants of this age seek comfort from a mother with whom they have formed a strong attachment, but are also more likely to show anger to her than to any other person. She is protested to when she appears not to have given the protection or comfort normally expected of her.

CONCLUSIONS

The expressions of infants that I have briefly described have the same patterns or forms of movement as those by which adults communicate states of motivation and emotion. The infant expressions may have a profound emotive effect on adults—they are felt as emotional. Moreover, these same movements are exquisitely sensitive to the affectional quality of the responses they elicit from adults—the infants feel adult emotions. It would appear that the early months build visual and auditory awareness of emotions on the foundation of an inherent sensitivity to the primary affective code. When the interplay of expressions between a mother and infant, or a stranger and infant, are studied in their totality, it becomes clear that the coordination for this behavior is achieved within the mental relationship or engagement between the two feeling subjects. Thus, the expressions become manifestations of an empathic awareness and mutual control. This awareness is based on a sensitivity to *rhythmic patterns in movement* by some process that couples inherent pacemakers or clocks in infant and adult. It is also receptive to the *forms of emotion,* and this must be due to a neural image of the expressive apparatus that can detect species of affect in another, while transmitting it to the perceiver's own motor system. No other explanation can be given for the capacity neonates have to imitate expressions (Field et al., 1982).

Figure 6.1 attempts to chart what may be called the *field of emotions* in the infant and to show how it functions to regulate interpersonal engagements in relation to the infant's consciousness of objects in the first year of life (cf. Trevarthen, 1979b, 1982a, 1982b, 1983). A newborn infant is severely limited in the coordination and regulation of body movements and both peripheral and central structures for perception are imperfectly formed. Vision, in particular, undergoes elaborate differntiation in the first 3 weeks after birth. This special immaturity suffices to explain why newborns, although they are capable of discriminating and resonating to features and expressive movements of the human face and vocal system, and though they show subtle affective responses to body contact, rhythmic stroking, and holding, are turned in on themselves—they actively withdraw from visual engagement with others. They express affect along an axis between sad or agitated distress and calm, inturned or diffusely broadcast pleasure, yet they also emit a rich variety of expressions indicative of more complex emotions. Their inwardness explains why the visible and audible expressive behaviors of neonates appear fragmentary and imperfectly controlled. By 2 months, however, facial, gestural, and vocal expression of an infant's feelings are highly coordinated with attending, and they soon become measured in their responsiveness to facial, gestural, and vocal signals from a principal caretaker. The infant seeks to interact by watching an adult's face while listening to the voice. Learning of voice features that begins *in utero* (Spence & De-Casper, 1982) favors preferential engagement with the mother, at least in the first

A

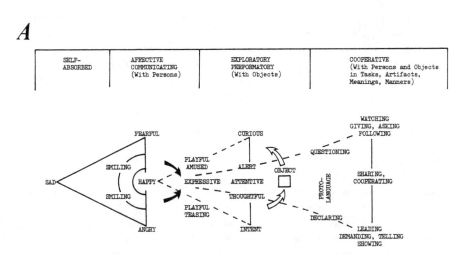

B

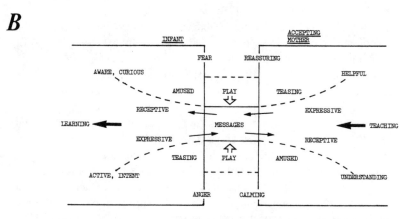

FIG 6.1.   A. Diagram of the field of emotions of an infant and its relations with motives for engagement with objects and for cooperation.

B. Maternal complementation of motives is regulated by affective states and facilitates development of cooperative behavior and teaching.

weeks, and in this period, too, the happy mother is in an erotic state that leads her to seek and stimulate emotional engagement with the infant in a clearer, more consistent manner than other persons do.

The complexity and efficiency of emotional communication in the second and third month, when the infant has just developed adequate visuo-manual coordination, indicates that emotions have first place in the behavioral systems that regulate psychological development of the child. The infant first explores the human affective environment and interacts with it by means of expressions before attempting to manipulate objects.

As shown in Fig. 6.1, early engagements with persons appear to be adjusted against a triangle of negative affect: sadness (eliciting comforting and care), fear (favoring withdrawal of the person causing fear and bringing the caretaker and reassurance to the infant) and anger (obtaining control or active rejection of the other), positive engagements being regulated by expressions of interest and happiness. Smiling has different forms depending upon the set of the upper lip and jaw, and a distinction between a more timid amused smile and an assertive, more aggressive one becomes clearer in the third month. When 2- to 3-month-old infants engage in face-to-face play they mirror a reciprocate smiling to obtain a coincidence of communicative motives or interaction of interpersonal initiatives with the partner (Trevarthen, 1979a, Fig. 8). Supported by affectionate, smiling speech from a partner they achieve a state of contented excitement in which they cease smiling and make a variety of other kinds of expression (including coos, and 'ahgoos', prespeech and gestures). These are emitted in bursts of a few movements lasting one or two seconds, sometimes coincidentally with a brief withdrawal of gaze from the partner's face. Thus, one may define a friendly expressive emotional state. Mothers reply to such behavior as if it constitutes real speech messages (Trevarthen, 1979a; Sylvester-Bradley & Trevarthen, 1978).

When exploratory and performatory behaviors of infants start to take up the impersonal or objective world in the third and fourth months, expressions of cognitive involvement with reality (interest, intention, orientation, curiosity, surprise, and recognition) partly displace affective expressions in communication, and they lead interpersonal interactions in new directions (Trevarthen, 1983). The baby develops a sense of humor and joins in games in which the interpersonal collaboration centers on sharing of pleasure in experience and action (Trevarthen & Hubley, 1978; Trevarthen, 1979b). First steps in development of the concepts or representations of objects of manipulation are taken in this context where other familiar and loved persons appreciate and react to the infant's expressions of "pleasure in mastery," "serious intent," and distress at failure when oriented to things and attempting to gain cognitive and motoric control of the experience of repeating events (Papousek, 1967; Watson, 1972). The baby may react emotionally to the mother's voice or her actions while looking away from her face and by showing more aggressive pleasure in interacting with her expressive playfulness. Games and gentle teasing lead the mother to present the baby with culturally ritualized chants, action games, and nursery rhymes, which are strongly rhythmical with simple repeating patterns of climax and suspense (Trevarthen, 1983). The traditional rhymes merely activate in memorable and verbalized form the kinds of adult behavior that are most successful in engaging the 3-month-old's sense of measured conflict and the pleasure it evokes. Happy expressiveness (in shouts, laughter, and vigorous gestures) is regulated by teasing, infant and mother alternately becoming more assertive or more passive and defensive.

In later infancy, affective and orientational signaling assists in the keeping and limiting of relationships, reinforcing a developing cooperative awareness in which the infant and familiars share knowledge of a common world of objects and events (Hubley & Trevarthen, 1979; Trevarthen, 1979b; Trevarthen & Hubley, 1978). Language and other culturally significant skills develop within or on top of this shared awareness in relationships and are at first dependent upon mutual learning of intimate conventions in nonverbal signalling (Trevarthen, 1983).

Similtaneously with the emergence of imitation of gestures or acts on objects, infants over 9 months start to employ vocalization and gesture in deliberate adjustment to the interest of a partner. Thus, they gain a power to transmit clear messages about their needs, wishes, wants, curiosity, disagreements, irritation with well-specified orientation to others' awareness. Such behavior has been called performing "acts of meaning" (Halliday, 1975) or exhibiting "intention to communicate" (Bretherton & Bates, 1979). The utterances and hand movements of the infant are now becoming marked by emotions in a way that corresponds with inflections and gestures of adult conversational behavior. The illocutionary force of a 1-year-old's nonverbal questions, statements, refusals, demands, etc., is defined by the affective quality of signaling behavior. Evidently, this development in the use of affect is responsible for authors describing many emotions as appearing for the first time at this age. More correctly, it is the communicative use of affective expression that is changed. The same expressions have been used with less focus on the intentions and awareness of others, but with adjustment to their affective responses, since the infant was 2- or 3-months-of-age.

In summary, the affective functions that gain expression so rapidly in early weeks, starting to control engagements between the infant and other persons from birth, remain at the center of all aspects of cognitive and behavioral growth where caretakers have a facilitatory and teaching role.

It is clear that what counts for the infant to develop into a confident sharer of experience and activity is the quality and dependability of affective control in relationships to one or a few adults, not any nonmental factor like blood relationship or nutritional support. The mother's importance depends on her consistency of affection and is neither entirely permanent nor obligatory. As the infant gains in mobility and social awareness, a consistent code of emotional signaling guides him or her through the formation of new relationships and the adjustment of ties with siblings and other persons for whom the infant maintains feelings of preference, or aversion.

This evidence from infancy indicates that the original and key function of human emotions is to regulate the mental representations of interpersonal contacts and relationships. Emotional expressions that are capable of affecting the approach and withdrawal of other persons and communications with them also relate to and interact with expressions of cognitive effort or mastery of purely objective events, but the expressions of interpersonal feeling remain distinct in form and function from all manifestations of the subject's cognitive control of impersonal phenomena. Humans express affect in relation to cognitive effort and its success, or mental tension and its release, because their mastery of objects is always at least partly cooperative with persons. This explains why, for example, infants smile or laugh, vocalize and gesture, when they play with objects or solve mental problems (Trevarthen, 1979a, 1983; Trevarthen, Murray & Hubley, 1981).

Other less psychological correlates of emotion can easily be separated from the interpersonal. Thus, physiological regulation either of cerebral arousal or blood circulation, release of hormones and breathing, are coupled with emotional states simply because the brain and body are necessarily involved in behaviors that accompany interpersonal contacts. Emotions are not to be identified with or reduced to such brain and body states at any stage of development.

Finally, it should be emphasized that it is the essential adaptive biological function of emotions in human life to set up and regulate interpersonal engagements and mental cooperation (intersubjectivity). This cooperative awareness is superordinate to and prior in the development of more general adaptive functions that involve animate cooperation, such as reproduction, regulation of gene flow in populations of the species, exploitation of food resources, or defense of the individual or group. The emotional processes of infants clearly are not needed to regulate reproduction or any feeding or defense behavior on which survival of the group depends. They are needed to regulate development of human consciousness.

ACKNOWLEDGMENTS

Research on which this report is based was funded by the Social Science Research Council of the U.K. and The Spencer Foundation of Chicago. I am deeply appreciative of the contributions made by my associates Lynne Murray, Benjamin Sylvester-Bradley, Penelope Hubley, Helen Marwick and Kevan Bundell.

REFERENCES

Ainsworth, M.D.S. The development of infant-mother attachment. In B.M. Caldwell & H.N. Riccuiti (Eds.), *Review of Child Development Research, Vol. 3.* (Chicago: University of Chicago Press).

Ainsworth, M.D.S., & Wittig, B.A. Attachment and exploratory behavior of one-year-olds in a strange situation. In B.M. Foss (Ed.), *Determinants of infant behaviour, Vol. 4.* London: Methuen, 1969.

Bates, E. *Language and context: The acquisition of pragmatics.* New York and London: Academic Press, 1976.

Bateson, G. A theory of play and fantasy. *Psychiatric Research Reports, Series A,* 1955, *2,* 39–51.

Blehar, M.C., Lieberman, A.F., & Ainsworth, M.D.S. Early face-to-face interaction and its relation to later mother-infant attachment. *Child Development,* 1977, *48,* 182–194.

Bowlby, J. The nature of the child's tie to his mother. *International Journal of Psychoanalysis,* 1958, *39,* 1–23.

Brazelton, T.B., Koslowski, B., & Main, M. The origins of reciprocity: The early mother-infant interaction. In M. Lewis & L.A. Rosenblum (Eds.), *The effect of the infant on its caregiver.* New York and London: Wiley 1974.

Bretherton, I., & Bates, E.The emergence of intentional communication. In I.C. Uzgiris (Ed.), *New directions for child development, Vol. 4,* San Francisco: Jossey-Bass, 1979.

Bridges, K.M.B. Emotional development in infancy. *Child Development,* 1932, *3,* 324–341.

Bruner, J.S. The ontogenesis of speech acts. *Journal of Child Language,* 1975, *2,* 1–19.

Charlesworth, W.R., & Kreutzer, M.A. Facial expressions of infants and children. In P. Ekman (Ed.), *Darwin and facial expression.* New York and London: Academic Press, 1973.

Darwin, C. *The Expression of Emotion in Animals and Man.* London: Methuen, 1872.

Darwin, C. A biographical sketch of an infant. *Mind,* 1877, *2,* 285–294.

Dore, J. *The development of speech acts.* The Hague: Mouton, 1975.

Field, T.M., Woodson, R., Greenberg, R., & Cohen, D. Discrimination and imitation of facial expressions by neonates. *Science,* 1982, *218,* 179–181.

Fraiberg, S. *Clinical studies in infant mental health: The first year of life.* London: Tavistock, 1980.

Halliday, M.A.K.*Learning how to mean: explorations in the development of language.* London: Arnold, 1975.

Hubley, P., & Trevarthen, C. Sharing a task in infancy. In I. Uzgiris (Ed.), *Social interaction during infancy, new directions for child development, 4,* 1979.

Izard, C.E. On the ontogenesis of emotions and emotion-cognition relationships in infancy. In M. Lewis & L.A. Rosenblum (Eds.), *The development of affect.* New York: Plenum Press, 1978.

Laver, J. *The phonetic description of voice quality.* London: Cambridge University Press, 1980.

Lewis, M., & Brooks, J. Infants' social perception: A constructivist view. In L.B. Cohen & P. Salapatek (Eds.), *Infant perception: From sensation to cognition, Vol. 2.* New York: Academic Press, 1975.

Lewis, M., & Brooks, J. Self-knowledge and emotional development. In M. Lewis & L.A. Rosenblum (Eds.), *The Development of Affect.* New York: Wiley, 1978.

Murray, L. *The sensitivities and expressive capacities of young infants in communication with their mothers.* Thesis for Doctorate of Philosophy, University of Edinburgh, 1980.

Murray, L., & Trevarthen, C. Emotional regulation of interactions between two-month-olds and their mothers. In T. Field and N. Fox (Eds.), *Social Perception in Infants.* Norwood, N.J.: Ablex, 1983.

Oster, H., & Ekman, P. Facial behaviour in child development. In A. Collins (Ed.), *Minnesota symposia on child development (Vol. 11.)* New York: T.A. Crowell, 1977.

Papoušek, H. Experimental studies of appetitional behaviour in human newborns and infants. In H.W. Stevenson, E.H. Hess, & H.L. Rheingold (Eds.), *Early behavior comparative and developmental approaches*. New York: Wiley, 1967.

Peiper, N. *Cerebral Function in Infancy and Childhood*. New York: Consultants Bureau, 1963.

Piaget, J., & Inhelder, B. *The psychology of the child*. London: Routledge and Kegan Paul, 1969.

Plutchik, R. *Emotion: A psychoevolutionary synthesis*. New York: Harper and Row, 1980.

Robertson, J. Mother-infant interaction from birth to twelve months: two case studies. In B.M. Foss (Ed.), *Determinants of infant behaviour* (Vol. 3.) London: Methuen, 1963.

Snow, C.E. The development of conversation between mothers and babies. *Journal of Child Language*, 1977, *4*, 1–22.

Spence, M.J., & De Casper, A.J. *Human fetuses perceive maternal speech*. Paper delivered at the International Conference on Infant Studies. Austin, Texas, March 1982.

Spitz, R.A. *No and yes: On the genesis of human communication* New York: International Universities Press, 1957.

Sroufe, L.A. Socioemotional development. In J. Osofsky (Ed.), *Handbook of infancy*. New York: Wiley, 1978.

Stern, D.N. The goal and structure of mother-infant play. *Journal of the American Academy of Child Psychiatry*, 1974, *13*, 402–421.

Stern, D.N., & Gibbon, J. Temporal expectancies of social behaviours in mother-infant play. In E. Thoman (Ed.), *Origins of the infant: Social responsiveness*. New York: Lawrence Erlbaum Associates, 1980.

Sylvester-Bradley, B. Negativity in early infant-adult exchanges and its developmental significance. In P. Robinson (Ed.), *Communication in development*. London: Academic Press, 1981.

Sylvester-Bradley, B., & Trevarthen, C. Baby talk as an adaptation to the infant's communication. In N. Waterson & C. Snow (Eds.), *The development of communication*. New York: Wiley, 1978.

Tatam, J. *The effects of an inappropriate partner on infant sociability*. Dissertation for M.A. Hons, University of Edinburgh, 1974.

Trevarthen, C. Early attempts at speech. In R. Lewin (Ed.), *Child alive*. London: Temple Smith, 1975.

Trevarthen, C. Descriptive analyses of infant communication behaviour. In H.R. Schaffer (Ed.), *Studies in mother-infant interaction: The Loch Lomond Symposium*. London: Academic Press, 1977.

Trevarthen, C. Communication and cooperation in early infancy. A description of primary intersubjectivity. In M. Bullowa (Ed.), *Before speech: The beginnings of human communication*. London: Cambridge University Press, 1979. (a)

Trevarthen, C. Instincts for human understanding and for cultural cooperation: Their development in infancy. In M. von Cranach, K. Foppa, W. Lepenies, & D. Ploog (Eds.), *Human ethology*. Cambridge: Cambridge University Press, 1979. (b)

Trevarthen, C. Review of: *The making and breaking of affectional bonds* by John Bowlby. *British Journal of Psychiatry*, 1980,*137*, 390.

Trevarthen, C. The primary motives for cooperative understanding. In G. Butterworth & P. Light (Eds.), *Social cognition: Studies of the development of understanding*. Brighton: Harvester Press, 1982. (a)

Trevarthen, C. Basic patterns of psychogenetic change in infancy. In T. Bever (Ed.), *Dips in learning*. Hillsdale, N.J.: Lawrence Erlbaum Associates, 1982. (b)

Trevarthen, C. Interpersonal abilities of infants as generators for transmission of language and culture. In A. Oliverio and M. Zapella (Eds.), *The behaviour of human infants*. London and New York: Plenum 1983.

Trevarthen, C., & Hubley, P. Secondary intersubjectivity: Confidence, confiding and acts of meaning in the first year. In A. Lock (Ed.), *Action, gesture and symbol:* The emergence of language. London: Academic Press, 1978.

Trevarthen, C., Murray, L., & Hubley, P. Psychology of infants. In J. David & J. Dobbing (Eds.), *Scientific foundations of clinical paediatrics*. London: W. Heinemann Medical Books (2nd edition), 1981.

Tronick, E., Als, H., Adamson, L., Wise, S., & Brazelton, T.B. The infant's response to entrapment between contradictory messages in face-to-face interaction. *Journal of the American Academy of Child Psychiatry, 1978, 17, 1–13.*

Tronick, E., Als, H., & Brazelton, T.B. Early development of neonatal and infant behaviour. In F. Falkner & J.M. Tanner (Eds.), *Human growth (Vol. 3)*. New York: Plenum Press, 1979.

Watson, J.S. Smiling, cooing and the game. *Merrill-Palmer Quarterly, 1972, 18, 323–339.*

Wolff, P.H. Observations of the early development of smiling. In B.M. Foss (Ed.), *Determinants of Infant Behaviour (Vol. II)*. London: Methuen, 1963.

III

PSYCHOLOGICAL AND ETHOLOGICAL APPROACHES

Ethological and psychological approaches might be expected to address most directly questions about the nature and function of emotion. Historically, psychology is the discipline which focuses most on emotion, and most of the general theories of emotion have emanated from psychologists. It would be beyond the scope of this volume to try to represent most or even many of those theoretical approaches. Similarly, it would be impossible to fairly represent the role that ethologists have played in investigating emotional behavior, (even though emotion as a term was shunned by many ethologists until recently). Thus, by necessity, the contributions in this section present only a sample, of these approaches, not a representative sample, but what the editors judge to indicate important and diverse approaches.

Perhaps the only common concern in these contributions is the role of emotion in the adaptation of the organism to the physical and social environment. Stretching the point, one could argue that almost all theories of emotion regard emotion as an adaptational response. However, they differ in terms of the specific conditions under which the adaptation occurs. For example, disruption theories of emotion postulate that emotion is the response of the organism to a blocking or interruption of ongoing behavior or execution of plans. Most of the theorists included in this volume would think of emotion as an adaptive response in a broader sense. But even here, there are major differences in terms of where the emphasis is placed.

The first three contributions in this section are reprints of up to date statements of theoretical positions by three major figures in the area of emotion: Tomkins, Plutchik, and Lazarus. Silvan Tomkins considers the affect system the primary motivational system that can amplify any other state, particularly drive states of the organism. Robert Plutchik, who adopts a strongly ethological approach, stresses the evolutionary continuity of emotion with instinctive behavior patterns in animals, dealing with the key survival issues posed by the environment. Richard Lazarus stresses the importance of cognitive evaluation processes in establishing the meaning of events and stimuli for the organism in transaction with the environment and the way in which the organism is able to cope with such situations. Each of these theorists focuses on a different aspect of the adaptive function of emotion. Each differs in terms of the structural mechanisms that are postulated to subserve the specific adaptive functions considered. All of these theories have had major impact on theorizing and research in the area of emotion as the next chapters show.

One particularly salient issue is the role of cognition in emotion. A lively controversy was started when Robert Zajonc, in a paper in 1980, claimed that cognition is not necessary for emotional evaluation and that there may be an affective judgment system that is more basic and primary than the cognitive system. (Note similarity on this point to both Plutchik and Tomkins). A short version of his argument is included in the contributions in this section. During the conference which formed the basis for this volume, Lazarus and Zajonc argued about this issue. Given the importance of the issue, the exchange of arguments was prepublished in the *American Psychologist* and is reprinted here.

Adopting a thoroughly functional approach in his contribution, Klaus Scherer proposes a component process model of affective states to deal with some of these problems. It is suggested that the process of change in the states of several organismic subsystems is to be observed over time, using a descriptive facet system to assess these states. In addition, Scherer proposes a process model of stimulus evaluation that focusses on different types of stimulus evaluation checks arranged in hierarchical order to help clarify issue of the cognitive versus non-cognitive evaluation.

The role of cognition is again taken up in the contribution by Howard Leventhal. He also believes that much of the controversy can be traced back to the problems of defining cognition and proposes his own theory that postulates three different levels of processing (sensory motor, schematic, conceptual) as a more detailed conceptualization of the processing of external and internal information in the course of emotion. The chapter by Leventhal demonstrates the complexity of the relationships between the various components of emotion: cognition, expression, physiological processes, and experience. Leventhal's perceptual motor theory is a dynamic model that, in the tradition of Tomkins, attempts to argue that the earliest emotional experience is produced by expressive motor activity. In this model the motor system is divided into volitional and automatic components and the interaction between them in the central nervous system is hypothesized to be the source of emotional feelings, with feedback from the periphery playing a secondary role.

Paul Ekman, whose view of emotion has also been influenced by Tomkins, traces the development of his work focusing upon four issues of relevance to any theory of emotion. He describes both empirical findings and theory which explains universals and cultural differences in emotional signals. The possibility that emotion signals differ in noticeable ways from other uses of the signaling equipment is considered. He reports new evidence and theory regarding emotion-specific physiological activity, and connections between voluntary facial movements and involuntary physiological activity. And, he reexamines the startle reaction, raising the question of how reflexes differ from emotions. His chapter concludes with a proposal of some of the characteristics that might distinguish emotion from moods, attitudes and sentiments.

The final contribution in this section is an example of a purely ethological approach. Here, the basic issues of both the role of cognition in emotion and the role of emotional expression are addressed in a novel way. On the basis of recent experimental evidence, Peter Marler presents the argument that contrary to the belief that most animal signalling is purely affect-based, there may be important elements of referential signaling, involving cognitive components, in many animal communication systems. In discussing a number of examples, such as the role of deception and dissimulation, Marler shows the tremendous complexity of the issues concerning the interactions between cognition, emotion, and communication. This chapter is a strong demonstration of the value of comparative approach to emotion. It forces us to extend concepts and functions that seem self-evident in the human case to different species of animals where may implicit, underlying assumptions may no longer be so defensible.

7 Affect Theory*

Silvan S. Tomkins
University of Pennsylvania

AFFECTS AND DRIVES

I view affect as the primary innate biological motivating mechanism, more urgent than drive deprivation and pleasure, and more urgent even than physical pain. That this is so is not obvious, but it is readily demonstrated. Consider that almost any interference with breathing will immediately arouse the most desperate gasping for breath. Consider the drivenness of the tumescent, erect male. Consider the urgency of desperate hunger. These are the intractable driven states that prompted the answer to the question, "What do human beings really want?" to be: "the human animal is driven to breathe, to sex, to drink, and to eat." Yet this apparent urgency proves to be an illusion. It is *not* an illusion that one must have air, water, and food to maintain oneself and sex to reproduce oneself. What *is* illusory is the biological and psychological source of the apparent urgency of the desperate quality of the hunger, thirst, breathing, and sex drives.

Consider these drive states more closely. When someone puts their hand over my mouth and nose, I become terrified. But this panic, this terror, is in no way a part of the drive mechanism. I can be terrified at the possibility of losing my job, of developing cancer or of losing my spouse. Fear or terror is an innate affect, which can be triggered by a wide variety of circumstances. Not having enough air to breathe is one of many such circumstances. But if the rate of anoxic deprivation becomes slower, as, for example, in the case of wartime pilots who

---

*The modifications in theory presented here are taken from my book, *Affect, imagery, consciousness,* Vol. 3, New York: Springer, 1982.

refused to wear oxygen masks at 30,000 ft, then there develops, not a panic, but a euphoric state; and some of these men met their deaths with smiles on their lips. The mile and its feedback are the affect of enjoyment, in no way specific to slow anoxic deprivation.

Consider more closely the tumescent male with an erection. He is sexually excited, we saw. He is indeed excited, but no one has ever observed an excited penis. It is a man who is excited and who breathes hard, not in the penis, but in the chest, the face, the nose, and the nostrils. But such excitement is in no way peculiarly sexual. The same excitement can be experienced, without an erection, from mathematics—beauty bare—to poetry, to a rise in the stock market. Instead of these representing sublimations of sexuality, it is rather that sexuality, in order to become possible, must borrow its potency from the affect of excitement. The drive must be assisted by affect as an *amplifier* if it is to work at all. Freud, better than anyone else, knew that the blind, pushy, imperious Id was the most fragile of impulses, readily disrupted by fear, by shame, by rage, by boredom. At the first sign of affect other than *excitement,* there is impotence and frigidity. The penis proves to be a paper tiger in the absence of appropriate affective amplification.

The affect system is, therefore, the primary motivational system because without its amplification, nothing else matters, and with its amplification, anything else *can* matter. It thus combines urgency and generality. It lends its power to memory, to perception, to thought, and to action no less than to the drives.

The relationship we have postulated between the drive system and the affect system must also be postulated between both of these and nonspecific amplifying systems, such as the reticular formation. This and other amplifier circuits serve both motivational and nonmotivational systems. The words "activation" and "arousal" have tended to confound the distinction between amplification from affects and the nonspecific amplification of any neural message, be it a sensory, motor, drive, or affect message. *Amplification* is the preferable, more generic term, because it describes equally well the increase or decrease in gain for any and every kind of message or structure. Analogic amplification is now restricted to the affect system. The terms *activation* and *arousal* should be abandoned because of their affective connotations.

It is clear from the work of Sprague, Chambers, and Stellar (1961) that is possible, by appropriate anatomical lesions, to produce a cat that is active by virtue of intact amplifier structure but shows little affect and, conversely, to produce a cat that is inactive and drowsy but responds readily with affect to mild stimulation.

Both drives and affects require nonspecific amplification, but the drives have insufficient strength as motives without concurrent amplification by both the affects and the nonspecific amplification. Their critical role is to provide vital information of time, of place and of response, i.e., where and when to do what, when the body does not know how to otherwise help itself. When the drive signal is activated, we learn first when we must start and stop consummatory activity. We become hungry long before our tissues are in an emergency state of deficit, and we stop eating, due to satiety, long before the tissue deficit has been remedied.

But there is also the information of place and of response—where to do what. When the drive is activated it tells us a very specific story—that the "problem" is in the mouth in the case of hunger, farther back in the nose and throat and chest if it is an oxygen drive, in the urethra if it is the urination drive, at the anal sphincter if it is the defecation drive. This information has been built into the site of consummation, so the probability of finding the correct consumatory response is very high. That this information is as vital as the message *when* to eat can be easily demonstrated:

Let us suppose that the hunger drive were "rewired" to be localized in the urethra and the sex drive localized in the palm of the hand. For sexual satisfaction the individual would first open and close his hand and then reach for a wide variety of "objects" as possible satisfiers, cupping and rubbing his hand until orgasm. When he became hungry, he might first release the urethra and urinate to relieve his hunger. If this did not relieve it, he might use his hands to find objects that might be put inside the urethra, depending on just how we rewired the apparatus. Such an organism would be neither viable nor reproductive. Such specificity of time and place of drive system, critical though it is for viability, is, nevertheless, a limitation on its general significance for the human being.

It is the affects, rather than the drives, that are the primary human motives. This primacy is demonstrated, first, by the fact that the drives require amplification from the affects, whereas the affects are sufficient motivators in the absence of drives. For example, one must be excited to be sexually aroused, but one need not be sexually aroused to be excited. It is quite sufficient to motivate any man, to arouse either excitement or joy or terror or anger or shame or contempt or distress or surprise.

Second, in contrast to the specificity of the space-time information of the drive system, the affect system has those more general properties. which permit it to assume a central position in the motivation of man. Thus, the affect system has generality of time rather than the rhythmic specificity of the drive system. Because the drive system is essentially a transport system, taking material in and out of the body, it must impose its specific temporal rhythms, strictly. One cannot breathe only on Tuesday, Thursday and Saturday, but one could be happy on Tuesday, Thursday and Saturday and sad on Monday, Wednesday, and Friday.

In contrast to the necessary constraints of a system that enjoys few degrees of freedom in transporting material in and out of the body, there is nothing inherent in the structure of the affect mechanism to limit its activation with respect to time. One can be anxious for just a moment or for half an hour, for a day, for a year, or a lifetime, or never, or only occasionally now, though much more frequently some time ago, or conversely.

There are structures in the body that are midway between the drive and affect mechanism. Thus the pain receptors on the back of my hand are as site-specific as any drive. If I were to place a lit cigarette on the skin of my hand, I would experience pain. But the pain mechanism is similar to the affect mechanism in its time generality. There is nothing in the nature of pain receptors that requires that they be stimulated rhythmically or that they ever be stimulated and nothing that would prevent them from being stimulated whenever the person had an accident.

The affect system also permits generality or freedom of object. Although one may satisfy hunger by Chinese, American or Italian food, it must be some variety of edible object. Not so with any affect. There is literally no kind of object that has not been linked to one or another of the affects. In masochism man has even learned to love pain and death. In Puritanism he has learned to hate pleasure and life. He can invest any and every aspect of existence with the magic of excitement and joy or with the dread of fear or shame or distress.

Affects also are capable of much greater generality of intensity than drives. If I do not eat, I become hungrier and hungrier. As I eat I become less hungry. But I may wake mildy irritable in the morning and remain so for the rest of the day. Or, one day I may not be at all angry until quite suddenly something makes me explode with rage. I may start the day moderately angry and quickly become interested in some other matter and so dissipate my anger.

Not only are both intensity and duration of affect capable of greater modulation than is possible for drives, but so is their *density*. By affect density I mean the product of intensity times duration. Most drives operate within relatively narrow density tolerances. The consequence of too much variation of density of intake of air is loss of consciousness and possible death. Compared with drives, affects may be either much more casual and low in density or much more monopolistic and high in density. By virtue of the flexibility of this system, humans are able to oscillate between affect fickleness and obsessive possession by the object of their affective investments.

Not only may affects be widely invested and variously invested, but they may also be invested in other affects, combined with other affects, to intensify or modulate them and to suppress or reduce them. Neither hunger nor thirst can be used to reduce the need for air, as a child may be shamed into crying or may be shamed into stopping his crying.

The generality of time, object, intensity, and density of the affect system are not the *consequence* of learning but rather the structural, innate features of the affect system that make learning possible. In contrast to the drive system with its insistence on air, food, and water, it is *possible* to live a lifetime without ever experiencing fear or joy because the affect mechanism has these structural degrees of freedom that the drive mechanism lacks. Further, in contrast to the customary antithesis between the innate and learned motives, I base the possibility of learning on just these very general features built into the structures and programs of the affect system.

The basic power of the affect system is a consequence of its freedom to combine with a variety of other components in what may be called a *central assembly*. This is an executive mechanism upon which messages converge from all sources, competing from moment to moment for inclusion in this governing central assembly. The affect system can be evoked by central and peripheral messages from any source and, in turn, it can control the disposition of such messages and their sources.

The affect system provides the primary blueprints for cognition, decision, and action. Humans are responsive to whatever circumstances activate the varieties of positive and negative affects. Some of these circumstances innately activate the affects. At the same time, the affect system is also capable of being instigated by learned stimuli and responses. The human being is thus urged by nature and by nurture to explore and to attempt to control the circumstances that evoke his positive and negative affective responses. It is the freedom of the affect system that makes it possible for the human being to begin to implement and to progress toward what he regards as an ideal state—one that, however else he may describe it, implicitly or explicitly entails the maximizing of positive affect and the minimizing of negative affect.

INNATE AFFECT ACTIVATORS

I turn now to an examination of the specific affects I have postulated, how they are activated and some of the consequences of that theory of activation.

I now distinguish nine innate affects.[1] The positive affects are as follows: first, *interest* or *excitement,* with eyebrows down and stare fixed or tracking an object; second, *enjoyment* or *joy,* the smiling response; third, *surprise* or *startle,* with eyebrows raised and eyes blinking. The negative affects are the following: first, *distress* or *anguish,* the crying response; second, *fear* or *terror,* with eyes frozen open in fixed stare or moving away from the dreaded object to the side, with skin pale, cold, sweating, and trembling, and with hair erect; third, *shame* or *humiliation,* with eyes and head lowered; fourth, *contempt,* with the upper lip raised in a sneer; fifth, *disgust,* with the lower lip lowered and protruded; sixth,

---

[1]Data from the Polarity Scale (Tomkins & Izard, 1965) revealed that differential magnification of contempt was correlated with normative ideology and that disgust was correlated with humanistic ideology. Originally, contempt and disgust were treated as variants of a unitary response, thus making for eight affects in the original theory, rather than nine.

anger, or *rage,* with a frown, clenched jaw, and red face. These facial and skin responses are not meant to represent an exhaustive description of the primary affects but rather a representative sample of the more prominent features.

If these are innately patterned responses, are there also innate activators of each affect? Consider the nature of the problem. The innate activators must include the drives as innate activators but *not* be limited to drives as exclusive activators. The neonate, for example, must respond with innate fear to any difficulty in breathing but must also be afraid of other objects. Each affect had to be capable of being activated by a *variety* of unlearned stimuli. The child had to be able to cry at hunger or loud sounds as well as at a diaper pin stuck in his flesh. Therefore, each affect had to be activated by some general characteristic of neural stimulation, common to both internal and external stimuli and not too stimulus-specific like a releaser. Next, the activator had to be correlated with biologically useful information. The young child must fear what is dangerous and smile at what is safe. The activator had to "know the address" of the subcortical center at which the appropriate affect program is stored, not unlike the problem of how the ear responds correctly to each tone. Next, some of the activators had to be capable of nonhabituation, whereas others had to be capable of habituation, otherwise a painful stimulus might too soon cease to be distressing and an exciting stimulus never be let go—such as a deer caught by a bright light. These are some of the characteristics built into the affect mechanism's activation sensitivity. The most economical assumption on which to proceed is to look for communalities among these varieties in the characteristics of the innate activators of each affect. This I have done, and I believe it is possible to account for the major phenomena with a few, relatively simple, assumptions about the general characteristics of the stimuli that innately activate affect.

I account for the differences in affect activation by three general variants of a single principle—the density of neural firing, or stimulation. By density, I mean the number of neural firings per unit of time. The theory posits three discrete classes of activators of affect, each of which further amplifies the sources that activate them. These are *stimulation increase, stimulation level,* and *stimulation decrease.* Thus, there is a provision for three distinct classes of motives: affects about stimulation that is on the increase, about stimulation that is steady, about stimulation that is on the decrease. With respect to density of neural firing, or stimulation, then, the human being is equipped for affective arousal for every major contingency. If internal or external sources of neural firing suddenly increase, he will startle or become afraid, or become interested, depending on the suddenness of the increase in stimulation. If internal or external sources of neural firing reach and maintain a high, constant level of stimulation, which deviates in excess of an optimal level of neural firing, he will respond with anger or distress, depending on the level of stimulation. If internal or external sources of neural firing suddenly decrease, he will laugh or smile with enjoyment, depending on the suddenness of the decrease in stimulation.

The general advantage of affective arousal to such a broad spectrum of levels and changes of level of nerual firing is to make the individual care about quite different states of affairs in different ways. It should be noted that, according to my views, there are both positive and negative affects (startle, fear, interest) activated by stimulation increase; only negative affects are activated by a continuing. unrelieved level of stimulation (distress, anger); and only positive affects are activated by stimulation decrease (laughter, joy). This latter, in my theory, is the only remnant of the tension reduction theory of reinforcement. Stimulation increase may, in my view, result in punishing inasmuch as it activates the cry of distress or anger, depending on how high above optimal levels of stimulation the particular density of neural firing is. A suddenly reduced density of stimulation is invariably rewarding, whether, it should be noted, the stimulation reduced is itself positive or negative in quality. Stated another way, such a set of mechanisms guarantees sensitivity to whatever is new, to whatever continues for any extended period of time, and to whatever is ceasing to happen. In Fig. 7.1, I have graphically represented this theory.

Thus, any stimulus with a relatively sudden onset and a steep increase in rate of neural firing will innately activate a startle response. As shown also in Fig. 7.1, if the rate of neural firing increases less rapidly, fear is activated, and if the rate increases still less rapidly, interest is innately activated. In contrast, any sustained increase in the level of neural firing, as with a continuing loud noise, would innately activate the cry of distress. If it were sustained and still louder, it would innately activate the anger response. Finally, any sudden decrease in stimulation that reduced the rate of neural firing, as in the sudden reduction of excessive noise, would innately activate the rewarding smile of enjoyment.

Such a neural theory must be able to account for how the "meaning" in such neural messages operates without the benefit of a homunculus who "appraises"

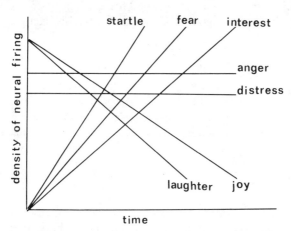

FIG. 7.1.   Model of the innate activators of affect.

every message before instructing the individual to become interested or afraid. It is clear that any theory of affect activation must be capable of accounting for affect that is triggered in either an unlearned or a learned fashion. Certainly the infant who emits his birth cry upon exit from the birth canal has not "appraised" the new environment as a vale of tears before he cries. Equally certain he will later learn to cry at communications telling of death of a beloved person and this does depend on meaning and its appraisal. It is my view that theories (e.g., Arnold 1960, or Lazarus this volume) that postulate such appraisal as a necessary condition for affect activation are more embarrassed by unlearned activation than my theory is embarrassed by the learned activation of affect, which I propose can activate affect *only* through the general profiles of neural firing I have postulated. Thus, the novelty of information adequate to trigger interest and the final laughter to a new joke depends on the rate of acceleration of information in the first case and in the rate of deceleration in the second case. If we hear the same information a second time, there is a sense in which it may be appraised as essentially a repetition, but because we now see it coming, there is neither interest nor enjoyment because the gradients of neural firing are now much flatter because compressed, than when the information was first received. Similarly with the startle response, a pistol shot is adequate as an unlearned activator but so is the sudden appearance of a man with two heads. In such a case I would suggest that the rate of neural firing from the conjoint muscular responses of the double-take and the very rapid recruitment of information from memory to check the nature of the apparent message also have the requisite square-wave profile of neural firing called for in my model. In short, "meaning," operates through the very general profiles of acceleration, deceleration, or level of neural firing as these are produced by either cognitive, memorial, perceptual, or motor responses. Any such responses singly or in concert can, through their correlation between meaning and the profiles of neural firing, "innately" fire innate affect programs by stimuli, or responses that are themselves learned may.

ROLE OF THE SPECIFIC AFFECTS

Let us consider now some of the consequences of the affect theory for each of the specific primary affects. We shall begin with startle, fear, and interest, which differ, with respect to activation, only in the rate at which stimulation or neural firing increases.

Startle

Startle appears to be activated by a critical rate of increase in the density of neural firing. The difference between startle (or surprise in its weaker form) and interest is a difference in the steepness of the gradient of stimulation. The same stimulus, therefore, may evoke surprise or interest, depending on the steepness of the rise of stimulation (which in turn depends on numerous factors, prominent among which is the degree of unexpectedness). Thus, a gun shot will evoke startle rather than interest. An unexpected tap on the shoulder by someone who is not seen will also evoke startle rather than interest. In the case of the gun shot, the suddenness of increase of stimulation was primarily in the auditory stimulus itself.

The general function of the startle response we take to be that of a circuit breaker, or interrupter mechanism, which resets the central assembly. This mechanism is similar in design and function to that in a radio or television network that enables special announcements to interrupt any ongoing program. It is ancillary to every other affect because it orients the individual to turn his attention from one this to another. Whether, having been interrupted, the individual will respond with interest, fear, joy, distress, disgust, shame, or anger will depend on the nature of the interrupting stimulus and on the interpretation given to it. The experience of surprise itself is brief and varies from an essentially neutral quality in its milder form to a somewhat negative quality in its more intense form as the startle response. Whatever its quality, positive or negative, it is frequently confused with the affect that immediately follows it. The surprise of seeing an unexpected love object is an overall positive experience. The surprise of seeing a dreaded person is an essentially negative experience. In its intense form, it is an involuntary massive contraction of the body as a whole, which momentarily renders individuals incapable of either continuing whatever they were doing before the startle or of initiating new activity for the duration of the startle response.

If startle, fear, and interest differ with respect to activation only in the rate at which stimulation or neural firing increases, then we can account for the unstable equilibria that there seem to be among them. First, it would illuminate the familiar sequences of startle. fear, interest. The same object that first startles quickly passes over into fear and then, somewhat less quickly, is transformed into interest or excitement.

Fear

Study of the fear affect has led to the conclusion that the fear experience in infancy should have minimal aftereffects upon repetition. D. M. Levy (1960) found that in the first six months of life, infants did not cry upon seeing the same doctor about to give them an injection for the second time in their life. Even as late as a year of age, if the interval between inoculations exceeded two months, there was no memory cry. There was a rising frequency of memory cries with age, starting with 1% at six months of age and rising to 20% at a year. There is nothing in the visual stimulus of doctor or needle that would innately activate fear, according to our model. Because memory and recognition are primitive in the first year we should expect fear to be limited to only those stimuli that produce the requisite density of neural firing. The pain of the needle does cause crying, but the sight of the needle again produces no apparent affect.

Our second conclusion about fear is that we should expect a great variety of sudden internal events to be capable of activating fear. These include the feedback of sudden muscular contractions, as in avoidance responses, the rapidly accelerating construction of future possibilities via imagery or cognition, the rapid change of rate of any internal organ or system, such as the heart, circulatory system. respiration, endocrine system, and so on.

Thus it follows that any radical change of the internal environment by drugs can either increase or decrease the threshold for fear by increasing or decreasing the general neural rate of firing. We would suggest that the time-honored effect of alcohol on the release of inhibitions occurs through its relaxation of the skeletal musculature and of the blood vessels lying close to the skin. The muscles relax and the face becomes warm and tingles from vascular relaxation. The combined effect is to reduce radically the possibility of activating fear. A warm bath is similarly disinhibiting, and hydrotherapy has been used successfully to control acute anxiety through essentially similar mechanisms.

Interest

With respect to interest and excitement, while it is sufficiently massive a motive to amplify and make a difference to such an already intense stimulation as that from sexual intercourse, it is also capable of sufficiently graded, flexible innervation and combination to provide a motive matched to the most subtle cognitive capacities. Rapidly varying perception and thinking is thereby combined with varying shades of interest and excitement, which wax and wane appropriately with the operation of the analyzer mechanisms. The match between excitement and the drives is a different match from that between excitement and cognition. Because the latter is a process that is much more rapid, and much more variable in time, it necessarily requires a motivational system that is matched in speed, gradation and flexibility of arousal, combination, and reduction. It must be possible to turn excitement on and off quickly, to grade its intensity, and, above all, to combine it with everchanging central assemblies. In contrast even with other affects, such as fear and anger, interest must have both more and less inertia. It must not necessarily remain activated too long once aroused, but it must also be capable of being sustained indefinitely if the object or activity so demands it.

Interest is also a necessary condition for the formation of the perceptual world. In learning to perceive any new object, the infant must attack the problem over time. Almost any object is too big a bit to be swallowed whole. If it is swallowed whole it remains whole until its parts are decomposed, magnified, examined in great detail and reconstructed into a new more differentiated object. There is thus created a variety of problems in early perception. The object must be perceived in some detail, but it must also be perceived in its unity. Attention must steer a middle course between extreme distractibility from one aspect of an object to some other aspect of an adjacent object, and extreme stickiness and compelled attention to the same object, as in the case of a deer caught and immobilized by a light or an animal fascinated by the eyes of a cobra. Attention must stick long enough both to achieve detail and to move on to some other aspect of the object, not to every competing stimulus in the field. In order to make such graded and differential sampling possible, there must be the continuing support of interest or excitement to the *changing* sampling of the object.

In order to shift from one perceptual perspective to another, from the perceptual to the motor orientation and back again, from both the perceptual and the motor to the conceptual level and back again, and from one memory to another, one must, at the very least, maintain a continuing interest in all of these varying transactions with what is the same object. Without such an underlying continuity of motivational support, there could indeed be no creation of a single object with complex persectives and with some unity in its variety.

Interest is also a necessary condition for the physiological support of long-term effort. Excitement lends more than spice to life. Without zest, long-term effort and commitment cannot be sustained, either physiologically or psychologically. What constitutes a clogging of the zest for work can be transformed into a major stasis when the individual, through sudden changes in circumstances, comes face to face with the awareness that he cannot fulfill himself in his work. When the individual knows what he wants but must renounce his central aims, this crisis has dramatic physiological consequences. (See Alexander & Portis. 1944).

Distress

In comparison with startle and fear, the affect of distress appears to be based, not on an increase of density of stimulation, but rather on an absolute level of density of stimulation or neural firing, which deviates in excess of an optimal level of neural firing. Thus, pain characteristically produces crying in the infant. The suddenness of pain is not the critical feature of the activation of distress. Either sudden or prolonged pain is equally capable of activating distress. Thus, a sudden stab of pain elicits a sudden scream of distress, and prolonged pain ordinarily produces prolonged crying. In contrast to fear, it is the total quantity or density of stimulation through crying. It is the quantity rather than the quality of stimulation that appears to be critical.

Distress-anguish is a fundamental human affect primarily because of the ubiquity of human suffering. Anxiety, by contrast, is properly an emergency affect. When life and death hang in the balance, most animals have been endowed with the capacity for terror. This is appropriate if life is to be surrendered only very dearly. The cost of terror is so great that the body was not designed for chronic activation of this affect. A human being who responds as if there were justification for being chronically terrorized would properly be diagnosed as ill.

It seems very likely that the differentiation of distress from fear was required in part because the coexistence of superior cognitive powers of anticipation, with an affect as toxic as fear, could have destroyed man if this were the only affect expressing suffering. What was called for was a less toxic, but still negative, affect, which would motivate human beings to solve disagreeable problems without too great a physiological cost or too great a probability of running away from the many problems that confront the human being and which would permit anticipation of trouble at an optimal psychic and biological cost. Such, we think, is the human cry of distress.

If distress is activated by a general continuing level of nonoptimal neural stimulation, then we can account for the fact that such a variety of stimuli, from both internal and external sources, can produce the cry of distress in the infant and the muted distress response in the adult. This variety ranges from the low-level pains of fatigue, hunger, cold, wetness, loud sounds, and overly bright lights to the cry itself as a further stimulus.

The crying response is the first response the human being makes upon being born. The birth cry is a cry of distress. It is not, as Freud supposed, the prototype of anxiety. It is a response of distress at the excessive level of stimulation to which the neonate is suddenly exposed upon being born.

The general biological function of crying is, first, to communicate to the organism itself and to others that all is not well, doing this for a number of alternative distressors, second, to motivate both the self and others to do something to reduce the crying response with a degree of toxicity that is tolerable for both the organism that cries and for the one who hears it cry.

Because the cry is an auditory stimulus, it can be heard at a distance, which provides a considerable safety factor for the otherwise helpless infant. It is also a much more distinctive stimulus for purposes of communication than are the various thrashing-about movements of which the neonate is capable. It is conceivable that, in the absence of the auditory cry, the human mother would be quite as unable to detect the distress of the neonate as is the chick's mother when she sees but is prevented from hearing the cry. This is also likely because of the number of alternative ways in which the cry can be activated. A mother who could detect distress if a diaper pin were sticking into the infant might be unable to do so if the infant were distressed at being alone, in the absence of a distress cry, since much of the thrashing about of the infant is very similar whether the infant is happy or unhappy.

What the distress cry gains in specificity as a distinctive communication, it sacrifices somewhat because it is a sign of so many possible different distressors. When a mother hears an infant cry, she characteristically does not know what it is crying about. It might be hungry, or cold, or in pain, or lonely. She must try each of these in turn to find out, and even then the test does not always remove the ambiguity. Because infants will stop crying for many reasons, quite unrelated to what started them, the mother may easily misdiagnose the nature of the distressor. For example, an infant who is hungry may stop crying upon being picked up but start again when it is put down. The mother at this point cannot be sure whether the child is crying from hunger or loneliness.

The degree of ambiguity is a necessary consequence of the generality of activation of the distress response. In lower forms, the cries are more specific in nature. It is an unanswered question of how specific the cries of the human neonate may be.[2]

Although the number of alternative activators of the cry creates some ambiguity concerning its significance, it is this multiplicity of activators that makes the cry a response of such general significance. It enables general suffering and communication of such suffering. It is as important for the individual to be distressed about many aspects of its life, which continue to overstimulate it, and to communicate this as it is to be able to become interested in anything that is changing.

Although the communication of distress to the mother is primary during infancy because of the infant's helpless dependency, the significance of communication of distress to the self increases with age. Just as the human drive signal is of value in telling the individual when he is hungry and when he should stop eating, so the distress cry is critical in telling the individual himself when he is suffering and when he has stopped suffering. Awareness that all is not well, without actual suffering, is as unlikely as would be the awareness of the threat of a cigarette burning the skin that had no pain receptors. This is to say that, over and above the motivating qualities of pain or of the distress cry, there are important informational characteristics that are a consequence of their intense motivating properties. The cry not only has information for the self and others about a variety of matters needing alleviation, but it also motivates the self and others to reduce it.

Both the nonoptimal level of stimulation and the distress cry may be masked or reduced in awareness or in general by competing stimulation, which is more intense and more sharply increasing in intensity, and by the affects of startle, fear, or excitement, which may be activated by such competing stimulation. Despite such competition, the coupling of distress and its activators enjoys the

---

[2]One method of answering such a question would be to record a sample of the cries of a neonate during its first week. Then, at moments when the infant was not crying, subject it to a distributed series of playbacks of its past cries and record the fresh crying that the infant emitted in response to hearing itself cry. The infant should cry to the sound of its own cry, because the cry is a quite contagious response. One could then examine the degree of correlation between each cry used as a stimulus and the contagious response to that cry. If the neonate does emit distinctively different cries, then it might respond differentially to its own distinctive cries; therefore the variance between pairs of cries should exceed that within pairs of cries.

competitive advantage of endurance in its claim upon consciousness. Both the activator and the distress cry are long-term motivators, requiring no novelty to keep the individual in a perpetual bind.

Anger

Anger is the other affect that is activated by the absolute density level of stimulation. It is our assumption that anger is activated by a higher density level of stimulation than is distress. Hence, if a source of stimulation, say pain, is adequate to activate distress and both pain and distress continue unrelieved for any period of time, the combination of stimulation may reach the level necessary to activate anger. This is also why frustration may lead to anger. Further, either distress alone or pain alone might be sufficiently dense to activate anger. Thus, a slap on the face is likely to arouse anger because of the very high density of receptors on the surface of the face. In contrast, a stab of pain elsewhere in the body may lack both the requisite density and the duration to activate more than a cry of distress. This principle would also account for the irritability produced by continuous loud noise that tends to recruit widespread muscle contraction, which, added to the distress affect, could raise the density of stimulation to that necessary for anger. The role of distress and anger in the mother-infant relationship is complex. The infant's crying is capable of innately activating the distress of the mother, and so enlisting the aid of the mother and strengthening commitment to her child. But this very combination of the loud crying of distress of the child and the evoked distress of the mother is also quite capable of innately activing anger sufficient to attenuate the tie to the infant and, in the extreme case, lead the mother to destroy the child.

Joy

In contrast to stimulation increase and stimulation level, there is also the affect that operates on the principle of stimulation reduction. The *smile of joy* is based on such a mechanism. The smile of joy is innately activated in our view by any relatively steep reduction of the density of stimulation and neural firing. Thus, sudden relief from such negative stimulations as pain, fear, distress, or agression will produce the smile of joy. In the case of pain, fear, and distress, the smile of joy is a smile of relief. In the case of sudden anger reduction, it is the smile of triumph. The same principle operates with the sudden reduction of pleasure, as after orgasm or the completion of a good meal, there is often the smile of pleasure. Further, the sudden reduction of positive affect, such as excitement, also activates the smile of joy, in this case usually the smile of recognition or familiarity. In all of these cases, it is the steepness of the gradient of stimulation reduction that is critical. A gradual reduction of pain may pass into indifference. A gradual reduction of distress, similarly, may provide no secondary reward of joy. For a steep gradient reduction in density of stimulation to be possible, it is, of course, necessary that there be a prior level of high density of stimulation. This means that a reduction of weak pain stimulation that is sudden enough may nonetheless not involve a sufficient reduction in density of stimulation to activate the smiling response. Under such conditions, whatever reward value there may be in the cessation of pain stimulation is not enhanced by the incremental reward of the smiling response. Further, it means that many familiar objects in the environment may be too familiar to evoke enough, even momentary, excitement to evoke the smile of joy at the recognition of the familiar and the reduction of very weak interest. In order to enjoy seeing someone or something familiar, one must first have been sufficiently interested so that the sudden reduction of this interest will constitute a sufficient change in density of stimulation to evoke the smiling response.

This theory of activation of the smiling response enables us to account for phenomena as disparate as the joy of relief from pain and the joy of the infant at the sight of the mother. The mother's face is one of the few objects in the environment with sufficient variation in appearance to produce both excitement at its sudden appearance and the smile at the sudden reduction of this excitement when the face is recognized as a familiar one. This would account for the smile, observed by other investigators, such as Piaget, at the sudden perception of familiar toys or at somewhat expected and somewhat unexpected "effects" produced by the child's own efforts.

The second principle of activation of the smiling response is based on our theory of memory. Simply stated, the visual sight of a smiling face can be learned to become a "name", i.e., a message capable of retrieving from memory a specific trace at a specific address. In this case, it retrieves the stored memory of how the individual experienced the feedback from the muscles of his own face when he smiled in the past. This retrieved past experience can also become a "name" of a stored program, which translates these perceived "awarenesses" into their equivalent motor messages, i.e., a set of impulses that instruct the facial muscles to contract in such a way that the feedback from the contracted facial muscles is equal to the experienced set that initiated this motor translation.

We do not wish at this point to enlarge on subtle distinctions, except to note that the conscious experience of the smile of another face may activate retrieved awareness of one's own past smiles, which may then either retrieve a stored program in the manner just indicated or directly innervate the innate program of the smiling response via the subcortical centers. The difference in these two routes would be that in the former case a "learned" smile would be activated and in the latter it would be an "unlearned" smile.

We are attempting here to distinguish learning that utilizes preformed programs from learning and memory that may produce identical responses on a purely learned basis, which bypasses the innate programs while it mimics them.

It is, in part, the difference between the "OH!" of surprise and the same "OH" of an actor reading his lines. In either event, and by either route, the smile of another person is capable of evoking the empathic response. Such mimesis is quite different from the activation by sudden stimulation reduction and somewhat confounds the empirical investigation of the smiling response.

The third way in which the smiling response may be activated is through memory, or learning. It is not necessarily the case that any experience that produced the smile of enjoyment in the past will be capable of activating the same affect upon being recalled. Emotion remembered in tranquility need be no more motivating than the toothache that has just stopped aching, which can be recalled with relative calm. Any affect requiring any degree of uncertainty for activation is all but impossible to repeat exactly, even when the circumstances, in fact or in memory, are duplicated exactly. No joke is ever quite as funny on repetition. Although the smile is an affect that can be emitted to the familiar, it also depends on stimulation reduction, which, apart from pain, distress, or anger, requires some novelty if excitement is to be activated sufficiently so that its reduction constitutes an adequate stimulus for the smile.

How then is memory, or anticipation, likely to evoke the smile of enjoyment? Any recollection, or anticipation, that produces a present affect sufficiently intense and suddenly reduced either through remembered, imagined, or antici- pated consequences may evoke the smile of joy. Such would be the case if I anticipated meeting someone who excited me and whom I had not seen for many years. If this generated present excitement, the shock of recognition, in visualiz- ing such a reunion, might sufficiently reduce the excitement so that the smile of joy might be evoked. Similarly, if the recollection of such a meeting first arouses excitement that is suddenly reduced, the smile of joy may be activated in what may be called "postication." If the anticipated or posticipated encounter gen- erates fear, distress, or shame that is reduced in the imagination by appropriate counteractive measures, one may smile in joy. The crushing retort to the insuf- ferable opponent, even when it occurs too late for the battle proper, may bring joy to the heart of the defeated, whose anger is suddenly reduced by the imagined discomfiture of the adversary. The recollection of past defeat in attempting problem solving, which may occasion present distress or shame, can evoke the smile of joy if suddenly there is an expectation of a solution and with it a rapid reduction of the distress or shame. The same smile of joy may occur in the midst of difficulties if the individual simply imagines to have heroically solved the problem.

Smiling creates a *felicité à deux* similar to and also different from that created by the enjoyment of sexual intercourse. In sexual intercourse, the behavior of each is a sufficient condition for the pleasure of each individual for himself and at the same time for the please of the other. This dyadic interaction is inherently social inasmuch as the satisfaction of the self is at the same time the satisfaction of the other.

In the smiling response, as we see it first between the mother and her child, there is a similar mutuality, except that it is on the affect level rather than through mutual drive satisfaction, and it operates at a distance rather than requiring body contact. The difference in this respect is as profound a change in the structure of motivation as was involved in the development of perception with the appearance of distance receptors compared with proximity receptors.

Because the infant will smile at the face of the mother and thereby reward itself, and because the mother will in turn smile at the smile of the infant and thereby reward herself, concurrent smiling is mutually rewarding from the out-set. Later, when the child's development is sufficiently advanced, both parties to this mutual enjoyment are further rewarded by the awareness that this enjoyment is shared enjoyment. This is mediated through the eyes. Through interocular interaction both parties become aware of each other's enjoyment and of the very fact of communion and mutuality. Indeed, one of the prime ways in later life that the adult will recapture this type of communion is when he smiles at another person, who smiles back at him and at the same time the eyes of each are arrested in a stare at the eyes of the other. Under these conditions one person can "fall in love with" another person. The power of this dyadic posture is a derivative of an earlier unashamed fascination-and-joy smile. The power of the earlier experience is essentially innate: the match between the stimulus characteristics of the human face and the conditions necessary for innately arousing the reciprocal affects of interest and joy biologically equips the infant, no less than the mother, to be joyous in this way.

More often than not, mutual awareness of each other's smile will include visual awareness of each other's face, including the smile but with the eyes as figure against the rest of the face as ground. One may look at the other's eyes, but with limited awareness. Because socialization ordinarily places restrictions on the direct intent stare into the eyes of another, adult communion ordinarily excludes prolonged interocular interaction as being excessively intimate. Despite this exclusion there is a deeply rewarding sense of communion made possible by mutual awareness of each other's face in mutual smiling. Awareness of mutuality is achieved without interocular interaction even though this exclusion somewhat attenuates the intimacy of this experience.

The general biological significance of social responsiveness and therefore of any affect supporting such characteristics is manifold. First, because the human infant is the most helpless of animals, it is important that he attract the care of the mother. This is guaranteed first by the distress cry, which creates an *infelicitéà deux* and prompts the mother to child. The child must be free to explore the world and yet to feel safe in doing so. To the extent to which he must have body contact to feel joy and love, the infant is not free to satisfy his curiosity in the world about him. He would also be restricted in the kind of social responsiveness which would be possible for him. Thus to be a few feet away from the mother or any other familiar person, to engage in conversation, or to engage in any of the adult variants of human communion, for example, to lecture, to act, to perform before an audience, all of these would constitute frustration unless the smiling-enjoyment response could be emitted to visual stimuli that were at some distance from the child.

The equation of oral interest with every type of human dependence and interdependence has masked the critical role both of the face and of the distance receptors in human communion. Both the face and tongue are organs of exquisite subtlety of expressiveness. We do not think it accidental that Freud sat behind the patient so that facial interaction was minimized. He shared the almost universal taboo on intimate facial interaction and overweighted the role of the mouth as an instrument of hunger, in symbolizing all human communion. We are arguing that the smile in response to the human face makes possible all those varieties of human communion that are independent of eating and of touching another.

The purely social wishes of the human being are diverse. They are derivatives of numerous affects complexly organized to create addictions to particular kinds of human communion. Although the smile of joy is perhaps the central affect in such a matrix, it is by no means the exclusive base of social responsiveness. Humans characteristically are excited by other human beings as well as made joyous by them. They are, on the negative side, distressed, frightened, ashamed, and angered by the deprivation of human interaction as well as by a variety of inappropriate responses from other human beings.

Social enjoyments are so diverse partly for the same reason that the objects of human excitement are so diverse. Anything that can capture the interest of a human being can also produce the smile of joy. Among this larger set of interests is a very large subset of social interests and enjoyments. Every time and in every manner in which one human being has excited another, either party independently or both can become candidates for social enjoyment. Add to this all the possible transformations that the imagination of an intelligent animal permits and the outcome is a very broad spectrum of social enjoyments.

Although I argued for the existence of nine innate affects, the theory of the innate activators of affect omitted shame, contempt, and disgust. I do not believe these three are innate affects in the same sense as the six already described. They have motivating, amplifying properties of affects but have somewhat different characteristics and mechanisms.

Contempt, Disgust, and Shame

Contempt and disgust are innate defensive responses, which are auxiliary to the hunger, thirst, and oxygen drives. Their function is clear. If the food about to be ingested activates contempt, the upper lip and nose are raised and the head is drawn away from the apparent source of the offending odor. If the food has been taken into the mouth, it may, if disgusting, be spit out. If it has been swallowed and is toxic, it will produce nausea and be vomited out, either through the mouth or nostrils. The early warning response via the nose is contempt; the mouth or stomach response is disgust. If contempt and disgust were limited to these functions, we should not define them as affects but rather as auxiliary drive mechanisms. However, their status is somewhat unique in that contempt, disgust, and nausea also function as signals and motives to others as well as to the self of feelings of rejection. They readily accompany a wide spectrum of entities that need not be tasted, smelled, or ingested. Contempt and disgust appear to be changing more in status from drive-reducing acts to acts that also have a more general motivating and signal function, both to the individual who emits it and to the one who sees it.

Just as contempt and disgust are drive auxiliary acts, I posit shame as an innate *affect auxiliary* response and a specific inhibitor of continuing interest and enjoyment. Like disgust, it operates only after interest or enjoyment has been activated and inhibits one or the other or both. The innate activator of shame is the incomplete reduction of interest or joy. Such a barrier might arise because one is suddenly looked at by one who is strange, or because one wishes to look at or commune with another person but suddenly cannot because he is strange, or one expected him to be familiar but he suddenly appears unfamiliar, or one started to smile but found one was smiling at a stranger. The response of shame includes lowering the eyelid, lowering the tonus of all facial muscles, lowering the head via a reduction in tonus of the neck muscles, and a unilateral tilting of the head in one direction.

Shyness, shame, and guilt are identical as affects, though not so experienced because of differential coassembly of perceived causes and consequences. Shyness is about strangeness of the other; guilt is about moral transgression; shame is about inferiority, but the core affect in all three is identical, though the coassembled perceptions, cognitions. and intentions may be vastly different.

Biologically, disgust and contempt are drive auxiliary responses that have evolved to protect the human being from coming too close to noxious-smelling objects and to regurgitate these if they have been ingested. Through learning, these responses have come to be emitted to biologically neutral stimuli, including, for example, disgusting and dirty thoughts. Shame, in contrast, is an affect auxiliary to the affect of interest-excitement. Any perceived barrier to positive affect with the other will evoke lowering of the eyelids and loss of tonus in the face and neck muscles, producing a head hung in shame. The child who is burning with excitement to explore the face of the stranger is nonetheless vulnerable to shame just because the other is perceived as strange. Characteristically, however, intimacy with the good and exciting other is eventually consummated. In contrast, the disgusting other is to be kept at a safe distance permanently. The reason for distinguishing disgust more sharply from contempt than I had done before, arose primarily from data in connection with my ideological polarity theory, which I shall now describe briefly.

POLARITY THEORY

I have been concerned for some time with a field I have called the *psychology of knowledge,* an analog of the sociology of knowledge. It is a concern with the varieties of cognitive styles, with the types of evidence that the individual finds persuasive and, most particularly, with his ideology. I have defined *ideology* as any organized set of ideas about which humans are at once most articulate, ideas that produce enduring controversy over long periods of time, that evoke passionate partisanship, and about which humans are least certain because there is insufficient evidence. Ideology therefore abounds at the frontier of any science. But today's ideology may tomorrow be confirmed or disconfirmed and so cease to be ideology. In a review of 2,000 years of ideological controversy in western civilization, I have detected a sustained recurrent polarity between the humanistic and the normative orientations appearing in such diverse domains as the foundations of mathematics, the theory of aesthetics, political theory, epistemology, theory of perception, theory of value, theory of child rearing, theory of psychotherapy, and personality testing.

The issues are simple enough. Is man the measure, an end in himself, active, creative, thinking, desiring, loving force in nature? Or must man realize himself, attain his full stature, only through struggle toward, participation in, and conformity to a norm, a measure, an ideal essence basically prior to and independent of man? This polarity appeared first in Greek philosophy between Protagoras and Plato. Western thought has been an elaborate series of footnotes to the conflict between the conception of man as the measure of reality and value versus that of man and nature as alike unreal and valueless in comparison to the realm of essence that exists independently of space and time. More simply, this polarity represents an idealization of man—a positive idealization in the humanistic ideology and a negative idealization in the normative ideology. Human beings, in Western civilization, have tended toward self-celebration, positive or negative. In Oriental thought another alternative is represented, that of harmony between man and nature.

I have further assumed that the individual resonates to any organized ideology because of an underlying ideo-affective posture, which is a set of feelings that is more *loosely* organized than any highly organized ideology.

Some insight into these ideological concepts held by an individual may be obtained through use of my *polarity scale.* The polarity scale assesses the individual's normative or humanistic position on a broad spectrum of ideological issues in mathematics, science, art, education, politics, child rearing, and theory of personality. Following are a few sample items from the scale. The normative position will be A, the humanistic B. The individual is permitted four choices: A, B, A and B, and neither A nor B.

1. A. Numbers were discovered.	B. Numbers were invented
2. A. Play is childish	B. Nobody is too old to play.
3. A. The mind is like a mirror.	B. The mind is like a lamp.
4. A. If you have had a bad experience with someone, the way to characterize this is that it leaves a bad smell.	B. If you have had a bad experience with someone, the way to characterize this is that it leaves a bad taste in the mouth

I have assumed that the ideo-affective posture is the result of systematic differences in the socialization of affects. For example, the attitudes toward distress in the items above could be a consequence of the following differences in distress socialization. When the infant or child cries, the parent, following his own ideo-affective posture and more articulate ideology, may elect to convert the distress of the child into a rewarding scene by putting his arms around the child and comforting him. He may, however, amplify the punishment inherent in the distress response by putting himself into opposition to the child and his distress. He will require that the child stop crying, insisting that the child's crying results from some norm violation and threaten to increase the child's suffering if he does not suppress the response. "If you don't stop crying, I will really give you something to cry about." If the child internalizes his parent's ideo-affective posture and his ideology, the child has learned a very basic posture toward suffering, which will have important consequences for resonance to ideological beliefs quite remote from the nursery and the home. This is exemplified by the following items from the polarity scale: "The maintenance of law and order is the most important duty of any government" versus "Promotion of the welfare of the people is the most important function of a government."

The significance of the socialization of distress is amplified by the differential socialization of all the affects, including surprise, enjoyment, excitement, anger, fear, shame, contempt, and disgust. I have outlined elsewhere (Tomkins, 1979) a systematic program of differential socialization of each of these affects, which together produce an ideoaffective posture that inclines the individual to resonate differentially to ideology. In the preceding example, excitement and enjoyment are implicated along with distress, anger, shame, fear, contempt, and disgust, as it is the relative importance of the reward of positive affects versus the importance of the punishment of negative affects that is involved in law and order versus welfare.

What is less obvious is that similar differences in ideoaffective posture influence such remote ideological options as the following items from the polarity scale: "Numbers were invented" versus "Numbers were discovered"; "The mind is like a lamp which illuminates whatever it shines on" versus "The mind is like a mirror which reflects whatever strikes it''; ''Reason is the chief means by which human beings make great discoveries'' versus ''Reason has to be continually disciplined and corrected by reality and hard facts''; ''Human beings are basically evil.'' The structure of ideology and the relationships among the socialization of affects, the ideoaffective postures, and ideology are more complex than can be discussed here. I wish to present just enough of this theory to enable the reader to understand the relationship of the theory to the face.

I have assumed that the humanistic position is one that attempts to maximize positive affect for individuals and for all their interpersonal relationships. In contrast, the normative position is that norm compliance is the primary value and that positive affect is a *consequence* of norm compliance, not to be directly sought as a goal. Indeed, the suffering of negative affect is assumed to be a frequent experience and an inevitable consequence of the human condition. Therefore, in any interpersonal transaction, the humanist self-consciously strives to maximize positive affect insofar as it is possible.

The first hypothesis concerning the face is that humanists would smile more frequently than the normatively oriented, both because they experienced the smile of enjoyment more frequently during their socialization and because they internalized the ideoaffective posture that one should attempt to increase positive affect for the other as well as the self. The learned smile does not always mean that the individual *feels* happy. As often as not, it is a consequence of a wish to communicate to the other that one wishes him to feel smiled upon and to evoke the smile from the other. It is often the oil that is spread over troubled human waters to extinguish the fires of distress, hate and shame. It was known from previous investigations with the stereoscope (Tomkins & Izard, 1965) that when one presented humanists and normatives with two pictures of the same face (one of which was smiling and one of which was not), the humanists tended to suppress the nonsmiling face significantly more often than did the normatives. Vasquez (1975) confirmed that humanist subjects actually smile more frequently while talking with an experimenter than do normative subjects. There is, however, no such difference when subjects are alone, displaying affect spontaneously.

The second hypothesis is that humanists would respond more frequently with distress and normatives would respond more frequently with anger. The rationale for this is that when an interpersonal relationship is troubled, the humanist will try to absorb as much punishment as possible and so display distress rather than anger; anger being more likely to escalate into conflict is a more blaming extrapunitive response than distress. It was assumed that the normative subjects would more frequently respond with anger because they are more extrapunitive, more pious and blaming, and less concerned with sparing the feelings of others, as their internalized models did not spare their own feelings. This hypothesis was not confirmed, but neither was it reversed. This failure may have arisen because the differences in polarity scale scores were not as great as I would have wished. In part, this was a consequence of a strong humanistic bias among college students at the time of testing and because of the reluctance of known normatives to volunteer for testing. This is consistent with prior research, including my own, which indicates that volunteers are more sociophilic and friendly.

The third hypothesis is that humanists would more frequently respond with shame and that normatives would respond less frequently with shame but more frequently with disgust and contempt. The rationale is that shame represents an impunitive response to what is interpreted as an interruption to communion (as, e.g., in shyness) and that it will ultimately be replaced by full communication.

In contrast, contempt and disgust are responses to a bad other and the termination of intimacy with such a one is assumed to be permanent unless the other one changes significantly. These hypotheses were confirmed for shame and disgust but not for contempt. Humanistic subjects, although displaying affect spontaneously, did respond more frequently with shame responses than did normative subjects, whereas normative subjects displayed significantly more disgust responses than did humanistic subjects.

In conclusion, it was predicted and confirmed that humanistic subjects respond more frequently with smiling to the good other and with shame if there is any perceived barrier to intimacy. The normative subjects smile less frequently to the other and emit disgust more frequently to the other who is tested and found wanting. The differences represent a correlation between cognition and affect, as affect is displayed on the faces of those who differ significantly in what they believe about the world in which they live.

MAJOR CHANGES IN MY THEORY OF AFFECT

The theory presented in *Affect, imagery, consciousness* (Tomkins, 1982) has since been developed and modified in four essential ways. First, the theory of affect as amplification I now specify as analogic amplification. Second, I now believe that it is the skin of the face, rather than the musculature, that is the major mechanism of analogic amplification. Third, a substantial quantity of the affect we experience as adults is pseudo-, backed-up, affect. Fourth, affect amplifies not only its own activator but also the response to both that activator and to itself.

Analogic Amplification

The theory of affect as amplification was flawed by a serious ambiguity. I unwittingly assumed a similarity between electronic amplification and affective amplification, such that in both there was an increase in gain of the signal. If such were the case, what was amplified would remain essentially the same except that it would become louder. But affects are separate mechanisms, involving bodily responses quite distinct from the other bodily responses they are presumed to amplify.

How can one response of our body amplify another response? It does this by being similar to that response, but also different. It is an analog amplifier. The affect mechanism is like the pain mechanism in this respect. If we cut our hand, saw it bleeding, but had no innate pain receptors, we would know we had done something that needed repair, but there would be no urgency to it. Like our automobile that needs a tune-up, we might well let it go until next week when we had more time. But the pain mechanism, like the affect mechanism, so amplifies our awareness of the injury that activates it that we are forced to be concerned, and concerned immediately. The biological utility of such analogic amplification is self-evident. The injury, as such, in the absence of pain, simply does not hurt. The pain receptors have evolved to make us hurt and care about injury and disease. Pain is an analog of injury in its inherent similarity. Contrast pain with an orgasm, as a possible analog. If, instead of pain, we always had an orgasm to injury, we would be biologically destined to bleed to death. Affect receptors are no less compelling. Our hair stands on end and we sweat in terror. Our face reddens as our blood pressure rises in anger. Our blood vessels dilate and our face becomes pleasantly warm as we smile in enjoyment. These are compelling analogs of what arouses terror, rage, and enjoyment.

These experiences constitute one form of affect amplification. A second form of affect amplification occurs also by virtue of the similarity of their profiles, in time, to their activating trigger. Just as a pistol shot is a stimulus that is very sudden in onset, very brief in duration, and equally sudden in decay, so its amplification affective analog, the startle response, mimics the pistol shot by being equally sudden in onset, brief in duration, and equally sudden in decay. Therefore, affect, by being analogous in the quality of the feelings from its specific receptors as well as in its profile of activation, maintenance, and decay, amplifies and extends the duration and impact of whatever triggers the affect. Epileptics do not startle, according to Landis and Hunt (1939). Their experienced world is different in this one fundamental way. If epileptics had in addition lacked fear and rage, their world would have become even more different than the usual humanly experienced world. They experience a pistol shot as sudden but not startling. A world experienced without any affect at all because of a complete genetic defect in the whole spectrum of innate affects would be a pallid, meaningless world. We would know that things happened, but we could not care whether they did or not.

By being immediately activated and thereby coassembled with its activator, affect either makes good things better or bad things worse, by conjointly simulating its activator in its profile of neural firing and by adding a special analogic quality, which is intensely rewarding or punishing. In illustrating the simulation of an activating stimulus, e.g., a pistol shot by the startle response, which was equally sudden in onset, equally brief in duration, and equally sudden in decay. I somewhat exaggerated the goodness of fit between activator and affect to better illustrate the general principle. Having done so, let me now be more precise in the characterization of the degree of similarity in profile of neural firing between activator and affect activated. I presented a model of the innate activators of the primary affects in which every possible major general neural contingency innately activates different specific affects. As I explained earlier, increased gradients of rising neural firing activate interest, fear, or surprise as the slope of increasing density of neural firing becomes steeper. Enjoyment is activated by a decreasing gradient of neural firing; distress is activated by a sustained level of neural firing, which exceeds an optimal level by an as yet undetermined magnitude; and anger is also activated by a nonoptimal level of neural firing but one that is substantially higher than that which activates distress. Increase, decrease, or level of neural firing are in this model the sufficient conditions for activating specific affects. Analogic amplification, therefore. is based upon one of these three distinctive features rather than all of them. It so happens that the startle simulates the steepness of the gradient of onset, the brief plateau of maintenance, and the equally steep gradient of decline of profile of the pistol shot and its internal neural correlate, but that is not the general case. Analogic simulation is based on the similarity to the adequate activator, not on all of its characteristics. Thus, it is the decay alone of a stimulus that is simulated in enjoyment. If one places electrodes on the wrist of a subject, permits fear to build, and then removes the electrodes suddenly, we can invariably activate a smile of relief at just that moment. This amplifies (or makes more so) the declining neural stimulation from the reduction of fear. Therefore, enjoyment amplifies by simulating decreasing gradients of neural stimulation. Interest, fear, and surprise amplify by simulating increasing gradients of neural stimulation. Distress and anger amplify by simulating maintained level of simulation.

Locus of Analogic Amplification

The second modification in my theory concerns the exact loci of the rewarding and punishing amplifying analogs. From the start, I emphasized the face and voice as the major loci of the critical feedback experienced as affect. The voice I still regard as a major locus and shall discuss its role in the next section.

The significance of the face in interpersonal relations cannot be exaggerated. It is not only a communication center for the sending and receiving of information of all kinds, but because it is the organ of affect expression and communication, it is necessarily brought under strict social control. There are universal taboos on looking too directly into the eyes of the other because of the likelihood of affect contagion, as well as escalation, because of the unwillingness to express affect promiscuously, and because of concern lest others achieve control through knowledge of one's otherwise private feelings. Humans are primarily voyeuristic, not only because vision is their most informative sense, but because the shared eye-to-eye interaction is the most intimate relationship possible between human beings. There is, in this way, complete mutuality between two selves, each of whom simultaneously is aware of the self and the other. Indeed the intimacy of sexual intercourse is ordinarily attenuated, lest it become too intimate, by being performed in the dark. In the psychoanalytic myth, the crime of the son is voyeuristic by witnessing the "primal scene" and Oedipus is punished, in kind, by blindness.

The taboo on the shared interocular experience is easily exposed. If I were to ask you to turn to another person and stare directly into their eyes while permitting the other to stare directly into your eyes, you would become aware of the taboo. Ordinarily we confront each other by my looking at the bridge of your nose and your looking at my cheek bone. If our eyes should happen to meet directly, the confrontation is minimized by glancing down or away, by letting the eyes go slightly out of focus, or by attenuating the visual datum by making it background to the sound of the other's voice, which is made more figural. The taboo is not only a taboo on looking too intimately but also on exposing the taboo by too obviously avoiding direct confrontation. These two strategies are taught by shaming the child for staring into the eyes of visitors and then shaming the child a second time for hanging his head in shame before the guest.

Only the young or the young in heart are entirely free of the taboo. Those adults whose eyes are caught by the eyes of the other in the shared interocular intimacy may fall in love on such an occasion or, having fallen in love, thereby express the special intimacy they have recaptured from childhood.

The face now appears to be still the central site of the affect responses and their feedback, but I have now come to regard the skin, in general, and the skin of the face, in particular, as of the greatest importance in producing the feel of affect.

In *Affect, imagery, consciousness* (Tomkins. 1982, p. 244), I described the affect system as consisting of 13 components, beginning with the innate affect programs and including affect motor messages. My statement that I regard the face and voice as the central site of affect responses and their feedback must not be interpreted to mean that the whole affect system and its supporting mechanisms are found in the face. Analogically, one might argue for the importance of the thumb and fingers in human evolution without specifying that there is a forearm, biceps, body, and brain to support the thumb.

Further, it is now clear, as it was not then, that the brain is sensitive to its own synthesized chemical endorphins, which serve as analgesics and thus radically attenuate pain and all the negative affects recruited by pain on both innate and learning bases.

My original observations of the intensity of infantile affect, of how an infant was, for example, seized by his own crying, left no doubt in my mind that what the face was doing with its muscles and blood vessels as well as with its accompanying vocalization was at the heart of the matter. This seemed to me to be the major phenomenon, not an "expression" of anything else. I then spent a few years in posing professional actors and others to simulate facial affect. A correlation of + .86 was obtained (Tomkins & McCarter, 1964) between the judgements of trained observers as to what affects they saw on the faces of these subjects as presented in still photographs and what we had intended these sets of muscular responses to represent. This success was gratifying, after so many years of indifferent and variable findings in this field, but it was also somewhat misleading in overemphasizing the role of innately patterned facial muscular responses in the production of affect. I was further confirmed in these somewhat misleading results by the successes of Paul Ekman and Carroll Izard. Ekman, Sorenson, and Friesen (1969), using some of my photographs, were able to demonstrate a wide cultural consensus, even in very primitive remote preliterate societies. Izard (1969), using different photographs but the same conceptual scheme, further extended these impressive results to many other literate societies.[3] The combined weight of all these investigations was more impressive, but I continued to be troubled by one small fact. The contraction of no other set of muscles in the body had *any* apparent motivational properties. Thus, if I were angry, I might clench my fist and hit someone, but if I simply clenched my fist, this would in no way guarantee I would become angry. Muscles appeared to be specialized for action and not for affect. Why then was the smile so easily and so universally responded to as an affect? Why did someone who was crying seem so distressed and so unhappy? Further, from an evolutionary point of view, we know that different functions are piled indiscriminately on top of structures that may originally have evolved to support quite different functions. The tongue was an organ of eating before it was an organ of speech. The muscles of the face were also probably involved in eating before they were used as vehicles of affect, thought we do not know this for a fact. It is, of course, possible that the complex affect displays on the human face evolved primarily as communication mechanisms rather than as sources of motivating feedback. My intuition was, and still is, that the communication of affect is a secondary spin-off function rather than the primary function. This is not, however, to minimize its importance as communication.

The primary inportance of motivating feedback over communication would appear to have been the case with a closely related mechanism, that of pain. The cry of pain does communicate but the feeling of pain does not. It powerfully motivates the person who feels it in much the same way that affect does. That someone else is informed of this is, however, not mediated by the pain receptors in themselves, but by the cry of distress that usually accompanies it. I, therefore, began to look at affect analogs such as pain and sexual sensitivity and fatigue for clues about the nature of the motivating properties of the affect mechanisms.

---

[3]Izard's results were not quite as good as Ekman's, for, I think, two reasons: first, his photograph selection was guided primarily by empirical criteria rather than theoretical choice, i.e., if subjects agreed that a face showed interest, it was retained, despite the fact that the clue to such consensus might be that the subject was depicted staring at some object. Second, the critical distinction between innate and backed-up affect was not observed in Izard's picture selection.

I soon became aware of a paradox: three of the most compelling states to which the human being is vulnerable arise on the surface of the skin. Torture via skin stimulation has been used for centuries to shape and compel human beings to act against their own deepest wishes and values. Sexual seduction, again via skin stimulation, particularly of the genitals, has also prompted human beings to violate their own wishes and values. Finally, fatigue to the point of extreme sleepiness appears to be localized in the skin surrounding the eyes. This area will sometimes be rubbed in an effort to change the ongoing stimulation and ward off sleepiness. But in the end, it appears to be nothing but an altered responsiveness of skin receptors, especially in the eyelids, that makes it impossible for the sleepy person to maintain the state of wakefulness. He cannot keep his eyes open, though he may be powerfully motivated to do so. I then found further evidence that the skin, rather than "expressing" internal events, did, in diving animals, lead and command widespread autonomic changes throughout the body in order to conserve oxygen for the vulnerable brain. When the beak of a diving bird is stimulated by the water as it dives for fish, this change produces profound general changes, such as vasoconstriction within the body as a whole. Investigators somewhat accidentally discovered that similar changes can occur in a human being by putting his face in water (without total immersion of his body). Then I examined (at the suggestion of my friend Julian Jaynes) the work of Beach (1948) on the sexual mechanism in rats. Beach, examining the structure of the penis under a microscope, found that sensitive hair receptors of the skin of the penis were encased between what resembled the interstices of a cog wheel when the penis was flaccid. When there was a blood flow that engorged the penis, the skin was stretched smooth and the hairs of the receptors were no longer encased, but exposed, and their exquisite sensitivity changed the animal from a state of sexual quiescence to one of total sexual arousal. The relevance of such a mechanism for an understanding of the affect mechanism now seemed very clear. It had been known for centuries that the face became red and engorged with blood in anger. It had been known that in terror the hair stood on end and the skin became white and cold with sweat. It had long been known that the blood vessels dilated and the skin felt warm and relaxed in enjoyment. The face as penis would be relatively insensitive in its flaccid condition, its specific receptors hidden, encased within surrounding skin. When, however, there were massive shifts in blood flow and temperature, one should expect change in the positioning of the receptors, and pursuing the analogy to its bitter end, the patterned changes in facial muscle responses would serve as self-masturbatory stimulation to the skin and its own sensitized receptors. The feedback of this set of changes would provide the feel of specific affects. Although autonomic changes would be involved, the primary locus would now be seen to be in specific receptors, some as yet to be discovered. Changes in hotness, coldness, and warmth would undoubtedly be involved, but there may well be other, as yet unknown, specific receptors, which yield varieties of experience peculiar to the affect mechanism.[4] One implication of such a shift in theory is to render contemporary experimentation with the feedback of voluntarily simulated facial muscle responses as an inadequate test of the dynamics of the innate affect mechanism. (See Tourangeau & Ellsworth, 1979, and Tomkins, 1981 for my objections.)

Backed-up Affect

The third modification of the theory concerns the role of breathing and vocalization of affect. I have not changed my opinion that each affect has as part of its innate program a specific cry of vocalization, subserved by specific patterns of breathing. Rather, it is the implications of this aspect of the theory that took some years to understand. The major implications, which I now understand, concerns the universal confusion of the experience of backed-up affect with that of biologically and psychologically authentic innate affect. An analog may help in illustrating what is at issue. Let us suppose that all over the world human beings were forbidden to exhale air but were permitted and even encouraged to inhale air, so that everyone held their breaths to the point of cyanosis and death. Biologists who studied such a phenomenon (who had also been socialized to hold their breath) would have had to conclude that the breathing mechanism represented an evolutionary monstrosity devoid of any utility. Something similar to this has, in fact, happened to the affect mechanism. Because the free expression of innate affect is extremely contagious and because these are very high-powered phenomena, all societies, in varying degrees, exercise substantial control over the unfettered expression of affect, and particularly over the free expression of the cry of affect. No societies encourage or permit individuals to cry out in rage, excitement, distress, or terror whenever and wherever they wish. Very early on, strict control over affect expression is instituted, and such control is exerted particularly over the voice in general, whether used in speech or in direct affect expressions. Although there are large variations among societies and between different classes within societies, complete unconditional freedom of affect vocalization is quite exceptional. One of the most powerful effects of alcohol is the lifting of such control so that wherever alcohol is taken by large number of individuals in public places, there is a typical raising of the noise level of the intoxicated, accompanying a general loosening of affect control.

There are significant differences in how much control is exerted over voice and affect from society to society, and Lomax (1968) showed a significant

---

[4]It would suggest that thermography would be one major avenue of investigation. I pursued this possibility about 10 years ago and was disappointed at the relative inertia of the temperature of the skin. It may, however, be that advances in the state of the art in recent years may permit a more subtle mapping of the relationships between changes in skin temperature and affect.

correlation between the degree of tightness and closure of the vocal box as revealed in song and the degree of hierarchical social control in the society. It appears that more permissive societies also produce voice and song in which the throat is characteristically more relaxed and open.

If all societies, in varying degrees, suppress the free vocalization of affect, what is it that is being experienced as affect? It is what I have called *pseudo-* or backed-up, affect. It can be seen in children who are trying to suppress laughter by swallowing a snicker, by a still upper lip when trying not to cry, or by tightening their jaw trying not to cry out in anger. In all of these cases, one is truly holding one's breath as part of the technique of suppressing the vocalization of affect. Although this is not severe enough to produce cyanosis, we do not, in fact, know what are the biological and psychological prices of such suppression of the innate affect response. I would suggest that much of what is called stress is indeed back-up affect and that many of the endocrine changes reported by Frankenhaeuser (1979) are the consequence as much of backed-up affect as of affect per se. It seems at the very least that substantial psychosomatic disease might be one of the prices of such systematic suppression and transformation of the innate affective responses. Further, there could be a permanent elevation of blood pressure as a consequence of suppressed rage, and this would have a much longer duration than an innate momentary flash of expressed anger. Some years ago, French (1941) and the Chicago psychoanalytic group found some evidence for the suppressed cry of distress in psychosomatic asthma. The psychological consequences of such suppression would depend on the severity of the suppression, and I have spelled out some of these consequences elsewhere (Tomkins 1971, 1975). Even the least severe suppression of the vocalization of affect must result in some bleaching of the experience of affect and, therefore, some impoverishment of the quality of life. It must also produce some ambiguity about what affect feels like because so much of the adult's affect life represents, at the very least, a transformation of the affect response rather than the simpler, more direct and briefer innate affect. Such confusion, moreover, occurrs even among theorists and investigators of affects, myself included.[5] The appearance of the backed-up, the simulated, and the innate is by no means the same. Although this may be generally recognized so that typically we know when someone is controlling an affect or showing a pretended affect, with anger the matter is quite confused. Because of the danger presented by the affect and the consequent

---

[5]By this reasoning, the finding that observers across cultures will agree in identifying affect from facial expression does not tell us whether the faces utilized depicted innate or backed-up affect nor whether observers recognized the difference between the two. In these studies both controlled and innate responses were used as stimuli, but observers were not questioned about the difference between the two. It is my prediction that such an investigation would show a universal confusion just about anger, in which backed-up anger would be perceived as innate and innate anger would not be recognized as such.

enormous societal concern about the socialization of anger, what is typically seen and thought to be the innate is in actuality the backed-up. Finally, it is upon the discontinuity of vocalization of affect that the therapeutic power of primal screaming rests. One can uncover repressed affect by encouraging vocalization of affect, the more severe the suppression of vocalization has been.

Stimulus and Response Amplification

For several years I maintained that although affect has the function of amplifying its activator it does not influence the response to the activator or to itself. I portrayed the infant who was hungry as also distressed but saw the infant as in no way pushed in one direction or another in behavioral response to its hunger and distress. I was concerned to preserve the independence of the response from its affective precursor. It seemed that to postulate a tight causal nexus between the affect and its response would to limit severely the apparent degrees of freedom that the human being appears to enjoy and to come dangerously close to reducing both affect and the human being to the level of tropism or instinct. It seems to me now that my concern was somewhat phobic and resulted in my overlooking a powerful connection among stimulus, affect, and response. I now believe that the affect connects both its own activator and the response that follows by imprinting the latter with the same amplification it exerts on its own activator. Thus, a response prompted by enjoyment will be a slow, relaxed response in contrast to a response prompted by anger, which will reflect the increased neural firing characteristic of both the activator of angers as well as the anger response itself. What we, therefore, inherit in the affect mechanism is not only an amplifier of its activator but also an amplifier of the response that it evokes. Such a connection is in no way learned, arising as it does simply from the overlap in time of the affect with what precedes and follows it. It should be noted that by the response to affect I do not intend any restriction to observable motor responses. The response may be in terms of retrieved memories or constructed thoughts, which might vary in acceleration if amplified by fear or interest, in quantity if amplified by distress or anger, or in deceleration of rate of information processing if amplified by enjoyment. Thus, in some acute schizophrenic panics, the individual is bombarded by a rapidly accelerating rush of ideas, which resist ordering and organization. Such individuals will try to write down these ideas as an attempt to order them, saying upon questioning that if they could separate and clarify all of these too fast, overwhelming ideas, they could cure themselves. Responses to the blank card in the TAT by such schizophrenics concern a hero who is trying to put half of his ideas on one half of the card and the other half on the other side of an imaginary line dividing the card into two.

The great German philosopher, Immanuel Kant, likened the human mind to a glass that imprinted its shape on whatever liquid was poured into the glass. Thus, space, time, causality, he thought, were constructions of the human mind imposing the categories of pure reason upon the outside thing-in-itself, whose ultimate nature necessarily forever escaped us. I am suggesting that he neglected a major filtering mechanism, the innate affects, which necessarily color our every experience by producing a unique set of categorical imperatives, which amplify not only what precedes and activates each affect but also the further responses that are prompted by affect.

ACKNOWLEDGMENT

This chapter is a shortened version of a contribution to *Emotion in the Human Face*, edited by Paul Ekman and published by Cambridge University Press, 1982, pp. 353–395. Reprinted by permission.

REFERENCES

Alexander, F., and Portis, S. A psychosomatic study of hypoglycaemic fatigue. *Psychosomatic Medicine.* 1944, *6,* 195–205.
Arnold, M. B. *Emotion and personality.* New York; Columbia University Press, 1960.
Beach, F. A. *Hormones and behavior.* New York: P. B. Hoeber, 1948.
Ekman, P., Sorenson, E. R., & Friesen, W. V. Pan-cultural elements in facial displays of emotions. *Science,* 1969, *164*(3875), 86–88.
Frankenhaeuser, M. Psychoendocrine approaches to the study of emotion. In H. Howe (Ed.), *Nebraska Symposium on Motivation,* 1978, *(Vol. 26).* Lincoln: University of Nebraska Press, 1979.
French, T. M., & Alexander, F. Psychogenic factors in bronchial asthma. *Psychosomatic Medicine,* 1941, Monograph No. 2.
Izard, C. E. The emotions and emotion constructs in personality and culture research. In R. B. Cattell (Ed.), *Handbook of modern personality theory.* Chicago: Aldine, 1969.
Landis, C., & Hunt, W. A. *The startle pattern.* New York: Farrar, Straus & Giroux, 1939.
Levy, D. M. The infant's earliest memory of inoculation: A contribution to public health procedures. *Journal of General Psychology,* 1960, *96,* 3–46.
Lomax, A. *Folk song style & sulture.* Washington, D.C.: American Association for the Advancement of Science, 1968.
Sprague, J. M., Chambers, W. W., & Stellar, E. Attentive, affective, and adaptive behavior in the car. *Science,* 1961, *133,* 165–173.
Tomkins, S. S. A theory of memory. In J. Antrobus (Ed.), *Cognition and affect.* Boston: Little, Brown, 1971.
Tomkins, S. S. The Phantasy behind the face. *Journal of Personality Assessment.* 1975, *39.* 551–562.
Tomkins, S. S. Script theory: Differential magnification of affects. In H. E. Howe & R. A. Dienstbier (Eds.), *Nebraska Symposium on Motivation,* 1978, *(Vol. 26).* Lincoln: University of Nebraska Press, 1979.
Tomkins, S. S. The role of facial response in the experience of emotion: A reply to Tourangeau and Ellsworth. *Journal of Personality and Social Psychology.* 1981, *40*(2). 355–359.
Tomkins, S. S. *Affect, Imagery and Conciousness (Vol. 3. Cognition and Affect).* New York: Springer, 1982.

Tomkins, S. S.. & Izard, C. E. (Eds.) *Affect, cognition and personality.* New York: Springer, 1965.
Tomkins, S. S., & McCarter, R. What and where are the primary affects? Some evidence for a theory. *Perceptual and MOtor Skills,* 1964, *18(1)*, 119–158.
Tourangeau, R., & Ellsworth, P. C. The role of facial response in the experience of emotions. *Journal of Personality and Social Psychology,* 1979, *37,* 1519–1531.
Vasquez, J. *The face and ideology.* Unpublished dissertation, Rutgers University, 1975.

8
Emotions: A General Psychoevolutionary Theory

Robert Plutchik
Albert Einstein College of Medicine

Examination of both the recent and historical literature on emotions, suggests that there are four major traditions that have developed over the past century. These may be characterized as the evolutionary tradition, identified with Charles Darwin; the psychophysiological tradition, derived from the writings of William James; the neurological tradition, identified with Walter Cannon; and the dynamic tradition, stemming from the work of Sigmund Freud. The following paragraphs provide thumbnail sketches of the views of these four pioneers.

Darwin assumed that the process of evolution applied not only to an animal's structures but to its "mind" and emotions as well. In his 1872 book titled *The Expression of the Emotions in Man and Animals* he gave numerous illustrations of the basic continuity of emotional expressions from lower animals to humans. For example, he pointed out that the baring of the fangs of the wolf is related to the sneer of the human adult. Also. many species of animals, including humans, show an apparent increase in body size during rage, due to erection of body hair or feathers, changes in posture, or expansion of air pouches. According to Darwin, emotions increase the chances of survival by being appropriate reactions to emergency events in the environment. In addition. emotions act as signals of future actions or intentions. Darwin's contributions have had a major influence on the developing field of ethology.

The theory of William James, first published in 1884, was concerned with a kind of chicken-and-egg problem, that is, which comes first, the feeling of an emotion or the physiological changes that are associated with it. Although the conclusion drawn by James has been attacked on various grounds over the past century, the very ambiguity of the problem has prevented a definitive resolution. The value of the approach appears to be in the impetus it has given to the development of psychophysiological research which includes studies of autonomic physiology, lie detectors, and arousal.

Walter Cannon, a Harvard professor of physiology, was one of the severest critics of William James' theory (1929). He published extensively on the effect of autonomic impairements and brain lesions on emotional expressions in animals. He described emotions as emergency reactions concerned largely with the arousal of the organism for fight or flight, and proposed that the hypothalamus be considered the "seat" of the emotions, largely on the basis of "pseudo-rage" reactions that cats showed after various types of brain lesions. His work had a strong influence on the later generations of neurologists who have attempted to map the various areas of the brain associated with emotional reactions.

The dynamic tradition was launched by the work of Freud dealing with hysteria (1895). Hysterical patients with various kinds of paralyses or sensory losses could be "cured" by hypnosis combined with abreaction, that is, strong emotional expression. This led eventually to his theory of repressed emotions and his complex theory of drives, conflicts, personality development and psychotherapy. Freud concluded that emotions could be repressed, expressed, modified, distorted, or changed into derivatives of various types. From this point of view an emotion was a complex inference based upon certain classes of evidence. It was not synonymous with a verbal report of a supposed introspective state. The very idea of "psychoanalysis" implies an attempt to determine what are the theoretical elements of complex, disguised, emotional states.

The four traditions that have been briefly outlined here have had a major influence on contemporary conceptions of emotion. Yet, there have been few attempts to show how these approaches are related to one another, or how they may be integrated. To the extent that each approach deals with a valid concern, each approach must be incorporated into a general theory of emotion.

A STRUCTURAL, PSYCHOEVOLUTIONARY THEORY

Most people tend to think of emotions as subjective feelings of a certain kind; the kind for which labels such as angry, disgusted, and afraid are appropriate. However, there is considerable evidence to suggest that such verbal reports are too narrow a way to define emotion. I have already mentioned the views of the psychoanalysts who conceive of emotions as complex, inferred states, having many derivatives. The work of Davitz is also relevant (Davitz, 1969). He asked students to write brief descriptions of their emotional experiences. After summarizing and factor analyzing the data, it became evident that each emotional state was composed of many elements including physiological changes (e.g., "lost my appetite"), attitudes toward oneself (e.g., "feel insignificant"), and impulses to action (e.g., "feel like crying").

Another examples of the limitation of subjective reports as measures of emotion is found in the cross-cultural review of depression written by Marsella (1976). He reports that some languages have no terms for depression as such, and that other cultures do not label inner mood states. The more Westernized a culture, the more likely are psychological components, such as guilt, to be included in a description of depression.

A third example of a type of difficulty with verbal reports as measures of emotion may be found in some deception experiments. For example, in the well-known study by Schachter and Singer (1962) dealing with the interaction of environmental events and induced states of arousal, it was found that subjects in the Anger condition labeled themselves more "happy" than "angry." It was later learned that the subjects in the Anger condition actually felt angry, but were afraid to say this publicly for fear of losing some points on their final examination.

In summary, some of the evidence against the view that an emotion is nothing but a subjective feeling state revealed by verbal reports, is as follows:

1. Verbal reports of emotion may sometimes be deliberate attempts to deceive.

2. Repression may create false negative; that is, an observer may erroneously assume that no emotion exists because none has been reported.

3. Reports of emotion depend upon an individual's particular conditioning history, as well as his or her facility with words.

4. Emotions are generally believed to occur in young children, infants, the mentally ill, the mentally retarded, and in lower animals. Such beliefs must be based upon other classes of evidence than verbal reports of presumed inner states.

5. Emotions are rarely if ever experienced in a pure state. Typically, any given situation creates mixed emotions which are difficult to describe in any simple or unequivocal way.

It seems reasonable to conclude that an emotion is a hypothetical construct or inference based upon various classes of evidence. This evidence may include verbal reports about inner feelings, as well as expressive behaviors, and peer-group reactions, among others. This approach is exactly analogous to that taken in other parts of psychology or the physical sciences. Such terms as memory, perception, traits, atoms, genes, and DNA molecules are hypothetical constructs whose properties are inferred on the basis of various kinds of evidence.

An important implication follows from this conception of emotions as hypothetical constructs. One may validly describe emotions in terms of different types of languages. For example, we may identify emotions in terms of the common subjective language which includes words like happy, sad, angry, and disgusted.

TABLE 8.1
Three Languages That May Be Used To Describe Emotional States

Subjective Language	Behavioral Language	Functional Language
Fear, Terror	Withdrawing; Escaping	Protection
Anger, Rage	Attacking; Biting	Destruction
Joy, Ecstasy	Mating; Possessing	Reproduction
Sadness, Grief	Crying for Help	Reintegration
Acceptance, Trust	Pair Bonding; Grooming	Incorporation or Affiliation
Disgust, Loathing	Vomiting; Defecating	Rejection
Expectancy, Anticipation	Examining; Mapping	Exploration
Surprise, Astonishment	Stopping; Freezing	Orientation

Or, we may describe emotions in behavioral terms as the comparative psychologists or ethologists do. This language would include such expressions as: hitting, biting, running away, growling, crying, and vomiting. Still another way to describe emotions is in terms of the effects of the emotional reaction on the environment, that is, in terms of its function. From this point of view, the effect of fear and running away is to *protect* the individual. The effect of anger and attack is to *destroy* a barrier to the satisfaction of a need. The effect of sadness and crying is to try to produce a supportive reaction from other members of ones' group. These ideas can be illustrated in Table 8.1.

Several other important implications may be drawn from this table. For one thing, it is evident that emotions vary in *intensity,* as reflected by the distinctions we make between fear and panic, or irritation and rage. They also vary in degree of *similarity* to one another. We recognize, for example, that shame and guilt are more similar than are joy and disgust. Finally, emotions have the character of *polarity.* We recognize that joy is the opposite of sadness, and hate is the opposite of love.

There is one other important element that is needed before we can develop a structural model of the emotions. This is the concept that some emotions are fundamental, or primary, and others are derived or secondary, in the same sense that some colors are primary and others are mixed.

This notion of primary and secondary emotions and parallels between emotions and colors is an old one. Spinoza, Hobbes, Darwin, William James, and McDougall all proposed that certain emotions were primary and that all others were mixtures. In recent years the same general idea has been proposed by Cattell, (1946), and by Nowlis (1965) on the basis of their factor analytic studies, and also by Tomkins (1962) and Izard (1971) on other grounds. The fundamental questions, however, are: How many primaries are there and how shall they be labeled?

In order to provide theoretically useful answers to these questions, emotions must be conceptualized within the framework of evolution. Because the concept of emotions must apply to lower animals as well as humans, we must look for fundamental patterns of adaptation that can be identified at all phylogenetic levels as clues to the basic emotions.

All organisms, in order to survive and maintain their populations, must find and ingest food, avoid injury. and reproduce their kind. This is as true of lower animals as it is of higher ones. The nature of the environment creates certain functional requirements for all organisms if they are to survive. Any organism must take in nourishment and eliminate waste products. It must distinguish between prey and predator, and between a potential mate and a potential enemy. It must explore its environment and orient its sense organs appropriately as it takes in information about the beneficial and harmful aspects of its immediate world. And in organisms that are relatively helpless at birth and for a while thereafter, there must be ways of indicating the need for care and nurturance. The specific behaviors by which these functions are carried out will vary widely throughout the animal kingdom, but the basic prototype functions will remain invariant. Wilson (1975), the sociobiologist, points out the existence of certain general classes of adaptive behavior. In comparing termites and monkeys he notes the many similarities of function. For example, he points out that both types of animals are formed into cooperative groups that occupy territories. The group members communicate hunger, alarm, hostility, caste status or rank and reproductive status among themselves and they can distinguish between group members and nonmembers. There is also a division of labor.

Many ethologists have also identified basic categories of adaptive behavior. These include: consumption, approach, escape, exploration, aggression. curiosity, sex, expulsion, and play. In Van Hooff's factor analyses of sequential social behaviors in chimps (1973), at least five basic behavioral categories were identified. These were called: the play system, the aggression system, the submission system, the affinity system, and the excitement system. Various lists have been proposed by other ethologists.

The most extensive description of basic adaptive behavior patterns that are found at most phylogenetic levels, has been given by Scott (1958). His list follows:

Ingestive behavior. All organisms take in food in order to survive.
Agonistic behavior. All organisms become involved in a fight or flight struggle with other organisms.
Sexual behavior. Almost all organisms show sexual activity in one form or another ranging from contact and courtship to coition.
Shelter-seeking behavior. Many organisms tend to move about until they find environmental conditions that are favorable for survival.
Care-giving behavior. In many species nurturant behavior is provided by adult members of the group toward the young and relatively helpless members.
Care-soliciting behavior. The young of many species show various care-seeking

behaviors that tend to elicit care-giving behaviors from the adult members of the group.

Eliminative behavior. The elimination of waste products is essential for survival.

Allelomimetic behavior. In many species imitative behavior creates integrated group activity which increases chances for survival.

Investigative behavior. Exploratory behavior enables an organism to map its environment and increase its chances of survival.

I have proposed some modifications in this list (Plutchik, 1962). Care-giving and care-soliciting behavior are found only at relatively high phylogenetic levels. This is also true of shelter-seeking behavior. Allelomimetic behavior is found only in certain groups of animals. In an effort to achieve the greatest generality across phylogenetic levels, we may modify Scotts lists to product the following set of basic or prototype behavior patterns:

Incorporation. Behavior of food ingestion or the acceptance of beneficial stimuli from the outside world into the organism.

Rejection. Riddance behavior designed to expel something harmful that has already been incorporated.

Protection. Behavior designed to avoid danger or harm. This includes retreat, flight, or any behavior that increases the distance between the organism and a source of danger.

Destruction. Behavior designed to destroy a barrier that prevents the satisfaction of an important need.

Reproduction. Reproductive behavior may be defined in terms of approach, maintenance-of-contact tendencies, and exchange or mixing of genetic materials.

Reintegration. Behavior reaction to the loss of something important that has been possessed or enjoyed. It functions to regain nurturant contact.

Orientation. Behavior reaction resulting from contact with a new, strange or unevaluated object.

Exploration. Behavior designed to map a given environment.

These eight basic, prototype, patterns have several interesting characteristics. First, they all represent adaptive behavioral patterns, related to survival. Second, the behaviors that may be identified with each prototype have a function, which is indicated by its name. This, therefore, represents a functional language. In each case, the behaviors associated with a given prototype are designed to have an effect on some stimulus that creates an emergency situation. In Tolman's (1923) terms, these behaviors are not simply responses, but "responses-as-affecting-stimuli."

The third point worth emphasizing is that these prototypes can be conceptualized as polar opposites. *Incorporation* (taking in) is bipolar to *rejection* (expelling); *protection* (running away) is bipolar to *destruction* (attacking); *reproduction* (possessing) is bipolar to *reintegration* (losing); and *orientation* (stopping) is bipolar to *exploration* (starting). Finally, it is evident that each of these basic functional terms can be associated with a cluster of emotion words found in our subjective language as seen in Table 8.1.

In summary, there are several sources for the decision concerning which emotions are basic. One is the various analyses that have been published by psychologists, psychiatrists and ethologists. Another is the concern with achieving the maximum possible generality is defining basic adaptive (or prototype) behavior patterns across all phylogenetic levels. A third is the desire to achieve a systematic structural model.

Based on these various sources, I have suggested that there are eight basic adaptive reactions that are the prototypes, singly or in combination, of all emotions. The particular choice of these prototypes and their labels are justified on the basis of: (1) their parsimonious summarizing of a great deal of human and animal literature on the subject; (2) their ability to provide a basis for a structural model; (3) their ability to guide research; and (4) their ability to show relations among several disciplines traditionally considered as separate, such as emotions, personality and diagnoses.

The structural model implied by these considerations is shown in Fig. 8.1. Each "slice" of the emotion solid, which bears certain interesting relations to the color solid, represents a different primary emotion, with the vertical dimensions implying an intensity or arousal variable. The terms at the top represent maximal levels of arousal of each basic emotion dimension. The shape of the model implies that the emotions become less distinguishable at lower intensities. If we imagine taking successive cross sections, we keep duplicating the emotion circle with progressively milder versions of each of the primaries. Emotions placed near one another are more similar than are those that are further apart or are opposite.

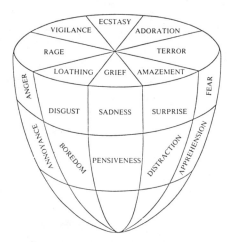

FIG. 8.1.   A multidimensional model of the emotions.

The question of relative similarity of the emotions is clearly an empirical one, and several studies have been reported which shed light on this issue. In 1957 Block published a paper on the phenomenology of emotions using the semantic differential as a method for measuring their connotative meanings. He asked college students to describe a series of 15 emotions using 20 semantic differential scales. Emotions such as anger, love, fear, and guilt were to be described on such scales as active-passive, good-bad, and tense-relaxed. Correlations were then computed between the ratings for each emotion and every other emotion to produce a matrix of correlations, which was then factor analyzed. Because most of the variance was accounted for by the first two factors, it was possible to plot the location of each emotion in a two dimensional space. The configuration was very close to a circle, which expressed the similarity relations among these particular emotion terms. Some time later I replicated this study with a larger sample of emotions words as well as semantic differential scales.

I conducted several studies with Schaefer (Schaefer & Plutchik, 1966), using an entirely different methodology that also confirmed the circular order of emotion terms. However, the most extensive and direct study of emotion similarity was carried out by Conte and myself, and was described in my book on emotion (Plutchik, 1980a). We used a modified method of paired comparisons and asked a group of judges to rate the relative similarity of over 140 emotion words to three reference terms. Our procedure was based upon the convention that emotions rated as similar are within 90 degrees of one another on a circle, and that emotions rated as dissimilar are between 90 and 180 degrees apart on a circle. Emotions rated as neither similar nor dissimilar (i.e., as independent) are exactly 90 degrees apart on a circle (i.e., are orthogonal).

On the basis of this method, angular locations were obtained for every emotion on the list. The emotion terms were found to be distributed around the entire circle with no appreciable gaps. Terms that are linguistically opposite such as affectionate and unaffectionate or obedient and disobedient were found to fall at opposite parts of the circle. In addition, clusters of related words fell near each other. For example, the terms *joyful, happy,* and *enthusiastic* are quite close to each other on the circle and at the same time, opposite to the cluster *gloomy, unhappy,* and *griefstricken.* The order of terms around the circle were verified by an entirely independent method based on the degree of similarity of semantic differential profiles. From these findings, the similarity order of emotions is pretty much as shown in Fig. 8.2. This is essentially a cross section of the emotion solid shown in Fig. 8.1.

What are some implications of this structural model? If we take seriously the parallels between the emotion solid and the well-known color solid and color wheel, several ideas are implied. On the basis of three primary colors plus variations in degree of brightness, all the colors observed in nature can be duplicated. A similar idea applies to emotions. If we ask groups of judges what

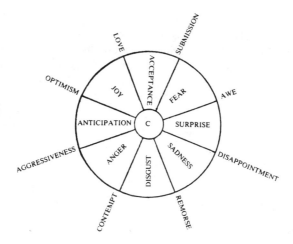

FIG. 8.2.   Primary dyads formed by the combinations of adjacent pairs of basic emotions.

would happen if they were to imagine the combination of two or more primary emotions, a fair amount of agreement can be obtained on the name of the mixture. An alternative to synthesis is analysis. Judges can be given long lists of emotion terms and asked to identify the possible primaries that comprise them. Considerable agreement is also found in this situation. The words outside the circle in Fig. 8.2 represent the mixtures of adjacent pairs of emotions, what I have called primary dyads.

EMOTIONS AND PERSONALITY

What is especially interesting about these mixed emotions is that the names given to them, such as *cheerful, spiteful,* and *hostile* are quite often words we used to describe personality. Conversely, personality trait terms such as *aggressive, friendly,* and *stubborn* are often used to describe transient emotional states. A series of studies reported in my book (Plutchik, 1980a) identified the emotion components of a large number of personality trait terms.

These lists of components have provided the basis for an interesting new test of personality/emotions, called the *Emotions Profile Index* or EPI. In this test, subjects are presented with pairs of trait or emotion terms such as *sociable-adventurous, cautious-gloomy,* or *quarrelsome-self conscious.* The subject is asked to choose the word from each pair that is most like him or herself. Each time a trait choice is made, the choice is scored for the underlying emotion components. Total scores are obtained for each of the eight basic emotions and compared to percentiles obtained from several normative populations. The EPI is useful as a clinical tool and has also been found to discriminate among a number of groups including: alcoholics, schizophrenics, drug addicts, manic patients, depressed patients, and asthmatics, among others. Its use has provided some new insights into the emotional dispositions that seem to be related to the risk of suicide.

The EPI is versatile and has been adapted for use with animals by Buirski, Kellerman, Plutchik, & Weininger, 1973. They selected a set of terms descriptive of emotional behavior, terms that could be used with animals. The emotion components were determined by consensus of a group of judges. The terms were coupled in all possible pairs and observers made ratings on the emotional behavior of baboons or chimpanzees. In the latter case (Buirski, Plutchik, & Kellerman, 1978), observations were made at the Gombe Stream Research Centre in Tanzania, East Africa, on 23 free-living chimpanzees, 13 males and 10 females. This Center had been established by Jane Goodall. Ratings were made by seven graduate students living at the camp, who were quite familiar with the day-to-day behavior of most of the chimps. Raters were asked to rate those chimps whose behavior they were most familiar with, in terms of the EPI scales. Most of the interjudge reliabilities were greater than $+.70$.

Figure 8.3 shows the average EPI profiles for the males and for the females. Significant sex differences were found for five of the eight emotions. For example, the female chimps were rated as more *timid,* more *depressed,* and more *trustful* than the males, whereas the males were judged as more *gregarious* and more *distrustful.* If we were interpreting the profiles in human terms, we would add that the females have more conflict in the area of socialization (i.e., the gain or loss of social contacts) and the males have more conflict in the area of passivity and aggression.

The dominance rank of each male was independently estimated from brief biographies of the animals. The rank position was then correlated with each of the eight EPI emotion dimensions. The set of correlations suggested that dominant animals tend to be *distrustful* and *aggressive,* whereas nondominant animals tend to be *timid, impulsive,* and *trustful.* The importance of this and other studies like it, is that it demonstrates the usefulness of a method for judging emotional dispositions (personality traits) in nonhuman primates that has reasonable reliability and theoretical generality. It enables direct comparisons to be made between different phylogenetic levels on emotion dimensions.

It is also important to mention that a number of other tests or scales for measuring emotions have been developed on the basis of the theory. For example, several mood scales have been published in addition to the EPI, as well as a scale for describing the emotional interactions between parents and their children (Plutchik, 1980a and Plutchik 1980b). Also available now are sets of scales based upon the theory, for measuring ego defenses (Plutchik, Kellerman, & Conte, 1979), and coping styles.

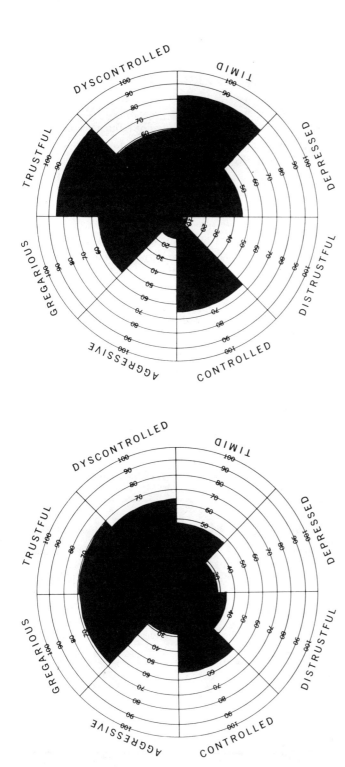

MALE CHIMPANZEES

FEMALE CHIMPANZEES

FIG. 8.3. Average emotion profiles for 13 free-living male chimpanzees and 10 female chimpanzees observed at the Gombe Stream Research Center in Tanzania, East Africa.

EMOTIONS AND COGNITIONS

Every organism must evaluate its environment in some way. This evaluation process represents the cognitive aspect of emotions, and it influences the type of response pattern that is actually observed. So-called cognitive approaches to emotion are mainly concerned with the identification of variables that influence the evaluation process in humans, but it should be emphasized that an evaluation is not an emotion. Evaluations are a part of the total process that involves an organism interacting with its environment in biologically adaptive ways.

How cognitions relate to emotions are illustrated in Table 8.2.

It is meant to show that the occurrence of certain stimulus events such as a threat by an enemy or the loss of a parent, is followed by a cognition (interpretation) such as "danger" or "isolation." Such cognitions may (or may not) be reflexive and unconscious, and are followed by introspective feelings such as fear or sadness that we usually think of as emotions. The feeling state is only one step in a chain of reactions and are followed, with a certain probability, by some kind of appropriate behavior. Such behaviors, if successful, lead to protection of the individual or reintegration with parent substitutes or other members of one's social group. The word emotion refers to this complex chain of reactions that has adaptive value for the individual in dealing with various kinds of life crises or survival problems.

In describing the complex chain of reactions called emotions, there are a number of viscissitudes that may befall the emotional sequence. For one thing,

TABLE 8.2
The Complex, Probabilistic Sequence of Events Involved in the
Development of an Emotion

Stimulus Event	Inferred Cognition	Feeling	Behavior	Effect
Threat	"Danger"	Fear, terror	Running, or flying, away	Protection
Obstacle	"Enemy"	Anger, rage	Biting, hitting	Destruction
Potential mate	"Possess"	Joy, ecstasy	Courting, mating	Reproduction
Loss of valued individual	"Abandonment"	Sadness, grief	Crying to be reunited	Reintegration
Group member	"Friend"	Acceptance, trust	Grooming, sharing	Affiliation
Gruesome object	"Poison"	Disgust, loathing	Vomiting, pushing away	Rejection
New territory	"What's out there?"	Anticipation	Examining, mapping, organizing	Exploration
Unexpected object	"What is it?"	Surprise	Stopping, alerting	Orientation

the initial cognition may be in error so that the threat is misperceived or misinterpreted. If the cognition is accurate, it is still possible for the feeling aspect of the emotional chain to be blocked, modified, or distorted by ego defenses such as denial or repression. However, even if the feeling is clearly present, appropriate action may or may not occur. This is simply because environmental or internal restraints may prevent the action. If someone is in prison, running away in the face of danger is impossible. Similarly, if one has strong feelings about the importance of bravery, one may not flee even if one's life is at stake. Finally, depending on whether appropriate behavior occurred that was effective, the goal or purpose of the chain of emotional reactions may or may not be served.

COGNITIONS ARE IN THE SERVICE OF EMOTIONS

Although there have been a number of recent cognitive approaches to emotion none have considered cognitions within a broad evolutionary framework. The basic point of view presented here is that cognitive capacities have evolved along with the evolution of the brain, and that cognitions have largely evolved in the service of emotions.

In a broad sense, we may say that the main function of a large brain and a highly developed cognitive system is to ensure survival. We may, however, describe the cognitive process in a more precise way. From the point of view of evolution, *cognition developed in order to predict the future.*

Cognitive activities are a form of map making. Cognition provides a model of the environment and codes information in a time-binding neural code. The development of abstract concepts denoting classes of events meant escape from the present. This increased ability to classify the environment made it possible for humans to develop foresight of future needs. The more precisely the environment could be assessed or mapped, the greater the capacity to make predictions about the likely course of external events and thus to initiate novel patterns of adaptive behavior.

In the most basic sense, any organism must predict on the basis of limited information whether there is food, a mate, or danger in its environment. Depending on the prediction made, the organism makes a decision to run, to attack, to play, or to mate. From this point of view, the complex processes of sensory input, evaluation, symbolization, comparison with memory stores, and the like—those processes we call cognitive—are in the service of emotions and biological needs. This idea is not new and has been made previously by Dember (1974) and by Neisser (1963). Dember pointed out that cognitive processes are instruments, or means to an end—in effect that the brain is the servant of the stomach and the sex organs. In my book (Plutchik. 1980a) and in an earlier publication (Plutchik, 1977), a schema is presented for describing the hypothetical part-processes that are involved in all cognitive events. This schema is based on the ideas that have been discussed about cognition as an evolving set of functions based upon brain mechanisms, which are designed to make maps, predict the future, and organize appropriate action.

EMOTIONS AND NEUROPHYSIOLOGY

At the Bad Homburg, Germany, conference on emotions, discussion with Karl Pribram led to the development of several new hypotheses. These hypotheses reflected our respective interests. The basic ideas are summarized in Table 8.3.

We assume that all organisms are faced with certain existential crises that may be defined as problems related to the existence of hierarchies, territoriality, identity, and temporality. Because individuals of all species differ in various ways, some have more rapid access to food. shelter, or sex than others. This generally leads to the establishment of hierarchical relations among the organisms with some individuals dominant and others submissive. Dominant animals tend to maintain their positions through the expression of anger whereas submissive animals maintain their positions through the expression of fear. Anger has a positive valence and represents a movement toward a stimulus. Fear has a negative valence and reflects a movement away from a stimulus.

In a related way one can anticipate what is likely to happen within one's own territory, while unexpected surprises are likely to occur outside of one's territory. Anticipation (and curiosity) represents a positive valence and an opening of one's boundary to new inputs. Surprise has a negative valence and is associated with a rapid closing of one's boundary to potentially unknown and threatening stimuli.

The problem of identity refers to the basic issue of who we are; or alternatively, to what group does one belong. Genetic survival requires that organisms recognize other organisms of their own type with whom they may mate. Those who are part of our group are accepted and taken in (a positive valence) whereas those who are not part of our group are rejected or expelled.

Temporality refers to the limited extent of the life of a single individual. The inevitability of death creates the problem of loss and separation and the disruption of social bonds. This leads to the affect of sadness, a negative valence. In contrast, the gain of social bonds leads to a feeling of joy or satisfaction.

Pribram (personal communication) suggests that all emotions and behavioral processes having a positive balance are associated with a ''Start'' process in the brain and a period of gradual activation. In contrast, all behaviors with a negative valence are associated with a ''Stop'' process in the brain and a rapid state of phasic arousal. The Start processes are appetitive in that they imply the desire for more input whereas the Stop processes are satiating in that they imply the desire for less input.

Pribram hypothesizes that the lateral hypothalamus and the basal ganglia are the neural structures involved in the appetitive Start processes. He further as-

TABLE 8.3

A Proposed Schema for Interaction of Emotion Systems
(Plutchik and Pribram, 1981)

Existential Crisis	Emotions	Behavioral Process	Valence
Hierarchy	Anger	Move Toward	+
Hierarchy	Fear	Move Away	−
Territoriality	Anticipation	Open Boundary	+
Territoriality	Surprise	Close Boundary	−
Identity	Acceptance	Take In	+
Identity	Rejection	Expel	−
Temporality	Joy	Gain	+
Temporality	Sadness	Lose	−

Neuro-psychology			Neuro-anatomy	Psycho-physiology	Neuro-chemistry
Start Process	Tonic Activation	Appetitive (Desire More)	Lateral Hypothalamus + Basal Ganglia	Heart Rate Deceleration, Negative Evoked Potential	Dopaminergic + Cholinergic
Stop Process	Phasic Arousal	Effort (Chronic)	Hippocampus	Heart Rate Acceleration	ACHT + Peptinergic + Enkephelons
		Satiety (Desire Less)	Medial Hypothalamus + Amygdala	GSR, Positive Evoked Potential	Noradrenergic + Serotonergic

211

sumes that these processes are reflected by heart rate decelerations and by negative evoked potentials, and that the underlying neurochemistry is dopaminergic and cholinergic.

The neural structures assumed to be the originators for Stop or satiety processes are the medial hypothalamus and the amygdala. GSR changes and positive evoked potentials reflect these processes and the underlying neurochemistry is noradrenergic and serotonergic.

Some actions are assumed to have no affective tone (neither positive nor negative) but to reflect muscular effort per se. The underlying neural structure for initiating such processes is assumed to be the hippocampus and the process is represented physiologically by heart rate accelerations. The neurochemistry is assumed to be ACTH, peptinergic, and enkephalon systems.

Overall, although these ideas are speculative, they represent a possible synthesis of ethological concepts with affect and neurophysiological concepts. They represent a testable set of interrelated hypotheses, which hopefully, will serve as a stimulus to research.

THE ANTECEDENTS OF EMOTION

The concept of antecedents of emotion is a complex idea. From a psychoevolutionary point of view, all emotions are triggered by events that have an important significance for the organism. Significant emotion-triggering events include such things as presence of a prey or predator, friend or enemy, mate or competitor, a novel occurrence, or symbols of these events.

The capacity to recognize such events has both a phylogenetic and an ontogenetic aspect. At lower phylogenetic levels genetic coding plays a relatively large role in the recognition of and reaction to these kinds of events. At higher phylogenetic levels genetic coding plays a smaller role in the recognition of and reaction to these emotion-triggering events and the vicissitudes of development and learning play a larger role.

An important point that needs to be emphasized is that the antecedents of emotion cannot be considered independent of the consequences of an emotion. This follows from the point of view that recognizes that emotions are adaptive reactions to significant stimuli in the life of an organism, and, that the emotional response functionally acts to influence the relation between the initiating stimulus and the organism. Scott writes that there are only a few classes of adaptive behavior found in most species and phylogenetic levels. These behaviors— agonistic, ingestive, sexual, care-soliciting, investigative, etc.—imply the presence of certain specific types of antecedents; e.g., threats, food, mate, young, novelty, etc. An emotional reaction such as fear and its associated behavior of flight acts to separate the individual from a source of danger. The emotion of anger and its associated attack behavior acts to destroy a barrier to the satisfaction of a need. The cry associated with loss of a significant other usually initiates succoring responses from other members of the social community. A similar point can be made for each of the primary emotions.

Although it is usually stated that there are a large number of events that can trigger emotional reactions in animals or humans there is an alternative viewpoint that may be proposed. This view claims that events per se do not produce emotions, but that only evaluated events (appraisals) produce emotions. The intervening link between a stimulus and the subsequent chain of events we call an emotion is the cognitive evaluation. It may be argued that only a small number of types of cognitive evaluations and their mixtures produce emotional reactions.

The ontogenetic argument about the antecedents of emotions claims that in higher animals and particularly humans, emotions and the stimuli that elicit them, are fortuitously related and that the relationship solely depends on the accidents of conditioning. However, it is important to recognize that the capacity to learn from experience is itself as much a product of evolution as any other species characteristic. Genetic programming determines the limits and nature of the modifications that each individual can undergo as a result of life experiences. For example, although the specific object, a duck, for example, becomes imprinted on is somewhat a product of chance, the timing of the response is under the strict control of the genetic structure of the duck. In other words, although the context may sometimes be determined by accidental experiences, the complexity of the stimuli that can be discriminated and the complexity of the responses that can be made are largely limited by genetic restraints (Plutchik, 1983).

In lower organisms the cognitions of the animal are quite limited. Breland and Breland (1966) have pointed out that the vast majority of the species of the earth use only very limited kinds of learning in their interactions with the environment. Most organism enter the world prepared to cope with it through the use of certain fixed sequences of behavior that are activated by particular species-specific stimuli, or "releasers." Moths find mates by responding to certain types of odors, most birds have fixed styles of nest building, and fighting behavior is often triggered by particular colors or movements of an animal.

Not all behaviors are equally conditionable, and some appear not be conditionable at all. For example, although it may take a pigeon days or weeks to learn to pull a string, a chicken can learn this task in a matter of minutes. This is probably due to the fact that the chicken normally eats by pulling worms from the ground, whereas pigeons normally peck at food. It is virtually impossible to get a chicken to vocalize for food reinforcement whereas other birds can easily be trained to do this. Similarly, efforts to train chimpanzees to use a vocal language have all failed. The Brelands suggest that the degree to which behavior patterns are rigid and relatively unchangeable depends on the phylogenetic level to which an animal belongs. It also depends on the size of the environmental niche of the animal. Animals that occupy only a small segment of the environment, such as rabbits do, show relatively more fixed behavior sequences than those animals, such as the raccoon, that occupy a broader environmental niche.

Universals that are observed are due to the existence of certain common problems with which all organisms must deal. Emotions are total body reactions to the various survival-related problems created by the environment. Emotions are attempts of the organism to achieve control over events that relate to survival. Emotions are the "ultraconservative" evolutionary adaptations that were found to be successful (like amino acids, DNA, and genes) in increasing the chances of survival of organisms. Therefore, they have been maintained in functionally equivalent form through all phylogenetic levels.

How are emotions related to other domains of interest? The following paragraphs briefly suggest the kinds of relations that exist between emotions and learning, motivation and social structure.

Emotion and Learning. There are three major influences of learning on emotion. First, an individual may learn to modify or inhibit some of the external expressive signs of emotion. Second, an individual's experience will affect which of the basic emotions are most likely to be evident in his day-to-day behavior, and also which are most likely to interact. Third, the reinforcement history of an individual may affect the strength and stability of the emotion mixtures that develop. The basic emotions are not learned, but are a direct expression of the genetic potentials of an individual.

Emotions enter into all problem-solving endeavors. Many problems are solved out of curiosity, some out of necessity (fear), some out of frustration, some out of a desire for approval, and some out of a combination of these (implied) emotions. The emotions act as energy sources that maintain the impulse (commitment) to solve the problem. When an individual is bored or indifferent to a problem, the problem will not be solved.

Emotion and Motivation. There are a number of distinctions that one can make between emotions and motivations

Emotions	*Motivations*
1. Aroused by external stimuli.	1. Aroused by changing internal states of the organism.
2. Aroused by the *presence* of a survival-related event.	2. Aroused by the *absence* of homeostatically significant stimuli.
3. There are few "natural" objects in the environment toward which emotions are automatically directed.	3. There are specific "natural" objects toward which motives direct the organism (e.g., food, water).
4. Induced after an object is seen or evaluated.	4. Induced before process of search is begun.
5. Depend on events in environment which may occur on a random basis.	5. Tend to have a rhythmic character.

Despite these differences between emotions and motivations confusion exists in the psychological literature. There are two major reasons. First, there are differences between primary and acquired motives, just as there are differences between primary and mixed emotions. Acquired motives often do not show a rhythmic fluctuation of intensity (the miser may be greedy regardless of the amount of money he accumulates), nor do they seem to occur as a direct function of recurrent deprivations. Whereas primary emotions are typically transient reactions to certain stimuli, mixed emotions are not usually transient, but may persist (as personality traits) and thus may not seem to be clearly dependent upon external stimuli for their appearance.

Second, although emotions are typically produced by external stimuli, internal stimuli may, under certain conditions, arouse emotional reactions. Severe deprivation of food may lead to internal pains and a reaction of fear. An individual deprived of sex may experience this as a frustrating condition and may react with anger. Thus internal stimuli may occasionally trigger emotional reactions.

Emotion and Homeostasis.   Homeostasis refers to the automatic adjustments made within the body to maintain the internal environment within narrow limits and thus ensure survival. One may speculate that emotions can be thought of as a kind of behavioral homeostatic process. In other words, when a survival-related emergency situation arises, emotions act to try to reestablish the conditions that existed before the situation arose. For example, if a threat occurs, the individual's fear directs him to carry out actions that will eliminate the threat and reduce the fear.

Emotion and Interpersonal Relations.   In a fundamental sense emotions influence all interpersonal relations, both on a moment-by-moment basis and in enduring relationships. This is true because emotions have derivative states and it is in the form of derivatives that emotions enter into all transactions.

This notion of derivatives of emotion is discussed more fully in my book *Emotion: A Psychoevolutionary Synthesis* (Plutchik, 1980a), so that only a brief summary is presented here. From the point of view of the theory, personality traits, diagnosis, ego defenses, and coping styles are derivatives of the basic emotions, and it is these characteristics of the individual that enter into interpersonal relations. Some examples follow.

A person who frequently shows fear (emotion language) eventually may be perceived as an anxious person (trait language). This person may also, if the condition is extreme enough, be labeled as a passive-dependent personality type (diagnostic language). In order to deal with his anxieties, this person may use repression or denial as ego defenses (ego defense language), and he may learn to cope with situations that make him anxious by avoiding them (suppression or minimization).

EMOTION AND SOCIAL STRUCTURE

A speculative, but interesting application of the psychoevolutionary theory of emotion concerns the relations between emotions and social institutions. The term "social institution" is used to refer to such broad social activities as marriage and the family, religion, education, science and technology. From this broad point of view it is evident that what is being considered are basic classes of social activities that are identifiable, in some form, in all human societies, large and small, primitive and sophisticated, in all parts of the world. The question that is being asked is: "Is there a connection between particular basic emotions and particular basic social institutions of the types listed above?"

The thesis of the following remarks is that such connections exist and that in a deep and fundamental sense, these social institutions evolved as a way of dealing with, or controlling, the form or expression of the different basic emotions. We are concerned here with the fact that certain types of life events have a high likelihood of eliciting certain emotions, and that as a result, certain social procedures, strategies, or institutions developed to handle the expression of these emotions.

The hypothesis is being proposed that there are classes of events that occur in all societies that have a very high probability of arousing certain emotions; social institutions are assumed to be ways of controlling the form of expression of these emotions. Table 8.4 summarizes the ideas implicit in this viewpoint.

One may argue that this notion is too simplistic. Social institutions obviously serve multiple functions and roles, particularly in more technologically advanced societies. However, this fact should not allow us to ignore the possibility that the universality of certain institutions suggests that they reflect universal human experiences.

In a fundamental sense, religions deal with the reality of death and loss, which in turn are associated with the emotions of fear and sadness. It is no accident that fear and sadness are typically highly correlated both in "normal" experiences of

TABLE 8.4
Basic Emotions and the Social Institutions Hypothesized to Deal with
Them

Emotion	Universal Experience	Institution
Fear	Death and Loss	Religion
Anger	Frustration and Inhibitions	Warfare (and Police)
Joy	Sexual Drives and Behavior	Marriage and Family
Sadness	Death and Loss	Religion
Disgust	Disease and Illness	Medicine
Acceptance	Mental Illness	Psychotherapy (Shamanism)
Surprise	Novelty	Sports and Games
Curiosity	Food Gathering, Preparation and Shelter	Science and Technology

daily life, and in psychiatric conditions as well. All societies provide inhibitions on its members and the resulting feelings of frustration and anger are handled both by inhibiting them (through police or its equivalent) or by expressing them in socially sanctioned ways (e.g., by warfare or certain types of sports). Sexual drives and behavior are socialized through the institution of marriage and the family. The emotion of disgust is one that tends to be associated with disease and illness. The special institution that has evolved to deal with this emotion is medicine in its various forms. Mental illness is also found to some degree in all social groups; this experience is usually handled by shamanism or some form of "psychotherapy." The key emotion in psychotherapy is acceptance. Novelty leads to surprises, and surprises appear to be important enough to lead to the evolution of social instructions that create surprises in systematic ways. This institution is the existence of games and certain sports. Finally, the need for food gathering and preparation and the need for shelter leads to the evolution of science and technology.

Although these ideas are obviously highly speculative, they may contain enough truth to justify their detailed examination. Even the effort to refute them may generate new insights.

What is an Emotion?

At this point I should like to conclude with an explicit definition of the term "emotion." In my earlier book on emotion (Plutchik, 1962), I defined an emotion "as a patterned bodily reaction of either destruction, reproduction, incorporation, orientation, protection, deprivation, rejection, or exploration, or some combination of these, which is brought about by a stimulus." This definition is correct as far as it goes, but is limited in that it emphasizes only the functional language of emotions. As has already been discussed an emotion can be described in terms of multiple languages that include subjective feeling, cognitions, impulses to action, and behavior. A fuller but more complex definition must take these elements into account. Therefore, in light of the psychoevolutionary structural theory of emotion, the following definition is proposed. An emotion is an inferred complex sequence of reactions to a stimulus, and includes cognitive evaluations, subjective changes, autonomic and neural arousal, impulses to action, and behavior designed to have an effect upon the stimulus that initiated the complex sequence. These complex reaction sequences may suffer various vicissitudes. which affect the probability of appearance of each link in the chain. These complex reactions are adaptive in the struggle in which all organisms engage for survival. At higher phylogenetic levels, the patterns of expression associated with each chain of emotional reactions serve to signal motivation or intent from one member of a social group to another. Finally, there are eight basic reaction patterns that are systematically related to one another and that are the prototype sources for all the mixed emotions and other derivative states that may be observed in animals and humans.

The theory that I have proposed does not answer all questions about emotions, but it does begin to demonstrate connections between apparently diverse areas of investigation and it suggests questions with which future research should be concerned. It provides a framework for examining or re-examining many problems in the field—for example: the ontogenesis of emotions, the relations between emotions and personality, the nature of emotion terms in natural languages, the influence of learning on the expression, inhibition, and mixing of emotions, the genetics of emotion, etc. The theory remains an evolving conception, subject to new data and insights.

REFERENCES

Block, J. Studies in the phenomenology of emotions. *Journal of Abnormal and Social Psychology,* 1957, *54,* 358–363.

Breland, K., & Breland, M. *Animal behavior,* New York: Macmillan, 1966.

Buirski. P., Kellerman, H., Plutchik, R., Weininger, R., & Buirski, N. A field study of emotions, dominance and social behavior in a group of baboons (Papio anubis). *Primates,* 1973, *14,* 67–78.

Buirski, P., Plutchik, R., & Kellerman, H. Sex differences, dominance and personality in the chimpanzee. *Animal Behavior,* 1978, *26,* 123–129.

Cannon, W. B. *Bodily changes in pain, hunger, fear and rage.* New York: Appleton, 1929.

Cattell, R. B. *The description and measurement of personality.* New York: Harcourt Brace Jovanovich, 1946.

Conte, H. R., & Plutchik, R. A circumplex model for interpersonal personality traits. *Journal of Personality and Social Psychology,* 1981, *40,* 701–711.

Darwin, C. *The expression of the emotions in man and animals.* London: Murray, 1872. Reprinted by University of Chicago Press, 1965.

Davitz, J. R. *The language of emotions.* New York: McGraw-Hill, 1969.

Dember, W. N. Motivation and the cognitive revolution. *American Psychologist,* 1974, *29,* 161–168.

Freud, S. *Studies in hysteria.* Leipzig: Deuticke, 1895. (First English translation by A. A. Brill.) Nervous and Mental Disease Publications, 1936.

Izard, C. E. *The face of emotion.* New York: Appleton-Century-Crofts, 1971.

James, W. What is emotion? *Mind,* 1884, *19,* 188–205.

Marsella, A. J. Cross-cultural studies of depression: A review of the literature. Paper presented at the Symposium on Cross-Cultural Aspects of Depression, International Association of Cross-Cultural Psychology, Tilburg, Netherlands, 1976.

Neisser, U. The imitation of man by machine. *Science,* 1963, *139,* 193–197.

Nowlis, V. Research with the mood adjective checklist. In S. S. Tomkins & C. E. Izard (Eds.), *Affect, cognition, personality.* New York: Springer, 1965.

Plutchik, R. *The emotions: Facts, theories and a new model.* New York: Random House, 1962.

Plutchik, R. Cognitions in the service of emotions. In D. K. Candland, J. P. Fell, E. Keen, A. I. Leshner, R. Plutchik, & R. M. Tarpy (Eds.), *Emotion.* Monterey, California: Brooks/Cole, 1977.

Plutchik, R. *Emotion: A psychoevolutionary synthesis.* New York: Harper and Row, 1980. (a)

Plutchik, R. Measurement implications of a psychoevolutionary theory of emotions. In K. R. Blankstein, P. Pliner, & J. Polivy (Eds.), *Assessment and modification of emotional behavior.* New York: Plenum, 1980. (b)

Plutchik, R. Emotions in early development: A psychoevolutionary approach. In R. Plutchik and H. Kellerman (Eds.), *Emotions in early development.* New York: Academic Press, 1983.

Plutchik, R., Kellerman, H., & Conte, H. R. A structural theory of ego defenses. In C. E. Izard (Ed.), *Emotions, personality and psychopathology.* New York: Plenum, 1979.

Schachter, S., & Singer, J. E. Cognitive, social and physiological determinants of emotional state. *Psychological Review,* 1962, *69,* 379–399.

Schaefer, E. S., & Plutchik, R. Interrelationships of emotions, traits, and diagnostic constructs. *Psychological Reports,* 1966, *18,* 399–410.

Scott, J. P. *Animal behavior.* Chicago: University of Chicago Press, 1958.

Tolman, E. C. A behavioristic account of the emotions (1923). In *Behavior and psychological man: Selected papers of E. C. Tolman.* Berkeley: University of California Press, 1958.

Tomkins, S. S. *Affect imagery consciousness, Vol. 1. The positive affects.* New York: Springer, 1962.

Van Hooff, J. A. R. A. M. A structural analysis of the social behavior of a semicaptive group of chimpanzees. In M. von Cranach and I. Vine (Eds.), *Social communication and movement.* New York: Academic Press, 1973.

Wilson, E. O. *Sociobiology: The new synthesis.* Cambridge: Harvard University Press, 1975.

9
Cognition, Emotion and Motivation: The Doctoring of Humpty-Dumpty

Richard S. Lazarus
James C. Coyne
Susan Folkman
University of California, Berkeley

The importance of cognitive processes in human adaptation is now generally accepted, and the cognitive orientation has experienced such a general resurgence in psychology that it has even been referred to as a "cognitive revolution" (Dember, 1974). Yet, "campaigners for a 'cognitive movement' can hardly afford to slacken their efforts now that their candidates have ostensibly assumed office" (Mahoney, 1977, p. 6). They have campaign promises to keep or apologies to make as they confront the basic problems of psychology from their special perspective. Undoubtedly, extreme idological positions will have to be softened or abandoned as cognitive theorists come to terms with important areas of inquiry they have previously ignored.

During the 19th century it was fashionable to separate cognition (reason) from emotion (passion) and motivation (will or volition). Few would still seriously subscribe to the view that the three are distinct and fundamental faculties capable of independent development, but their reintegration—the doctoring of the shattered Humpty-Dumpty—has proven to be a frustrating problem for a succession of theoretical frameworks.[1] Too often the problem has been settled with the accession of one of the three, the banishment of another, and a denial of any data

---

[1]Since writing this we have come across a related quote from Riegel (1979) concerning faculty psychology and modern experimental psychology. He writes:

> But not even all the King's horses and all the King's men could put Humpty-Dumpty together again, and thus, experimentalists were bound to fail in their attempts of putting meaning back into their psychology from which they had eliminated it so radically. Meaning is not something that can be added later to the system analyzed; rather, it is the most fundamental topic [p. 3].

that might embarrass this arrangement. Emotion has been assimilated into drive, motivation and emotion denuded of thought or taken over altogether by cognition. The "organism" that emerges from such conceptualizations is inevitably fragmented and incomplete. Furthermore, if the distinctions among the three concepts have been drawn too sharply and reified, so too has the distinction between the person to whom are ascribed the thoughts, emotions and motives, and the environment to which that person responds.

Our objective here is to struggle with the perennial problem of the interdependence of thoughts, emotion, and motivation, and their involvement in the person's ongoing relationship to the environment. In doing so we give our main attention to cognition and emotion, and will touch motivation only lightly.

Although we shall be raising doubts throughout about the tendency to separate and reify the cognitive, motivational, and emotional, this is also a good moment to affirm two ideas that are central to our perspective. First, there is no way to understand emotion without reference to the way a person construes or cognizes his or her relationship with the environment and, indeed, with the particular environmental context of the moment. Thus, we argue that cognitive activity has a pivotal significance for an emotional reaction. Second, as we have elsewhere (e.g., Coyne & Lazarus, 1980; Lazarus, 1981; Lazarus & Launier, 1978), we also make a case that how a person acts and reacts, whether adaptively or maladaptively, can only be understood from a transactional metatheoretical framework. In developing our arguments it is best to begin with a brief history of our current outlook.

THE BACKGROUND OF OUR PRESENT THINKING

Since the late sixties, the work of Richard S. Lazarus and his coworkers has been characterized by two main themes. First, the quality and intensity of an emotional reaction are determined by *cognitive appraisal* processes, that is, the person's continually reevaluated judgments about the significance of demands and constraints in ongoing transactions with the environment and about the options for meeting them. Second, cognitive appraisal processes underlie *coping* activities which, in turn, continually shape the emotional reaction by altering in various ways the meanings of ongoing relationships between the person and the environment, that is, by affecting appraisal itself via *reappraisal*. This emphasis on the pivotal significance of cognition in emotion and adaptation stemmed from a sense that its role had been understated in traditional drive-oriented views, and also from a belief that cognitive appraisal often represents a critical juncture in the person-environment transaction (Coyne & Lazarus, 1980). We frequently apply the term "causal" to cognition in discussing its role in emotional response and adaptation in general. In doing so, however, we intend a rather restricted meaning. We do not mean that cognition is a separate force or entity acting on emotional and adaptational processes; we consider cognition an integral part of them. Instead, we are calling attention to the vital necessity of invoking cognitive concepts in understanding how people come to respond in the manner that they do.

The research of the Lazarus group has progressed from laboratory studies of cognitive mediation to stressful films to the more naturalistic study of coping with anticipated surgery (Cohen & Lazarus, 1973), and, most recently, to a large-scale attempt to describe stress and coping processes over the course of a year in a sample of normal middle-aged adults (Coyne & Lazarus, 1979). This current study focuses on the flux and flow of the relationship of men and women to their environments by examining major life changes, minor daily hassles and uplifts, cognitive appraisals of stressful episodes, coping resources, patterns of emotion and adaptational outcomes. This shift in attention to natural settings and everyday life reflects a growing conviction that the most important theoretical issues are refractory to laboratory-derived data (Lazarus, 1981; Lazarus & Launier, 1978).

The early film studies generated substantial data in support of the notion that how a person appraises and copes with an environment can have an important bearing on emotional and adaptational outcomes. The findings also challeneged prevailing conceptions of emotion as motivator or drive, and called attention to limitations inherent in the treatment of emotion as an antecedent variable. Given our current interest in the relationships among cognition, emotion and motivation, it would be useful to return briefly to some of these studies, examine how the relationship between cognition and emotion was construed, and to contrast this with the then dominant view. We then note some disturbing tendencies of cognitive theorists falling prey to the same conceptual traps that characterized earlier views of emotion as drive or motivator, that is, as a causal antecedent of cognition and behavior.

Motion pictures were chosen as a source of stress because they did not depend on deception but relied on the natural tendency of people to react emotionally while watching others have a damaging experience (Lazarus, Speisman, Mordkoff, & Davison, 1962). In some of the studies, situational manipulations designed to influence the subject's appraisal of the film events predictably raised or lowered the level of emotional disturbance, as measured by self-report and autonomic indicators, while the film was being watched. Further analyses of the results of these and additional studies revealed that the effectiveness of these manipulations depended in part on the personality of the subjects (see Lazarus, Averill, & Opton, 1970, for a review). One study (Koriat, Melkman, Averill, & Lazarus, 1972) examined self-generated rather than situationally induced modes of emotional control. Subjects were instructed to detach themselves from the emotional impact of a film showing woodshop accidents or to involve themselves more fully, but in neither case were they given explicit instructions as to how to do this. It was found that people could indeed modulate their emotional states volitionally, as measured by self-report and heart rate.

These demonstrations that cognitive coping strategies could dampen or eliminate emotional response encouraged rejection of the then prevailing view of coping as the *result* of emotion. In the revised view, coping is treated not as a consequence but as having causal significance in the emotional response and as an integral component of that response. Emotions, from this perspective, are better regarded as a reflection of a person's ongoing appraisal of information with respect to its significance for well-being, rather than as being merely fortuitously conditioned to physical stimuli.

The focus on person and environmental antecedents of cognitive and self-regulatory processes opens up a multidirectional diversity in the theoretical handling of emotion. Treating emotion as a dependent variable, describable in terms of a set of self-report, behavioral, and physiological measures, also calls attention to discrepancies among measures of the same concept, and to more general issues inherent in the study of the topography of emotional response.

Still, the legitimacy of emotion as an antecedent variable too should not be totally rejected. There is, after all, an extensive body of older work showing the disruptive effects of emotion on cognitive functioning (e.g., Basowitz, Persky, Korchin, & Grinker, 1955; Child & Waterhouse, 1953; Sarason, 1972; Sarason, Mandler, & Craighill, 1952; for reviews and analysis see also Lazarus, 1966; Lazarus, Deese, & Osler, 1952). Particularly in the latest work of the Lazarus group, care has been taken to note that in adaptation there is constant interplay between cognitive appraisals, emotion, subsequent information-processing, reappraisals. and so on (Folkman, Schaefer, & Lazarus, 1979). For the purpose of hypothesis-testing or theoretical explanation, one can intervene in this sequence, designating one phase as an antecedent condition, and then examine its consequences (Coyne & Lazarus, 1980). For example, one can induce a positive mood state in a group of subjects and observe resulting differences in cognitive processes (Isen, Shalker, Clark, & Karp, 1978), or look first at commitments and observe their impact on thoughts and fantasy (Klinger, 1975).

At the same time, we must remain cognizant of the arbitrariness of the sequence that is observed—i.e., that it is relative to one's point of entry into the process. With alternative punctuations of the sequence, other, even reversed, "causal" patterns can be observed. For instance, the effects of cognitive processes on mood can also be studied by having subjects attend to negatively or positively valued aspects of themselves and then assessing their mood states (Teasdale & Fogarty, 1979). The major hazard, however, lies in our tendency to reify the *direction* of this relationship as going always one way or the other.

A second hazard is to treat emotion and cognition as theoretically and empirically *separable*. If one conceptualizes the above manipulations of emotion and cognition as one might a cue stick driving one of two billiard balls (cognition or emotion) into the other, one can generate all sorts of insoluble questions about how emotion can influence cognition, vice versa, or even about emotionless thought or thoughtless emotion, which our conceptual past history has frequently had us do. Taking their distinctiveness too seriously (as separate and independent billiard balls), one is left unprepared for the many circumstances in which emotion and cognition have the same referents and are neither theoretically nor empirically separable.

For example, anger refers not only to a disturbed physiological, subjective and behavioral state, but to cognitions about a hostile environmental agent; and fear involves not only actions (or impulses) of avoidance or flight but also an appraisal of a dangerous environmental agent which is the object of the fear. These emotions, cognitions, and impulses or actions are often best treated as interdependent and totally *fused* aspects of the person's relationship with the environment. This does not mean that these aspects are *always* fused. There can be attack without anger and anger without attack, or avoidance without fear and fear without avoidance. When there is this type of separation in life, it is because of some special additional process such as inhibition or defensive reappraisal. But the *full* experience of anger and fear includes at least three fused elements: the impulse to act, the cognitive appraisal of a relationship with the environment, and the physiological and subjective disturbance which defines these emotional states (Lazarus, 1966).

Whether or not theories of emotion take cognizance of the aforementioned problems, the separation of cognition and emotion and the designation of one as causal antecedent and the other as consequence is an important directive in the organization of theory and research that has far-reaching consequences. We should explore, therefore, what has happened in theory and research in the recent past when emotion was reified as an antecedent condition of cognition and action.

EMOTION AS ANTECEDENT

At the time of the original film studies (1960–1971), theoretical treatments of emotion focused almost exclusively on changes in behavior as a consequence of emotion. Attention was directed to emotion's arousing or motivational functions, and its substantive qualities and determinants were largely ignored. Emotion was generally fused (and sometimes confounded) with concepts of drive and activation (e.g., Duffy, 1934, 1941, 1962; Lindsley, 1951). Even later conceptualizations of emotion advertised as cognitive were not fully cognitive but emphasized a process of cognitive labeling of a diffuse state of activation (Schachter, 1966). Therefore, Schachter's two-factor theory (emphasizing both activation and cognitive labeling) seems to hold to the core concept of drive-activation, this being a necessary element in emotion. As a result, cognitive processes seem weakened as causal elements by being treated largely as labeling rather than a full process of appraisal of the significance of a social encounter for one's well-being.

We have argued that there is nothing inherently illogical or improper in treating emotion provisionally as an antecedent to some behavior of interest. Yet theorizing in this vein has been plagued by recurring problems (Lazarus, 1968). It became dominated by a set of five rather consistent imbalances and distortions:

1. Conceptualization of emotion as a drive, antecedent, or even as an intervening variable, directed attention away from its own determinants and, in particular, from any consideration of cognitive and motivational processes mediating between a stimulus situation and the observed reactions. The association between emotion and stimulus conditions was assumed to be acquired fortuitously, as a result of simple contiguity and drive reduction or reinforcement. Subsequent evocation of an emotion by these conditions was assumed to be automatic. Lost was any sense of emotion as a *relational* or *meaning-centered* concept that could be concerned with the significance of a person's ongoing transactions with the environment. Empirical questions as to the person and environmental variables that might influence these judgments (or appraisal processes)—and therefore the observed pattern of emotional response—were simply not articulated in theoretical analysis.

Over many years, a large variety of studies were designed to examine the effects of emotional arousal on laboratory task performance. Many of these studies were based on some variant of the Yerkes–Dodson Law (1908), suggesting an inverted U-shaped relationship between arousal and performance. Much research also emphasized the tendency of high arousal to interfere with the subject's ability to deal with task requirements (Child & Waterhouse, 1953; Easterbrook, 1959; Sarason, Mandler, & Craighill, 1952). Other such studies had a Hullian basis and, while also conceptualizing emotion as nonspecific arousal, attempted to delineate a systematic relationship between performance, drive, and habit strength (Spence & Farber, 1954; Spence & Spence, 1966). For example, to manipulate emotion or drive as an independent variable, subjects were given an ostensibly solvable task which was not in fact solvable. It was assumed that experimenter-induced failure would automatically induce emotional arousal or drive. Little attention was given to the constellation of experimental demands and person variables (e.g., motives, beliefs) that might make failure threatening, or to the cognitive processes involved in making the judgment that something important enough to create emotion was at stake for the experimental subject.

Conceptions of emotion as an antecedent condition involved more than a downplaying of the antecedents of emotion itself. Consistently and uncritically applied, a concentration on the consequences of emotion ultimately led to a default in the form of the theoretical judgment that the psychological processes mediating the emotional reaction were insignificant or even nonexistent.

2. Conceptualizations of emotion as an antecedent also downplayed questions of its measurement, focusing instead on limited aspects of concomitant and subsequent behavior. A variety of types of information can be used to infer the quality and intensity of emotional response. In conjunction with eliciting conditions, researchers can employ measures of physiological response, self-reported cognitions and feelings, and the patterning of behavior (e.g., avoidance, attack, facial expression). Yet, as Lazarus (1968) and others have noted, there is substantial lack of agreement among alternative indices of emotion:

> No single response component is capable of producing adequate inferences about any internal state, be it an emotion or some other conceptual entity. Motoric-expressive cues are unreliable because people wear masks. Self-report fails for similar reasons, and is also confounded with response sets, self-justifications, etc. Physiological changes can also be produced by conditions of nonemotional relevance [p. 204].

The patterning of response indices of emotion presents both theoretical and methodological challenges. Theoretically, it raises the possibility of identifying distinct emotional states with specific patterns of measurement (Lazarus, Kanner, & Folkman, 1980). Methodologically, however, one is faced with the need for multiple measures and a way of explaining discrepancies among them. Conception of emotion as an antecedent condition ignored these important and complex issues. Instead, limited performance measures were assumed to reflect the effects of emotion as a unidimensional state of arousal. The possibility that different patterns of emotion—as assessed by self-report, physiological, or alternative behavioral measures—might be associated with divergent performance impairments was not raised. Conceivably, a subject might perform poorly following a failure induction as a concomitant of being angry, anxious, depressed, bored, or simply indifferent. However, an equally logical possibility is that different patterns of emotion, say, anger as opposed to depression, both generated by failure induction, could have different performance outcomes, for example, different degrees of impairment or even similar impairment achieved in quite different ways. With only simple performance and emotion state measures. however, such possibilities could not be explored.

The lack of attention to the substantive characteristics of emotions by drive-related or activation conceptions reduced emotion to a narrow. unidimensional construct, an undifferentiated state of drive or arousal rather than a rich panoply of experiences, somatic patterns, and action patterns. Studies of experimenter-induced failure construed the subject's emotional state variously and vaguely as being frustrated, stressed, anxious, or simply aroused (Brown & Farber, 1951). No need for a choice among these possible labels, nor any sense of loss at not speaking of anger, fear, guilt, sadness-depression, jealousy, disgust, or some combination or sequence of them. The great importance attached to the drive or motivational properties of emotion led to the virtual disappearance of emotion as a substantive topic in psychology journals. Aspects of emotion that were not readily accommodated in these terms were neglected, as were positive emotions such as joy, love, and elation. Psychology suffered a severe form of tunnel vision.

3. Conceptualization of emotion as antecedent to behavior came to imply that it had a causal status with respect to the very behavior that served as its referent. Webb (1948) proposed explicitly that "emotion be defined as an inferred concept which results in a change in the organism's behavior [p. 332]." In too literally accepting the notion that it *results* in the behavior change, a false explanatory power was granted to the concept of emotion. It one accepts a causal status for an inferred variable, one ceases to look for further explanations of the behavior change in antecedent conditions. Yet emotion was a concept abstracted from the very behavior for which it was being proffered as a cause. As such it begged rather than provided an explanation. The legerdemain by which emotion passed from a description of a psychological and physiological state or process to an explanation of behavior took a number of forms.

One common approach was to administer a measure of emotionality such as the Manifest Anxiety Scale (Taylor, 1953) and relate subjects' scores to their performance on some laboratory task. The most parsimonious description of such a procedure is that a self-report measure is being correlated with concurrent behavior; one is examining the concordance of two alternative indices of anxiety. However, if one conceptually detaches the performance measure from the self-reported anxiety score, one can be easily led to accept that the anxiety score explains the observed difference in performance, a seemingly more profound observation than a simple correlation. When such explanations were presented, they were typically bolstered by references to presumed neurochemical events, yet little empirical support for this was available. Even if it had been, neurochemical data would only have provided a further dimension to emotion as an inferred organismic state, not a complete explanation for concomitant behavior.

Another variation of the tautological use of emotion as an explanation can be found in the experimental manipulation of emotional arousal itself, such as experimenter-induced failure. The effectiveness of the manipulation is usually judged by whether the subject's performance is impaired. When impairment was observed in such studies, it was taken as evidence of emotional arousal (e.g., anxiety), which in turn was invoked to explain the impairment.

Still a third variant has been to substitute the term "anxiety" for the superordinate term "emotion," and psychology soon seemed to be saying that anxiety was a dominant causal factor both in psychopathology (e.g., Dollard & Miller, 1950) and in positive adaptation (e.g., Davis, 1944). Anxiety became the "prime" emotion for all behavior. If any other emotions existed, for example, sadness-depression, anger, guilt, they were downplayed as intervening factors in adaptation and maladaptation, or relegated to somewhat esoteric work such as efforts to distinguish between guilt and shame (Ausubel, 1955), to psycho-analysis, or to other disciplines such as anthropology. And virtually no attention was paid to what might be called positively toned emotions (see Lazarus et al., 1980). The person, in this scheme, seems to become an anxiety-reducing machine, and anxiety reduction can serve him or her well (as in successful ambition) or badly (as in psychopathology).

4. With emotion thus conceptually detached from antecedent person and environment variables, mediating psychological processes, and even the differences in behavior it was intended to explain, doubts could be raised about the concept's scientific status. Some called for its elimination. Duffy (1934, 1941, 1962) argued, for example, that the concept was worse than useless. Duffy (1941) noted that the features of behavior for which emotion was invoked as an explanation were features of *all* behavior:

> All responses, not merely "emotional" responses, occur as adjustment to stimulating conditions. All responses, not merely emotional responses, occur at some particular energy level. All responses manifest discrimination, or response to relationships [p. 292].

In a highly influential paper, Brown and Farber (1951) also rejected emotion as a substantive concept suitable for scientific study. "Emotion is not a *thing* in the simple, naive sense that a chair or table is a thing [p. 466]." Even if scientific study does not require that a phenomenon be a "thing," Brown and Farber did raise legitimate questions about the particularly truncated concepts of emotion that emerged from its treatment as an antecedent variable. As Peters (1963) described it, theorists "had been erroneously led to treating emotion as a separate category or part of behavior, a force and an agent [p. 438]."

Problems associated with emotion as antecedent can be summarized in various ways. Such a conception offers little improvement over folk or naive psychological conceptions of emotion as a force seizing or overwhelming the person. However consistent with the phenomenology of emotion such explanations may be, they really do not extend our knowledge of the determinants of emotion, and are tautological at best. When it is detached from antecedent conditions and used to explain its own behavioral referents, emotion becomes an intervening variable without true explanatory power.

Refocusing on emotion as a *consequence*, one can open issues of its measurable antecedents and the substantive features of the behavior pattern to which it refers. A *cognitive* conception of emotion as consequence emphasizes the active processing of information inherent in an emotional reaction, and suggests attention to both person and environmental variables affecting such processes. A cognitive orientation to emotion reestablishes a linkage between emotion and its antecedents—not just environmental conditions but the various determinants of the individual's orientation to them.

One can legitimately speak of the cognitive determinants of emotion, but herein also lies the potential for conceptual mischief. Cognition, like emotion, is an inferred variable, and it can similarly be abused by making it an antecedent condition detached from its own measurable antecedents. and then employing it as the explanation for its sole referent. Like emotion, cognition can be treated as an elusive inner "thing" rather than a relational process. Instead of clarifying the structure of the person's transactions with the environment, the construct can be employed in a way that leaves the person lost in thought. Examples abound in the current cognitive literature.

COGNITION ÜBER ALLES

The triumph of cognition over both emotion and motivation as explanatory concepts has been both dramatic and thorough. Pervin (1979) has documented and qualified this with reference to changes in the *Psychological Abstracts* and the *Annual Review of Psychology*. By 1978, the number of entries in *Psychological Abstracts* listed in association with cognition had four times those under motivation. The concept of drive, which had often subsumed emotion in the past, was missing from the index for the first time in 1965, and although it reappeared in 1968, it was again missing for the period 1972–1978. Cognition had not even been a chapter heading in the *Annual Review* before 1966, but by 1978 the number of subheadings under it exceeded the combined total under emotion and motivation.

Yet now that cognition is in ascendancy, there are clear signs that the cognitive orientation is in danger of not fulfilling its promise of providing an understanding of the whole person as a "cognitive, conative, affective, biological and social individual" (McKeachie, 1976; cited in Pervin, 1979) in transaction with the environment.

WHITHER MOTIVATION?

As a concept, motivation has gotten its major impetus in psychology from the need to explain what pushed a quiescent, equilibrated organism into action. The obvious answer was a motivating force of some kind, which in the heyday of Freud and of associative learning theory—both based on the theme of tension-reduction and reinforcement—was conceptualized as drive (see Hull, 1943; Spence, 1956, 1958). All behavior represented efforts to reduce tension, and behavior that seemed to deviate from the principle (e.g., altruism, ambition) was viewed as merely a necessary detour. The main sources of drive energy were tissue needs or instincts, but other, acquired, drives became conditioned to these through chance reinforcement, that is, by virtue of their success in producing tension-reduction. Because many forms of human activity seemed as likely to add tension as subtract it, Allport (1937) introduced his concept of functional autonomy, and Dollard and Miller (1950) argued that even neurotic or maladaptive behaviors (e.g., defenses) were learned and survived because they reduced anxiety (a form of tension) and they persisted because the person never discovered that the threatening outcomes producing the anxiety were unrealistic.

We all know that what seemed like an elegant edifice, drive, and simple reinforcement theory, passed out of favor because it had to be shored up constantly by costly qualifications and the gradual addition of necessary complications in the form of mediating processes such as cognition. This is not the place to detail this interesting history in which several major personages such as McClelland, Harlow, Klein and White played important roles. At the same time, arousal theorists (e.g., Duffy, 1941, 1962: Lindsley, 1951; and Malmo, 1959), who contributed to the appeal of the drive concept by bringing together three key strands into a single arousal dimension, namely, physiological arousal, behavioral activation, and drive, were slowly losing ground to evidence of autonomic (physiological) specificity (Lacey, 1967; Lazarus, 1966; Mason, Maher, Hartley, Mougey, Perlow, & Jones, 1976; Shapiro, Tursky, & Schwartz, 1970). The fall of logical positivism as an ideological basis for an elegant theory also contributed to the demise of drive formulations.

Although there had been abundant treatments of motivation from a more cognitive point of view (e.g., Kelly, 1955; Murray, 1938), George Klein and Robert White managed to remain within the drive framework while modifying it in a cognitive direction. White's (1959) beautifully constructed argument that the infant is normally far less involved in feeding or obtaining oral stimulation than in examining and manipulating the environment (effectance motivation) was very influential in turning psychology away from a strictly drive formulation. And writing within the ego psychology tradition, Klein (1970) infused the concept of drive with cognitive activity, redefining it more or less as follows:

> It seems more economical to . . . think of drive as a construct which refers, on the one hand, to the "relating" process—the meaning—around which selected behavior and memories are organized, and in terms of which goal-sets, anticipations and expectations develop, and on the other hand, to those processes which accommodate this relational activity to reality. In this way drive is defined solely in terms of behavior and thought products . . .

Klein's concept of drive is obviously no longer drive in the Freudian or associative learning sense; while retaining its instinctual or tissue basis (primary or viscerogenic), it has been shifted toward means-ends and goal-related thought. Drive is now suffused with cognitive activity.

This shift away from tissue tensions and toward thought brought with it a corresponding shift away from a conceptualization of the person as normally quiescent and passive to one that is constantly active in seeking stimulation, to have an effect on the environment, to explore and understand, to interpret oneself, an organism for whom quiescence and homeostasis are foreign. Activity, per se, need no longer be explained (see also Piaget, 1952). As Miller, Galanter, and Pribram (1960) put it:

> Plans are executed because people are alive. This is not a facetious statement, for so long as people are behaving, *some* plan or other must be executed. The question thus moves from why *Plans* are executed to a concern for which plans are executed [p. 62].

But in the fervor to move away from the old-fashioned concept of drive, and toward the role of thought, we must not forget that the answer to Miller et al.'s question must still lie partly in motivational concepts. "which plans are executed" depends on personal agendas on the basis of which transactions with the environment are evaluated. To be benefited and thus to feel good, or to be harmed, threatened or challenged, means to have some personal stake in an outcome; the more significant the stake, the greater the potential for harm, threat, or challenge, or for a positive emotion in the case of a favorable outcome. In lower animals the stakes are mainly physical safety, survival, and comfort; in humans they involve long-range goals and commitments, and are largely symbolic. No matter how difficult the task of conceptualizing motivational concepts and understanding their developmental course, operation and behavioral consequences, or their interrelationships with thought and emotion, a motivational concept cannot be abandoned in the effort to understand stress and adaptation.

The term "commitment," above, illustrates what we are saying very well because it is a motivational concept heavily infused with cognitive processes. A commitment is a statement of what is important to the person (see Wrubel, Benner, & Lazarus, 1981), and it can be defined at many levels of abstraction. For example, one can be committed to an ideal such as parenting, or to a specific goal such as having three children. Klinger (1977) has described the importance of commitments in people's lives, explaining depression as a process of disengagement from commitments. What is important to a person parallels the idea of stakes in our earlier discussion of harm, threat and challenge. Without some such concept it would not be possible to understand the emotional response to a transaction.

Commitment illustrates the way cognition and emotion fuse in real life. To understand a commitment requires knowledge about its cognitive referent—i.e., commitment to what?—also about the strength with which it is held and the contexts in which it is relevant. The meaning and significance of stressful events and how they unfold is also carried by the concept of commitment, since this meaning includes what and how much can be gained, lost or endangered, as well as how much must be expended to prevent or live with the loss; it also implies a sense of other commitments that might remain to take up the slack. The meaning and significance of an encounter from a motivational standpoint is expressed in the kind and intensity of emotion experienced, for example, relief, exultation, or guilt at escaping loss, anger, or depression.

Why isn't it enough to say that motivation is a form of cognition and hence subsumable under the concept of cognition? Because we know that people hold to commitments with greater or lesser fervor; because striving occurs not merely in a directional sense but also with greater or lesser intensity and persistance; because some commitments never turn off as do short-term goal-oriented behaviors; in short, because commitments are a special form of thought characterized by something that might be called arousal. Yet, because committed people are not always aroused, even when they are in pursuit of their commitments, it is not enough to say that motivation can be subsumed, therefore under emotion or arousal. Their fervor is indeed related to emotion, often even fused with it, but as much in a dispositional sense as directly evident. Motivation does not reduce to emotion, though when it is most clearly in evidence the two concepts are very apt to be conjoined.

Although we cannot here fully resolve this problem of the lack of parallelism among the concepts of thought, emotion and motivation—indeed, with so much having been written on the concept of motivation, it would be arrogant to try in a few paragraphs—we are still firm in our assertion that it is not fruitful or even possible to speak of one without reference to the other in the natural context of human behavior. The shattered egg does not serve us, conceptually, because its pieces have no living existence as separable identities. We must try somehow to keep Humpty-Dumpty intact.

CONCLUDING REMARKS

The concepts of cognition, motivation, and emotion emphasize different but related aspects of the person's transactions. The cognitive revolution has righted some excesses and imbalances in previous theory and research. It called attention to the usefulness of the assumption that people not only process and appraise information about the nature of their relationship to the environment, but that they can exert considerable control over it. The importance of this point should not, however, distract us from the perspectives on the person-environment relationship provided by the concepts of emotion and motivation.

Emotion organizes our awareness that cognition and behavior are embodied, and that measures of the state of this body, whether physiological or subjective feelings, provide the important information about the state of the person-environment relationship. Motivation emphasizes that people have goals, plans, projects, and commitments that organize the person-environment relationship. Apparent inconsistencies in the person's behavior can be explained potentially with reference to their relevance to these motivational considerations. Furthermore, motivational variables set the terms for the way a person construes transactions by identifying the stakes and payoffs that influence cognitive processes, action impulses, and the emotional response.

Thoughts, emotions, and motives are inferred from observations of the person, and we have noted how they often have the same referents. How we partition these concepts and punctuate theoretical sequences is often a matter of theoretical and methodological convenience. Yet we cannot lose sight of the fact that cognition, motivation, and emotion are inferential processes, not entities, each with a separate and independent existence. For purposes of conceptual analysis, it is appropriate to distinguish among them. However, we must realize that in nature, that is, in the actual phenomena of human experience and action, they are usually fused and difficult to separate. To speak of such fusion is not a matter of conceptual sloppiness but a recognition of the necessity of putting the pieces back together into an organized whole.

In his classic work, Ryle (1949) warned of the insolubility of certain theoretical questions about the relations among presumed inner entities. If cognition and emotion, for example, are separate entities in relation to each other, one has to establish some tie between them. But one cannot conceptualize this tie as either cognitive or emotional without disturbing their status as separate entities. The solution, of course, is that *people* think and respond emotionally, rather than endure passively the interaction of thoughts and emotion.

It is this point, i.e., that activity and involvement with the environment characterize people rather than detached fragments of them, that might allow the cognitive perspective to reintegrate the person, as McKeachie (1976) proposed in his A.P.A. Presidential Address. To focus on cognitions, motives, and emotions as separable entities, linked in strict, one-way causal sequences, is to continue the conceptual confusion of the past, and to seriously distort their operation in the natural course of living. The pieces of poor Humpty-Dumpty cannot be allowed to lie separately and lifelessly on the ground, and however awesome the synthetic task, must surely be put back together again.

ACKNOWLEDGMENT

This is a shortened version of a chapter with the same title in R. W. J. Neufeld (Ed.), *Psychological stress and psychopathology*. New York: McGraw-Hill, 1982, pp. 218–239, by permission of the publisher.

REFERENCES

Allport, G. W. *Personality: A psychological interpretation.* New York: Holt, Rinehart & Wiiston, 1937.

Ausubel, D. P. Relationships between shame and guilt in the socializing process. *Psychological Review,* 1955, *62,* 378–390.

Basowitz, H., Persky, H., Korchin, S. J., & Grinker, R. R. *Anxiety and stress.* New York: McGraw-Hill, 1955.

Brown, J., & Farber, I. E. Emotions conceptualized as intervening variables—with suggestions toward a theory of frustration. *Psychological Bulletin,* 1951, *48,* 465–495.

Child, I. L., & Waterhouse, I. K. Frustration and the quality of performance: II. A theoretical statement. *Psychological Review,* 1953, *60,* 127–139.

Cohen, F., & Lazarus, R. S. Active coping processes, coping dispositions, and recovery from surgery. *Psychosomatic Medicine,* 1973, *35,* 375–389.

Coyne, J. C., & Lazarus, R. S. *The ipsative-normative framework for the longitudinal study of stress.* Paper presented at the 87th Annual Convention of the American Psychological Association, New York, September 1979.

Coyne, J. C., & Lazarus, R. S. Cognitive style, stress perception, and coping. In I. L. Kutash & L. B. Schlesinger (Eds.), *Handbook on stress and anxiety.* San Francisco: Jossey-Bass, 1980.

Davis, A. Socialization and adolescent personality. *Yearbook of the National Society for the Study of Education,* 1944, *43,* Part I, 198–216.

Dember, W. N. Motivation and the cognitive revolution. *American Psychologist,* 1974, *29,* 161–168.

Dollard, J., & Miller, N. E. *Personality and psychotherapy.* New York: McGraw-Hill, 1950.

Duffy, E. Emotion: An example of the need for reorientation in psychology. *Psychological Review,* 1934, *41,* 184–198.

Duffy, E. An explanation of emotional phenomena without the use of the concept of "emotion." *Journal of General Psychology,* 1941, *25,* 283–293.

Duffy, E. *Activation and behavior.* New York: Wiley, 1962.

Easterbrook, J. A. The effect of emotion on cue utilization and the organization of behavior. *Psychological Review,* 1959, *66,* 183–201.

Folkman, S., Schaefer, C., & Lazarus, R. S. Cognitive processes as mediators of stress and coping. In V. Hamilton & D. M. Warburton (Eds.), *Human stress and cognition: An information-processing approach.* London: Wiley, 1979.

Hull, C. L. *Principles of behavior.* New York: Appleton-Century-Crofts, 1943.

Isen, A. M., Shalker, T. E., Clark, M., & Karp, L. Affect, accessibility of material in memory and behavior: A cognitive loop? *Journal of Personality and Social Psychology,* 1978, *36*(1), 1–12.

Kelly, G. A. *The psychology of personal constructs.* (2 volumes). New York: Norton, 1955.

Klein, G. S. *Perception, motives and personality.* New York: Knopf, 1970.

Klinger, E. Consequences of commitment to and disengagement from incentives. *Psychological Review,* 1975, *82,* 1–25.

Klinger, E. *Meaning and void.* Minneapolis: University of Minnesota Press, 1977.

Koriat, A., Melkman, R., Averill, J. R., & Lazarus, R. S. The self-control of emotional reactions to a stressful film. *Journal of Personality,* 1972, *21,* 25–29.

Lacey, J. I. Somatic response patterning and stress: Some revisions of activation theory in psychological stress. In M. H. Appley & R. Trumbull (Eds.), *Psychological stress.* New York: Appleton-Century-Crofts, 1967.

Lazarus, R. S. *Psychological stress and the coping process.* New York: McGraw-Hill, 1966.

Lazarus, R. S. Emotions and adaptation: Conceptual and empirical relations. In W. J. Arnold (Ed.), *Nebraska symposium on motivation.* Lincoln: University of Nebraska Press, 1968.

Lazarus, R. S. The stress and coping paradigm. In C. Eisdorfer, D. Cohen, A. Kleinman, & P. Maxim (Eds.), *Models for clinical psychopathology.* New York: Spectrum, 1981.

Lazarus, R. S., Averill, J. R., & Opton, E. M., Jr. Toward a cognitive theory of emotions. In M. Arnold (Ed.), *Feelings and emotions.* New York: Academic Press, 1970.

Lazarus, R. S., Deese, J., & Osler, S. F. The effects of psychological stress upon performance. *Psychological Bulletin,* 1952, *49,* 293–317.

Lazarus, R. S., Kanner, A. D., & Folkman, S. Emotions: A cognitive-phenomenological analysis. In R. Plutchik & H. Kellerman (Eds.), *Theories of emotion.* New York: Academic Press, 1980.

Lazarus, R. S., & Launier, R. Stress-related transactions between person and environment. In L. A. Pervin & M. Lewis (Eds.), *Perspectives in interactional psychology.* New York: Plenum, 1978.

Lazarus, R. S., Speisman, J. C., Mordkoff, A. M., & Davison, L. A. A laboratory study of psychological stress produced by a motion picture film. *Psychological Monographs,* 1962, *76* (34, Whole No. 553), 1–35.

Lindsley, D. B. Emotions. In S. S. Stevens (Ed.), *Handbook of experimental psychology.* New York: Wiley, 1951.

Mahoney, M. J. Cognitive therapy and research: A question of questions. *Cognitive Therapy and Research,* 1977, *1,* 5–17.

Malmo, R. B. Activation: A neuropsychological dimension. *Psychological Review,* 1959, *66,* 367–386.

Mason, J. W., Maher, J. T., Hartley, L. H., Mougey, E., Perlow, M. J., & Jones, L. G. Selectivity of corticosteroid and catecholamine response to various natural stimuli. In G. Serban (Ed.), *Psychopathology of human adaptation.* New York: Plenum, 1976.

McKeachie, W. J. Psychology in America's bicentennial year. *American Psychologist,* 1976, *31,* 819–833.

Miller, G. A., Galanter, E. H., & Pribram, K. *Plans and the structure of behavior.* New York: Holt, 1960.

Murray, H. A. *Exploration in personality.* New York: Oxford University Press, 1938.

Pervin, L. A. *Are we leaving humans buried in conscious thought?: The cognitive revolution and what it leaves out.* Unpublished manuscript, 1979.

Peters, H. N. Affect and emotion. In M. H. Marx (Ed.), *Theories in contemporary psychology.* New York: Macmillan, 1963.

Piaget, J. *The origins of intelligence in children.* New York: International Universities Press, 1952.

Riegel, K. F. *Foundations of dialectical psychology.* New York: Academic Press, 1979.

Ryle, G. *The concept of mind.* London: Hutchinson, 1949.

Sarason, I. G. Experimental approaches to test anxiety: Attention and the uses of information. In C. D. Spielberger (Ed.), *Anxiety: Current trends in theory and research, Vol. 2.* New York: Academic Press, i972.

Sarason, S. B., Mandler, G., & Craighill, P. C. The effect of differential instructions on anxiety and learning. *Journal of Abnormal and Social Psychology,* 1952, *47,* 561–565.

Schachter, S. The interaction of cognitive and physiological determinants of emotional state. In C. D. Spielberger (Ed.), *Anxiety and behavior.* New York: Academic Press, 1966.

Shapiro, D., Tursky, B., & Schwartz, G. E. Differentiation of heart rate and blood pressure in man by operant conditioning. *Psychosomatic Medicine,* 1970, *32,* 417–423.

Spence, J. A., & Spence, K. W. The motivational components of manifest anxiety: Drive and drive stimuli. In C. D. Spielberger (Ed.), *Anxiety and behavior.* New York: Academic Press, 1966.

Spence, K. W. *Behavior theory and conditioning.* New Haven: Yale University Press, 1956.

Spence, K. W. A theory of emotionally based drive (D) and its relation to performance in simple learning situations. *American Psychologist,* 1958, *13,* 131–141.

Spence, K. W., & Farber, I. E. The relation of anxiety to differential eyelid conditioning. *Journal of Experimental Psychology,* 1954, *47,* 127–134.

Taylor, J. A. A personality scale of manifest anxiety. *Journal of Abnormal and Social Psychology,* 1953, *48,* 285–290.

Teasdale, J. D.. & Fogarty, S. J. Differential effects of induced mood on retrieval of pleasant and unpleasant events from episodic memory. *Journal of Abnormal Psychology,* 1979, *88,* 248–257.

Webb, W. B. Motivational theory of emotions. *Psychological Review,* 1948, *55,* 329–335.

White, R. W. Motivation reconsidered: The concept of competence. *Psychological Review,* 1959, *66,* 297–333.

Wrubel, J., Benner, P., & Lazarus, R. S. Social competence from the perspective of stress and coping. In J. Wine & M. Smye (Eds.), *Social competence.* New York: Guilford, 1981.

Yerkes, R. M., & Dodson, J. D. The relation of strength stimulus to rapidity of habit formation. *Journal of Comparative Neurological Psychology,* 1908, *18,* 459–482.

10 The Interaction of Affect and Cognition

R. B. Zajonc
The University of Michigan

This comment seeks to inquire into both the independence of affect of cognition and into the nature of their interaction. It derives from a recent article (Zajonc, 1980) which reviewed theoretical and empirical evidence suggesting that cognition and affect are separable, parallel, and partially independent systems. The main evidence for independence of affect of cognition came from studies on the so-called mere exposure effect (Zajonc, 1968), that is, the phenomenon of increasing preference for objects that can be induced by virtue of mere repeated exposures. The traditional theory associated with this phenomenon since the days of Titchener, held that positive attitude to the repeatedly exposed object was produced by the increasing awareness of recognition of the object as familiar. A series of studies in our laboratory (Kunst-Wilson & Zajonc, 1980; Matlin, 1971; Moreland & Zajonc, 1977, 1979; Wilson, 1979), however, has shown that neither objective recognition nor subjective impression of recognition are necessary for the exposure effect, and that liking for a stimulus object can be enhanced by virtue of repeated exposure alone, independently of whether the subject is able or unable to recognize it as familiar. These results were obtained with a variety of stimuli, different methods of presentation, and diverse measures of affect. Nevertheless. they were entirely consistent in showing the exposure effect as being entirely independent of recognition when measured either by subjective report or by objective sensitivity scores (d').

The results on the exposure effect have two implications, one specific and one general. In particular, they cast serious doubt on the classical explanation of familiarization and exposure effects. But they also have a much broader implication for they are in conflict with theories of emotion that invoke the mediation of cognitive processes as a necessary element in the generation of emotional states.

These theories derive from the Schachter-Singer (1962) position which holds that emotional states arise only if there is *both* some form of arousal and an appropriate cognitive attribution. Included in this class of theories would be Mandler's theory of emotions (Mandler, 1975) and Lazarus' theory of cognitive appraisal (Lazarus, 1966) all of which require extensive participation of cognitive processes. In a recent summary, Lazarus, Kanner, and Folkman (1980) write, for example, that "each emotion quality and intensity—anxiety, guilt, jealousy, love, joy, or whatever—is generated and guided by its own particular pattern of appraisal. . . . Learning, memory, perception, and thought—in short, cognitive activity—are always key causal aspects of the emotional response pattern [p. 192]."

The understanding of the affect-cognition interaction must be founded on our conceptions of emotion. The term "emotion" is not always clear and it is useful for the present purposes to distinguish between the "occurrence of emotion" and the "experience" and "expression of emotion." I suppose that by "occurrence of emotion" we must mean the *arousal* of autonomic, visceral, glandular, and neuromuscular processes by virtue of an efficient emotional stimulus. Normally, but not always, the arousal of these processes is accompanied by a *subjective* state which is the "experience of emotion." The *overt neuromuscular discharge* is the "expression of emotion." Efficient stimuli may be discovered by observing the association between the occurrence of stimuli and the emotional expression—an association that has some reliability over repeated occurrences. Thus, in cases where the stimulus situation previously known to have always brought about a standard emotional expression does not produce the given expression, we would know to measure autonomic and visceral states, as well as low amplitude EMG's, in an effort to determine whether the core emotional excitation has taken place.

There are actually two classes of theories about emotion. One class invokes cognition as a necessary factor (Lazarus, 1966; Mandler, 1975; Schachter & Singer, 1962). The other class emphasizes somatic factors and especially motor output (Ekman & Friesen, 1975; Izard, 1977; Tomkins, 1980). On the whole, these two classes of theories have also a different orientation and purpose. The cognitive theories of emotion are clearly more interested in the emotional *experience;* they seek to explicate the subjective manifestations of emotion. The motor theories of emotion, on the other hand, seek to describe the *expressions* of emotion and to explicate the *perception* of emotional expressions.

What conceptualization do these two classes of theories of emotion suggest for the study of the affect-cognition interaction? Theories that require the participation of autonomic and somatic processes (e.g., arousal) must cope with the question of *how* somatic processes make contact with mental processes so as to influence them. These theories must be precise about how it is that the physiological state associated with mood, for example, can influence the retention of mood-related information (Bower, 1980), or how hunger can influence the perception of ambiguous objects (Sanford, 1936, 1937). How is it that stomach contractions direct cognition to be particularly sensitive to food stimuli and how, moreover, do they influence information processing so that ambiguous stimuli are imagined as having food properties? Where in the organism (or in the individual as a psychological system) is the *contact* made between hunger and cognition such that the one can have an impact on the other?

Motor theories of emotion have not confronted the problem of affect-cognition interaction, and when they did they invoked a feedback process that generated cognitive (subjective) representations of the somatic states—representations that were now on the same conceptual level as the cognitions with which they could interact (Izard, 1971; 1977; Lanzetta, Cartwright-Smith, & Kleck, 1976; Laird, 1974). Somatic correlates of affect were tracked for their proprioceptive consequences, and these proprioceptions were transformed into cognitions. Thus, the interaction of affect and cognition was meant to be studied on the cognitive terrain.

Cognitive theories of emotions have a direct solution to the affect-cognition interaction by employing the cognitive components of affect.

Clearly, if we wish to understand what cognitive processes are implicated in emotion and how they are implicated we must also define what we mean by "cognition." I will understand by "cognition" those internal processes that are involved in the acquisition, transformation, and storage of information. These processes always derive from a transformation of some sensory input—immediate or temporally distal—according to a specifiable code. The code allows the input to be transformed into "representations." We sometimes mean by "cognitions" the products of the above processes, and there tends to be a confusion between "representations" and "cognitions" because they are often synonymous.

We can, thus, inquire into the minimal cognitive processes that participate as necessary elements in affect and emotion. Recall the distinction between "occurrence," "expression," and "experience" of emotion. Minimal cognitive processes, if any at all, are sufficient for the *occurrence* of emotion. Not a great deal more might be needed for the *expression* of these emotions. I am speaking, of course, about primitive and simple emotions. The prototypical case here might be the unconditioned aversive stimulus. Such stimuli are capable of evoking unconditioned escape and avoidance reactions that by definition require no prior experience, and which are automatic and instantaneous. If we understand by "cognition" some internal process that transforms sensory input (according to a given code) into particular forms of information, then we shall have to acknowledge that many cases exist (e.g., traumatic avoidance learning, opponent processes, taste preferences, etc.) that require no cognitive participation. The process in these cases is shortcircuited to such an extent that the sensory input alone—without a transformation—is capable of eliciting an escape or avoidance reaction (and the appropriate autonomic and visceral responses).

To *experience* an emotion, however, means to perceive oneself as having one and to be aware of having one. By definition then, the experience of an emotion must require cognitive processes. Thus, the occurrence of some complex emotions such as embarrassment or pride would require cognitive participation because the efficient stimulus situations must be processed for their meaning.

It follows from the above that if the affect-cognition interaction is viewed entirely at the cognitive or subjective level then we do not really analyze how emotion proper influences cognition (nor how cognition influences emotion), but how the *subjective representation of emotion* influences cognition (and how cognition influences the subjective representation of emotion).

There is an alternative locus, not necessarily mutually exclusive, for this interaction. Instead of looking at the subjective realm of experience in attempting to explicate this interaction, I am proposing to look at the neuromuscular realm, and specifically at the motor realm. The promise and advantages of this approach become clear below.

All theories of emotion, regardless of how heavy their cognitive component, take it for granted that the autonomic, visceral, and neuromuscular systems are significant elements of the emotional experience and expression. In contrast, however, contemporary theories of information processing have very little to say about the motor components of cognition. Yet it is an obvious fact that mental states are *accompanied* by overt and quasi-overt muscular activity. The overt activity is readily seen by an observer and the quasi-overt activity is systematically revealed by electromyographic studies (see, for example, Cacioppo & Petty, 1979; Jacobson, 1930, McGuigan, 1978; Sokolov, 1972). I have purposely italicized the predicate because it isn't at all clear, let alone obvious, what it is that muscular activity "accompanies."

There have been various attempts to specify the role of motor activity in mental processes (see Smith, 1969 for a good history) but they have proven not to be promising in the study of cognitive processes. It is generally believed today that the muscular and peripheral activity that takes place during cognitive processes is secondary and derivative. In a recent study, for example, Tourangeau and Ellsworth (1979) have argued that facial expressions themselves did not contribute to the emotions reported by the subject, whereas the nature of the eliciting stimulus (films) had powerful effects. These authors found no effects of facial expression on reported emotion or physiological measures of emotion. However, the experiment has been criticized (Izard, 1981; Tomkins, 1981) for using a voluntary simulation of facial expressions. Because the subjects had to hold their expressions for a duration of 2 minutes it is difficult to see what sort of emotion (besides tedium) might have been experienced by them. A fear expression does not last for more than a few seconds in response to a nonthreatening stimulus. Moreover, the expressions the subjects assumed were produced by instructing them to contract a number of specific muscles on the face. These muscular patterns followed the general pattern for the given emotions and represent something like the prototype or a central tendency for each emotion (Ekman, 1971). It is quite unlikely, therefore, that there were many individuals among the subjects for whom the muscular patterns corresponded exactly to their *own* customary and idiosyncratic expressions. Hence, we would not expect the motor patterns to have dramatic effects. We would also not expect these patterns of facial expressions to be stronger than the stimulus influences because there are a host of other bodily manifestations for a given emotion besides the contraction of four facial muscles.

It is generally believed that the essence of cognition will not be found in the muscles. The essence of cognition is believed to be either in the form of propositions (Anderson & Bower, 1973) or in the form of both propositions and images (Paivio, 1978). The evidence that these are in fact *the* contents of the mind is extremely thin (Kolers & Smythe, 1979), however, and the task of resolving whether they are pictures or propositions has been shown to be impossible (Anderson, 1978). Yet the controversy over the nature of cognitive representations has occupied many journal pages (see, for example Kosslyn (1981) and Pylyshyn (1981) who cite most of the literature of this debate). Curiously, almost none of these papers invoked the possibility of a contribution by the motor stratum. Piaget (1954), in contrast, assigned the internal motor activity a central and necessary role in cognitive representation.

Have we discarded the motor elements of mental states prematurely? Only a few moments of casual observation reveals that there is an enormous motor involvement during mental activity. And, more importantly, one can notice systematic differences with different activities. Most clear examples are to be found in attending and orienting. People looking at a photograph of a face or a painting engage a complex set of orienting acts that expose them to different features of the stimulus. The head tilts at a proper angle, their lenses accommodate for the proper distance, and the eyes roam over the various parts of the stimulus. But are they entirely inconsequential for the cognitive processes implicated in the recall or recognition memory of these stimuli?

Observers, in fact, do more than just orient efficiently to explore the various attributes and parts of the stimulus. They open their mouths, move their hands over their lips, shift their weight from one foot onto the other. They might smile at the photograph if it is a photograph of a smiling face or frown if it is angry. It is quite easy to understand why is it that the perceivers roam their eyes over the photograph or accommodate for the proper distance. But why do they open their mouths? Or why do they smile?

The function of muscular activity present during nonperceptual cognitive tasks, such as thinking, recalling, or imaging, is even less clear. Persons engaged in an arithmetic problem often purse their lips, bite their pencils, scratch their heads, furrow their brows, or lick their lips. When asked to suppress subvocalization, people find doing mental arithmetic impossible (Fryer, 1941). Why? What is "going on in the mind" the requires this rich muscular output? Why do people scratch their heads and rub their chins when they try to remember something? The violinist, Itzhak Perlman, in trying to play a difficult note raises his eyebrows (if it is a high note) and keeps them raised until the note has been played. In fact, his face and body perform a rich program of varied movements. Why, again? With few exceptions (Piaget, 1954) it has been generally believed that these motions are secondary and ancillary. But suppose that a good part of musical memory is in fact lodged in these movements. Suppose that they are significant. Looking at performing musicians, one is impressed with the possibility that they are engaged in a sort of matching process. It seems as if they had "*in* their eyebrows" or "*in* their tongue" a representation of the ideal tone that they wish to produce. They seem to accommodate their hands; they adjust their bows over the strings of the instrument and modulate finger pressure over the board to attain the closest match between the output and that ideal. This observation is equivalent to asserting that some significant part of musical representation is in the eyebrow, in the tongue, in the foot, or whatever muscles the musician is prone to engage. It may also be in the mind. But these contents are harder to observe and to manipulate.

Thus, the question to be raised is whether these movements are merely helpful to the musician (they rid the organism of excess energy, for example). or whether they represent essential cues and are integral parts of the representation of the music in memory. Of course, not all movement that occurs during thinking, recalling, or imaging is significant for affective or cognitive analysis. But some may well be. Clearly, it will be quite difficult to separate the relevant motor movements from noise. Not impossible, however. It appears intuitively that the aspects of motor activity that are significant for cognitive functions are also orienting behaviors. However, instead of deploying the sensory apparatus toward stimulus features, they deploy and search among motor patterns for representations and traces. The first may be termed *external orientation,* the second *internal orientations.* The logic of discovery of these aspects of motor activity that are significant for information processing would rely on finding motor acts that are present both during acquisition and retrieval or perception and imagery. Thus, for example, one could compare eye movements during the perception of a rotating figure and measure muscle potential from the muscles that were observed to have participated in the perceptual act.

Now, we cannot always expect a uniformity of a "motor code" across subjects such as we find for mental (cognitive) representations because these latter phenomena are closely allied to language. and hence uniform within a linguistic community. Perhaps it is the failure of discovering such a uniformity for motor processes that prompted psychologists to abandon motor theories of cognition and perception. Our work will have to rely, therefore, on within-subject comparisons rather than on between-subject comparisons.

If it is supposed that *all* cognition has a significant and essential neuromuscular correlate, then a distinct advantage for an affect-cognition theory is reaped.

For neuromuscular discharge is clearly a very significant and essential aspect of affect and emotion. Thus, a theory of affect-cognition interaction that focuses on the role of neuromuscular discharge that is involved in both processes is more likely to gain understanding of their interaction than a theory that seeks to translate affect into cognition, or one that limits itself to the subjective aspects of affect. Note that I neither deny the existence or the importance of representational states hypothesized by current cognitive theories. Nor do I argue that my approach is necessarily superior to any other, although I shall ask different questions than are cast in work pursued in the spirit of cognitive *imperialism*. It is clear to the students of cognition and of emotion, that progress in either field requires the simultaneous study of these. The current literature in both areas is a incontrovertible witness to this observation (Bower, 1981; Plutchik & Kellerman, 1980; Tomkins, 1980).

REFERENCES

Anderson, J. R. Arguments concerning representations for mental imagery. *Psychological Review,* 1978, *85,* 249–277.

Anderson, J. R., & Bower, G. H. *Human associative memory.* Washington, D.C.: Winston, 1973.

Bower, G. H. Mood and memory. *American Psychologist,* 1981, *36,* 129–148.

Cacioppo. J. T.. & Petty, R. E. Lip and nonpreferred forearm EMG activity as a function of orienting tasks. *Biological Psychology,* 1979, *9,* 103–113.

Ekman, P. Universal and cultural differences in facial expression of emotion. In J. K. Cole (Ed.), *Nebraska Symposium on Motivation,* Vol. 19. Lincoln: University of Nebraska Press, 1971.

Ekman, P., & Friesen, W. V. Unmasking the face. Englewood Cliffs, N.J.: Prentice-Hall, 1975.

Fryer, D. H. Articulation in automatic mental work. *American Journal of Psychology,* 1941, *54,* 504–517.

Izard, C. E. *The face of emotion.* New York: Appleton, 1971.

Izard, C. E. *Human emotions.* New York: Plenum, 1977.

Izard, C. E. Differential emotions theory and the facial feedback hypothesis of emotion activation: Comments on Tourangeau and Ellsworth's "The role of facial response in the experience of emotion". *Journal of Personality and Social Psychology,* 1981, *40,* 350–354.

Jacobson, E. Electrical measurements of neuromuscular states during mental activities: III. Visual imagination and recollection. *American Journal of Physiology,* 1930, *95,* 694–702.

Kolers, P. A., & Smythe, W. E. Images, symbols, and skills. *Canadian Journal of Psychology,* 1979, *33,* 158–184.

Kosslyn, S. M. The medium and the message in mental imagery: A theory. *Psychological Review,* 1981, *88,* 46–66.

Kunst-Wilson, W. R., & Zajonc, R. B. Affective discrimination of stimuli that cannot be recognized. *Science,* 1980, *207,* 557–558.

Laird, J. D. Self-attribution of emotion: The effects of expressive behavior on the quality of emotional experience. *Journal of Personality and Social Psychology,* 1974, *29,* 475–486.

Lanzetta, J., Cartwright-Smith, J., & Kleck, R. Effects on nonverbal dissimulation on emotional experiences and autonomic arousal. *Journal of Personality and Social Psychology,* 1976, *33,* 354–370.

Lazarus, R. S. *Psychological stress and the coping process.* New York: McGraw-Hill, 1966.

Lazarus, R. S., Kanner, A. D., & Folkman, S. Emotions: A cognitive-phenomenological analysis.

In R. Plutchik & H. Kellerman (Eds.), *Emotion: Theory, research, and experience*. New York: Academic Press, 1980.

McGuigan, F. J. Imagery and thinking: Covert functioning of the motor system. In G. E. Schwartz & D. Shapiro (Eds.), *Consciousness and self-regulation*, Volume 2. New York: Plenum Press, 1978.

Mandler, G. *Mind and emotion*. New York: Wiley, 1975.

Matlin, M. W. Response competition, recognition, and affect. *Journal of Personality and Social Psychology*, 1971, *19*, 295–300.

Moreland, R. L., & Zajonc, R. B. Is stimulus recognition a necessary condition for the occurrence of exposure effects? *Journal of Personality and Social Psychology*, 1977, *35*, 191–199.

Moreland, R. L., & Zajonc, R. B. Exposure effects may not depend on stimulus recognition. *Journal of Personality and Social Psychology*, 1979, *37*, 1085–1089.

Paivio, A. Images, propositions, and knowledge. In J. M. Nichols (Ed.), *Images, perception, and knowledge. The Western Ontario series in philosophy of science* (No. 8). Dordrecht, The Netherlands: Reidel, 1978.

Piaget, J. *The construction of reality in the child*. New York: Basic Books, 1954.

Plutchik, R., & Kellerman, H. (Eds.). *Emotion: Theory, research, and experience*. New York: Academic Press, 1980.

Pylyshyn. Z. W. The imagery debate: Analogue media versus tacit knowledge. *Psychological Review*, 1981, *88*, 16–45.

Sanford, R. H. The effects of abstinence from food upon imaginal processes: A preliminary experiment. *Journal of Psychology*, 1936, *2*, 129–36.

Sanford, R. H. The effects of abstinence from food upon imaginal processes: a further experiment. *Journal of Psychology*, 1937, *3*, 145–159.

Schachter, S., & Singer, J. Cognitive, social, and physiological determinants of emotional state. *Psychological Review*, 1962, *65*, 379–399.

Smith, M. O. History of the motor theories of attention. *Journal of General Psychology*, 1969, *80*, 243–257.

Sokolov, A. N. *Inner speech and thought*. New York: Plenum, 1972.

Tomkins, S. S. Affect as amplification: Some modifications in theory. In R. Plutchik & H. Kellerman (Eds.), *Emotion: Theory, research, and experience*. New York: Academic Press, 1980.

Tomkins, S. S. The role of facial response in the experience of emotion: A reply to Tourangeau and Ellsworth. *Journal of Personality and Social psychology*, 1981, *40*, 355–357.

Tourangeau, R., & Ellsworth, P. The role of facial response i.. the experience of emotion. *Journal of Personality and Social Psychology*, 1979, *37*, 1519–1531.

Wilson, W. R. Feeling more than we can know: Exposure effects without learning. *Journal of Personality and Social Psychology*, 1979, *37*, 811–821.

Zajonc, R. B. Attitudinal effects of mere exposure. *Journal of Personality and Social Psychology Monographs*, 1968, *9*(2, Part 2), 1–28.

Zajonc, R. B. Feeling and thinking: Preferences need no inferences. *American Psychologist*, 1980, *35*, 151–175.

11 Thoughts on the Relations Between Emotion and Cognition*

Richard S. Lazarus
University of California, Berkeley

Recent years have seen a major change in the way psychologists view emotion—the rediscovery that emotions are products of cognitive processes. The emotional response is elicited by an evaluative perception in lower animals, and in humans by a complex cognitive appraisal of the significance of events for one's well-being.

Although there are many other issues concerning the relations between emotion and cognition, my comments will focus on the role of thought in the emotional response. I will refer often to Zajonc's (1980) challenge to the assumption that cognition occurs prior to emotion. I use his views to illustrate widespread misunderstandings of what it means to speak of cognition as a causal antecedent of emotion; I also use his views as a point of departure for my argument that cognitive activity is a *necessary* as well as sufficient condition of emotion.

DO EMOTIONS REQUIRE COGNITIVE MEDIATION?

My own position on this question is a variant of a family of theories of emotion centered on the concept of cognitive appraisal. Campos and Sternberg (1981) state, for example, that "The recent history of the study of emotion has been dominated by approaches stressing cognitive factors. In theories of adult emotional response, cognitive appraisal now functions as the central construct" (p. 273). Its role is to mediate the relationship between the person and the environ-

---

ment. The appraisal process gives rise to a particular emotion with greater or lesser intensity depending on how the relationship is evaluated with respect to the person's well-being. Cognitive appraisal means that the way one interprets one's plight at any given moment is crucial to the emotional response.

Cognition and emotion are usually fused in nature (Folkman, Schaefer, & Lazarus, 1979), although they can be dissociated in certain unusual or abnormal states. For example, cognitive coping processes (cf. Lazarus, 1981) such as isolation and intellectualization (or detachment), which are aimed at regulating feelings, can create a dissociation between thoughts and feelings. Moreover, attack can occur without anger, and avoidance without fear. These latter conditions are also instances in which the usual link between thought and feeling has been loosened or broken. Yet such separations are less often a rule of living and more often a product of coping under special circumstances. The full experience of emotion (as opposed to sham rage, for example) normally includes three fused components: thoughts, action impulses, and somatic disturbances. When these components are dissociated we are left with something other than what we mean by a true emotional state. Our theories of emotion must reflect the normal fusion, and separating thoughts, action impulses, and somatic disturbances except under certain specifiable conditions (as was done in the old days of faculty psychology—which treated cognition, emotion, and motivation as independent entities) distorts rather than clarifies the structure of the mind (cf. Lazarus, Coyne, & Folkman, 1982).

One bit of fallout from the above analysis is the implication, often derived from statements of cognitive theory. that cognitive appraisal is a necessary as well as sufficient condition of emotion. Such a position has been criticized trenchantly by Zajonc (1980). He writes that affect is erroneously regarded in contemporary psychological theory as postcognitive, occurring only after extensive cognitive operations have taken place, and that in actuality affective judgments are fairly independent of, and even precede, the perceptual and cognitive activities on which they are said to depend. Zajonc argues that not only can affect occur without extensive perceptual and cognitive encoding—and even before—but that affect and cognition are controlled by separate and partially independent neural systems (see also Tomkins, 1981). Zajonc thus seems to be saying two things contrary to what I have argued: first, that the proposed directionality in which cognition determines affect is wrong and that the actual direction is affect to cognition; and second, that cognition and affect should be regarded as relatively independent subsystems rather than as fused and highly interdependent.

Building his argument. Zajonc cites a stanza of poetry from e. e. cummings (1973):

since feeling is first
who pays any attention
to the syntax of things
will never wholly kiss you. (p. 160)

He also cites Wundt's (1907) concept of affective primacy, and Bartlett (1932), Ittelson (1973), Osgood (1962), and Premack (1976) as having adopted the view that feelings come first. He states, for example:

> In fact, it is entirely possible that the very first stage of the organism's reaction to stimuli and the very first elements in retrieval are affective. It is further possible that we can like something or be afraid of it before we know precisely what it is and perhaps even *without* knowing what it is [p. 154].

The most serious mistake in Zajonc's analysis lies in his approach to cognition, which is characteristic of much of present-day cognitive psychology. In this approach information and meaning stem from the conception of mind as an analogue to a computer (Shannon & Weaver, 1962), a view illustrated also by the work of Newell and Simon (1961) and Weiner (1960). This conception has been rebutted by Dreyfus (1972), Polanyi (1958, 1966), and others, although the rebuttal has not affected the mainstream of cognitive psychology. The mainstream stance is that meanings for decision and action are built up from essentially meaningless stimulus display elements or bits and that systematic scanning of this display generates information. Thus, human cognition, like the operations of a computer, proceeds by serially receiving, registering, encoding, storing for the short- or long-run, and retrieving meaningless bits—a transformation to meaning that is called ''information processing.'' Meanings and their associated emotions, or hot cognitions as Abelson (1963) referred to them, are built through such processing. As Erdelyi (1974) and others (e.g., Neisser, 1967) have suggested, however, emotion can influence the process at any of its stages. With this in mind, it is not surprising that Zajonc might be troubled by the inplication that emotion lies at the end of a tortuous cognitive chain of information processing, and therefore find it necessary to suggest an independent system making possible rapid, nonreflective emotional reactions.

As many have argued (Folkman et al., 1979; Wrubel, Benner, & Lazarus, 1981), humans are meaning-oriented, meaning-creating creatures who constantly evaluate events from the perspective of their well-being and react emotionally to some of these evaluations. Zajonc is therefore correct in asserting that meanings are immediately inherent in emotionally laden transactions without lengthy or sequential processing, but for the wrong reasons. In my view, the concept of meaning defined by the traditional information processing approach subscribed to by Zajonc has a perfectly reasonable—and better—alternative.

We do not always have to await revelation from information processing to unravel the environmental code. As was argued in the New Look movement in perception, personal factors such as beliefs, expectations, and motives or commitments influence attention and appraisal at the very outset of any encounter. Concern with individual differences leads inevitably to concern with personal meanings and to the factors that shape such meanings. We actively select and shape experience and in some degree mold it to our own requirements (see also

Rychlak, 1981). Information processing as an exclusive model of cognition is insufficiently concerned with the person as a source of meaning.

The history of debate about the phenomenon of subception is instructive (see Eriksen, 1956, 1960, 1962; Lazarus, 1956; Lazarus & McCleary, 1951). In a controversial experiment, McCleary and I showed that by associating a set of nonsense syllables to the threat of a painful electric shock, subjects would later react with a galvanic skin response selectively to the shock-associated syllables, even when they had misperceived and misreported them. We referred to this phenomenon as "autonomic discrimination without awareness," or "subception," arguing that subjects somehow sensed the threat without consciously recognizing the syllables.

The debate sparked by this interpretation touched on many complex issues, but it mainly centered on a claim by Bricker and Chapanis (1953) and Eriksen (1956, 1960, 1962) that even though the subjects had misreported what had been flashed on the screen, they probably had registered perceptually some of the structural elements of the syllables and had, in effect, reacted automatically (emotionally) to "partial cues" of threat.

My response (Lazarus, 1956) was that it was reasonable to assume that perceptions are often global or spherical rather than built sequentially from structural elements and that emotionally relevant meanings (connotations) could be triggered by inputs whose full-fledged denotations had not yet been achieved. An anecdotal example might be that when people misperceive the word *cigarette,* they do not necessarily report a structural equivalent such as *pencil,* but a meaning equivalent such as *smoke* (cf. Werner, 1948). All this accords nicely with Zajonc's insistence that emotional or affective meaning comes early, even before one knows what the object or event is. However, I reject the assumption that this early presence means that it is detached from or independent of cognitive appraisal.

If one accepts the principle that meaning lies at the end of a seriatim cognitive processing, then accommodating the fact that we can react emotionally instantly, that is, at the onset of a transaction, forces us to abandon the idea that emotion and cognition are necessarily connected causally and to adopt the position that emotion and cognition are separate psychological systems. This is exactly what Zajonc does.

However, we do not have to have complete information to react emotionally to meaning. We can react to incomplete information, which in fact we do in most ordinary transactions. The meaning derived from incomplete information can, of course, be vague; we need to allow for this type of meaning as well as for clearly articulated and thoroughly processed meaning.

Zajonc actually appears ambivalent about the cognitive involvement in emotion, as displayed in the many qualifying phrases he uses in speaking of affect or feeling. In the abstract of his article, for example, he writes that "affective judgments may be *fairly* independent . . . of perceptual and cognitive operations commonly assumed to be the basis of these affective judgments. . . . Affective reactions can occur without *extensive* perceptual and cognitive encoding [p. 151, emphasis added]," and he refers to "affective judgments [p. 157]," implying that cognitive judgment is indeed involved in emotion.

Addressing some of Zajonc's statements from my perspective highlights the difference in our views. For example, he writes, "in fact, it is entirely possible that the very first stage of the organism's reaction to stimuli and the very first elements of retrieval are affective [p. 154]." This is acceptable if one adds that this is so only because evaluation or cognitive appraisal also begins at the start. In this connection it is noteworthy that earlier on the same page, Zajonc states, "In nearly all cases, however, feeling is not free of thought, nor is thought free of feelings." With this I agree wholeheartedly. Later Zajonc writes that for most human decisions

it is very difficult to demonstrate that there have actually been *any* prior cognitive processes whatsoever. One might argue that these are cases in which one alternative so overwhelmingly dominates all the others that only a *minimum* of cognitive participation is required and that is why the cognitive involvement preceding such decisions is so hard to detect. (p. 155, second emphasis added)

Where, then, are we left with respect to the question of whether cognitive mediation is a necessary condition for emotion? By and large cognitive appraisal (of meaning or significance) underlies and is an integral feature of all emotional states. Are there any exceptions? I think not, and I underscore qualifications by Zajonc such as "minimum cognitive participation" to reflect that emotion or feeling is never toally independent of cognition, even when the emotional response is instantaneous and nonreflective, as emphasized in Arnold's (1960) use of term *appraisal*. This is the real import of the expression "hot cognition." The thought and feelings are simultaneous. The only doubts I have are in the arena of phylogenetically based triggers or releasers of fear in humans such as those postulated by Hebb (1946). Perhaps humans are "instinctually" wired to react with fear to spiders, snakes, or strangeness. However, many of these tendencies (such as the sucking reflex) seem to disappear or at least go underground with an ontogenetic shift to higher mental processes, just as they seem to disappear or go underground with the phylogenetic accretions of the neocortex that only suppress or regulate but do not banish lower functions.

For all intents and purposes, therefore, meaning (in the sense of significance for well-being), whether primitive or advanced, is always an essential component of such reactions. Such meaning exists not merely in the environmental display, but inheres in the cognitive structures and commitments developed over a lifetime that determine the personal and hence emotional significance of any person-environment encounter.

SOME WIDESPREAD CONFUSIONS ABOUT
COGNITION

In his discussion of cognitive activity in emotion, Zajonc errs in his understanding of cognitive appraisal, displaying a confusion that is widespread and had
been dealt with much earlier in my original treatment of appraisal (Lazarus,
1966). The cognitive activity in appraisal does not imply anything about deliberate reflection, rationality, or awareness. Nevertheless, Zajonc (1980) writes:

> The rabbit cannot stop to contemplate the length of the snake's fangs or the
> geometry of its markings. If the rabbit is to escape, the action must be undertaken
> long before the completion of even a simple cognitive process—before, in fact, the
> rabbit has fully established and verified that a nearby movement might reveal a
> snake in all its coiled glory. The decision to run must be made on the basis of
> *minimal cognitive engagement*. (p. 156, emphasis added)

This would obviously have to be correct. It must be remembered, however,
that as a result of its neural inheritance and experience the rabbit already has
cognitive schemata that signify danger instantly at the sound of a slight rustle in
the grass or the sight of a dimly perceived shape. Although the schemata required
in human social affairs are apt to be far more complex and symbolic, the appraisal of danger does not have to be *deliberate*.

*Zajonc, like many others, also seems to erroneously equate cognition with
rationality.* He writes, for example:

> Unlike judgments of objective stimulus properties, affective reactions that often
> accompany these judgments cannot always be voluntarily controlled. Most often,
> these experiences occur whether one wants them to or not. One might be able to
> control the expression of emotion but not the experience of it itself. It is for this
> very reason that law, science, sports, education, and other institutions of society
> keep devising ever new means of making judgments ''objective.'' We wish some
> decisions to be more independent of these virtually inescapable reactions. [p. 156]

Such a statement implies that cognition is rational whereas feeling is irrational
and primitive, a view that goes back to classical Greek times and that was also
emphasized by the Catholic Church during the Middle Ages. Even today most
psychologists treat emotions as primitive, midbrain phenomena, whereas reason
is seen to reflect human phylogenetic superiority and as vulnerable to being
overwhelmed by the primitivizing effects of passion (see Averill, 1974). One of
the most influential of the cognitive behavior therapists, Ellis (1962), has argued
in accord with this centuries-old tradition that faulty belief premises underlie
psychopathology, creating distressing emotional states when the person reacts to
situations on the basis of such premises. The treatment is designed to help the
person give up the faulty beliefs so that he or she can operate more effectively

and with less misery. However, in my view even positively toned, healthy emotions such as joy, peacefulness, love, and certainly many human commitments which sustain morale, rest on shared or private illusions (Lazarus, 1983) and depend on beliefs whose accuracy is often irrelevant to the elicitation of the emotion. The point is that cognition cannot be equated with rationality. The cognitive appraisals that shape our emotional reactions can distort reality as well as reflect it realistically.

Finally, cognitive appraisal does not necessarily imply *awareness* of the factors in any encounter on which it rests. In this connection Zajonc writes about two different forms of unconscious processes: "One emerges where behavior, such as that occurring in discrimination among stimuli, is entirely under the influence of affective factors without the participation of cognitive processes [p. 172]." In this he includes perceptual defense and subliminal perceptions. The other form of unconscious process "is implicated in highly overlearned, and thus automatized, sequences of information processing; this form includes cognitive acts but has collapsed them into large molar chunks that may conceal their original component links [p. 172]." Zajonc assumes that the former type of unconscious process involves no cognitive activity (as in Freud's "primary-process" thinking); the latter is a primitive, automatized process without significant cognitive activity or reality testing. I would certainly agree that a person need not be aware of his or her cognitive appraisals and may utilize primitive logic, but I would argue against the idea that some appraisals (Zajonc refers to preferences) are noncognitive.

SOME FURTHER ISSUES ABOUT HOW EMOTION IS GENERATED

There are a number of phylogenetic and ontogenetic implications of this cognitive emphasis. For example, those who are less sanguine than I about the causal role of cognition in emotion often point to the startle response, since cognition is obviously absent or negligible in this reaction. I do not consider startle an emotion. Emotion results from an evaluative perception of a relationship (actual, imagined, or anticipated) between a person (or animal) and the environment. Startle is best regarded as a primitive neural reflex process. It signals that something has happened, and although it could precipitate a "true" emotional response, it is in itself merely a physiological response to an unanticipated change in stimulation, perhaps analogous to an eye blink in response to a sudden burst of light.

On the other hand, I am also convinced that some emotions depend more on cognitive activity, particularly of the symbolic sort, than others. For example, cognitive activity is apt to be more modest with respect to symbolic representation in fright than in anxiety. As Averill and I (Lazarus & Averill, 1972) have argued, anxiety always involves symbolic threats (probably to the self), is anticipatory, and occurs under conditions of ambiguity, whereas fright is immediate, concrete, and concerns survival-related dangers.

From this standpoint, then, in comparatively simple creatures there should be little symbolic representation in the appraisal process, although no living creature could survive unless it were able to distinguish harmful from nonharmful events. Perhaps the concept of releaser (i.e., a physical pattern that matches a neural engram and sets off an emotional escape or attack reaction) is now considered simplistic. However, the basis idea seems sound that in more primitive creatures there is greater dependence on rigid, built-in processes, whereas in higher creatures such as humans there is much more variability and dependence on learning and symbolic processes.

Probably all mammals meet the minimal cognitive requirements of emotion if one permits the concept of appraisal to include the type of process described by ethologists in which a fairly rigid, built-in response to stimulus arrays differentiates danger from no-danger. An evaluative perception, hence appraisal, can operate at all levels of complexity, from the most primitive and inborn to the most symbolic and experience-based. If this is reasonable, then it is also possible to say that cognitive appraisal is *always* involved in emotion, even in creatures phylogenetically far more primitive than humans.

A corollary of the above is that the child's capacity to experience particular emotional reactions depends on the development of an understanding of the social context and its significance. Complex and more symbolically based emotional reactions, such as indignation and guilt, probably emerge later in ontogenesis than more simple types of emotion such as anger and fear, although even anger and fear in humans can have highly complex and symbolic social and psychological determinants. The capacity for emotional richness seems similar in the very young child and the more primitive mammal. However, the capacities diverge as the human child acquires symbolic modes of thought and knowledge; the child's cognitive processes and social circumstances extend its capacity for emotional richness far beyond that of other mammals. By implication, particular emotions will enter into the child's repertoire only after the child has come to master their particular cognitive prerequisites.

From a cognitive perspective, we can also ask whether it is possible to speak meaningfully about universals in the generation of an emotional state. Across species the basic neurochemical makeup of animals is quite similar, especially if we take as our starting point MacLean's (1949, 1975) reptilian and mammalian brain, two of three systems of the "triune" brain that also includes the human cerebral cortex. These similarities provide a neural template that makes emotion in all species similar in some fundamental ways.

Of even greater interest to those who emphasize a social and cognitive perspective are the similarities and variations within the human species in the processes underlying the elicitation of an emotion. Here too, although people share some biological and social agendas, social and personal meanings vary and take on great importance. As Hochschild (1979) points out, every society has "feeling rules"—prescriptions and proscriptions about how people should feel and act in diverse social contexts. The society, then, provides a kind of template (see also Kemper, 1978) of human relationships and meanings on which the appraisal of the significance of an encounter for one's well-being depends. These shape not only impression management but how we actually feel. Further, within a species and within a society, commitment patterns and beliefs vary from individual to individual and group to group. Therefore, whatever their origins, there are both common and distinct agendas that shape appraisals of the significance of a particular transaction with the environment for the well-being of any given individual.

If, as I do, one regards emotion as a result of an anticipated, experienced, or imagined outcome of an adaptationally relevant transaction between organism and environment, cognitive processes are always crucial in the elicitation of an emotion. This idea has long been resisted by those disciplines most concerned with emotion as a feature of biological adaptation, perhaps because the concept of appraisal appears to emphasize individual differences and thereby requires complex, even individualized, rules about the determinants of appraisal. However, the search for such rules about how emotion is shaped by cognition in no way threatens the basic premises of the evolutionary-adaptational perspective that has long dominated the biological and social sciences. There is nothing in this perspective that requires reduction of all emotion to the lowest common denominator of comparatively simple animals and reptilian or mammalian brain structures. When such reduction occurs, it is at the expense of recognizing and investigating the primary role of cognition in emotion. It is about time we began to formulate rules about how cognitive processes generate, influence, and shape the emotional response in every species that reacts with emotion, in every social group sharing values, commitments, and beliefs, and in every individual member of the human species.

ACKNOWLEDGMENT

This contribution grew out of the discussions of the conference upon which this volume is based. It was first published in the *American Psychologist*, 1982, *37*, 1019–1024. © The American Psychological Association. Reprinted by permission.

I wish to thank my research colleague, Susan Folkman, and my secretary, Carol Carr, for providing substantial editorial advice on this article. I appreciate their skill and judgment.

REFERENCES

Abelson, R. P. Computer simulation of "hot cognitions." In S. Tomkins & S. Messick (Eds.), *Computer simulation of personality*. New York: Wiley, 1963.

Arnold, M. B. *Emotion and personality.* New York: Columbia University Press, 1960.

Averill, J. R. An analysis of psychophysiological symbolism and its influence on theories of emotion. *Journal for the Theory of Social Behavior,* 1974, *4,* 147–190.

Bartlett, F. C. *Remembering: A study of experimental and social psychology.* Cambridge, England: Cambridge University Press, 1932.

Bricker, P. D., & Chapanis, A. Do incorrectly perceived tachistoscopically presented stimuli convey some information? *Psychological Review,* 1953, *60,* 181–188.

Campos, J. J., & Sternberg, C. R. Perception, appraisal and emotion: The onset of social referencing. In M. Lamb & L. Sherrod (Eds.), *Infant social cognition.* Hillsdale, N.J.: Lawrence Erlbaum Associates, 1981.

cummings, e. e. *Complete poems* (Vol. 1). Bristol, England: McGibbon & Kee, 1973.

Dreyfus, H. L. *What computers can't do: A critique of artificial reason.* New York: Harper & Row, 1972.

Ellis, A. *Reason and emotion in psychotherapy.* New York: Lyle Stuart, 1962.

Erdelyi, M. H. A new look at the new look: Perceptual defence and vigilance. *Psychological Review,* 1974, *81,* 1–25.

Eriksen, C. W. Subception: Fact or artifact? *Psychological Review,* 1956, *63,* 74–80.

Eriksen, C. W. Discrimination and learning without awareness: A methodological survey and evaluation. *Psychological Review,* i960, *67,* 379–400.

Eriksen, C. W. Figments, fantasies, and follies: A search for the subconscious mind. In C. W. Eriksen (Ed.), *Behavior and awareness: A symposium of research and interpretation.* Durham, N. C.: Duke University Press, 1962.

Folkman, S., Schaefer, C., & Lazarus, R. S. Cognitive processes as mediators of stress and coping. In V. Hamilton & D. M. Warburton (Eds.), *Human stress and cognition: An information-processing approach.* London: Wiley, 1979.

Hebb, D. O. On the nature of fear. *Psychological Review,* 1946, *53,* 259–276.

Hochschild, A. R. Emotion work, feeling rules, and social structure. *American Journal of Sociology,* 1979, *85,* 551–575.

Ittelson, W. H. Environment perception and contemporary perceptual theory. In W. H. Ittelson (Ed.), *Environment and cognition.* New York: Seminar Press, 1973.

Kemper, T. *A social interaction theory of emotions.* New York: Wiley, 1978.

Lazarus, R. S. Subception: Fact or artifact? A reply to Eriksen. *Psychological Review,* 1956, *63,* 343–347.

Lazarus. R. S. *Psychological stress and the coping process.* New York: McGraw-Hill, 1966.

Lazarus, R. S. The stress and coping paradigm. In C. Eisdorfer, D. Cohen, A. Kleinman, & P. Maxim (Eds.), *Models for clinical psychopathology.* New York: Spectrum, 1981.

Lazarus, R. S. The costs and benefits of denial. In S. Breznitz (Ed.), *Denial of stress.* New York: International Universities Press, 1983.

Lazarus, R. S., & Averill, J. R. Emotion and cognition: With special reference to anxiety. In C. D. Spielberger (Ed.), *Anxiety: Current trends in theory and research* (Vol. 2). New York: Academic Press, 1972.

Lazarus, R. S., Coyne, J. C., & Folkman, S. Cognition, emotion and motivation: The doctoring of Humpty-Dumpty. In R. W. J. Neufeld (Ed.), *Psychological stress and psychopathology.* New York: McGraw-Hill, 1982.

Lazarus, R. S., & McCleary, R. A. Autonomic discrimination without awareness: A study of subception. *Psychological Review,* 1951, *58,* 113–122.

MacLean, P. D. Psychosomatic disease and the "visceral brain": Recent developments bearing on the Papez theory of emotion. *Psychosomatic Medicine,* 1949, *11,* 338–353.

MacLean, P. D. Sensory and perceptive factors in emotional functions of the triune brain. In L. Levi (Ed.), *Emotions: Their parameters and measurement.* New York: Raven, 1975.

Neisser, U. *Cognitive psychology.* New York: Appleton-Century-Crofts, 1967.

Newell, A., & Simon, H. A. Computer simulation of human thinking. *Science,* 1961, *34,* 2011–2016.

Osgood, C. E. Studies on the generality of affective meaning systems. *American Psychologist,* 1962, *17,* 10–28.

Polanyi, M. *Personal knowledge.* Chicago, Ill.: University of Chicago Press, 1958.

Polanyi, M. *The tacit dimension.* Garden City, N.Y.: Doubleday, 1966.

Premack, D. *Intelligence in ape and man.* Hillsdale, N.J.: Lawrence Erlbaum Associates, 1976.

Rychlak, J. F. Logical learning theory: Propositions, corollaries, and research evidence. *Journal of Personality and Social Psychology,* 1981, *40,* 731–749.

Shannon, C. E., & Weaver, W. (Eds.). *The mathematical theory of communication.* Urbana: University of Illinois Press, 1962.

Tomkins, S. S. The quest for primary motives. Biography and autobiography of an idea. *Journal of Personality and Social Psychology,* 1981, *41,* 306–329.

Weiner, N. The brain and the machine. In S. Hook (Ed.), *Dimensions of mind: A symposium.* New York: NYU Press, 1960.

Werner, H. *Comparative psychology of mental development* (Rev. ed.), Chicago: Follett, 1948.

Wrubel, J., Benner, P., & Lazarus, R. S. Social competence from the perspective of stress and coping. In J. Wine & M. Smye (Eds.), *Social competence.* New York: Guilford, 1981.

Wundt, W. *Outlines of psychology.* Leipzig: Englemann, 1907.

Zajonc, R. B. Feeling and thinking: Preferences need no inferences. *American Psychologist,* 1980, *35,* 151–175.

12 On Primacy of Affect

R. B. Zajonc
The University of Michigan

Only a few years ago I published a rather speculative paper entitled "Feeling and thinking" (Zajonc, 1980). The title also included the provocative postcolon suffix "Preferences need no inferences," deliberately suggesting an occasional independence of emotion from cognition. In this paper, I tried to make an appeal for a more concentrated study of affective phenomena which have been ignored for decades, and at the same time to ease the heavy reliance on cognitive functions for the explanation of affect. The argument began with the general hypothesis that affect and cognition are separate and partially independent systems and that although they ordinarily function conjointly, affect could be generated without a prior cognitive process. It could, therefore, at times precede cognition in a behavioral chain. I based this proposition on a number of diverse findings and phenomena, none of which alone could clinch the argument, but all of them taken together pointed to a clear possibility of an affective independence and primacy, first advanced by Wundt (1907) and later reiterated by others (e.g., Izard, in press). Lazarus (1982) takes a very strong issue with all of this, and almost categorically rejects the likelihood of the independence of affect of cognition, let alone the possibility of an affective primacy. In this paper, I review Lazarus' position and contrast it with mine.

Lazarus employs in his argument two definitions—one for emotion and one for cognition. All of his inferences are based on these two definitions. Central to Lazarus' position is his definition of emotion for which he requires cognition as a necessary precondition. On the basis of this definition alone, therefore, the argument is unassailable. If Lazarus insists on his definition, and he has all the right to so insist, we must agree with him that indeed affect cannot be independent of cognition because *by definition* cognition is a necessary pre-condition for affective arousal.

Because, for Lazarus, cognition is an ever-present prior element of affect and since the presence of cognitive functions cannot always be documented, a rather special definition of cognition is required. Thus, Lazarus' definition of cognition and of cognitive appraisal also include forms of cognitive appraisal that cannot be observed, verified, or documented. Because the emotional reaction is *defined* as requiring cognitive appraisal as a crucial pre-condition, it must be present whether we have evidence of it or not. If cognitive appraisal of a given emotional excitation cannot be documented then, according to the definition, it must have nevertheless taken place, albeit at an unconscious level or in the form of most primitive sensory registration. Therefore, Lazarus' proposition cannot be falsified.

Perhaps because the argument is circular, more need not be said. However, there are important reasons to say more. Whether or not cognitive appraisal is always necessary for emotion should not be settled by definitions alone. Empirical facts should contribute to the formulation of these definition and if we wish to understand how cognition and emotion interact, it is important to know what is true. Assuming that cognitive appraisal is always a necessary precondition of emotion, preempts research on the matter. It is my preference to leave the question of cognitive appraisal open for empirical research, postponing the task of precise and extensive definitions of both processes until we know more about them. Solving problems by definition is not an incentive for further study. It is a useful temporizing maneuver that allows us to proceed with our work for a while, pretending that one aspect of our problem had already been solved. But we can pretend just so long. At some point of theoretical development, we must look to the empirical side of the problem and confront each element of our definition with empirical reality and theoretical consistency. This point of theoretical development has now been reached, I believe. Of course, the question that is contested here cannot be *fully* resolved unless we have a full understanding of consciousness. Such an understanding is at the moment beyond our reach. But we have learned just about enough about cognition and emotion to move beyond definitional disputes. There are sufficient number of conflicting results which I pointed out in my paper (Zajonc, 1980), and a sufficient number of suggestive experimental results that need to be integrated. Questions about the independence and primacy of affect can now be seriously asked at the empirical level. I offered the notion of affective independence and primacy as an hypothesis to be empirically verified—not as a definition to be disputed. Above all, however, defining affect as heavily dependent on cognition, should make it rather clumsy to study the interaction of cognition and emotion, and especially those forms of emotion where the latter influences cognition (in such phenomena, for example, as phobia and prejudice).

"WIDESPREAD MISUNDERSTANDING"

Lazarus (this volume) bemoans a "widespread misunderstandings of what it means to speak of cognition as a causal antecedent of emotion." (p. 247). According to Lazarus, "Cognitive appraisal means that the way one interprets one's plight . . . is crucial to the emotional response." (p. 247). But "cognitive appraisal" need not be a deliberate, rational, or conscious process. (p. 253). We "do not have to have complete information to react emotionally to meaning." (p. 250). Perceptions that are "global or spherical" (p. 250) will suffice. In this respect, however, Lazarus mistakenly assumes that I equated intention, rationality, and awareness, with cognition *in general,* or with cognitive appraisal *in particular.* This is not so. I selected some examples in which deliberate, rational, or conscious processes could be shown to be clearly unnecessary for the generation of affect. I selected these examples on purpose. If we could agree that *these* forms of cognition are not necessary for an emotional arousal, then part of our problem had been solved. Now we only need to determine whether the forms of cognition that are hidden from the cognizer are necessary antecedents of emotion. What remains to be analyzed is the requirement for an unconscious cognitive appraisal, because Lazarus and I agree that cognitive processes which are unintentional and irrational but conscious are unnecessary for emotional arousal. My definition of cognition (Zajonc, 1980, p. 154) required some form of transformation of a present or past sensory input. "Pure" sensory input untransformed according to a more or less fixed code, is not cognition. It is just "pure" sensation. Cognition need not be deliberate, rational, or conscious. But it must involve some minimum "mental work." This "mental work" may consist of operations upon sensory input that transform it into a form that may become subjectively available, or it may consist of the activation of items from memory.

The essence of the question that we are concerned with can be stated as follows. If there is a detectable emotional response but there is, at the same time, no detectable antecedent cognitive process, did such a cognitive process take place nevertheless, albeit at the unconscious level? Lazarus' (this volume) position is that it was there but we couldn't document it. "Are there any exceptions?" asks Lazarus (p. 251). "I think not," he answers himself.

Now, there are a host of theories, in and outside of psychology, that assume entities and processes that cannot be observed given current state of the art. However, these unobservable processes are postulated because otherwise the explanation of the phenomena under investigation would be impossible. Moreover, they are postulated only when they do not conflict with empirical evidence. Neither is true of emotions. Many emotional phenomena can be explained and have been explained without invoking cognitive processes of any kind (e.g., Izard, 1977; Tomkins, 1962). And conflict with empirical reality is in fact created if we assume a cognitive appraisal for every emotion. The facial feedback theory of emotion (Darwin, 1955; Izard, 1971; Tomkins, 1962), gaining increasing empirical support (Duncan & Laird, 1977; Laird, 1974; Laird, Wegener, Halal, & Szegda, 1982; Lanzetta & Orr, 1980; Rhodewalt & Comer, 1979; Zuckerman, Klorman, Larrance, & Speigel, 1981), requires no assumptions about prior cognitive appraisal, and appraisal of the kind Lazarus postulates would play havoc with the opponent process theory of affect (Solomon, 1980).

For Lazarus, "cognitive appraisal (of meaning or significance) underlies and is an integral feature of all emotional states [p. 251]." Thus, all three aspects of emotional reaction—bodily processes, overt behavioral expression, and subjective experience, need cognitive appraisal as a necessary precondition. This is not so, I believe, and I shall try to show why not.

EMPIRICAL BASIS OF AFFECTIVE PRIMACY

There are various phenomena that cannot be ignored when one questions the independence of affect from cognition. At the moment, the best single explanation for these phenomena is the assumption that affect can be aroused *without* the participation of cognitive processes and that it may, therefore, function independently for those circumstances; provided we mean by "cognition" something more than pure sensory input. I have reviewed some of this evidence elsewhere (Zajonc, 1980; Zajonc, Pietromonaco, & Bargh, 1982). However, it did not impress Lazarus. I briefly summarize these findings and phenomena—some of them not mentioned in my previous paper (Zajonc, 1980)—that need a comment from those theoreticians who assume all of affect to be always postcognitive and always depending on appraisal.

1. Affective reactions show phylogenetic and ontogenetic primacy. Izard (in press) reviewed the evidence on ontogenetic primacy of emotion and the picture that emerges from his extensive examination of the literature is quite convincing. Thus, if emotion precedes cognition at some level of the individual's development, then at that level of development no cognitive appraisal is necessary (or even possible) for the arousal of an affective reaction. Note that in the *Feeling and Thinking* paper I hypothesized the *independence* of affect *of* cognition (see Zajonc, 1980). At the formal level, therefore, affect could be simultaneous or secondary and still independent of cognition. This hypothesis requires no demonstration that affect is primary. Nor must affect be *always* primary. If evidence can be uncovered about the primacy of affect in only one situation, the independence hypothesis would be confirmed.

2. Separate neuroanatomical structures can be identified for affect and cognition. Izard (in press) writes, for example:

The case for considering emotions as a separate system seems fairly well established at the neurophysiological-biochemical level. At this level it is well known that some brain structures, neural pathways, and neurotransmitters are relatively more involved than others with emotion expression, emotion experience or feelings, and emotion-related behaviors. The limbic system is sometimes referred to as the "emotional brain," and the fact that at least one limbic structure, the hippocampus, has been strongly implicated in information processing (Simonov, 1972) and memory (O'Keefe & Nadel, 1979) suggests that there are brain mechanisms specially adapted for mediating emotion-cognition interactions.

(a) Emotional reactions are likely to be under the control of the right brain hemisphere, while cognitive processes are predominantly the business of the left hemisphere (Cacioppo & Petty, 1981; Schwartz, Davidson, & Maer, 1975; Suberi & McKeever, 1977). This evidence is not strong, but it is very suggestive. In a recent review of work on lateralization, Tucker (1981) concluded that the two hemispheres do participate differentially in cognitive functions and in emotion, and that cognitive activity would not be possible without the independent neurophysiological processes that give rise to emotion.

(b) Emotional features of speech are apparently controlled by the right hemisphere, while semantic and lexical aspects are on the left. Ross and Mesulam (1977) found a number of patients with lesions in the right hemisphere, directly across from Broca's area. All these patients produced intelligible speech, but it was speech that was totally devoid of emotional inflections and other affect-dependent prosodic parameters.

(c) A *direct* pathway from the retina to the hypothalamus has been demonstrated in a large number of species (Nauta & Haymaker, 1969). On the basis of an extensive review, Moore (1973) concluded that "a retinal projection to the suprachiasmatic nuclei is a regular feature of the mammalian visual system [p. 408]." Because the hypothalamus plays a central role in the arousal and expression of emotion, the retinohypothalamic tract allows the organism to generate an emotional reaction from a purely *sensory* input. No mediation by higher mental processes is apparently required. Thus, it is possible that rapidly changing light gradients, such as those that arise with looming objects, could generate fear reactions directly. Other studies show that direct aggression can be elicited by the electrical stimulation of the hypothalamus (Flynn, Edwards, & Bandler, 1971; Wasman & Flynn, 1962), and other efferent projections have been found issuing from the suprachiasmatic nuclei (Stephan, Berkley, & Moss, 1981). These findings would imply that pure sensory input—requiring no transformation into cognition—is capable of bringing about a full emotional response, involving visceral and motor activity, and there is no reason why subjective feeling could not follow as well. Required only is a specific form of activity at the retina—produced perhaps by a looming object or a rapidly changing illumination gradient. For many species, efficient stimuli exist that are capable of eliciting fixed action patterns by virtue of an automatic process that short-circuits even "global or spherical" perceptions. Extremely small changes in retinal excitation can produce these reactions (Goodale, 1982; Ingle, 1973). Newborn infants respond in this manner to a host of stimuli, and with over-learning all sorts of other stimuli may acquire the ability of eliciting emotional reactions automatically, short-circuiting cognitive appraisal that initially may have been a necessary part of the emotional reaction.

(d) Some olfactory and gustatory stimuli, when of sufficient amplitude, produce clear overt emotional reactions and they produce them immediately and directly (Steiner, 1974). And these response are universal across cultures and require no learning.

3. Appraisal and affect are often uncorrelated and disjoint.

(a) Affective judgments of persons are characterized by a primacy effect, whereas appraisal information is more likely to display recency effect (Anderson & Hubert, 1963; Posner & Snyder, 1975).

(b) Weights associated with trait adjectives that contribute to liking judgments of hypothetical individuals are uncorrelated with the recall of these adjectives (Dreben, Fiske, & Hastie, 1979).

(c) Multidimensional space for preferences cannot be decomposed to reveal descriptive dimensions. The dimensions generated by similarity judgments of an array of objects (e.g., hues, soft drinks) are independent of the dimensions generated by comparisons of preferences among these objects (Cooper, 1973; Nakashima, 1909; Premack & Kintsch, 1979).

(d) If cognitive appraisal is a necessary determinant of affect, then changing appraisal should result in a change in affect. This is most frequently not so, and persuasion is one of the weakest methods of attitude change (Petty & Cacioppo, 1981).

4. New affective reactions can be established without an apparent participation of appraisal.

(a) Taste aversion can be established even when the possible association between food (CS) and the delayed nauseous UCS is obliterated by anesthesia (Garcia & Rusiniak, 1980). The UCS is administered and takes its effect when the animal is unconscious. Therefore, the appraisal, if it takes place at all, must make a rather remote connection between the ingested food and the nausea that occurred during anesthesia (and has probably been only vaguely registered). It is highly unlikely that any sort of appraisal process, even unconscious, could have been involved when the animal rejected the CS food following conditioning.

(b) Lazarus and McCleary (1951) have found that subjects are able, without awareness, to make autonomic discriminations (GSR) among nonsense syllables. Lazarus insists that in their experiment *some* form of appraisal occurred prior to the emotional excitation, but there is no evidence that such was the case in fact.

The argument is simply that appraisal occurred because, by definition, it must have occurred (Lazarus, this volume, p. 251).

(c) Preferences for stimuli (tones, polygons) can be established by repeated exposures, degraded to prevent recognition (Kunst-Wilson & Zajonc, 1980; Takenishi, 1982; Wilson, 1979). Interestingly, Mandler (personal communication) reports that he was unable to obtain the above effects. Yet, Seamon and his colleagues replicated the results without difficulty (Seamon, Brody, & Kauff, 1983a, 1983b). In one of their first studies they demonstrated that the affective discrimination, obtained in the absence of recognition memory, was subject to lateralization effects. Thus, affective preferences were best for stimuli presented in the right visual field, and recognition memory was best for stimuli shown in the left visual field. A subsequent study (Seamon, Brody, & Kauff, 1983b) has shown that affective discriminations in the absence of recognition memory can be made by the subject even when the test follows the initial exposure by as long as one week.

(d) In blind tests, smokers are unable to identify the brand of cigarettes they customarily smoke, but when asked which cigarettes of those tasted they like best, they unknowingly point to their own brand (Littman & Manning, 1954).

5. Finally, there are affective states that can be induced by drugs, hormones, or electrical stimulation of the brain. An individual who is given valium, concealed in his food, will change his mood, whether he knows about it or not. He may have all sorts of explanations for this change. and it is possible, as Schachter and Singer (1962) have shown, that some qualities of the valium-induced state may be altered by cognitive input. But in the final analysis, at least some—very significant—aspects of the change in the emotional state will be caused directly by the valium, regardless of what information the subject is given and what appraisal he is offered afterwards.

FACTS OR DEFINITION

These are facts, not conjectures, and they have to be somehow explained. If we define affect as requiring cognitive appraisal as a necessary precondition, then we must discover for all the above findings and phenomena where and how cognition could possibly enter. Of all of these, Lazarus mentions only autonomic discrimination without awareness (Lazarus & McCleary, 1951). The effect is explained by assuming "that emotionally relevant meanings (connotations) could be triggered by inputs whose full-fledged denotations had not yet been achieved [p. 2|51]." This argument may be quite correct, and one is tempted to suppose that some cognitive work took place because we deal with lexical material. But we must not prejudge the case. Marcel (1980) and Fowler, Wolford, Slade, and Tassinary (1981) have demonstrated that semantic features of words are accessible earlier than perceptions of physical stimulus properties of words, and they are accessible under viewing conditions so impoverished that even simple detection is at a chance level.

Experiments that use semantic material presented at levels that do not allow the subject to identify the stimuli or even to detect them, may be questioned because we are tempted to assume that in some unknown ways, the meaning of the stimuli becomes accessible to the subject *prior* to his affective reaction. But affective reactions are established without awareness to such stimuli as food (Garcia & Rusiniak, 1980), tone sequences (Wilson, 1979), Japanese nonsense words (Takenishi, 1982), or geometric figures (Kunst-Wilson & Zajonc, 1980; Seamon, Brody, & Kauff, 1983a, 1983b). Especially intriguing are the Garcia-Rusiniak data just described because in their case the conditioned stimulus is presented at optimal level while the noxious UCS is given much later and under anesthesia. The fact that the animal subsequently avoids the food in question (CS) is significant because it suggests that all sorts of cognitive appraisal processes must have been circumvented. Perhaps, if the experiment were conducted with humans, when asked why they refused the food, some of the subjects might have said that they did not find it appetizing in the first place. But we could not tell whether these appraisals came *before* rejecting the food and they caused rejection, or whether they came *afterwards* as a justification.

Nowhere in Lazarus' (1982) paper is there any empirical evidence even suggestive of the fact that cognitive appraisal must precede affect. The argument is based entirely on definition, and as such it becomes circular when applied to the explanation of the kinds of results that I discussed here and previously. Given Lazarus' definitional stance, there is no empirical evidence that can be marshalled to show that appraisal is *not* necessary. There is always the possibility that some appraisal took place, even if there is no evidence that it did.

INDEPENDENCE OF AFFECT OF COGNITION

If cognition is not a necessary condition for emotion then there must be instances where affective reactions are primary in the course of behavior. What are they?

The individual is never *without* being in some emotional state. Emotional reactions may have chronic or phasic character (mood), tonic character, (e.g., jealousy), or acute character (e.g., surprise or mirth). The chronic state may be overlayed by the tonic arousal, and tonic state may be altered by an acute reaction. No emotional reactions occur in vacuum. They manifest themselves as changes in the emotional state characterizing the organism at the given time.

What are the first steps in the course of a change from one emotional state to another? Clearly, one of such conditions is cognitive activity. One may recall a sad event or be reminded of an impending unpleasant obligation. As a result, one's mood changes. But there are other reactions that cause the individual suddenly to change the focus of attention or to become generally alert. I have represented the course of such behavioral changes as having an early affective trigger (Zajonc, 1980, Fig. 5). What makes the frog shift attention from a lily pad to a snake is not the perception of the snake itself. What shifts the frog's attention is a particular form of change in the environment, perhaps a change in the light pattern caused by a movement of the lily pad that differs from the patterns of the previous few minutes. There may have been perhaps a minute change in the ripple patterns of the water, or in a reflection that was sensed peripherally. A sensorimotor program is activated, muscles tense, and there is readiness for flight. Emotional state changes radically as a result of this minimal sensory input that needs not be transformed into meaningful information. The neuroanatomical structures necessary for such a cognition-free reaction are available and the relevant motor processes are also available (Goodale, 1982; Ingle, 1973). The retinohypothalamic fibers that lead from the retina project to the suprachiasmatic nucleus, and can directly activate hypothalamic neurons (Moore, 1973). In turn there are all sorts of projections from the hypothalamus and from the suprachiasmatic nucleus (Stephan, Berkley, & Moss, 1981) that participate in such typical emotional reactions as recruitment of carbohydrate from the liver, transfer of blood from the abdomen to the heart, lungs, and limbs, piloerection, and at the behavioral level, retraction of the lips, exposure of canines, or freezing.

CONCLUSION

The question of affective primacy must be settled on empirical grounds. If one insists that cognitive appraisal is always a precondition to emotion, one is forced to allow cognition to be reduced to such minimal processes as the firing of the retinal cells. Thus, if we accept Lazarus' position, all distinctions between cognition, perception, and sensation disappear.

Lazarus (1982) says that we do not need complete stimulus information to react emotionally. There can be no disagreement about that. However, the question is not how much information the organism requires from the environment but *how little work it must do on this information* in order to produce an emotional reaction. Perceptions that are "global or spherical" will suffice, insists Lazarus. I ask what forms of cognition *will not* suffice? It is this question that Lazarus must answer if he wishes to hold fast to the proposition that cognitive appraisal is a necessary condition for all emotional states. His argument cannot generate clear answers. He cannot declare that cognitive participation in emotion must be such as to allow for an appropriate emotional response because that is simply begging the question. Nor can he assert that cognitive participation must be such as to allow for stimulus identification, because research—including Lazarus' own classic work—has shown that emotion can be generated without identification. Lazarus argues that although there was no conscious identification there was some form of unconscious identification. But we can't be sure, can we?

It is a critical question for cognitive theory and for theories of emotion to determine just what is the minimal information process that is required for emotion. Can untransformed pure sensory input directly generate emotional reactions? The answer is likely to be yes because the patttern of various findings seems to point in that direction. At the simplest level, any physical stimulus if sufficiently intense produces an escape reaction. There is no doubt, therefore, that the organism is hard-wired for particular classes of reactions—at the grossest level, for approach and avoidance—to particular classes of stimuli. There is some property of afferent excitation—perhaps the extent of neural firing—that selects between approach and avoidance reactions. If other stimuli or situations can acquire this property, they too will select between approach and avoidance, and the new process will become "hard-wired." There is no reason why afferent excitation deriving from stimuli that acquired affective potential by virtue of a cognitive process, must retain their affective potential only by retaining the cognitive element and reinstate that element on all subsequent encounters of the stimulus. Affective reactions may become autonomous and rid themselves of the cognitive mediators (Zajonc & Markus, 1982). Neutral stimuli that acquire emotional significance through an initially extensive cognitive process, may eventually become able to select between approach and avoidance on the basis of very rudimentary sensory process that involves no mental work—a process that short-circuits cognition and links the response to sensation in a most direct fashion. If it is possible to react emotionally on the basis of pure sensory input in one case, then it is possible to so react in other cases as well.

If cognitive appraisal must be involved in all affect, then a completely new view must be taken of a variety of phenomena that I described here. The emotional system becomes subordinated to complete cognitive control. Such a system has a questionable adaptive value. In contrast, if we assume that there may be conditions of emotional arousal that do not require cognitive appraisal, we shall dedicate our research to the questions of what these conditions are and how they differ from those that do require appraisal. Should it turn out that not all emotion depends on appraisal, we may wish to enquire what is the precise role that appraisal plays in the natural history of emotional reactions—when it enters as a significant element of these reactions—and what is its role in the three manifestations of emotional states: bodily process, overt expression, and subjective feeling.

ACKNOWLEDGMENT

This work was supported by Grant BS-8117477 from the National Science Foundation. I wish to thank Pam Adelmann and James L. Olds for drawing my attention to the literature on retinohypothalamic tract.

REFERENCES

Anderson, N. H., & Hubert, S. Effects of concomitant verbal recall on order effects in personality impression formation. *Journal of Verbal Learning and Verbal Behavior*, 1963, *2*, 379–391.

Cacioppo, J. T., & Petty, R. E. Lateral asymmetry in the expression of cognition and emotion. *Journal of Experimental Psychology: Human Perception and Performance*, 1981, *7*, 333–341.

Cooper, L. G. A multivariate investigation of preferences. *Multivariate Behavior Research*, 1973, *8*, 253–272.

Darwin, C. R. *Expression of the emotions in man and animals.* New York: Philosophical Library, 1955.

Dreben, E. K., Fiske, S. T., & Hastie, R. The independence of evaluative and item information: Impression and recall order effects in behavior-based impression formation. *Journal of Personality and Social Psychology*, 1979, *37*, 1758–1768.

Duncan, J., & Laird, J. D. Cross-modality consistencies in individual differences in self-attrbution. *Journal of Personality*, 1977, *45*, 191–196.

Flynn, J. P., Edwards, S. B., & Bandler, R. J., Jr. Changes in sensory and motor systems during centrally elicited attack. *Behavioral Science*, 1971, *16*, 1–19.

Fowler, C. A., Wolford, G., Slade, R., & Tassinary, L. Lexical access with and without awareness. *Journal of Experimental Psychology: General*, 1981, *110*, 341–362.

Garcia, J., & Rusiniak, K. W. What the nose learns from the mouth. In D. Muller-Schwarze & R. M. Silverstein (Eds.), *Chemical signals.* New York: Plenum Press, 1980.

Goodale, M. A. Vision as a sensorimotor system. In T. E. Robinson (Ed.), *A behavioral approach to brain research.* New York: Oxford University Press, 1982.

Ingle, D. Two visual systems in the frog. *Science*, 1973, *181*, 1053–1055.

Izard, C. E. *The face of emotion.* New York: Appleton-Century-Crofts, 1971.

Izard, C. E. *Human emotions.* New York: Plenum, 1977.

Izard, C. E. The primacy of emotions in human development and in emotion-cognition relationships. In C. E. Izard, J. Kagan, & R. B. Zajonc (Eds.), *Emotions, cognition, and behavior.* New York: Cambridge University Press, in press.

Kunst-Wilson, W. R., & Zajonc, R. B. Affective discrimination of stimuli that cannot be recognized. *Science*, 1980, *207*, 557–558.

Laird, J. D. Self-attribution of emotion: The effects of expressive behavior on the quality of emotional experience. *Journal of Personality and Social Psychology*, 1974, *29*, 475–486.

Laird, J. D., Wegener, J. J., Halal, M., & Szegda, M. Remembering what you feel: The effects of emotion on memory. *Journal of Personality and Social Psychology*, 1982, *42*, 646–657.

Lanzetta, J. T., & Orr, S. P. Influence of facial expressions on the classical conditioning of fear. *Journal of Personality and Social Psychology*, 1980, *39*, 1081–1087.

Lazarus, R. S. Thoughts on the relations between emotion and cognition. *American Psychologist*, 1982, *37*, 1019–1024.

Lazarus, R. S., & McCleary, R. A. Autonomic discrimination without awareness: A study of subception. *Psychological Review*, 1951, *58*, 113–122.

Littman, R. A., & Manning, H. M. A methodological study of cigarette brand discrimination. *Journal of Applied Psychology*, 1954, *38*, 185–190.

Marcel, T. Conscious and preconscious recognition of polysemous words: Locating the selective effects of prior verbal context. In R. S. Nickerson (Eds.), *Attention and performance VII.* Hillsdale, N.J.: Lawrence Erlbaum Associates, 1980.

Moore, R. Y. Retinohypothalamic projection in mammals: A comparative study. *Brain Research*, 1973, *49*, 403–409.

Nakashima, T. Contribution to the study of the affective processes. *American Journal of Psychology*, 1909, *20*, 157–193.

Nauta, W. J. H., & Haymaker, W. Retino-hypothalamic connections. In W. Haymaker, E. Anderson, & W. J. H. Nauta (Eds.), *The hypothalamus.* Springfield, Ill.: Charles C. Thomas, 1969.

O'Keefe, J., & Nadel, L. Precis of O'Keefe and Nadel "The hippocampus as a cognitive map" (and open peer commentary). *The Behavioral and Brain Sciences,* 1979, *2,* 487–533.

Petty, R. E., & Cacioppo, J. T. *Attitudes and persuasion: Classic and contemporary approaches.* Dubuque, Iowa: Wm. C. Brown, 1981.

Posner, M. I., & Snyder, C. R. R. Facilitation and inhibition in the processing of signals. In P. M. A. Rabbitt, & S. Dornic (Eds.), *Attention and performance V.* New York: Academic Press, 1975.

Rhodewalt, F., & Comer, R. Induced-compliance attitude change: Once more with feeling. *Journal of Experimental Social Psychology,* 1979, *15,* 35–47.

Ross, E. D., & Mesulam, M. M. Dominant language functions of the *right* hemisphere: Prosody and emotional gesturing. *Archives of Neurology,* 1977, *36,* 144–148.

Schachter, S., & Singer, J. Cognitive, social, and physiological determinants of emotional state. *Psychological Review,* 1962, *65,* 379–399.

Schwartz, G. E., Davidson, R. J., & Maer, F. Right hemisphere lateralization for emotion in the human brain: Interaction with cognition. *Science,* 1975, *190,* 286–288.

Seamon, J. J., Brody, N., & Kauff, D. M. Affective discrimination of stimuli that are not recognized: Effects of shadowing, masking, and cerebral laterality. *Journal of Experimental Psychology: Learning, Memory, and Cognition,* 1983 (a)

Seamon, J. J., Brody, N., & Kauff, D. M. Affective discrimination of stimuli that are not recognized: II. Effect of delay between study and test. *Bulletin of the Psychonomic Society,* 1983 (b)

Simonov, P. V. On the role of the hippocampus in the integrative activity of the brain. *Acta Neurobiologiae Experimentalis,* 1972, *34,* 33–41.

Solomon, R. L. The opponent-process theory of acquired motivation: The costs of pleasure and the benefits of pain. *American Psychologist,* 1980, *35,* 691–712.

Steiner, J. E. Innate discriminative human facial expressions to taste and smell stimulation. *Annals of the New York Academy of Science,* 1974, *237,* 229.

Stephan, F. K., Berkley, K. J., & Moss, R. L. Efferent connections of the rat suprachiasmatic nucleus. *Neuroscience,* 1981, *6,* 2625–2641.

Suberi, M., & McKeever, W. F. Differential right hemispheric memory storage for emotional and nonemotional faces. *Neuropsychologia,* 1977, *15,* 757–768.

Takenishi, M. *Stimulus recognition plays some role in exposure effects.* Paper presented at the 46th Meeting of the Japan Psychological Association, Kyoto, July 1982.

Tomkins, S. S. *Affect, imagery, consciousness, Vol. I.* New York: Springer, 1962.

Tucker, D. M. Lateral brain function, emotion, and conceptualiization. *Psychological Bulletin,* 1981, *89,* 19–46.

Wasman, M., & Flynn, J. P. Direct attack elicited from hypothalamus. *Archives of Neurology (Chicago),* 1962, *6,* 220–227.

Wilson, W. R. Feeling more than we can know: Exposure effects without learning. *Journal of Personality and Social Psychology,* 1979, *37,* 811–821.

Wundt, W. *Outlines of psychology.* Leipzig: Englemann, 1907.

Zajonc, R. B. Feeling and thinking: Preferences need no inferences. *American Psychologist,* 1980. *35,* 151–175.

Zajonc, R. B., & Markus, H. Affective and cognitive factors in preferences. *Journal of Consumer Research,* 1982, *9,* 123–131.

Zajonc, R. B., Pietromonaco, P., & Bargh, J. Independence and interaction of affect and cognition. In M. S. Clark & S. T. Fiske (Eds.), *Affect and cognition: The Seventeenth Annual Carnegie Symposium on Cognition.* Hillsdale, N.J.: Lawrence Erlbaum Associates, 1982.

Zuckerman, M., Klorman, R., Larrance, D. T., & Spiegel, N. H. Facial, autonomic, and subjective components of emotion: The facial feedback hypothesis versus the externalizer-internalizer distinction. *Journal of Personality and Social Psychology,* 1981, *41,* 929–944.

13 A Perceptual Motor Theory of Emotion

Howard Leventhal
University of Wisconsin—Madison

The goal of this chapter is to provide a concise overview of the Perceptual Motor Theory of emotion. This theory is in the tradition of the theories advanced by Ekman (Ekman, Friesen, & Ellsworth, 1972), Izard (1971), and Tomkins (1962, 1963, 1980), but differs from them in a number of ways that will become apparent. The theory I am presenting is intended to be comprehensive, and in addition to presenting this model, I address three issues of concern to emotion theorists: (1) the relationship of emotion to cognition, (2) the relationship of subjective feeling to expressive behavior, and (3) the issue of emotion control. I begin my exposition with a number of basic assumptions about the substance of emotion. Next, I present the perceptual motor model and show how it applies to the three basic questions. Due to space limitations I do not justify all of my points or marshall a complete array of evidence for each. Detailed arguments and references can be found elsewhere (see Leventhal, 1980; Leventhal & Mosbach, in press).

Basic Assumptions About the Nature of Emotion

Laymen agree that the term "emotion" refers to subjective feelings. Psychologists agree only that there is disagreement about the meaning and referents of the term. These disagreements reflect their varied theoretical approaches. Behaviorists are unable to accept a definition of emotion as experience, and cognitive theorists are unable to accept a definition of emotion as overt behavior. I have adopted a perceptual frame of reference which treats emotion as an experience. Emotion is like other perceptual experiences, such as the experience of distance or of objects, and as such it is private and can only be studied through indicators.

The indicators for emotion are verbal and instrumental responses, expressive responses, and autonomic responses. All three types of indicator response are used in the study of emotion. None of the three types of response is itself "the emotion," as "the emotion" is an hypothetical construct. Emotion is an experience that is real but cannot be directly observed. As is the case with all behavioral indicators, those for emotion (verbal reports, expressive reactions, and autonomic responses) are responsive to environmental and organismic states in addition to that of emotion. Hence, each of the indicators of emotion is fraught with potential for bias.

This state of affairs might lead to despair, until we recognize that the study of perception has advanced despite its reliance on indicators and lack of direct access to the perceptual phenomena under study. It is my judgment that verbal report and its related response methods (rating scales, check lists, etc.) is the best of the available indicators for the study of emotion in adult subjects. This is particularly true at the early stage of the research enterprise. Verbal report is particularly suited for assessing the many facets of emotional and perceptual experience. The early Gestaltists were clearly aware of this virtue of verbal report. Its utility is even greater with the advent of procedures for the analysis of multidimensional data (e.g., cluster analysis, factor analysis, multidimensional scaling). Other types of indicator responses will become more useful as our theoretical and methodological questions become more precise.

Disagreement between indicators has also plagued the study of emotion. Inconsistency of this sort is a particularly serious problem if the investigator treats the underlying phenomenon of emotion as though it is identical to his/her operational measures. On the other hand, if the investigator views his measures as reflections of several, underlying hypothetical variables only one of which is emotion, disagreement between verbal reports and expression, or between expression and autonomic response, become problems to be studied in relation to emotional experience, and not the insoluable conundrums they would otherwise seem to be.

THE PERCEPTUAL MOTOR SYSTEM

While emotional experience is the phenomenon under study, it is not the primary target for conceptual elaboration. Although we must identify the attributes of emotion, such as its qualities (fear, anger, disgust, joy, shame, etc.), and its intensive attributes, our major task is to conceptualize the system that constructs emotional experiences. The model I am presenting, therefore, is a theory of the mechanisms that are active in the construction of emotional experience. The model must be designed to account for the basic facts of emotional phenomena. Among these facts are the following:

1. Emotions are universal: People from widely differing cultures express and identify a common set of core emotions (Ekman & Friesen, 1975). This universality is seen in the development of emotion in the normal and blind infant.

2. Emotions are differentiated. Emotional differentiation begins at birth and continues with maturation. Learning also produces differentiation. Learning affects the generalization of emotions to new situations (i.e., to new, perceived cues and to abstract ideas). Learning affects the nature of the emotional experience itself. New blends and new types of emotions appear with development. Learning also affects the organization or relationship among the indicators of emotion, or how emotion expresses itself in behavior.

3. Emotions appear to alter the organization of the behavioral system as a whole. They structure or focus all components of the processing system toward a common goal. This "tightness" of organization has been commented on before (e.g., Leeper, 1948), but has not been discussed within the context of the present theory. As we shall see, the present theory adds a new dimension to the idea of emotional integration.

This list accounts for only some aspects of emotional phenomena, for which a theory must account. I have listed other aspects elsewhere (Leventhal, 1980, 1982). In the following section I present my view of the processing system.

THE PROCESSING SYSTEM

I have proposed an emotional processing mechanism which is one of two parallel routes within a larger system for the mediation of adaptive behavior. The other route is an objective processing mechanism. Each pathway of this larger system is organized as a series of steps or stages and as an hierarchy of processing levels. They are conceptualized as an active, processing system that mediates between stimulus situations and response. The stage hypothesis suggests that stimulus information is progressively elaborated upon in the process of generating responses. The first stage or step involves the reception and interpretation or coding of information which results in the construction of perceptual-interpretation or REPRESENTATION of the stimulus situation, and the construction of a subjective emotion, or EMOTIONAL REPRESENTATION of the situation. The second stage involves the generation and execution of action plans to cope with (i.e., in some way alter or control) the perceived situation and with the emotional reaction to it. Thus, there is problem based and emotion based coping (Leventhal, 1970). The third stage involves setting criteria and evaluating the outcome of coping efforts. We have called this an APPRAISAL stage (Leventhal, 1970, 1980, 1982; Leventhal & Nerenz, 1982; Leventhal, Meyer, & Nerenz, 1980). In this system, therefore, emotion is constructed in the first stage of

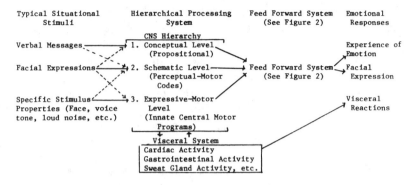

FIG. 13.1. Model of the Hierarchical Processing System for the construction of emotional reactions.

processing, stimulus reception and interpretation. The system is recursive and fast acting. It rapidly cycles through representation, coping, and appraisal, and each of the two latter stages can influence both the problem and emotion aspect of the representation.

The stage property of the system is of less importance to our present discussion than is hierarchical organization. The hierarchical property postulates that emotional processing, or the creation of an emotional representation or experience, is a product of a multilevel system, all parts of which are usually simultaneously active and congruent in their emotional output (see Fig. 13.1). It is not necessary that the levels act congruently. Indeed, we can best observe and learn about these separate systems when they act differently or are in conflict with one another.

I have suggested three levels to the hierarchy that constructs emotional experience (i.e., the representation stage of emotion): (1) sensory-motor processing, (2) schematic processing, and (3) conceptual processing. All three levels connect stimulation and emotional experience. Each is a route to the generation of emotional experience. The sensory motor system is essentially an "innate" route that generates "primitive" or partially formed emotions. The schematic and conceptual are memory systems. They represent different ways of abstracting and storing memories of the prior conditions that elicit emotion and a memory of the emotion itself. The three pathways are also responsive to different stimuli that elicit emotion. I elaborate briefly on each.

Sensory-Motor Processing

I view the sensory-motor system as the elementary core of emotional processing. I have labeled it a sensory motor system because the activity of this "innate" motor system is noticeable in the newborn's receptivity to specialized, interpersonal cues (e.g., tones of voice, the human face) and his/her attentive and expressive reactions to these cues (see summary of work by Brazelton and others in Leventhal, 1980). The most dramatic demonstration of innate facial reactions to similar expressive displays in adult models has been reported by Field, Woodson, Greenberg and Cohen (1982). They exposed 76 neonates (mean age of 36 hours) to an adult who modeled happy, sad, and surprised expressions over a series of trials and found the neonates imitated the expressive reactions (i.e., the neonate's expression was judged by an observer who was blind to the model's expression) on 76% of the surprise trials, and 58% and 59% of the happy and sad trials, percentages well in excess of chance.

The variety of expressive reactions produced just hours after birth provide fairly strong evidence to the preprogrammed nature of expression and its associated set of emotional experiences, though evidence for the latter half of this assumption is lacking. These motor reactions or motor categories can be said to form a basic vocabulary of emotional response and experience. Thus, expressive activity in early infancy suggests the presence of an emotional state and its associated emotional experience. The state is also accompanied by autonomic changes and, in some instances, by simple, instrumental actions (e.g., the infant's arm and leg cycling when he/she is confronted by another person).

I view these early emotional reactions as simple, assimilative responses. They are motor meanings as are all sensory motor reactions (Piaget, 1954). These early, motor based feelings are simple as they lack clear associations to well-structured objects or events, or to well-structured patterns of coping. The infant does not conceive of his or her feeling states as dependent on specific images, or more elaborate notions of others, as he or she does not have specific or abstract memory structures to attach to emotional states. The infant also has yet to acquire a host of well-structured action-plans to cope with emotion provoking situations. In summary, the emotional states activated by sensory-motor processing are in many ways like simple reflexes as they are not yet linked to a complex set of environmental experiences (situational expectations) nor are they associated with a complex set of problem-solving behaviors (response expectations). They appear, however, more complex than simple reflexes as they seem to be dependent on elaborately patterned stimulation and involve the joint action of several muscle groups.

Schematic Emotional Processing

Repeated elicitation of sensory motor emotions in conjunction with the perception of and reactions to specific environments leaves a storehouse of nonverbal, perceptual-motor memory structures. Initially, these memories are of concrete episodes. Hence, they record in considerable detail impressions of the specific situations that aroused strong emotion. Linked to these detailed impressions of the eliciting situation is a record of the emotional feeling itself, which is a motor memory of expressive and autonomic reactions. It also includes motor memories of instrumental reactions that are regularly associated with the prior image, feeling, and expressive and autonomic reactions. These schematic structures are similar to conditioned responses. The association between the components of the emotional schemata, (i.e, the record of the stimulus, the emotional experience, and the expressive and autonomic reactions, but not that of the coping responses), seems to be much tighter and better integrated than most other associative processes. One might speculate that these structures form cortical "columns" such that the neural representations of the separate components are closely related in space. This association would be tighter and more difficult to undo than that typically found between emotional reactions and instrumental behaviors.

Emotional schemata, like other perceptual memories, are abstract. They become abstract because repeated exposure to specific types of emotionally provocative situations, such as repeated loving or repeated angry encounters with a parent, are blended into an average or prototypic experience (Posner & Keele, 1968, 1970). Although prototypes or schemata are abstract, they are not abstract in the same way as signs or symbols. Schemata are averages of actual stimulus and response conditions. They are elicited by stimuli which have features of both specific eliciting episodes and of the average of these episodes. They are not elicited by stimuli that stand in a "remote" or arbitrary relationship to the experienced setting.

Schematic processing is also conceived as rapid and automatic. It resembles recognition and intuitive preference, not reasoning, because there is no need for the eliciting stimulus or the choice process to enter conscious awareness. Attention is required only to bring the eliciting stimulus into the receptor field. Once a component of the schemata is activated, the other components are activated instantly.

It is also clear that development leads to transformations in schemata. The initial schemata are likely to be highly closely tied to perception and concrete. With time, however, they become richer and more operational or free from perception, just as schemata of the physical world change from pre-operational to concrete operational form. Both types of cognition organize perceptual experience, though the concrete operational concept is better able to generalize across a class of situations generating a common emotional experience despite a wide range of transformations in the elicitating situations.

Elsewhere, I have cited five types of evidence for schematic, emotional processing (Leventhal, 1980; Leventhal & Mosbach, 1982). These include the role of imagery in emotion (as seen in behavioral therapies such as desensitization), the intrusion of emotionally relevant imagery into ongoing problem solving activity, the generalization or intensification of a subsequent emotional state by autonomic arousal from a prior emotion, the observation of vivid imagery in the dreams of paradoxical sleep, and a variety of data suggesting the right cerebral hemisphere is particularly well suited to the processing of holistic, patterned information. The phenomenon of phantom pain, however, has played the most important role in the development of our concept of schematic processing (see the discussion in Leventhal, 1980, 1982; Leventhal & Everhart, 1979; Melzack, 1973). Phantom body parts are often experienced after amputation, and these phantoms can be extremely painful. The occurrence of pain in the phantom limb strongly suggests that emotions can be stored in perceptual (schematic) memory. The pain stored in a phantom is often closely related to some prior emotionally distressing experience. For example, the pain of a sprained ankle appeared in the phantom of a soldier whose leg was amputated after a severe case of gangrene. The milder pain from the sprain, not that from his gangrenous wound, inhabited the phantom because it was perceived as responsible for his subsequent injury, infection, and amputation. It is also likely the sprain was more closely attended to and worried about. The attention and worry about fear of injury, imprinted this pain in the schematic memory. Phantom pain has one other important property; the arousal of negative emotion, such as anxiety and distress due to negative life events, may reactivate a dormant phantom. This last observation supports the hypothesis that emotional schemata are tightly integrated structures of eliciting situations, subjective feelings, and expressive and autonomic activity.

Conceptual Processing

We have defined two components of conceptual processing: (1) One that stores information *about* past emotional episodes which can be accessed to talk about emotional experiences, and (2) One used for the voluntary performance of emotional acts. Both of these processing components make use of a propositional, memory network in which specific elements are logically related. Propositional storage is more abstract than schematic storage. It can be applied to, or used to interpret, emotional situations even though these situations undergo a very wide range of transformations.

Due to its greater abstractness, propositionally stored information does not change much after exposure to new, emotional experiences. Minor, and sometimes major, differences in the content and form of a specific episode are ignored as the episode need only match the memory structure in some abstract features to be conceptualized as emotional, and similar to prior episodes. Propositional storage also permits more flexible or thoughtful response to emotional experience and aids in the short- and long-term control of this experience. Conceptual processing is also voluntary and effortful, and makes demands on conscious, attentional capacity (Posner & Snyder, 1975).

We have suggested that conceptual memories are formed when the individual reflects upon his or her emotional experiences. The self-conscious review and formulation of the nature of an emotionally evocative situation, and the nature of one's feelings, leads to the formation of abstract, conceptual memory structures

about (rather than of) the emotional episode. Similarly, self-reflective and deliberate review and practice of the motor aspects of emotional episodes plays a
crucial role in the formation of conceptual codes for the performance and control
of emotional reactions. Because in many cultures it is unusual to engage in
extensive self-observation and practice of expressive responses, people frequently lack voluntary control of automatically generated (through schematic
processing) emotional reactions. Hence, most conceptual processing involves
voluntary action that is nonemotional. We can tell ourselves what to read, where
to look, and decide to approach objects and people in order to engage in voluntary, instrumental actions. Because of this, emotional control is usually achieved
indirectly, through the exercise of voluntary actions which alter emotional feelings and responses. Practice in emotional responding can help to develop direct
control over emotional reactions. For example, Lang and his associates (Lang,
1979; Lang, Kozak, Miller, Levin, & McLean, 1980) instruct subjects to imagine walking with heart beating, hands trembling and sweating, in response to
emotionally provocative stimuli, and have found this response training increases
the consistency between autonomic reactions and experienced fear. Response
training seems valuable in preparing subjects for desensitization treatment as
desensitization proceeds more smoothly if the autonomic, subjective, and instrumental levels of the emotional response are congruent. Response training seems
especially helpful for male subjects, as males are much less likely to show
congruity between their autonomic responses and their subjective feeling states
than females.

Elsewhere (Leventhal, 1980; Leventhal & Mosbach, 1982; Safer, 1981), we
have reviewed a substantial amount of evidence on sex differences that show a
higher level of consistency between indicators of emotion (autonomic, expressive, and verbal report) for female than for male subjects. Female subjects
also show evidence of both schematic (perceptual memory codes) and conceptual
competence in making judgments of the emotional value of stimuli. Safer (1981)
found that females were equally accurate in identifying facial expressions of
emotion in the left and right visual fields (right and left hemispheres respectively), whereas males could match the accuracy of females only in the left visual
field (right hemisphere). Because right hemispheric functions are pattern oriented, they would seem to parallel the type of automatic processing we have
identified with emotional schemata. On the other hand, left hemispheric functions are generally sequential and voluntary in nature and would seem to parallel
the type of processing we have identified as conceptual. Such gender differences
may occur because females are far more likely than males to rehearse and
observe themselves in emotional poses and, because the left hemisphere can
function automatically with emotional material if the individual is highly practiced. It is reasonable that females would show both greater consistency between
indicator responses of emotion (autonomic, expressive, and subjective) and show
conceptual processing skill when assessed with more subtle methods such as

tachistoscopic judgments of emotional expressions selectively exposed in the right and left visual fields.

APPLICATION OF THE MODEL TO BASIC PROBLEMS

Our goal in this section is to show how our model would answer questions about the relationship of emotion to cognition, expressive action, memory, and self-control. In asking these questions we are addressing the issue of how the processing system operates when generating an emotional experience. There are four fundamental issues that need be kept in mind regardless of the particular question we pose. These are the following:

1. The emotion system operates as a whole. All stages (feeling, coping, and appraisal) and all levels (sensory-motor, schematic, and conceptual) are typically involved in generating emotional experience.
2. There is influence across the levels of the processing hierarchy from the top down (conceptual to the schematic and sensory motor), and from the bottom up.
3. The system, across stages and across levels, moves toward an integrated state, (i.e., toward a common focus or a common theme).
4. Other, nonemotional processing may proceed along similar lines, and in parallel to emotional processing.

Emotion is not unique, as many if not all of the properties of processing emotion are observable in the processing of other types of information.

These four points suggest there will be no simple answers. Because emotional experience and behavior are generated by the operation of a complex system, any part of the system could be primarily responsible for eliciting subjective emotion at a given point in time. Moreover, any part of the system could elicit subjective emotion by first activating some other level of processing which would then activate emotion. For example, conceptual processes could elicit subjective emotion by first activating schemata and then emotion. Hence the relationships between emotion and cognition, emotion and expressive behavior, and emotion and the problem of self-control will be complex. Examining these relationships will force us to consider for each, the system as a whole, influences across levels (top to bottom and bottom to top), the tendency toward integration, and the relationship of emotion to parallel, nonemotional processes.

Emotion and Cognition

The role of cognition in the experience of emotion moved to center stage with the publication of Schachter and Singer's (1962) classic study on the ability of cognition to define the type of emotion felt during a state of physiological arousal. Arousal provided the turbulence necessary for an affective experience, but it was cognition that was necessary to label, and give the emotion its distinctive hue or quality. As I have pointed out elsewhere (Leventhal, 1974, 1979, 1980), Schachter was restating a position that had been raised at least twice before in this century (see Russell, 1927; Sully, 1902). On both prior occasions, as in the present, the key point was the absence of evidence that body reactions (autonomic or expressive responses), were sufficient to generate emotional experience or the experience of different emotion qualities.

The model proposed here shares the assumption of other theorists operating in a Darwinian framework (e.g., Ekman, Izard, Tomkins), as it views emotion as a fundamental property of experience. From this perspective, cognition is not necessary to define the quality of emotion, as the quality of emotion can be determined by organized activity in neurochemical and motor areas of the central nervous system, (i.e., by sensory-motor processing). By cognition, we mean a broad class of events including abstract thought and perception of identifiable or meaningful objects. Thus, neither conceptual nor schematic processing, is the ingredient that is necessary to define specific and differentiable emotional qualities, as the sensory-motor system can provide this differentiating information. But, even if emotion can be generated by processes that are *independent* of what we ordinarily label cognition, is emotion processed or generated in this way in most life situations? Or is emotion (nearly) always elicited by cognition or followed by some form of cognition?

My early work on fear communications led me to postulate that emotion was processed in parallel to "cold" or nonemotional, cognitive processes (Leventhal, 1970). Most recently, Zajonc (1980) has argued that preferences, or emotionally based choices, occur independent of inferences or cognitively based recognition or reasoning. His argument is based on findings showing that subjects become increasingly favorable toward repeatedly heard or seen words and pictures even when they do not report recognizing the items they prefer or like. Preferences are seen to be independent of cognition.

What does our perceptual motor model say about the connection of emotion to cognition? First, it should be clear that the emotion processing system can generate emotions without the participation of cognitive processes (i.e., without perception or cognition initiating emotion), or without perception or cognition following the arousal of emotion. It should be clear that there are few cases where this degree of independence can be seen. One case would be in earliest infancy. The neonate may experience emotion without prior or subsequent cognitive experience. This possibility is seen in the Field et al. (1982) studies mentioned earlier. Even in this case, however, cognition is absent only in the sense that no prior *learned* memory schemata is needed to elicit the expressive (and presumably subjective) emotional reaction. Perception, mediated by "innate" sensory motor events, is necessary for the expressive reaction. It is likely this is only a once in a lifetime state of affairs, as it is only in the very earliest days that the infant will lack both schematic and conceptual memory. Schematic or perceptual memories will be formed with the infant's earliest emotional experiences, and these concrete, memory schemata (cognitions) will then participate in most if not all emotional responding either as antecedents or consequences of the activation of emotional responses (or components of such responses such as induced, autonomic arousal).

Another possible case would involve the use of drugs to directly stimulate sensory-motor emotional processing. These drugs would have to act selectively on specific, emotion generating structures. Because there is no reason to believe that systemically administered drugs act so precisely as to evoke sensory-motor processes dedicated solely to the production of basic emotions such as joy, fear, or anger, we should have to concede that this case is more likely confined to thought experiments than reality. The Schachter and Singer study and replications following it, illustrate the difficulty of eliciting an emotion with a drug. Inasmuch as drugs spread throughout the body and nervous system, there is no reason to believe they will activate only a single, emotional processing network.

It is clear that under nearly all conditions, emotion is accompanied by cognition. Emotion is either elicited by cognition or it generates cognition (by activating schematic memory) once aroused. Even in earliest infancy, emotion is generally elicited by the perception of environmental events. How then, can someone like Zajonc argue that preferences are independent of cognition? Zajonc's (1980) argument is only sensible if cognition is defined as conscious, propositional thinking, or conscious recognition. All other cognition, such as perceptual categorization and nonconscious cognitive enrichment, are by his definition, noncognitive. From the perspective of the perceptual motor theory, Zajonc's approach represents a play on words. We believe emotion is linked to cognition at nearly every step of emotional processing from the initiation through the maintenance and termination of an emotional experience. Emotion is elicited by cognition and emotion activates cognition. The cognitions involved range from simple sensory and perceptual cues (events that are perceived but not necessarily coded in acquired schematic or conceptual structures), to cognitions that code the identity or features of the object and codes that identify the event despite major transformations in specific features. All levels of cognition can be associated with emotion, but it is perceptual codes that are most strongly linked to affective experience. These codes need not have verbal tags to increase their accessibility to consciousness and aid "recognition."

If the type of emotional preference described by Zajonc is close to perception as I have argued, it should be susceptible to influence from other perceptual and sensory-motor processes. In an unpublished study, Leventhal and Panagis (1975) examined the possibility of interaction using Zajonc's repetition paradigm. Subjects listened to lists of three syllable nonsense terms. The list consisted of two nonsense terms that were repeated 20 times each, two repeated 10 times each, two 5 times each, and two repeated only once. The items were described as words from the Thai language and subjects were asked to listen to the words and attend to their sound rather than try to memorize them. They were told this was preparation for actual learning, which would follow. After listening to a list, they were exposed to a second list of words. This second list contained both the items they had previously heard and other nonsense words to which they had not been exposed. They rated each item on this second list for recognition and liking. If the typical findings repeat, subjects should give more positive liking ratings to the words used most frequently on the first list, yet show no sign of recognizing the items.

This description of the data is, however, incomplete. We used two items at each frequency level (20, 10, 5, and 1), varying the tone of voice in which *one* of the items was read on each of its repetitions. Thus, for one group of subjects, the first list they heard contained one item at each frequency of repetition read in a neutral tone of voice and the other item at the matching frequency read in a laughing, affectively positive, tone of voice. In another list, listened to by yet another group of subjects, one item at each frequency level was read in a neutral tone of voice and the other in a negative, angry tone of voice. Finally, in a third group, one item at each level was read in a positive tone of voice while the other item was read in a negative tone of voice. A control group heard all of the items read in a neutral tone of voice. We expected the strong tonal qualities of the positively and negatively read words would activate emotion through sensory-motor processes, and that this tonally generated emotion would disrupt the preference effects.

Our expectation that tonality would disrupt preference was based on the following logic. Given that subjects had not paid close attention to the items, the schemata formed with repeated exposure, would be less well defined. Hence, when an affective or emotional quality was added to the schemata by the tone of the voice, it would be linked to all schemata in the list rather than to items read in that tone of voice. In the list read in both happy and angry voice tones, the two emotional tones would cancel each other and interfere with any feeling of "liking" or preference for the most frequently repeated items. The results supported this conclusion as there was absolutely no increase in preference with more frequent exposure to the words in the positive–negative list. Thus, repetition does use a cognitive-emotional store, and that memory store can access and be disrupted by other types of emotional (tone of voice) information.

In summary, Zajonc (1980) uses an arbitrary definition of cognition when he argues for a separation of cognition and emotion. The perceptual motor theory, on the other hand, sees emotion intimately intertwined with various types or levels of cognition. This does not imply these various types of cognition are always linked to emotion. The total processing system is parallel, and, there are cognition-emotion structures (which include sensory-motor, schematic, and conceptual processing) for processing different emotions, and for processing non-emotional experiences.

Emotion and Expression

James' (1890) formulation, "In all cases of intellectual or moral rapture . . . unless there be coupled a bodily reverberation . . . unless we actually laugh . . . thrill . . . or tingle . . . our state of mind can hardly be called emotional at all [p. 470–471]," initiated a history of research and controversy respecting the precise function of expressive behavior in emotion. Is outer expression an indicator of inner emotional experience, or is outer expression necessary for the occurrence of inner experience? The perceptual-motor model postulates that emotion is a centrally experienced and centrally generated phenomenon, and that expression is an outer reflection of an inner emotional state. The model specifies that the relationship of outer expression to emotional experience is complex. First, it is clear that outer emotional expression is frequently produced by inner emotion, as the two are linked in sensory-motor processing and in emotional schematic memory. Thus, there are two routes by which outer expression can initiate, strengthen, or sustain inner experience, the activation of sensory-motor processing or the activation of schematic processing. In most instances, outer expression is preceded by the activation of an inner emotional state such as a stimulus situation that evokes an expressive-motor process (for example, laughter initiating feeling and expression) or a schematic structure (the smiling face of a parent evokes a perceptual memory of positive feeling, expression, and autonomic response). The issue that has concerned investigators is whether emotional experience is altered by artificial or indirect methods of creating expressions such as by posing facial expressions, moving muscles touched by a pointer, hiding or showing expressions to a camera, or intensifying expressions with irrelevant (canned laughter) stimulation.

Our model suggests that artificially induced expressions are unlikely to intensify a spontaneously induced emotion (or weaken that emotion if opposite to it in expressive pattern) unless the artificially induced expression is itself spontaneous. Spontaneous induction of supplemental expression is likely to use the emotional processing machinery. Thus, if we use canned laughter or jokes to evoke additional expressions of laughter, both the "artificial" or secondary induction procedures and the induced laughter will activate sensory-motor and schematic processing that promote central, emotional states. These new affective states are likely to add to existent affective experience. Our model suggests that using voluntary methods for intensifying expressive behavior will have little effect on emotional experience and may have the paradoxical effect of reducing the intensity of emotional experience even when the voluntary expression is the same as that elicited spontaneously.

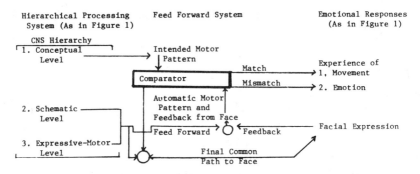

FIG. 13.2.   The Feed Forward System.

To understand the last hypothesis requires an exposition of our model of the central motor system. As has been suggested by Ekman (Ekman, Roper, & Hager, 1980), and others, we have proposed that emotional expressions, as is the case with all motor reactions, can be generated by automatic (involuntary) and deliberate (voluntary) processing. There are parallel tracts for expression (pyramidal and extrapyramidal pathways: Meyers, 1976). We have also accepted the hypothesis of separate, central, templates for involuntary and voluntary motor action. We have then added the hypothesis that the discharge of central, involuntary motor templates has two functions: (1) creating expressive movement, and (2) feeding forward into a system that creates conscious experience of movement. We have suggested that the latter system compares the spontaneous motor pattern to existent templates for intended motor action, and if there is no intended or voluntary template to match the spontaneous pattern, the spontaneous pattern is felt as an emotion (See Leventhal, 1979, 1980 for more detail).

The workings of this system are pictured in Fig. 13.2. The key to understanding this part of our model is to recognize that experience of both movement and emotion takes place in the voluntary motor system. It is the voluntary motor system that must access consciousness to be aware of the consequences of motor activity. This is the system that feels or senses movement and checks it against intentions. When movement feedback matches intention, it is felt as movement not as emotion. When it does not check against intention, it is experienced as involuntary movement. Either the feed-forward motor discharge or the feed-back motor pattern, of an automatic reaction can be felt as an emotion if its pattern is that of an emotional response. But if an individual generates an intentional expressive pose whose pattern is the same as that of the emotion, the intended motor template will match either the feed-forward or the feed-back pattern. In that instance, the automatic motor reaction will be sensed as completing an intended movement and it will be felt as a movement and not as an emotion. For example, if a hostess deliberately adopts a smiling expressive set while greeting her guests, she may feel little positive emotion when greeting either liked guests or disliked guests, as the feed-forward and feed-back signals from any spontaneous emotional, motor discharge will always match against her intended "smile," motor template. Thus both automatic and voluntary processes occur in the emotion system, but only when their output disagrees is the subjective experience of an emotion generated.

The feed-forward model of motor interaction further complicates our view of the emotion generating system. This increased complexity helps us generate a set of predictions respecting the way interactions between emotional and nonemotional motor processes alter subjective affect. This is only one of a number of potential interactions, but it is an important one as it leads us into our next topic, the control of emotional reactions.

The Control of Emotion

The majority of our emotional reactions are initiated by external stimuli and internal cognitions that activate schematic processing. These emotional reactions are provoked whether or not we expect or want to feel them. This is the source of most of the inconsistency we experience between how we feel and how we want to feel. Although we can, and often do, change our minds about how we want to feel, more often than not we try to control or change our feelings. Control is typically initiated by what we have been calling conceptual (volitional) coping. Two major sets of tactics are available to the conceptual coper for controlling the automatic, expressive-motor and schematic processing systems. These are: (1) Regulating stimulation, and (2) Regulating motor responses.

Regulating motor responses. I have discussed the regulation of emotion through the interaction of volitional and automatic motor codes. There is only one point to add here. I believe that parallel codes of expressive motor reactions can and do develop in both the automatic and volitional motor system. Practice is clearly important for developing these volitional codes (e.g., Lang, 1979). What is unclear is precisely what features of the automatic code are recoded or stored in the voluntary system. Identifying and rehearsing the critical features of the automatic code is likely to be crucial for the direct exercise of emotional control via self-regulation of expressive responding. Of course, other motor procedures exist for controlling emotional reactions, the most obvious being to alter the eliciting situation.

Regulating stimulation. People can push away from or avoid a stimulus to reduce its power to provoke emotion, or they can assimilate or take in a stimulus and enhance the clarity of their memory codes for categorizing it. Blocking, or avoiding stimulation is generally associated with stimuli that provoke negative affects such as fear, pain, distress, disgust, or anger. Taking in or assimilating information is generally associated with stimuli that provoke positive affects, for example, joy, sexual feelings, or hunger. The differences in strategies for regulating negative and positive emotion is likely to affect the schematic (and conceptual) memory systems linked to each. For example, stimuli arousing positive emotion are likely to become associated with one another regardless of their logical relatedness because the individual is motivated to sustain positive feelings by approaching and thinking about a wide variety of positive events. Stimuli arousing negative emotions, on the other hand, seem less likely to be joined in a common network, as avoidance motivation is unlikely to bring negative memory structures in contact with one another. Avoidance, therefore, is very likely to be selected as a strategy for reducing negative emotion.

It is also true that strong autonomic reactions frequently accompany, and are noticed when an individual experiences negative emotions. It is likely, therefore, that autonomic cues will play an important role in evoking negative emotional schemata and negative images, and serve as an associative link between ideas that are otherwise unrelated. Just this process would seem to be at work in studies conducted by Zimbardo and his colleagues (Marshall & Zimbardo, 1979; Maslach, 1979). It is also likely that some portion of the success of relaxation and stress-control procedures in reducing unpleasant emotions can be attributed to the suppression of autonomic reactions that serve as cues to frightening and stressful imagery. Drugs that suppress the occurrence or the experience of autonomic cues may prevent the elicitation of a wide range of negative, emotional memories for the very same reason.

Another way of controlling the automatic processing of emotion is to direct attention to the features of the emotion provoking stimulus. Careful attention to the features of a noxious stimulus appears to facilitate experiencing the stimulus as an objective event. We have conducted approximately a dozen studies which investigated the experience of ischemic pain and distress produced by either immersing the hand in cold (2° or 7°C) water or blocking the circulation by tightening a blood pressure cuff about the arm. The subject is exposed to the stimulus for 6 to 7 min and rates the amount of distress he or she feels at 30 sec intervals for the first 2 minutes, and at minute intervals thereafter. Subjects are given different instructions prior to exposure to the noxious stimulus. The primary experimental instructions directed the subject's attention to the objective features of the noxious stimulus and provided information about what he or she would feel (e.g., coldness, pins and needles, and numbness). These instructions were compared to instructions where subjects were told to pay attention to color slides, to think positive thoughts, or were given information about the procedures to be used in the experimental setting. The findings are quite consistent: Subjects who attend to and analyse the component features of the stimulus report substantial reductions in distress in comparison to subjects in the control condition. It is unlikely this difference is due to response bias as the subjects attending to specific sensations report equally high levels of distress during the first 1 to 2 min of exposure. Differences between the groups appear in the last half of the exposure period (the final 3 to 4 min). The beneficial effects of sensation monitoring also carry over from a first to a second trial. Subjects who monitored during the first trial report very low levels of pain and distress on the second trial even when they are instructed not to monitor on that later trial (Ahles, Blanchard, & Leventhal, 1981; Shacham, 1979). In contrast, blocking or ignoring the noxious event produces a reduction in pain experience only during the time the subject actively tries to distract him or herself. It does not carry over to later trials.

It is important to note that the effects of sensation monitoring are counterintuitive. Subjects regard monitoring as a very poor way of adapting to stress. Even after subjects have monitored and reported low levels of distress in the final minutes of exposure to a noxious stimulus, they will rate monitoring as an ineffective strategy at the close of the experimental session. None of these effects should be surprising. People know they will feel a stressor when they attend to it, and the results of their early reports are clearly in agreement with this. Lacking the opportunity to compare their feelings after a substantial period of monitoring to their feelings after a similar period without monitoring, they cannot readily form the verbalizeable abstraction that monitoring was beneficial. They are not aware of the build up of inhibitory reactions in the automatic processing systems that are responsible for their experiencing a decline in distress.

We have conducted a number of studies in patient populations illustrating the beneficial effects of sensation information and monitoring. These studies add to our understanding of emotional control as they suggest that an accurate view of the stimulus promulgated by monitoring can help direct effective, problem oriented coping. For example, expectant mothers were less distressed, frightened, and angry during the latter stages of childbirth (the time they were actively pushing), if they had monitored their contractions from the time of admission. The monitoring gave them information about these stressful events which facilitated coordination of their breathing and pushing.

Finally, our most recent studies suggest that chronically ill patients learn that "waiting and watching" is an effective way of coping with unalterable, and stressful disease. This strategy seems highly effective for managing long-term distress. The key to its success appears to be familiarization with and the formation of an objective schema of the noxious event. For example, in cancer patients the lessening of surprise, and the reduction of struggling to change unalterable events decreases distress. Our data suggest that ineffective coping adds to distress (Nerenz, Leventhal, & Love, in press). These findings parallel those reported by Weiss (1971) in his studies comparing laboratory rats exposed to identical electrical shocks, one of whom could control (successfully cope with) the stimulus. The coper did not develop ulcers. The control rat exposed to equal amounts of shock developed ulceration and the extent of the ulceration was related to the frequency with which it attempted to (unsuccessfully) regulate exposure to shock.

We have now covered two ways in which responding can regulate emotion: (1) by anticipating the pattern of automatic, expressive actions, and (2) by learning the objective features of a stimulus so one can guide coping reactions to minimize the situation's impact. It should be clear that the distinction between "stimulus" control tactics and "response" control tactics is somewhat artificial, as the organism must respond in particular ways to control informational input. Thus, subjects must pay attention to the features of a noxious stimulus to benefit from the inhibition of automatic, emotional responding, or they must think of happy thoughts to successfully block out of consciousness the experience of a short-lived, noxious stimulus. It is also evident that we can replace the term "noxious" by terms such as "tempting," "disgusting," and "happy." The tactics can be applied to a wide variety of affects, though they may not operate in identical ways across the full spectrum of emotions.

CONCLUSIONS: EMOTION AS A SYSTEM

Our discussion of emotion and cognition, emotion and expressive behavior, and the control of emotion, reflects the systems property of the perceptual motor model. The complexity of the link of emotion to cognition reflects the tri-level hierarchy of the processing system. The complexity of the levels requires that we distinguish between different types of cognition and recognize that we cannot begin to answer questions about the linkage of emotion to cognition if we treat cognition and emotion as unitary constructs! There are several types of process to be called "cognitive," and in parallel to them are several types of process in the system that generates emotion.

We face a similar complexity when we attempt to answer questions about the relationship of expressive behaviors to subjective emotion. We must distinguish between different types of expressive activity, spontaneous and voluntary, and examine the complex ways in which they can interact (e.g., feed-forward and feed-back in relation to volitional, motor templates). Finally, when we address the issues related to the control of emotion, we can try to organize our answers by discussing methods of control that are stimulus oriented and those that are response oriented, but quickly realize that stimulus-oriented techniques also involve responding! Taking in information requires a higher level of self-instruction to attend and the directing of attention to stimulus features: this is action. Attention, directed by high-level conceptual activity, affects processing or schema formation, or sensory-motor inhibition, at lower levels: This is stimulus control and it can produce effects that are contrary to common sense notions of behavior. Systems are complex and flexible. They can produce seemingly contradictory outcomes. The contradictions are resolvable, however, if we understand the situations in which the processing occurs and the history of the processing system. This includes the knowledge base (primary vocabulary or expressive-motor processing, emotion schemata, and emotion concepts) that is brought to the situation. The complexity of the model also makes it evident that single issue hypotheses will provide little understanding of emotional processes.

Finally, it is clear that emotions have many functions and contribute to a wide range of activities. They are not different in this regard from perception and memory. Two functions given relatively little attention are the role emotion plays in providing information about the status of our processing systems and its role in organizing and integrating the behavioral machinery, so that both automatic and deliberative processes aim at common goals. The first function suggests that emotions act as gauges that provide an ongoing, moment by moment read-out of the state of the organism as it is engaged in problem solving. These broadly experienced subjective states tell us how we feel about events, how their representation strikes us, how we expect to feel about them later on, what outcomes we anticipate, and how well we expect to cope. Emotions are like states of energy and fatigue, vigor and hopelessness, and are clues to the functioning of the system (its stages and levels). Weiner and his colleagues (Weiner, 1981) have made this point by suggesting that emotions are like a spectrum reflecting the arrangement of the cognitive (regulative) system in specific situations.

The second function suggests that emotions serve to integrate across the levels of the processing hierarchy. We have seen a dramatic illustration of this in our study of the development of anticipatory nausea in patients undergoing cancer chemotherapy. Patients receiving these noxious medications experience nausea and sometimes vomiting. The nausea rapidly conditions to taste (from the medications) and then may condition to concrete cues (needles, the nurse) in the immediate treatment situation. If the patient is also anxious while receiving his or her injections, the combination of taste and anxiety leads to the spread of the conditioning to a much wider range of cues, both concrete (sights of the hospital) and abstract (the thought that tomorrow requires a visit to the hospital). Simple, emotional reflexes (e.g., sensory elicited nausea), are integrated with concrete and abstract memory structures in the presence of fear and anxiety. Emotions play a critical role in organizing the regulative system so that its coping stage meshes with the demands of the environmental representation, and its lowest, automatic levels of processing are directed to the same ends as the highest, conceptual levels of processing. It may seem as if the emotional animal is decorticate. Not so. The emotional animal is using its cortex (higher level conceptual skills) in the service of a goal that is common to its schematic-perceptual processes, and primitive, sensory-motor processes.

REFERENCES

Ahles, T.A., Blanchard, E.B., & Leventhal, H. Cognitive control of pain: Attention to the sensory aspects of the cold pressor stimulus. *Cognitive Therapy and Research*, 1983, 7, 159–178.

Ekman, P., & Friesen, W. *Unmasking the face: A guide to recognizing the emotions from facial cues*. Englewood Cliffs, NJ.: Prentice-Hall, 1975.

Ekman, P., Friesen, W., & Ellsworth, P. *Emotion in the human face: Guidelines for research and integration of the findings*. New York: Pergamon, 1972.

Ekman, P., Roper, G., & Hager, J. Deliberate facial movement. *Child Development*, 1980, *51*, 886–891.

Field, T.M., Woodson, R., Greenberg, R., Cohen, R. Discrimination and imitation of facial expressions by neonates. *Science*, 1982, *218*:4568, 179–81.

Izard, C.E. *The face of emotion*. New York: Appleton-Century-Crofts, 1971.

James, W. *The principles of psychology* (Vols. 1 and 2). New York: Henry Holt and Co., 1890.

Lang, P.J. A bio-informational theory of emotional imagery. *Psychophysiology*, 1979, *16*, 495–512.

Lang, P.J., Kozak, M.J., Miller, G.A., Levin, D., & McLean, A. Emotional imagery: Conceptual structure and pattern of somato-visceral response. *Psychophysiology*, 1980, *17*, 179–192.

Leeper, R.W. A motivational theory of emotion to replace "Emotion as a disorganized response." *Psychological Review*, 1948, *55*, 5–21.

Leventhal, H. Findings and theory in the study of fear communications. In L. Berkowitz (Ed.), *Advances in Experimental Social Psychology* (Vol. 5). New York: Academic Press, 1970.

Leventhal, H. Emotions: A basic problem for social psychology. In C. Nemeth (Ed.), *Social Psychology: Classic and contemporary integrations*. Chicago: Rand McNally, 1974.

Leventhal, H. A perceptual-motor processing model of emotion. In P. Pliner, K. Blankenstein, & I.M. Spigel (Eds.), *Perception of emotion in self and others* (Vol. 5). New York: Plenum, 1979.

Leventhal, H. Toward a comprehensive theory of emotion. In L. Berkowitz (Ed.), *Advances in Experimental Social Psychology* (Vol. 13). New York: Academic Press, 1980.

Leventhal, H. The integration of emotion and cognition: A view from the perceptual-motor theory of emotion. In M.S. Clark & S.T. Fiske (Eds.), *Affect and cognition: The 17th annual symposium on cognition*. Hillsdale, N.J.: Lawrence Erlbaum Associates, 1982.

Leventhal, H., & Everhart, D. Emotion, pain and physical illness. In C. Izard (Ed.), *Emotions and psychopathology*. New York: Plenum, 1979.

Leventhal, H., Meyer, D., & Nerenz, D. The commonsense representation of illness danger. In S. Rachman (Ed.), *Medical Psychology* (Vol. 2). New York: Pergamon, 1980.

Leventhal, H., & Mosbach, P. The perceptual-motor theory of emotion. In J.T. Cacioppo & R.E. Petty (Eds.), *Social psychophysiology*. New York: Guilford Press, 1983.

Leventhal, H., & Nerenz, D.R. A model for stress research and some implications for the control of stress disorders. In D. Meichenbaum & M. Jaremko, (Eds.), *Stress prevention and management: A cognitive behavioral approach*. New York: Plenum, 1982.

Marshall, G.D., & Zimbardo, P.G. Affective consequences of inadequately explained physiological arousal. *Journal of Personality and Social Psychology*, 1979, *37*, 953–969.

Maslach, C. Negative emotional biasing of unexplained arousal. *Journal of Personality and Social Psychology*, 1979, *37*, 953–969.

Melzack, R. *The puzzle of pain: Revolution in theory and treatment*. New York: Basic Books, 1973.

Meyers, R.E. Comparative neurology of vocalization and speech: proof of a dichotomy. *Annals of the New York Academy of Sciences*, 1976, *280*, 745–757.

Nerenz, D.R., Leventhal, H., & Love, R. Factors contributing to emotional distress during cancer chemotherapy. *Cancer*, in press.

Piaget, J. *Construction of reality in the child*. New York: Basic Books, 1954.

Posner, M.I., & Keele, S.W. On the genesis of abstract ideas. *Journal of Experimental Psychology*, 1968, *77*, 353–363.

Posner, M.I., & Keele, S.W. Retention of abstract ideas. *Journal of Experimental Psychology*, 1970, *83*, 304–308.

Posner, M.I., & Snyder, C.R. Attention and cognitive control. In R. Solso (Ed.), *Information processing and cognition: The Loyola Symposium*. Hillsdale, N.J.: Lawrence Erlbaum Associates, 1975.

Russell, B. *An outline of philosophy*. New York: Meridian Books, 1960. (Originally published, 1927).

Safer, M.A. Sex and hemisphere differences in access to codes for processing emotional expressions and faces. *Journal of Experimental Psychology: General*, 1981, *110*, 86–100.

Schachter, S., & Singer, J. Cognitive, social, and physiological determinants of emotional state. *Psychological Review*, 1962, *69*, 377–399.

Shacham, S. *The effects of imagery monitoring, sensation monitoring and positive suggestion on pain and distress*. Unpublished doctoral dissertation, University of Wisconsin, Madison, 1979.

Sully, J. *An essay on laughter*. London: Longmans, Green, 1902.

Tomkins, S.S. *Affect, imagery, consciousness (Vol. 1). The positive affects*. New York: Springer, 1962.

Tomkins, S.S. *Affect, imagery, consciousness (Vol. 2). The negative affects*. New York: Springer, 1963.

Tomkins, S.S. Affect as amplification: Some modifications in theory. In R. Plutchik & H. Kellerman (Eds.), *Emotion: Theory, research and experience*. New York: Academic Press, 1980.

Weiner, B. *The emotional consequences of causal ascriptions*. Unpublished manuscript, University of California, Los Angeles, 1981.

Weiss, J.M. Effects of coping behavior with and without a feedback signal on stress pathology in rats. *Journal of Comparative and Physiological Psychology*, 1971, *77*, 22–30.

Zajonc, R.B. Feeling and thinking: Preferences need no inferences. *American Psychologist*, 1980, *35*, 151–175.

14 On the Nature and Function of Emotion: A Component Process Approach

Klaus R. Scherer
University of Giessen

Plato's early division of the human psyche into cognition, emotion, and conation has profoundly affected virtually all scientific approaches to the study of human nature and human behavior. This trichotomy has seemed so appropriate that its adequacy has rarely been challenged. The issue of the supremacy of cognition over emotion, or vice versa, has powerful implications for the scientific view of human nature, and has been the subject of perennial debates in philosophy, psychology, and the social sciences. As with many other theoretical issues concerning human behavior, there seem to be cyclic changes in what is considered to be fashionable, or even acceptable. in scientific thought during particular historical periods. and rational views of human nature have alternated with irrational views throughout the centuries. Behaviorism, and particularly the ''cognitive revolution'' in the 1960s, led to the predominantly cognitive and rational view of human behavior which is popular in the social and behavioral sciences today in contrast to the instinctivist and irrationalist views that dominated psychology and the social sciences during the 19th and early 20th centuries. Thus, today the image of man is no longer that of an individual enslaved by his passions, but rather that of a philosopher making decisions on the basis of logical deduction and inference. In this tradition, emotion is seen as a regrettable flaw in an otherwise perfect cognitive machine.

Needless to say, an extremely cognitive view of human functioning is just as inadequate as an extremely affect-oriented one. A radically cognitive view of man as pure logician is bound to neglect important features of human functioning and risks developing into an elegant but improbable theoretical edifice. However, the pendulum seems to swing back. In anthropology, ethology, philosophy, psychology, and sociology there has recently been a notable increase in the number of publications concerned mainly with emotion and affective behavior.

Unfortunately, this renewed interest in emotion has had little effect so far in righting the balance in a direction of more fruitful views of human nature, and more complex approaches to behavioral research. One of the major obstacles to progress in this area has been the problem of arriving at a definition and a concept of emotion acceptable to most psychologists. While it is generally difficult for psychologists to reach consensus on working definitions and ways of operationalizing the phenomena they study, they nonetheless often work with definitions that allow them to communicate with each other on work in progress, and are able to reach at least an implicit understanding. For example, while I know of no officially sanctioned and universally shared definition of cognition, most "cognitive psychologists" seem to agree they are dealing with very similar phenomena. In the study of emotion, such an implicit understanding has mostly been absent, leading at times to proposals that the concept be abolished altogether as misleading (e.g. Duffy, 1941). However, this situation is slowly changing.

There now seems to be a growing consensus among emotion theorists that emotion is best treated as a psychological construct consisting of several aspects or components: a) the component of cognitive appraisal or evaluation of stimuli and situations, b) the physiological component of activation or arousal, c) the component of motor expression, d) the motivational component, including behavior intentions or behavioral readiness, and e) the component of subjective feeling state. Judging from a number of recent surveys of emotion in the literature, there seems to be a fair amount of agreement that the concept of emotion should encompass all of these components, rather than just some of them (see Averill, 1980; Izard, 1977; Lazarus, Averill & Opton, 1970; Leventhal, 1979; Plutchik, 1980).

This convergence of opinion in terms of emotion as a psychological construct does not mean, of course, that we have reached a stage where emotion theorists would subscribe to a consensual textbook treatment of emotion as a psychological phenomenon. On the contrary, some of the central issues in emotion theory and research have crystallized in recent years and continue to provoke lively argument and dissension among scholars in the field. In this chapter I will deal with three major points of dissension which I consider to be of particular importance in terms of the further development of emotion theory. These issues concern 1) the functions of emotion, 2) the definition of emotion and the need for a descriptive framework, and 3) the role of cognition in emotion. In each case I will give only a fairly cursory review of earlier treatments of these issues and point to some of the opposing views, since the scope of this chapter prohibits an extensive historical review. Rather, I will outline some preliminary theoretical ideas which I have been examining while trying to develop the theoretical framework for my empirical work on the vocal nonverbal expression of emotion (Scherer, 1979a,c, 1981a,b).

THE FUNCTIONS OF EMOTION

As far as the functions of emotion are concerned, there seems to be a major split between theorists who view emotion exclusively as "disruption" or "interruption" of coordinated behavior sequences and those who view emotions as primarily adaptive, motivational mechanisms.

Pribram (1967), Mandler (1975), and others take the interruption of ongoing behavior sequences with a resultant direction of attention towards the cause of the interruption to be the major criterion for defining emotion. This view has been very pervasive in the social and behavioral sciences and may have led to a somewhat one-sided notion of emotion. For example, Simon (1967) argued that emotions could easily be represented in computer simulations of behavior by an interrupt system that would call upon corrective subroutines if the major program ran into difficulties.

Much of our experience with affect, however, seems to contradict the notion of emotion as interruption. For example, increased interest and pleasure during the course of a successful behavioral routine would seem to be supportive rather than interruptive. The notion of an interrupt system usually implies relatively extreme and mostly negative emotions that are incompatible with an ongoing plan of behavior. Yet, mild emotional states, such as pleasure or weak anxiety, can be superimposed on plans and behavior sequences without necessarily interrupting them. Whether emotional processes interrupt, disturb or adaptively support cognitive or behavioral sequences depends on the specific situation, the nature of the task, the degree of arousal and other factors, but does not constitute an adequate criterion for describing emotion.

I view emotion more broadly as the interface between an organism and its environment mediating between constantly changing situations and events and the individual's behavioral responses. The major aspects of this process are threefold: first, evaluation of the relevance of environmental stimuli or events for the organism's needs, plans or preferences in specific situations; second, the preparation of actions, both physiological and psychological, appropriate for dealing with these stimuli; and finally the communication of reactions, states, and intentions by the organisms to the social surround (Scherer, 1979b, 1981b,c, 1982).

In terms of evolutionary history, the flexibility of the behavioral adaptation of organisms to their environment is largely due to the emotion system. Emotions "decouple" the behavioral reaction from the stimulus event by replacing rigid reflex-like stimulus response patterns or instinctive innate releasing mechanisms.

As higher species evolve, they develop a need for increasingly complex information processing together with greater flexibility and variability of behavioral inventories. To accomplish this, the organism requires a mechanism to allow for an adequate adaptation of its behavior to changing external and internal stimuli. This is achieved by the process of emotion. In organisms capable of emotion, rigid releasing mechanisms are replaced by cognitive evaluation processes for stimuli and events. Reflex-like reactions are replaced partly by physiological activation, providing the energy required for an adequate response, and partly by the preparation of behavioral plans with high probability of occurrence but a certain latency. This decoupling of stimulus and response provides important advantages in that the flexibility of behavior is increased enormously (see also Tomkins, 1962, pp. 111–115). Most importantly, this mechanism makes possible the constant re-evaluation of complex stimuli and/or situations without much time delay since preparation of the behavioral reaction is part of the emotion process. Consequently, in line with Arnold (1960) and Lazarus (1968), I have postulated in recent papers (Scherer, 1979b, 1981b,c, 1982) that one of the major functions of emotion consists of the constant evaluation of external and internal stimuli in terms of their relevance for the organism and the preparation of behavioral reactions which may be required as a response to those stimuli.

A directly related function of emotion is the facilitation of learning. Emotional reactions provide an important intraorganismic signal system which is very important in enabling the organism to acquire new behavior patterns and to avoid maladaptive behavior. As Mowrer (1960) and other learning theorists have pointed out, emotion is a major prerequisite for learning. According to this view, negative emotions signal distress or pain and thereby produce avoidance reactions whereas positive emotions signal success and reward. The classical learning theory paradigm for emotion has not been widely accepted because the nature of the processes through which emotion interacts with cognition, motivation, and behavior was not spelled out in detail. Recent work in cognitive psychology is beginning to shed some light on the nature of the association between emotion, experience, and memory. Most pertinent is Bower's (1981) associative network theory which is an attempt to model the role of emotion in memory and learning.

The development of emotions as a mechanism for decoupling stimulus and response is particularly important for socially organized species. Because of the component of motor expression and because the intended behavioral reaction is often visible in rudimentary form in the pattern of motor expression, both the reaction and the behavioral intention of the individual are communicated to the social surround. This not only allows other organisms to predict the most likely behavior of the emoting organism and to plan their behavior accordingly, it also provides feedback about the likely reaction of others to the intentional movement or expression, allowing in turn appropriate changes in one's own behavioral plans.

Darwin (1872) was one of the first to point out the important role of emotional communication for social behavior. He put great emphasis on the fact that particular types of functional expression of emotion in the form of intention movements seem to have been selectively developed in the course of evolution for purposes of communication. Using the conceptual tools of modern biology and ethology, Leyhausen (1967) makes a very convincing case for the role of "impression" in shaping "expression" given the adaptational significance of communication. Unfortunately, this important functional aspect of emotion has been largely neglected in most theories of emotion to date.

It is interesting to speculate about the possibility that specific components of emotion are specialized to serve particular functions. A tentative juxtaposition of functions and components shows that this may well be the case:

Functions	Components
Evaluation of environment	Cognitive stimulus processing
System regulation	Neurophysiological processes
Preparation of action	Motivation and behavior tendencies
Communication of intention	Motor expression
Reflection and monitoring	Subjective feeling state

I believe that as in the case of growing consensus on the definition of emotion as a psychological construct consisting of several components there will be more of a convergence of opinion on the nature of emotion if a functional, rather than a conceptual or structural, approach is adopted. The most serious source of dissension concerns the issue of how many psychological states should be regarded as bona fide emotions and how these can be distinguished from each other.

ON THE DEFINITION AND DESCRIPTION OF AFFECTIVE STATES

Even a superficial perusal of the scientific literature on emotion yields an enormous number of verbal labels used to refer to emotional states. There have been several attempts to produce comprehensive lists of emotion related labels (Averill, 1975; Davitz, 1969; de Rivera, 1977). Most of these have listed well over 500 English terms without attempting to be exhaustive and without listing longer expressions. A similar attempt using German words (Scherer, 1983a), and trying to eliminate synonyms, yielded well over 200 such terms. In glancing through the entries of such lists, the problem of differentiating and clearly delineating emotions from other psychological states becomes immediately obvious: Do labels such as "impressed," "adventurous," "careless," "determined," "doubtful," "awed," "pensive," "reckless" characterize emotional states? If not, what are the psychological categories that can subsume these states?

Our language allows for the differentiation of a huge number of psychologically relevant states that seem to go unlabeled and uncategorized by most psychological taxonomies. In spite of the current distinction between "state" and "trait" we do not have a comprehensive theory of "psychological states." It is possible that the difficulties encountered in developing a satisfactory field of emotion research are largely due to the lack of an adequate "psychological state" theory. Apart from the lack of theory, we have a serious terminological problem: Which generic term are we to use for states of the organism that have both organic and psychological components, only some of which we will want to call emotions? I suggest the term "affective states" as such a generic term. The original meaning of the Latin root "afficere" seems perfectly suitable to denote the various types of states to be subsumed under such a term: (1) to bring somebody into a bodily or organic state, condition or disposition, (2) to bring somebody into a mental or psychological mood, to excite or stimulate or to move or touch, (3) to attack, weaken or exhaust someone (Menge, 1908). "Affective" thus appears to be a suitable generic term for a psychological state construct implying several different components (setting aside the term's meaning of "strong emotion" which seems to be popular in naive parlance).

The term "emotion" could then be used to refer to clearly delineated, intensive patterns of affective processes. In order to factor out special states to be called emotions from the steady flow of affective processes, we need a descriptive system that allows us to plot all relevant features of affective states systematically. Such a descriptive system will eventually enable us to draw up a taxonomy of emotions that will both answer the question of how to separate emotions from nonemotions, and also provide a classification of different emotions. A short survey of existing emotion theories shows (Scherer, 1983a) that none of the present theories of emotion satisfactorily distinguishes emotions from other affective states nor offers a consistent classification of different emotions, quite apart from settling the issue of the overall number of emotions. Given the heavy emphasis that many theorists of emotion place on fusions or blends of primary emotions, this problem is particularly salient (Izard, 1971, 1977; Plutchik, 1962, 1980, this volume; Tomkins, 1962, 1963, this volume).

Psychology needs to develop a conceptual system along the lines of analytic chemistry which allows the researcher to determine the components of even the most complex affective blends. Even though we usually refer to affective *states*, implying a static concept, we know very well that contrary to the fairly stable compounds studied by analytic chemistry, we are dealing with dynamic, constantly changing affective *processes*. We face the problem of having to describe the states of various components of the organic and psychological systems without neglecting the dynamic process of change from one stage to the next. In addition, we need to identify recurring patterns of change that are generally labeled using emotion terms.

To illustrate the basic idea, let us look at an emotional episode in the life of a simple animal, a member of the species of *Organismus simplicissimus,* an imaginary mammal feeding on small insects but occasionally catching worms (a great delicacy, particularly when they are fat and juicy). Figure 14.1 lists the respective changes in the different subsystems of the organism which are considered to be components of affective states. The figure shows the way in which the cognitive evaluation of environmental events changes the states in other subsystems, the persistence of such states after novel input (because of the sluggishness of some of the subsystems), and the way in which the newly instigated changes blend with and gradually supersede former states. What is less obvious in this example, but needs to be emphasized, is the fact that all components influence each other, e.g., cognitive states can be affected by earlier physiological, motivational, or expressive states. The emphasized state descriptions in Fig. 14.1 represent the emotions of joy and anger defined (in terms of a psychological construct) as a patterned sequence of states in different subsystems over a period of time.

This is an oversimplified example of a descriptive approach to a taxonomy of affective states which I call a *component process model.* This term is based on the notion that dynamic affective processes can be conceptualized as patterns of state changes in the relevant subsystems of an organism. In other words, the *process of affect* is seen as a sequence of complex, multisystem micro-states in which changes in the state of one subsystem have lawful effects on consequent changes in other subsystems.[1] The term "component process model" implies that the construct involves both several interrelated and interdependent components reflecting the states of the different subsystems of the organism and that the dynamic nature of the component state changes is central to its definition.

Once a descriptive system that permits us to determine all relevant features of the varying states of organismic subsystems is developed, it should be possible to identify recurring patterns of state changes over time, as shown by the pattern in Fig. 14.1. According to the growing consensus on the relevant components of emotion (see earlier), the following component states would have to be assessed by such a descriptive system: motivation, perceptual/cognitive information processing, motor expression and behavior, central and autonomic changes, and finally a component of consciousness or subjective feeling state.

I have developed a preliminary version of the descriptive system designed to systematically describe the states of the subsystems of an organism over time (Scherer, 1983b). This approach is cast in the form of a facet system amenable to the methodological procedures advocated by facet theorists (Borg, 1981; Gutt-

---

[1]Because of the established usage of terms like "affective state," I use the word "state" both in that sense of a "macro-state" (which is really a process), and in the sense of a steady state as a "static" micro-state. We need a "theory of states" to get around the conceptual problems here.

TIME ------>

COMPONENTS	1	2	3	4	5	6
Cognitive	Seeing a worm	Evaluating it as very fat	*Seeing worm disappear*	*Attribute to neighbor snatching it*	*Judging neighbor to be weaker*	Seeing novel object
Physiological	Visceral changes	Salivation	*Orienting reflex*	*ANS arousal*	*ANS arousal*	*ANS arousal* + orienting
Motivational	Wanting to catch and eat	Wanting to feast	Wanting to feast + search	*Wanting to feast + retrieve*	*Wanting to feast + fight*	*Wanting to fight* + explore
Expressive	Open mouth	Smile	Raised eyebrows	*Frown*	*Bared teeth*	*Bared teeth* + raised eyebrows
Feeling	Appetite	Anticipatory enjoyment	Anticipatory enjoyment + surprise	*Frustration*	*Anger*	*Anger* + interest

Note: Underlined state descriptions are postulated as components of joy, italicized descriptions as components of anger.

FIG. 14.1. Component process model of affective state changes in "organismus simplicissimus."

TABLE 14.1
Descriptive Facet System for
Affect States—Major Subsystems

Support system
    Neuroendocrine state
    Autonomic state

Action system
    Neuromuscular state

Information system
    State of perception/memory/prediction/evaluation
    of situations, relationships, facts, events/actions

Executive system
    Motivational state
    State of planning/decision making

Monitoring system
    State of consciousness
    State of attention

---

man, 1957). Space considerations prohibit a more detailed description of the role of facet theory and methodology in this approach. I will therefore use the term "facet" but not the facet notation to discuss the descriptive system. The terms "category" or "feature" can be used to convey the basic meaning of "facet" in this context for those less familiar with facet theory. Basically, I am trying to provide a systematic listing of the features, qualities, attributes, characteristics, or facets of affective states that need to be assessed or described in order to provide a comprehensive characterization of an affective state.[2]

Table 14.1 shows five functionally defined subsystems of an organism together with a breakdown of the types of states that need to be described within each of these subsystems. Again, space permits only a brief indication of the implications inherent in this list, such as hierarchical relationships between the subsystems including feedforward, feedback, and control processes. Clearly, we need much more progress in the study of psychological functioning before such a discussion can profitably begin. I am assuming, however, that there is some consensus on the utility of assuming such functional subsystems.

The facet system attempts to bring together systematically those features, attributes, characteristics or facets of the components reflecting the various subsystems described which can be seen as useful in distinguishing different affective states. Clearly, serious problems exist in the choice of level for such facets

---

[2]A note on terminology: I use "subsystem" to refer to functionally defined systems in the *organism*, "component" to refer to that part of the *psychological construct* of emotion that reflects states of a particular subsystem, and "facet" to refer to specific *characteristics* or *features of components* that can be empirically determined.

(e.g., functional versus structural, microscopic versus macroscopic, etc.). In developing the preliminary facet system, my approach has been to cull from the relevant literature all those parameters that can contribute to describe and distinguish different types of affective states. For example, for the support system I have used the literature on the essential characteristics of autonomic system changes, such as the distinction between sympathetic and parasympathetic system states. For the executive system, I based my approach on work examining types or classes of motives in order to develop facets reflecting the salience of particular motivational states during specific periods of time, and also used decision theory to propose facets relevant to states of decision making. A number of useful descriptive systems exist for the motor system, particularly for motor expression. Ekman & Friesen's (1978) Facial Affect Coding System (FACS) is a good example of such a system, allowing a comprehensive description of facial movement (see Ekman, 1982).

The choice of appropriate facets for the perceptual-cognitive information processing system is particularly difficult. At the same time, the nature of the facets for this component is of particular importance, since the type of emotion resulting seems to be strongly determined by cognitive evaluation processes. Table 14.2 shows the list of facets proposed for the information processing subsystem in my preliminary version of the facet system. The types of facets and their arrangement has been strongly influenced by the hierarchical model of stimulus evaluation checks in the process of emotion which I suggested earlier

TABLE 14.2
Information System Facets

Occurrence of event
   Time, expectation, probability, predictability

Evaluation of outcome
   Intrinsic pleasantness
   Goal relevance, conduciveness
   Justice/equity

Attribution of causation
   Agent
   Motive/cause
   Legitimacy

Evaluation of coping potential
   Ability to control event or consequences
   Power to change event or outcome
   Capacity to cope with consequences

Comparison with external or internal standard
   Conformity to cultural expectations or norms
   Consistency with real and/or ideal self-image

TABLE 14.3
Elements for the Facet
"Evaluation of outcome"

0	irrelevant
1	expectations exceeded
2	expectations met
3	no concrete expectations, outcome conducive to goals
4	no concrete expectations, outcome not conducive to goals
5	expectations not completely met
6	expectations not met
7	outcome completely contrary to expectations

(see Scherer, 1981c, 1982, and p. 306ff. below). A long-term cross-cultural study aimed at assessing the major features of emotion-producing situations has also had a major influence here.[3] In addition, classification schemes suggested in the literature (Davitz, 1969; de Rivera, 1977; Kemper, 1978; Roseman, 1979) have been used to complement the list of relevant facets. As a concrete example of the possible elements in a particular facet, Table 14.3 shows the decisions to be made in assessing the state of the information processing system for one such facet ("evaluation of outcome").

At our present state of knowledge the development of facets for the monitoring system and for describing subjective feeling states is particularly difficult. In Table 14.1 I list attention deployment and state of consciousness as preliminary facets for the monitoring subsystem. In addition, I suggest defining subjective feeling state theoretically as "the awareness of the respective states of all other subsystems of the organism." Most likely, the elusive nature of the concepts of consciousness or awareness will continue to frustrate hopes for progress in theory and research in this domain.[4]

Assuming that valid coding of the various facet elements in this descriptive system is possible for small units of time, the sequence of element codes for the individual facets will yield an exhaustive description of dynamic changes in

---

[3] A general "component coding system" for emotion antecedent situations was developed jointly by Verena Aebischer, Gilles Benejam, Jacques Cosnier, Heiner Ellgring, Dino Giovannini. Eva Huber, Pio Ricci-Bitti, Angela Summerfield. Harald Wallbott and myself in the framework of an intercultural project on emotion antecedents, expression and regulation supported by the European Laboratory of Social Psychology in Paris. In the course of this project, descriptions of emotion antecedent situations, emotional reactions in the different subsystems of the organism, and attempts at regulation and control have been obtained from more than 1.200 subjects in 6 countries (see Scherer, Summerfield, & Wallbott, 1983).

[4] A more extensive discussion of the facet system in its present form would clearly exceed the space available. The preliminary version of the system (Scherer, 1983b) can be obtained from the author who would welcome comments, criticism, and further suggestions.

affective states. One could develop a much more complex sequence pattern of state changes analogous to the example of *Organismus simplicissimus* in Fig. 14.1, using the comprehensive facet system proposed for the human organism and, at the same time, attempt to describe patterns of state changes (as symbolized by the pattern in Fig. 14.1) that could form the basis for labeling a state with a particular emotion term.

What are the potential uses of such a facet system? One immediately obvious application is the comprehensive and relatively objective description of affective states of organisms, including infrahuman organisms, for a variety of purposes (although it will obviously be difficult to assess some of the information required). Further, it could be useful for organizing or coding subjectively reported affective experiences. In a number of recent studies (Averill, 1982; Boucher & Brandt, 1981; Scherer, Summerfield & Wallbott, 1983) subjects were asked to report past events that led to emotional reactions and to describe their physiological and nonverbal responses. The facet system proposed here could provide a coding scheme to organize both the evaluation of free responses and structure the development of fixed response questionnaires.

On particularly important area for the application of the facet system is the study of the relationships between affective processes, as described by patterns of changes in the states of organismic subsystems, and the verbal labels that are commonly used to refer to such changes. It seems to me that one major hindrance to progress in theory and research on emotion has been the difficulty of getting beyond the semantics of emotion terms. Quite a few theories are based on meaning analyses of emotion terms or on statistical analyses of similarity judgments of emotion terms (e.g., Davitz, 1969; Plutchik, 1980). Although the semantic space of emotion terms is an interesting topic in itself, it should not be the sole basis for a comprehensive psychological theory of emotional processes. We know that linguistic labels are imprecise and capture only specific aspects of phenomena, mostly those that are immediately relevant for speakers in a particular context. The facet system might make it possible to study the conditions under which particular linguistic labels are used more carefully. This could be done by using the facet system to analyze subsystem state changes in behavioral episodes which are given a particular emotional label, either by the person experiencing the affect or by outside observers. Another possibility would be to construct accounts of affective processes and get subjects to label these using standard emotion terms. The results of such studies are likely to shed more light on the nature of the similarity judgments and the underlying dimensions for emotion terms. Obviously, it would be highly interesting to conduct such studies in the framework of crosscultural comparisons to assess how different languages encode emotion-relevant subsystem states and/or their changes.

Finally, and this brings us back to the starting point of the discussion, the facet system might help to settle some basic questions: the definition and delineation of emotion, and the question of the number of distinct emotions, including a taxonomy of different emotional states. It will be difficult to obtain a consensus among emotion theorists on the criteria required to call an affective state or process an "emotion." It may be that constructing a facet system that presents an inventory of possible criteria is helpful at least in defining the issues about which one can disagree. This question is not independent of the problem raised earlier, concerning the use of emotion terms in naive psychology. Given the widespread usage of the words "emotion" and "affect," it seems pointless to strive for a scientific concept of "emotion" that is widely divergent from the everyday use of that word. Therefore, I would argue for an inductive approach to the problem, trying to use a descriptive system such as the facet system proposed here, to determine how theorists differ in the use of the concept of emotion and how this relates to popular use of the word. This approach would provide a basis for reaching agreement on a shared scientific definition for the concept of "emotion."

It would be possible to solve the problem of the number of emotions and provide a taxonomy in a similar way. The facet system allows not only a clearer description of the kinds of taxonomies that seem to be inherent in the semantic distinctions provided by emotion terms in our language, but can also be used to construct a number of scientific taxonomies. Obviously, there is no natural classification or taxonomy but rather a wide variety of potential classifications depending on which facets or combination of facets are used as criteria for constructing a classification. For example, for some purposes different states of the *support* system, e.g., states of sympathetic versus parasympathetic dominance, would be of primary importance in distinguishing affective states, whereas in other situations it would be more important to consider different facets of the *information processing* system, such as states resulting from the blocking of a goal or action sequence versus states following the achievement of goals. One of the possible outcomes of such an analysis is that the apparent differences between discrete emotion theories, dimensional theories, and cognitive theories could turn out to be differences that are based mostly on the differential use of facets or elements of facets in distinguishing affective states. Rather than attempting to find the ultimate classification of emotions, it might be more useful to determine a classification that is best suited for a particular purpose.

It must be stressed that a systematic description using the facet system proposed here is not an aim in itself. It provides the basis for developing functional models and theories and guides the design of empirical studies of the factors involved in emotional processes. For example, the important issue of the relationships between the different components of emotion (see chapters by Ekman and Leventhal) would benefit from a more comprehensive and systematic description of the elements involved in each component and the relevant state changes that occur over time. Again, the purpose of such a facet system is to provide a blueprint of the important elements involved in an emotional process as a basis for the development of functional models of emotion. Empirical tests of such functional models can help to continuously expand and refine the descriptive system and evaluate its usefulness. As an example of the kind of theoretical approach that could be studied with the help of such a descriptive framework, I now present a functional model of the precognitive and cognitive processes involved in the course of an emotion. In terms of the component process approach the following model postulates a hierarchical sequence of state changes in one component, the information processing system.

A PROCESS MODEL OF STIMULUS EVALUATION

As a number of contributions in this volume show (see chapters by Lazarus, Zajonc, Leventhal), the role of cognition in emotion is a hotly debated topic. I do not think, however, that our knowledge is increased by categorizing certain information-processing events as cognitive and denying this label to others. Although we still lack a clear understanding of the process by which internal and external stimuli are evaluated, I do not believe that much is gained by discussing whether one or two systems are involved, nor which one is the more dominant or more basic. My own efforts in this area have been restricted to an attempt at understanding what the nature of the stimulus evaluation process might be, adopting a functional, rather than a structural approach.

In an earlier paper (Scherer, 1981c) I suggested that this process of evaluation consists of a very rapidly occurring sequence of hierarchically organized stimulus processing steps. In other words, I suggest that the evaluation of the relevance of any external or internal stimulus (or the interpretation of the meaning of a stimulus event) registered by an organism's sensorium is established by a sequence of specific checks in terms of hierarchically ordered criteria. Given the function of emotion as a mechanism for survival, the sequence of evaluative checks must obviously be organized in such a way that criteria most relevant to the survival of the organism are checked first in order to prepare the organism for emergency action.

I now describe a sequence of such stimulus evaluation checks (SEC) which would seem minimally necessary for adequately evaluating or appraising emotion producing stimuli. It is important to note that these stimuli can consist of external events or situations as well as of one's own behavior or even internally generated sensations or memories.

The first SEC consists of an evaluation of the *novelty* or unexpectedness of the stimulus, and is very closely related to the orientation reflex (see Pribram, this volume, p. 23). It is quite possible that this first check is at least partly independent of higher cortical functions and may be a direct result of neural firing patterns (see Tomkins, 1962, this volume). Thus, a startle reaction to a sudden loud noise may be the immediate result of such a very basic novelty check. On the other hand, for less sudden and extreme stimuli there may well be higher cortical functions involved in checking the stimulus against expectations in memory using some kind of schematic processing. This first evaluative check is clearly involved in emotions such as boredom and surprise, although later SECs may affect the particular form of these emotions. This check must occur first and must be very fast, since the survival of the organism may depend on a quick reaction to an unexpected event. One of the effects of a novelty evaluation might be to speed up processing of the following SECs.

The second SEC consists of the evaluation of the *intrinsic pleasantness* or unpleasantness of a stimulus which causes the organism to experience pleasure or distress. It is important to stress that this check has to do with the *inherent* pleasantness or unpleasantness of a stimulus, and is not dependent on its relevance to the goals of an organism at that particular moment. The pleasantness/unpleasantness evaluation is one of the major aspects of almost all studies of emotional meaning or expression, independent of whether their focus is on verbal labels or nonverbal expression. Similarly, this type of appraisal is central to most theories of emotion. To what extent this check is independent of higher cortical functions is an interesting question (cf. Zajonc's 1980 postulate of a phylogenetically older affective evaluation system which according to his view functions independently of cognitive evaluation).

The third SEC performs the evaluation of the *goal/need conduciveness* of the stimulus, i.e., the appraisal of the extent to which the introduction of that particular stimulus or event will advance or hinder the attainment of a specific goal, or the satisfaction of a need, high in priority for the organism at that particular time. I believe that this aspect of goal conduciveness must be clearly distinguished from the evaluation of the inherent pleasantness or unpleasantness of a given stimulus. Even intrinsically pleasant stimuli can interrupt ongoing plans and thus be evaluated negatively by the organism in terms of goal attainment. If the result of the goal relevance SEC indicates an interruption of ongoing plans, fear or anger may be the result. Stimuli which further goal attainment on the other hand, will lead to a state of contentment. If the organism's expectations are exceeded, delight or joy will be the resulting state.

The fourth subcheck determines the *coping potential* of an organism with regard to the outcome of a past or future event and its consequences for the organism. It consists of four subchecks: 1) the causation check, which serves to determine the agent and the motive or cause of an event, 2) the control check, determining to which extent any activities of the organism can affect the consequences (which requires information about causation), 3) the power check, evaluating the relative power with respect to obstacles or adversaries, and 4) the adjustment check, assessing the ease with which the organism can adjust to conditions changed by uncontrollable events. Sadness would seem to be the result of uncontrollable negative events, whereas anger and fear represent the high and low power outcomes, respectively.

While all of the SECs discussed so far are likely to be present in many species of animals, certainly in the higher developed mammals, there seems to be a fifth SEC for humans (and possibly chimpanzees), *a norm/self compatability check.*

This SEC consists of a comparison of stimuli, particularly one's own actions or the actions of others and their results, with external and internal standards such as social norms and various aspects of the real or ideal self-concept. For example, if one's own behavior does not conform to social norms or if it is not compatible with one's self-concept, embarrassment, shame, or guilt may result.

The assumption underlying this sequence of stimulus evaluation checks is that each consecutive SEC further differentiates the emotional state of the organism. I assume that our verbal labels for emotions characterize the outcome of particular checks. In some cases, the label may describe the outcome after a specific SEC, e.g., startle or surprise may be appropriate verbal descriptions of the result of the first SEC, the novelty check. However, in most cases, the emotional state is further differentiated by the subsequent SECs. Thus, surprise will be positive or negative, depending on the inherent pleasantness and/or the goal relevance of the stimulus. Also, the outcomes of consequent SECs can quickly supersede the result of earlier SECs, as for example, in the case of anger replacing surprise after the agent of an unexpected hindrance is discovered.

Given the assumption of a hierarchical sequence of SECs in the model presented so far, it is important to address the issue of whether the evaluation process passes through all the steps or SECs at every time. Clearly, this may not always be the case. Rather, the assumption is that the process passes through the SECs always in the same hierarchical order but that some of the steps may be skipped and the process short-circuited. Since one of the underlying postulates of the model is that the evaluation process is continuous, the skipping of steps is most likely to occur with *re-evaluations* of stimuli, evaluations that have already once passed through the evaluation sequence. In such a case, the novelty and pleasantness SECs may be bypassed and a "loop" of repeated coping and norm-consistency checks activated. Also, with "own behavior" or a memory of an event as the stimulus to be evaluated, the novelty check may not seem particularly appropriate. Furthermore, some SECs may only be activated if certain conditions hold, e.g., the goal/plan conductiveness check if there are indeed salient goals or plans against which events need to be evaluated. However, even in these cases, one could conceive of the evaluation process passing through all the steps with a predetermined outcome on some of them (and a resulting increase in the speed of processing).

The preceding discussion of the emotions as possible outcomes of individual SECs or sequences of SECs has been rather superficial and no attempts have been made to outline the antecedent evaluation processes in more detail for any one of the "classic" emotions. This remains to be done in future work. Table 14.4 shows a first attempt to use the facet system to hypothetically specify some of the relevant elements of the primary facets in the area of information processing for selected emotions that might be the outcome of such hierarchical SEC sequences. The presence of some of the elements specified seems necessary (but not sufficient) for the particular emotion to occur, others may or may not be

present. The entry "irrelevant" indicates that the facet does not play an antecedent role for that emotion, the entry "open" means that several elements of that
particular facet are possible antecedents for the respective emotion in question.
For example, "agent" in the case of anger could be "self," "other," or even
"chance." I want to stress that the entries in Table 14.4 reflect my personal
hypothetical estimate as to which elements of specific facets are likely to be
involved as antecedents of the states referred to by the respective labels. Much
empirical work will be required to check the adequacy of this conjecture. We are
currently involved in a cross-national questionnaire study of emotional experience which promises to furnish data that could be used for this purpose (Scherer,
Summerfield & Wallbott, 1983).

The tabular representation shown in Table 14.4 has the advantage of allowing
us to represent much more complex configurations of elements than flow charts,
decision trees, or structure diagrams. Also, by specifying the elements that
characterize an affective state, many different subtypes of an emotion normally
subsumed by one emotion term are possible. For example, depending on the
specific elements in the facets "goal relevance" and "justice" on the one hand,
and "agent" and "motive" on the other, one could distinguish between "just
anger" and "blind anger." Similarly, if one adds the autonomic and motor
expression subsystems, "hot" and "cold" anger should be clearly distinguishable.

An important question to consider is the extent to which the models outlined
above are at variance with discrete emotion theories such as those put forward by
Tomkins (1962, this volume) and Izard (1977). Clearly, the notion that human
emotional states are the complex results of a series of stimulus evaluation checks
appraising particular dimensions of stimulus meaning and may be characterized
by different component processes is well suited for explaining the large number
of highly differentiated emotional states which we seem to experience and are
often unable to describe verbally. The differentiatedness and complexity of the
resulting states is further increased, of course, by the fact that the emotional
reactions to an earlier part of the stimulus evaluation process in turn become an
input to the ongoing evaluation process. At least in humans, this situation is
further complicated by psychological defense and attempts at controlling emotion. The latter, incidentally, frees behavioral reaction even further from stimulus control. At the same time, since particular types of outcomes of the stimulus
evaluation process seem to reoccur reliably for many species there could be a
number of discrete emotions as *modal* outcomes of stimulus evaluation processes. Presumably, these modal outcomes are the bases for the verbal labels of
emotional states that are universally found in many different language families
all over the world.

One of the major advantages of the model suggested here is that it allows a
novel theoretical approach to blends or mixtures of emotions. Most discrete
emotion theories (e.g., Izard, 1977; Plutchik, 1980) can be described as "palette

TABLE 14.4
Hypothetical Information System States Required as Antecedents for Selected Emotions

Stimulus Evaluation checks (SEC)	Facets	Fear	Anger	Joy	Shame	Disgust	Sadness
Novelty	Expectation	unexpected	open	expected	open	open	open
Intrinsic Pleasantness	Pleasantness	open	open	pleasant	open	very unpleasant	unpleasant
Goal/Need Conduciveness	Relevance	highly relevant	highly relevant	relevant	relevant	irrelevant	relevant
	Conduciveness	obstructive	obstructive	conducive	open	irrelevant	obstructive
	Justice/Equity	open	unjust	just	unjust	irrelevant	irrelevant
Coping Potential	Agent	other	open	open	self	open	open
	Motive/Cause	malevolent or chance	open	benevolent or chance	egoistic or malevolent	open	open
	Control	low	low	low	low	low	low
	Power	low	high	high	low	low	low
Norm/Self Compatibility	Norm Compatibility	open	low	high	low	low	irrelevant
	Self Compatibility	open	open	high	highly inconsistent	irrelevant	irrelevant

theories," which imply a blending of basic emotions like that of a painter mixing basic colors on a palette. The alternative conceptualization that I would advocate on the basis of the component process model could be called a "kaleidoscope theory": a unique mixture of color and light resulting from the way in which the kaleidoscope pieces—the facet elements—fall or arrange themselves in a particular case. In other words, if outcomes of SECs (described by facet elements) that are specific to the "typical" evaluation process for several different "pure emotions" (those that can be easily characterized by a linguistic label) occur simultaneously, this may result in "hybrid" emotions with fairly special or singular characteristics. This theoretical notion implies that we do not have to postulate functionally homogeneous mechanisms constituting basic discrete emotions that are evolutionarily fixed, but can conceive of a much more flexible system capable of generating many different kinds of emotional states without clear boundaries.

At first glance, this may seem to contradict our experience of the functional unity and discreteness of emotions such as anger, fear, joy, etc. Yet, some of that apparent unity may be due to the fact that experience is affected by the availability of linguistic labels that by definition impose a large degree of separateness and discreteness on those sections of reality they describe. On the other hand, the regularity inherent in any environment results in the regular recurrence of specific combinations of facet elements and thus provides a good deal of discreteness. For example, perceptions of the achievement or the blocking of goals are constantly recurring states in the information processing subsystem that lead to predictable changes in states of other subsystems.

Furthermore, I do not want to imply that the state changes in different subsystems are totally variable or could occur in all possible combinations and sequences. On the contrary, in line with many recent findings in ethology and biology, as well as in developmental psychology, I am inclined to believe that there is some degree of "prewiring," innately determined links between changes in one subsystem and correspondent changes in other subsystems (like strings between some kaleidoscope pieces). A good deal of this prewiring is evolutionarily continuous and adaptive. The sequence of stimulus evaluation checks which I have outlined above may well be an example of such a prewired sequence of changes in the states of the information processing subsystem. The assumption is. as explained earlier, that the order in which the individual evaluation checks are activated is biologically predetermined and that the operation of later checks is based on the outcome of earlier checks. Thus, this notion is consonant with many of the ideas that have been expressed by Izard (1971, 1977). Plutchik (1962, 1980, this volume) and Tomkins (1962, 1963. this volume) on the one hand and psychoanalytically oriented researchers (Emde. 1980, this volume) on the other hand. One big difference is that it does not require, and even calls into question, the existence of a small number of functionally homogeneous *mechanisms* in the form of basic emotions.

One particularly important implication of this difference concerns the assumptions about the nature of the physiological and expressive components of discrete emotional states. Representatives of a discrete emotion theory seem to postulate a relatively invariable unitary pattern of changes in these subsystems, based upon innate neural pathways, all of which are collectively activated when the appropriate antecedent conditions for one of the basic emotions occur. My position is that such innate neural pathways exist only for the outcomes of the individual SECs. Elsewhere (Scherer, 1984a), I have suggested a *componential patterning model* for the changes in the support and action systems, assuming that the states of these subsystems are consecutively modified by the outcomes of the successive SECs. Based on functional considerations, a number of specific changes in physiological processes and expressive behavior can be predicted to follow particular outcomes.

Roughly, the following effects are to be expected. A positive outcome of the novelty check is likely to result, in addition to the frequently described orienting response, in straightening the posture, raising eyelids and eyebrows for scanning, interrupting ongoing locomotion and instrumental action, and deep inhalation. A pleasant outcome of the intrinsic pleasantness check should lead to autonomic sensitization of the sensory organs, and oro-facial changes maximizing taste and smell sensations. Further effects should consist in faucal and pharyngeal expansion resulting in clear, harmonic vocal sounds, and instrumental and locomotor approach behavior. An unpleasant outcome, on the other hand, should result in autonomic desensitization of the sensory organs and defense reactions, including oro-facial actions to close the orifices, or to expel noxious matter. This involves faucal and pharyngeal constriction (giving rise to narrow, pressed vocal sounds), as well as a closing-in, shrinking posture, and instrumental and locomotor distancing or avoidance behavior.

A positive outcome of the goal conduciveness check should produce a shift to the trophotropic side of the ergotropic-trophotropic balance (see Pribram, this volume, p. 15; Whybrow, this volume, p. 65) and a balanced tone in the striated musculature, as well as comfort and rest behavior. A negative outcome, a mismatch between actual and desired state, on the other hand, should produce ergotropic dominance—increasing arousal or activation. This will be accompanied by strongly increased tonic innervation of the musculature as well as phasic task-dependent innervations. The corresponding facial behavior is the frown (corrugator activity) which has been frequently linked with "something difficult or displeasing encountered in a train of thought or action" (Darwin, 1872/1965, p. 222). The voice is tense with high pitch and strong high-frequency harmonics.

A negative outcome of the control subcheck of the coping potential SEC will result in trophotropic dominance and general hypotension of the musculature with slumping posture, slow movement, flaccid facial tone, and a lax, muffled-sounding voice. If events or outcomes are still controllable, but if flight seems to be the only option (negative outcome of the power subcheck), ergotropic dominance increases to energize the emergency reaction of the organism. Increased adrenaline secretion is responsible for redirection of blood flow to the muscles of the peripheral organs (for running or protecting; leading to trembling if not used in movement), peripheral vasoconstriction to reduce bleeding (with a resulting drop in skin temperature), and an increase in respiratory rate. The voice is hypertense, with very high pitch, voicing irregularities, and high-frequency resonance (sounding harsh or shrill). A positive outcome of the power check, encouraging dominance assertion, produces increased noradrenaline secretion which, because of its thermogenetic effects, may be responsible for anger feeling "hot". Blood flow is redirected to the head and chest to support threat displays and fighting responses. Consequently, the facial musculature will show preparatory biting patterns and tensing of the muscles in the neck and around the mouth; the voice, because of deep breathing and chest register phonation, will be rather loud and full, with relatively low pitch (for details and a review of the relevant literature see Scherer, 1984a,b).

Clearly, these predictions are highly speculative, particularly since there is very little pertinent research evidence. While details will have to be revised as data become available, it is expected that the componential patterning mechanism will be borne out by future work, i.e. the postulate that the outcome of each consecutive SEC will modify the states produced by the preceding SECs, with the final pattern being the net result of these cumulative changes (with the added effects of control, impression management, and deception attempts, of course).

If these notions are correct one should be able to predict which types of emotional states should occur in particular species (provided that the information processing capacity of a species can be specified). Because the SECs are sequentially ordered in terms of increasing complexity of the processing system, one would expect that only some of the highest developed species, such as primates, are equipped for the whole range of emotions, whereas simpler species may be restricted to very basic, undifferentiated emotional states. This is very much in line with Hebb's (1949) early claim that homo sapiens is the most emotional species of all, a characteristic that tends to be masked by highly developed systems of emotional regulation and control.

In the same vein, one can attempt to predict the appearance of different emotions in ontogenetic development based on the unfolding cognitive capacities of the infant. Table 14.5 shows estimates of first appearances of specific emotional expressions based on observations reported in the relevant literature (see Scherer, 1979b, p. 238; cf. also Emde, this volume, p. 90). In the second column of Table 14.5 I list the SECs I believe to be necessary for the specified emotion to appear as a result of stimulus processing. This sequence seems to correspond roughly to the major stages in cognitive development as described by Piaget and others (cf. Sroufe, 1979; this volume).

In general, the study of the ontogenetic and phylogenetic development of the emotions seems of the utmost importance in attempting to settle some of the

TABLE 14.5
Stimulus Evaluation Prerequisites for the Ontogenetic Development of Emotion

Emotional Expression	Age of Onset (in months)	Stimulus Evaluation Checks (SECs) required				
		Novelty	Intrinsic pleasantness	Goal/need conduciveness	Coping potential	Norm/self-concept compatibility
Startle	0	x				
Displeasure	0	•	x			
Surprise	1–3	•	•	x		
Joy	3–5	•	•	x		
Anger	4–6	•	•	x	x	
Fear	5–9	•	•	x	x	
Shame/guilt	12–15	•	•	•	•	x
Contempt	15–18	•	•	•	•	x

Note: X indicates that the respective SEC is a necessary prerequisite for the occurrence of a particular emotion (albeit not necessarily sufficient); • indicates that the SEC is available but may not be centrally involved in determining which emotion will occur as a result of the stimulus evaluation sequence. (Reproduced from Scherer, 1982, p. 561.)

issues raised earlier. Again, I believe that a facet system of the kind proposed in this chapter could be useful in designing developmental and comparative studies of affective processes. It should be possible to look at different ontogenetic and phylogenetic steps in relation to the presence and/or importance of specific facets for a particular organismic subsystem, and the degree of differentiation of the elements. For example, it would be interesting to examine the notion that in the course of development more and more facets become pertinent as the cognitive capacities of the organism mature.

As previously pointed out, I believe that there is a high degree of parallelism between the ontogenetic, the phylogenetic and the microgenetic development, or sequence, of these steps. Consequently, in terms of the facets of the information processing system shown in Table 14.2, I would expect that the capacity of the system to deal with such facets develops in such a way that the earlier facets in the table develop first and the others follow step by step. However, in addition to this kind of vertical increase in complexity and greater differentiation, there is probably also a degree of horizontal complexity and differentiation. In other words, there may be rudimentary forms of information processing relative to each of the facets at different phylogenetic and ontogenetic stages. For example, goal relevance could be checked by feature recognition in a very simple organism whereas it may involve complex utility estimates in humans.

CONCLUDING REMARKS

In this chapter, I was only able to sketch some of the lines of thought I have been following in my work on emotion. The models I have outlined here are scarcely more than blueprints at the present time and obviously need much further thought and elaboration. The reason I venture to publish some of these preliminary ideas is my hope that critical feedback from colleagues will prevent me from being drawn into too many blind alleys. One of the major problems of the approach, particularly with the component process model and the facet system, is that it requires much more knowledge about psychological processes than we have so far accumulated. Although I realize the potential danger in this, I think that there is also a potential benefit. Namely, the possibility that the phenomenon of emotion might serve as a rallying, or focusing point to coordinate progress in different areas of psychology.

At the same time, the construct proposed here and the models suggested for its empirical study require a rather formidable research effort. In the long run, fragmentary studies of the individual components of emotion, such as physiological arousal, facial expression, or subjective feeling states in isolation, are unlikely to yield a major contribution to our understanding of the process of emotion. A long-term series of studies in which the phenomenon of emotion is studied in terms of all the components and levels described earlier using modern methodology is necessary. In recent years there has been definite progress in the development of appropriate techniques, notably for the assessment of motor expressive behavior (see Scherer & Ekman, 1982). All of these methods, whether they be measurement of autonomic arousal, of EEG patterns, or of verbal and nonverbal, vocal and nonvocal behavior require a fairly substantial investment in terms of the researcher's time and effort. Unfortunately, the present climate as far as research support is concerned, is not very conducive to such investment, nor is, for the most part, the academic climate, with its emphasis on quick publication rather than long term efforts. In addition, a phenomenon like emotion with its many components and their complex interaction, cannot be adequately studied unless interdisciplinary groups of researchers combine their different approaches to study it jointly. If such research efforts were to materialize, one could reasonably hope that after the next cyclic change in scientific thought on the role of passion and rationality in human nature, one would not have to start again from scratch.

ACKNOWLEDGMENT

This contribution is based on a number of papers presented at various meetings (Scherer, 1981c, 1982, 1983a), some parts of which are reproduced verbatim here. I am deeply indebted to a number of colleagues who have provided me with very thoughtful comments on the material presented in this chapter, particularly Jens Asendorpf, Joseph Campos, Paul Ekman, Phoebe Ellsworth, Robert Emde, Jurek Karylowski, Richard Lazarus, Robert Levenson, Howard Leventhal, Robert Levy, Peter Marler, Robert Wyer, and to Ruta Noreika for carefully editing the manuscript.

REFERENCES

Arnold, M. B. *Emotion and personality. (Vol. 1). Psychological aspects.* New York: Columbia University Press, 1960.

Averill, J. R. *A semantic atlas of emotional concepts.* JSAS Catalogue of Selected Documents in Psychology, 1975, *5,* 330.

Averill, J. R. A constructivist view of emotion. In R. Plutchik & H. Kellerman (Eds.), *Emotion. Theory, research, and experience (Vol. 1).* New York: Academic Press, 1980.

Averill, J. R. *Anger and aggression: An essay on emotion.* New York: Springer, 1982.

Borg, I. *Anwendungsorientierte multidimensionale Skalierung.* Berlin: Springer, 1981.

Boucher, J. D., & Brandt, M. E. Judgment of emotion: American and Malay antecedents. *Journal of Cross-Cultural Psychology,* 1981, *12,* 272–283.

Bower, G. H. Mood and memory. *American Psychologist,* 1981, *36,* 129–148.

Darwin, C. *The expression of the emotions in man and animals.* London: Murray, 1872. (Reprinted, Chicago: University of Chicago Press, 1965.)

Davitz, J. R. *The language of emotion.* New York: Academic Press, 1969.

de Rivera, J. A structural theory of the emotions. *Psychological Issues,* 1977, *10,* No. 4, Monograph 40.

Duffy, E. An explanation of "emotional" phenomena without the use of the concept "emotion." *Journal of General Psychology,* 1941, *25,* 283–293.

Ekman, P. Methods of measuring facial action. In K. R. Scherer, & P. Ekman, (Eds.), *Handbook of methods in nonverbal behavior research.* Cambridge: Cambridge University Press, 1982.

Ekman, P., & Friesen, W. V. *Manual for the facial action coding system.* Palo Alto, Calif.: Consulting Psychologists Press, 1978.

Emde, R. N. Toward a psychoanalytic theory of affect: I. The organizational model and its propositions. In S. I. Greenspan, & G. H. Pollock (Eds.), *The course of life: Psychoanalytic contributions toward an understanding of personality development* (Vol. 1) *Infancy and early childhood.* Washington, D.C.: NIMH, 1980.

Guttman, L. *Introduction to facet design and analysis.* Proceedings of the 15th International Congress of Psychology in Brussels. Amsterdam: North-Holland, 1957.

Hebb, D. O. *The organization of behavior.* New York: Wiley, 1949.

Izard, C. E. *The face of emotion.* New York: Appleton-Century-Crofts, 1971.

Izard, C. E. *Human emotions.* New York: Plenum, 1977.

Kemper, T. D. *A social interactional theory of emotions.* New York: Wiley, 1978.

Lazarus, R. S. Emotions and adaptation: Conceptual and empirical relations. In W. J. Arnold (Ed.), *Nebraska Symposium on Motivation (Vol. 16).* Lincoln: University of Nebraska Press, 1968.

Lazarus, R. S., Averill, J. R., & Opton, E. M. Towards a cognitive theory of emotion. In M. B. Arnold (Ed.), *Feelings and emotions.* New York: Academic Press, 1970.

Leventhal, H. A perceptual-motor processing model of emotion. In P. Pliner, K. Blankstein, & I. M. Spigel (Eds.), *Advances in the study of communication and affect: Perception and emotion in self and others.* New York: Plenum Press, 1979.

Leyhausen, P. Biologie von Ausdruck und Eindruck (Teil 1). *Psychologische Forschung,* 1967, *31,* 113–176.

Mandler, G. *Mind and emotions.* New York: Wiley. 1975 (2nd ed. 1980).

Menge, H. *Lateinisch-Deutsches Schulwörterbuch.* Berlin: Langenscheidt, 1908.

Mowrer, O. H. *Learning theory and behavior.* New York: Wiley, 1960.

Plutchik, R. *The emotions: Facts, theories, and a new model.* New York: Random House, 1962.

Plutchik, R. *Emotion: A psychoevolutionary synthesis.* New York: Harper & Row, 1980.

Pribram, K. H. Emotion: Steps toward a neuropsychological theory. In D. C. Glass (Ed.), *Neurophysiology and emotion.* New York: Rockefeller University Press and Russel Sage Foundation, 1967.

Roseman, I. *Cognitive aspects of emotion and emotional behavior.* Paper presented at the 87th Annual Convention of the American Psychological Association, New York, September 1979.

Scherer, K. R. Nonlinguistic vocal indicators of emotion and psychopathology. In C. E. Izard (Ed.), *Emotions in personality and psychopathology.* New York: Plenum, 1979. (a)

Scherer, K. R. Entwicklung der Emotion. In H. Hetzer, E. Todt, I. Seiffge-Krenke, & R. Arbinger (Eds.), *Angewandte Entwicklungspsychologie des Kindes- und Jugendalters.* Heidelberg: Quelle und Meyer, 1979. (b)

Scherer, K. R. Personality markers in speech. In K. R. Scherer & H. Giles (Eds.), *Social markers in speech.* Cambridge: Cambridge University Press, 1979. (c)

Scherer, K. R. Vocal indicators of stress. In J. Darby (Ed.), *Speech evaluation in psychiatry.* New York: Grune & Stratton, 1981. (a)

Scherer, K. R. Speech and emotional states. In J. Darby (Ed.), *Speech evaluation in psychiatry.* New York: Grune & Stratton, 1981. (b)

Scherer, K. R. Wider die Vernachlässigung der Emotion in der Psychologie. In W. Michaelis (Ed.), *Bericht über den 32. Kongress der deutschen Gesellschaft für Psychologie in Zürich, 1980.* Göttingen: Hogrefe, 1981. (c)

Scherer, K. R. Emotion as a process: Function, origin and regulation. *Social Science Information,* 1982, *21,* 555–570.

Scherer, K. R. Prolegomina zu einer Taxonomie affektiver Zustände: Ein Komponenten-Prozess-Modell. In G. Lüer (Ed.), *Bericht über den 33. Kongress der Deutschen Gesellschaft für Psychologie in Mainz, 1982.* Göttingen: Hogrefe, 1983. (a)

Scherer, K. R. *A facet system for describing psychological states.* Unpublished manuscript, University of Giessen, 1983. (b)

Scherer, K. R. *Toward a dynamic theory of emotion: The component process model of affective states.* Manuscript submitted for publication. University of Giessen, 1984. (a)

Scherer, K. R. *Componential patterning of vocal affect expression.* Manuscript submitted for publication. University of Giessen, 1984. (b)

Scherer, K. R., & Ekman, P. (Eds.) *Handbook of methods in nonverbal behavior research.* Cambridge: Cambridge University Press, 1982.

Scherer, K. R., Summerfield, A. B., & Wallbott, H. G. Cross-national research on antecedents and components of emotion: A progress report. *Social Science Information,* 1983, *22,* 355–385.

Simon, H. A. Motivational and emotional controls of cognition. *Psychological Review,* 1967, *74,* 29–39.

Sroufe, L. A. Socioemotional development. In J. D. Osofsky (Ed.), *The handbook of infant development.* New York: Wiley, 1979.

Tomkins, S. S. *Affect, imagery, consciousness (Vol. 1). The positive affects.* New York: Springer, 1962.

Tomkins. S. S. *Affect, imagery, consciousness (Vol. 2). The negative affects.* New York: Springer, 1963.

Zajonc, R. B. Feeling and thinking: Preferences need no inferences. *American Psychologist,* 1980, *2,* 151–176.

15 Expression and the Nature of Emotion

Paul Ekman
University of California, San Francisco

INTRODUCTION

There is little agreement about a definition of emotion. Not all of those who study emotion even think it necessary to make their own definition explicit. None have explained how they distinguish the boundaries of emotion, how emotion differs from reflex, motive, mood, or attitude. The last half of this chapter proposes ten characteristics which can help in beginning to define what distinguishes emotion from other psychological states. These characteristics are based in part on my earlier work, (with Wallace V. Friesen) on universals in facial expression. I will summarize that work before describing our current research—on voluntary and involuntary expression, emotion-specific autonomic nervous system activity, and startle reactions—which is the other source for my ideas about the characteristics that distinguish emotion.

CROSS CULTURAL STUDIES OF EXPRESSION

For more than 100 years scientists argued about whether facial expressions are universal or specific to each culture. On one side Darwin (1872/1965), and, more recently, Lorenz (1965) and Eibl-Eibesfeldt (1972), argued that facial expressions are innate, evolved behavior. On the other side, Birdwhistell (1970). Klineberg (1940), LaBarre (1947), Leach (1972), and Mead (1975), argued that facial expressions are instead like a language, socially learned, culturally controlled, and variable in meaning from one setting to another.

When Friesen and I began our study of facial expression we fortunately were able to borrow from Carleton Gajdusek (1963), over 100,000 feet of film he had taken of two preliterate New Guinea cultures in the late 50s and early 60s, before these peoples had contact with the outside world. These New Guineans did not show any expressions we had not seen before; there were no unique facial expressions. Although the people looked very exotic in their dress and other aspects of their behavior, their facial expressions were totally familiar and, as best we could tell when we could see enough of the social context to check our judgments, our interpretations of their expressions were correct. Their facial expressions were not a foreign language. After studying these films we set out to explore systematically the possibility of universality in facial expression.

Our best known experiments involved showing photographs of facial expressions to observers in different cultures and asking them to check from a list the emotion they saw. Observers in five cultures gave the same interpretation of each face. (This and our other cross cultural studies are reported in detail and compared to previous cross cultural studies of expression by other investigators in Ekman, 1973.) Quite independently of us, Carroll Izard (1971) did exactly the same experiment, with different photographs of facial expressions and a somewhat different list of emotion terms, and obtained very similar results.

Although pleased that we were able to obtain strong evidence of universality in expression which fit our impressions from viewing the New Guinea films we were perplexed about how wise people, anthropologists such as Weston La Barre and Margaret Mead who had studied many cultures, had come to the opposite judgment about facial expression. We came up with the notion of *display rules* (Ekman & Friesen, 1969a) to reconcile our findings with their observation of cultural differences. Display rules are overlearned habits about who can show what emotion to whom and when they can show it. Examples of display rules in many Western cultures are: males should not cry; females (except in a maternal role) should not show anger; losers should not cry in public and winners should not look too happy about winning. We presume that these display rules are learned early in childhood as well as later, that they vary with social class and ethnic background within cultures, as well as across cultures.

We designed an experiment to show that display rules are responsible for the frequent observation of cultural differences in facial expression. Within a single experiment we hoped to show universality both in facial expression and cultural differences due to display rules. We contrasted Japan with the United States because of the observations of how Orientals are "inscrutable" and because of the anthropological data, which translated into our terms, suggested that Japanese have very different display rules, particularly about not displaying negative affect in the presence of an authority.

A subject sat alone in a room, watching positive (scenery) and negative (surgical) films while a hidden video camera recorded facial expressions. We had one set of subjects in Berkeley, California, and another set of subjects in Tokyo. When we measured each and every movement of the face we found nearly identical facial muscle movement at nearly identical points in the film, regardless of culture. The correlations between the expressions shown by Americans and Japanese were above .90. Culture made no difference. In the second part of the experiment, we brought a scientist into the room with the subject, an American in Berkeley, a Japanese scientist in Tokyo. Our hypothesis was that display rules would operate in Japan, causing the subject to mask negative affect with a smile. In the United States the presence of an authority might lead college students, (during the rebellious 1960s), to amplify negative affect, certainly not to conceal it. Measurement of the facial movements showed no overlap in the facial behavior of the Japanese and Americans.

In this single experiment we had shown how facial expressions are both universal and culturally different. In private, when no display rules to mask expression were operative, we saw the biologically based, evolved, universal facial expressions of emotion. In a social situation, we had shown how different rules about the management of expression led to culturally different facial expressions.

There was still a loophole, one which Ray Birdwhistell was quick to exploit, in our evidence of universals in facial expression. All the people we had studied had shared visual input. Instead of evolution being responsible for pan-human facial expressions it might be the television tube and the silver screen. Birdwhistell argued that people had learned from watching John Wayne and Charlie Chaplin, which expressions signify which emotion.

We went to New Guinea to close this loophole. We studied a visually isolated people, who had not seen the television screen, movies, photographs, magazines, and few, if any, outsiders. We did two types of studies. We could not do a typical emotion judgment study because the people could not check emotion labels off from a list. Instead we told the subject a story, such as, "A man has learned that his child has just died," and asked the subject to choose from three expressions the photograph that showed that man. These visually isolated subjects picked for the child-died story the photograph that had been judged as sad in literate cultures; the angry one for the "about to fight" story, and so on. Incidently, we got the idea for the task from a report by Dashiell (1927) about how to measure the judgment of emotional expression in children who could not yet read. Our second study turned the design around. We read a story to the subject and asked him to show it to us on his face. When we measured the New Guinean posed expressions we found they moved the same muscles for each emotion as do people in literate cultures.

VOLUNTARY AND INVOLUNTARY EXPRESSION

When people follow display rules to manage an expression do they totally succeed, or is some leakage detectable? How completely can expressions be masked? Can people who deliberately put on feelings they don't actually experience do so in a way that is convincing to others? Can one tell from the expression itself that it is false, or is that only learned from the context in which it occurs, if at all. More generally these are questions about how well voluntary efforts can inhibit involuntary expression and the extent to which voluntary action can duplicate action brought about involuntarily.

Work in clinical neurology (Meihlke, 1973; Myers, 1976; Tschiassny, 1953) has shown that different neural pathways are involved in voluntary and involuntary facial expression. Certain types of brain lesions result in a patient being unable to smile on request. but able to smile if happiness is spontaneously aroused. Lesions in another part of the brain produce the reverse pattern. The patient can smile on request but not spontaneously. The fact that different neural pathways are involved in voluntary and involuntary expression does not prove or even make it more likely that voluntary and involuntary expressions would differ in appearance, but it at least makes the question a reasonable one to ask.

Part of the problem encountered in asking such a question resides in the over simplification of the voluntary—involuntary dichotomy. There are many different voluntary expressions, and many types of involuntary expressions, each probably varying in the underlying neural substrates that are involved. We have conducted three studies, each examining a different type of voluntary expression. First let us consider the most deliberate of voluntary expressions, facial movements performed on request.

We contrasted these movements our subjects performed when we asked them to move specific muscles with unplanned, spontaneous emotional expression. We (Ekman, Hager, & Friesen, 1981) have extensive data comparing requested smiles with smiles in response to a joke. We found a significant difference between the two in the extent of asymmetry. Deliberate smiles more often than spontaneous ones were asymmetric; and, among those which were asymmetrical, the deliberate more often than the spontaneous were stronger on the left side of the face (with subjects who are right handed). Because most current thinking about hemispheric specialization claims that the right hemisphere, which controls the left side of the face, is implicated in emotion, one might wonder why the deliberate was stronger on the *left* not the right side of the face. Our a posteriori position is that the right hemisphere does not direct emotional expression, but instead manages and modulates it. In any kind of cortically modulated facial behavior, whether it is a requested action or a speech-accompanying piece of facial behavior, there will be more asymmetry than in either reflexive or more spontaneous emotional behavior.

Let me turn to a study of another kind of voluntary movement, this time a *false* expression. A false expression is put on the face deliberately to mislead the person viewing it into thinking an emotion is felt when it is not. One of our studies of false expression (Ekman, Friesen, & Simons, submitted) compared spontaneous startle reactions, reactions to a blank pistol shot, with the subjects' expressions when we told them that we were going to count from ten to zero and when we reached zero there would be no gunshot but they were to act in such a way that anyone looking at them would think the gun had been fired. Fine grained measurement with our Facial Action Coding System (FACS) (Ekman & Frieson, 1976, 1978) revealed many markers of the false startle. The latency is too long. It seems that no one can put a startle on their face within a 100 msec. which is the hallmark of a genuine startle. The deliberate startles also are asymmetrical, tending to be stronger on the left side of the face.

A third study examined still another type of voluntary expression, what we call a *referential* expression. By this we mean an expression which refers to an emotion that is not felt at the moment. The person who sees a referential expression knows that the person showing it is mentioning an emotion which is not felt. The person who sees a false expression, however, often is misled. The referential expression that we have most closely examined is what we (Ekman & Frieson, 1982) call a *miserable smile*. This smile is put on to acknowledge being miserable. Anyone who sees it does not think the person making it is happy. Suppose the dentist tells a patient that a root canal is needed, which is going to hurt a lot and cost a lot of money. A good patient will greet such news with a miserable smile. It is a "grin and bear it" smile. It lets the other person know one is not going to show the distress or fear that one feels. It acknowledges one's misery.

There are many ways in which such deliberate, miserable smiles are marked. They are often either too short or too long, held on the face much longer than genuine smiles. Also, they tend not to have the involvement of the muscle around the eyes. Darwin was the first to propose that in genuine smiling not only do the lip corners go up but the orbicularis oculi muscle, which circles the eye, is contracted as well. Miserable smiles are often abrupt in onset and offset, appearing to jump on and off the face. A fourth way in which miserable smiles differ from genuine ones is in the addition of other muscular actions—lip pressing or chin muscle action, for example—which are not present in the genuine, uncontrolled happy expression. From a semiotic viewpoint, the miserable smile must be a transformation of the genuine smile signal which still resembles it. The message of something positive must be conveyed, yet the smile must look sufficiently different not to confuse the observer into thinking the person is actually happy.

Our three studies suggest that there are multiple facial clues to distinguishing between voluntary and involuntary expressions. Actions that are usually present when the emotion is felt are absent. Actions usually absent when emotion is felt are present. There is more asymmetry. Timing differs in a number of ways; the expression may be too short or too long in duration, onset or offset may be abrupt. Which type of marking occurs we believe depends on which type of voluntary expression occurs.

Many questions remain about the differences between voluntary and involuntary expressions. One of them is detectability. We can detect differences between voluntary and involuntary facial expression, but to do so we spent enormous amounts of time, looking essentially with a microscope, in repeated, slowed motion. Are the signals apparently different without such analyses? Can people tell? We believe the referential expressions (such as the miserable smile) are performed in such a way as to be readily distinguished from the felt expression. But we do not yet know how well it is possible to detect the false expression when it is seen in real time embedded in the flow of behavior.

Are there individual differences in the ability to disguise emotional expression, to put on false expressions. Again we believe there is but it is not well understood. If there are such individual differences, is that ability a skill that can be developed by anyone? And if there is such a skill, is it general across emotions or are people adept in disguising one emotion but not in disguising another?

Is the ability to falsify an emotion, to put on an expression not felt, correlated with the ability to inhibit emotion, to conceal what is felt? The neurologists tell us that these involve different neural substrates. If you are good at one are you good at the other?

FACIAL EXPRESSION AND THE AUTONOMIC
NERVOUS SYSTEM

Let me turn now to another question, a very old one in the history of psychology: whether or not Autonomic Nervous System (ANS) activity differs or is the same for each emotion. William James (1890), Ax (1953) and others suggested that each emotion has a different pattern of ANS activity. Cannon (1927), Schachter and Singer (1962), and others suggested that the ANS activity varies with just the extent but not the nature of emotional arousal. In the last decade with the growth of cognitive psychology the prevalent model of emotion (e.g., Mandler, 1975). stemming from the Schachter and Singer's study, holds that it is only differentiated cognitions, particular expectations, which produce the experience that each emotion differs in feeling. ANS activity is necessary, but probably contributes little or nothing to the impression that each emotion differs in feeling. People interpret any awareness of ANS changes strictly in terms of their cognitions.

We (Ekman, Levenson, & Friesen, 1983) used voluntary facial actions to explore different patterns of ANS activity for each emotion. Previous attempts to demonstrate emotion-differentiated ANS activity foundered for three reasons. First, most experiments only studied a couple of emotions; usually with only one or two ANS measures. We studied six emotions and used four ANS measures.

A second flaw in past studies has been the failure to recognize that embarrassment may have confounded their attempts to elicit different emotions. Being in an experiment with electrical leads attached to various places on one's body is not a neutral situation. We suspect most subjects were embarrassed, and if embarrassment has it's own pattern of ANS activity that feeling would overlay the experimental attempts to produce different emotions. While the experimenter might think he was eliciting fear at one point and anger at another, the social psychology of the situation might be that embarrassment was contaminating both. We eliminated this problem by our choice of subjects. They were people who are not self-conscious about having their faces, ANS, or emotional life carefully scrutinized in public. They were people who work at our laboratory, who are well accustomed to having their facial expressions filmed, and also trained actors.

A third flaw in past studies of whether ANS activity varies with different emotion has been the failure to verify that pure emotions were sampled. If blends of two emotions are obtained rather than pure emotions, this could produce undifferentiated ANS activity even if each of the single emotions contained in the blend actually produces a different pattern of ANS activity. Most investigators have blithely assumed that all subjects would produce but a single emotion, and would do so when they were supposed to. If, for example, subjects were asked to imagine fear at one point and anger at another, investigators presumed that is just what happened, failing to recognize the need to verify that they had obtained samples of single emotions. Our experience suggests that people typically experience blends of emotion. If subjects are asked to imagine fear they are likely to generate fear blended with surprise, or fear blended with distress. The problem is no different if emotion is elicited by showing a stress-inducing film. Our studies of self-report and expression when subjects watch films of accidents, surgery or mutilation, found that more than one emotion was typically elicited. Fear, disgust, distress, surprise often occurred within the same subject, often in rapid sequence, merging one on top of another. Because of the likelihood of obtaining blends it is necessary for the investigator to verify by some means that the subjects have indeed generated a single emotion when the experimenter wanted them to do so. We dealt with this problem by using new emotion eliciting techniques, chosen because they are likely to elicit pure emotion samples. And, we further verified that blending did not occur.

We told our subjects to voluntarily move particular patterns of facial movement, hypothesizing that such deliberate performances of facial actions would turn on the autonomic nervous system. We did not ask people to produce emotions; we did not say "look afraid" or "look angry" but instead we told them particular muscles to move on their face. For fear, for example, the instruction was: raise your brows, while holding them raised pull your brows together, now raise your upper eyelid and tighten the lower eyelid, now stretch your lips horizontally. Each of the subjects received six different instructions; each instruction involved a combination of muscle movements, the combinations chosen both on the basis of theory and evidence as to which expressions signal which emotions universally. The instructions were for the muscle movements involved in fear, anger, surprise, disgust, sadness and happiness. Each set of instructed facial movements was specific to one and only one emotion. We did not trust our subjects to do what we said but we scored the facial movements they made and we analyzed the data using only the performances where people indeed did make the muscle movements as instructed.

We found differential activity on both skin temperature and heart rate, distinguished among emotions. Figure 15.1 shows that the ANS activity differed not just between positive and negative emotions, but also noted were different patterns of ANS changes for anger versus disgust, and either anger or disgust as compared to fear or surprise. When we analyzed all the data regardless of whether the subjects had actually been able to perform each set of facial muscle actions in each instruction, the results were much weaker. The specified set of muscle movements must be performed to produce the clearly differentiated patterns of ANS activity. There was no difference in the results between the people at our laboratory and the actors.

The changes in ANS activity produced by the directed facial actions task were not trivial. Heart rate increases of up to 25 beats per minute for anger and 22 beats per minute for fear were observed. There are no larger differences in ANS activity reported in the experimental literature.

We replicated our findings of emotion-differentiated ANS activity using a Stanislavski technique, in which the subjects were asked to remember and relive

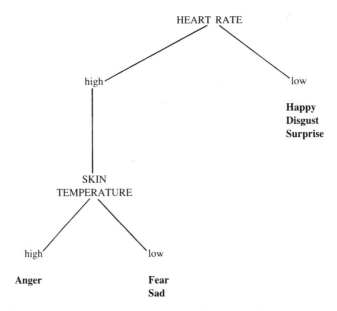

FIG. 15.1.   Decision tree for discriminating emotions in Direct Facial Action Task.

emotions. We verified through self-ratings that the subject experienced but one emotion, not a blend. The findings differ in some details but the main effects were the same. Positive emotions could be distinguished from negative emotions, and differences in the pattern of ANS changes distinguished among negative emotions.

This study raises two important issues for any theory of emotion. The first issue is what is the role of emotion-differentiated ANS activity as compared to cognition in the experience of emotion? The second question is how could voluntary facial movement from the motor cortex turn on hypothalamicly directed autonomic nervous system changes?

The first issue. There is now evidence of three differentiated emotion systems. Strong evidence for differentiation in cognition and in facial expression, and more tentative evidence, which I believe our present studies will strengthen, of emotion specific activity in the autonomic nervous system. (We suspect the voice is also differentiated for each emotion, but the evidence for that is not yet available. See Scherer, Chapter 14.) With three emotion-differentiated systems the question is how do they interrelate? We believe that they must be interconnected. Our experiment suggests that changing one (face) changes another (ANS). I presume that usually these three systems operate consistently, and that interrelated variations in each are what produce the color and unique quality of each and every emotional experience.

When are they discrepant? Are they ever discrepant outside the psychologist's laboratory? I suspect that we will have to work hard to make them discrepant. If they are discrepant is cognition always the master in determining subjective experience? I suspect not. Whether cognition will override the autonomic nervous system patterning in determining a person's impressions as to which emotion is occurring will depend on the strength of the cognitive process, how fixed and strong the expectations might be, and the strength and nature of ANS activity. There may be individual differences as well.

We are not throwing out, nor denying the importance of cognitive processes in the experience of emotion. We are only suggesting that cognition is a part of an integrated, differentiated package. The autonomic nervous system activity may be more differentiated and play more of a role in emotional experience than some of the cognitive theorists have presumed.

Let me turn to the second issue raised by our study: How is it that a voluntary muscle action produces autonomic nervous system activity of any kind let alone differentiated autonomic activity? We can not yet rule out the possibility that cognitive mediation was necessary to produce the ANS activity. Our subjects might have attached a label to the facial instructions they received, and it might have been the label not the directed facial actions that produced each pattern of ANS activity. We do not think that was the case and our next studies will evaluate the role of this and other cognitive mediators. We believe that there is a direct, central connection between the pathways leading from the motor cortex that direct facial muscle activity and hypothalamic areas involved in the direction of ANS activity. but learning about that will also take further research.

The fact that voluntary facial action produced emotion-specific patterns of ANS activity has many implications. Clinicians might wonder whether voluntary facial action instructions could be used therapeutically. If somebody is anxious, will giving them the instructions for a nonanxious face change their ANS activity, and make them feel less anxious? If they are depressed can directed facial actions make them happy, or if manic, can they be toned down, just by giving them a set of directed facial muscle movements? We doubt that directed facial actions have much therapeutic value, but we do plan to investigate the related question of whether deliberate facial actions can influence ANS changes which were aroused spontaneously by an emotional event.

Our results may help explain why people seek social interaction to pick up their mood when they are feeling rather emotionless. Putting on a polite expression, going to a social gathering in which one has to smile and be polite, may actually change how one feels. Our evidence suggests that putting on such an expression will actually start to produce the physiological changes that are part and parcel of a happy or an excited experience.

Our study may also help to explain why advertisers so often show us people smiling with their products. It may well be a nice conditioning experiment. Because people usually imitate smiles they see, even in advertisements, presenting a product with a smile may cause the viewer to experience positively toned ANS changes in association with the advertiser's product.

DISTINGUISHING EMOTION FROM REFLEX

Our recent study of startle reactions has raised anew the question about whether startle is an emotion or a reflex (Ekman, Friesen, & Simons, submitted). Averill (1980) and Lazarus (1982) said startle cannot be an emotion because cognition does not play a causal role in eliciting it. Bull (1951), Lindsley (1951). Plutchik (1962), Tomkins (1962) and Woodworth and Schlosberg (1954) all classified startle as an emotion not a reflex. Landis and Hunt (1939) in their pioneering study of startle reactions took an intermediate position, considering startle to be "preemotional" as it is simpler in organization and expression than true emotions.

We examined subjects facial and bodily responses in four conditions: when they did not know when a blank pistol would be fired; when they knew exactly when the pistol would be fired; when they attempted to inhibit their startle response; and, when they attempted to simulate a genuine startle response. Some of our findings on the simulated condition were reported earlier in discussing the differences between voluntary and involuntary expressions. Now let us compare our findings on startle with what is known about emotions such as fear. anger, or surprise.

In some respect startle resembles emotions. There is a uniform facial appearance in startle, apart from from intensity variations or attempts to control the expression, as there is in emotions such as happiness, surprise or fear. While startle has a very brief latency and duration, beginning within 100 msec. and gone within 500 msec., surprise also is brief, although startle is much briefer than surprise.

In a number of ways, however, startle differs from emotions, including surprise. Startle is very easy to elicit. It is highly reliable; for every subject it was the initial response to the gunshot. By contrast, there is no single elicitor for any emotion which, at least in the adult, will always call forth the same initial emotional response. The startle response can not be totally inhibited, whereas the little evidence available suggests that emotions can be. When subjects were told exactly when they would be startled and instructed that they were to inhibit any sign of being startled, none succeeded. Although the muscular actions that form the startle pattern were diminished. they did not disappear. Our studies of deception have shown that some subjects can succeed totally in eliminating any sign of felt emotion, even though that emotion is quite severe. And, we found that no one could simulate the startle correctly; everyone failed to produce the very brief latency which is the hallmark of a startle. There is no comparable clear-cut marker of simulated expressions for the emotions. The only candidate would be the finding (described earlier), that deliberate facial actions are more asymmetrical than genuine ones; but asymmetries are not always present and even when they are evident they are typically subtle in appearance.

In sum, we believe startle differs in so many ways from what characterizes emotions that it should not be considered an emotion. Yet, this evaluation should remain tentative, because the information about just what characterizes any emotion is in many respects conjectural, not, as with startle, based on careful descriptive study. This very fact—that so much more is known about startle than about any emotion—may be further proof that startle is not an emotion. It is so easy to study, regular in occurrence, and reliably elicited in a laboratory.

CHARACTERISTICS OF EMOTION

Our studies of emotional expression may help in distinguishing the boundaries of emotion, how an emotion differs from a reflex, mood, emotional trait, or emotional disorder.[1] The distinctions I wish to draw among these affective phe-

---

[1]Still another boundary state which needs to be distinguished from emotion is what I term *emotional plots*. Such a plot specifies the particular context within which specific emotions will be felt by specific persons, casting the actors and what has or is about to transpire. Mourning specifies two actors, the deceased and the survivor, something about their past relationship, the survivor was attached to the deceased, and the pivotal event, one of the actors died. The survivor is likely to feel distress, sadness, and perhaps fear and anger. Jealousy and infatuation are examples of other emotional plots in which there is more than one live actor. Elsewhere (Ekman & Matsumoto, in prepara-

nomena are partly, but imperfectly, expressed in language. Distress is an emotion, feeling-blue a mood, melancholic an emotional trait, and depression the related emotional disorder. A similar set of distinctions is implied by the words: fear (emotion), apprehensive (mood), timorous (trait), and anxiety state (disorder); or by joy (emotion), euphoric (mood), happy-go-lucky (trait), and mania (emotional disorder, with the emotion of excitement as well); or by anger (emotion), irritable (mood), and hostile (trait). There is no English word for an emotional disorder in which anger is principally implicated, although people who are chronically violent may represent such an entity.

Language suggests but cannot provide the bases for discovering how emotions differ from these other affective phenomena. Any one language reflects only those distinctions recognized by a particular culture. Language tells us what features of an emotion are symbolically represented in awareness, subject to discussion, consensual check, likely to be governed by display and feeling rules (Ekman, 1971; Hochschild, 1983). An emotion ignored (Levy, Chapter 19) or denoted by only one or two words in one language may be highly differentiated in another language, with terms which denote variations in intensity, antecedents, extent of control, etc.

I propose to distinguish the boundaries of emotion by focusing not on language but upon the patterned changes in expression and physiology which are distinctive for emotion. I will suggest how emotion differs from either a reflex or a mood in terms of how these patterned changes are organized and brought into action by particular kinds of information processing. I will emphasize less how emotion differs from either emotional traits or emotional disorders, treating those boundaries more fully elsewhere (Ekman & Matsumoto, in preparation). While the ten characteristics which I describe emphasize expression, it is *not* because I believe expression is the most important feature in characterizing any affective phenomena. Physiological and cognitive activity are important also, as is the influence of the social context and the subjective experience. But, expression is what I know most about, and what is most readily accessible for study.

1. There is a Distinctive Pan-Cultural Signal for Each Emotion

Earlier in this chapter I reviewed our evidence of such a distinctive facial expression for fear, surprise, anger, disgust, distress, and happiness. The evidence of universality is weaker for surprise and still weaker for interest, contempt and shame. If there is no distinctive universal facial expression associated with a given state, which functions as a signal, I propose that we not call that state an emotion. This does not mean that an expression must always be visible or audible, for emotional expressions can be inhibited (see Characteristic 7).

tion) the distinction between emotional plots and other affective states are described more completely. Also see Clanton and Smith, 1977; and Gordon, 1981 for related but different treatments of emotional plots; Plutchik, 1980 for a different set of distinctions among emotions, moods, traits and disorders).

Furthermore, even without inhibition, an expression may be too weak to be noticeable when emotion is elicited by imagery or memory (Characteristic 9 discusses various routes for calling forth an emotion). Also, the mere presence of an emotional expression does not itself establish the presence of an emotion, for emotional expressions can be simulated (Characteristic 8). I believe that no *single* characteristic is sufficient to establish emotion, but a set of characteristics is required, organized, as I will describe, into a coherent pattern. Nevertheless the requirement that there be a pan-cultural signal has some utility in distinguishing the boundaries of emotion.

Although reflexes have a distinctive pan-human pattern of motor behavior, they do not function as signals. A reflex such as the startle is too brief—less than half a sec—to have much value as a signal. Many other reflexes occur in parts of the body which are not sufficiently visible to have signal value. Moods do not have a particular facial expression, at least none that is universal and none that has signal value. A person who is in an irritable mood, for example, does not show an irritable signal, but instead irritability is marked by when and how anger occurs. When irritable a person is more than usually likely to: (a) become angry, the threshold for eliciting anger is lower; (b) stay angry, the duration is extended, the person cannot as readily turn anger off; (c) recycle anger, almost as if anger is calling forth more anger; and, (d) appear angrier, manifesting intense displays. There might be enduring, distinctive, but very subtle changes in muscle tonus for each mood, but there is no evidence as yet, and they would not, in any case, be sufficiently clear to function as signals.

Much of what I suggest in regard to the role of emotion signals in moods, is also relevant to emotional traits and emotional disorders. There is no distinctive signal for an emotional trait, nor for an emotional disorder; instead, both are marked by how often and when particular emotional signals occur. A hostile person chronically shows anger, not just when in an irritable mood. A hostile person becomes angry about matters that do not usually elicit anger in others, and when a hostile person is angry, the anger expression and the social consequences of the anger are likely to be more severe than is so when a non-hostile person is angry. Hostile characters also may be less able to dampen anger expressions, and they may have a longer recovery time. Hostile characters are known to others by their anger, it is what is salient about them, central to the organization of their personality, just as sadness is for the melancholic character.

While the idea that there is no distinctive signals unique to moods or emotional traits is based only on examples, I do have evidence (Ekman & Friesen, 1974; Matsumoto, Ekman & Friesen, in prep) to support the idea that there are no distinctive universal expressive signals in any of the emotional disorders. Our studies of depression and mania found no unique, pathognomic facial or bodily expressions unique to them, but only the emotional expressions. What was distinctive was not the signal but the high saturation of the signal. As I describe later (Characteristic 4), in the emotional disorders particular emotions are *flooded*.

2. Distinctive Universal Facial Expressions of Emotion Can Be Traced Phylogenetically

I accept Darwin's view that facial expressions of emotion have evolved, and are universal in humans because they are part of our biological inheritance. There is some evidence of similar distinctive expressions in other primates for fear and anger, possibly also sadness and happiness, although there is argument about both of these (Chevalier-Skolnikoff, 1973; Redican, 1982). Disgust has not been carefully studied in nonhuman primates. It is not certain whether surprise can be seen separately from fear in nonhuman primates, but there are doubts about that also from some of the human studies in preliterate cultures. This characteristic of emotional expressions—that the signal can be traced phylogenetically—does not add to our ability to distinguish the boundaries of emotion, but it is relevant to note because it explains the basis for universality which is a distinctive characteristic. Any emotional expression that cannot be traced phylogenetically is not likely to be pan human. While I expect there are such culture-specific emotional expressions, my attempts to identify them have failed.

3. Emotional Expressions Involve Multiple Signals, Involving the Voice as Well as the Face

Scherer (1981) says that there has not been sufficient research to yet determine whether the voice conveys only the difference between positive and negative states, or provides the differentiated information about specific emotions available from facial expression. Since facial expressions require visual attention, the young infant would be at quite a disadvantage if vocalizations, which have the advantage over facial expressions of being able to reach a disattending caretaker, did not at least signal positive/negative states (see Engle, 1963). Presumably, that would be sufficient to capture attention, and then the face could provide the more precise information about which emotion is occurring. Yet, I expect that further work will confirm Tomkins (1962) proposal that vocal expressions are just as emotion-specific as facial expressions.

I propose that if the vocalization does not occur with the facial expression of emotion the emotional experience is weak, or some attempt (deliberate or habitual), has been made to manage the expression. Vocalization is not necessarily part of the package of events found in a reflex. We observed none in the startle. Moods, emotional traits, and emotional disorders, will, I presume, show a high saturation of vocal as well as facial signals of particular emotions.

4. There Are Limits on the Duration of an Emotion

Although emotions do vary in duration, and those variations, as I describe below, have signal value, I suggest that there may be absolute limits in the total duration of an emotion. Our studies of facial expression suggest that the great majority of expressions of felt emotions last between ½ second and 4 seconds, and those that are shorter or longer are mock or other kinds of false expressions (Ekman & Friesen, 1982).[2] Even such false expressions are rarely less than ⅓ of a second or more than ten seconds. We have never seen a facial expression held for minutes, let alone hours. Spasms would occur if contractions of the facial muscles were maintained for many minutes.

While many of the changes in the autonomic nervous system that occur during emotion may last longer than facial expression, as may be so also of the neurohormonal activity, I nevertheless propose that certain limits on duration is a distinguishing characteristic of an emotion. Even the autonomic nervous system changes probably do not endure for many hours. And yet, in the language of the layman, that is what is meant by a mood. It is bizarre to speak of being in an irritable mood for a fraction of a second. Moods refer to longer time spans than emotions, and reflexes to shorter time spans.

A person is identified as having an emotional trait if a particular emotion or set of emotions chronically reappears. It is not a matter of a few hours or a day or two. An emotion must characterize that person over an entire life epoch, or perhaps over many life epochs. Nearly everyone may on occasion have an irritable mood, but for the hostile person, anger is more than an occasional matter. Obviously it is more than simply the duration or frequency of emotion episodes which distinguishes an emotional trait from a mood or an emotion—the style of behavior, and the organization of personality must be considered—but duration is of significance. It is not certain how the anger manifest by a hostile person differs from the anger manifest when a nonhostile person is in an irritable mood, or how the sadness manifest by a melancholic person differs from the sadness shown when a nonmelancholic person is in a blue mood, etc. Would it be accurate to say that a hostile person has many irritable moods, or does the expressive and physiological activity characterizing moods and emotional traits differ fundamentally?

In an emotional disorder, such as depression, mania, or anxiety states, duration is important in a different way. It is not that the relevant emotions chronically reappear over a life epoch, but instead that particular emotions are *flooded*. What I mean by a flooded emotion is that: (a) nearly anything that happens will set off the emotion, it is called forth by events that rarely would elicit it; (b) the

---

[2]Not all emotions may have the same time envelope. All who have considered surprise have noted that it is the briefest of emotions, rarely lasting more than a second or two, although, as with any emotion, the unfolding of events may cause one to be surprised many times in a short period of time. I hypothesize that happiness, disgust and distress each have a larger time envelope within which they can vary. Each of these emotions can be as brief as surprise, but each may also last much longer. Distress may be a special case, since when it endures for long periods it is converted into sadness, which after a period of time may then revert back into distress. I believe that anger or fear have a time envelope which extends further than happiness, disgust, or distress. Although fear or anger can be as brief as any other emotion, they may also last much longer.

emotion appears to recycle frequently reappearing with no evident elicitor; (c) once called forth the emotion is intense; (d) the person cannot modulate, or deamplify the emotional expression or experience; and, (e) the reiteration of the emotion continues over time periods long enough to seriously interfere with fundamental life tasks such as eating, sleeping, working, and the usual emotional demands of polite social interaction. In depression, which is the disorder I have studied, the flooded emotions appear to be distress and fear.

5. The Timing of an Emotional Expression Reflects the Specifics of a Particular Emotional Experience

While the characteristic just described asserts limits on the total duration of an emotion, within those limits variations in timing do occur which are related to the particulars of an emotional experience. We (Ekman, Friesen, & Ancoli, 1980) found evidence that the duration of an emotional expression was correlated with the person's report of the strength of the emotional experience. And, that was so in regard to both positive and negative emotions.

Other aspects of the timing of an emotional expression also may be related to the strength of the emotional experience, or to the nature of the eliciting event, or to attempts to manage the expression. We distinguish *latency* (from the moment of stimulation to the point when an expression begins), *onset* (the period from latency until the performance reaches its maximal level), *apex* (the period during which the expression is maintained at maximal strength), and *offset* (from the end of apex until the expression disappears). Latency, onset, apex, and offset may each reflect multiple influences. Presumably the stronger the stimulus the shorter the latency and onset, and the longer the apex and offset. It also seems apparent that the events calling forth an emotion may have a given time course which influences the timing of the expression. For example, a slowly developing pattern of insults might produce a longer onset than an abrupt, clear, explicit insult. Finally, attempts to manage an expression may cause the onset period to become longer than it otherwise would be as a person struggles to contain the expression, or it may curtail the apex if the person succeeds in wiping out the expression, or cause the offset to appear abrupt.

On the basis of our research on the startle, we expect that the latency and onset and duration of the actions in a reflex are fixed, and unlike emotion do not vary with the nature of the experience. Moods may be characterized by alterations in onset and offset times. It seems reasonable to suppose that when irritable, for example, the onset of anger will be shorter and the offset longer than it usually is for that person. Our language suggests that emotional traits are also manifest in these different aspects of the timing of an emotion. A hot-head has a short latency and/or onset for anger; a sulker has a long anger apex and/or offset. It is not certain whether hot-heads and sulkers refers to two different traits, or if these terms instead refer to consistencies in style, without implying that the emotion is central in personality organization. It would be interesting to learn whether there are parallel distinctions about timing for other emotions, and to examine how languages differ in whether individual differences in the timing of emotional experiences are represented.

6. Expressions Are Graded in Intensity, Reflecting Variations in the Strength of Felt Experience

Our evidence (Ekman, Friesen, & Ancoli, 1980) suggests that facial expressions of emotion as well as reflexes (Ekman, Friesen, & Simons, submitted) vary in the strength of muscular action and that is an index of the strength of the experience. We had hoped that emotions and reflexes would differ in this regard, but they apparently do not. I have already explained how more intense emotional experience and expression would be expected to characterize particular emotional traits and emotional disorders.

It is important to note exceptions to this congruence between the intensity of felt emotion and the intensity of expression, instances when emotions can be felt strongly but there is little or no apparent expression. One obvious instance is when someone attempts, either deliberately or through well established habit, to deamplify or totally inhibit the expression of emotion. The emotion may still be felt quite strongly, although the subjective experience should differ from when no attempt is made to diminish expression. Another exception is suggested by experiments in which people imagined an event or remembered and relived one. While people often report intense feelings in these circumstances, their expressions are usually too weak to be signals, detectable only by electromyography. This suggests that congruence between the intensity of felt emotion and the intensity of emotional expression may not be general, but limited only to those occasions when an emotion is brought forth by appraisal of an event. Work is needed to determine whether there might still be some relationship between the intensity of feeling and intensity of expression when remembering or imagining an emotional event occurs naturally rather than to meet an experimental request.

7. Emotional Expression Can Be Totally Inhibited

Our studies of people who followed instructions to conceal their reactions to stress inducing films (Ekman & Friesen, 1974; Ekman, Friesen, O'Sullivan, & Scherer, 1981; Ekman, Friesen, & Scherer, 1976) found that about ten percent of them were able to eliminate any facial leakage, avoiding detection even by our most microscopic measurement. While I believe that expression can be inhibited, I agree with Tomkins (Chapter 7) that the efferent impulses for a patterned facial expression will always be produced when an emotion is called forth. Those efferent impulses may not result in a visible expression if: (a) the arousal is very slight; (b) attempts to inhibit were very successful; (c) the emotion was called forth by imagining or remembering an event. In each of these instances the nonvisible expression may still be detectable electromyographically. No one yet knows whether inhibition can take place *centrally*, preventing the efferent impulses from reaching the peripheral expressive equipment.

We suspect that some emotions are harder to inhibit than others. It seems obvious that it is harder to inhibit any emotion when it is very intense. Perhaps it is also difficult to inhibit emotions when they are felt only slightly because people are less alert to the onset of such feelings or the need for inhibition. We know there are marked individual differences in the ability to inhibit emotional expression, but we were unsuccessful in identifying the personality characteristics of skillful inhibitors of expression. Nor did we, nor has anyone, determined whether such individual differences are general across the range of emotions and across situational contexts. Quite apart from individual differences, the nature of the social context should influence the ease of inhibiting emotional expression. For example, in some situations people expect they may have to inhibit expression of their true feelings. We have hypothesized (Ekman, 1981; Ekman & Friesen, 1969b) that it is harder to inhibit some modes of expression than others: harder to inhibit signs of emotion in the voice than in facial expression, harder to inhibit facial expressions than signs of emotion in body movement.

If we can generalize from our study of the startle reaction, in which people could not inhibit the appearance of the startle, this may be another characteristic which distinguishes reflexes from emotion. If there is no neurological disorder, and the reflex has not been repeatedly called forth in a short time period, I expect that people typically cannot inhibit all evidence of it. There has been no study of whether people can inhibit signs of a mood. Earlier I suggested that mood has no distinctive signal, but is saturated with the appearance of particular emotions. I hypothesize that when a strong mood occurs the ability to inhibit any sign of the relevant emotion is at least partially impaired. For reasons explained earlier, it seems reasonable to propose that one way an emotional trait or emotional disorder can be manifest is in decreased evidence of inhibiting or deamplifying the expression of the relevant emotion(s).

8. Emotional Expressions Can Be Convincingly Simulated

Earlier, in discussing the startle, I suggested that the inability to simulate the expression probably means that the expression is a reflex, not an emotion. Not everyone can voluntarily move all of the facial muscles which are found in the universal expressions of every emotion (Ekman, Roper, & Hager, 1980). And, many people become so embarrassed when trying to simulate an emotional expression that they fail because the embarrassment overrides their attempts to deliberately move their facial muscles. The difficulties we found with the attempts to simulate the startle were not these, however. People could make the movements, and they were not embarrassed, but they could not produce the movements fast enough and assembled in the correct order.

Although emotions can be convincingly simulated that does not mean that they occur without flaws. We have found a number of markers of whether an emotional expression is felt or not, including the particular muscles deployed, duration, coordination of the muscular movements, and the symmetry of the expression (Ekman & Friesen, 1982). It is interesting to note that these signs of whether an expression is felt or false can be detected by others, although in the social interactions we have studied they often are not (Ekman, in press).

It seems reasonable to propose that moods make it more difficult to simulate convincingly the expression of an unfelt emotion. The more *dissimilar* the unfelt emotion is from the emotion involved in the mood, the harder it will be to simulate. We (Ekman & Friesen, 1975, 1978) found certain pairs of emotions to be quite similar in the facial muscles deployed in their expressions: fear and surprise; anger and disgust; and, to a lesser extent, fear, and distress. If distinctive vocal signals are found for each of these emotions I expect analysis of the vocal signals would yield parallel similarity pairings. It would be a very neat package indeed, if these similarities noted in expression could be observed also in the extent of overlap among emotions in the patterning of autonomic and central nervous system activity.

Even if the similarities are limited just to the facial expressions, when irritable it should be much easier to simulate disgust than fear, when apprehensive it should be easier to simulate surprise than anger, etc. In a related vein, we found that depressed patients could not convincingly simulate happiness or anger (Ekman & Friesen, 1974). It is less certain whether an emotional trait impairs the ability to simulate convincingly emotions most dissimilar from the emotion involved in the trait.

9. There Are Pan-Human Commonalities in the Elicitors for Each Emotion

Part of the informational package provided by an emotion signal is to tell others something about what has just happened to the person who shows the expression. (Also included is some idea of what sensations that person may be feeling and what that person is likely to do next.) Although what calls forth an emotion is not the same for a child and adult, nor for a given person in different social roles, nevertheless there is some commonality in the eliciting circumstances for each emotion. Theorists disagree about how much commonality.

Those who take an evolutionary view of emotion have proposed that those commonalities in what elicits each emotion cut across our species, although there is disagreement in how they characterize this. Tomkins (Chapter 7) proposed that it is the density of neural firing generated, not any specifics in the stimulus situations, which distinguishes the elicitors for each emotion. We (Ekman & Friesen, 1969a) initially proposed few universals in the elicitors of each emotion, but revised our position after Boucher (1981) obtained evidence of commonalities in emotion antecedents across many cultures, literate and nonliterate, both Western and non-Western. We then proposed (Ekman, 1977; Ekman & Friesen, 1975) universal, abstract, *prototypic* situations as the elicitors for each emotion, such as loss of an important object for sadness, an unexpected event for surprise, etc. Scherer's (Chapter 14) recent evidence of commonalities in the antecedents of emotions across Western Europe fits well with our predictions.[3]

Despite this disagreement about the nature of the universal emotion elicitors, I agree with Tomkins that there is considerable generality in the stimuli which can, through experience, come to call forth an emotion. For example, almost any object can become the object of such psychological investment that a person will become distressed about the loss of it; a person can be taught to view almost any social act as repulsively disgusting, threateningly fearful, provocatively angering, etc. Experience fills in the details, sharpening and elaborating the universal prototypic elicitors for each emotion. I also agree with Tomkins that many, although not all, elicitors can bring forth emotional reactions near immediately. I have referred to this as *automatic* appraisal (Ekman, 1977) to distinguish it from the *extended* appraisal which has interested many cognitive psychologists.

In automatic appraisal an event is instantly matched with one of the prototypic situations, thereby immediately setting off emotion-specific changes in expression and physiology. This matching function may be determined genetically (e.g., sudden loss of physical support eliciting fear) or through repeated experience (e.g., entering a crowded room producing fear). Extended appraisal occurs when the antecedent event is not well established, it does not obviously match any of the prototypic situations, or is in some way baffling, requiring a more extended process of problem solving for its evaluation. External events such as social actions or physical events, and memories, or images of such events, fantasy, or perception of change in organismic state may elicit emotion via automatic or extended appraisal. By my reasoning the argument between Lazarus (Chapters 9 and 11) and Zajonc (Chapters 10 and 12) is due, in part, to each focusing upon a different type of appraisal, *both* of which occur in emotional experience.

The elicitors for a reflex are much more specific than for an emotion, and should be much less influenced either by immediate social context or longer term learning. In discussing the startle reaction I mentioned that the ability to call forth the startle so reliably, to specify a stimulus which would always succeed, makes the startle attractive to the experimenter, but also suggests it is a reflex not an emotion.

---

[3]Too little work has examined the array of emotion elicitors. While it is important to ask people their beliefs about this, (Scherer, Chapter 14) that is no substitute for actually examining the circumstances in which emotions are elicited. Now that there are precise methods available for measuring the physical properties of emotional expressions in face and voice, developmental and cross cultural studies should be able to carry out the necessary but time consuming descriptive studies of the contexts in which emotions are seen to occur.

Little is known about what calls forth a mood, particularly as compared to emotions. I suspect moods can be produced in two different but related ways: (1) a change in the biochemical state of the organism, resulting from tiredness, exertion, diet, disease, and a variety of other noninterpersonal events; (2) the repeated elicitation of a particular emotion over a short time period. For example, irritability may be a consequence of tiredness (termed ''cranky'' in children); or, a person may become irritable if that person has repeatedly been provoked to anger within a short period of time. My presumption is that the second route turns into the first, that if anger is experienced often enough in a short enough time period a threshold is crossed, and a toxic state is generated, producing the biochemical changes which mediate the mood state. With anger this threshold may be crossed more quickly if the expression had to be dampened repeatedly, and if the person felt unable to cope with the source of the anger. It is not as clear that those considerations are as relevant with other moods. The likelihood of generating a positive mood may not be increased if joy repeatedly had to be dampened, nor would the ability to cope with the source of the joy be likely to increase the likelihood of producing a positive mood. Even among negative moods dampening an emotional expression may not be an antecedent. Whether fearful experiences generate an apprehensive mood would not seem to depend on whether the fearful expression had to be dampened.

I suspect that emotional traits also have a dual origin, both biologically and interpersonally based. Work now, such as that by Kagan (personal communication) is relevant to understanding how that may occur. It is beyond the scope of this discussion to review the arguments about what causes the emotional disorders, except to note again that the division is between those advocating biological and interpersonal factors. No matter which, the level and complexity of what is involved is far different than with an emotion.

10. There is a Pan-Human, Distinctive Pattern of Changes in the Autonomic and Central Nervous System for Each Emotion

Our study of ANS activity described earlier is but a first step. Many of our findings on the ANS activity distinctive for anger were quite independently uncovered by Lakoff and Kovecses' (1983) analysis of the language of anger referent words. Presuming that our finding of emotion-specific ANS activity replicates, I propose that if there is no distinctive pattern of ANS activity we not call that state an emotion. This does not mean that discovering a distinctive pattern of ANS activity is sufficient to establish emotion. ANS activity occurs with a variety of phenomena not considered emotional, as for example with pain or sexual arousal.

There must also be a variety of central nervous system changes which characterize each emotion (see Davidson, Chapter 2). I suspect that there are distinctive patterns of physiological activity which mark both moods and reflexes but that they not only differ from each other but also from that which is found for emotion. I will not here attempt to specify how the physiological activity which accompanies particular emotions might differ for individuals with particular emotional traits or emotional disorders.

* * * * * *

The ten characteristics I have described are not of equal importance in distinguishing the boundaries of emotion. Duration is, for now, the most useful in distinguishing among all the affective phenomena. Research may soon show that these distinctions can be as readily made by the type and extent of ANS and CNS activity.

Three general assumptions about emotion have been implied in my discussion. (1) Emotion has evolved to deal with fundamental life tasks. (2) To be adaptive quite different patterns of activity would have evolved for each emotion, so that *what* occurs (in expression or physiology), and *when* it occurs (the events which call forth emotion) is emotion-specific, different for anger, fear, distress, happiness, etc. (3) There is coherence; for each emotion there are interconnected patterns in expression and physiology linked to the appraisal of prototypic situational events.

The ten characteristics are not all that distinguishes emotion, although it does include much of what has been found by emotion researchers in the last decade. I have not discussed the subjective experience of emotion, nor developmental factors. I left out how collateral cognitive activity (such as expectations and memories), and social contextual factors differentially come into play, distinguishing not only among the emotions, but also between emotions and the other affective states. Hopefully, what I have described will aid in sharpening the argument about the nature of emotion, exposing areas of agreement and disagreement, and most importantly, provoking questions for theoretical consideration which are amenable to empirical study.

ACKNOWLEDGMENT

Part of this chapter was reported in 1980 at the Conference on the Nature and Function of Emotion in Bad Homburg, Germany. Portions were also presented to the German Congress of Psychology in 1982 and are printed in the proceedings of that meeting. The preparation of this chapter was supported by a Research Scientist Award from the National Institute of Mental Health. The research reported was supported by a grant (MH 11976) from the National Institute of Mental Health and the John D. and Catherine T. MacArthur Foundation.

All of the research reported and the interpretations are the produce of collaborative research over the past 20 years with Wallace V. Friesen.

REFERENCES

Averill, J. R. A constructivist view of emotion. In R. Plutchik & H. Kellerman (Eds.), *Emotion: Theory, research and experience*. New York: Academic Press, 1980.

Ax, A. F. The physiological differentiation between fear and anger in humans. *Psychosomatic Medicine*, 1953, *15*, 433–442.

Birdwhistell, R. L. *Kinesics and context*. Philadelphia: University of Pennsylvania Press, 1970.

Boucher, J. D., & Brandt, M. E. Judgment of emotion from American and Malay antecendents. *Journal of Cross Cultural Psychology*, 1981, *12*(3), 272–283.

Bull, N. The attitude theory of emotion. *Nervous and Mental Disease Monographs* No. 18, 1951.

Cannon, W. B. The James-Lange theory of emotion: A critical examination and an alternative theory. *American Journal of Psychology*. 1927, *39*, 106–124.

Chevalier-Skolnikoff. S. Facial expressions of emotion in nonhuman primates. In P. Ekman (Ed.), *Darwin and facial expression: A century of research in review*. New York: Academic Press. 1973.

Clanton, G., & Smith, L. G. *Jealousy*. Englewood Cliffs, N.J.: Prentice-Hall, 1977.

Darwin, C. *The expression of the emotions in man and animals*. London: John Murray. 1872. Chicago: University of Chicago Press, 1965.

Dashiell, J. F. A new method of measuring reactions to facial expression of emotion. *Psychology Bulletin*. 1927, *24*, 174–175.

Eibl-Eibesfeldt, I. Similarities and differences between cultures in expressive movements. In R. A. Hinde (Ed.), *Nonverbal Communication*. Cambridge University Press, 1972.

Ekman, P. Cross-cultural studies of facial expression. In P. Ekman (Ed.), *Darwin and facial expression: A century of research in review*. New York: Academic Press, 1973.

Ekman, P. Biological and cultural contributions to body and facial movement. In J. Blacking (Ed.), *Anthropology of the body*. London: Academic Press, 1977.

Ekman, P. Mistakes when deceiving. *Annals of the New York Academy of Sciences*, 1981, *364*, 269–278.

Ekman, P. *Clues to deceit*. Hillsdale, N.J.: Lawrence Erlbaum Associates, in press.

Ekman, P.. & Friesen, W. V. The repertoire of nonverbal behavior: Categories. origins, usage, and coding. *Semiotica*, 1969, *1*, 49–98. (a)

Ekman, P., & Friesen, W. V. Nonverbal leakage and clues to deception. *Psychiatry*, 1969, *32*, 88–105. (b)

Ekman, P., & Friesen, W. V. Detecting deception from body or face. *Journal of Personality and Social Psychology*, 1974, *29*(3), 288–298.

Ekman, P., & Friesen, W. V. *Unmasking the face: A guide to recognizing emotions from facial clues*. Englewood Cliffs, N.J.: Prentice-Hall, 1975.

Ekman, P., & Friesen, W. V. Measuring facial movement. *Journal of Environmental Psychology and Nonverbal Behavior*, 1976, *1*(1). 56–75.

Ekman. P., & Friesen, W. V. *The facial action coding system (FACS): A technique for the measurement of facial action*. Palo Alto. Calif.: Consulting Psychologists Press, 1978.

Ekman, P., & Friesen, W. V. Felt, false, and miserable smiles. *Journal of Nonverbal Behavior*, 1982, *6*(4), 238–252.

Ekman, P., & Matsumoto, D. *Characteristics which describe emotion*. Manuscript in preparation.

Ekman, P., Friesen, W. V., & Ancoli. S. Facial signs of emotional experience. *Journal of Personality and Social Psychology*, 1980, *39*(6), 1125–1134.

Ekman. P., Friesen, W. V., O'Sullivan, M., & Scherer, K. Relative importance of face, body, and speech in judgments of personality and affect. *Journal of Personality and Social Psychology*, 1980. *38*. 270–277.

Ekman, P., Friesen, W. V., & Scherer, K. Body movement and voice pitch in deceptive interaction. *Semiotica*, 1976, *1*(1), 56–75.

Ekman, P., Friesen, W. V., & Simons, R. C. *The boundary between emotion and reflex: An examination of startle.* Manuscript submitted for publication.

Ekman, P., Hager, J. C., & Friesen, W. V. The symmetry of emotional and deliberate facial action. *Psychophysiology*, 1981, *18*(2), 101–106.

Ekman, P., Levenson, R. W., & Frieson, W. V. Autonomic nervous system activity distinguishes between emotions. *Science*, 1983, *221*, 1208–1210.

Ekman, P., Roper, G., & Hager, J. C. Deliberate facial movement. *Child Development*, 1980, *51*, 886–891.

Engle, G. L. Toward a classification of affects. In P. Knapp (Ed.), *Expression of emotions in man.* New York: International University Press, 1963.

Gordon, S. L. The sociology of sentiments and emotion. In M. Rosenberg & R. H. Turner (Eds.), *Social psychology,* New York: Basic Books, 1981.

Hochschild, A. *A managed heart.* Berkeley: University of California Press, 1983.

Hunt, W. A. Recent developments in the field of emotion. *Psychological Bulletin*, 1941, *38*(5), 249–276.

Izard, C. E. *The face of emotion.* New York: Appleton-Century-Crofts, 1971.

James, W. *The principles of psychology* (2 vols.). New York: Henry Holt, 1890.

Klineberg, O. *Social psychology.* New York: Henry Holt, 1940.

LaBarre, W. The cultural basis of emotions and gestures. *Journal of Personality*, 1947, *16*, 49–68.

Lakoff, G., & Kovecses, Z. The cognitive model of anger inherent in American English. *Berkeley Cognitive Science Report No. 10.* University of California, Berkeley, 1983.

Landis, C., & Hunt, W. A. *The startle pattern.* New York: Farrar, Straus & Giroux, 1939.

Lazarus, R. S. Thoughts on the relations between emotion and cognition. *American Psychologist*, 1982, *37*(9), 1019–1024.

Leach, E. The influence of cultural context on nonverbal communication in man. In R. Hinde (Ed.), *Nonverbal communication.* Cambridge: Cambridge University Press, 1972.

Lindsley, D. B. Emotion. In S. S. Stevens (Ed.), *Handbook of Experimental Psychology.* New York: Wiley, 1951.

Lorenz, K. *Evolution and modification of behavior.* Chicago: University of Chicago Press, 1965.

Mandler, G. *Mind and emotion.* New York: Wiley, 1975.

Matsumoto, D., Ekman, P., & Friesen, W. V. Depression and facial affect. In preparation.

Mead, M. Review of Darwin and facial expression. *Journal of Communication*, 1975, *25*(1), 209–213.

Meihlke, A. *Surgery of the facial nerve.* Philadelphia: Saunders, 1973.

Myers, R. E. Comparative neurology of vocalization and speech: Proof of a dichotomy. *Annals of the New York Academy of Sciences*, 1976, *280*, 745–757.

Plutchik, R. *The emotions: Facts, theories, and a new model.* New York: Random House, 1962.

Plutchik, R. *Emotion: A psychoevolutionary systhesis.* New York: Harper and Row, 1980.

Redican, W. K. An evolutionary perspective on human facial displays. In P. Ekman (Ed.), *Emotion in the human face.* Second Edition. New York: Cambridge University Press, 1982.

Schachter, S., & Singer, J. Cognitive, social, and physiological determinants of emotional state. *Psychological Review*, 1962, *69*, 379–399.

Scherer, K. R. Speech and emotional states. In J. Darby (Ed.), *Speech evaluation in psychiatry.* New York: Grune & Stratton, 1981.

Scherer, K. R. Methods of research on vocal communication: Paradigms and parameters. In K. R. Scherer & P. Ekman (Eds.), *Handbook of methods in nonverbal behavior research.* New York: Cambridge University Press, 1982.

Schwartz, G. E., Weinberger, D. A., & Singer, J. A. Sadness, anger, and fear following imagery and exercise. *Psychosomatic Medicine.* 1981, *43,* 343–364.

Tomkins, S. S. *Affect, imagery, consciousness (Vol. 1. The Positive Affects).* New York: Springer, 1962.

Tschiassny, K. Eight syndromes of facial paralysis and their significance in locating the lesion. *Annals of Otology, Rhinology, and Laryngology,* 1953, *62,* 677–691.

Woodworth, R. S., & Schlosberg, H. *Experimental psychology,* Revised edition. New York: Henry Holt, 1954.

16 Animal Communication: Affect or Cognition?

Peter Marler
Rockefeller University

The phenomenon of affect is widespread in the animal kingdom. It plays a role in the control of behavior at many levels, ranging from individual maintenance of internal physiological stability to the emergence of patterns of social interaction, as they are influenced by the temperament of individual members (Scherer, 1982). There is a wide spectrum of comparative variation on these themes, and, by rights, research on affect in animals should be a rich source of insights into its nature and functional significance. Yet, with a few exceptions, this has not been a productive approach (see Candland, 1977, p. 54). One obvious reason for the failure to exploit comparative approaches to research on affect is the virtual impossibility of identifying emotional states unequivocally, and the difficulty of distinguishing them in a reliable way from states that are primarily based not on activities of the autonomic nervous system but on cognitive activities of the brain.

Skepticism about the scientific status of the distinction between affective and nonaffective signaling reflects more than a pedantic concern with terminology. It is an issue that must be faced by every ethologist or comparative psychologist who chooses to explore affective phenomena in animals. Language and thought have traditionally provided yardsticks for separating affect from nonaffective aspects of human communication. Despite the inapplicability, by definition, of this distinction in animals, it has nevertheless led to the virtual equation of certain nonlinguistic human behaviors with emotion or affect, such as facial expressions, with the further presumption that such phenomena are more primitive and animal-like than language (e.g., Jurgens, 1979). As a further nonsequitur, many or all animal communicative behaviors, such as vocalizations of the rhesus macaque, are assumed to be purely affective in nature (e.g., Lancaster, 1975; Luria, 1981; Myers, 1976; Robinson, 1976).

To judge by the evidence that is accumulating, the view of animal signal production as purely affective is erroneous. It is increasingly evident that we have greatly underestimated the extent of cognitive contributions to the behavior of animals in general, and communicative behavior in particular (Cheney & Seyfarth, 1982; Griffin, 1981; Menzel & Johnson, 1976). The aim of this paper is to review evidence that some animal communicative behavior is quite inconsistent with the affective interpretation, and comes closer to human language behavior than has been supposed. This is not to assert that any animal has language, which is by definition a human attribute. Rather, a case will be made that some of the cognitive underpinnings of language necessary for symbolic representation are also manifest in some animals. The particular focus is on representational signaling in the natural communicative behavior of nonhuman primates.

THE SEMANTICS OF ALARM CALLS IN MONKEYS

Among the many communication signals that monkeys employ in the course of their daily lives, there are sets of alarm calls for announcing the presence of danger. Often, the signals warn them of a predator that eats monkeys, either as infants or as adults. According to the traditional view, such calls are direct reflections of the degree of anxiety that the predator evokes, and nothing more. It is easy to show, however, that the monkeys would be ill-served by an alarm call that did no more than mirror the degree of apprehension, fright, or terror of the caller.

Consider the circumstances of the vervet monkey, whose alarm-calling behavior has been the subject of intensive research. Vervets are endangered not by one predator, but many (Seyfarth, Cheney, & Marler, 1980a,b). A response that, with one predator, optimizes the chances of escape, could be catastrophic with another. At Amboseli in Kenya two major predators of vervet monkeys are leopards and eagles. Leopards typically hunt by ambush, lurking within dense cover and capturing monkeys that approach too close. Thus, dense cover is quite the wrong place to retreat to when leopards are about. Once a leopard is in pursuit of a monkey the only safe refuge is up in the canopy of a tree, on branches that are too slender to carry a leopard's weight. A typical response of vervets to a hunting leopard is in fact to rush into the upper branches of the nearest large fever tree.

Now consider the threat posed by a hunting monkey-eating eagle. Eagles strike either by stooping from a great height, or by flying in rapidly over the tree tops. In either case, they are moving at great speed, and could easily break a wing if they were to plunge after a monkey crouching in the heart of a tree or bush. On the other hand, a monkey out on the open savanna, or in the topmost branches of a tree can be seized and carried off without any risk of damaging collisions. Thus, the safest refuge for a monkey from an eagle attack is within dense cover, and it is there that vervets retreat when an eagle threatens.

If monkeys had but one alarm call that announced dangers of varying degrees of intensity, but without any specification of the *kind* of danger, the eagle/leopard problem would confront them with a serious dilemma. A signal that served as a peremptory command to rush to dense cover would be effective if the predator was an eagle, but disastrous in the case of a leopard.

Natural dilemmas such as this generate intense selection pressures for the evolution of repertories of alarm signals that represent different predators and specify distinct responses. Do monkeys possess the perceptual and cognitive capacities for adaptive responses to selection pressures of this type? The evidence indicates that they do, and the consequence has been adaptive changes both in the specificity of the neural processes that underlie the perception and categorization of predators, and in the production of vocal signals to represent them. Vervet monkey alarm calls can serve as a model of the kind of evolutionary forces that press a species toward signal/referent relationships that are much more specific than would be possible with purely affective signaling behavior (Seyfarth & Cheney, 1982).

Struhsaker (1967) first described the varied and complex responses of wild vervet monkeys to danger. He found that they employ different escape strategies for different predators. As a group-living species, they respond on a collective rather than an individual basis, with a repertoire of several distinct alarm calls that seemed to play a part in these group responses. Precautions vary according to the type of predator, and Struhsaker had a strong impression that on hearing the alarm appropriate to a given predator, they were compelled to the same alternative set of responses, apparently irrespective of whether or not they themselves had seen the predator.

In natural experiements of this kind, however, it is hard to be sure just what role an alarm call plays. It might only serve as an alerting signal, leading others to search for the source of danger. Alternatively, the response might be to look at the signaler, to observe and interpret its other ongoing escape behaviors, to follow its line of gaze and thus locate and identify the predator, only then selecting the appropriate escape strategy. Finally, we should entertain the possibility, rejected out of hand by the majority of those who comment on animal signaling behavior, that alarm calls function in truly representational fashion. This would imply that production of a particular alarm call is associated with the evocation of the mental concept of a particular class of dangers or predators, and that on hearing the alarm call an equivalent conception is evoked in the minds of companions. They in turn adopt the escape strategy most appropriate for their own individual circumstances.

The problem in observational field studies is that, with the rapidity of natural escape responses, it is impossible to distinguish between these various alternatives. That members of a troop of vervet monkeys tend to respond to a leopard or an eagle as a group is clear, despite the fact that some members, at least initially, could not have seen the predator.

The only sure way to demonstrate the role of alarm calling in this pattern of social contagion is to shift from observational study to experiment. With modern techniques of tape recording and sound spectrography it is a relatively straight-forward matter to conduct playback experiments on vervet monkeys living in their natural environment, using as stimuli alarm calls that have been recorded from known individuals in specified circumstances, with an acoustic structure that has been characterized in advance. Recordings can be presented in naturalis-tic fashion and, to maintain the illusion that a predator may actually be present, the presentation can be made to a subgroup of monkeys from which the recorded caller is temporarily absent. To permit detailed analysis of the responses of all animals, sound cinematography can be used, with the additional advantage that the moment of call playback is recorded on the sound track, permitting measure-ment of the timing of responses of different group members.

Such experiments have now been conducted with three vervet monkey alarm calls, given to eagles, leopards, and snakes, all of which pose a significant threat to them in nature (Seyfarth & Cheney, 1980; Seyfarth, Cheney & Marler, 1980a,b). The monkeys responded differently to the calls in the absence of any predator. Playback of the "leopard alarm call," which is loud, short, tonal, and typically produced in a rapid series on both exhalation and inhalation, caused vervets to run up into trees. By contrast, "eagle alarm calls," which are low-pitched, staccato grunts, caused vervets to run into dense cover, out of trees, and most interestingly, to look up into the sky as though searching for the silhouette of an eagle. "Snake alarm calls," which are high-pitched chutters, caused the animals to look down onto the ground, often going up onto their hind legs to get a better view around them in the long grass. In each case, the vervets responded as though the call had made them aware of the presence of a particular predator.

Even the most ingenious advocate of affective interpretations of animal sig-naling would find it difficult to explain, either the occurrence of alarm calling, or the patterns of responsiveness to different alarm calls. We know that adult vervets give specific calls to specific predators (Seyfarth & Cheney, 1980). More often than not, Amboseli vervets give leopard calls to leopards and not to lions, and eagle calls to martial eagles and not to storks or vultures or even other species of eagle. Although fear is undoubtedly a component in the response to both types of predator, for a purely affective interpretation of this behavior, signal/referent relationships as specific as this would require us to postulate particular *kinds* of fearfulness, distinct for each predator. Also the vervets would have to agree on which kind of fearfulness was appropriate for each predator (Premack, 1975).

The only other alternative is that variations in affect *intensity* evoked by different predators suffice to explain the evocation of distinct alarm calls, but we know of no evidence to support this view. At some level, notions of arousal are of course a necessary component in any interpretation of behavior (Duffy, 1962; Schneirla, 1959), including alarm calling. The intensity of alarm responses does vary in a meaningful way according to the seriousness of the immediate threat. However, the specificity of vervet alarm-calling behavior invites a different kind of interpretation, appealing to processes not of emotion but of cognition and connotation. If we also take account of the absence of any iconic component in alarm-calling behavior, such as might be invoked if alarm calls resembled sounds of predators, for example, the arbitrariness of the relationship between signal and referent satisfies yet another criterion for symbolic behavior.

Shifting attention now to the *responses* that vervet alarm calls evoke in others, affect intensity considerations are no help in understanding the specific aspects of the reactions of others on hearing a particular alarm call, such as looking up into the sky. Although there might be differences in the overall intensity of responses evoked by snake alarm calls than by eagle alarms, there is no reason to couple such differences to searching the grass in one case and looking up into the sky in the other.

In an experimental approach to this question, the intensity of alarm call stimulation was varied in one series of experiments by creating two sets of recordings, one very short, the other about ten times longer. If the differences in response to eagle and snake calls were simply matters of stimulus intensity, use of strong stimuli of one type should blur the difference from the response evoked by weak stimuli of another type. No such effect was found (Seyfarth *et al.*, 1980a,b).

The possibility that the affective "arousability" of different classes of responding individuals might vary was also considered, especially in relation to age and sex. Assuming young animals to be more nervous than adults, and postulating that, for example, looking up is associated with greater fear than looking down in the grass, young animals should be more prone than adults to scan the sky in response to the same alarm call. Although the frequency of production of some calls does vary between males and females, and between old and young, no indication was found that these considerations blurred the distinctions between the major categories of response evoked by the various alarm calls in different subjects.

We are led to the conclusion that the depreciation of animal signals as nothing more than manifestations of emotion or affect is misplaced. Although vervet monkeys show every sign of possessing emotions, there seems no more reason to invoke affect to explain highly differentiated alarm calling than for other kinds of behavior. Although affect is clearly involved in much of what a monkey does, by itself it can explain only a fraction of what is going on. As already indicated, the only way out of the dilemma would be to invoke a different emotion for each alarm call, and for every other signal behavior as well, thus relieving the concept of emotion of any explanatory value whatsoever.

AFFECT, COGNITION, AND THE PROBLEM OF
SPECIFICITY

What kinds of judgments have underlain the widespread but evidently mistaken view that affect reigns supreme in animal behavior? Why are we so ready to infer that the chain of events linking experience of a referent with the production of a signal correlated with that referent is radically different from the sequence to which we as humans are subject when a linguistic label is produced for an external referent? The key issue here is the tendency to underestimate the specificity of the stimulus-response relationships that are involved. Previously it had been thought that in animals the relationships between external situations and signal production are typically highly generalized. No doubt this misconception stemmed from an inability to distinguish one call type from another and from a failure to analyze responses to signals with sufficient precision. Reliance on purely observational studies may have furthered such misinterpretations, encouraged by the many uncontrolled variables that impinge on animals in nature as they interact with one another and with their environments. The result is a great deal of apparently meaningless variation in the ways in which they behave. With refinements in techniques for acoustical analysis, and the new insights that derive from a shift of emphasis from observation to experimentation, we can now begin to appreciate the particularity of the interrelationships between the acoustic structure of the sound signals of animals and the referents that they represent. Thus, much of the apparently random variability actually consists of adaptive responses to constantly changing conditions and changing needs, and is not a consequence of the imprecise and generalized control of behavior by the emotions.

The Problem of Referential Specificity

The theme of *specificity* is, I believe, a major source of misunderstanding in differentiating what we are accustomed to thinking of as symbolic or representational signaling on the one hand, and "affective" signaling on the other. There are several aspects to this specificity.

The most important is referential specificity. In the production of the leopard call by adult vervets, leopards are by far the most frequent referent, but calling to other predators does take place. A vervet monkey may give the leopard alarm call to lions or hyenas. Suppose that this was more common. A large, apparently ill-defined class of referents would hardly seem consistent with the notion of cognitive labeling. Instead it smacks of a generalized emotion. However there are implied guesses here as to what is referred to. The lack of specificity might be taken to suggest some confusion on the monkey's part as to the predator's identity. This is highly improbable, and there is ample evidence to the contrary. Monkeys in the wild are highly attuned to stimuli from specific predators, and it could hardly be otherwise if they are to survive. In any case, lions and perhaps even hyenas could on occasion be a threat. When monkeys use a leopard call for a lion, perhaps they are doing something more sophisticated than we give them credit for. How do we know that they are not first accurately identifying the predator, then assessing the nature of the hazard, and finally selecting an alarm call on the basis of that assessment, rather than the taxonomic identity of the predator?

The way in which vervets respond to playback of leopard calls would be consistent with such a cognitive interpretation. Certainly there is nothing sloppy about their perceptual processing of predators. This is clear from the data of Seyfarth and Cheney (1980) on eagle alarm calling, where the association with particular species is precise, at least in adult monkeys, despite the presence of more than 20 species of eagle. Monkeys often make a correct identification when a bird is a tiny speck in the sky, long before a human observer is even aware that an eagle is present.

To be sure, there are occasions when the animals appear to make mistakes. At least some of the lack of referential specificity in vervet alarm calling is attributable, however, not to adult animals but to infants and juveniles. An adult may give a leopard alarm to another carnivore. An infant may give it even to an antelope grazing under the tree in which the monkeys are feeding. A snake alarm, normally restricted to species that endanger vervets, may be given by an infant to a mouse running in the grass.

Of particular interest is the referential specificity for the production of eagle calls. In adult vervets at Amboseli this call is given almost exclusively to eagles, mostly just to one species, the martial eagle, as shown in Fig. 16. 1. Juvenile monkeys will give the call not only to martial eagles, but to other eagles as well, and on accasion to non-raptors such as vultures or spoonbills. In infants, this trend toward loss of specificity is even more exaggerated. Eagles are no longer the primary referents for eagle calling. Instead the call may be given to a wide variety of bird species and even, on one occasion to a falling leaf.

Infant monkeys do in fact give the alarm calls to a much wider array of referents than is the case with adults. The ontogenetic sequence suggests that specific responsiveness is something they have to learn. As they pass from infancy through adolescence to adulthood, the relation between referents and signals gradually becomes more highly focused. In each case they begin with a large and imprecisely defined set, finally coming to focus on particular species, corresponding with the major real-life representative of the class that threatens vervets in the place where they live.

One immediately begins to wonder what kinds of experience guide this sharpening of referential specificity. Perhaps there is something equivalent to adult tutelage, or maybe maturation is involved? A fair guess at present is that adult calling is a reinforcer for the calling of infants. If an infant sights an appropriate

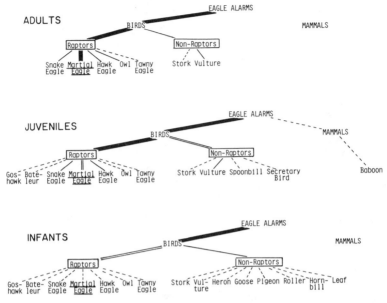

FIG. 16.1.   A diagrammatic representation of stimulus objects evoking "eagle alarm" calls in wild vervet monkeys. Results for adult, juvenile and infant monkeys are given separately so that a developmental sequence can be discerned. Only the species connected by lines were effective. The width of the lines gives a rough index of the relative frequency of elicitation of alarm calling. In adult vervets, martial eagles were the major referent for eagle alarm calling. Reproduced from "Monkey Responses to Three Different Alarm Calls: Evidence of Predator Classification and Semantic Communication," Seyfarth, et al., *Science*, Vol. 10, pp. 801–803, Fig. 1, November 14, 1980. Copyright 1980 by the AAAS.

predator for a call and then vocalizes, to be joined by a chorus of adults, that linkage is more likely to be perpetuated than an inappropriate one in which adults do not take part.

Note that we are not addressing other questions about the development of communication by alarm calls such as the ontogeny of call structure and the development of call responsiveness. While calls develop innately so far as we know, it is likely that the mode of responsiveness to the alarm calls of others is influenced by learning. Here we are only concerned with the development of the referential specificity of alarm call production.

Although young monkeys initially display a great deal of apparent confusion about what name to use for what animal, they certainly do not behave like a tabula rasa, at least at 2 or 3 months, which is the youngest age at which observational data of this kind can be gathered. Inspection of the many different stimulus situations in which eagle calling occurs in infants reveals that all have something in common, namely an object moving above them in free space. Correspondingly they do not give eagle calls to a leopard, though a leopard call may be given to other large ground-living quadrupeds. Similarly there is a certain degree of specificity in the large class of stimuli evoking infant snake calls. The young are in fact behaving as though their brains already contain some instructions for the analysis and classification of predatory animals. The rules are adequate for dividing them into lumped classes, while insufficient as yet for the separate classification of different species of predator.

Although the developmental work on alarm calling remains to be done, these findings are consonant with what animal ethologists have discovered in other perceptual domains (Marler, Dooling & Zoloth, 1980), and with the increasing referential specificity that one observes in the early word usage of children. It appears that rather unspecific, generalized, so-called "innate release mechanisms" set the path of perceptual development of the young organism on certain species-specific trajectories. These innate perceptual mechanisms are shared by members of the species, to be subject to change, adjustment, refinement or erasure in the face of individual experience. By the time a monkey is mature, whether giving alarm calls or responding to them, its brain must be generating complex cognitive schemata for predators and calls, for which the term "connotation" does not seem inappropriate (Marler, 1978). What I have in mind here is equivalent to the term "reference" that Ogden and Richards (1923) use for "the concept which mediates between the word or expression and the referent" (Lyons, 1977, p. 175).

Although the referential specificity of these vervet alarm calls as used in adulthood is impressive, it should not be inferred that all animal signals have an equivalent degree of specificity. This is certainly not the case. Within the vervet alarm call repertoire there are signals other than those discussed here with more generalized referents, serving more to bring companions to the alert than to evoke specific escape strategies. Probably animal signals run the full gamut, some with a high degree of referential specificity, others with generalized referents, as in language.

Even with generalized referential specificity, it is not clear that we should feel compelled to adduce affective interpretations of the behavior to the exclusion of cognitive, symbolic contributions. There must be *some* cluster of features that leads a group of referents to be treated as a category in the first place, however unspecific it is (Marler, 1982). Moreover, even if there were a set of referents that was large and highly generalized from one point of view such as taxonomic identity, it might be highly specific from another such as the nature of the hazard that they pose. Until we have a better understanding of how animals perceive the world, how they rank the salience of its many features, and how they assess the implications for their own future plans, we are ill advised to guess at the degree of referential specificity actually involved in any given case (Marler, 1982). Meanwhile, it seems advisable to view variations in referential specificity as irrelevant to the differentiation of affective and nonaffective behavior.

Motor Specificity

For symbolic signaling we require an ability to perform the motor act of signaling separately from all of the other behaviors that constitute the adaptive cluster of responses to the particular referent. Thus if an alarm call is truly a referential symbol it should be potentially dissociable from acts of fleeing. A truly symbolic food call should be potentially separable from acts of eating. If an animal were incapable of such separation, and the signal proved to be inextricably bound up with the set of other reactions to the referent, we would be inclined to favor the interpretation that the essential substrate for the call is not cognitive, but a gross motivational complex, perhaps affective in nature (cf. Lancaster, 1975).

We must proceed with care here. An alarm caller that did not itself flee would not survive long. The question is not whether the two are commonly intermingled, but whether calling is *potentially* dissociable from the other behaviors. Vervet monkey alarm calling is of interest in this context. We have noted that playback of the alarm calls evoked the full array of normal, vigorous escape responses with, however, one interesting exception. Rarely did any of the respondents give alarm calls themselves (Seyfarth et al., 1980a). In a natural predator encounter there is typically a chorus of calling as first one then another animal joins in broadcasting the alarm. In the alarm call playback experiments, responses were uncannily silent. Conversely, Seyfarth and Cheney (1982) have noted that solitary male vervets alarmed by a leopard may withhold alarm calls, while performing other components of the escape response, suggesting voluntary control of call production.

Here then is a case where the call can be dissociated from the other components of alarm behavior. Presumably the chorusing that one normally hears is a consequence of one animal after another, alerted by the calling, locating the predator and only then becoming an alarmist itself. The extent of the chorus will thus reflect the number of independent judgments about the certainty of the predator identification and the immediacy of the threat, adding another dimension to the communicative system.

In the laboratory the calls of monkeys can be brought under experimental control quite independently of their normal antecedents and accompaniments, as has been shown successfully with vocalizations of the rhesus monkey and some other species (Sutton, 1979; Sutton, Larson, Taylor, & Lindeman, 1973; Wilson, 1975). Many animal signals are produced independently of their normal accompaniments in the course of play behavior. Thus the capacity for independent production of some animal signals is clearly present.

To the extent that we see signals as bound up with other behavioral complexes, this binding is probably in turn a reflection of functional requirements rather than limited cognitive capacities. Monkeys do not, so far as we know, use signal production as a vehicle for reflective rehearsal of past or contemplated future events. There is typically an immediacy to their communication stemming from the caller's own involvement in basic functional requirements for survival. In many circumstances, display of an ability to dissociate signals from other motor components would be of little service, and perhaps hazardous. The witholding of a signal in the absence of an audience, as in solitary vervets, constitutes one exception. There is also always the possibility of prevarication. Ethologists are currently showing increasing interest in the possibility of deception and lying in animal communication, again assuming some ability to separate signal and affect. Even if the ability for such dissociation were not present, it is by no means clear that lack of motor specificity is a reliable criterion for affective signaling in our own species. With signal components that usually appear as part of a coherent complex, a degree of individuation seems to be perfectly possible, to judge from the work of Ekman and others on the capacity to use visual signals from the face and body for affective prevarication (Ekman & Friesen, 1969, 1974).

Closely related to motor aspects of signal production is the issue of physiological specificity. The emotions are associated with activities of limbic brain mechanisms known to be involved in some nonhuman primate sound production (Myers, 1976), though probably not to the exclusion of other cortical areas as well (Steklis & Raleigh, 1979). Although human symbolic and affective signals typically act in concert (Lamendella, 1977), a criterion for purely symbolic signaling is the potential dissociation from the generalized physiological manifestations of emotion associated with actual perception of the referent, including autonomic components (Marin, 1976). We can discuss a predator without necessarily experiencing the autonomic arousal that would accompany an actual confrontation. As already indicated, this ability to maintain specific physiological linkages between production states and signaling behavior, without the involvement of generalized emotions, is less rare in animals than has been supposed, though it is questionable whether any behavior other than that which is purely reflexive is totally free of affect. As Zajonc (1980) points out, it is doubtful whether human cognitive behavior could proceed very far without the kind of appraisal and evaluation that affective mechanisms provide.

Animal communicative behavior appears to be strongly focused on the here-and-now. While past experience clearly bears on present communicative behavior, I know of no well-documented cases of animals actually signaling about past events in the absence of some reminder, either referential or contextual. At issue is the degree of temporal linkage between the immediate perception of a referent, and signaling about it.

One could argue that human affective behavior is more closely tied to the present than our symbolic behavior, although this temporal specificity obviously breaks down in neuroses and affective disorders. Whereas referential perception and signaling are readily dissociable in time in our own symbolic behavior, they appear to be much more closely tied in animals. Does this mean that animals never think about predators when there are none present? I doubt it. They probably have predators constantly in mind as they move from place to place, relying on recollections about when and where the most recent hazards were encountered in choosing one route over another. If they do not produce predator-specific signals in the absence of predators, this probably reflects no lack of ability on their part. Rather one suspects that there are sometimes specific prohibitions on proceeding from completion of memory circuits about a referent to the production of a referential signal, suggesting barriers of the kind an actor must overcome in simulating the expression of an emotion that he does not experience. The fact that simulations can and do occur implies that the prohibitions are relative rather than absolute, but nonetheless real for that.

Simulation and deception are not unknown in animal behavior, but if an animal were to call frequently with no external cause, this would obviously place the functional value of the entire communicative system in jeopardy—that is, unless a second set of signals was added to indicate when alarm is "not-serious," as does sometimes seem to occur with playful versions of certain behaviors. Research is urgently needed on the role of such "meta-signals" in animal communication.

More than any other feature, I believe it is the temporal interdependence of signal production and the perception of referents that leads us almost intuitively to separate affective expression from purely symbolic signaling, where the temporal linkage between signal and referent is so much looser. However we may again be mistaken if we conclude from such coherence that animals lack the ability for temporal dissociation of signal and referent. The potential conditionability of animal signals is relevant here, though the crucial question is whether one is conditioning the action alone, or the underlying concept as well. Answers will be difficult to come by, but not impossible. An experimental demonstration that production of a conditioned alarm call is accompanied by lowering of thresholds to respond to the actual predator that it is supposed to represent would suggest conditioning both of call and of concept, for example.

One may ask whether the temporal linkage of referent and signal is a necessary feature of all affective signaling. Certainly in our own case it is commonplace for the memories of an event to work us into a rage or a state of despair long after it first happened. Furthermore the greater inertia of the emotions as compared with cognitive states is such as to make the time relations between referent perception and affective signaling inherently somewhat unspecific. Thus, while the temporal relationships that characterize most animal signals and their referents are highly constrained, it is not clear that this implies an affective basis for them. Rather the temporal interdependence appears to be an adaptive phenomenon, related to the use of communication by animals, not for reflective discourse, but for coping with concerns that are urgent and immediate, for signaler as well as for respondent.

Where then does this leave us in the search for criteria for distinguishing affective from nonaffective signal production in animals? One begins to wonder about the status of the dichotomy. Could it be that affective and symbolic signal production depends ultimately on similar cognitive underpinnings? It seems conceivable that affective and symbolic processing normally functions in parallel, each with its own sets of positive and negative feedback relations, with different degrees of specific connectivity, but finding roots in the same set of brain mechanisms for stimulus classification and appraisal. One might even argue that, in higher vertebrates, all true signaling behavior is underlain by both kinds of events, affective and symbolic, the emphasis varying from situation to situation, sometimes greatly favoring cognitive contributions, and at other times favoring affect. This interpretation would not be inconsistent with the new view of the signaling behavior of animals that is emerging.

COGNITION AND EMOTIONAL THEORY

This point of view on animal affect and cognition converges with prevailing viewpoints on human affective behavior (Plutchik & Kellerman, 1980). Although not universally accepted (e.g., Zajonc, 1980), most modern theorizing about human emotions assumes the necessary participation not only of autonomic elements but also a strong cognitive component (Arnold, 1970; Candland, 1977; Izard, 1971; Plutchik, 1977, 1980; Pribram, 1967; Schachter, 1975). This is not, of course to deny that autonomic effects are crucial both in the genesis and the maintenance of most emotional states. But it does appear that the strongest form of the James/Lange theory of emotion, that emotion is no more than a reflection of the body's state of arousal, is untenable.

As long ago as 1906 Sir Charles Sherrington emphasized the intimate and perhaps obligatory co-involvement of cognitive and emotional events. He conjectured that "Mind rarely, probably never, perceives any object with absolute indifference, that is, without feeling." In other words, affective tone is a constant accompaniment of sensation. It seems no less appropriate to invoke the interplay of cognition and affect in the behavior of monkeys than in our own species (Sherrington, 1900, p. 974, quoted in Blumenthal, 1977, p. 102). This is the prevailing view in most recent work on the subject, as exemplified by the studies of Schachter and Singer (1962) who, in one of the few experiments on the problem, found that the quality of experience associated with injections of adrenaline was fundamentally determined by the subject's cognitive appraisal of the situation. Although subject to criticism, the major thrust of this study—that cognition shapes the quality of emotional experience—is widely accepted.

So, the nature of the dichotomy between affect and cognition that many presume is by no means clear. Another dichotomy one could invoke is that between the *idea* of a referent, and *feelings* associated with that referent. But again the heart of the matter in both cases is the mental conception or image or schema of the referent that we and other animals must consult in its perceptual identification or recall. After consultation of a mental schema other correlates may then follow, including labeling by a verbal or some other signal, as well as images associated with the first by varying degrees of proximity or abstraction. There is also an appraisal of importance or salience—what it means to us in a different sense than just putting a label on it. All of these considerations contribute to the emotion or feeling associated with a referent, including the verbal component or at least some aspects of it. Again the ideas and the feelings associated with a referent are closely related, and perhaps in a causal way. It is thus not quite clear what is implied if one wants to associate animal signals more with feelings than with ideas.

One of the difficulties here is in deciding how global the pattern of physiological response to a referent must be before it merits status as an emotional manifestation. What do we find if we persevere in refining and subdividing systems of emotion? How many distinct qualities do there in fact seem to be? And how do they fit in a system of social communication?

One obvious component is that of activation or arousal, with inactivity or depression at one pole, and high arousal at the other. Another is that of strong attentiveness at one pole and distractedness or inattentiveness at the other. Norbert Wiener (1948) has pointed out the rich communicative potential of a combination of external signs of arousal and the indexical information that derives from following another person's gaze to determine what they are looking at, always assuming that deception or manipulation are not involved. Visualizing an encounter with a member of a strange culture and with an unknown language, he suggests that . . .

> Even without any code of sign language common to the two of us, I can learn a great deal from him. All I need to do is to be alert to those movements when he is showing the signs of emotion or interest. I then cast my eyes around, perhaps paying attention to the direction of his glance, and fix in memory what I see or hear. It will not be long before I discover the things which seem important to him, not because he has communicated them to me by language, but because I myself have observed them.

Thus with no other signaling elements than signs of arousal and the indexical property of eyes and where they are looking, such behavior has rich communicative potential. A directly parallel theme, that we should not underestimate the potential of affective signaling, is echoed by Premack (1975).

Consider two ways in which you could benefit from my knowledge of the conditions next door. I could return and tell you, 'The apples next door are ripe.' Alternatively, I could come back from next door chipper and smiling. On still another occasion I could return and tell you, 'A tiger is next door.' Alternatively, I could return mute with fright, disclosing an ashen face and quaking limbs. The same dichotomy could be arranged on numerous occasions. I could say, 'The peaches next door are ripe' or say nothing and manifest an intermediate amount of positive affect since I am only moderately fond of peaches. Likewise, I might report, 'A snake is next door,' also an intermediate amount of affect since I am less shaken by snakes than by tigers [p. 591].

Premack goes on to develop the differences between two kinds of signaling, referential (= symbolic) and affective (= exited or aroused), suggesting that information of the first kind consists of explicit properties of the world next door while information of the second kind consists of affective states, that he assumes to be positive or negative and varying in degree. Premack continues,

Since changes in the affective states are caused by changes in the conditions next door, the two kinds of information are obviously related. In the simplest case we could arrange that exactly the condition referred to in the symbolic communication be the cause of the affective state [p. 592].

Again developing the communicative implications, Premack indicates that as long as there is some concordance between the preferences and aversions of communicants then a remarkable amount of information can be transmitted by an affective system. While he explicitly restricts himself to "what" rather than "where" one may note, harking back to the Wiener quotation, that incorporation of an indexical component in the signal—pointing or looking—not only indicates where, but also adds a highly specific connotation—one particular apple tree.

The dimensions of emotional behavior incorporated by Wiener and Premack in their examples of affective communication have long been accepted as major axes along which emotions are organized, in systems that go back to Wundt. These involve three dimensions, one the hedonic dimension of pleasantness and unpleasantness, an arousal dimension, and a dimension of attentiveness.

There are some who would go further. The widely quoted system of emotions developed by Plutchik (1977, 1980) suggests a further subdivision of the hedonic dimension into what we can distinguish as dimensions of social engagement and disengagement on the one hand, and object acceptance or rejection on the other. This is a system with some appeal to an ethologist in that it provides niches for a significant proportion of the major classes of behaviors that comprise the natural repertoires of animals.

What I find intriguing about this effort to press the fractionation of emotional state further is that the view of behavioral organization it leads to begins to merge with a classification of groups of behaviors on the basis of drive states. If we push the process of fragmentation still further we eventually arrive at a relationship between signal production and internal states in which the latter are so narrowly specified that they coincide with the states that generate single actions. The difficulty one has in placing a firm boundary between the global internal states that are supposed to underlie emotional expressions and the specific states that underlie the production of a referential signal suggests that symbolic and affective signaling can be viewed as extremes on a continuum, characterized by the variations in specificity and temporal interdependence of referent and signal I have outlined. As such, they may prove to differ more in degree than in kind.

One place to look for confirmation or refutation of this hypothesis would be in signalling behaviors that we unhesitatingly accept in ourselves as being emotional or affective in nature. To what extent do they spread across the same continuum? Are all affective expressions inextricably bound up in a matrix of other emotional manifestations? Can so-called affective expressions be dissociated from their more typical emotional substrates? Actors presumably have such an ability. Studies of affective facial expressions are especially illuminating in this regard (Ekman & Oster, 1979; Ekman, Roper & Hager, 1980).

Suppose one hypothesized that affective expressions are less inextricably related to underlying emotional states than has been supposed. Kraut and Johnston (1979) sought to test such a notion by recording the incidence of smiling in pairs of situations in one of which the level of pleasure or happiness would be judged greater than in the other. The situations selected were behavior in a bowling alley, with good scores or poor ones, the audience at a hockey game, with the scoring going in favor of the home team or against it, and behavior as people walked along a street in pleasant weather or when it was excessively hot and humid.

In all cases there was a small increment in smiling in the more pleasant of the two situations. However the overwhelming correlation for smiling was not with happiness or unhappiness, but with occurrence or nonoccurrence of social interaction. Thus in the bowling situation people tended to remain impassive while facing the pins, irrespective of whether they were doing well or poorly. However smiling was frequent as they turned to interact with companions watching the game. The same was true in the other situations, leading the authors to conclude that there is a strong and robust association of smiling with a social motivation and an erratic one with emotional experience. This is not to say that smiling is completely uninvolved with emotion, as emerged from the negative correlation between smiling and signs of anger, inferred from other affective and verbal behaviors recorded in the course of the study. But it seems that smiling is not inextricably linked with situations associated with happiness.

Among possible criticisms, one might assert that these were not emotion-producing situations. However they were selected because they seemed to be potent in this regard, and many of the other behaviors recorded seem to imply that feelings ran high and that people were not especially inhibited. Another possible interpretation is that in these social situations subjects were masking their emotional expressions as Ekman and Friesen (1969) demonstrated in some social situations, perhaps to confuse their audience or to comply with what were felt to be normative pressures. Ekman has in fact proposed that in America the smile is often used to hide or mask negative emotional facial expressions. Again, people were quite highly expressive in these situations, and it is not obvious that they were in a mood to mask their feelings.

A further, potentially more cogent criticism is that there may be more than one kind of smile (cf. Ekman, Friesen & Ancoli, 1980), and that the social appeasement smile, according to the interpretation favored by Kraut and Johnston (1979), may in fact be a different one from that associated with happiness. More research is needed to clinch this issue. Finally the authors suggest that while smiling does not necessarily represent the expression of happiness, it may be a display for the communication of happiness. In other words they suggest that it may serve as a symbol for happiness. This proposal again makes one wonder where we stand with regard to the distinction between affective and symbolic signaling. The uncertainty is especially germane to animals in view of the impression I and others have obtained that much of what these authors report about human smiling might also be true for the grimace of nonhuman primates. Again there is evidence of some dissociation of the expression from its underlying affect, and a capacity for voluntary use. Certainly the association of smiling with presence of an audience or recipient suggests a relationship with the intent to communicate, a condition which I suspect would also be satisfied by the nonhuman primate equivalent. Thus, even with an affective expression as elementary as smiling, it is clear that a pure, "affect" interpretation is hard to sustain. There has to be a strong cognitive component, although the reference, if there is such, must be concerned with social intentions rather than semantic in the sense of a correlation with some external referent.

Studies of the success people have in concealing or falsifying emotional manifestations also suggest more flexibility than one might suppose in the relationship between affective state and affective expression. Ekman and his colleagues have shown that when nurses were shown an unpleasant film and told to convince another observer that they were viewing a pleasant film, they were evidently reasonably successful in falsifying the information presented by their face, but less successful in concealing cues from other parts of the body, especially the hands (Ekman & Friesen, 1974). Studies of prevarication suggest that there is more ability to withhold the linguistic aspects of speech than nonlinguistic aspects such as variations in fundamental frequency, although this could be in part a result of the fact that normal life offers less opportunity for practice in the nonlinguistic mode. Facial movement is in general more manageable than movement of the body. The position of the voice in this hierarchy of affective withholdability is still moot, however (Scherer, personal communication).

It is not clear whether there is a hierarchy of physiological automaticity, as it were, or whether the hierarchy reflects people's awareness of the vehicles that others are responding to in judging the extent of simulation of affect. Thus, contrary to what one might have supposed, Robert Krauss and his colleagues at Columbia found that you can make better judgments about whether a person is lying by listening to a tape of an interview than by actually conducting the interview yourself (Streeter, Krauss, Geller, Olson, & Apple, 1977). This suggests that facial movements may be easier to suppress or simulate than what we say or how we say it, although other interpretations are possible. It might be harder to suppress our response to facial movements, irrespectively of how well they can be simulated. And it may take a lot more concentration to extract the vocal information, becoming easier if you are not distracted by the plethora of information available in a face-to-face interview. In any event, it is clear that degrees of simulation of emotional expression are possible, with patterns of signaling behavior that, at least in the older literature, were unhesitatingly accepted as affective and nonsymbolic.

The picture that emerges is one of varying degrees of coupling between affective signals and the underlying affective substrate, close and perhaps virtually obligatory in some cases and loose or nonexistent in others. To the extent that one must appeal in the latter case to cognitive mechanisms for nonaffective production the way is open to introduce symbolic contributions to the operation of a great deal of affective signaling.

This is the very conclusion towards which animal studies are now pointing. A strong case can be made that some animal signals possess the attributes of symbols. We have probably been mistaken in assuming that the nonsymbolic or affective mode is somehow more primitive than the symbolic one. The efficient use of affect is probably predicated on prior access to cognition. The intermingling of cognition and affect in signaling behavior, whenever it was achieved in the course of animal evolution, greatly enriches its communicative content. A signaling system totally devoid of affect would be significantly impoverished. Achievement of the kind of facultative blending of cognition and affect I am proposing here must have been a significant evolutionary advance. This interpretation leads in turn to a novel position on the origin of language. It implies that man did not invent a new symbolic mode of operation, but rather that he enriched and elaborated a system already operating in animals. As neurobiology advances, we should soon be able to broach direct studies of the physiology of mental processes. If the approach presented here is valid, it should be possible, with carefully chosen subjects, to study symbolic processing just as well in animals as in man.

In trying to decide which components of animal signaling are equivalent to human affect we must proceed with care. It is no longer obvious what people mean when they interpret animal behavior as purely emotional in nature. Do they intend to exclude that component of affective behavior that is almost universally viewed as cognitive? Affect probably cannot exist independently of cognition. In any case, we have clear and growing evidence that cognitive events are important in animal signaling behavior. Thus the task that confronts us is rather like that which the student of speech grapples with in trying to dissociate the affective from the purely linguistic content (Ekman, Friesen, Ancoli, 1980; Scherer, 1981, in press; Williams & Stevens, 1979). Comparative studies have only just begun to deal with issues of semanticity, and it is still premature to judge how widespread the symbolic use of animal signals will prove to be. Yet, it is also clear that parallels with human emotion are present in animals, and that, at many levels, understanding them is vital to the further analysis of animal behavior. Similarly, a new generation of animal studies may lead in turn to a reappraisal of the possibility of symbolic, representational use of human, nonlinguistic signaling behaviors, especially of the face, that have hitherto been viewed as purely affective and nonrepresentational in nature.

ACKNOWLEDGMENTS

Field work on vocal communication in vervet monkeys, conducted in collaboration with Robert Seyfarth and Dorothy Cheney was supported by a grant from the National Science Foundation (BNS 16894) with supplementary funding from the following: NIMH MH07446, a grant from the Wenner-Gren Foundation, a NSF National Needs postdoctoral fellowship and National Geographic Society Grant No. 1767. I am indebted to Drs. Cheney and Seyfarth for permission to reprint Fig. 16. 1 and, together with Drs. Harold Gouzoules, Sarah Gouzoules and Klaus Scherer, for insightful criticisms of the manuscript.

REFERENCES

Arnold, M. B. Perennial problems in the field of emotion. In M. Arnold (Ed.), *Feelings and emotions*. New York: Academic Press, 1970.

Blumenthal, A. L. *The process of cognition*. Englewood Cliffs, N.J.: Prentice Hall, 1977.

Candland, D. K. The persistent problems of emotion. In D. K. Candland, J. P. Fell, E. Keen, A. I. Leshner, R. M. Tarpy, & R. Plutchik (Eds.), *Emotion*. Monterey, Calif.: Brooks/Cole, 1977.

Cheney, D. L., & Seyfarth, R. M. How vervet monkeys perceive their grunts: Field playback experiments. *Animal Behaviour*, 1982, *30*, 739–751.

Duffy, E. *Activation and behavior*. New York: Wiley, 1962.

Ekman, P., & Friesen, W. V. Nonverbal leakage and clues to deception. *Psychiatry*, 1969, *32*, 88–106.

Ekman, P., & Friesen, W. V. Detecting deception from the body or face. *Journal of Personality and Social Psychology*, 1974, *29*, 288–298.

Ekman, P., Friesen, W. V., & Ancoli, S. Facial signs of emotional experience. *Journal of Personality and Social Psychology*, 1980, *39*, 1125–1134.

Ekman, P., Friesen, W. V., & Scherer, K. Body movements and voice pitch in deceptive interactions. *Semiotica*, 1976, *16*, 23–27.

Ekman, P., & Oster, H. Facial expressions of emotion. *Annual Review of Psychology,* 1979, *30,* 527–534.

Ekman, P., Roper, G., & Hager, J. C. Deliberate facial movement. *Child Development,* 1980, *51,* 886–891.

Griffin, D. R. The question of animal awareness. New York: The Rockefeller University University Press, 1981.

Izard, C. *The face of emotion.* New York: Appleton-Century-Crofts, 1971.

Jurgens, U. Neural control of vocalization in nonhuman primates. In H. D. Steklis & M. J. Raleigh (Eds.) *Neurobiology of social communication in primates.* New York: Academic Press, 1979.

Kraut, R. E., & Johnston, R. Social and emotional messages of smiling: An ethological approach. *Journal of Personality and Social Psychology,* 1979, *37,* 1539–1553.

Lamendella, J. T. The limbic system in human communication. In H. Whitaker & H. A. Whitaker (Eds.), *Studies in neurolinguistics.* New York: Academic Press, 1977.

Lancaster, J. B. *Primate behavior and the emergence of human culture.* New York: Holt, Rinehart & Winston, 1975.

Luria, A. R. *Language and Cognition* (J. V. Wertsch, Ed.). New York: Wiley, 1981.

Lyons, J. *Semantics. Vol. 1.* Cambridge: Cambridge University Press, 1977.

Marin, O. S. M. Neurobiology of language: An overview. In S. R. Harnad, H. D. Steklin, & J. Lancaster (Eds.), *Origins and evolution of language and speech.* New York: The New York Academy of Sciences, 1976.

Marler, P. Affective and symbolic meaning: Some zoosemiotic speculations. In T. A. Sebeok (Ed.), *Sight, sound and sense.* Bloomington: Indiana University Press, 1978.

Marler, P. R. Avian and primate communication: The problem of natural categories. *Neuroscience & Biobehavioral Reviews,* 1982, *6,* 87–94.

Marler, P. R., Dooling, R. J., & Zoloth, S. Comparative perspectives on ethology and behavioral development. In M. H. Bornstein (Ed.), *Comparative methods in psychology.* Hillsdale, N.J.: Lawrence Erlbaum Associates, 1980.

Menzel, E. W., & Johnson, M. K. Communication and cognitive organization in humans and other animals. In S. R. Harnad, H. D. Steklin, & J. Lancaster (Eds.), *Origins and evolution of language and speech.* New York: The New York Academy of Sciences, 1976.

Myers, R. E. Comparative neurology of vocalization and speech: Proof of a dichotomy. In S. R. Harnad, H. D. Steklis, & J. Lancaster (Eds.), *Origins and evolution of language and speech.* New York: The New York Academy of Sciences, 1976.

Ogden, C. K., & Richards, I. A. *The meaning of meaning.* London: Routledge & Kegan Paul, 1923.

Plutchik, R. Emotions, evolution and adaptive processes. In M. B. Arnold (Ed.), *Feelings and emotions.* New York: Academic Press, 1970.

Plutchik, R. Cognitions in the service of emotions. In D. K. Candland, J. P. Fell, E. Keen, A. I. Leshner, R. M. Tarpy, & R. Plutchik (Eds.) *Emotion.* Monterey, Calif.: Brooks/Cole, 1977.

Plutchik, R. A general psychoevolutionary theory of emotion. In R. Plutchik & H. Kellerman (Eds.), *Emotion, theory, research, and experience* (Vol. 1). New York: Academic Press, 1980.

Plutchik, R., & Kellerman, H. (Eds.). Theories of emotion. In R. Plutchik & H. Kellerman (Eds.), *Emotion, theory, research and experience* (Vol. 1). New York: Academic Press, 1980.

Premack, D. On the origins of language. In M. S. Gazzaniga & C. B. Blakemore (Eds.), *Handbook of psychobiology.* New York: Wiley, 1975.

Pribram, K. H. Emotion: Steps toward a neuropsychological theory. In D. Glass (Ed.), *Neurophysiology and emotion.* New York: The Rockefeller University Press and Russell Sage Foundation, 1967.

Robinson, B. W. Limbic influences on human speech. In S. R. Harnad, H. D. Steklis, & J. Lancaster (Eds.), *Origins and evolution of language and speech.* New York: The New York Academy of Sciences, 1976.

Schachter, S. Cognition and peripheralist-centralist controversies in motivation and emotion. In M. S. Gazzaniga & C. B. Blakemore (Eds.), *Handbook of psychobiology.* New York: Wiley, 1975.

Schachter, S., & Singer, J. Cognitive, social and physiological determinants of emotional state. *Psychological Review*, 1962, *69*, 379–399.

Scherer, K. R. Speech and emotional states. In J. Darby (Ed.), *Speech evaluation in psychiatry.* New York: Grune & Stratton, 1981.

Scherer, K. Emotion as a process: Function, origin and regulation. *Social Science Information* Beverly Hills: Sage, 1982, *21*, 4/5, 555–570.

Scherer, K. R. Nonlinguistic vocal indicators of emotion and psychopathology. In C. E. Izard (Ed.), *Emotions in personality and psychopathology.* New York: Plenum, in press.

Schneirla, T. C. An evolutionary and developmental theory of biphasic processes underlying approach and withdrawal. In M. R. Jones (Ed.), *Nebraska Symposium on Motivation.* Lincoln: University of Nebraska Press, 1959.

Seyfarth, R. M., & Cheney, D. L. The ontogeny of vervet monkey alarm calling behavior: A preliminary report. *Zeitschrift für Tierpsychologie*, 1980, *54*, 37–56.

Seyfarth, R. M., & Cheney, D. L. How monkeys see the world: A review of recent research on East African vervet monkeys. In C. T. Snowdon, C. H. Brown, & M. R. Petersen (Eds.), *Primate communication.* New York: Cambridge University Press, 1982.

Seyfarth, R. M., Cheney, D. L., & Marler, P. Vervet monkey alarm calls: Semantic communication in a free-ranging primate. *Animal Behavior*, 1980, *28*, 1070–1094. (a)

Seyfarth, R. M., Cheney, D. L., & Marler, P. Monkey responses to three different alarm calls: Evidence of predator classification and semantic communication. *Science*, 1980, *210*, 801–803. (b)

Steklis, H. D., & Raleigh, J. J. Behavioral and neurobiological aspects of primate vocalization and facial expression. In H. D. Steklis & M. J. Raleigh (Eds.), *Neurobiology of social communication in primates.* New York: Academic Press, 1979.

Streeter, L. A., Krauss, R. M., Geller, V., Olson, C., & Apple, W. Pitch changes during attempted deception. *Journal of Personality and Social Psychology*, 1977, *34*, 345–350.

Struhsaker, T. T. Auditory communication among vervet monkeys (*Cercopithecus aethiops*). In S. A. Altmann (Ed.), *Social communication among primates.* Chicago: University of Chicago Press, 1967.

Sutton, D. Mechanisms underlying vocal control in nonhuman primates. In H. D. Steklis & M. J. Raleigh (Eds.), *Neurobiology of social communication in primates.* New York: Academic Press, 1979.

Sutton, D., Larson, C., Taylor, E. M., & Lindeman, R. C. Vocalization in the rhesus monkey: Conditionability. *Brain Research*, 1973, *52*, 225–231.

Wiener, N. *Cybernetics.* New York: Wiley, 1948.

Williams, C. E., & Stevens, K. N. Emotions and speech: Some acoustical correlates. In S. Weitz (Ed.), *Nonverbal communication,* 2nd Ed. New York: Oxford University Press, 1979.

Wilson, W. A., Jr. Discriminative conditioning of vocalizations in *Lemur catta. Animal Behaviour*, 1975, *23*, 432–436.

Zajonc, R. B. Feeling and thinking. Preferences need no inferences. *American Psychologist*, 1980, *35*, 151–175.

IV SOCIOLOGICAL AND ANTHROPOLIGICAL APPROACHES

Many of the contributions in this volume stress the important role of emotion for social interaction and social organization. However, the author often focused on emotion as an individual phenomenon with adaptive value for the individual. While granting that the individual's interaction with significant others is important, most authors did not focus specifically on the functions of emotion on the level of social organization itself. This is the proper domain of sociology and anthropology. It was not possible to represent all such approaches to emotion in this volume, for interest in emotion is burgeoning in these disciplines. The contributions that are included represent three different perspectives: (1) the sociological model of relationships and social interaction outcomes that determine emotional processes, including their effect on the organism, (2) the role of emotion as expressed by individuals for social structure and social change in society, and (3) the role of emotion in culture, both in terms of cultural definitions of emotional phenomena and the regulative function of emotion in society.

The first of these issues is addressed by Theodore Kemper in his model on power and status as the two most important dimensions to describe relationships and the outcomes of interaction. Kemper proposes a scheme whereby a large number of different emotions can be predicted on the basis of a power and status relationship between individuals. He tries to show how this fact can be traced down to the physiological level.

Whereas Kemper's approach tends to be microsociological, Randall Collins in his chapter adopts a macrosociological point of view, examining the societal functions of emotion. Collins conceives of emotion as a form of social energy that subserves repeated patterns of face-to-face interaction, which Collins considers as equivalent to social structure. Collins argues that emotion as a factor on the microsociological level of conversation and interaction plays a major role for macrosociological phenomena such as social change because of a "market economy of emotional energy."

The anthropologist Robert Levy, finally, presents a fascinating account of the role of emotion in non-Western societies. As in the case of comparative analysis in animal species, comparative analysis of different cultural traditions yields major insights into features of emotion that tend to remain hidden when one focuses exclusively on one's own sociocultural environment. In addition to again raising a number of issues central to the study of emotion, such as cognitive evaluation of antecedent events, and the expression of emotion, Levy discusses at length the way that emotion itself is cognized in a particular cultural group and how this treatment of the emotion effects regulation and control. Levy proposes that the *feeling* which is an essential part of the emotion sequence mobilizes a cultural system of definitions and interpretations, and marks a transition between a private kind of knowing and a more public communal one. These two kinds of knowing have different structures, different relations to learning and to culturally defined reality.

17

Power, Status, and Emotions: A Sociological Contribution to A Psychophysiological Domain

Theodore D. Kemper
St. John's University

Sociologists have generally eschewed systematic inquiry into the emotions. This is understandable, in as much as sociologists ordinarily concern themselves with patterns of group organization and social structure. The emotions, on the other hand, are physiological and psychological phenomena, experienced-by and measured-in individual organisms. Even social psychology—which deals with the effects of social patterns on individuals—has concerned itself little with emotions per se, though many of the results of social psychological experiments are pertinent to the study of emotions (Kemper, 1978, Ch. 5). This can be seen most clearly when the dependent variables are liking, satisfaction, anxiety, anger, and the like. Nonetheless, social psychologists have initiated relatively little systematic inquiry from a strictly social perspective.

Even where the social has seemed to play a part in psychological investigations of emotion, it has been scanted and left relatively undefined. In perhaps the most widely known instance of this—Schachter and Singer's (1962) investigation of "cognitive, social and physiological determinants of emotional state"—the social appears not in its own right as a set of definite categories associated with specific emotions, but rather in the weak form of "social comparison processes." Young (1961) and Lazarus, Averill, and Opton (1970) have also endorsed the desirability of a social approach to emotions, but have not specified what the social must include.

Lazarus (1968) and Jacobs, Skultin, and Brown (Jacobs, 1971) have attempted a somewhat more focused approach to the social in the realm of emotions. Their advance over previous formulations in psychology was to articulate emotions with patterns of reinforcement. As reinforcements frequently, though not always, originate in the social environment, a social basis for emotion is

369

implicit in their formulations. Lazarus (1968), for example, proposed that anxiety resulted from noxious stimuli, and depression from actual or potential deprivation of positive reinforcements. Jacobs (1971) and his colleagues, building on the work of Mowrer (1960), proposed that positive and negative reinforcement contingencies were linked to emotions as follows: (1) danger signal on: fear; (2) danger signal off: relief; (3) safety signal on: security; (4) safety signal off: apprehension; (5) reward expectation: elation; (6) termination of reward expectation: disappointment; (7) signal that there will be no reward: frustration; and (8) termination of no-reward signal: hope.

Although some of the contingency states are not social, e.g., where expectations are involved, some do allow for interesting hypotheses about the connection between events in the social environment and the ensuing emotions. However, the Jacobs approach—as is true of virtually all reinforcement theories—provides no translations into the conceptual and theoretical language of social analysis. For example, what is a "danger signal," or a "safety signal?" Doubtless such translations can be attempted, though they have not been to date. There is a danger, however, that they may not be. This is because there is a strong tradition in psychology of defining the stimulus only in terms of its impact on the organism. As Arnold (1967) put it in discussing stress: ". . . there is a genuine advantage in starting our analysis from the contending or stress emotions rather than from stress itself. . . . In starting from emotion we save ourselves the difficulty of finding a criterion of stress. . ." [p. 126] (see also Izard, 1972, p. 73; John, 1973, p. 320; Korchin, 1967, p. 140). Additionally, there is the problem of defining the stimulus independently of its effect. Unless this is done, the social environmental stimulus has no separate analytic status, hence the solution adopted by Arnold. But without that status the social remains a stepchild in the study of emotions.

At this juncture the sociologist becomes an interested party, for it is precisely the sociologist in the division of labor of the sciences who is most concerned with the definition, conceptualization, and elaboration of the categories of the social environment: social class, bureaucracy, normative order, division of labor, hierarchy, power, status, and the like. There are relational or organizational concepts. They are properties of relationships or of groups. They are not properties of individuals, nor are they measurable in individuals in the manner of, let us say, motives, abilities, or emotions. Sociological terms allow us to examine the social environment and its effects on emotion more immediately than the abstract language of reinforcement theory. We can move quite directly from social class to emotion, or from power to emotion without the mediation of abstract reinforcement concepts.

Indeed the central contribution of a sociological approach to emotions is the specification of a comprehensive model of the social environment, as is detailed below. This allows for the formulation of empirically-based hypotheses linking variations in the social environment with varying emotions. More importantly, the presently most adequate sociological model of the environment also invites the surmise that a particular formulation of the psychophysiological properties of emotion—namely the so called Funkenstein hypothesis (Funkenstein, 1955)—may be correct.

POWER AND STATUS AS SOCIAL ENVIRONMENT

A remarkable convergence of theoretical and empirical work in the social sciences has gone relatively unremarked. I refer here to the oft-repeated findings that two central dimensions characterize social relationships between human actors. (See Kemper 1978, 1981 for review of evidence for two dimensions.) The two dimensions are variously named but they refer unmistakably to relations of *power* and *status*. Power implies the ability to overcome the resistance of others when others do not wish to comply (cf. Weber, 1946, p. 181). Relationships can be *structured* in terms of power, so that there is a probability that in specified domains each actor can achieve his or her will to a certain extent despite the resistance of the other. There is also *process* power: this entails all the acts designed to overcome the resistance of the other, both actually and prospectively, including physical and verbal assaults, deprivations, threats, and the like.

Status refers to the compliance that actors voluntarily accord each other, unaccompanied by threat or coercion. As with power there are structural and processual aspects. Status structure in relationship indicates the probability of voluntary compliance with the desires and wishes of the other, whether actually or prospectively. As process, status entails the range of friendly, congenial, supporting, rewarding, ultimately, loving behavior that actors voluntarily accord each other. (See Kemper 1978, 1981, for extended discussion of structure and process in power and status, including love as the most intense form of status conferral.)

The particular utility of the power and status dimensions is that they permit the heuristic assumption that *all* social relations can be located in a two-dimensional power-status space, and that changes in social relations may be understood as changes in the power and status positions of actors. Actors relate to each other in structures of power and status, and in their interactions with each other express or change the relationship structure by acts that signify particular levels of power and status.

Granted this view of relationship, the following proposition is possible: *A very large class of human emotions results from real, anticipated, recollected, or imagined outcomes of power and status relations* (Kemper, 1978). This means that if we wish to predict or understand the occurrence of many human emotions we must look at the structure and process of power and status relations between actors. This approach encompasses both the distressful emotions—anger, depression, guilt, shame, anxiety—as well as the positive emotions—happiness, security, pride, righteousness, and love (Kemper, 1978, provides details on these emotions).

One important assumption about power and status relations is that they are cross-culturally valid (cf. Triandis, 1972), hence universally applicable in the prediction of emotions. However, three things are not universal:

1. The specific cultural signifiers of particular levels of power and status outcomes. For example, Krout (1942, reproduced in Hinde, 1979, p. 60) indicates 15 different ways, distributed across 20 different cultures, of displaying *humility,* a condition expressing very low power-and-status for self, often in combination with accord of very high status (and probably very high power) to the other. Hence different concrete behaviors in different cultures may elicit and signify certain emotions.

2. Also not universal are the power and status levels of particular social positions, especially as defined by ascriptive category. For example, preliterate societies tend to respect older men for their wisdom and knowledge of the society's traditions. In modern societies, older men are ceded far less status.

3. Finally, specific social organizational and social structural patterns may exacerbate or inhibit the production of certain emotions. Marx (1964) proposed the link between capitalism and alienation. Blauner (1964) showed how this link is mediated by a particular form of technology and division of labor. Levy (1973, and chapter 19, this volume) reported the "hypocognition" of certain emotions among Tahitians (this means there is a limited vocabulary for these emotions). Depression is one of the hypocognated emotions, apparently rarely experienced among Tahitians. Why? Because, we see, in Levy's discussion, that the social organizational pattern does not frequently produce the kind of status-loss outcomes that are associated with depression (see Kemper, 1978).

Universality of emotion does not mean that all societies experience the same amounts of different emotions. That would require that the social organization and the social structure of the societies be the same. Universality of emotions means that when particular social relational outcomes occur, the same emotions will result—regardless of how often such social relational outcomes occur in the society over-all.

I turn now briefly to three sociologically relevant considerations about emotions: their evolutionary survival value, emotions in the societal social structure, and emotions in interpersonal and micro-interaction.

A fundamental idea about emotions is that they have evolutionary survival value (Darwin, 1873; Hamburg, Hamburg & Barchas, 1975; Lazarus & Averill, 1972; Plutchik, 1980). This truism about emotions is ordinarily taken to reflect the distinctly biological property of emotions, from which sociological interests are ordinarily excluded. However, when we examine the biological survival value of emotions, we see that biological survival entails not merely the survival of organisms, but the preservation of patterns of social organization, or perhaps change of pattern to a more adaptive form. This does not mean that all emotions in all instances are adaptive for group survival. But where groups and their particular structures do survive or adapt, emotions have played a significant part. For example:

Fear and anger energize flight or fight in the face of danger or threat from others. Love and attachment emotions help sustain commitment to pregnant women and to infants who can't forage or protect themselves; also to aged parents and other elder members of the group who may have wisdom to offer. Respect, and loyalty permit allegiance to leaders who manifest respect-worthy qualities that augment the survival prospects of the group. Guilt and shame allow for the exercise of relatively unsupervised self-control of impulses to aggression, malfeasance, and irresponsibility.

Durkheim (1965) emphasized the importance of religious sentiments (awe, respect, fear) in imparting a necessary force to moral commitments to other members of society. Further, Durkheim valued the "emotional effervescence" (today we would call it arousal or excitation) that simple physical communion and common activity engender in people, giving them a sense of solidarity, security and strength via the identification with a larger social entity. (One thinks here of Zajonc's [1965] "social facilitation" of performance in the presence of others.) Hammond (1978) suggested that for Durkheim, emotions replace in humans the missing regulatory mechanism of instinct. Without emotions, presumably, humans would not bind themselves with sufficient constancy to any particular social-moral pattern, shunning others even if these are immediately instrumental i.e., immediately rewarded. Via emotions, commitments to symbolic forms of even the most self-abnegating kind are possible (Weber, 1947, also recognized this in his category of *Wertrational* action.) Hence it may be seen that emotions have not simply biological, but social survival value.

At the same time as we see the sociological facet of the biological phenomenon—the emotions—we must not proceed as far as have the sociobiologists in this area (e.g., Wilson, 1975). Sociobiologists presume to discover underlying biological processes and structures that support *particular* patterns of social organization, e.g., in relations between the sexes, hierarchy in society, etc. My proposal about the sociological relevance of the emotions is different. I view the emotions as capable of supporting extremely broad, even opposite, forms of social organization. Despite the great variability of cultural patterns and forms of societal organization, the same emotions undergird them. Hence we do not have direct biological determination of social patterns, but a case where social patterns—of whatever type—rely upon emotions for stability and support.

We may define *social structure* in society as a more or less stable distribution of power, status, and resources (usually wealth). Some have more, some less. Marx (1964) and Weber (1946) pointed out that these are potential bases of group formation, e.g., social classes and status groups, more or less conscious of their common interests and certainly aware of their standing relative to each other in the social structural dimensions. Two kinds of emotions are of interest here:

Integrating emotions, which bind groups together, e.g., loyalty, pride, love; and *Differentiating* emotions, which maintain the differences between the groups, e.g., fear, anger, contempt, envy. Collins (1975, and chapter 18, this volume) has significantly developed our understanding of how social groups depend on the integrative emotions to arm them for the battle with other groups and how this is accomplished. deTocqueville (1835/1945) wrote of the emotional qualities of security and aloofness in stable, unthreatened aristocracies; on the other hand, he saw envy as the predominant emotion of democracy, where certain social differences are leveled.

Actual or threatened change in social structure—the previous arrangements of power, status, and wealth—produces extremely intense emotions. History records some of the most terrible cruelties and, we must assume, hatreds to have occurred at such times. Threatened groups are not only fearful, the fear may become a virtual paranoia. Groups on the rise may indulge themselves in the most extravagant confidence and hope. Nostalgia and depression are peculiarly appropriate for groups who sense their decline. Chekov was an exquisite literary recorder of the emotions of this phenomenon. Those already declassé maintain self-esteem through privately expressed contempt for the *nouveaux riches*. The succeeding class of parvenus or commissars must ride for some time a crest of extraordinary optimism and self-aggrandizement, even megalomania (see Kemper, 1978, p. 545). Bensman and Vidich (1962) detail systematically the possibilities here.

At the microinteraction level—interpersonal, moment-to-moment, etc.— emotions should operate both to integrate and differentiate, just as they do in the larger social structure. This is because the same descriptive categories can be applied at both levels: power, status, resources. Interaction consists of doing technical things together (cooperation in some form of divided labor), and of power and status relations. Emotions flow from the outcomes of the power and status relations (Kemper, 1978). As in larger social structures, integrative emotions—love, loyalty, liking, respect—bind individuals together; differentiating emotions—anger, fear, envy, jealousy—drive them apart.

Moment-to-moment interaction and the ensuing emotions appear to be guided by three principles: First, there is *reciprocity*. This means that behaviors of one kind from actor A are likely to be followed by behaviors of a specific kind from actor B, with greater than chance probability. We may infer that the emotions evoked in B by the original actions of A provide some push for actor B's response. That response releases an emotion in turn in A, which leads to the start of another round in the interaction cycle. There are few studies that carry the analysis past the first round, or even calculate the relative likelihoods of response to a given action from among a set of possible responses even in the first round. The most stable empirical generalization from these studies is that there is greater reciprocity of negative (punishing, hurting, controlling, rejecting, i.e., power) behaviors than of positive (approving, supporting, loving, i.e., giving status).

The gradient of avoidance of the bad appears to be less steep than the gradient of approach to the good. The result has been found in studies by Rausch (1965), Rausch, Barry, Hertel, M. Swain (1974), Shannon and Guerney (1973), Wills, Weiss, and Patterson (1974), Gottman, Markman, and Notarius (1977) and in a computer simulation of interaction by Loehlin (1965).

But the data also show a certain variability according to whether the interaction proceeds in the negative direction in the first place. This brings us to the second principle: *prior structure effects,* that is the influence on interaction and emotions of the existing social and personality structure. Gottman *et al.* (1977) found among distressed couples—those with a history (i.e., structure) of high-power, low-status interaction—that communication of disagreement was accompanied by negative affect; among the nondistressed by neutral affect. Among distressed couples messages sent with positive intent were more likely to be received as negative. Rausch *et al.* (1974) report similar findings. Among nondistressed couples, there was greater chance of power behavior from one partner to be answered with conciliatory or status behavior. Among distressed couples, power behavior was virtually always met with counterpower. Even among strangers disagreements are remembered more than agreements (Gormly, Gormly & Johnson, 1971). But yet more important, there is an interaction effect between number of agreements and number of disagreements and liking for the other. *When there is a high number of agreements,* disagreements cumulate to produce less liking for the other. This effect is not found when the number of agreements is low (Gormly *et al.,* 1971).

It's as if we can stand the "fly in the ointment" less than we can stand having less ointment. This suggests an hypothesis about the probably intensity of conflict among couples who match each other's standards for desirability in love relationships (see Kemper, 1978, Chaps. 12, 13) at the 90% level as opposed to those who only meet each other's standards 60%. I would predict more intense anger, disappointment, and conflict in the high-match group. This is similar to the greater intensity of fraticidal conflict (see Coser, 1956).

Personality structure also moderates the meaning and emotional effects of interaction. Noblin, Timmons, and Kael (1966) found that mild praise (evoking satisfaction, pride) improved the performance of psychoanalytically-defined oral types, whereas with criticism (evoking shame, depression) it declined. The opposite effects were found for anal types: criticism improved performance, while praise depressed it. In a related study, Baxter, Lerner, and Miller (1965) found that identification (respect, liking, loyalty) with either a rewarding or punishing instructor-model depended on childrearing background. High authoritarian childrearing led to identification with the punishing model, low authoritarian childrearing led to identification with the rewarding model.

A third principle of microinteraction that appears less distinctly is that of *devolution.* In interaction, things very often start well and end badly, or go downhill. Rausch (1965) found that interaction sequences tended to devolve over five exchanges from about 90% friendly to about 70–75% friendly. Loehlin's (1965) computer simulation of dyadic interaction found that even when his "personalities" were both essentially "positive" they reached a harmonious conclusion in a sequence of interactions only with some difficulty. A pair of "negatives," or one positive and one negative personality ineluctably ended their interaction in conflict and disharmony. Love relations appear to be particularly vulnerable to movement into high-power sequences (Kemper 1978, Chaps. 12, 13). Integrative emotions tend to be replaced by differentiating emotions in a somewhat predictable way (Houseknecht & Macke, 1981; Swensen, Eskew, & Kohlhepp, 1981).

I turn now to a final, perhaps astonishing, sociological interest in the domain of emotions, namely the physiological.

SOCIOLOGY, PHYSIOLOGY, AND EMOTIONS

I have spoken thusfar of the intimate involvement of social relations in the determination of emotions, bringing into focus the sociological contribution. On the nether side, so to speak, emotions are constituted also by physiological activity: hormonal and neurochemical processes that dilate blood vessels, engorge the stomach, contract arterial vessels, and so on. It would appear that here the sociological interest in emotions must stand aside, in fact, simply disappear. Yet there is evidence to suggest that sociological and physiological patterns in emotion may be integrated in a single theoretical structure allowing each disciplinary perspective to shed light on the other.

The possible conjunction of sociological and physiological interests in emotion occurs in terms of what is known as the *specificity* issue. Lange (1885/1967) and James (1893) proposed that we experience emotions when we become aware of certain bodily processes that follow upon some event (real or imagined): we are caught in a foolish error and we feel our face flush; we unexpectedly see the person we love and our heart skips a beat; we become aware that we are being followed on a dark street and our bowel feels suddenly loose. All these specific physiological accompaniments of different felt-emotions may seem plausible enough to common sense, but they did not to the great physiologist Walter Cannon (1929)—at least not in the precise way formulated by the James and Lange approach.

Lange and James were arguing that specific visceral processes were related to specific emotions. Cannon on the other hand demurred from this, taking what is known as the antispecificity position. Based on his own long series of experiments with cats (in which he appeared to find that certain more or less identical physiological processes underlay such "emotions" as pain, hunger, fear, and rage), and apparently corroborated in the work of others with humans, Cannon argued that visceral processes were not distinct enough to permit discrimination of subjectively different emotions.

There is also an up-to-date version of the Cannon position, viz., the famous study by Schachter and Singer (1962), in which experimental subjects appeared to feel widely different emotions under supposedly identical conditions of physiological arousal, thus making it appear that in conditions of uncertainty only imitation or social comparison processes rather than underlying physiological differentiation give rise to different felt-emotions. Indeed, Cannon and Schachter and Singer (helped also by the work of Levi [1972] and Frankenheuser [1976] essentially derailed the specificity approach.

Yet a sociological perspective on these psychophysiological matters offers an astonishing counter-hypothesis: specificity theory is the heuristically more valuable approach here. There are three reasons for this.

First, Cannon's analysis was undertaken prior to the discovery of norepinephrine (noradrenalin), a chemical neurotransmitter in the sympathetic nervous system that is different in emotional effect from epinephrine (adrenalin), which Cannon assumed underlay all emotional arousal. (Epinephrine and norepinephrine both activate the sympathetic nervous system, but in somewhat different ways [Sternbach, 1966].) Additionally, Cannon himself worked with cats, not humans. Although comparative results are heuristically useful, they can not be taken as conclusive for humans. Finally, although pain, fear, and rage are different emotions as experienced by humans, perhaps they are not different enough as experienced by cats. I believe, therefore, that Cannon's own results cannot be translated simply into the conclusion that there are no *distinct* physiological states associated with particular emotions.

Second, an important series of studies, mainly from the 1950s, did find differential physiological processes for different emotions (e.g., Ax, 1953; Cohen & Silverman, 1959; Elmadjian, Hope, & Lamson, 1958; Funkenstein, 1955; Funkenstein, King, & Drolette, 1957; Graham, Cohen & Shmavonian, 1967; J. Schachter, 1957). The principal result of this body of work, widely known as the Funkenstein hypothesis, is that fear and/or anxiety is associated with increased secretion of epinephrine and anger with increased secretion of norepinephrine.

Most important, the Funkenstein hypothesis allows for a direct link between the physiological processes in emotion and the sociological dimensions of interaction. Because deficit of own power (or excess of other's power) is the social relational condition for fear or anxiety, and because loss of customary, expected, or deserved status (other as agent) is the basic relational condition for anger, it seems entirely compatible to suppose that specific social relational conditions are accompanied by specific physiological reactions, with the felt-emotions as the psychological mediators between the two. Furthermore, the fact that only two neurochemical substances appear to differentiate the power emotion (fear) from the status-loss emotion (anger) suggests that two may be a correct estimate of the number of separate dimensions of relationship. Yet, the sociological finding that there are two underlying dimensions of relationship provides support in turn for the existence of two neurochemicals in specific emotional processes (see Kemper, 1978, for a full treatment of this issue).

There is much to be gained from viewing the two findings as mutually supportive theoretically as well as concretely in the occurrence of emotions. It makes sense, I believe (and a close analysis of the problem of emotions demands it), that there be some kind of integration between the social relations we enact and the cognitive-somatic-autonomic accompaniments of the interaction.

There is a third argument favoring specificity theory. Schachter and Singer's (1962) experiment—treated now as a classic—appeared to refute the work of the previous decade, especially the Funkenstein hypothesis. Schachter and Singer supposedly showed that anger and euphoria, never previously linked to the same type of physiological arousal, were possible emotions after injections of epinephrine, depending on the subject's interpretation of the supposed prevailing social situation: namely whether a confederate of the experimenters' was displaying anger or euphoria in the presence of the physiologically-aroused subject.

In a very detailed analysis of the Schachter and Singer experiment (Kemper, 1978), I believe I have shown that the common interpretation of its results is quite probably erroneous. Schachter and Singer viewed their crucial findings as stemming from the social comparison with the actions of the confederate. They failed to consider how their different experimental conditions also created different *power and status relationships with the experimenters themselves,* and that the interpretation of these relationships can better explain the results than can the interpretation based on the actions of the confederates. Indeed, viewed from this relational perspective, Schachter and Singer's results can be seen to *confirm* rather than refute the Funkenstein hypothesis (Kemper, 1978). Stein (1967) and Plutchik and Ax (1967) also doubt Schachter and Singer's interpretation of their own work.

Recent attempts to replicate Schachter and Singer's findings have produced seemingly mixed results: Maslach (1979) and Marshall and Zimbardo (1979) failed to obtain the same findings. Schachter and Singer (1979) in rebuttal claim the experiments were methodologically flawed, a charge which Maslach and Marshall and Zimbardo reject. On the other hand, Erdmann and Janke (1978) appear to confirm Schachter and Singer for the emotions anger and happiness, but not for anxiety. Yet even here there are ambiguities. Unlike what Schachter and Singer intended in their experiment, Erdmann and Janke provided their subjects with a direct *relational* stimulus—the kind they thought would ordinarily make a person angry, happy, or anxious. But these stimuli must have been very weak indeed, as the control groups in the anger and happiness conditions showed *no* emotional effects. Nonetheless, the experimental groups, surreptitiously fed ephedrine (like epinephrine it mimics arousal of the sympathetic nervous system), did react as predicted, with amplified anger or happiness. However, the ephedrine, which differs importantly from epinephrine by stimulating the central nervous system, could simply have heightened the perception of the weak relational stimulus; thus subjects were reacting to the stimulus *appropriately,* rather than "finding" it in the actions of others as they presumably searched for an explanation of their physiological arousal, as Schachter and Singer would claim.

Additionally, ephedrine acts physiologically through potentiating the release of norepinephrine as well as inhibiting norepinephrine reuptake (Bergesen, 1979, p. 130; Sapeika, 1972, p. 145). This bears directly on the experience of anger (one of Erdmann and Janke's experimental conditions), because, according to the Funkenstein hypothesis, this emotion is particularly associated with norepinephrine. Indirectly, Erdmann and Janke's happiness condition is also connected with norepinephrine. Low concentrations of norepinephrine in the brain are associated with depression (Kety, 1972). Although very high concentrations of norepinephrine are associated with rage, ephedrine absorption may have countered depressive tendencies sufficiently to produce the higher happiness outcome in that experimental condition. Although one must retain a tentative stance toward this explanation, it is important to see that the substantial reliance of Schachter and Singer (1979) on Erdmann and Janke as supporting their own position may be unwarranted. Even more recently, Manstead and Wagner (1981) have cast serious doubt on the Schachter and Singer position by reviewing the logical and empirical grounds of support for it.

Lest it appear that the integration of sociological and physiological concerns has been accomplished here too facilely, and that the integration proposed is too tight, some further comments are in order.

Issac Newton supposedly said about his work: "*Hypotheses non fingo,*" which translates roughly into: "I don't speculate." By this he meant that he based his conclusions only on data. Of course, he violated his own prescription, which gives the rest of us a little elbow-room. I do *fingo hypotheses,* namely that there is a relationship between psychophysiology and social relations. That is, the things that we are able to do in interaction with each other are in the flesh, so to speak, articulated with specific psychophysiological mechanisms that dovetail with the behavioral and intentional details of social relations.

The overall articulation takes place through power-fear-epinephrine and status (withdrawal)-anger-norepinephrine. When power and status relations are satisfactory, I suppose the sympathetic (SNS) and the parasympathetic nervous systems (PNS) to be in balance. When strong power and/or status satisfactions are experienced, I suppose the PNS system to dominate. It too has its specific neurotransmitter, namely acetylcholine. Ergo, I see integration between psychological systems, and sociological systems.

Yet, clearly, the specificity issue is more complicated than I have made out. An important problem in specificity theory is that while only two or three neurotransmitters have been specifically linked to emotions, there seem to be more than two or three emotions. I wish to propose two possibilities here. One is that different emotions activate neurotransmitters differently via central nervous system (CNS) differentiation. But the SNS or PNS activation that gives the feeling of the emotion still depends on the actions of the two or three available transmitters. The paradigm is: Social relations and their outcomes produce differnetial CNS activity which in turn produces differential messages to modulate the SNS and the PNS, which in turn produce differentially experienced body sensations of emotion. In this view, SNS and PNS are integrated in perhaps the manner that Gellhorn and Loufbourrow (1963) and Gellhorn (1967) have suggested. Their work approaches the degree of complexity that probably prevails in these systems (and their interactions) to produce the emotions we experience. The governing mechanism, however, would be at the CNS level. Importantly, though, my major speculation involving the integration of social relations, emotions, and physiology, would remain in tact.

The second possible loophole to escape from the many-emotions-limited-physiology dilemma follows a line of thought that may be found in the work of Izard (1972) and Plutchik (1980). Their view is that many experienced emotions are actually compounds of simpler emotions. For example, according to Izard disgust is comprised of disgust, anger, contempt, distress, and surprise; guilt includes distress, fear, interest, shyness, among other emotions. Proceeding along this line, the following may hold: All socially provenanced emotions result from outcomes in power-status relations. If the outcomes are "bad" they involve basically fear or anger. And the Funkenstein hypothesis shows the connection with epinephrine and norepinephrine respectively. Other "bad" emotions, e.g., guilt, shame, depression, are compounded in some way with fear and/or anger as a constituent, hence they also will display specificity effects. Taking this line, specificity theory would be salvaged on the basis of *classes* of emotions distinguished by a common neuroendocrine substrate, i.e., either epinephrine, norepinephrine, or acetylcholine (in the case of positive emotions). Most important is that the over-all integration of social relations and psychophysiology would be preserved.

CONCLUSION

As may be gleaned from this cursory overview of sociological interests in the area of emotions, there is a considerable field of inquiry that may be launched into emotions from the social context. It is important to recognize that the central sociological contribution is the formulation of a model of social relations that can capture the nuances of interactional structure and change. The power-status model does this, both at the level of the interpersonal as well as at the societal level. Most encouragingly, the approach to social relations via power and status has been able to shed some light on the longstanding controversy over specificity at the psychophysiological level. But, it should be recognized, the psychophysiological pattern—at least as described in the Funkenstein hypothesis—lends support to the sociological formulation of two dimensions of relationship. Should this integration of two very different levels of analysis and discourse prove to be tenable over the course of the many researches that must yet be undertaken to support it, the science of emotions will have taken a significant step forward.

REFERENCES

Arnold, M. B. Stress and emotion. In M. H. Appley & R. Trumbull (Eds.), *Psychological stress.* New York: Appleton-Century-Crofts, 1967.

Ax, A. F. The physiological differentiation between fear and anger in humans. *Psychosomatic Medicine,* 1953, *15,* 433–442.

Baxter, J. C., Lerner, M.J., & Miller, J. S. Identification as a function of the reinforcing quality of the model and the socialization background of the subject. *Journal of Personality and Social Psychology,* 1965, *2,* 692–697.

Bensman, J., & Vidich, A. Business cycles, class, and personality. *Psychoanalysis and Psychoanalytic Review,* 1962, *49,* 30–52.

Bergesen, B. S. *Pharmacology in nursing,* 14th Ed. St. Louis: Mosby, 1979.

Blauner, R. *Alienation and freedom.* Chicago: University of Chicago Press, 1964.

Cannon, W. B. *Bodily changes in pain, hunger, fear and rage.* 2nd edition. New York: Ronald, 1929.

Cohen, S. I., & Silverman, A. J. Psychophysiological investigations of vascular response variability. *Journal of Psychosomatic Medicine,* 1959, *3,* 185–210.

Collins, R. *Conflict sociology.* New York: Academic, 1975.

Coser, L. *The functions of social conflict.* New York: Free Press, 1956.

Darwin, C. *The expression of emotions in man and animals.* New York: Appleton, 1973.

Durkheim, E. *Suicide.* (Translated by George Simpson.) New York: Free Press, 1951. (Originally published 1897.)

Durkheim, E. *The elementary forms of the religious life.* (Translated by Joseph Ward Swain.) New York: Free Press, 1965. (Originally published 1915.)

Elmadjian, F., Hope, J. M., & Lamson, E. T. Excretion of epinephrine and norepinephrine under stress. *Recent progress in hormone research.* New York: Academic, 1958.

Erdmann, G., & Janke, W. Interaction between physiological and cognitive determinants of emotions: Experimental studies on Schachter's theory of emotions. *Biological Psychology,* 1978, *6,* 61–74.

Frankenhaeuser, M. Experimental approaches to catecholamines and emotions. In L. Levi (Ed.), *Emotions: Their parameters and measurement.* New York: Raven, 1976.

Funkenstein, D. The physiology of fear and anger. *Scientific American,* 1955, *192,* 74–80.

Funkenstein, D., King, S. H. & Drolette, M. E. *Mastery of stress.* Cambridge, Mass.: Harvard University Press, 1957.

Gellhorn, E. *Principles of autonomic-somatic integration.* Minneaoplis: University of Minnesota Press, 1967.

Gellhorn, E., & Loofbourrow, G. N. *Emotions and emotional disorders: A neurophysiological study.* New York: Harper, 1963.

Gormly, J., Gormly, A., & Johnson, C. Interpersonal attraction: Competence motivation and reinforcement theory. *Journal of Personality and Social Psychology,* 1971, *19,* 375–380.

Gottman, J., Markman, H., & Notarius, C. The topography of marital conflict: A sequential analysis of verbal and nonverbal behavior. *Journal of Marriage and the Family,* 1977, *37,* 461–477.

Graham, L. A., Cohen, S. I., & Shmavonian, B. M. Some methodological approaches to the psychophysiological correlates of behavior. In L. Levi (Ed.), *Emotional stress: Physiological and psychological reactions. I. Medical, industrial, and military applications.* New York: Elsevier, 1967.

Hamburg, D. A., Hamburg, B. A., & Barchas, J. D. Anger and depression in perspective of behavioral biology. In L. Levi (Ed.), *Emotions: Their parameters and measurements*. New York: Raven, 1975.

Hammond, M. Durkheim's reality construction model and the emergence of social stratification. *The Sociological Review*, 1978, *26* (New Series), 713–727.

Hinde, R. A. *Towards understanding relationships*. New York: Academic, 1979.

Houseknecht, S. K., & Macke, A. S. Combining marriage and career: The marital adjustment of professional women. *Journal of Marriage and Family* 1981, *43*, 651–661.

Izard, C. E. *Patterns of emotions*, New York: Academic, 1972.

Jacobs, D. Moods—emotion—affect: The nature of and minipulation of affective states with particular reference to positive affective states and emotional illness. In A. Jacobs & L. B. Sachs (Eds.), *The psychology of private events*. New York: Academic, 1971.

James, W. *Principles of psychology*. New York: Holt, 1893.

John, E. R. Where is fancy bred? In M. Hammer, K. Salzinger, & S. Sutton (Eds.), *Psychopathology: Contributions from the social, behavioral, and biological sciences*. New York: Wiley, 1973.

Kemper, T. D. *A social interactional theory of emotions*. New York: Wiley, 1978.

Kemper, T. D. Social constructionist and positivist approaches to the sociology of emotions. *American Journal of Sociology* 1981, *87*, 336–362.

Kety, S. S. Norepinephrine in the CNS and its correlations with behavior. In A. G. Karcsmar & J. C. Eccles (Eds.), *Brain and human behavior*. New York: Springer, 1972.

Korchin, S. Comments on Arnold. In M. H. Appley & R. Trumbull (Eds.), *Psychological stress*. New York: Appleton-Century-Crofts, 1967.

Krout, M. H. *Introduction to social psychology*. New York: Harper and Row, 1942.

Lange, C. G. The emotions: A physiological study. In C. G. Lange & W. James, *The emotions*. New York: Hafner, 1967. (Originally published 1885.)

Lazarus, A. A. Learning theory and the treatment of depression. *Behavior Research and Therapy*, 1968, *6*, 83–89.

Lazarus, R. S., & Averill, J. S. Emotion and cognition: With special reference to anxiety. In C. D. Spielberger (Ed.), *Anxiety: Current trends in theory and research* (Vol. 2). New York: Academic, 1972.

Lazarus, R. S., Averill, J. S., & Opton, E. M., Jr. Toward a cognitive theory of emotions. In M. Arnold (Ed.), *Feelings and emotions*. New York: Academic, 1970.

Levi, L. Sympathoadrenomedullary responses to 'pleasant' and 'unpleasant' psychosocial stimuli. In Stress and distress in response to psychosocial stimuli: Laboratory and real life studies in sympathoadrenomedullary and related reactions. *Acta Medica Scandanavica*. Supplementum 528. Stockholm: Almquist and Wiksell, 1972.

Levy, R. *Tahitians: Mind and experiences in the Society Islands*. Chicago: University of Chicago Press, 1973.

Loehlin, J. C. 'Interpersonal' experiments with a computer model of personality. *Journal of Personality and Social Psychology*, 1965, *2*, 580–584.

Manstead, A. S. R., & Wagner, H. L. Arousal, cognition and emotion: An appraisal of two-factor theory. *Current Psychological Reviews* 1981, *1*, 34–54.

Marshall, G. D., & Zimbardo, P. G. Affective consequences of inadequately explained physiological arousal. *Journal of Personality and Social Psychology*, 1979, *37*, 970–988.

Marx, K. *Selected Writings in Sociology and Social Philosphy*. T. B. Bottomore and M. Rubel (Eds.), New York: McGraw-Hill, 1964.

Maslach, C. Negative emotional biasing of unexplained arousal. *Journal of Personality and Social Psychology*, 1979, *37*, 953–969.

Mowrer, O. H. *Learning theory and behavior*. New York: Wiley, 1960.

Noblin, C. D., Timmons, E. O., & Kael, H. C. Differential effects of positive and negative verbal reinforcement on psychoanalytic character types. *Journal of Personality and Social Psychology,* 1966, *4,* 224–228.

Plutchik, R. *The emotions: A psycho-evolutionary synthesis.* New York: Harper and Row, 1980.

Plutchick, R., & Ax, A. F. A critique of determinants of emotional state by Schachter and Singer (1962). *Psychophysiology,* 1967, *4,* 79–92.

Rausch, H. L. Interaction sequences. *Journal of Personality and Social Psychology,* 1965, *2,* 487–499.

Rausch, H. L., Barry, W. A., Hertel, R. K., & Swain, M. A. *Communication, conflict, marriage.* San Francisco: Jossey-Bass, 1974.

Sapeika, N. *Actions and uses of drugs.* Amsterdam: A. A. Balkema, 1972.

Schachter, J. Pain, fear, and anger in hypertensives and normotensives: A psychological study. *Psychosomatic Medicine,* 1957, *19,* 19–29.

Schachter, S., & Singer, J. E. Cognitive, social, and physiological determinants of emotional state. *Psychological Review,* 1962, *69,* 379–399.

Schachter, S. & Singer, J. E. Comments on the Maslach and Marshall–Zimbardo experiments. *Journal of Personality and Social Psychology,* 1979, *37,* 989–995.

Shannon, J., & Guerney, B., Jr. Interpersonal effects of interpersonal behavior. *Journal of Personality and Social Psychology,* 1973, *26,* 142–150.

Stein, M. Some psychophysiological considerations of the relationship between the autonomic nervous system and behavior. In D. C. Glass (Ed.), *Neurophysiology and emotion.* New York: Rockefeller University Press and Russell Sage Foundation, 1967.

Sternbach, R. A. *Principles of psychophysiology.* New York: Academic, 1966.

Swensen, C. H., Eskew, R. W., & Kohlhepp, K. A. Stage of family life cycle, ego development, and the marriage relationship. *Journal of Marriage and Family* 1981, *43,* 841–851.

Tocqueville, A. de. *Democracy in America.* New York: Vintage, 1945. (Originally published 1835.)

Triandis, H. C. *The analysis of subjective culture.* New York: Wiley, 1972.

Weber, M. From Max Weber: *Essays in sociology.* H. Gerth & C. W. Mills (Eds.), New York: Oxford University Press, 1946.

Weber, M. *The theory of social and economic organization.* New York: Oxford University Press, 1947.

Wills, T. A., Weiss, R. A., & Patterson, G. R. A behavioral analysis of the determinants of marital satisfaction. *Journal of Cross-Cultural Psychiatry,* 1974, *42,* 802–811.

Wilson, E. C. *Sociobiology: The new synthesis.* Cambridge: Harvard University Press, 1975.

Young, P. T. *Motivation and emotion.* New York: Wiley, 1961.

Zajonc, R. B. Social facilitation. *Science,* 1965, *149,* 269–274.

18 The Role of Emotion in Social Structure

Randall Collins
San Diego, California

How important are the emotions in society? I would argue that they are quite fundamental. This is especially so if one conceives of emotion as a form of social energy, which can take any state ranging from completely passive inactivity on through strong affectual arousal. The crucial mid-range of this continuum is a series of variations in social confidence, which manifest themselves in feelings of solidarity—membership in social groups. At their stronger levels, such feelings of confidence are important in the organization of property and authority.

Emotional energy not only upholds the social structure, but is produced by it. That is, social social structure *is* nothing more, on the most fine-grained empirical level, than repeated patterns of face-to-face interaction. These interactions have a *ritual* quality, which reproduce, increase, or decrease the emotional energies of individuals. Both the statics of repetitively reenacted social structure and the dynamics of social change are crucially mediated by the social production of emotions.

The following sociological theory of *interaction ritual* is based on the theories of Emile Durkheim (1947, 1954) and Erving Goffman (1959). I have suggested elsewhere (Collins, 1975, pp. 90–111) that it is consonant both with Darwinian animal ethology and with recent developments in cognitive micro-sociology, especially ethnomethodology. I have also attempted to show (Collins, 1975, pp. 49–89) how a variety of both hierarchic and egalitarian interactions produce the different emotional tones and cognitive propensities that make up the varieties of class cultures. The "marketplace" of such ritual interaction makes up social networks.

A fuller version of this discussion may be found in Collins (1981b).

EMOTION AS A MICRO BASIS OF MACRO-SOCIOLOGY

Both neo-rationalist self-criticisms (Heath, 1976) and micro-sociological evidence (Garfinkel, 1967) agree that complex contingencies cannot be calculated rationally, and hence that actors must largely rely on tacit assumptions and organizational routine. But the actual structures of the social world, especially as centered around the networks upholding property and authority, involve continuous monitoring by individuals of each other's group loyalties. Because the social world can involve quite a few lines of authority and sets of coalitions, the task of monitoring them can be extremely complex. How is this possible, given people's inherently limited cognitive capacities?

The solution must be that negotiations are carried out implicitly, on a different level than the use of consciously minipulated verbal symbols. I propose that the mechanism is *emotional* rather than cognitive. Individuals monitor others' attitudes towards social coalitions, and hence towards the degree of support for routines, by feeling the amount of confidence and enthusiasm there is towards certain leaders and activities, or the amount of fear of being attacked by a strong coalition, or the amount of contempt for a weak one. These emotional energies are transmitted by contagion among members of a group, in flows that operate very much like the set of negotiations that produce prices within a market.

The underlying emotional dynamic, I propose, centers upon feelings of *membership in coalitions*. Briefly put: property (access to and exclusions from particular physical places and things) is based upon a sense of what kinds of persons do and do not belong where. This is based, in turn, upon a sense of what groups are powerful enough to punish violators of their claims. Authority is similarly organized: It rests upon a sense of which people are connected to which groups, to coalitions of what extensiveness and what capacity to enforce the demands of their members upon others. Both of these are variables: There is no inherent, objective entity called "property" or "authority," but only the varying senses that people feel at particular places and times of how strong these enforcing coalitions are. There may also be memberships groups who make little or no claims to property or authority: purely "informal" or "horizontal" groups, like friends and acquaintances, whose solidarity is an end in itself as far as its members are concerned.

The most general explanation of human social behavior encompasses all of these. It should specify: What makes someone a member of a coalition? What determines the extensiveness of a coalition, and the intensity of bonds within it? How do people judge the power of coalitions? The answers to these questions, I am suggesting, determines the way in which groups of friends and other status groups are formed; the degree to which authority and property routines are upheld; and who will dominate others within these patterns. The basic mechanism is a process of emotional group identification that may be described as a set of interaction ritual chains.

A Theory of Interaction Ritual Chains

From a micro-translation viewpoint, all processes of forming and judging coalition memberships must take place in interaction situations. The main activity in such situations is conversation. But no one situation stands alone. Every individual goes through many situations: indeed, a lifetime is, strictly speaking, a chain of interaction situations. (One might also call it a chain of conversations.) The people one talks to also have talked to other people in the past, and will talk to others in the future. Hence an appropriate image of the social world is a bundle of individual chains of interactional experience, criss-crossing each other in space as they flow along in time. The dynamics of coalition membership are produced by the emotional sense individuals have at any one point in time, due to the tone of the situation they are currently in (or last remember, or shortly anticipate), which in turn is influenced by the previous chains of situations of all participants.

The *manifest* content of an interaction is usually not the emotions it involves. Any conversation, to the extent that it is taken seriously by its participants, focuses their attention upon the reality of its contents, the things that are talked about (Goffman, 1967, pp. 113–116). This may include a focus upon practical work that is being done. What is significant about any conversation from the point of view of social membership, however, is not the content, but the extent to which the participants can actually maintain a common activity of focusing upon that content. The content is a vehicle for establishing membership. From this viewpoint, any conversation may be looked upon as a ritual. It invokes a common reality, which from a ritual viewpoint may be called a "myth": in this case, whether the conversational "myth" is true or not is irrelevant. The "myth" or centent is a Durkheimian sacred object. It signifies membership in a common group, for those who truly respect it. The person who can successfully become engrossed in a conversational reality becomes accepted as a member of the group of those who believe in that conversational entity. In terms of the Durkheimian model of religious ritual, (Durkheim, 1954/1912; cf. Goffman, 1967), a conversation is a cult in which all believers share a moral solidarity. In fact, it *creates* the reference point of moral solidarity: those who believe are the good; defense of the belief and hence of the group is righteousness; evil is disbelief in, and even more so attack upon, the cognitive symbols that holds the group together. The cognitive symbols—however banal, particularized, or esoteric the conversational content may be—are important to the group, and defended by it, because they are the vehicle by which means the group is able to unify itself.

Not all conversations, however, are equally successful rituals. Some bind individuals together more permanently and tightly than others; some conversations do not come off at all. Among those conversations that do succeed in evoking a common reality, some of these produce a feeling of egalitarian membership among the conversationalists, while others produce feelings of rank differences, including feelings of authority and subordination. These types of variability, in fact, are essential for producing and reproducing stratified social order. Conversational interaction ritual, then, is a mechanism producing *varying* amounts of solidarity, varying degrees of personal identification with coalitions of varying degrees of impressiveness.

What, then, makes a conversational ritual succeed or not, and what kinds of coalitions does it invoke?

I suggest the following ingredients. (1) Participants in a successful conversational ritual must be able to invoke a common cognitive reality. Hence they must have similar *conversational* or *cultural resources*. A successful conversation may also be inegalitarian, in that one person does most of the cultural reality-invoking, the others acting as an audience; in this case we have a domination-and-subordination-producing ritual. (2) Participants must also be able to sustain a common emotional tone. At a minimum, they must all want to produce at least momentary solidarity. Again, the emotional participation may be stratified, dividing the group into emotional leaders and followers.

These two ingredients—cultural resources and emotional energies—come from individuals' chains of previous interactional experience, and serve to reproduce or change the pattern of interpersonal relations. Among the most important of the things reproduced or changed are feelings about persons' relationships to physical property, and to the coercive coalitions of authority. How individuals are tied to these is the crucial determinant of which coalitions are dominant or subordinate.

Conversational Resources.   Particular styles and topics of conversation imply memberships in different groups. At any point in time, the previous chain of interaction rituals that have been successfully negotiated have made certain conversational contents into symbols of solidarity. The range of these has been discussed elsewhere (Collins, 1975, pp. 114–131). For example, shop talk invokes membership in occupational groups, political and other ideological talk invokes contending political coalitions, entertainment talk invokes groups with various tastes, general discussion invokes different intellectual and nonintellectual strata, while gossip and personal talk invoke specific and sometimes quite intimate memberships. Again, it is not important whether what is said is true or not, but that it can be said and accepted as a common reality for that moment, that makes it an emblem of group membership.

Conversational topics have two different types of implications for reproducing the social structure. Some conversational topics are *generalized*: they refer to events and entities on some level of abstraction from the immediate and local situation. Talk about techniques, politics, religion, entertainment are of this sort. Their social effects, I would suggest, are to reproduce a sense of what may be called status group membership: common participation in a horizontally-organized cultural community who shares these outlooks and a belief in their importance. Ethnic groups, classes to the extent that they are cultural communities, and many more specialized cultural groups are of this type. Successful conversation on these topics brings about a generalized sense of common membership, then, although it invokes no specific or personal ties to particular organizations, authority, or property.

Other conversational topics are *particularized*: They refer to specific persons, places, and things. Such talk can include practical instructions (asking someone to do something for someone at a specific time and place), as well as political planning about specific strategies (as organizational politics), and gossip and personal narration. Some of this particularized talk serves to produce and reproduce informal relations among people, i.e., friendships. But particularized talk, paradoxically enough, also is crucial in reproducing property and authority, and hence organizations. For, as argued earlier, property and authority structure exist as physical routines, whose micro-reality consists of people taking for granted particular people's rights to be in particular buildings, giving orders to particular other people, and so on. In this sense, property and authority are reenacted whenever people refer to *someone's* house, *someone's* office, *someone's* car, as well as whenever someone gives an order to do a particular thing, and the listener acknowledges the reality, at least for that moment, of that order. Again, it is worth pointing out that orders are not always carried out; but it is the situation in which the *communicative* ritual occurs that is crucial for maintaining the structure, as a real social pattern, not the actual consequences for practical action.

Of course, as indicated, even the degree of *ritual* compliance is a variable, and we must inquire into the conditions that make people respect and enact organizational communications less and more enthusiastically, or even rebel against them. This brings us to the second ingredient of rituals, emotional energies.

Emotional Energies.   Emotions affect ritual membership in several ways. There must be at least a minimal degree of common mood among interactants if a conversational ritual is to succeed in invoking a shared reality. The stronger the common emotional tone, the more real the invoked topic will seem to be, and the more solidarity will exist in the group (cf. Collins, 1975, pp. 94–95, 153–154). Emotional propensities are thus a prerequisite for a successful interaction. But the interaction also serves as a machine for intensifying emotion, and for generating new emotional tones and solidarities. Thus emotional energies are important results of interactions at any point in the ritual chain. The emotional solidarity, I would suggest, is the payoff that favorable conversational resources can produce for an individual.

If successful interactional rituals (IRs) produce feelings of solidarity, stratification both within and among coalitions is a further outcome of emotional flows along IR chains. As noted, conversational rituals can be either egalitarian or asymmetrical. Both types have stratifying implications. Egalitarian rituals are nevertheless stratifying in that insiders are accepted and outsiders are rejected; here stratification exists in the form of a coalition against excluded individuals, or possibly the domination of one coalition over another. Asymmetrical conversations, in which one individual sets the energy tones (and invokes the cultural reality) while the others are an audience, are internally stratified.

The most basic emotional ingredient in interactions, I would suggest, is a minimal tone of positive sentiment towards the other. The solidarity sentiments range from a minimal display of nonhostility, up to warm mutual liking and enthusiastic common activity. Where do such emotions come from? From previous experiences in IR chains. An individual who is successfully accepted into an interaction acquires an increment of positive emotional energy. This energy is manifested as what we commonly call confidence, warmth, and enthusiasm. Acquiring this in one situation, an individual has more emotional resources for successfully negotiating solidarity in the next interaction. Such chains, both positive and negative, extend throughout every person's lifetime.

Let us consider the variations possible within this basic model. The main conditions which produce emotional energy are these:

1.   Increased emotional confidence is produced by every experience of successfully negotiating a membership ritual. Decreased emotional confidence results from rejection or lack of success.

2.   The more powerful the group within which one successfully negotiates ritual solidarity, the greater the emotional confidence one receives from it. The power of a group here means the amount of physical property it successfully claims access to, the sheer size of its adherents, and the amount of physical force (numbers of fighters, instruments of violence) it has access to.

3.   The more intense the emotional arousal within an IR, the more emotional energy an individual receives from participating in it. A group situation with a high degree of enthusiasm thus generates large emotional increments for individuals. High degrees of emotional arousal are created especially by IRs which include an element of conflict against outsiders: either an actual fight, a ritual punishment of offenders, or on a lower level of intensity, symbolic denunciation of enemies (including conversational griping) (see Collins, 1974).

4.   Taking a dominant position within an IR increases one's emotional energies. Taking a subordinate positions within an IR reduces one's emotional energies; the more extreme the subordination, the greater the energy reduction.

Interactions as Marketplaces for Cultural and Emotional Resources

Why will a particular person, in any given interactional situation, achieve or fail to achieve ritual membership? And why will particular persons dominate or be subordinated in an IR? These result from a combination of the emotional and cultural resources of all the participants in any encounter. These in turn result from the IR chains that each individual has previously experienced. Each encounter is like a marketplace, in which these resources are implicitly compared, and conversational rituals of various degrees of solidarity and stratification are negotiated. Each individual's "market" position depends on the emotional and cultural resources they have acquired from their previous interactions.

The several kinds of emotional and cultural resources interact. Because emotional energies result from success or failure in previous IRs, having high- or low-cultural-resources also contributes to high- or low-emotional-energies. To a lesser extent there is an effect in the opposite direction: the more emotional energy (confidence, social warmth) one has, the more one is able to gain new cultural resources by successfully entering into new conversations; at the opposite extreme, a person with low emotional confidence may be "tongue-tied," unable to use even what cultural resources they have.

Both cultural and emotional resources change over time. But they change in different rhythms. Generally speaking, I would suggest that emotional energies are much more volatile than cultural resources, and that they can change in both positive and negative directions. If one encounters a series of situations in which one is highly accepted or even dominating, or in which the emotions are very intense, one's emotional energy can build up very rapidly. The rhythms of mass political and religious movements are based upon just such dynamics. On the contrary, if one goes through a series of ritual rejections or subordinations, one's energies can drop fairly rapidly.

Cultural resources, on the other hand, are fairly stable, and they change largely in a positive direction. But here we must pay attention to the distinction between generalized and particularized cultural resources. Generalized resources usually grow over time, and at a slow rate. Individuals may forget some of the generalized information they possess, but since it is often reproduced as common conversational topics repeated in their usual encounters with other people, loss of generalized cultural capital is probably confined to those occasions in which someone leaves their habitual milieu of conversational partners for a long time. And even so, there is a considerable lag; the power of memory makes generalized cultural resources a stabilizing force in social relations.

Particularized cultural resources, on the other hand, are potentially more discontinuous. Particularized conversational actions (giving a specific order, asking practical advice, negotiating a strategy regarding a particular issue in organizational politics, joking with friends, etc.) are evanescent. The particular bonds which they enact are permanent only to the extent that those particularized actions are frequently reproduced. Particularized cultural resources are especially important as the micro-basis of organization, authority, and property, as well as of close personal ties. The relationship of people to particular physical objects that constitute property is enacted, over and over again in ordinary and taken-for-granted encounters, in IRs that have a particularized content. The same is true of the micro-reproduction of authority and of organizations.

Particularized conversational resources differ from generalized conversational resources, and from emotional resources as well, in that one acquires them not only in one's *own* conversations, but that they also circulate independently of oneself. When other people talk particularistically about some individual, they are constituting her/his reputation. One's reputation, then, is a particularized conversational resource that circulates in *other people's conversations*. For the micro-translation of macro structures, the most important kind of reputations that circulate are simply the parts of talk that identify someone by a particular title ("the chairman," "his wife") or organizational membership ("he is with G.E."), or which tacitly give someone a reputation for certain property and authority ("I went in his office"; "She sent out a memo directing them to . . ."). Particularized conversation, both as enacted and as circulated secondarily as reputations of other people, is what principally constitutes the social structure of property and authority.

Compared to generalized conversation, particularized conversation is potentially quite volatile, although much of the time it simply reproduces itself and hence reproduces social routines. Most of the time the same people are placed into organizational and property-maintaining routines, by both the particularized conversational rituals in which they take part, and those in which they are conversational subjects. But this flow of particularistic cultural resources *can* shift quite abruptly, especially on the reputational side. On a small and local scale, this happens quite frequently: a new person enters a job, a familiar one leaves a place—the old round of particularized conversational enactments and reputations suddenly stops, and a new particular social reality is promulgated. Most of the time these particularized items of conversation reinforce the bedrock of physical routine, which human cognitive capacities require us to rely upon to such a great extent. But by the same token, the particular structure of organizational behavior, including very large organizational aggregates such as the state, is potentially very volatile: it is not upheld by generalized rules or generalized culture of any kind, but by short-term, particularized interaction rituals, and these can abruptly take on a new content. This micro-basis of property and authority, then, implies that these routines alternate between long periods of relatively stable micro-reproduction, and changes in dramatic episodes of upheaval or revolution.

If we ask, then, what causes the variations in this pattern—when will particular individuals move in or out, and when will the whole pattern of property and authority be stable or shift—we find a market-like dynamic. Particular individuals enact the property and authority structure because their previous IR chains give them certain emotional energies and cultural resources, including the resource of reputation for belonging in certain authority rituals and particular physical places. The relative value of these resources may shift from encounter to encounter, as the combinations of different individuals varies. If one begins to encounter persons whose emotional and cultural (including reputational) resources differ as greater or lesser than what one is used to, one's own capacity to generate ritual membership and conversational dominance will shift up or down. Hence one's emotional energies will undergo an increase or decrease. If these energy shifts reach the point at which one is motivated to, and capable of, shifting one's physical and ritual position in the pattern of property and organizational authority, then one's reputation and one's other particularized conversational resources will abruptly shift. Generalized cultural resources, finally, may build up across a long series of interactions, but this occurs relatively slowly.

IR situations are market-like, but it is worth stressing that the mechanism by which individuals are motivated by their market positions is not one of rational calculation. As noted earlier, a fundamental difficulty in rationalistic social exchange models is that there is no way for individuals to compare disparate goods that have no common metric, nor is it possible to multiply these values times the different metric of a scale of probabilities of attaining them. But if individuals are motivated by their emotional energies as these shift from situation to situation, then the sheer amount of emotional energy is the common denominator deciding the attractiveness of various alternatives, as well as a predictor of whether an individual will actually attain any of them. Individuals thus do not have to calculate probabilities in order to feel varying degrees of confidence in different outcomes. Disparate goods do not have to be directly compared, but only the emotional tone of situations in which they are available. Nor do actors have to calculate the value of their various cultural resources (generalized and particularized) in each situation. These resources have an automatic effect upon the conversational interaction, and the outcomes are automatically transformed into increments or decrements of emotional energy.

The fundamental mechanism, then, is not a conscious one. Rather consciousness, in the form of cultural resources, is a series of inputs into each situation that affects one's *sense* of group memberships available of varying degrees of attractiveness. It is possible, of course, for individuals sometimes to consciously reflect upon their social choices, perhaps even to become aware of their own cultural and emotional resources vis-à-vis those of their fellows. But choices consciously made, I would contend, would be the same as choices made without reflection. One's sense of "choice" or "will" nevertheless rests upon the accretion of energies—one's degree of self-confidence—which is the product of a larger dynamic.

Another long-standing difficulty of social exchange theories is answered by the IR chain model: Why do people repay a gift? Self-interest is not a sufficient explanation, as an exchange is only rewarding to the extent that individuals *already* know there will be reciprocity. Hence theorists have felt it necessary to fall back upon such claims as "what is customary becomes obligatory" (Blau, 1964) or to invoke an alleged "norm of reciprocity" (Gouldner, 1960; cf. Heath, 1976). Both these formulations beg the explanatory question: in both cases, the customariness of the behavior is just what remains to be explained, and to call this customariness a "norm" is only a description of it. The IR chain model, instead, proposes that feelings of solidarity within a social coalition are fundamental. If two individuals feel a common membership, then they will feel a desire to reciprocate gifts, because the gift and its reciprocation are emblems of continuing their common membership. This model has the advantage of making gift-giving and reciprocation into a variable instead of a constant: Individuals will reciprocate to the extent that a particular coalition membership is attractive to them in terms of its emotional dynamics. Similarly, they will feel like giving gifts or not because of the same range of circumstances. Hence the variables already described should account for the degree to which reciprocity is actually practiced (see Mauss, 1967).

Macro-structural Effects

The preceding model suggests that large-scale social changes are based on micro-mechanisms of one or more of the following kinds: large scale changes in the amount or distribution of (1) generalized cultural resources; (2) particularized cultural resources; (3) emotional energies.

(1) The *generalized cultural resources* across a large population can shift due to the introduction of new technologies of communication, or by more individuals specializing in the production and dissemination of generalized culture. Writing implements, mass media, and educational and religious organizations of varying size, have introduced new cultural resources, or increased their distribution, in societies at various times in history. One can picture at least two kinds of structural effects of this. The distribution of the expanded culture may be concentrated in particular populations; hence these will be able to raise their level of success in IRs at the expense of the others, forming new organizational ties and thereby eventually developing emotional and reputational advantages over others. A second kind of effect occurs when the whole population uniformly receives an increase in generalized cultural resources; the sheer degree of mobilization, of efforts to negotiate new IR connections, should increase throughout the society. Although no one gains relative to others, the overall process should increase the amount of organization-building generally in that society. It can be suggested that early phases of this process contribute to economic booms, and to the growth of political and/or religious movements; later phases, however, if generalized cultural currency becomes continuously expanded, may involve a devaluation of the cultural currency, with ensuing contraction of political and economic activity (Collins, 1981a).

(2) *Particularized cultural resources* define individuals relative to particular physical properties and authority coalitions. What can change the whole structure of these resources? The volatile aspect of particularized culture, I would suggest, is especially important in the reputations of the individuals who ritually enact the most powerful coalitions. Most reputational talk, as indicated, is local and repetitive. But rapid upheavals in personal reputations characterize important shifts in political and religious power. A person becomes powerful (or "charismatic") when a dramatic event, usually involving success in a conflict, makes large numbers of people focus upon him/her. The widespread and rapid circulation of their new reputation gives them the self-reinforcing power of commanding the largest, and therefore dominant, coalition in that society. Conversely, powerful persons fall usually because of dramatic events—scandals or defeats in conflicts—which suddenly circulate their *negative* reputation.

The movement of such particularized cultural resources, then, suggests several implications for the dynamics of social change. Such changes are discontinuous, and alternate with periods of routine. They depend on dramatic events that are highly visible to many people. The most dramatic events, I would contend, are conflicts, and especially violent ones. It is for this reason that wars are so important in mobilizing revolutions and other rapid social changes. Politics itself is a master determinant of the property system and so many other routine aspects of social life, because politics consists of continuously organized coalitions mobilized to engage in conflicts. These coalitions gain their power from broadcasting the dramatics of their own conflicts in ways favorable to themselves, thereby creating particularized reputations for various individuals as powerful, villainous, or impotent. Politics, as the struggle over reputation, rests upon control of the means of reputation management.

(3) *Emotional energies* are the most crucial mechanism in all of these processes. Shifts in both generalized and particularized cultural resources have effects upon people's actions in micro-situations because they affect their emotional energies. The reputation shift of a political leader, for example, is truly effective only when the rumors carry an emotional impact, a contagion of feelings throughout the society as to where the dominant coalition now resides.

Hence the market attractiveness of that coalition increases, all the more so to the extent that it spreads fear for the danger to those people who remain outside of it. Conflict, war, and politics, in the preceding account, can be regarded as quintessentially emotion-producing situations. The stronger the conflict, the more emotional energy which flows through the networks of micro-interaction constituting the macro-structure. Periods of rapidly changing reputational resources become particularly important for the organization of social networks to the extent that they are vehicles for strong emotional contagion.

There are also conditions that change the entire level of emotional energy in a society. Parallel to the introduction of new communications technology and generalized-culture-producing specialists, one can think of the historical introduction of new emotion-producing "technologies," including shifts in the numbers of emotion-producing specialists. From this viewpoint, changes in material conditions are most important because they change the numbers of people who can assemble for ritual purposes, or because they change people's capacities for impression management or dramatization (Collins, 1975, pp. 161–216, 364–80). Such technologies of dramatization have ranged from the massive architecture and lavish religious and political ceremony of the Pharoahs through the various styles of political display of today. The history of religions can be seen similarly as a series of inventions of new social devices for generating emotions, ranging from the shaman's magic ritual, to congregational worship, to individual meditation and prayer. In this perspective, shifts among tribal, patrimonial-feudal, and bureaucratic forms of organization are shifts among diverse sources of emotional impression-management. The various combinations of these emotional technologies available at any given time, and their degree of concentration or dispersion among the populace, are crucial factors in the struggle for power in any particular historical society.

ACKNOWLEDGEMENT

Portions of this chapter originally published in *American Journal of Sociology*, 1981, *86* (March). Copyright 1981 University of Chicago Press, Chicago. Reprinted by permission.

REFERENCES

Blau, P. M. *Exchange and power in social life*. New York: Wiley, 1964.
Collins, R. Three faces of cruelty: Towards a comparative sociology of violence. *Theory and Society*, 1974, *1*, 415–440.
Collins, R. *Conflict sociology*. New York: Academic Press, 1975.
Collins, R. Crises and declines in credential systems. In *Sociology since midcentury*. New York: Academic Press, 1981. (a)
Collins, R. On the micro-foundations of macro-sociology. *American Journal of Sociology*, 1981, *86*, 984–1014. (b)
Durkheim, E. *The division of labor in society*. Glencoe, Illinois: Free Press, 1947. (Originally published, 1893.)
Durkheim, E. *The elementary forms of the religious life*. Glencoe, Illinois: Free Press, 1954. (Originally published, 1912.)
Garfinkel, H. *Studies in ethnomethodology*. Englewood Cliffs, N.J.: Prentice-Hall, 1967.
Goffman, E. *The presentation of self in everyday life*. New York: Doubleday, 1959.
Goffman, E. *Interaction ritual*. New York: Doubleday, 1967.
Gouldner, A. W. The norm of reciprocity: a preliminary statement. *American Sociological Review*, 1960, *25*, 161–178.
Heath, A. *Rational choice and social exchange*. Cambridge: Cambridge University Press, 1976.
Mauss, M. *The gift*. New York: Norton, 1967. (Originally published, 1925.)

19 The Emotions in Comparative Perspective[1]

Robert I. Levy
University of California, San Diego

Different approaches to emotion suggest different kinds of questions. In addition to a consideration of a number of the issues which are introduced in the preliminary list of "Questions about Emotion," this chapter raises some additional questions: What is the relation of awareness, feeling and emotion (401–403)? What are the characteristics which might identify emotion as a sub-set of feeling (401–403)? Do different cultures define which feelings should be considered as emotions (400–410)? Might emotion be considered most centrally among humans, at least, as an indicator of the relation of "the self" to the social world (402–409)? Are there emotions which are emphasized in some cultures and not in others (403–404)? What are the differences in the types of knowing involved in the initial appraisal, on the one hand, and in cognitive evaluation in response to the "feeling of emotion", on the other, (404–409)? What is the cultural and cognitive function of the feeling phase of emotion; might it be considered as a trigger for the mobilization of culturally provided cognitive and definitional systems (406–407)? What are the limits to the cultural variability of the forms and types of specific emotions (409)? Why is emotional expression generally understandable across cultures (410–411)?

---

[1]This paper is a somewhat revised version of an article, "On The Nature and Function of the Emotions: an Anthropological Perspective," which appeared in *Social Science Information*, 21, 4⁄5 (1982), pp. 511–528. Another version of it, further developing certain themes and emphasizing the relation of various emotions to the problem of the meaning of "culture," appears as a chapter "Emotion, Knowing and Culture," to appear in *Culture and its Acquisition,* edited by Robert LeVine and Richard Schweder, in preparation.

What does the experience and discipline of anthropology bring to the consideration of the problem of the nature and function of the emotions? That experience begins with the examination of various phenomena in some radically "non-Western" community. In such communities the historically derived systems of meaning that influence the formation, interpretation, and contexts of the phenomenon in question may vary greatly from those in which the phenomenon is usually studied (that is, by nonanthropologists). An emphasis on the systems of meaning that characterize a particular community, the "culture" (to use that protean word in one of its senses) of the community, provides some comparative perspective on the nature of emotions in their varied relations to such systems of meaning, as well as something of their variable and universal features.

Anthropologists tend to study small, isolated and highly integrated communities. This gives them a bias towards the consideration of systematically organized contexts (ultimately the community itself—and occasionally the community as embedded in some still larger system) as the proper method of understanding the phenomenon under consideration. This often leads to what has been called (by Clifford Geertz) "thick description," a clinical, "idiographic," approach in which the interrelated influences bearing on the phenomeon in which one is interested are described in great detail. One can stop at this descriptive stage, the production of an "ethnography," but most, although not all, anthropologists hope that more general theory may be developed based on such descriptions.

My discussion of the "nature and function of emotion" in this paper is based primarily on my own studies in a small, relatively isolated Tahitian village (Levy, 1973), informed by perspectives from the later study of a Hindu City in Nepal. I started in these places with "psychological ethnography," studies of phenomena related to personal style and integration, usages and meanings of the body, personal implications of the supernatural, self and identity, motivation, cultural influences on cognition, moral controls, fantasy, etc., and, of relevance here, "feeling." I tried to describe these things as interrelated elements in the personal, "psychological systems" of individuals, and in relation to the transactions of individuals with larger, more public cultural and social systems.

ANTHROPOLOGICAL APPROACHES TO EMOTION

Before turning to some considerations on emotions deriving from my own studies, I should say a few words about my impressions of the study of emotion in earlier anthropological studies. (For a review of "Cross-Cultural Perspectives on Emotion," with an emphasis on facial expression see Izard 1980a.) The phenomena of emotion were not of central concern in themselves. Clyde Kluckhohn, for example, in a forty-seven page review of "Culture and Behavior" (in *Hand-*

book of Social Psychology, edited by Gardner Lindzey in 1954) gave only one and one-half pages to "affect," mostly supporting the emphasis vital to the cultural relativism of the day that although "there may well be a sense in which emotions, as biological events, are the same the world over . . . the expression of emotions and the circumstances arousing particular emotions vary culturally." In the second edition of the same handbook (1969) the new review of psychologically relevant anthropological studies by George DeVos and Arthur Hippler dealt with emotion primarily as an element in "expressive affective symbolic behavior," that is, as expressed in such forms as folklore and art in various cultures.

As most psychological studies in anthropology were influenced by one or another form of psychoanalytic theory, emotion was usually attended to in such studies as clues for the understanding of a psychodynamically conceived "personality organization." Robert LeVine in his classic monograph on this approach to "Culture, Behavior and Personality," as his 1973 study was entitled, wrote, "The commonly observable bodily symptoms (such as weeping, blushing, trembling) of intense affective reactions can provide a series of anchor points from which to begin the comparative study of affective experience . . . . Discovering the diverse cultural and psychological contexts in which these symptoms occur (or are narrowly avoided) should yield comparable information relevant to the understanding of personality structure and development."

The interest in "personality" represented by LeVine, the beginnings of which date back to the 1920s, was pushed from central stage in the anthropology of "mind" in the last 15 or 20 years by a concern with narrowly conceived problems of "cognition," of the ways in which aspects of social life are represented and effected in codes and in systems of classification. This intellectualist approach to the organization of human experience and action, which has taken various forms within anthropology (see, for example, Bilmes & Boggs, 1971), was stimulated by similar emphases in sociology, linguistics, psychology, philosophy and literary criticism.

"Emotion" was entirely peripheral to the concerns of this approach. As a recent polemic against French structuralism, which profoundly affected one sector of American and European anthropology, put it, "It is Lévi-Strauss's stated view that because human emotions and impulses are difficult to explain, they can have no part in any theory of human nature; they belong to the world of the body and as such have no interest for anthropology, whose exclusive concern, in Lévi-Strauss's view, is with the mind. It is to a condition of passionless mental purity that he seeks to reduce human nature" (Webster, 1981.)

Recent work by younger anthropologists has emphasized the socially constructed "person" as a significant focus of anthropological analysis, and has emphasized the cultural shaping and conceptualizing of various emotions as part of this construction. (For example Kirkpatrick, 1980; Levy & Rosaldo, 1983; Lutz, 1980; Rosaldo, 1980;) As Catherine Lutz (1980) phrased it, "An anthropological theory of the person in culture must take account of the fundamental and organizing role of the emotions in behavior, thought, and meaning systems. A psychological theory of the emotions must take account of the evidence from many cultures indicating that emotions are conceptualized, experienced, and expressed in various ways [p.1].''

TAHITIAN FEELINGS

I will turn to some material on some specific "emotions" in a Tahitian village as a basis for some speculations on the nature of emotion, and the relation of culture and emotion.[2] In anthropological writings one must be prepared progressively to refine one's vocabulary in terms of the specific forms manifested by the culture under study, and of one's developing theoretical schemas for dealing with these forms. But here I will start with such terms as "emotion," "anger," "sadness" in ordinary English usage. In comparing Tahitian terminology, conception and action in regard to various (in Western conception) emotions, one striking matter is that there is a great difference in the cultural visibility of different emotions. Various forms of anger, for example, are named; there are separate words for irritability, for rage, for the ordinary feeling of anger. There is doctrine about what stirs anger up in personal relations, how it works in the individual, what to do about it and how to evaluate it. It is, relative to some other emotions, *hypercognized*, that is there are a large number of culturally provided schemata for interpreting and dealing with anger.

There are other emotions for which these cultural "amplifiers of human ratiocinative capacities" (as Jerome Bruner [Bruner, Oliver, and Greenfield, 1966] has called them) are minimal; sadness is an example. "There are words for severe grief and for lamentation. There are, however, no unambiguous terms which represent the concepts of sadness, longing, or loneliness . . . . People would name their condition, where I supposed that [the body signs and] the context called for 'sadness' or 'depression,' as 'feeling troubled' (*pe'ape'a*, the generic term for distrubances, either internal or external); as 'not feeling a sense of inner push' (*'ana'anatae*, inner push or enthusiasm); as 'feeling heavy' (tōiaha); as 'feeling fatigued' (haumani); and a variety of other terms all referring to a generally troubled or subdued bodily state. *These are all nonspecific terms, which had no implications of any external [social] relational cause about them, in the sense that 'angry' implies an offense or a frustration.*'' (Levy 1973, p.

---

[2]It is important to note that I am here sometimes concerned with comparative differences in *specific emotions,* and sometimes with differences (or similarities) in comparative *emotion in general.*

305.Italics for the purposes of the present paper.) Let us call such under-schematized emotional domains *hypocognized*.[3] Another Tahitian example of a hypocognized domain of feeling is "guilt," which contrasts with the elaborated system of naming, classification and doctrine having to do with "shame," or more properly "shame/embarrassment."

One of the consequences of hypocognition, is that the felt disturbance, the "troubled feelings" can be interpreted in various ways that are not "emotional" (in ways that I will define). Thus the troubled feelings that persist too long after the death of a loved one, or that occur after some loss that cultural theory says is trivial and easily replaceable is in the village often interpreted as illness, or as the harmful effects of a spirit. Note that there are two kinds of knowing involved: the "unconscious" knowing, which identified certain events as a loss and *produced* a felt organismic response, a feeling, and a later knowing, which entailed the culturally patterned *evaluation and response to that feeling.*

I would like to discuss a number of considerations bearing on the theory of emotions and of the relation of emotions to "culture" suggested by such data.

FEELING, EMOTION, KNOWING AND CULTURE

Feeling

In dealing with what I took to be "sadness' as, say, "fatigue," the Tahitians were in some important sense accepting the "feeling" but denying that it was an "emotion." "Emotion" can be thought of as a sub-set of "feeling"; a sub-set whose members share certain critical features. Feeling, from a common sense and introspective point of view, involves *awareness* plus some kind of pressure towards action. That is, one is aware of the visual field, without "feeling" the visual forms of which one is aware. When the light is too bright, when the visual image is "moving" in some sense, questions of feeling arise. Living creatures make all kinds of adjustment and responses to the external (and internal) environment without any awareness. Small degrees of oxygen deprivation are, for example, automatically adjusted to by nonconscious shifts in respiration. But if such responses are not sufficient then, in higher animals at least, something new happens, the "self" (or some analogue or anticipation of it) becomes aware of discomfort, of a feeling, which then mobilizes a program of action, which in turn, requires some sort of information and understanding of the environment.

---

[3]As Sylvan Tomkins has pointed out (personal communication) a distinction has to be made between cultural hypocognition and the cultural mislabeling of an emotion. I think the two, both being attempts to ignore and to distort the relational significance of an emotion, are usually associated.

One decides now to open a window, or to leave the room; for an animal in pain, to seek a safe shelter. "Feeling" here is a signal from some prior, nonconscious system of internal adjustment and external adaptation that something new is required—something that requires the coordination of many physiological responses in action and that requires complex information beyond that sufficiently prepackaged through evolution. At the moment in humans when "self," learning, understanding, and programs become involved as they do in "It is stuffy in here, therefore what I must do to make myself more comfortable is to open the window," then historically derived learned systems for interpreting the world, differing systems of local culture which are shared in large degree by the members of different groups, become highly significant.[4] "Feeling" mobilizes in an individual relevant learned knowledge, and much of that knowledge is specific to specific "cultures." But my topic here is not feeling in general, not pain, itching, or nausea, but a sub-set, "emotion." I shall, using Tahitian materials, suggest what I take to be the nature of that sub-set, and shall then consider something of "culture" in its relation to "emotions."

Emotion

I have asserted that Tahitians do not recognize all of the responses that would seem to be "emotions" from a cross-cultural point of view as "emotions" (although they do recognize the great majority). But what does it mean to recognize, or conceive of a "feeling" as an "emotion." Tahitian does not have any general term for "feeling" or "emotion," but the *class* that I am calling "emotions" has special features in Tahitian usage. Asked to describe such matters as anger, desire, fear, etc., villagers say that their "place" is in "the intestines," referring to those sensations in the abdomen that are one element in the complex specific emotion. These feelings can arise spontaneously in "the intestines," or they may be stirred up by some thought from the head, or by something that is "seen by the eyes," or "heard by the ears." The feeling can lead to action directly, but this usually produces a bad result. It should first be thought over in the head, the seat of proper judgment prior to taking action.

In ordinary speech Tahitians discard such differentiated description and say, "I am angry," "I am afraid." In contrast they say of pain, "My tooth hurts," etc., and of itching, 'My leg is itching." These verbal distinctions, of course, are the same as ours. The Sino-Tibetan speaking Newars whom I studied in Nepal made similar verbal distinctions. Anger, desire, fear, etc. involve, then the "I," the "person," rather than a part of the person. But there are other "feelings"

---

[4]One assumes that everywhere one learns in the same way to deal with many aspects of the physical and social world. This includes the universal cognitive orientations and skills which concerned Piaget. But a great deal of the "reality" with which individuals in various groups must deal is locally constructed, and involves a historical process and specific local adaptations and inventions.

that also involve the whole person, which Western common sense thought rejects as "emotions." Tahitians, like us and like Newars, do say, *I* am exhausted, " "*I* am sick." When "sadness" is (mis)interpreted by Tahitians as "illness," the condition of the total "I" is still at issue.

In sickness, exhaustion, etc., however, there is an emphasis on something wrong in the relation of a person to his own body, to his internal environment, to the physical support of the "I." But in an "emotion," say anger, there is an emphasis on something wrong in the relationship of the person to his external physical and social context, the world of actions, plans, and socially defined meanings. The difference between the nonemotional "My foot hurts me," and the emotional "I am angry with him because he stepped on my foot," involves in the second case a relationship with another. The emotions are feelings that are connected with the external relationships of the self, of "I." And this self in humans, and social animals, is intimately constructed out of group processes and interpersonal relations.

So we may say, tentatively, that the class of feelings which Tahitians deal with as "emotions" (1) involves the whole "person" (a complex psychosocial creation) and (2) implies something about the relation of the person-as-a-whole to his or her environment, especially to the other persons (or personified elements) in that environment.

When an "emotional feeling" is dealt with as a "nonemotional feeling" it may be done either by ignoring the awareness of an external relational cause as when loneliness is interpreted as sickness, or by denying that the whole person is involved and focusing on a part of the reaction—the hypochondriac's "My heart is acting peculiarly," which also blunts the relational information proposed by "I am afraid."

The Emotion of Unclassifiable Situations

There is an "emotion" that is very common in Tahitian villages, and rare among adult Westerners, and which has some bearing on the idea of emotion as a feeling that is a response to the meaningful external relationships of a person. This is the emotion of the uncanny. Uncanny feelings are not localized in the abdomen, but are felt in the head and on the skin. One feels the head swelling, the hair standing up on the head, and the flesh crawling. This occurs in those situations where it is unclear whether the ordinary categories of orientation in the spacio-temporal world are still operating—at twilight, in the brush, in the presence of phenomena that dissolve clear categorizations, such as fires that glow without heat, people with peculiar faces. Bruner, Goodnow, and Austin (1956) have noted that "When an event cannot be . . . categorized and identified, we experience terror in the face of the uncanny. And indeed, 'the uncanny' is itself a category, even if only a residual one [p. 12]." But the Tahitian response is not terror. The uncanny sensation (or emotion) may turn into terror, but it is felt as and interpreted as something different from fear. Not all difficulties in categorization lead to a sense of the uncanny. That boderline emotion seems to derive from difficulty in making those categorizations that help anchor us (i.e., our selves) in "common-sense" reality—in familiar kinds of time, space, scale, and causal and logical contexts.

The Initial Appraisal[5]

The hypocognized emotions illustrate an interesting problem. A Tahitian responds to the emotional feelings[6] produced (in the viewpoint of an outside observer) by the loss of something he cared about in accordance with local cultural schemata as, say, the effect of spirits on his body. The emotional feeling has produced in itself a problem for (secondary) cognitive evaluation (following Schachter & Marañon; see Mandler, 1975), and in accordance with local cultural schemata he evaluates the emotion in (again from some transcultural viewpoint) a peculiar fashion.

But in some sense the individual must "know" that he has undergone a loss. This, the result of an initial appraisal of an eliciting situation, is what generates the emotional feeling in the first place. That is, if we take emotions as involving the responses of a "person" to a mostly social environment, the first phase that will result in the production of an emotional feeling involves some kind of first order knowledge. Someone is frustrating me, hurting me, becoming detached from me, is sexually receptive, etc. This entails elementary knowledge of some kind about relationship, and operates, in its first phase at least, out of awareness. It is this knowledge that generates the emotional feeling, which then in turn mobilizes the culturally influenced system of percepts, concepts, words, values, etc., a second order knowledge which is usually fully conscious, or preconscious

---

[5]I am following Paul Ekman in considering emotional responses as being composed of components and phases. He suggests (Ekman, 1977, 1980a and in other works) a schema including (1) *elicitors,* "events which are appraised quickly as the occasion for one or another emotion"; (2) an *appraisal system* "which determines when the affect program becomes operative" and "which attends to those stimuli (external or internal) which are the occasion for activating the affect program"; and (3) an *affect program* "that directs emotional responses," some of which are modified and controlled through *display rules,* "the conventions, norms, and habits that develop regarding the management of emotional response." For my present purposes I segment the sequence somewhat differently: (1) The initial appraisal of an eliciting situation (the two are logically connected); (2) the "emotional feeling" which enters into awareness as a result of the initial appraisal, (3) the cognitive evaluation motivated by that feeling (a "secondary" cognitive evaluation if the initial appraisal is considered to be "cognitive"), and (4) the expression of the emotion as involuntary symptom or intended communication.

[6]I am using the awkward "emotional feeling" to designate the component of feeling in the emotional sequence. This suggests the question of whether or in what way "emotional feelings" in themselves might be a special class of feeling, as the whole emotional sequence is a sub-class of the feeling sequence.

in the sense that it can be brought into awareness by an effort of will.[7] What is the relation to "culture" of the first order knowledge of the initial appraisal on the one hand and of the second order knowledge of the cognitive evaluation following the feeling signal on the other? We are told that in animals, at least, the appraisal is "sunk" into deep neurological structures. A decorticate cat, for example, is said to show its greatly augmented rage only to "appropriate objects" (e.g., Grastyán, 1974). This suggests, of course, that some aspects of knowledge about relationship are evolutionarily learned and in some cases "prewired."

There is, in humans (and, probably, in some sense in many animals) in addition to the possibility of phylogenetically determined understandings of the meanings of relationship, some kind of "cultural" influence on primary appraisal (the appraisal of the eliciting situation) but this seems to be significantly different, both in its structure and the way it is learned, from the influence of "culture" in secondary appraisal (the appraisal of the feeling response to the eliciting situation).

For example, learning involved in primary appraisal seems in comparison to learning involved in secondary appraisal to be relatively random in relation to the systems of values and definition which give some coherence to a community and which define its morality and its common sense. Cultural learning theory has tended to focus on "socialization," the components of a child's experience that train him for acceptable adult behavior and understanding. It was assumed (particularly by the "Culture and Personality" school) that this entailed very early learning sequences. Often associated with this was the usually unstated assumption that all learning in a culture is shaped towards the specific adaptive requirements of the adult society.

An alternative possibility was clearly stated by Ernest Schachtel (1949) in an essay "On Memory and Childhood Amnesia." Some of the rich and diverse understandings of childhood experience, he wrote, are filtered out by a "process [which] leaves the culturally unacceptable or unusable experiences and the memory thereof to starvation by the expedient of providing no linguistic, conceptual, and memory schemata for them and by channeling later experience into the experience schemata of the culture. As the person, in the process of education, gradually comes to live more and more exclusively within the framework of the culturally and conventionally provided experience schemata, there is less and less to remind him of the possibility of trans-schematic experience [p. 47]." In the relatively random experiences of children with others within a culture, a great variety of relational lessons are learned (including whatever may be necessary to

---

[7]Such phenomena as "consciousness" and "effort of will" involve the presence of a sub-system of mind, the self. This self is a social product, and to some degree a variable product of different historical and social circumstances (see Levy & Rosaldo, 1983).

complete "prewired" inherited "knowledge"). Later learning must operate to modify and control this primary knowledge. The two phases may well be in some way related to the primary and secondary appraisals which precede and follow the signal of feeling.

As the members of the group conceive of the growing child as more and more of a "person," as more and more of a morally responsible actor, various sequential educational devices—the progressive learning of language, the correction of language to adult standards, the emphases on moral learning and responsibility, the sequences of educational rites of passage with their powerful symbolic transformation of orientation, serve to transform the first "rich and diverse" understandings in a culturally coherent direction. The "starved schemata" are left as a basis for creativity, dreams, humor, and transcultural understanding.

But insofar as the forms of a culture *do* systematically affect the early learning that may modify the primary appraisal this would seem to operate in large part by affecting the person's *reactivity* to the eliciting situation, his sensitivity to loss, frustration, etc. Such learning, as "temperament" does, affects the reactive base that the defining, evaluative, and programmatic schemas of culture must deal with during the secondary evaluation. The learning that affects the primary assessment phase probably involves the shape of experience rather than doctrines about experience. As a crude example one would expect a child with only one mothering, nurturant person to experience temporary separations from that person as a dangerous loss in comparison with a child who had a number of substitute nurturant people at hand. The first child would react to later losses of loved ones differently than the second. He or she would appraise eliciting situations more vigorously and extensively than would the second. For the first child the class of eliciting situations would be wider, and the import of a given one more serious. But in both, once the emotional feeling of sadness signalled the need for a secondary cognitive evaluation the same learned cultural program would be used. *Insofar as most people in a community shared similar shapings of experience there would be similarities in this reactivity, in contrasts to some other community.*

The Response to "Emotional Feeling"; The Secondary Cognitive Evaluation

Howard Leventhal (1980) has distinguished similar components of knowing in relation to emotion. He categorizes what I have called the primary phase as involving perceptual memories or "schemata" and distinguishes them from conceptual memories associated with social labels and discursive processes. "The schematic and conceptual systems attach different types of cognitive processes to emotion. The schematic is in some sense the more primary and important; it integrates specific situational perceptions (*episodes*) with autonomic, subjective, expressive and instrumental responses in a concrete, patterned, im-

age-like memory system. The conceptual system is more sequential and volitional in nature and corresponds more closely to social labeling processes [p.
160]." Furthermore, Leventhal states, the processing of the conceptual system
has to do with *"the conclusions we draw about our feelings*—our guesses as to
what internal events and actions make up emotion as well as the causes and
consequences of emotion. Although these beliefs are based on information
gleaned from sensory motor and schematic processing, there is no reason to
assume that they accurately reflect the mechanisms, responses, eliciting conditions or consequences of emotional processing [p. 181, italics added]."

Once the intense and compelling phase of feeling[8] follows the primary appraisal, the processes of secondary evaluation, of cognition per se, become
prominent. Here cultural systems and their private components and versions
become centrally influential for naming, classifying, interpreting, directing.

Although the ethnography of recent decades has been concerned with cultural
systems of classification in various groups of various domains other than emotions it should be noted that the pragmatic consequences of "ethno-classifica-
tions" vary greatly depending upon what is being classified. The Tahitians for
example have namings, classification, and doctrine concerning thinking. But the
Tahitian *theory* of thinking does not affect thinking and its outcome. The Tahitian theory of specific emotions, on the other hand, has a great effect on the total
emotional sequence. *Among psychological processes it is possible that "emotional feelings" are uniquely sensitive to intellectual and cultural definitional
schema.* This is implied in considering them as signals for activating the cultural
definitional system (both in the "actor" and the observers of his act) in regard to
problems of person-environmental relationship.

The analysis of these secondary systems of dealing with various emotions in a
particular community entails the "thick description" of functions of the various
emotions within the community, their relationship to various other cultural values and forms (e.g., the underplaying of emotions of loss in Tahiti seem logically
related to the exchange system), their relation to other emotions and to a full
variety of psychological constructs. Here, I note only some miscellaneous features of evaluation which may have some comparative interest.

Hypercognition and Hypocognition.   I have discussed this earlier. In Tahiti,
and presumably in other "simple" communities some domains (for Tahiti—
anger, shame, fear, for example) are "hypercognized"; some others (for Tahi-

---

[8]Does the emotional feeling in itself vary across cultures? Izard (1980b) has claimed that "the
experimental component of emotion is a quality of consciousness or feeling, and at this level the
emotion state is invariant across cultures." This is not a closed issue. Some *dimensions* of emotional
feeling may well vary cross-culturally, their intensity perhaps—the data on pain is suggestive here
(e.g., Levy, 1975: 308–314). But the *qualitative* character of the emotional feeling probably has
everywhere the same form.

ti—sadness, guilt) are "hypocognized." Both of these can be considered as methods of control, but matters that are controlled by not being known, and those that are controlled by being known in obsessive detail would seem to imply different kinds of process, and to have different psychological and social implications.

Comparative Ways of Controlling Emotion.   I have argued that culturally influenced cognitive evaluation responding to the awareness of feeling of a certain quality acts as a system of control and integration affecting the projects, discharges, and internal readjustments consequent to that feeling and the associated arousal state. This cognitive control works best in what Goffman (1961) has called *Total Institutions,* which include isolated, traditional simple societies, albeit reinforced even in such societies by additional redundant controls (Levy, 1978).

But there are other ways of dealing with emotion besides cognitively, much of psychoanalytic theory is involved with this. In a complex society and culture such as the Newars of Nepal where there is, for example, compared to the Tahitian language, an enormous vocabulary (derived from Persian, Sanscrit, Nepali, and various Sino-Tibetan sources), there is a nuanced terminology for expressing and reflecting on almost any emotional possibility. In situations of such complexity controls do not work primarily through culturally accepted elementary definitions of situations. Types of control systems have to be developed, which involve special elaborations of moral controls, of dramatic and compelling symbolic processes, and of special kinds of internal controls. The question of the specific sociocultural variations in emotion-control methods that may be related to other aspects of community structure is still to be investigated.

The Importance of the Feeling Itself in the Cognitive Evaluation.   There are two issues here for which comparative data might be of interest. First is the relative weight given to eliciting situations versus the feeling itself in the secondary cognitive evaluation. When a Tahitian says "I knew there must have been a ghost near by because I had gooseflesh" he is apparently, with due regard for rhetoric, evaluating the situation primarily from the feeling. When he says, "I knew that what I felt for her was love because she treated me so kindly" he is using the situation as his main reference for evaluation.

The first example brings us to a second question about the relation of feeling to a specific cognitive evaluation, the question of whether the feeling response has in itself a *special shape* which can be read for specific, differential information, whether something more than a generalized arousal is involved. Uncanny emotion seems to have this specific form for Tahitians, and is experientially differentiated from, say, abdominal feelings. I did not inquire as to whether my Tahitian informants felt other sensations beyond the abdominal ones, which helped them differentiate anger from, say, fear. One can guess that there were, for example, other feelings which helped them differentiate "desire" and its various sub-types. The question of differential emotional feeling and how it might enter into evaluation could well be investigated in cross-cultural studies.

The Limits on the Possibilities of Cultural Definition.   In comparative studies of color naming it seems that color categories in various cultures have the same "central reference"; that is, what we recognize as the purest, the ideal yellow, red, green and so forth are the same colors that are so named in other cultures, provided they have a name for the category at all. What differs are the boundaries within which the central term (e.g., yellow) applies—the point at which a greenish yellow becomes a yellowish green (Berlin & Kay, 1969). My Tahitian and Newar studies suggest that in some similar fashion the central tendencies named by various emotional terms are probably universal, but that the borders of the categories may differ. There are also, as in color naming, situations where two or more categories which are separated in one culture (although they seem in some sense closely related, or semantically "adjacent") are in another differentiated.

That is, whatever the cultural peculiarities in the relations and associated meanings of Tahitian emotional terms I had little trouble in recognizing, say, *ri'ari'a* as "fear," *riri* as "anger," *hina'aro* as "desire," *oa'oa* as "happiness," ha'ama as shame. That is, if an emotion was recognized and named at all its "central tendency" seemed to be universally human.

There are, however, in Tahiti differences from English in boundaries, and in condensations of categories. Thus *ri'ari'a* ("fear") also includes mild aversion to certain foods. The categories that we differentiate as "embarrassment" and "shame" are named as one category in Tahiti (and widely, perhaps universally throughout Polynesia) and are also so grouped by the Newars. On the other hand the sub-categories of the various emotional domains are divided in different ways. The Tahitians, for example, distinguish verbally *ri'ari'a*, fear, as a present experience ("I am afraid now because the dog is biting me"), from *mata'u*, anticipatory fear ("I fear that the dog might bite me"; "I am afraid of dogs").

The Relation of Emotions to Other Aspects of the Person

Here there are very many matters that vary, of course, from individual to individual and from group to group. Here emotions become an element in some larger analysis of "personality" or "mind." Here is where the clinical approach of a psychological anthropology can provide complex description and subtle models. I wish to comment on only one issue, the relation of feeling to action, of emotion to motivation.

Tahitians seem to be comparatively dependent on the strength of emotion (including an inner sense of drive, energy and enthusiasm) for the performance of a range of tasks. They are anxious and concerned when the inner sense of "enthusiasm" decreases. This seems to be related to the relative weakness of other motives for performance, e.g., those related to "guilt." (Perhaps related to this is that Tahitian "depression," as seems to be the case for much of the non Judeo-Christian world, seems to be manifested by apathy, and lack of initiative, rather than by agitation and self hatred. It seems to involve problems with the level of arousal rather than in the nature and force of conscience.)

The Expression of Emotion

Although the Tahitians and the Newars have specific features in their style of emotional expression that can be related to other features of their personal organization and of their cultural system, and which provide part of the subject matter for psychological ethnography, I wish here to make some comments on expressive "universals." Aside from one or two temporarily confusing gestures expressive behavior in both places was not difficult for me to understand.

Because of a traditional anthropological emphasis on cultural relativism and on the specific coding of communication within various groups, what is now perhaps most interesting about the expression of emotion are those universal features that Ekman (e.g., Ekman, 1980b) and others have helped to document. Much of this, of course, is species specific and biologically rooted behavior, but I would like to suggest an additional dimension concerning the cross-cultural comprehensibility of expressive behavior.

I must preface this with some remarks on the aspect of the social significance of emotional expression. Emotionally expressive behavior often has the communicative function of showing the *relationship of an actor to his culturally constituted act*. That is, one acts like a chief by accepting cultural guides for the role, guides that help determine its legitimacy and acceptability to others. But the expression of emotion, or its obvious inhibition, which indicate a proud, anxious, happy, depressed, hesitant, overeager, angry or whatever chief is a meta-message about an actor's relation to his socially coded behavior. Even if the role calls for some emotional expression in itself, there will still be expressive messages illuminating the relation of the actor to that conventional emotion.

As the first appraisal segment of the emotional response indicated to a person his own relationship to his external world, now through expression the person is transmitting information to others about that relationship. This is in part the direct *expression* of the emotion in the person who is "having it," but the observer is also the recipient of a *communication*, a message intended for another.

These expressive/communicative signs include paralinguistic behaviors, which in this case can be said to signal the *relation of the speaker to his utterance*, such relations as irony, direct quotation, doubt, reference to the uncanny (the universal paralinguistics of the telling of ghost stories), insincerity—as well as the more properly emotional angry, anxious, seductive, depressed, enthusiastic (etc.) relations.

It was thought that aside from those paralinguistic signs of emotion universally produced by gross organismic influences on the production of speech, the other information about the relation of the speaker to his utterance was culturally coded in the same arbitrary way that, for example, "vache" had come to stand for a French cow. In a pioneering study of paralinguistic behavior, *The First Five Minutes*, Pittenger, Hockett, & Danehy (1960) asserted that paralinguistic habits "show variation from culture to culture and from region to region. They are as much the product of experience as are one's language habits [p. 185]." But, in fact, in learning non-European languages a Westerner must painfully learn the arbitrarily coded semantics and syntax of the language, but has (in my experience) little trouble understanding the relational aspects of the language, its paralinguistic forms, once he has mastered its semantics and syntax. The reason for this is that such relational patterns are "analogically" coded, rather than "digitally" coded. In Peirce's language they are "iconic," resembling in some features their referent, rather than "symbolic," that is, arbitrarily related to their referent by convention. Thus, for example, once one knows what the standard intonation pattern of a declarative sentence is in a particular language, one can recognize the analogical meaning of an *unresolved* intonation which indicates a question, or the cautious articulation of the sentence that indicates doubt. It is possible that some of the universals in the expression of emotion in general, not only its vocal features, are "universal" in that they are analogically mediated (instead of by arbitrary code), and can be read by all humans, as well as by many other animals.

REFERENCES

Berlin, B. & Kay, P. *Color terms: Their universality and evolution.* Berkeley: University of California Press, 1969.

Bilmes, J. & Boggs, S. Language and communication: The foundations of culture. *In Perspectives on cross-cultural psychology.* New York: Academic Press, 1979.

Bruner, J., Goodnow, J., & Austin, G. *A study of thinking.* New York: Wiley, 1956.

Bruner, J., Oliver, R., & Greenfield, P. *Studies in cognitive growth.* New York: Wiley, 1966.

Ekman, P. Biological and cultural contributions to body and facial movement. In J. Blacking (Ed.), *The anthropology of the body*, A.S.A. Monograph 15. London: Academic Press, 1977.

Ekman, P. Biological and cultural contributions to body and facial movement in the expression of emotion. In A. O. Rorty (Ed.), *Explaining emotion*, Berkeley: University of California Press, 1980. (a)

Ekman, P. *The face of man. Expressions of universal emotions. In a New Guinea Village.* New York: Garland STPM Press, 1980. (b)

Goffman, E. *Asylums.* Garden City: Doubleday Anchor, 1961.

Grastyán, E. "Emotion," in *The Encyclopedia Britannica*, 15th Edition. Chicago: Encyclopedia Britannica, Inc., 1974.

Izard, C. Cross-Cultural Perspectives on Emotion and Emotion Communication. In H. Triandis (Ed.), *Handbook of cross-cultural psychology.* Boston: Allyn and Bacon, 1980. (a)

Izard, C. *Emotions in personality and culture.* Unpublished discussion of a panel on Emotions in Personality and Culture, American Anthropological Association Annual Meeting, Washington, D.C., Dec. 1980. (b)

Kirkpatrick, J. *The Marquesan notion of the person.* Ph.D. Dissertation, Department of Anthropology, University of Chicago, 1980.

Leventhal, H. Towards a comprehensive theory of emotion. In *Advances in exprimental social psychology* (Vol. 13.). New York: Academic Press, 1980.

LeVine, R. *Culture, behavior and personality.* Chicago: Aldine, 1973.

LeVine, R., & Shweder, R. *Culture and its acquisition,* In preparation.

Levy, R. I. *Tahitians: Mind and experience in the Society Islands.* Chicago: University of Chicago Press, 1973.

Levy, R. I. Tahitian gentleness and redundant controls. In A. Montague (Ed.), *Learning non-aggression.* New York: Oxford University Press, 1978.

Levy, R. I., & Rosaldo, M. (Ed.) *Self and emotion,* a special edition of *ETHOS,* Fall, 1983, pp. 129–209.

Lutz, C. *Emotion, ethnopsychology, and parental goals on Ifaluk Atoll.* Paper presented to the American Anthropological Association, Washington, D.C., December 1980.

Mandler, G. *Mind and emotion.* New York: Wiley, 1975.

Pittenger, R. E., Hockett, C., & Danehy, J. *The first five minutes.* Ithaca: Paul Martineau, 1960.

Rosaldo, M. *Knowledge and passion: Ilongot notions of self and social life.* Cambridge: Cambridge University Press, 1980.

Schachtel, E. On memory and childhood amnesia. In Patrick Mullahy (Ed.), *A study of interpersonal relations.* New York: Hermitage Press, 1949.

Webster, R. *The Observer Review.* London: February 1, 1981.

Author Index

Numbers in *italics* indicate pages with complete bibliographic information.

A

Abelson, R. P., 249, *255*
Abrams, R., 41, *55*
Acuna, C., 31, *56*
Adamson, L., 87, 92, 93, *107*, 144, *157*
Adey, W. R., 19, *34*
Ahles, T. A., 287, *289*
Ainsworth, M., 116, 118, 119, *127*, 132, 149, *155*
Ajuriaguerra, J. D., 40, *56*
Akert, K., 44, *55*
Akil, H., 21, 22, *36, 37*
Akiyama, Y., 83, *106*
Alexander, F., 173, 192, *194*
Alford, L. B., 40, *55*
Allport, G. W., 231, *235*
Als, H., 87, 92, 93, *107*, 131, 144, *157*
Ancoli, S., 335, *342*, 361, 363, *363*
Anders, T., 82, 98, *102*
Anderson, B. J., 86, 93, *106*
Anderson, N. H., 264, *269*
Anderson, J. R., 243, *245*
Andrew, R. J., 79, *102*
Apple, W., 362, *365*
Arend, R., 119, *127*, 124, *127*

Arnold, M. B., 17, *34*, 98, 100, *102, 170*, *194*, 251, *256*, 296, *316*, 357, *363*, 370, *381*
Asnis, G., 68, *71*
Austin, G., 403, *411*
Ausubel, D. P., 229, *235*
Averill, J. R., 223, *235, 236*, 252, 253, *256*, 294, 297, 304, *316*, 328, 341, 369, 372, *382*
Ax, A. F., 324, *341*, 377, 378, *381, 383*

B

Bagshaw, M. H., 23, 31, *34, 36, 37*
Bailey, C. J., 25, *36*
Bailey, P., 31, *38*
Bandler, R. J., Jr., 263, *269*
Baranovskaya, O. P., 44, *55*
Barchas, J. D., 372, *382*
Bard, P., 14, *34*
Bargh, J., 262, *270*
Barry, J., 31, *37*
Barry, W. A., 375, *383*
Bartlett, F. C., 249, *256*
Basowitz, H., 224, *235*

413

Subject Index